Cesare Zavattini's Neo-realism and the Afterlife of an Idea

Cesare Zavattini's Neo-realism and the Afterlife of an Idea

An Intellectual Biography

David Brancaleone

BLOOMSBURY ACADEMIC
NEW YORK · LONDON · OXFORD · NEW DELHI · SYDNEY

BLOOMSBURY ACADEMIC
Bloomsbury Publishing Inc
1385 Broadway, New York, NY 10018, USA
50 Bedford Square, London, WC1B 3DP, UK
29 Earlsfort Terrace, Dublin 2, Ireland

BLOOMSBURY, BLOOMSBURY ACADEMIC and the Diana logo are trademarks
of Bloomsbury Publishing Plc

First published in the United States of America 2021
This paperback edition published 2023

Cover design: Namkwan Cho
Cover photograph © Biblioteca Panizzi Archivio Cesare Zavattini,
Comune di Reggio in Emilia

A catalog record for this book is available from the Library of Congress.

ISBN: HB: 978-1-5013-1697-5
PB: 978-1-5013-7735-8
ePDF: 978-1-5013-1698-2
eBook: 978-1-5013-1700-2

Typeset by Deanta Global Publishing Services, Chennai, India

To find out more about our authors and books visit www.bloomsbury.com and
sign up for our newsletters.

Contents

Acknowledgements

I wish to thank Katie Gallof, my publisher at Bloomsbury Academic, for all her support at every stage of this dual publishing project, this *Intellectual Biography* and a separately published two-volume companion, *Selected Writings*. My thanks to all the anonymous peer reviewers of both.

Cesare Zavattini's eldest son, Arturo, granted unlimited and unconditional access to all papers, contained in the vast Zavattini Archive, which his father donated to the Panizzi library of Reggio in Emilia, from the late 1970s on. Arturo also gave me many rare books, a sizeable part of the Zavattini corpus, as well as of the relevant secondary literature. Arturo also helped shape my outlook, to consider the total Zavattini, and namely, the important relation between his writings, be they cinematic, literary or a combination of both, and his other forms of artistic expression, as well as to consider Zavattini the publisher and the editor.

I was helped by film historian and critic Mino Argentieri, by director Francesco Maselli, by film historian and critic Lorenzo Pellizzari and by director Fernando Birri, all of whom granted me interviews and allowed me to film and record them. Lorenzo Pellizzari, an early reader of this project in its preliminary stages, provided valuable information on the Festival of Porretta Terme. My thanks to Max Le Cain, the editor of *Experimental Conversations*, where initial research and translation was encouraged and published.

Professor Laura Rascaroli drew my attention to the relation between Zavattini's ideas and *Tercer Cine*, to Zavattini's diary form of cinema. At the Panizzi archive, Giorgio Boccolari, former head archivist, fielded many queries and provided expert advice. The keeper of the Zavattini Archive of Reggio Emilia, Roberta Ferri, facilitated access, including long-distance, seamlessly coordinating Italian inter-library loans. My thanks also to Antonietta Vigliotti, Annalisa De Carina, Monica Leoni, Elisabetta Pini and Peppe, who lent me *Emigrantes* (1948), directed by Aldo Fabrizi. Laura Pompei, of the Ufficio Acquisizione e Digitalizzazione materiali bibliografici e archivistici, at the Biblioteca Chiarini in the Centro Sperimentale di Cinematografia di Roma, gave advice and practical help with bibliographic research in accessing the Chiarini library and its archival holdings, unpublished correspondence by Guido Aristarco and Siegfried Kracauer, sending articles, and sourcing an important unpublished, and only recently bequeathed letter written by Mario Verdone and addressed to Zavattini, and facilitating contact with his son, Carlo Verdone.

The staff of the Archivio Audiovisivo del Movimento Operaio supported this project at the outset, by providing easy access to their film and paper archives, to the production papers for Zavattini's scenarios, to unpublished correspondence and other writings, to digital copies of all fifteen surviving free newsreels as well as to other very rare documentaries of the era. Paola Scarnati, who worked with Zavattini on behalf of the Communist Party's production house UNITELEFILM, in the 1970s, was instrumental in establishing contact with Zavattini's son Arturo. My thanks to her colleague Letizia Cortini, who insisted with me that the project should be grounded on sound philological methodology and on original archival research, given the untapped wealth of archival holdings in Reggio Emilia.

Claudia Brugnoli of the Alma Mater Studiorum, of the University of Bologna, provided Ernesto de Martino's 'Realismo e folclore nel cinema italiano' (1952), and Marianna Montesano at the Biblioteca delle Arti, Sezione Spettacolo 'Lino Miccichè', Università di Roma Tre, sent me a digital copy of the inaugural issue of *Cine cubano* (1960).

Finally, I would like to thank my home institution, the Limerick Institute of Technology, for supporting travel costs over the past eight years, and enabling this kind of long-term research, and for supporting two Erasmus grants which have allowed me to teach in the Rome film school and at Reggio University Media Studies department. *Dulcis in fundo*, my deepest gratitude to the two As in my life.

Introduction

Cesare Zavattini is well known as the author of famous screenplays for major post-war classics, recognized as milestones of cinema history, namely, *Sciuscià*, *Bicycle Thieves*, *Miracle in Milan* and *Umberto D*. Less generally known is the fact that he was also, during a life that spanned most of the twentieth century, a driving force of Italian Modernism in the Milan of the 1930s, a public intellectual, a theorist, a painter, a tireless lobbyist and organizer for change within the film industry, a campaigner against colonialism and for peace, who, jointly with the documentarist Joris Ivens, was awarded the 1955 Lenin Peace Prize by Moscow (at the height of the Cold War), a man of letters, and a poet.

This biography is for anyone interested in cinema and its histories, who may or may not be a specialist in the field. Everything is spelt out. The biography assumes that the general reader, the student and the film historian, all have one thing in common: they share the same curiosity about cinema and its fate, and Cesare Zavattini's life's work tries to change that fate, a testament to ethical and political cinema. The bias towards his contribution to Italian, European and World Cinema is in keeping with the Bloomsbury Academic film studies publishing series, where this *Intellectual Biography* and its companion, two-volume *Selected Writings*, are situated.

It was only in 2006 that the first scholarly biography was published in Italian.[1] After his death in 1989, an exhibition in honour of his life achievement was held at the Centre Georges Pompidou, from 5 December to 7 March 1991. A similar retrospective exhibition, *Cesare Zavattini: una vita in Mostra*, took place in Italy, from 21 May to 27 June 1997, containing informative essays on his many achievements in different fields of activity.[2] In 2006, Orio Caldiron, the author of a very informative anthology of Zavattini's scenarios, asked this question: 'How many Zavattinis are there?'[3]

Stefania Parigi answered Caldiron's question, by demonstrating how the filmmaker, the short story writer and master of humour, the theorist and pioneer of cinema, and the painter all coexisted in the same person, in a number of intriguing ways.[4] It might come as a surprise, for example, to know that some of his gags in the Neo-realist *Miracle in Milan* were originally jokes, written as early as 1927, several years before Zavattini became a screenwriter in the early 1930s.

In Italy, his literary comic streak is still mistaken for Surrealism, but, as in this telling example, it is closer to a nonsense tradition of writing, with a peculiar, Italian genealogy, partly rooted in the popular tradition of *scemenze* (illogical statements, literally, the thoughts of an idiot), partly in Aldo

Palazzeschi's Florentine Futurism, partly in Massimo Bontempelli's whimsical realism, but also in Laurence Sterne's wit. The outcome, Zavattini's minimalist prose, with undercurrents of gentle irony, sometimes spilling over into satire, is quintessentially Modernist. His short stories or advocate of visual culture in Italy? *Raccontini*, as he called them, were collected in three books in the 1930s and early 1940s, which provide a different model to the kind of literature in vogue, during the years of Fascist dictatorship. They were a runaway success on publication, sold out immediately, and went into several reprints. His first book came out ten years before Elio Vittorini's anthology of American literature in translation, *Americana* (1941), which was later credited for its vibrant influence in renewing Italian prose, after the war.

To dwell for a moment on Caldiron's question, 'How many Zavattinis are there?', in addition to the screenwriter, one must acknowledge the film theorist, the desk editor, the film editor, unofficially working in the cutting room, the editorial director; indeed, the publisher who knew how to turn an ailing publication into a whopping bestseller. Someone who understood what dizzy layouts could do for a magazine, when they broke out of the typographic grid with photographs, or what could be achieved through judicious commissioning of illustrations from major artists and designers of the day, such as Saul Steinberg, Bruno Munari or one of the Rationalist architects from the *Domus* circle. The person who knew how to launch a successful campaign and cajole his authors and artists, not to mention his publisher, was the very same acclaimed author of literary texts. And, in 1939, Zavattini became a painter who exhibited his work in public and won prizes. This man, who spent hours, even days, at the moviola, was also the campaigner for socially engaged cinema; not to mention a tireless campaigner for world peace, which involved endless phone calls, meetings, letters, discussions and organizing. What about Zavattini the cinematic ethnographer? What about the advocate for Outsider art in Italy? What about Zavattini the pioneer and advocate of visual culture in Italy? This *Intellectual Biography* has always kept in mind the various areas of his endeavours, while concentrating on Zavattini the filmmaker.

Inevitably, to write about Zavattini has also entailed taking on the vast historiography concerning cinematic Neo-realism, to establish how the movement or non-movement, depending on points of view, has been 'framed', bearing in mind all the questions along the way.[5] As Judith Butler explains:

> To call the frame into question is to show that the frame never quite contained the scene it was meant to limn, that something was already outside, which made the very sense of the inside possible, recognizable. Something exceeds the frame that *troubles* our sense of reality; in other words, something occurs that does not conform to our established understanding of things.[6]

Trinh T. Minh-ha asks this question: What is left out of the frame? In relation to Zavattini, the fact of the matter is that most of his activities have been ignored, which has inevitably affected the way he has been 'framed'.[7]

Consequently, this *Intellectual Biography* seeks to tease out some, if not all, of these Zavattinis, as different as their pursuits, or as parts of a composite, complex, character, all feeding into a contribution towards disparate fields and various spaces of public intervention. Francesco Casetti rightly wonders in timely fashion about *il cinema a venire*, the cinema to come. Yet, we also need to reassess the cinema that has been, *il cinema che è stato*, in this expanded sense suggested earlier.[8] Henri Lefèbvre or Michel de Certeau, cited by Casetti, can also be used, not in a literal sense of pondering over new physical and virtual cinematic spaces, but to explore existing cinematic space, understood in Lefèbvre's and de Certeau's ethnographic sense, of space of Self and Other, taken as the space within and without the frame, both equally cinematic spaces, a crucial area of Zavattini's contribution to film theory and practice.

Much of Zavattini's thought travels outside the existing cinematic frame or across different media. Take the colossal Reggio Emilia Zavattini Archive. Zavattini doubled up as a competent archivist of his life work. He collected and stored everything, even hotel telephone messages on slips of paper, visiting cards, all his notes, even lowly press cuttings, and scribbles on the back of an envelope. Almost all this material, comprising his private archive, still exists, and, thanks to his eldest son, Arturo Zavattini, was made available to the author in its entirety. The thousands and thousands of letters from and to Zavattini complement the entire collection of scenarios, treatments and film paperwork, adding to vast expanses of box files tracing his journeys, his conferences, what I would call his interventions which are the organizing principle underlying both this biography and the two, separately published anthologies, contained in the companion, two-volume, publication, Zavattini, *Selected Writings*, which were produced alongside it.[9] Since this biography builds on the research, translations and interpretation of these selections and ordering of texts – each preceded by an extensive critical and contextual frame of reference – here is some further detail about the *Selected Writings*. Volume One provides a substantial anthology of scenarios, incorporating Caldiron's selection, but adding to it, where deemed necessary, encompassing the full arc of Zavattini's enterprise, from the 1930s until the 1980s. Volume Two translates the core texts published in *Neorealismo ecc.* (1979), which is the only published anthology of Zavattini's writings, interviews and conference papers concerning Neo-realism, and includes many additions to that central corpus, and namely, a significant selection of Zavattini's pre-war literary prose, as well as other texts deemed useful to the reader, in terms of the filmmaker's critical interventions in the public sphere. Editorial choice and organization followed consultation with, and advice from, that anthology's editor, the late Mino Argentieri.

The main reason for publishing the two anthologies of Zavattini's writings is that because English is the modern *lingua franca*, it is necessary to close the gap between Italian scholarship, which provides a student, a researcher or a general reader with a significant library of published texts, and scholarship abroad. Working on a biography alongside editing and translating a large selection of Zavattini's writings has brought the author much closer to the driving preoccupations of the filmmaker's life, by virtue of having to grapple with his thought, to grasp it, with consideration for its original context, then translate into a cogent English equivalent, and, when necessary, attend to the many particularities and niceties of philological textual criticism.

One example: some of the files and press clippings in the Zavattini Archive made it possible to effect a reconstruction of the major 1955 Mexico Conference. Why? For the simple reason that there are no other records. Another example. On more than one occasion, Zavattini's marginal, handwritten notes in unpublished production papers shed a different light on his relations with the director Alessandro Blasetti. The same is true of his relations with Giuseppe De Santis, as their correspondence bears out, and, of course, with Vittorio De Sica.

A selection of Zavattini's Cinematic Diary was originally published in periodicals, then collected as *Straparole* (1967), and translated into English, over forty years ago, by William Weaver, as *Sequences from a Cinematic Life* (1971), which is long out of print. However, even when it was in print, any reader who was unfamiliar with twentieth-century Italian history and culture would have been challenged, faced with no introduction or notes to situate the cross-section of Italian film history, emerging from even the most superficial reading of *Straparole* or, for that matter, of the later *Diario cinematografico* (1979). This state of affairs suggests, in the English-speaking world, scarce curiosity, concerning the vast majority of his scenarios, the ones written before, during and after the years associated with historic Italian Neo-realism.

Such a lack of interest can partly be explained by a similar response to the ideas of Siegfried Kracauer or André Bazin, since the 1960s, both mistaken for naïve realists, until relatively recently.[10] This raises a knotty problem which cannot be avoided, and namely, how Neo-realism has been situated within film history. This issue is still complicated by old debates about the *realism* of Neo-realism, dating from the 1960s and 1970s. They coincided with the rise of post-structuralism, and its problematizing of 'the real'. The aesthetic validity of historic Neo-realism was partly critiqued in relation to its degree of adequation, or lack of it, as a screen image in respect of the material world. Such a critique pointed out, for example, inconsistencies in doing away with sets, studios and professional actors: on criticizing re-enactments.[11] But paradigms eventually change, as Alfred Kuhn's *The Structure of Scientific Revolutions* (1962) has shown.[12]

The project as a whole is dedicated to Ansano Giannarelli, a documentary film director, who worked on more than one of Zavattini's ambitious projects. In 2009, Giannarelli envisaged the kind of international project this book seeks to carry out. It is worth citing him directly:

It would be an amazing project to reconstruct Zavattini's thought about diverse aspects of cinema (and thus including also what nowadays we call 'documentary'). For this to be done thoroughly and with extreme accuracy, such an undertaking would require a re-reading of his extensive production: from his interviews (both radio recordings and those recorded on film),

to the public statements, the conference speeches, the diaries published in *Cinema Nuovo* and other journals, to the book reviews and the prefaces for catalogues and other books, and also the projects, treatments, screenplays (including all his annotations) and Zavattini's narrative writing.

Because Zavattini is not a systematic and rigorous thinker. Rather, he extracts the theoretical implications from practice, but not in the same way as Eisenstein and Pudovkin, who shared this approach. Zavattini was chaotic, seemingly casual, and extremely prolific. He is, in a sense, closer to Vertov, with whom he shares a strong association of ideas: Zavattini is probably the most important film theorist Italy has ever had.[13]

Another valuable methodological pointer, as to how to tackle a biography about Zavattini, was suggested a few years ago by a book written by film historian Gian Piero Brunetta, who confirmed the validity of Giannarelli's plan for multidisciplinary research methodology. In relation to the sphere of cinema, Brunetta speaks of 'parallel filmographies' of ideas which, for whatever reason, never went any further than expressing an idea, but may be, in some instances, more interesting than what he calls an 'effective' filmography.[14] This book has considered such parallel filmographies, which allow a historian to piece together known and previously unknown areas of Italian film history. These are, as he puts it, 'Sometimes independent, sometimes connected'.[15]

Inevitably, as intimated earlier, to write about Zavattini has required a sustained enquiry into Neo-realism, to observe how Neo-realism has been 'framed'. Zavattini would have agreed, insisting on breaking out of the frame, by pointing the camera elsewhere: towards the social, the here and now. This is how he put it:

I guess that if Christ had a cine-camera to hand, he wouldn't make up parables, however marvellous these might be, but, censorship permitting, he would show us who the good and the bad are *right now*, and he would confront us with close-ups of those who make their neighbour's daily bread, and of their victims, taste a little too bitter.[16]

As for the world-famous Zavattini, the screenwriter and principal theorist of Neo-realism, this biography contextualizes his interventions outside the frame, reconstructing the three main conferences on Neo-realism, bringing back to life the debates of the day to situate his ideas, and thus adopting a stance comparable to what is meant by Michael Baxandall by 'the period eye'.[17] In particular, Zavattini's thought has been pieced together and contextualized, from intervention to intervention, making use of interviews, conference papers, his gargantuan correspondence – mostly unpublished, his field research, his published Cinematic Diary, his campaigning for an ethical, popular and critical cinema. Bearing in mind existing historiography, this biography pieces together his thoughts and interventions within the cinema, a site of theory and practice, drawing together the many threads of his *praxis* of cinema.

Discussions about Neo-realism tend to be about a purely historic phenomenon, often dwelling on the number of films defining the Neo-realist canon, often centred on when the movement began, when it finished or if it is even to be considered a movement at all, or just a film style or perhaps a genre, as opposed to considering it a broader phenomenon, in terms of film theory, film philosophy and film history. This biography contributes to recent re-evaluations of Neo-realism, which have striven to investigate its relevance to contemporary film theory and practice today, and to evaluate its impact beyond the conventional framework of national cinema. The 2008 conference, 'Ripensare il Neorealismo', suggested it was time to reconsider.[18] Post-structural or post-Modernist tenets have been challenged in recent years, by new perspectives. Recent attempts are being made towards a re-evaluation of Neo-realism (albeit without ever questioning the consensus of understanding regarding *mimēsis*), addressing its impact, beyond a conventional framework of national cinema.

A groundbreaking anthology, *Italian Neorealism and Global Cinema* (2007), showed the spread of Neo-realist ideas across continents and began to question the physical, geopolitical and temporal boundaries of the movement.[19] Geoffrey Newell-Smith's *Making Waves* (2012) distinguished between the first Neo-realist new wave and subsequent new waves, which latter he considers heavily indebted to Neo-realism. Nowell-Smith has overturned existing orthodoxies and reductive approaches which reduced Neo-realism to a style recipe, dictated only by external circumstances (location shooting, non-professional actors, loose plot and so on).[20] In this respect, in terms of Neo-realism and its influence on global cinema, four of the chapters trace the direct transmission of Zavattini's idea of cinema to Spain, Mexico, Cuba and Argentina, drawing on the author's case study, *Zavattini, il Neo-realismo e il Nuovo Cinema Latino-americano* (2019).[21]

Even before *Umberto D.* (1952) – generally considered a canonical Neo-realist film – was screened, Zavattini had begun to formulate an ethnographic, socially engaged non-fiction cinema, which drew on investigative journalism and on Ernesto de Martino's innovative ethnography, based on the Marxian notion of the human being as a social being, and being as an inter-being, as a guiding principle for interaction. This biography traces the genealogy of this idea of cinema in Zavattini's works and its development, beginning with his scenario *Italia mia*, up until the late 1960s and early 1970s, when it reached its ultimate expression in putting into practice grassroots cinema, a 'guerrilla cinema', 'by the many, for the many', as he put it.

Early days

1.1 Luzzara

Cesare Zavattini was born in Luzzara in 1902, a place that was always shrouded in fog during long cold winters. The town is situated less than a kilometre from the banks of the river Po, in Reggio Emilia. His family owned a coffee bar and a bakery. This place was often mistaken for somewhere else, as Zavattini remembered: 'My hometown, Luzzara on the shores of the Po, is so common. Even if you write "Luzzara", the mail will be sent to Suzzara, a nearby town.' Petrarch, who spent a night there, stated that it was marshland inhabited by frogs.[1] While his mother was giving birth to Zavattini, the village band began to play outside the door.[2] When his grandfather stepped out to have a quiet word, the musicians moved up the road.

Zavattini lived in Luzzara until he was six, surrounded by the constant chatter in the family-owned patisserie, with its two large mirrors, advertising *Bitter Pastore* and *Cordial Campari*, and its velvet seating and white furniture, decorated with gold arabesques. In the billiards room, the Zavattinis occasionally had their meals. He remembered the rows of shiny liqueur bottles behind the bar; the cakes and extra treats on the menu, such as rice and *tartoufes*, veal cutlets *alla milanese*. The first moving image he ever witnessed was at the age of five, in 1907: he saw dogs chasing after rats in a *Pathé Journal* documentary.[3] The monochrome shapes on the large screen made a huge impression on him. The projector ran on petrol, and Zavattini remembered its pungent smell in the makeshift picture house set up in the village square. He became a regular visitor, because his parents ran a makeshift coffee bar inside. The following year, he was sent to Bergamo to stay with an uncle and his daughter, Silvia. From then on, he only saw his parents during the summer holidays.[4] Silvia taught in a primary school and Zavattini became her surrogate son. Her mothering was also influential in another respect, her atheism.[5]

It was during the years he spent in Bergamo with Silvia and his uncle that the two loves of his life, cinema and literature, developed. In Bergamo he witnessed the early years of cinema. There were two cinemas in town, the *Teatro Sociale*, in *Bergamo alta*, the hilly side of the town, and the *Cinema Nazionale*, at the other end. Nick Winters, Nick Carter, Nat Pinkerton, Petrosino and Max Linder were all regular characters who appeared on the screen at the *Nazionale* and whose photographs were on display at the newsagents, in illustrated magazine supplements. As for literature, he was moved to tears listening to Silvia reading verses like: 'Stronger than God's love is a mother's love.'[6] He also shed tears when she recited Pascoli's 'La cavalla storna', from his collection *Canti di Castelvecchio*.[7] This poem, on the school curriculum to this day, is about the murder of Ruggero Pascoli, the poet's father. In a flashback, a riderless horse and trap makes its return to the Pascoli homestead where the poet speaks through the character of Ruggero's wife. Pascoli heightens the tragedy of loss, using the plain music of children's rhymes to convey the expression of strong emotion. Almost unbearable.

There were children's stories – Carlo Collodi's *The Adventures of Pinocchio*. Once the characters came to life, when he saw *Pinocchio* in Silvia's puppet show, for her infants' class, based on the *Pinocchio* drawings by Attilio Mussino. Cesare would use a torch to read in bed under the blankets, adventure stories, whether by Alexandre Dumas or by Emilio Salgari, or detective stories by Maurice Leblanc, featuring the character of Arsène Lupin or the goings on of the fictional characters in the illustrated supplements linked to the detective films he and his friends saw at the *Nazionale* cinema.[8] Then his father introduced him to the theatre, giving him Pietro Goldoni's comedies in Venetian dialect.[9] And to a theatre of sorts, a theatre of attractions, belonged the performances of an actor called Fregoli, whom he watched for the first time in 1912. Fregoli was famous for his sudden costume changes, constantly taking his audience by surprise, switching from male character to female character, from the representation of an old man to that of a child. What particularly enchanted Zavattini was when Fregoli let the audience into his secrets, laying bare the illusion, to reveal his tricks. Two years later, in 1914, he and his middle school classmates joined one of several packed interventionist demonstrations, in protest at the Italian government's reluctance to get involved in the First World War.[10] Little did he know at the time, that in later life he would become an ardent pacifist.

However, by 1917, Silvia had had enough of her ward's insubordination and sent him back to Luzzara. In the meantime, his parents' financial difficulties were so severe that they were forced to let the coffee bar in Luzzara and take up employment elsewhere, near Rome, to run a factory canteen and a hotel.[11] Zavattini was enrolled in the second year of high school in Rome, at a *Liceo Classico*, the kind of college where you learn Latin and Greek and some history of philosophy. But Zavattini hardly attended. Like Collodi's *Pinocchio*, that year, he played truant, spending most of his time enjoying himself. What fascinated him weren't the archaeological sites of ancient Rome, but the world of show business, of famous comedians in the revues and variety shows, such as the great Petrolini, Armando Gil, Pasquariello, Lyda Borelli, Za la Mort and many other performers. He couldn't stay away from the attractions of light entertainment. He spent all the money his mother sent him on whatever performance was on offer. He attended the *Sala Umberto* shows day in and day out; from matinées, to afternoon and evening performances. When he wasn't gambling, he liked to spend his time on streetcars, just for the sheer excitement of watching Rome pickpockets at work.

By the end of his first year in the capital city, his parents, Arturo and Ida, who had been assuming their son had progressed to the next year of college, began to wonder about his studies. They sent one of his aunts to see how he was getting on. It turned out that he had to repeat the year. 'He doesn't like studying? Fine. Then get a job!'[12] But his illiterate mother interceded and persuaded Zavattini's father, Arturo, that if they really wanted their son to be a lawyer, he had to be given a second chance. So they decided to send him to Alatri, near Frosinone, not far from where they were working.

1.2 Alatri

His move to Alatri, far from serving as a punishment, led to even greater personal freedom, for now he could stay in a *pensione*, a small guesthouse, which provided lodgings to students. The custom was that boarders had to stay in after dark. But not Zavattini. Since there were no cabaret reviews to keep him entertained in Alatri, he devoted much of his time to gambling.[13]

Yet the reason he was in Alatri was school, but school was boring. He remembered his unsmiling Italian teacher, Ezio Lopez Celly, reading Guido Gozzano's 'Invernale' from *I colloqui* (1911), surprising for the way in which this poem freezes a small event, an incident, a dare among two young skaters on a lake, or Sergio Corazzini's melanchonic poems, copied out in the teacher's notebook, in his slow deliberate voice – perfectly suited to Corazzini's self-commiseration and sense of loss in, for example, the opening lines of his famous 'Desolation of the poor sentimental poet', which begins:

> Why do you call me a poet? I am no poet. I am nothing more than a young child who is crying. Can you not see? I have only tears to offer the Silence.[14]

'Something like a momentous earthquake happened that night, when I was seventeen. Herds of cells shifted around, or entirely changed their substance.'[15] He had come across a consignment of books in his local grocery store which had been delivered to the wrong address. It included Giovanni Papini's *Un uomo finito* (1913) (*Finished Man*). Many years later, he told Papini: 'I read it in a single night. What a cataclysm! From the next morning, a new life began for me.'[16] Zavattini's reference to 'a new life' ('*vita nuova*') suggests that he remembered the book well enough to drop a hint to the author who had used the conversion analogy several times.[17] The hint references the famous *Incipit* of the *La Vita Nuova* ('The New Life'), written by medieval poet Dante Alighieri, which charted the poet's conversion from self-centred love to disinterested love.[18] A triple conversion then: Dante's, Papini's, Zavattini's. For Zavattini it marked a new direction and sense of purpose. No more gambling, no more aimlessness; instead, the realization of what writing can express, of the ways in which it can convey a distinctly personal voice, addressed at oneself, but also at an audience of readers.

But what was it about this book which could make such a lasting impression on him? Doubtless, the country boy from Luzzara would have appreciated statements such as: 'The words I choose and prefer, my words, have to be as hard as granite, dry as stones, sparse.'[19] From the very beginning of his career as a writer, in his humorous stories, Zavattini adopted a personal tone and linguistic register, apparently informal, seemingly spontaneous. This is exactly what *Finished Man* had to offer. There was no other contemporary literary model for such a literary style. Papini's book charts a work in progress, taking on the form of an ongoing confession, leading to a conversion, but not a religious one.[20] *Finished Man* showed Zavattini how anti-rhetorical writing could be, when it adopted the tone of a seemingly intimate, touching diary; comprising a candid account of how an autodidact can fall in love with learning – a diary of reflections and reminiscences, for example, how, as a child, Giuseppe Garibaldi, the hero of the fledgling Italian state, and the writers, Alfieri and Plutarch, became Papini's imaginary friends and rescued him from loneliness.[21]

In Papini, he found someone who could sound openly confessional: 'I feel the need to confess out loud';[22] 'I'm no longer a victim.'[23] *Finished Man* carries the urgency of self-expression in a reflection and justification of a person's life choices. Papini refers to 'the diary of my dreams'.[24] He can sound candid: 'I'm ignorant.'[25] He also knew how to sound prophetic: 'In a world in which everyone only thinks about eating and making a living, about enjoying themselves and being in control, there needs to be someone, sometimes, who looks at the world anew, who makes us see the extraordinary in ordinary things, mystery in banality, beauty in waste.'[26] Papini is never mentioned by Zavattini in this regard, but it is undeniable that Zavattini later adopted and expanded upon the diary-form he discovered by chance, at the age of seventeen, in Papini.

1.3 Parma: Zavattini, writer and journalist

Two years later, in June 1921, Zavattini passed his school-leaving final exams and returned to his hometown, Luzzara. He then enrolled in the faculty of law at Parma University. It was this move to Parma that brought him into direct contact with budding and established writers. Not that it was an equal partnership, for he had everything to learn from his new acquaintances. This is something he later acknowledged. As far as he was concerned, the population of Parma comprised only eight people he felt very close to, all of them writers.

Ugo Betti was one of them. He'd fought in the Great War and was practising as a judge when Zavattini met him. But he was also writing poetry – the book *Il re Pensieroso* (1926) – and writing for the theatre. His first play was *La padrona* (1926). What he and Zavattini had in common was a respect for ordinary people. Unlike Zavattini, however, rather than pitting fantasy against reality, in startling and unprecedented ways, Betti faced the reader with ethical dilemmas. What they shared is apparent from Betti's Introduction to *La padrona*:[27]

> At night, as I listen to the silence which little by little stills the humble dwellings all around me, my heart fills with sadness. I know only too well what a painful burden the day has been for my neighbours; I look at the books that helped while away so many lonely hours. But now I come to understand that these writers sought only to shine a light on their intellect and subtlety, while everything else was but a pretext.[28]

Zavattini and his friends would often go to Betti's home in Parma to listen to him reading his plays and engage in endless discussion about his idea of the theatre; for example, in *La padrona*, the dramatic tension caused by a situation in which a young woman is dying from cancer, after her mother's death, while her father is busy remarrying a beautiful, sensuous woman. Pietrino Bianchi introduced Zavattini and his friends to Gino Saviotti, his schoolteacher at the Liceo Romagnosi, where Saviotti taught Italian literature and Latin.[29] They convinced Saviotti to go to the cinema for the first time. They watched a French adaptation of a novel by Émile Zola, and went again and again, to watch Chaplin's comedies and films starring Greta Garbo. It was Saviotti who gave Zavattini access to his own contacts of established writers and to a prestigious literary review, for Saviotti was also the opinion columnist for *La Fiera Letteraria*. Saviotti also edited the Parma review *Pagine critiche* and was the author of two books on art and aesthetics: *L'arte e la critica* (1924) and *Il pensiero estetico ed il gusto* (1925). Betti and Saviotti were influential members of their literary circle and Zavattini's first mentors and informal teachers. Zavattini later wrote to Saviotti, thanking him for the real education he had received in the literary discussions at his home: 'to G. S. in whose home I attended university.'[30] 'In those days, my ignorance was equal to my enthusiasm', Zavattini admitted to Saviotti much later.[31]

But the reason why Zavattini was in Parma was to attend law school. Then, in June 1922, he secured a position as an instructor at the Maria Luigia, a boarding school where he supervised homework and gave private lessons. That year, particularly the summer months, represented a critical moment in Italian politics. During the first six days of August, hundreds of Fascist Black Shirts descended on Parma. In a concerted action, their comrades were taking over local government all over the country, meeting little or no resistance. This was the only episode of fierce armed opposition against the Fascist coup taking place all over Italy. Italo Balbo and his Fascist militants arrived by train to destroy the new working-class union and quash the general strike, called for 1 August to protest and oppose Fascist nationwide aggressions. Barricades were put up on 3 August, when the town braced itself against the Black Shirts.

While all this was happening, on 4 August, Zavattini was moving house from the outskirts of San Pancrazio to Via Mazzini, near the Ponte di Mezzo, the bridge that spans the new Parma centre and the old Parma district, known as Oltretorrente.[32] There is no mention of this dramatic episode in Zavattini's reminiscences, spread across letters and articles, yet it was happening on his doorstep. His side of the town was sealed off from the bridge by the Fascists who tried repeatedly, but unsuccessfully, to break through to the working-class Oltretorrente, on the other side of the river. The shops closed down and the city was deserted. They attacked again and again, but met such a strong resistance by the population, though vastly outnumbered, that by 5 August the locals were regaining control of their town. The following day, the *squadristi* conceded defeat and left the city in drips and drabs, while lorries drove through the two sides of the city, Parma Vecchia and Parma Nuova, decorated with fluttering red flags and Italian tricolours.[33]

Long before and after this event, the working-class quarter of Oltretorrente had been, and continued to be, a regular meeting place for anarchists and socialists. This is where Zavattini's third mentor, Sebastiano Timpanaro Senior, held court. Timpanaro was an anti-Fascist intellectual, a physicist and a philologist. At the time, Timpanaro was already editing the first critical edition of Galileo Galilei's works, while teaching physics at Parma University. Timpanaro was also a contributor to *La Fiera Letteraria, Letteratura, Pan,* and the very prestigious Modernist *Solaria.*

Among Zavattini's students at the Maria Luigia boarding school were Attilio Bertolucci and Pietrino Bianchi, both far more interested in writing than Zavattini at the time, and both very knowledgeable about contemporary Italian literature. They were only fourteen, but they had already read Virginia Woolf, Marcel Proust and stories by James Joyce. Bertolucci had also read Eugenio Montale's first collection of poetry, *Ossi di Seppia* (1925), published by Piero Gobetti, and still hot off the press.[34] And yet it was a fair exchange: while they had read far more than he had, he possessed the confidence to make new contacts and knew how to make use of them; he was a natural. When Zavattini read Attilio Bertolucci's early poems, he realized that this boy was a poet, endowed with great talent, and gave him frequent feedback, encouraging him to publish the poems in a range of literary magazines and, eventually, as a collection in book form, entitled *Sirio* (named after a soap brand of the time), published by their mutual friend Alessandro Minardi.

Sebastiano Timpanaro, the founder of *L'Arduo,* a literary review which attracted contributions by Piero Gobetti, among others, was the lynchpin between Zavattini's Parma circle and Gobetti's open opposition to Fascism.[35] And Timpanaro is most likely the influence that led Zavattini to take out a subscription to Gobetti's *La Rivoluzione liberale* when it was first published.[36] Nothing more is known about Zavattini's political allegiance in these years. But it is a fact that Gobetti and Antonio Gramsci were among the very few who understood the dynamics of contemporary Italian politics and were able to communicate its complexities in a cogent and accessible way. Gobetti inspired his readers to take action and renew Italy's political and cultural life.[37] In his earlier *Energie Nove* ('New Energies'), Gobetti had spelled out the problems Italy faced immediately after the Great War.[38] That first issue of *La Rivoluzione liberale* Zavattini purchased contained a manifesto tackling the Italian crisis and its root causes: first, the fact that Italian political liberalism and its leader, Giolitti, were not up to the task; second, that there was a lack of freedom; third, that Italian citizens lacked a social consciousness and, finally, the need for a competent technological class, to run the country effectively.[39] Gobetti's political project put up a stiff intellectual resistance to the rising Fascist dictatorship. When harassment, house searches, imprisonment and repeated confiscations of *La Rivoluzione liberale* made it virtually impossible to distribute his review, Gobetti had to close it down. But he then founded *Il Baretti*, in December 1924.[40] *Il Baretti* resisted the aesthetics of *La Ronda* review, which tended to reduce literary criticism to a discussion of stylistic choices. Gobetti was most likely another source of mentorship for Zavattini in these years. Gobetti was a very supportive editor towards new writing, poetry or prose, and literary criticism. *Il Baretti* attracted the philosopher Benedetto Croce, poets such as Umberto Saba and Eugenio Montale, and the critics Sergio Solmi and Natalino Sapegno. It also published monographic studies, such as one on Proust by Giacomo De Benedetti.[41]

In the meantime, the regime was also being criticized from a different quarter: the Left-wing satirical paper *Il Becco Giallo*, a favourite of Zavattini's and his friends. Zavattini later recalled how the Fascist squads prowling around Parma assaulted anyone they encountered reading *Il Becco Giallo*.[42] After confiscations and harassment, *Il Becco Giallo* was also forced to close down in 1926.

Zavattini, Bianchi and Bertolucci would rush to Parma railway station to be the first to read Telesio Interlandi's lead article in *Il Tevere*, the review Interlandi edited, and to look out for the latest contributions by the hermetic poet Giuseppe Ungaretti or the prose writer Ercole Patti. Once, the three of them went to Milan, and, in Piazza San Carlo, stood for ages in front of the red neon sign of *La Fiera Letteraria*, a literary review they admired and whose editor, Enrico Falqui, would soon begin to publish scores of Zavattini's book reviews.[43]

In 1926, the headmaster at Maria Luigia boarding school encouraged Zavattini to contribute an article to the anti-Fascist provincial daily paper, *La Gazzetta di Parma*. On 29 April, after sitting an exam in Civil Law Zavattini dropped out from his law degree course, despite the fact that his academic record shows that he had passed most of the examinations required to complete a degree. The degree was well within reach, but he had come to realize that a legal career was not for him.[44] On 19 August 1926, he filed his first article.[45] In the meantime, Gobetti had escaped to Paris, but after the last of several severe beatings, he died of his injuries.

Zavattini's career as a journalist and writer took off when Priamo Brunazzi, the editor-in-chief of *La Gazzetta di Parma*, appointed him the editor of the daily paper's cultural page three. Zavattini immediately brought in his former students and friends Bianchi, Bertolucci and Minardi. His first editorial task was to convince Brunazzi that their idea of turning the cultural page into a virtual literary circle was worthwhile. He got his way.[46]

In addition to commissioning articles and developing a Modernist approach to the cultural page, Zavattini invented and wrote a range of new features, including one entitled 'Dite la vostra' ('Express your Opinion') begun in October 1927, as well as other contributions on other pages.[47] This is where the first signs of Papini's unusual approach to writing, a mixture of philosophical musings and personal confessions, appear, since Zavattini devised a very personal literary or better, anti-literary, style of writing, in which the Italian mainstream style of narrative writing was rejected outright, in favour of compression. He condensed his content into a few lines, telling a story or an anecdote, and conveyed dialogue by a quip or two, eschewing the kind of high drama he heard Ugo Betti declaim within their literary circle, which was more in tune with the period.

The recently published anthology of Zavattini's early writing shows how, by comparison with Achille Campanile, a leading comic writer of the day, Zavattini's eye is constantly on the lookout for genuine news stories, comments in the media, not excluding the radio, or taken from press agency reports, which, however insignificant they might have seemed to others, Zavattini considered symptomatic of 1920s modernity and its shortcomings. His approach subverted the stories with a touch of the absurd, creating distance and conveying more than a merely amused and amusing gaze on contemporary Italy, owing something to the *Becco Giallo* brand of Italian popular humour. Zavattini also used humour as a weapon for an ethical and social critique which afforded him the freedom to single out, not only cinema myths and the star system but also the seedy side of journalism, censorship, hypocrisy in marriage, mass tourism, sex, changes of gender and even animal rights, and succeed where *Il Becco Giallo* had failed. For, somehow, he managed to avoid incurring the restrictions of Fascist censorship.[48]

On 14 March 1927, Attilio Bertolucci and Pietro Bianchi persuaded him to watch Charlie Chaplin's *Goldrush*. This was when Zavattini came to the realization of what else cinema could be, besides pure entertainment.[49] The very next day, he published an admiring review in *La Gazzetta di Parma*, pointing out how 'Chaplin's well-known mask had revealed profound human qualities'.[50]

1.4 Zavattini's 'Holliwood' in *La Gazzetta di Parma*

It was in these Parma years that the cinema became a focus for his journalism. He published 'Holliwood', a nightmarish representation of an industrial machine which grabs reality to then recycle it into a simulacrum.[51] But is it a simulacrum? The word, as Jean Baudrillard has shown, denotes something that appears to be real, to the point of resembling a real object, but is, in fact, unreal.[52] Zavattini's Hollywood is presented as an unreality, in relation to the everyday world, but one which is, paradoxically, a reality in itself. In that first standalone story, published in 1928, the narrator is presented as an objective eyewitness, a journalist, who has travelled to 'Holliwood' to file his story. Try as he might, time and again, he fails to reach the hotel where he is staying. At each attempt, he barges into a studio set.[53] The entire space is taken up by the cinematic stage. Two policemen forbid him to cross the set, in order to get to his hotel, because *The Deserted City* is being filmed.

'Holliwood' is one large, deserted set, with the exception of the cameraman shooting *The Deserted City*. Two hours later, he is allowed to leave, only to bump into extras wearing animal skins on the set of *The Barbarians' Escape*. The narrator and journalist is now part of the crowd and also being filmed, which prompts the screenwriter to add an intertitle saying 'precursor' (literally, someone running ahead of everyone else). When he finally makes it to the hotel, he discovers that the forecourt is the scene of another film, *A Revolution*. He is told he mustn't cross the square. So, he persuades two stretcher bearers to carry him across, with the agreement of the director who adds an intertitle: 'Dead man.' The stretcher bearers slip and fall, but the journalist convinces the director to change the intertitle to: 'Dead?' And when he gets up, another intertitle answers the question: 'No!' He finally reaches the hotel lobby, only to be told that they're shooting *Lonely Women*. Can he please get out of the shot? His presence makes them change the title to: *Almost Lonely Women*. He thinks he's going mad. He runs back to the railway station, barely in time to catch the train. They're shooting another film on location: *The Emigrant Arrives*. It's not too much of a problem to add the rubric: *Painful Departure*.

This early stab at writing rehearses humour and parody, to bring out the underlying nature of the dream factory, couched in the terse language of a news report, pretending to give his readers an authentic account. The reality of experience blurs into the unreality of the studio set. Zavattini later remarked in a letter to Bertolucci: 'I can see more and more clearly what a formidable publicity machine Hollywood is and how nobody can avoid the pervasive attractions of advertising.'[54]

But in these early years, Zavattini also appreciated the potential of cinema as non-fiction. This is clear from one of his stories, inspired by Buster Keaton's film *The Cameraman* (1928), entitled 'Rodenstack and Co.' It features a reporter endowed with such extraordinary powers that he is able to capture amazing moments of everyday life, at the very instant they are happening, and turn real events into amazing stories, in a blurring of non-fiction and fiction.[55]

This was also the thrust of Russian filmmaker Dziga Vertov's *Man with a Movie Camera* (1929). But in Zavattini's literary version, the camera obeys its master. He tells the reader that instead of putting good middle-class Italian families in the frame, the camera will focus on bootleggers, Wall Street stock market agents – significantly, Zavattini published his story the year after the 1929 Wall Street Crash – and also, he adds, on a Pirandello-style enquiry into ourselves, as well as on Hollywood studios screen tests. Zavattini imagines an early morning take of the metropolis, shot from the dizzying top of a building. In this story, the reader becomes a character in what Zavattini himself describes as a 'documentary' (*un documentario*). He tells the reader: 'you're in the story, and you don't even know it.' Somehow, through a subterfuge, even a trial behind closed doors ends up in Rodenstack's frame. Using high angle or low angle shots, Zavattini shares his appreciation of what the modern photographer can do. His imagined filmmaker films what goes on in the street, where he can witness 'the scene of the crime' (*il luogo del delitto*). Somehow, he has an instinct for news events. He may even be on the spot before the event takes place. He might even influence a situation, just when it is unfolding, using photography to show the two sides of an argument, and how ugly the opponents' behaviour is, there and then.

This is when, in the late 1920s, Zavattini's idea of a filmmaker finding the extraordinary in the ordinary, filming in the street, focussing on real events, and the concept of cinema as a means of self-reflection for the viewer, who is considered a participant, first crops up in his early fiction.

1.5 From Parma to Florence

On 30 June 1928, *La Gazzetta di Parma* was to cease publication. This happened after the daily was taken over by a pro-Fascist newspaper, the *Corriere Emiliano*. That evening, Minardi, Zavattini and Bianchi leaned over the balcony of Minardi's home after dinner, awaiting the first copies of the final edition, and discussed their future, well into the night.[56]

Not long after dropping out of university, Zavattini received a letter instructing him to report to *La Fortezza* army barracks in Florence. He was no longer in a position to defer his military service. In the interim, having lost his job at the newspaper, he went home to Luzzara, to serve the tables in the family *trattoria*. In a letter to Ugo Betti, he reflected: 'Farewell Parma. The truth is that our group was a really good one.'[57]

The whole Parma group disbanded: apart from Zavattini going to Florence, Saviotti was transferred to a school in Genoa, Timpanaro was also transferred to Florence and judge Betti was transferred to a new job in Rome.[58] Although Parma was a provincial town, in those years it was a hub of cultural debate. The Parma years provided Zavattini with a crucial formative experience in his cultural education; Parma was where he first developed his anti-Fascist views; Parma was where he became a journalist; and Parma was where the late flowering of Futurist ideas influenced his own very particular brand of absurdist, nonsensical humour, closer to Italian Futurism than to any kind of French Surrealism.[59]

Florence was the living museum of Renaissance art treasures, churches, buildings, paintings and statues. However, not once during his ten months of military service in a sapper regiment was Zavattini tempted to visit Michelangelo's *David* at the Uffizi Gallery or any of the other major artistic Florentine artistic attractions. But Florence was no less lively a centre of contemporary intellectual life than Parma. It was also where Papini's Futurist *Lacerba* had been published. But, more importantly, it was where some of the best writers of the day lived and worked. These anti-Fascists had already formed a Gobetti-influenced cultural circle, before Zavattini's arrival.

Zavattini spent most of his time in the army barracks where he was assigned to administrative duties.[60] However, this enabled him to read over 100 books and review them during office hours. When he was found out, his punishment was to be appointed the regiment's courier.[61] Falqui guaranteed a steady flow of novels to be reviewed, most of them of a very low standard, which Zavattini reviewed and immediately sold off for a couple of liras each to Sergeant Gervasoni.[62] Most of his book reviews were written and published in these years spent in Parma and Florence. He later disowned them, but at the time, they were accepted for publication in *La Fiera Letteraria*, a highly esteemed literary magazine. Book reviewing provided a practical and economical focus for developing his skills as a critic of sorts, who had strong misgivings about most contemporary output.

Yet, some of his book reviews are as short as they are sharp-witted. Enter Zavattini the hatchet man. One review is only three sentences long: 'Justice means justice. Which triumphs. All the rest is clear and moving.' Another, only two: 'Fragments of a gentle soul. But don't persist.' He criticizes a writer who relies too heavily on unusual typography and remarks that the author of a Preface has been unkind to the novelist whose book he is prefacing, for offering him encouragement and recommending his book. Another one contains this observation: 'verse and prose which keeps chugging along like those depressing trains our Gieppi takes;[63] their hyperbolic chimneys making a lot of noise and too little progress.' Elsewhere, he makes throwaway observations: 'Compared to this writer, Salgari was a genius, or Verne.'

Sometimes only wit can convey his exasperation in, for example, reviewing a booklet by an author 'who took seven years to write a thirteen-page work of art in 13-point type. Diderot could do it, but not the author of *Vagabondi*.'[64] Most, but not all, of his book reviews are damning. The hatchet man knew when to cast aside his weapon. He was also the first, or, perhaps, one of the first, to review and acclaim Alberto Moravia's first novel, which he praised for the important contribution it was.[65] As Zavattini later admitted, his Parma friends helped him to include some literary references, but he himself was convinced of the novel's worth. Zavattini liked Moravia's novel and, as he later put it quite candidly: 'to tell the truth, all I could say about a book was: I like it or I don't.' But, to his regret, swayed by other writers, he toned down his review.[66] Zavattini sent Falqui his review of Moravia's novel, stating: 'I really would like to be the one to review *The Indifferent*', adding that he was willing to re-write it entirely, if the editor felt it was required. But by then, his review had been accepted.[67]

Florence's major attraction for the young Zavattini was 'the poet Eugenio Montale and the other members of the literary journal *Solaria*, whose circle met in the Caffé Giubbe Rosse'.[68] Montale's poetry reviews appeared on the same page of *La Fiera Letteraria* as Zavattini's book reviews, and his first collection of poems, *Ossi di Seppia*, had earned him instant recognition.[69] When Zavattini first went to meet the *Solariani*, he met Montale in person, in the company of Rafaello Franchi. They discussed Alberto Moravia's work, whom they also admired and whose novel they were in the middle of reading. Zavattini mentioned Bertolucci's first collection of poems, *Sirio*, which Franchi reviewed in *Solaria* in December.[70] He told Alessandro Minardi, one of his Parma friends: 'I really enjoy myself in their company. They're very unpretentious and friendly.

We shall see.'[71] This is how Elio Vittorini, one of the regulars, described the bar at the time:

> Why it is that this small bourgeois coffee house has become so indispensable to the lives of writers and artists based in Florence, I have no idea. It's uncomfortable, it's dark, with long corridors that remind you of waiting rooms in provincial railway stations; it's freezing cold and funereal in winter, populated by people who spit under the table, brandishing local newspapers. Once it was a good haunt, I've heard. Once, that is, in the days of [Giovanni] Papini and [Ardengo] Soffici.[72]

After seven in the evening, the stuffy, crowded, bar of the Giubbe Rosse regularly attracted no fewer than twenty writers and painters, Italians and foreigners alike. Among the regulars were Alessandro Bonsanti, one of *Solaria*'s editors, and Vittorini, who said Italo Svevo's melancholic smile still lingered in some of the bar's mirrors. From time to time, the bar's fame also attracted other writers: Umberto Saba and Sergio Solmi among the poets, the novelist Guido Piovene, seeking support from fellow writers, and Valéry Larbaud. These were 'people who graced them with an hour of their humanity', as Vittorini put it. The Caffè Giubbe Rosse was the best refuge in Florence for contemporary writers, including Alberto Moravia, Aldo Palazzeschi, the academic Mario Praz, Gianna Manzini, the novelist whose work Zavattini admired, even the flamboyant editor of *La Fiera Letteraria*, Enrico Falqui, who would come down from Milan dressed in startling blue, pink or orange suits. Vittorini had the impression that the whole of Italy made a beeline for the Giubbe Rosse.[73]

As for *Solaria*, it was the best and the most significant literary review of the time. It was also the only one to have followed the example of Piero Gobetti's *La Rivoluzione liberale* and *Il Baretti*. Indeed, it was in the pages of *Solaria* that many of Gobetti's distinguished former contributors had gathered. *Solaria* defied Fascism by adopting the same editorial line and critique of literary formalism, a critique which had characterized Gobetti's reviews and which contributed to form Zavattini's. Far from being provincial, *Solaria* adopted Gobetti's international Modernist scope, in its appreciation of the poetry of T. S. Eliot and Rainer Maria Rilke, its championing of Marcel Proust, André Gide, James Joyce, D. H. Lawrence and Ernest Hemingway.[74] As for Italian novelists, it promoted the work of Italo Svevo, little known at the time, but of central importance within twentieth-century Italian literature.[75] Years later, Elio Vittorini summed up the literary group:

> And so it was that I became a member of *Solaria*. The word *Solariano* meant, in the literary circles of the day, anti-Fascist, Europeanist, universalist, anti-traditionalist. Giovanni Papini insulted us from one end of the spectrum and [Roberto] Farinacci from the other.[76]

To put it differently, *Solaria* attracted the disapproval of both Fascists and Catholics. For, in the meantime, Papini had converted to Catholicism.

When Zavattini first met the *Solariani*:

> They noticed me and my green, uncomfortable, army bicycle come into
> the Giubbe Rosse. The very first time was in the spring of 1929 at Piazza
> Emanuele, where the famous coffee bar was situated. They were sitting
> round an iron table having a friendly discussion. The first words I heard
> were about a short story by [Alberto] Carrocci (*Narciso*, I think).
>   – Now it is time for him to choose, Right or Left.
>   Then Carrocci turned up. Nervous, disgruntled, but civilized. They were
> also, talking about someone's upcoming journey to Rome, to see [Emilio]
> Cecchi. Then they mentioned names I had never heard of: Hölderlin,
> Jouandaux ...[77]

He wrote to his friend Bertolucci that 'one evening in the Giubbe Rosse is equal
to a month's worth of reading'.[78]

> In among the tables of the coffee bar, all I can see are foreign books being
> exchanged, some in Italian translation, others not. What names! We'll talk
> about it later. I listen patiently, but, you see, among men of letters, you're
> *always* a bore when you talk, never when you listen.[79]

By October 1929, he had been welcomed into the circle, which admired
those witty four-line book reviews of his, published in *La Fiera Letteraria*.
Eventually, he was able to overcome his stuttering and shyness and read out a
few of his published short stories, already acclaimed by critics. In December,
Montale told him: 'When you first came, you were so very humble. But look
at you now. You're streets ahead of all of us. You're a Trojan Horse of a
kind' and Rafaello Franchi said: 'I'm getting envious: for the past week, all
we ever talk about is Zavattini.'[80] Once Montale invited Zavattini to dinner
at *Da Aglietti*, where he tasted caviar and Chianti for the first time.[81] On
16 December 1929, Zavattini wrote to a friend that 'Montale says that many
of my stories are prose poems, either in terms of form or of expressing a frame
of mind'.[82] The poet was right.

Solaria invited Zavattini to publish three of his brief short stories or *raccontini*,
which were being regularly published in a range of Italian magazines. His stories
duly appeared in the December edition of 1929, *Avventura*, *Nome* and *Se potessi*
('Adventure', 'Name', 'If I could'). 'Name' builds on vigorously stating one's
name, only to deny it in the next breath. His humour produces an afterthought,
inviting the reader to reflect on the power of persuasive, theatrical rhetoric, a
gentle satire of Fascism, in all probability. 'Adventure' is the tale of a man who
succumbs to the allure of a siren, but then resorts to deception, by resorting to
a children's game, Blind Man's Bluff, to return to the real world, with barely
a suggestion of allegory, a rejection, be it of fantasy, of art for art's sake, or of
literary escapism. The *Solaria* circle also encouraged him to publish a collection
of them in *Solaria* itself, in book form, but he decided against it.[83] Many of
Zavattini's stories debunk journalism and the workings of reportage, adopting

an evidence-based style, using whimsical reflection to subvert it. Sometimes, his humour touches a deeper chord which outlives the duration of a joke.

Zavattini's absurdist, colloquial, but terse and heavily compressed writing is certainly at odds with the kind of fragmentary and precious art prose that *La Ronda* had supported. Neither did it follow *Solaria*'s 'Dostoyevsky + durational narrative style + poetic aura', announced as an ideal in the first issue of the literary review in 1926. But it is absolutely Modernist, and at odds with the prevailing *Ronda* art prose which it sometimes evokes, only to then deride it. Later, when Zavattini collected and edited his stories to form a book, *Parliamo tanto di me* (1931) ('Let's Talk about Me'), three *Solaria* regular contributors reviewed it very favourably: Elio Vittorini, who pointed out that 'the book's humour emerges in short stoppages, ever so slight laughter, as if such things were almost ridiculous, but only for the brief moment in which their absurdity is made apparent'.[84] Sebastiano Timpanaro Senior (welcomed into the *Solaria* circle in October 1929, after his move from Parma to Florence) also noted the rhythm and the poetry in the prose, its subtle humour and its underlying melancholy. Timpanaro too rejected out of hand any comparison between Achille Campanile and Zavattini, in agreement with Vittorini's reading, and Rafaello Franchi's. Zavattini was unique, and not under the influence of Campanile's humour.[85]

Zavattini's time in Florence came to an abrupt end, when his father's ailing health suddenly took a turn for the worse. Being the sole provider for his extended family at the time, he was exonerated from completing his military service. He went home to Luzzara, where he spent months 'wiping tables with his cloth, uncorking bottles of Lambrusco, and balancing four plates in one hand'.[86] While he was back home, he made a selection of his best *raccontini*, with a view to bringing them out in book form, but not for *Solaria*. Initially, the title was to be *Viaggio nell'Aldilà* (*Journey to the Afterlife*), a clear indication of the proposed structure, based on Dante's *Divine Comedy*, to locate his stories in abstract time and space.

Editorial director and screenwriter in Milan

2.1 Milan, the Modernist publishing Mecca

Zavattini decided to look for work in Milan, already the epicentre of an ever-expanding Italian book and magazine publishing industry in the so-called industrial triangle. He arrived one afternoon, on 31 March 1930.[1] He had visited Milan during his Parma years, encouraged by one of his mentors, Gino Saviotti, and was already contributing to *Secolo XX*, a weekly magazine published by Rizzoli and edited by Filippo Piazzi, the editorial director, who introduced him to Enrico Cavacchioli, who edited *Il Secolo Illustrato* and *Novella*, which had already published some of Zavattini's stories.

Although Zavattini's reputation as a writer preceded him, when he went for a job as an editor at Rizzoli, Cavacchioli submitted him to a writing test on the spot: a story for *Novella*. He rose to the challenge and was offered a permanent job for a generous 2,000 liras a month. However, a telegram informed him that his father wouldn't last very long, so he had to leave town:

> [He] lay in bed with a bloated stomach, caused by all the Fernet Brancas and Bitter Camparis. Just before he died, I read him two or three stories from the book, and he'd laughed.[2] It happened one afternoon in June 1930.
>
> People came and went, and the moon went back to its place behind the shutters. The room was at peace again and despite the smell of Lysoform, I could go back to my literary reviews. No event was so important as to put me off completely from writing reviews, which had to get to Rome on time. They were never late on my account, never, in three years.[3]

Only a few hours earlier, his father had got out of bed clutching a gold chain, in a confused attempt to placate the creditors. The Zavattini family inherited a paltry fifty liras in cash and a mountain of debts. So they were forced to close down the tavern, despite the landlady's protests, and La Gabellina, their small hotel in the Appennine Mountains, as well as their Luzzara bakery and bar.[4] They were left with nothing. Even the furniture was taken away in part payment for their bankruptcy. Meantime, the locals would walk past his window and see him scribbling away and gossip that he'd hidden away a lump sum, which led them to the conclusion that the Zavattini family's bankruptcy had to be pure nonsense.[5]

As luck would have it, Zavattini's family was taken in by relatives, who were also bakers and Cesare, Olga and their two sons went to Milan, thanks to a loan from one of his friends.[6] On his return to Milan, he discovered that Cavacchioli had been fired, and that the prospect of a job had vanished into thin air. He told the Rizzoli editors he was willing to accept any job. The best they could do was to offer him a proofreading post for 600 liras a month for one of their titles, *Il Secolo Illustrato*. It represented half the living wage. He started on 15 October 1930, proofreading the galleys of a novel by a writer called Brocchi.[7]

However, he supplemented his day job with a constant flow of articles written after work, for *Secolo XX*, *Novella*, *Il Secolo Illustrato*, *Commedia* and *Piccola*. In those days, there were times when he and his family were entirely dependent on one of his articles getting into print.[8] However, as he put it:

> The smell of printing ink given off by the roto-gravure press at Rizzoli's printworks in Piazza Carlo Erba, the huge rolls of paper, the bulk of the press, very attentive printers, all these impressions, gave him the feeling that he'd landed on his feet and that he'd never do without again.[9]

Zavattini described his new life in Milan to the editor of *L'Italia Letteraria*, Enrico Falqui:

> My life? Going around from time to time to Savini, to Bagutta, having a chat with whoever drops into the publishers. Milan is a city, but you have to pretend to be less intelligent than you really are. I often think about the peace and quiet of Florence with nostalgia. I get strange postcards from there covered in signatures.[10]

2.2   Editing the Bompiani Literary Almanacs

To get his collection of stories into print as a book, Zavattini needed a publisher. In those days, Rizzoli, Zavattini's employer, published only magazines, so Zavattini decided to look elsewhere. His friend, Giovanni Titta Rosa introduced him to Count Valentino Bompiani, who had just started publishing the year before, in 1929, specializing in contemporary narrative literature.[11] Bompiani remembered their first meeting:

> When Zavattini came to see me, I didn't know him personally nor had I heard of him. This large, shy person didn't inspire any confidence. He sat down and was silent, methodically pulling at his eyebrows. He pulled out of a pocket or perhaps from a sleeve, a roll of press clippings.[12]

Bompiani's first response was to tell him to edit the clippings and come back to see him when he had. Later, Bompiani came up with the title and helped shape the book into its final form. Zavattini's meeting with this publisher soon led to Zavattini's involvement in editing and producing a Bompiani *Literary Almanac*. In an article published in 1942, Zavattini remembered:

> In those days, my time was split in half: I spent the daytime with Rizzoli, and the evenings with Bompiani. On any given morning, twenty people would come and see me at my desk. I liked that. [...] I was barely in time to finish my dinner, when I had to go to Via Durini and get there five minutes early. Bompiani would be bang on time. The doorway loomed large, but his office was cramped and had a low ceiling. Just two rooms. Bompiani had only recently started his publishing enterprise and we often had to work until two in the morning, because the *Almanac* was really hard work and required such humiliating patience.[13]

The *Almanac* was an annual publication, partly a commercial vehicle to attract publicity, but also, as a contract between Bompiani and Zavattini makes clear, an ambitious Modernist project.[14] Zavattini told Falqui that this 'high print run publication will be another venture of mine'.[15] The print run for the *Almanac* was 10,000 copies.[16] It is the first striking example of Zavattini's activity as a desk editor, but also as a publisher, one equipped with a Modernist vision, which he shared with Bompiani, who, in those years, was the first to publish Vittorini's novels and other new writing.

The three editions of the *Almanac* published in 1931, 1932 and 1933 were paperback format, and numbered over 500 pages each. Their glossy sections feature highly imaginative layouts, closer to mass-produced magazine publishing, combining text and photographic images in many imaginative ways. Even some of the plain paper pages feature line drawings or headlines, set in among the text. These pages open up the space, breaking out of the grid. The first glossy page, 'The Almanac behind the Scenes' ('Retroscena dell'Almanacco'), presents the reader, not without a gentle touch of editorial irony, with a startling behind-the-scenes montage of snippets taken from letters to the editors, praising or criticizing the previous *Almanac*.

The *Bompiani Almanac* for 1932, edited entirely by Zavattini, brought European and American experimental and fashion photography to Milan, publishing portraits by Edward Steichen, by the Dadaist Man Ray, who was also a fashion photographer working for the American *Vogue*, and Surrealist portraits by Maurice Tabard, a French Surrealist photographer, and by freelance fashion photographer and artist, George Hoiningen-Huene, based in Paris, originally published by Condé Nast magazine publishers. Experimental photographic portraits in double exposure appeared in this first *Almanac*.[17]

Zavattini and Bompiani also appropriated American visual culture, including photographs by the Modernist Edward Steichen, and originally published by Condé Nast magazine publishers, giving them new captions alongside the credits, and relating the images to characters in contemporary Italian literature. What is striking about some of these photographs is that they are experimental and in a few cases Surrealist, for example, featuring eyes and faces inside cracked open eggs.

In the following *Bompiani Almanac*, the glossy double-page spreads reveal a tighter structure. Montage and large headlines appear in capitals under the strapline: 'Atmosphere 1933' ('Atmosfere 1933'). Each has a subtitle, for example, 'They've Elected Roosevelt' or 'Sex Appeal', with a montage by Bruno Munari, a Modernist illustrator and designer, and line drawings by the sculptor Marino Marini. The glossy photography reveals more Surrealist scenes: mannequins and dolls, experimental shots, a child shot from below looking like a frog and on the same page as an illustration of a frog in the bottom right-hand corner. They adopted Modernist typography, making shapes out of type. Yet Zavattini was unhappy with the results, as he told Falqui:

> At least I can see clearly enough to whisper in your ear: 'it's ugly. Just like last year's, and the one from the year before. Or, if it's less ugly, that doesn't mean it isn't ugly all the same.'[18]

Zavattini told Bompiani that he was prepared to edit the next *Bompiani Almanac* only on condition that all the editorial decisions would be his and his alone, so that the end product would stand up to European scrutiny.[19] He then increased the format, from paperback to magazine size, and changed the text-to-image ratio. The new *Almanac* would be two-thirds the photographic image. Apart from the review of the new writing of the previous year, it would be exclusively news-based and would include commissioned photographs of writers photographed in the street and artists in their studios.[20] This was Modernist design.

2.3 Zavattini at Rizzoli

As for his daytime job at Rizzoli publishers, when his first collection of short stories or *raccontini*, *Parliamo tanto di me*, came out, one of Rizzoli's team asked Angelo Rizzoli if he knew who the author was: 'Did you know that you employ a proof reader who is a successful writer?' Angelo Rizzoli was so impressed that he invited his employee to lunch, but didn't give him a more favourable contract.[21] In addition to his proofreading job, in 1931, the publisher gave him a magazine to edit, *Il Secolo Illustrato*.[22] That year, a typical week also involved writing short stories and articles for *Il Secolo XX*; *Cinema Illustrazione*, *Piccola*, *La Massaia*, *La Gazzetta del Popolo*.[23]

When Giuseppe Marotta, the editor of *Cinema Illustrazione* was fired, as Zavattini found out from Marotta himself, Rizzoli offered Zavattini Marotta's job, but denied him an official promotion to journalist status and the corresponding salary. However, by 1934, Zavattini was carrying out the work of an editor-in-chief on a number of Rizzoli's popular magazines: *Piccola, Lei, Novella, Cinema Illustrazione* and *Il Secolo Illustrato*. While working at Rizzoli, he was given the additional responsibilities of a commissioning editor. In all but name, he was a publisher.

His inner circle of friends and contributors included, among others, poets Salvatore Quasimodo, Leonardo Sinisgalli, and Alfonso Gatto; the architect Edoardo Persico; the designer Bruno Munari; the illustrator Mino Maccari; the sculptor Arturo Martini; the cartoonist Saul Steinberg; the publisher Giovanni Scheiwiller; and the critic Sergio Solmi.[24] These were all people Zavattini had to keep chasing for their editorial contributions. Once he was so desperate to secure a commissioned drawing which Martini had promised him, but which never seemed to materialize, that, faced with an imminent deadline, he tracked down the sculptor at midnight in Via S. Radegonda and persuaded him to do the drawing on the spot.[25] Edoardo Persico was a particularly interesting Modernist who moved to Milan around the same time as Zavattini. Persico was also an anti-Fascist, and had contributed several articles to Gobetti's *Il Baretti*. Like Zavattini, he too was interested in the interdisciplinarity of the arts and literature and their relation with the new industrialized mass society.[26] Together with Giuseppe Pagano, Persico co-edited the architectural magazine *Casabella*, a magnet for what was going on internationally and, according to Victor Pevsner, the most beautiful and the most intelligent architectural journal in the world.[27] In a clear reference to the Fascist and Nazi rhetoric of scale, Pagano asked: 'Can we save ourselves from false traditions and monumental obsessions?'[28] At the time, *Casabella* stood for the kind of Modernist anti-rhetorical style to be found in the Bauhaus-style Bocconi Milan University, in Luigi Figini and Gino Pollini's industrial BBPR Group design (e.g. their radio-gramophone design of 1933) or Franco Albini's radio of 1936.

This was the Milanese Modernist milieu to which Zavattini belonged. The rise of mass publishing and the emergence of industrial design and architecture were all part of a new visual culture to which he contributed.[29] Zavattini saw the potentialities of the new popular media and visual culture, of illustrated journalism, photography and illustration, of cinema and radio, and was daring enough to experiment with them and persuade his publisher to invest in his ideas.

Since his move to Milan, and throughout the period of his employment by Rizzoli, Zavattini also did radio broadcasts at EIAR, the national radio, with a rubric entitled 'Parliamo tanto di me' ('Let's talk a lot about me'), echoing his bestselling first book by the same title, rejecting the bombastic mainstream approach to radio broadcasting, by taking mundane issues seriously and serious issues lightly, as one film historian has put it.[30] Radio, alongside cinema, was a new mass medium at the time. His interventions on radio involved a series of conversations with the listeners, like fireside chats, intimate and direct, something very unusual at the time, because it was at variance with 1930s formality. In one of them, he broke the anonymity and feigned objectivity of the new medium with a theatrical scream, followed by musings about the new medium and his role as a broadcaster, adopting a Pirandellian story-within-the-story approach. His endless conversations in Parma, with playwright Ugo Betti, to discuss Betti's plays and the use of dialogue, stood him in good stead. Zavattini experimented with the new medium to see if the personal touch, ordinary language, and the absurd, could be applied.

2.4 Zavattini's Hollywood at Rizzoli

In Milan, Zavattini soon produced a regular fictional feature, based on what he'd originally published in *La Gazzetta di Parma*. His new version ran from 1930 to 1934, as 'Letters from Hollywood'.

> For years, I wrote 'Letters from Hollywood'. I invented everything from A to Z, weddings of actors who were already married, fires, thefts, divorces, quarrels. It was all made up. I once wrote: *'In the evening, after leaving the studios, the stars get into their powerful automobiles and have a good time in New York'* which is thousands of kilometres from Hollywood.[31]

In his daily job, Zavattini was editing high print run illustrated film magazines, inventing stories and combining fact with fiction to create a fictional version of Hollywood for the Italian public. All Rizzoli's magazines were illustrated with photographs and stills from press packs sent by American agencies to promote the cinema, their cinema, Hollywood.

Writing as Giulio Tani, one of his many pseudonyms, Zavattini mused: 'Hollywood is as immortal as the dreams and the weaknesses of men.'[32] It was the closing sentence to the full-page regular feature 'Recentissime' ('The Most Recent'), which reveals his ambivalence towards Hollywood and 'Ultimissime' ('The Latest'), a compilation of invented gossip. He also edited the Letters page. After Marotta's departure, Zavattini revolutionized the overall look, design and layout of *Cinema Illustrazione*. It featured photographic portraits of the stars from the studios, to help promote their new films and create a false perception, or *glamour*, around actors and actresses, commodifying stage performance into a mythology. The stars also appeared in photo-stories, providing the reader with an illustrated scenario, which was then published in instalments. Zavattini's full-page features counterbalanced the promotion of the Hollywood mythology with a hilarious sendup which slotted in perfectly with the rest of the magazine, thanks to the unifying design style, characterized by the same big splash typography, layout and use of photographs.

In the provincial cultural climate of Fascist Italy, Zavattini drew on the medley of facts, news, and gossip, to be found in what was, essentially, promotional material churned out by the film studios about their upcoming releases and distributions abroad. His features were a cross between what is known in the magazine publishing industry as 'advertorial' matter, and what seemed to be a genuine journalist's reportage from Hollywood, following a 'From Your Own Correspondent' slant, apparently non-fiction, camouflaged in the same editorial structure, to mimic filed reports, supposedly written on the spot.

His allegorical Hollywood equals the unreality of the real Hollywood. It is an invented reportage, a representation of an ideal representation of reality, entirely imagined by Zavattini, and a serious reflection on *mimēsis*. The invented fires, thefts, divorces, interviews with stars, impresarios and middlemen are all grist to the mill of his humour, aimed at demythologizing Hollywood's star system and the so-called dream factory. He crafted his lookalike features, in the idiom and editorial structure of press releases, a combination of facts, quotes and lively descriptions. His fictive reporter is akin to an outsider observing with detachment urban modernity. Zavattini transforms himself, as if he were a Fregoli onstage, into a Baudelairean *flâneur*. For example, in one of the Hollywood stories, Erich Von Stroheim throws money from his hotel window and agrees to give an interview to the imaginary reporter, inviting him to appear in one of his films. The fictive Von Stroheim claims that only the depiction of reality could possibly be the way forward for contemporary cinema, adding that René Clair was doing exactly the opposite.[33]

Thus, Zavattini puts words into the mouth of his Hollywood actors and actresses, whose names coincide with their genuine real-world counterparts. One of the stories packs in references to Greta Garbo, Rodolfo Valentino, Barbara Stanwick, Buster Keaton, Norma Shearer and Richard Dix, all reinvented characters, simulacra of simulacra.[34] These names serve as signifiers of an ideal life in a fantasy world, which his narrative disrupts, by using comedy as a lethal weapon. They no longer signify that world, but a different practice of filmmaking, which has little in common with Hollywood's mainstream film industry. It is only when you read the text that you begin to realize how Zavattini appropriates language, style and structure, and repurposes them for his own ends. It seems no different to the practice of what was later described by Guy Debord and the Situationists as *détournement*, or, more recently, as 'culture jamming'.

In a feature entitled 'Rottami' ('Burned Out'), he describes unemployed men selling apples on the roadside. One of them recognizes Louis Sassoon, Zavattini's imagined reporter, and invites him to write about the real story of Hollywood in exchange for an apple:

> Extras work like manual labourers. They go in at 7am, change into their workers' togs, and are on standby until 5pm. They issue instructions with a whistle. Our bosses are more stupid than a Prussian corporal. They say: 'Shout! Fight! Run away! Destroy everything!' And we go ahead and do it.[35]

He answers the reporter's question:

> What do you specialize in? Unfortunately, I'm neither blind, nor a hunchback, nor a midget, nor deformed nor disfigured. I don't even have the looks to be

a janitor or a waiter: I'm the extra to make up a crowd, one of a crowd, in a fake crowd. Is there anything more humiliating?

Another fictional reportage features Wynne Gibson: 'To be an artist, you have to experience life', the Hollywood actress tells the press reporter, thus serving as a mouthpiece for Zavattini's cinema of the real.[36] This story opens with an interview, the bread and butter of many a press release, creating a strong impression of an authentic statement of what the star is quoted as saying. Fictional Wynne complains that actresses begin too young and too soon to have an experienced life and to know how to portray it in their work. She goes on to say that the world of cinema forces them to see life in such a way that has little or no resemblance to the real world. Their screen performances are unique, but flawed, since they portray conventional stereotypes. The reporter narrates how Wynne had decided to live in incognito for ten days, in an attempt to experience what it was like to be an ordinary person. Working as a typist, a shop assistant and in a bar, she witnessed the lives of others, their joys and suffering, quite divorced from the 'standard' screenplays she was used to performing. In another story, Zavattini appropriates King Vidor, whose film *The Crowd* (1928) he admired. Vidor is made to say what Zavattini wants the reader to hear.[37] The director tells the Italian reporter that the reason film directors are unable to make the films they would like to make is the fault of producers and of the public. Vidor is made to say:

> My ideal would be a film that describes a day in the life of a man, from the moment he gets up to when he goes to bed. I'm talking about the man in the street. The length of the film should be the same as the length of my hero's day. And the whole thing should be faithfully reproduced.[38]

In 'A terribly honest article makes Joan change her mind', his imagined reporter cites an imagined source by the name of 'Trottenam'.

> It has taken years and years, lies, sacrifices, noble enterprises – some less noble – and all the passion of a nation and the credulity of all nations, to create a myth: Hollywood, and to let rivers of gold fill the coffers of state and populate dreams all over the world. We have succeeded in idealizing mediocre men like Ramon Navarro, mediocre women like Marlene Dietrich. But on condition we don't see them too close up. Or else their disappointments and shortcomings would really begin to show.[39]

This was how Zavattini put the distinction between fiction and non-fiction to the test and problematized Hollywood, while at the same time generating humour, at the expense of Hollywood's self-glamourized image, and drawing attention to some of the concerns about mainstream cinema he was to voice in his post-war interviews and articles.

2.5 From Rizzoli to Mondadori

In 1934, Zavattini convinced Angelo Rizzoli to diversify from printing exclusively popular illustrated magazines on a rotary press, by breaking out into fiction. The first book Rizzoli published was on Zavattini's recommendation, inaugurating a new series, *I giovani*, edited by Zavattini. It was a novel by Carlo Bernari, entitled *Tre operai* (1934) (*Three Workers*), set in Naples. This, the first Neo-realist novel, offered an alternative to mainstream Italian prose writing. The prose of *Tre operai* is akin to Vittorini's writing. The book is set in Naples, which Bernari frees from its customary fictional stereotype and colourful backdrop. It is about two male workers and a woman who are faced with the problems of survival, after the defeat of the workers' revolts in the early 1920s, unemployment and disillusionment after the victory of Fascism. On its publication, Mussolini wrote to the Italian periodical press, demanding that it should not be reviewed, since it was 'a Marxist book', but he didn't go as far as preventing its publication.[40] Nevertheless, the regime's reaction caused Zavattini to panic and destroy several boxes of correspondence and other potentially incriminating documents he had filed away. From the very beginning, possibly as a result of his legal training, he maintained a private archive. In Florence, he had shared the Left-wing views of the Giubbe Rosse circle, and in Parma his mentors Betti and Saviotti were socialists, as were his extended family in his hometown.

In 1936, Zavattini came up with a new magazine for Rizzoli, *Il Bertoldo*. His plan was to compete with *Marc'Aurelio*, the twice-weekly satirical periodical published in Rome.[41] It was Zavattini who appointed *Il Bertoldo*'s new editor, Giovanni Guareschi, a former student of his at the Maria Luigia boarding school who also became a good friend during his Parma days.[42] However, just when *Il Bertoldo* was approaching its launch, the problems between Zavattini and Angelo Rizzoli came to a head.[43] Apart from being underpaid, and not being recognized as a publisher in all but name, there was also the fact that his boss was unwilling to invest in many of his new ideas. For example, Zavattini recommended the purchase of the ailing *Le Grandi Firme* ('Articles signed by Famous Writers') and turning it into a weekly publication.[44] That publishing proposal consisted in modernizing the magazine, by overhauling its content, increasing its format up to illustrated magazine dimensions, printing in photo-gravure for large print runs, and making its layout more flexible to accommodate a more imaginative use of images, in short, changing not only its look and feel but its content and ensuing identity altogether. But Rizzoli decided not to go ahead with the acquisition. The same happened with another magazine titled *Il Milione*. But the main problem Zavattini faced was his status and a salary which did not reflect the range of his responsibilities as the publisher and editorial director which he'd become in practice, if not in title. Consequently, when Rizzoli refused to give him a new contract, Zavattini joined the journalists' union. No soon as Rizzoli heard about this, he told him to resign from the union immediately, which Zavattini refused to do and then Rizzoli fired him on the spot. Twenty-four hours later, Alberto Mondadori hired him. Zavattini recalled:

> We had large offices in the brand-new building at San Babila, telephones, Dictaphones, megaphones, the magazine titles in neon flashed in the windows. Outside my office, a red light flashed when I was busy.[45]

Proposals from freelancers were either suitable or unsuitable for their publications. What was Zavattini looking for? 'The event. I was looking for events for my clients and nobody could change my mind.'[46] The point to any story had to be rooted in facts, or events; literary style came second. This was journalism as he practised it.

Zavattini's editorial vision comes across in the kind of advice he gave one of the editors of *Marc'Aurelio* – despite the fact that it was in direct competition to Mondadori's periodicals. *Marc'Aurelio* was one of three highly successful 1930s fortnightly illustrated magazines, the other two belonging to Rizzoli (*Il Bertoldo*) and to Disney-Mondadori (*Il Settebello*). MAD would be an example of an equivalent in English, with its mixture of zany prose, regular features and outright jokes, accompanied by any number of cartoons. Founded in 1931, *Marc'Aurelio* was so successful that it came out twice a week and somehow escaped the Fascist regime's censorship which had suppressed its predecessor *Becco Giallo* in 1926. *Marc'Aurelio* inherited many of its writers. A number of filmmakers began their careers at *Marc'Aurelio*, including Federico Fellini, Ettore Scola and Mario Camerini.[47]

The fact that Zavattini was Mondadori's editorial director didn't stop him from being a regular contributor to the competition, namely, *Marc'Aurelio*. For example, he invented a regular piece entitled *Cinquanta righe* (*Fifty lines*), which he kept up throughout his career at Mondadori, from 1936 to 1940.

> You told me: 'I'm giving you the space for fifty lines or so, every Wednesday. You can write what you like'. Then you left, after placing me under lock and key. Fifty lines! There are so many things I can do in this space; this is real happiness: I can feign deep sorrow for the demise of a lizard and fill so many lines with exclamations of suffering. I can write that Homer was a small alabaster swan. O heart, O soul, there is nothing else that I desire more than this small white space, where I can even piss in a beautiful autumn afternoon. [...] Fifty lines! Let me take my friends by the hand and dance around this half column my elders have put at my disposal. Let me contemplate it like the peasant his field. Three thousand lines a year, my God! What a dream, what sweet folly.[48]

Zavattini's valuable professional advice to *Marc'Aurelio* suggests that he cared a great deal about their future and success. In 1937, he suggested that the editors commission high-profile writers, offering to help *Marc'Aurelio*, by sharing his own contacts with the editorial team. He also suggested that they introduce interviews, which they then did. He later told them that the way they had followed his advice wasn't going to help keep up their circulation figures. Their approach to interviews was wrong: they should be interviewing the man in the street, feeling the pulse of everyday life. Now that would make the magazine more cutting edge.[49]

He subsequently gave them technical advice. He had no doubt that Vito De Bellis could improve the magazine's quality. They had to modernize and Zavattini knew how. What he proposed was nothing less than a remake, suggesting that the editor change the overall layout and design; that he reverse the balance between image and text, by including more cartoons; and that he publish shorter articles, connoting a new snappy editorial style for *Marc'Aurelio*.[50] Zavattini made it clear that he was alarmed by the prospect that the competition, included his own, would destroy *Marc'Aurelio*, especially in light of the fact that *Il Bertoldo*, his former employer's comic magazine, had switched to colour and adopted a typographic style that was very pleasing to the eye. Even implementing just these two changes could tip the balance in *Marc'Aurelio*'s favour, regardless of the magazine's content. It would help if they commissioned only the best writers, including himself and Achille Campanile (who, incidentally, also worked for Mondadori publishers). Branding, by using their names, would increase their recognition value and the public's ongoing allegiance to the magazine. They could use name dropping as a regular feature of writing, to highlight how contemporary and well informed a magazine *Marc'Aurelio* was. They could create more reader participation, by launching a writers' competition to invent a new comic character; going so far as to suggest luring a successful contributor away from Rizzoli's *Il Bertoldo*.

Three months later, he came up with further ideas for *Marc'Aurelio*, which were also adopted; a full sixteen-page pull-out section, envisaged as an independent publication from the rest of the magazine. He suggested they design a separate masthead and cover page, entitled *The Forbidden Book* (*Il libro proibito*). *The Forbidden Book* would employ humour, to touch on censorship throughout the world, but aimed at innocuous films, at invented court cases held behind closed doors, directed at imagined secret police stories, cooking up jokes and photographs which were anything but forbidden. Such suggestions provided his own recipe for a bullet-proof critique under a Fascist regime. What made it so funny? That it would be related to entirely innocent endeavours, using the nonsense technique of mismatching a general idea and its particular example.[51]

What comes as a surprise is that Zavattini knew Rizzoli planned to demolish *Marc'Aurelio* altogether, by employing its entire pool of contributors in one fell swoop. His support is extraordinary, and his advice is revealing for the extent to which it shows in practice how he operated as a publisher and a pre-war Italian press mogul, in this case, to the benefit of the competition. *Marc'Aurelio* mattered to him and he wanted it to survive.

2.6 Zavattini, Disney-Mondadori and other comics

As the reader will have gathered, by comparison with other writers of his generation, Zavattini was far from prejudiced against popular culture. A case in point is his involvement in science fiction comics, after he was sacked and was hired by Mondadori publishers. Illustrated science fiction was first imported into Italy in the shape of the adventures of the superhero Flash Gordon, in 1934. These became an immediate success in children's comics, leading to original comics by Italian writers.[52] When Disney-Mondadori was established in 1935, the new company took over the Italian version of *Mickey Mouse*, *Topolino*, from Nerbini publishers, who had never acquired the rights from Walt Disney.

In 1942, Zavattini remembered that, back in 1936, Federico Pedrocchi, 'a tall, dark, a man of few words who worked on the periodicals published by Mondadori, came into my office and said: "I need a story"'. Zavattini was his boss, but had no background in comics. However, in his position as editorial director, he oversaw the full range of Mondadori magazine publishing.[53] With one foot on his desk, 'American style', Zavattini dictated the first story of this kind to his secretary, inventing what he thought would be a one-off, *Saturn against Earth* (*Saturno contro la Terra*), illustrated by Giovanni Scolari.[54] When it sold out, he was asked to create a series, which he did. It lasted until 1946, was translated into English and published in the United States, by Future Comics in the 1940s.[55] Nor was *Saturn against Earth* the only scenario for comics Zavattini wrote. He also created *Zorro from the Metropolis* (*Zorro della metropoli*), *La compagnia dei sette* (*The Company of Seven*) and *The Mystery of Airport Z*.

2.7 From publisher to editorial director

Le Grandi Firme (*The Great Writers*) was another publishing success story of his. After his proposal to purchase the magazine had been accepted, he turned what was a boring looking anthology of new writing, which showcased short stories, into one of his biggest successes as a publisher. He did so without trashing the content. He commissioned the best high-profile writers for stories and interviews. He increased the format to large magazine dimensions. He replaced the film star photographic cover with an invented female character, a Vargas-like leggy character, drawn by Boccasile, which immediately boosted sales. Zavattini introduced photography, interviews and reportage, combined with photojournalism. And once again, he counterbalanced fame with a focus on ordinary people, whom Zavattini considered far from ordinary. He commissioned excellent writing to complement the everyday stories and illustrated them with photography. The centrefold was devoted to photo-reportage and headline-size titles and text. Culture and visual culture could combine forces. In 1930s Italy, this overall concept was both bold and innovative. The images told the story and the sales increased tenfold.

It is hardly surprising, then, that Rizzoli subsequently regretted sacking Zavattini. In 1937, he offered him 100,000 liras a year, an astronomical salary, considering that he was on 30,000, plus 2 per cent on magazine sales. But he turned down the offer.[56] Mondadori was so worried that he would lose him to the competition that he doubled his salary. The difference between the two publishers was that, whereas Rizzoli had ignored Zavattini's advice, Mondadori followed it. For example, Mondadori purchased *Il Settebello*, a satirical magazine, well placed to become stiff competition to *Il Bertoldo*. Its title was borrowed from the name of a popular Italian card game, suggesting its playful content. It began its life in Rome in 1933, where it was published by an editorial team which used anonymity to protect itself from censorship or worse.[57] It had survived several confiscations but had decreased its extent from eight pages to six. Zavattini's move brought Mondadori into the flourishing popular market of weekly and twice-weekly satirical magazines, alongside *Marc'Aurelio* and Rizzoli's rival *Il Bertoldo*. The trouble with the old *Il Settebello* was that it hadn't kept up with the times. The writing was so dense on the page that it overshadowed the illustrations. It contained few cartoons and a back page of sport. After Mondadori's acquisition, the cover was printed in full colour, the amount of text drastically reduced, and contained more cartoons, more features and a flexible layout. The new editorial formula created by Zavattini was a commercial success.

Zavattini followed his own advice given to De Bellis a year earlier. He introduced 'The Diary of a Shy Person' ('Diario di un timido'), on the last page and a Letters page. With the introduction of interviews with high-profile figures such as Massimo Bontempelli, Zavattini modified the conventional formula for humour-based magazines, based on a combination of jokes, witty stories and cartoons. There was sugar and spice, a literary element, but also journalism. The additional twist consisted in his idea of interviewing ordinary people going about their business.

> OUR MAJOR REPORTAGE. In this section of the magazine, each week we'll offer the public a piece of authentic journalism about a real event. Not the kind of events covered by the rest of the press. We are going to cover events which are extremely important for those people who live through them; events which could happen to all of us. Names and other information are all authentic.[58]

Bruno Munari, the designer who had worked with Zavattini since the first *Bompiani Almanac*, invented illustrations of improbable, Heath-Robinson-like machines for *Il Settebello*.[59] Mino Maccari delighted in expressionist caricatures of people and Vito Boccasile produced sexy Vargas lookalikes. Zavattini invited Saul Steinberg, a Romanian artist living in Italy, whom he had pinched from *Il Bertoldo* and other magazines, to join the salaried editorial staff.

'The Lady Janitor' ('La portinaia') is a typical example of Steinberg's humorous drawings for *Il Settebello*. In some ways, they translate into images the nonsensical humour of some of Zavattini's observations in his short stories. The Lady Janitor is a huge woman with eyes all over her body, on her arms, ears, dress. She is a nosey parker, who spends her time spying on everyone living in the apartment block. Often Steinberg's people move in the surreal urban space of modernity. However, Steinberg didn't last long at Mondadori. Zavattini's friend and protégée was fired that same year by Mondadori. By September 1938, there is no trace of his work. He was Jewish. That year Fascist racial laws went into force, denying Jews the freedom to work in Italy, regardless of whether they were Italian citizens or not. It was Italy's loss and the gain of the United States where Steinberg found refuge and worked for *The New York Times* and *The New Yorker* from then on with brilliant results.[60]

While *Marc'Aurelio* was supportive of the regime, *Settebello* wasn't. In fact, it turned Fascist rhetoric into a joke.[61] It did so by substituting the vague, idealist, language of the regime with a documentary-based approach. This was an early example of Zavattini's approach to criticality: describing the real world in fine detail, rejecting the generic concept of mass audience, in favour of the specific individual and specific social fact. This is borne out by the new feature containing interviews, presented as interviews with famous people. '*I nostri grandi servizi*' ('Our High-profile Reportages'). The joke was that the people they interviewed weren't famous. It was an idea Zavattini had first suggested to *Marc'Aurelio*. But it was more than a joke: it takes an established practice in journalism (based on the notion that celebrities aren't the only interesting people) and subverts it, by suggesting ordinary people as newsworthy candidates, but also using visuals to make the point that everyday events constitute history. For example, among the 'Letters' page, there is one addressed to none other than Luigi Freddi, the director of the *Direzione Generale per il Cinema*, the Fascist censorship board as of 1934 (and later hired by the Christian Democrats after the war).

The letter to Freddi concerns a group visit to the state-owned Rome film studios Cinecittà, inaugurated by Mussolini himself in 1935. Zavattini's narrative plays on mainstream expectations and myths about the cinema, to undermine them. His character sees the stars, the directors, the cameramen and sound technicians on a sunny day, but decides to abandon the group and wander behind the scenes and the stage sets, in among the extras to where a worker is constructing the façade of a house.

> 'Excuse me, Sir', he said, hat in hand, 'could you give me your autograph?' At the same time, some elderly ladies, who had just come down from Milan, were passing by, chasing after Camillo Pilotto who was in formal dress. 'But I'm Antonio Drei, the carpenter'. I insisted and he wrote his signature on a postcard. I asked him about his family, his thoughts, his diet, the make of his bicycle. 'Take a photograph of me next to Antonio Drei', I begged. And the photographers did as I asked, as fast as if they were in Hollywood. I was moved. Earlier, I'd been stopped by a Leica next to Mastrocinque, next to Vivi Gioi and earlier still, I'd asked Mario Camerini so many questions, and other screen personalities, taking my time over it.
>
> But now I was deeply moved, talking to Antonio Drei, one of the best workers in the world. [...] Now you'll understand, dear Freddi, why, at one point, I called out to all my colleagues who were there at the Quadraro – Boccasile, Manzi, Nando, Maggio, Baracco, Walter. We held hands and danced in a circle around Antonio Drei and asked him for his autograph and

his news and we are going to publish his image in the magazine, and blow it up, as big as Blasetti's and Laura Nucci's.

Zavattini's upside-down world has been interpreted as an example of what Mikhail Bakhtin called 'the carnivalesque'.[62] Zavattini described his technique in an interview given many years later, as a means of criticizing Fascist values:

> I was reading an article the other day which said chronicle is history. Well, I've been saying so for the past twenty years and more. To give you an example, when back in 1938, in *Il Settebello*, during the Fascist regime, I came up with the idea of an enormous title which read: 'Mr Giuliani has had a salary rise' – you get it, don't you? – it already encapsulated the whole concept of the value of a single person, of totally overturning established values. [...] The problematic of Neo-realism cannot be understood unless one understands this total reversal of values.[63]

The bestselling *Settebello* had been tolerated by the regime. But eventually, it requested it change its name. This was a subterfuge to close it down, by simply replacing it at the newsstand with a title its readers wouldn't recognize.[64] Alberto Mondadori won a reprieve, by promising to the Fascist Minister Alfieri he would change the content and include propaganda-like features about Italian foreign policy, using anecdotes and aphorisms.[65] Other Mondadori publications were targeted and closed down by the Fascist regime, including Zavattini's successful *Le Grandi Firme* (*The Great Writers*).

In 1939, Zavattini embarked on an entirely separate creative endeavour: painting. Most of his paintings are Modernist self-portraits. Hardly surprising, given that ever since his Parma days he had been in contact with visual artists, who were part of the same cultural milieu. Some of his Parma friends were professional artists and, later, in Milan, as a publisher, he commissioned illustrators and sculptors, as well as architects and designers. He also knew painters from the *Scuola romana*. For the rest of his life, he found the time to paint, and exhibit his work in public, and develop a collection of tiny portraits by contemporary Italian artists, all ten centimetres by eight.

In June 1939, while Zavattini was still the editorial director, Alberto Mondadori invested into launching *Tempo*, a *Life* magazine lookalike, in terms of typographic style, layout, use of photography and the way images were cropped, including colour features, and even a 'Letters' page.[66] This was the first mass-produced illustrated Italian weekly to use the photographic image not as mere illustration, but as a vehicle to convey information to its popular readership. It was modern, in the way it did not depend exclusively on syndicated features, but commissioned teams of journalists and photographers to work in tandem. The Fascist Ministry of Culture, known as *Minculpop*, closed other Mondadori publications, but never *Tempo*, which was pressurized to become a very effective medium of Fascist propaganda, both at home and abroad. If *Life* showed the American way of life, *Tempo* visualized the ideal Fascist way of life.

Zavattini's contributed to *Tempo* articles, film and theatre reviews, and a regular series of short stories, later collected in a book entitled *Io sono il diavolo* (1941) (*I am the Devil*). But he also launched a *Tempo* supplement, revolving around high-profile artists and writers across a range of disciplines, from architects to visual artists, poets, photographers, typographic designers, fashion designers and even scientists, to convey the modernity of E42, the international exposition scheduled for 1942 in what was to become a new district of Rome, EUR, the construction of which had only just begun.[67] He also proposed a photographic competition in which readers were invited to submit fifteen photographs pertaining to everyday life, from the ordinary to the extraordinary. They had to be event-based, as 'a kind of an interesting and self-evident event, conceived with reportage and chronicle in mind'.[68]

However, Zavattini objected to the magazine's pro-German stance, clearly conveyed in a special issue entirely devoted to 'Germania'. Alberto Mondadori himself, the man who ultimately made all the decisions, allowed this new Modernist magazine to become a propaganda vehicle for Fascism, coming out with editions in French, Spanish, Greek and other languages.[69] Soon, Zavattini resigned from Mondadori too. One would like to think that *Tempo* was the cause. It may have been a concomitant cause, but there were other reasons too. One was that Zavattini felt that his position as an editorial director was undermined by Alberto Mondadori, who had the final say. He continued after the war to work in publishing, as an independent writer and in several capacities. But his decision to leave Milan seems mostly motivated by his plan to work for the cinema, which had its base in Rome. He had reason to believe it was worth the risk and was prepared to forego his lucrative salary and position.[70]

Zavattini's early fiction and diary

3.1 The short story trilogy

It is essential to concentrate on Zavattini as a writer of fiction, in order to understand his screenwriting, especially the comic vein in the film *Miracle in Milan*, based on his scenario, published almost ten years before the film was made, and later expanded into a short story. His screenwriting developed alongside his activity and cultural influence in Italian visual culture, his pioneering work in Italian mass media, in terms of print culture, photography, documentary journalism under a Fascist regime. As well as Zavattini the journalist and publisher we must also consider Zavattini the writer of fiction.

Reading his trilogy *Parliamo tanto di me* (1931) (*Let's Talk a lot about Me*), *I poveri sono matti* (1937) (*The Poor Are Mad*) and *Io sono il diavolo* (1941) (*I am the Devil*), one gets the impression these books could not have been authored by one and the same person: a writer who was also a journalist, a desk and series editor, and eventually an influential editorial director. How could the storyteller coexist with the media-savvy journalist, someone who is curious about real people with names and surnames, taken as individuals, and curious about modern Italian society, developing in the industrial triangle of northern Italy?

In fact, Zavattini embarked on both careers at the same time: fiction and journalism, during his Parma days, when he started as a staff editor and soon became editor-in-chief. In the late 1920s and early 1930s, Zavattini was one of several writers publishing amusing stories, his main rival being Achille Campanile. In 1930, he watched a play by Campanile in Milan. In private, after the show, Zavattini remarked that the play was heavily derivative, dependent on the ideas of comic actor and satirist Ettore Petrolini. In his opinion, it was no better than Campanile's prose, which Zavattini considered 'an empty shell'; adding that, in repeating himself endlessly, even Campanile's parody of stereotypes had become a stereotype.[1] However, it is worth noting that Zavattini's comic writing shared Campanile's brevity, his prose's clearly discernible rhythm and its sharp wit. Like Campanile, he strikes a singular note within the pompous sounding, rhetorical Italian prose of the Fascist era. There is, however, a crucial difference. Zavattini's writing voice is layered, always suggesting that there's more, in a pause between the words, in the negative space of an image, in an ellipsis which conjures up what is absent.

In his first book, a selection of previously published short stories, *Parliamo tanto di me* (1931), there are so many underlying themes: destiny and chance; ghosts; news stories; the relation between individuals and the crowd; the rich and the poor; open-ended stories, word play, envy and literary success, melancholy, family, hints of autobiography. Zavattini himself appears twice as a character: first as himself, the author, in the Preface, with a verbal self-portrait, briefly and ironically describing his physical appearance and immense ambition as a young writer. He also features as his comic alter ego, Cesare Cadabra. Cadabra's first name coincides with Zavattini's, while his invented surname conjures up the figure of a magician, and the Abracdabra spell, the conjurer of words. In one instance, Cadabra is the storyteller who is so amusing that the devil, in charge of a group of the damned, refrains from punishing them for their sins, for as long as Candelabra entertains them.

To give the stories a cohesive thread, Zavattini gave his book a fragile structure in the form of a journey into the Underworld (Hell, followed by a one-page visit to Purgatory and Paradise, where children make such a din that they disturb the peace of the other resident souls). The author-witness imagines that he is accompanied by a guide, not Virgil, Dante's guide in most of the *Divine Comedy*, but a knowledgeable spirit. From the perspective of the 'Other' world, the real world of the living and its habits is constantly under observation, the distance creating distanciation, or a sense of abstraction, enabling the narrator to express the wonder and the absurdity of everyday life, in as many ways as the many situations he invents.

His characters, characterized by their mostly monosyllabic names ending in a consonant, sound more American than Italian: Tab, Rok, Mack, Morgan. In an Italian-speaking context, such blatantly foreign names create a sense of distance from any semblance of Italian identity; the geography is vague, abstract, and the place names contribute to make Zavattini's comic world entirely alien from contemporary Italy under Fascist rule. His version of time and of space is out of history, an abstract place devoid of props or time-bound events. Where the novel form explains, Zavattini's anti-novel, in which the narrative is compressed into the *raccontino*, jerks the attention of the reader with a break, an ellipsis; a sudden change of register; or even an unexpected switch of topic. Zavattini's first book was widely reviewed and acclaimed. In addition to the *Solaria* reviews mentioned earlier, it also attracted the attention of esteemed literary critics, such as Massimo Bontempelli, Guido Piovene, Adriano Tilgher and his friend and early mentor, Sebastiano Timpanaro.[2]

While his first book was effectively a montage of texts, originally published in a wide range of magazines, as Zavattini himself admitted to Falqui, his second book, *I poveri sono matti* (*The Poor Are Mad*), comprises a sequence of stories, featuring lower-middle-class employees, while the third, *Io sono il diavolo* (*I am the Devil*), consists of standalone stories and characters.

I poveri sono matti is more cohesive than his first book, since the same characters appear in different situations. Nevertheless, each narrative is self-contained; there is no progression in terms of a plot gradually reaching a conclusion and climax. Bat, the main character, is a journalist, like Zavattini and, in this parallel universe, also has to contend with his boss, his colleagues and the world around him. In this second volume, the author dispenses with an Underworld framework. The everyday is suspended by simple, deceptively child-like, syntax, which creates an abstract space in which any observation, reflection or action gives the reader pause for thought. In one story, Bat dreams of his funeral. His boss is in attendance, along with his grieving family and friends. They follow his boss, instead of following Bat's hearse; the grim joke being a comic critique of society.

'Le Ore' ('The Hours') is a non-story about Bat's struggle with writing.[3] Everything conspires against him, not only his colleagues and their gossip but even his own mind, when he tries to deal with the pressure and his growing awareness of the passing of time. Each moment brings another thought jangling in his head, awaiting its turn to make a sentence, and each thought draws him further and further away from writing, culminating in the appearance of his wife telling him it is time to leave. In another rejection of conventional narrative, 'Fra quattro minuti' ('In Four Minutes' Time'), so negligible an event takes place as to be almost meaningless. Bat sets off to work, but lingers to watch his children and their friends at play. He decides to defy time, convention and conformist routine, by walking on, past his office. As he does so, he experiences something new: nothing more than the distant sound of chairs scraping the floor of the office, as he walks away.[4] All it takes is a telling, tiny detail to suggest the habit pattern of the mind.

Such non-events flourish in this second book. Each one has the makings of a thought, suspended in a neutral, timeless space. Yet time is often mentioned, as is the final end-time of death. It's late at night in the last story, 'Lo stabilimento' ('The Press Works'). Bat is walking home after going to the cinema.[5] He walks past his office window, thinks about what the end of the world would be like as the wind blows and dust obscures the streetlights, when the printers knock off their shift, then watches them walking past and flying up and away out of his sight. He goes home, remembers his deceased father, while he is climbing the stairs, and imagines his colleagues Dod or Evans in his place. Then his wife reaches out, they make love and fall asleep.[6] These kinds of stories disrupt the banality of the everyday by inserting and combining elements which are fable-like, enchanting, in their candid nature, with others that are not.

At the time, there was nothing comparable in Italian literature, which made it hard for critics to classify Zavattini's prose writing. There is one notable exception. Someone who had the measure of *I poveri sono matti* was Giovanni Papini, co-founder of the Futurist review *Lacerba*, and *La Voce*. Papini wrote to Zavattini to say that the critics who had interpreted his book as comic prose had misunderstood him:

I find a tragic poet in this book. One who employs the seemingly grotesque, only to depict more effectively painful, melancholic, frightening, everyday reality. There's something remotely Kafkaesque and Joycean, but pared down to a most elementary and sombre form, and by so doing, more Italian, more lyrical.[7]

His third book, *Io sono il diavolo* (*I am the Devil*), lacked the light humour and gentle irony of the first two volumes, which had attracted the generic *umorista*, to denote a comic writer. In the third, there is a greater shift from the comedy of life to the tragedy of life, seen through an ironic and distancing gaze. In a conference given in 1942, Zavattini made a clear distinction between the light humour of the first book, by comparison with the other two.[8] Several critics have explained such a radical change by referencing Luigi Pirandello, Franz Kafka, Alberto Moravia and even the former *Solariano*, the poet Eugenio Montale.[9]

The prose of *Io sono il diavolo* gets under your skin: sometimes there is a sense of reading someone's private thoughts, carefully wedged into strange, but telling stories, each presenting a minimalist plot and barely sketched characters who keep changing. The recurring element is the situation, as an entity, despite the fact that nothing much happens; a non-event, one drawn from an imaginary kind of everyday life, which is given literary status. One is led to think that lived experience is always just beyond our reach. But the illusion of verisimilitude is regularly interrupted, by the insertion of the impossible, creating a juxtaposition of abstracted situations, vague descriptions of places and thoughtful asides, startling the reader through discontinuity between thoughts about being with a capital B, being in an abstract sense of the word, on the one hand, and a specific description about empirical being in a place and time, on the other.

'La corriera per Man' ('The Coach bound for Man') and 'Fegato' ('Liver') take the reader one step closer to real life. 'The Coach bound for Man' relates to an episode from Zavattini's life. The protagonist Antonio chooses not to get on the coach that would take him to his brother's funeral.[10] His reasons are not explained. By omitting them, and recounting the event, as if it were a normal occurrence, this simple story becomes bizarre. In the other autobiographical story, 'Liver', there is a graphic description of his father's agony and death. The last moments of his father's suffering are distilled by memory first, then by his literary craft. Narrator and author coincide, and the thin veil of fiction gives way to a memory of a situation, as strange as it was real, the unforgettable sight of his father in pain, their conversations, the waiting and the agony of it all.[11] These provenly autobiographical stories reveal how the Modernist compression Papini referred to serves to isolate the original event from its real occurrence and real place, and float it, so to speak, into the unreal time of narration. Thus, while these two stories have an origin in the author's biography, they contribute to the sense of loss, uncertainty, and doubt one finds, for example, in 'Allegria' ('Joy'), a nightmarish, first-person narrative, which opens with a paragraph of nonsense. Words are picked out as signifiers, but are alienated from the usual signified, and instead put on display, as empty objects of contemplation on a plinth. As the story of a non-event progresses, the narrator's 'I' becomes his worst enemy, when he imagines someone called G.M. and his fantasy becomes a reality.[12] As they struggle and look into each other's eyes, he realizes that his enemy looks like him and even thinks like him. 'Un fatto di cronaca' ('A News Story') would never make the news; the story of a murder that almost happened. The plot is so tenuous as to be almost non-existent: Giulia is waiting for her unfaithful husband in the stairwell, to kill him. She hears footsteps, the sounds of a man, watches him climb the stairs to his lover's apartment and, after a long silence and hesitation, puts down her weapon.[13] Vittorio goes to the police station to report his problem, but is too afraid of other people. It is winter and snowing in the city. And 'Tram' ('Trolley car') invents the kind of situation that features in Charlie Kaufmann's film *Anomalisa* (2015), but is over, in the space of a printed page of text. Carlo climbs on an empty trolleybus. It fills up with ten people who all look like him. They all realize they have the same features. They stare. They have an altercation, a fight and shame ensues, when they part.[14] With minimal details each outlandish situation is outlined, dwelling on the psychology of the imagined moment.

3.2 Zavattini's abstract humour

What kind of humour is it? An important aspect of humour is the reflective thinking it can provoke, by suggesting a disruption of the normal state of affairs, thought to be the outcome of a shift from *sensus communis* to *dissensus communis*.[15] *Sensus communis*, or common sense, guarantees the norm, but may be challenged by an alternative rationality that is suggested by humour. In this sense, humour reveals a critical faculty, capable of provoking a distancing effect in the reader, by inviting us to contemplate conventional behaviour in our shared, everyday experience.[16] This abstracting of behaviour, however transient or apparently insignificant it might be, distilled into something worthy of our consideration, highlights areas of our experience which are normally invisible to us, or which we tend to overlook.[17] Such a shared social world often becomes the target for humour. Where does one situate Zavattini's comic writing, specifically within an Italian cultural context? Well, two writers stand out, the playwright Luigi Pirandello and the writer Massimo Bontempelli.[18]

Pirandello wrote a dissertation on the critical potential of humour. His theory of the workings, meaning and purpose of humour, is helpful to understand these stories.[19] Pirandello argued that humour, using reflection, can 'deconstruct' (*scomporre*) the line of thinking 'constructed' by the writer.[20] Its deconstruction can be so disruptive as to place the totality, the sense, into doubt. Humour, by comparison with other kinds of writing, concerned exclusively with the body, Pirandello states, also engages with its shadow, and may sometimes be more interested in the shadow than the body to which it belongs, 'to the point of picking out all the shadow's jokes'. Its purpose is to pick out details from the 'material reality' of everyday life, in preference to the 'idealizing synthesis of art'.[21] Humour perceives that which is hidden from view: the opposite, *il contrario*, of what is taken to be the case. Reflection, induced by humour, enables us to see the dialectical opposition between idealism (*idealtà*) and reality (*realtà*). Humour has the power to bring societal illusion and pretence into the open, through deconstruction.[22] It can cast a shadow of doubt over what is normally understood as a self-evident situation, through the effect of alienation, 'intrinsic to reflection'.[23]

One is reminded of the theatre of Bertolt Brecht. In an Italian context, Umberto Eco has already argued that Pirandello's reflexive mode anticipates Brecht's *verfremdungseffekt*, or 'alienation effect'.[24] By 'rhetoric', Pirandello meant society's code or system of rules.[25] Humour, according to Eco, transgresses existing codes and discourse, to put it in structuralist and post-structuralist terms.[26] Furthermore, taken as a semiotic sign, a humorous statement may evoke a serious external one, equally familiar to the reader and the writer. Others have argued that, whatever its content, the meaning of humour will be an interaction between mind, culture and the real world.[27]

A frequent cause for humour in Zavattini's short stories is incongruity, that is to say, some kind of mismatch or discrepancy between signifier and its normal or usual signified, such that the reader is surprised, because her expectations do not match with the content. This is effectively a way of subverting expectations – however slightly – through suggesting that an alternative perception to the norm is plausible.[28]

Because defamiliarization, distancing, in which 'the ordinary is made extraordinary and the real surreal', is a recurring feature of *Parliamo tanto di me* and of Zavattini's second and third books in the trilogy, some critics have labelled his humour Surrealist, something which he has denied, drawing a distinction between practising an intuitive form of Surrealism and Surrealism proper.[29] In the third book, *Io sono il diavolo*, even a news feature can become absurd, otherworldly, as in 'In via Trestelle'. It recounts the tragic story of a boy, Vermicello was his real name, who fell into a sink hole and could not be saved. No parody, no word games, only plain, unadorned, syntax. Eventually, everyone gives up the rescue attempts, except his parents and a man wearing a hard hat who says: 'I don't think that nothing can be done. I refuse to believe it.' Humour subverts the event and provokes reflection beyond the passing moment in time of a news story. Zavattini said:

> I invented situations and behaviour with a tendency to see contradictions in ideas more than in things. Within my own narrows scope, closer to Nonsense than a critical and satirical kind of observation of events, I elaborated on the surprises provided by thought and logic.[30]

3.3 Zavattini's magic realism

It is tempting to explain Zavattini's prose in terms of Surrealism. But not only did he deny it, he was also never part of the kind of Italian artistic or literary circle of writers and artists who are known to have been in touch with the French Surrealist avant garde, such as Giorgio De Chirico and his brother Alberto Savinio, nor is there any sense in which Zavattini's approach to language is remotely similar to the work of André Breton or to the Surrealist group he founded in 1924.

Zavattini's fictional prose is, rather, a form of 'magic realism', as the Italian philologist Gianfranco Contini defined it in 1946, long before Gabriel García Márquez credited Zavattini for his influence. The Colombian had met Zavattini in Rome, while attending the Scuola Sperimentale di Cinema where he studied both film direction and screenwriting.[31] Zavattini's magic realism was a formative influence on the imaginary Macondo, in his *One Hundred Years of Solitude* (1967). García Márquez said as much: 'No one has ever suspected that *Miracle in Milan* is the most probable source of "magic realism" in the Latin American novel?'[32] The Colombian watched the film in 1955, in the company of Feranndo Birri, and left the theatre feeling that his perception of the world had been altered and that it was possible to change the world. On another occasion, García Márquez also remarked: 'I'm a son of Zavattini.'[33]

Gianfranco Contini included in *Italie magique* (1946), an anthology he published in Switzerland, a selection of Italian writers, with one thing in common: what Contini called 'magic realism', borrowing the phrase from the writer Massimo Bontempelli.[34] Contini gave Palazzeschi pride of place, while affording Bontempelli only a few pages, and negligible space to Zavattini.[35] Indeed, Palazzeschi's eighty pages dominate *Italie magique*, by comparison with only two short stories by Bontempelli, despite the fact that in Italy it was Bontempelli who had theorized Italian magic realism and irony – its organizing principle – in the 1920s.[36]

Bontempelli claimed in *Eva ultima* (1924) that an unexpected or inexplicable detail, object or person 'produces a *new reality* in a banal world'.[37] In *Mia vita, morte, miracoli* (1938), Bontempelli stated that his intention was to invent a new reality, using unchangeable elements of human life, to construct imaginary situations and simplified characters 'in which our real existence would seem like a fable'.[38]

Contini's *Italie magique* is important because it singles out this ironic line in pre-war Italian literature, which Contini, in 1944, was the first to identify as a well-defined tendency, involving what he called 'the deformation of reality'.[39] The anthology contains four of Zavattini's stories, all from *Io sono il diavolo*, though Contini's brief introduction does mention the earlier two books in the trilogy. This is how he characterizes Zavattini's prose:

> He composes surreal and humorous sketches, deliberate and sometimes superfluous, in acid prose that is somewhat polemical – ground down, like the abrasion of broken fragments of glass. He takes certain bourgeois themes, tender compassion for himself and for others, to an extreme. His humour subverts goodness into cruelty and provokes some unsettling spiritual feelings.[40]

This characterization shows precious little sympathy for Zavattini's unique form of the comedic. It seems a rather unfair portrait. Zavattini had recently published *Totò il Buono*, a development of a story written for the cinema and published in 1940. This short novel harks back to his earliest collection of stories, *Parliamo tanto di me*. Suffice it to say that it is the culmination of Zavattini's early abstract and poetic humour, held together by a structure which takes the reader aside, effortlessly drawing attention to the story within the story, then back to the main plot. An even greater sense of wonder and delight, the combination of realism and nonsense, permeates *Totò il Buono* to make it qualify as an important work of magic realism, which was later to inform the story and screenplay of the film *Miracle in Milan* (1950), directed by Vittorio De Sica.

However, this said, regardless of his personal bias in favour of the former Futurist Aldo Palazzeschi, Contini's portrait of early 1940s Italian mainstream literature has the merit of identifying two diametrically opposed tendencies: magic realism and existential realism, with a view to drawing a clear line between Italian magic realism ('*surréel sans surréalisme*') and French Surrealism.[41]

When a copy of Contini's rare book (first published in a small print run) was eventually rediscovered and translated into Italian in the late 1980s, in the new Postscript, not only did Contini stand by his original idea but he also included Italo Calvino among the magic realists.[42] Needless to say, at the time of the reprint, Contini was unfamiliar with Calvino's 1940s short stories, which were only published posthumously, in 1994, as part of Calvino's complete works. Internal evidence clearly shows that these early stories of his are related to Zavattini's unique model of comic prose. What is more, Calvino himself made a direct connexion in his 1940s correspondence, in which he refers to Italian humour of the 1930s and to its main figures: Massimo Bontempelli and Cesare Zavattini. Furthermore, in a letter addressed to Eugenio Scalfari of 1942, Calvino recommended that his close friend Eugenio Scalfari read Zavattini's books, stating that if he, Calvino, had read him earlier, he would have been a better writer.[43] What is more, the following year Calvino wrote that his own *raccontini* were inspired by a writer, whom he considered superior to Elio Vittorini, Zavattini.[44] As for the Bontempelli ascendency, Calvino privately confirmed his filiation from '*la linea bontempelliana*' ('the Bontempelli line'), in 1968, in a letter to Luigi Baldacci, stating that Bontempelli was the most prominent Italian narrator before the war, and that anything Bontempelli wrote fitted into magic realism, setting the tone for any new writer publishing comic prose, including Dino Buzzati, Nicola Lisi and Zavattini, before the war.[45]

Indeed, it is true to say that Calvino's literary genealogy actually began within Zavattini's milieu of comedy and satire, in *Marc'Aurelio* and *Il Bertoldo*.[46] Calvino confirmed the element of irony and humour expressed in Contini's analysis, evoking that same cultural climate of 1930s humour in those comic magazines, particularly *Il Bertoldo*, conceived by Zavattini himself who was, as shown earlier, also involved in its development, editorial decisions and commissioning strategies. Calvino realized that *Il Bertoldo* debunked official Fascist rhetoric and stereotyped situations, using a particular brand of *Il Bertoldo-style* irony, which departed from the earlier expression of Italian humour in *Guerin Meschino* and *Il Travaso delle idee*. He places this development within the emergent cultural industry which developed in Milan, where several writers were trying to codify a sustainable form of humour that had to avoid outright satire wherever there was any hint of life in contemporary society, to survive Fascist censorship. As Calvino puts it:

> The most it could do within the official culture of the time, to escape totalitarian language, was to open up a unique space for a surreal type of comedy, largely based on the use of language, rather than word play and inversions of meaning, logical, but absurd.[47]

Finally, in addition to Calvino's clear understanding of a little-studied strain of Italian pre-war humour, one finds Zavattini's direct influence on Calvino in twenty-six *raccontini* or short stories, published in 1994 as *Raccontini giovanili*, a title taken from one of the manuscripts, *Raccontini di dopodomani* (*Very Short Stories of the Day after Tomorrow*). The word *raccontini* is of course a borrowing from Zavattini, as are the kind of stories themselves, coeval with Contini's survey *Italie magique*.[48] It will therefore come as no surprise then that, for example, Zavattini's sense of the absurd features in *Passatempi* ('Pastimes') and *L'uomo che chiamava Teresa* ('The Man who called Teresa'), and that Zavattini's type of destabilizing humour is also apparent in *Il lampo* ('The Flash') and *Vita incerta* ('Uncertain Life'). This latter deals with the way life escapes easy categorization. Or indeed, *Il funerale* ('The funeral'), a typical and recurring theme in Zavattini's short stories, ever since his first collection of stories, *Parliamo tanto di me*, which features a drawing by Zavattini himself of a funeral procession. Zavattini also wrote an experimental story 'Il funeralino' ('The Child's Funeral'), which became the closing episode of the film *L'oro di Napoli* (1954). It is almost an abstraction, conforming to Pirandello's overturning of normality. While Calvino's funeral is comic through displacement, Zavattini's *Funeralino* is almost tragic, through the displacement of the gravity of death, challenged by the levity of life. In both, the world is turned upside down. Vintage Zavattini.[49] What is more, the very idea for Calvino's running mourners trying to keep up with the ever-faster pace of the horse-drawn hearse is taken from Zavattini's *Totò il Buono*.

3.4 From fiction to non-fiction and autobiography

Zavattini began to publish a public diary, in *Primato* magazine and in *Tempo*.[50] He expanded the diary form elsewhere into an intensely autobiographical, soul-searching, part fiction, part non-fiction form of address in *Ipocrita 1943* (*Hypocrite 1943*) begun in 1941.[51] However, Zavattini's authorial voice comes across much earlier, in short flashes, ever since he started writing short stories to later feature on the opening page of his first book, with an expression of the young writer's optimism and ambition, written in the first person, and on the closing page, with a fleeting mention of his father. However, with few exceptions, none of these three books could be described as directly autobiographical, since the author's presence is mostly restrained and always one step removed from the fictional narrative.

Hypocrite 1943 was started after *Io sono il diavolo*, but takes Zavattini in another direction altogether, autobiographical writing, conveyed through a thinly disguised fictional persona. It is prefaced by a few words in italics: 'At some time in 1943, someone kept his diary. Only the following notes have survived. No one has ever heard what happened to this miserable person. *Parce sepulto.*'[52] *Hypocrite 1943* plays with the thin line between the fictional persona and the author's genuine preoccupations of the time in what reads like an introspective diary, with roots in Giovanni Papini's autobiographical layered diary of philosophical reflections, *Finished Man*.

Verisimilitude acts as a filter confusing the reader with a narrative voice which belongs to someone with whom the reader would never wish to identify, someone who is willing to expose himself, in all his pettiness, and failings, in a confessional mode of writing which is in no way characteristic of Fascist declamatory prose of certainty. *Hypocrite 1943* conveys the character's uncertainty and doubt, but also his moral bankruptcy. Each paragraph is reduced to a standalone reflection. There's a monologue with a God who doesn't exist: 'Give me a sign. We're alone. Convince me. Make a chair speak. You can take a year of my life in exchange.' 'Listen to me. You still have time. I shan't close the door behind me. Rather, I shall look up at the sky. Show yourself from a crack in the sky.'[53] Zavattini's alter ego is not a nice person and knows it full well: 'I could go on talking about me about me about me', he says, echoing the title of his first book. But now it is an ironic thought, since the times and context had changed. But it is also unclear which 'I' is speaking, and this ambiguity adds to the constant questioning and doubting of the narrator who openly confesses his most intimate thoughts. The overall sense of uncertainty, changing times, self-criticism even, can be ascribed to the author, while the names, Antonio, Giulia, Maria, Carla and all the others, point to fictional characters, part of the literary screen dividing fiction from non-fiction. The book is an experiment in using a confessional register. God is often the interlocutor, but a silent one, for, as the text makes clear, he doesn't exist. But rather than posing the question of the existence of God, as a non-character and a non-being, God seems to represent an idea of ultimate goodness, by comparison with the narrator's self-loathing:

> I shall write a press communiqué. I hereby state that the undersigned no longer has anything in common with himself. He is an Other. No one can stop me from making a clean break. I shall let the words come out of my mouth at random.[54]

If *Hypocrite 1943* exposes a harsh inner gaze, through a fictional or semi-fictional persona, a sense of uncertainty and a confessed inability to deal with reality,

Riandando (*Looking Back*) is a wartime diary which combines a fragile sense of self with a factual and shocking record of what the writer actually saw and heard around him in the last stages of wartime conflict in Rome.[55] *Riandando* (*Looking Back*) is a documentary-style diary, which also marks a turning point. This wartime diary survived the war, but only after heavy editing, to the point of turning narrative prose into short aphorisms, featuring a heightened sense of reality, devoid of any fictional filter, conveying an emotionally powerful gaze onto the outside world. The prose compression of the *raccontini* also features here: *Looking Back* really is Zavattini's private diary, duly edited down into a small book, and only published in 1967.[56] In different ways, *Hypocrite 1943*, *Looking Back* and his Cinematic Diary all correspond to Contini's classification of existential realism or, perhaps more accurately, a form of phenomenological realism, in dialectical opposition to his earlier magic realism.

3.5 Zavattini's Cinematic Diary

In the same years, Zavattini began publishing his *Diario cinematografico*, his Cinematic Diary, which was to become a regular outlet for public reflection, but also his literary stomping ground for planning and public relations. Diaries tend to be published posthumously, but Zavattini's diary is an exception. It came out in instalments, from the 1940s to the mid-1980s. In the 1970s, he also broadcast in diary-style on national radio. The diary form serves many functions for Zavattini. One is to work out an idea from scratch, record inspiring moments for what they say about people and situations; to share with his readers the point of departure of his films. It often shares even the creative process itself. What stands out clearly from reading his diary in its entirety is how observation and field research are crucial to his screenwriting.

Zavattini's Cinematic Diary is an extraordinary literary work in its own right, with multiple functions, a sounding board for launching campaigns against censorship, for trying out a scenario, for reflecting on recent events and current affairs, recounting current debates, launching them or inviting them, all seamlessly interwoven with broadcasts, interviews, drafts for conferences, its author's views on matters which went beyond the personal sphere and which shed light on the development of his aesthetic and on his work in cinema, constantly shifting from detail to background, from story to argument, and from argument to reflection.[57]

Zavattini's diary-style voice, adapted to carry philosophical reflections, harks back to his early years, when he chanced upon Giovanni Papini's *Finished Man*, and took to his intriguing first-person narrative, and Papini's philosophical turn of phrase, mingling registers of experience, bringing together in a literary montage, his private life and his intellectual development. Zavattini acquired a similar range of approaches to writing, sometimes intimate, sometimes reflective, sometimes even confessional, developing an anti-rhetorical register in diary-style texts already during the last years of Fascist rule, compressing different linguistic registers within the same paragraph through severe editing, and, as Papini had done before him, expressing a similar attention to the everyday as a phenomenon worth investigating.

At first, his Cinematic Diary began to appear in film journals, in *Cinema*, in *Bis*, then in *Cinema Nuovo* for ten years, and later in the 1960s, in the Communist magazine *Rinascita* and finally the daily *Paese Sera*. Yet this crucial creative activity is the least known outside Italy and one of his great legacies. In 1967, Zavattini published a collection of texts, based on his regular diary articles previously published in periodicals, as *Straparole*. In 1979, a new edition came out, this time with the title *Diario cinematografico*, or 'Cinematic Diary'. It contains humour, introspection, private life stories, the early stages of an idea for a script, observations from everyday life and also forms a moving and inspiring self-portrait of this filmmaker.

At the heart of Zavattini's diary is his approach to the real; that attentiveness which led to either transcribing or re-creating real-world stories. At one stage, he came up with the proposal of a 'Diary of Italians'. In May 1948, Zavattini published extracts from five diaries which had been given to him by children living nearby, four years earlier. Thirteen-year-old Franco calls his diary 'the diary of sincerity'. In his presentation of their diaries Zavattini associates the diaries with screenwriting:

> These are the boys of via Merici with whom I'd like to make a film; but one with neither beginning nor end, along the lines of private thoughts, with me as the protagonist. A film which doesn't follow the rules of the cinema game and makes use of the freedom the Lord has given us.[58]

In November 1954, Zavattini wrote about how, just after the war, he walked the streets of Rome starting conversations with people from all walks of life and began to commission them to keep a diary and give it to him. For example, he spoke to a removals man who was resting on a bench, a street sweeper, a janitor, a bus driver, a mechanic, a housekeeper; not all the people he asked agreed straight away. They tried to put him off, claiming that they couldn't write; or that they were afraid of their partner, or of the tax man, or of the employer; or just that there was nothing to say because life was always the same. A bus driver told him that he felt that a diary would be useful, only if he wrote down everything truthfully. And a mechanic found that he was glad to review the day half an hour before going to bed at night. One homeless person told Zavattini how he struggled to get any sleep; 'the minute you close your eyes a car shrieks to a halt and you have to get up'.[59]

Valentina Fortichiari, the editor of the second edition of his diary, noted in her Preface to Zavattini's *Diario cinematografico* (1979) that the word 'everything', *tutto*, was a recurring feature in Zavattini's writing and talking: 'diary as everything', 'man as the sayable all', 'do all, say all'.[60]

Central to Zavattini's idea of the diary is less a confessional mode and its genealogy leading far back in time to Augustine's *Confessions*, rather, the idea of finding the link between the personal dimension of life and the social one, a line of the social being, explored by several contemporary thinkers, such as Roy Bhaskar, a philosopher of science; David Harvey, a political geographer; the educationalist Paulo Freire; or by Zavattini's friends, including the ethnographer Josué De Castro, the poet and anthropologist Danilo Dolci and the peace theorist Aldo Capitini.

Early screenwriting

4.1 *Five Poor Men in a Motorcar*

Cinema features from early on in Zavattini's life. In the 1920s, his journalism about cinema took an ironic, sometimes sarcastic stance. By comparison, his early writing *for* the cinema was comic, drawing on American screwball comedies. He particularly admired Charlie Chaplin and Buster Keaton. His very first attempt was *La fuga* (*The Escape*):

> I wanted to write about an escape. Someone is running away, because suddenly something alarms him, though it's not clear what that might be. His escape triggers a chase with more and more people joining in. It comes to an abrupt halt after generating an hour and a half of events.[1]

He wrote these lines in 1933, for the production house Cines.[2]

The following year, he wrote a comic story in collaboration with Andrea Rizzoli, called *Cinque poveri in automobile* (*Five Poor Men in a Motorcar*). Its original title was *Poveri in auto* (*Poor people in a Car*). The scenario was along the lines of Ernst Lubitsch's *If I had a Million* (1932).[3] Angelo Rizzoli, the publisher, purchased the scenario, but his choice of director, Mario Camerini, turned it down, claiming that it lacked a story and that the idea didn't go anywhere. After the war, Mario Mattòli made it into a film. Five working-class men win a motorcar in a lottery. Each episode charts their day of driving it, before they sell it. The film is about different kinds of love, from the passionate love of adultery to fatherly love, and compassion. It ends with an accident which puts paid to their dreams. The poor remain poor.[4] As has often happened, the film had a different ending, in which the poor share the proceeds of the sale.

Five Poor Men in a Motorcar takes everyday-life situations as an inspiration for its humour, instead of the abstract, timeless, space of his Nonsense *raccontini*. Zavattini's gaze, from the beginning, both in his literary writing, his journalism and his cinema, expresses the subaltern's gaze with not a hint of condescension.

4.2 *I'll Give a Million*

The chase structure of *The Escape* also underlies, among other films, *Buoni per un giorno* (literally, *Good for a Day*) the earliest version of what became the story, screenplay and film *Darò un milione* (*I'll Give a Million*). The first draft was written in collaboration with Giaci Mondaini, a friend and a cartoonist, who belonged to the same circle of comic illustrators Zavattini commissioned for several publications. But Mondaini dropped out. Then the story was published in *Quadrivio*.[5]

A millionaire called Gold wants to know what it is like to be penniless for a day: 'I'm bored. Today I want to go around dressed as a beggar. If I meet someone who thinks I'm poor and who does something kind, unexpected, imaginative even, I'll give that person a million.'[6] As the news travels on the grapevine, people all over town bend over backwards to show kindness to strangers who are beggars. The funfair is populated by middle-class people providing a beggar, whom, they hope, is the millionaire in disguise, a typically childish form of entertainment. The film combines Zavattini's type of humour with a love of American slapstick, fast-moving, comedy (his published story even mentions a film by Chaplin, as an example) in a seemingly endless string of gags. In one scene, Zavattini envisaged a shot, showing a poster of the Tiller girls and a close-up of their legs shifting from still image to animation and dance: pure fantasy for the fun of it. In another scene, he borrowed an idea from his *raccontini*, when two policemen in a chase reach a park and act out of character, playing 'Cuckoo', instead of pursuing a suspect, and, in yet another, an escalator conveys the characters up to the clouds.

Rizzoli purchased the story and chose Mario Camerini to direct it. The publisher had just produced Max Ophüls's *La signora di tutti* (1934) (*Everybody's Woman*). As far as Zavattini was concerned, relations with Camerini went downhill from then on. They had diverging views about the nature of comedy. Camerini leaned heavily towards sentimental realism, while Zavattini sought to bring to the silver screen his absurdist, minimalist stories, the light touch and new Italian humour of his *raccontini*. The producer Rizzoli agreed with Zavattini that Buster Keaton, who lived in Paris at the time, would have been an ideal choice for the main role, but Camerini rejected the idea outright. Nor would he countenance Macario or Totò. For the character of Bim, the beggar, he cast instead a character actor, Luigi Almirante. But one good thing happened on set. While filming the final scene, Zavattini and De Sica met for the first time in Verona.

Zavattini spent that summer of 1935 in Rizzoli's villa in Canzo, where he fought tooth and nail for his ideas, but he was outnumbered. Camerini brought in other writers as reinforcements, Mario Soldati and Ercole Patti, and the three of them completely rewrote Zavattini's story, which became the kind of full-blown sentimental and psychological comedy which Camerini was looking for. Soldati even suggested that they do away with the beggars from the script, but Zavattini held his ground.[7] 'It has been reduced to a sickly sweet story', he complained to his friend, Bompiani.[8] In the event, 70 per cent of Zavattini's treatment was cut.[9] And yet, the story attracted Hollywood, and specifically Darryl F. Zanuck who purchased the foreign rights and produced *I'll Give a Million* (1938), which was directed by Walter Lang. In the Hollywood version, the main story is replaced by a subplot in Zavattini's original script. Bim meets Anna, the newspaper vendor. His beggars, which Zavattini had struggled to keep in the frame, were almost entirely written out of the script, achieving what Camerini's writing team had only dared to suggest.[10]

4.3 *Everyone Should Have a Rocking Horse*

In 1938, Zavattini made another attempt at applying his unique comic vain to a gentle satire, *Diamo a tutti un cavallo a dondolo* (*Everyone Should Have a Rocking Horse*), also intended as a 'gag-film', a *film-trovata*, organized around a succession of gags, rather than a linear narrative.[11] But the script didn't get past the treatment stage, written in collaboration with Ivo Perilli. De Sica purchased the rights.

The recurring theme in this and other 1930s scripts by Zavattini is the opposition between poverty and wealth, mediated by his kind of humour to create a poetic allegory. Zavattini's gaze, from the beginning, in his literary writing, his journalism and his cinema, expresses the subaltern's gaze, with no trace of condescension. The subaltern is always a political subject, whether in a comedy, a satire, or a drama: an individual and a member of a family and of a community.

As Zavattini pointed out in an interview, in a sense, a film was made from *Everyone Should Have a Rocking Horse*, since this type of comedy, with borrrowings from his *raccontini*, migrated to the scenario and novella *Totò il Buono* (*Totò the Good*), which later became *Miracle in Milan* (1950), including the supernatural.[12]

Magic combines to filter the real world in this story, just as it would in *Miracle in Milan*. The protagonist, the factory worker Gec, wants to meet his boss, Bot, to suggest to him that his workers would be much happier, if they were all given a toy to play with. When Gec hears the other workers arguing, he blows a whistle and suggests they all whistle too. They do, get distracted, and the argument ends. When the creditors knock on his door, Gec hides behind a carnival mask. He tries to persuade his boss at the balloon factory to give away balloons. Whenever a worker makes a mistake, the balloons lift him up and away forever and whenever workers are angry, they go to a special room, where they can shout to their heart's content.

However, Fascist censorship accused Zavattini of inciting class warfare and vetoed the film's production, unless he changed the ending, so that the capitalist factory owner Bot and the factory worker Gec would make up their differences, thus avoiding a conflictual ending.[13] Censorship acted as a deterrent. As a result, the film was never made, but anyone who has seen *Miracle in Milan* will recognize that the screenwriter was drawing on his 1930s humour and poetic gaze.[14]

4.4 Comedy in theory

In 1936, in an article in *Il Tevere*, Zavattini made the audacious claim that Italian cinema could make better comic films than anyone else, provided it drew on the new comic talent of Campanile, Patti, Marotta, Rossi, Mosca of *Il Bertoldo* and himself.[15] Traditional comedy, moralizing and sentimental as it was, could be replaced by going in a new direction, less realist or more abstract.[16] To give the new writers more clout, he had created a short-lived association of comic writers, called *Umoristi Associati*.

He also gave an interview to the magazine *Cinema*, in which he said that working on *I'll Give a Million* was 'a nightmare'.[17] But the interview goes further than an expression of personal creative frustration, revealing as it does the problems emerging in the relations of production in the film industry, between writers, producers and directors. Zavattini's advice to prospective screenwriters was to take control of the means of production, by becoming a director of photography, the director and the protagonist.[18] In his *Cinema* interview, he reconstructed the sequence of events that had led to his story for *I'll Give a Million* being bowdlerized and reflected on the reasons why that had happened and, finally, discussed how to avoid the same thing happening again. His clash with Camerini was due to the importance the director gave to the plot and to sequencing. He was told that his story lacked a plot. Its fantastic elements had to be scrapped because they lacked the realism that Camerini sought to achieve in his films. A staircase could not be allowed to become a xylophone, and cartoon animation inserts were equally undesirable. His poetry of the everyday was neither acceptable nor understood. Zavattini was interested in exposing the reasons why Camerini thought that there was nothing funny in his story and why he believed it needed a plot. The reason was Camerini's traditional understanding of comedy, seen as light sentimental realism, as in his *Uomini, che malscalzoni!* (1932) (*What Scoundrels Men Are!*), which was to dominate pre-war Italian comedy. Such an approach was worlds apart from the subtle comedy Zavattini wanted to establish in Italy, built around gags.

In a 1936 interview, Zavattini cited Chaplin's silent movie *A Dog's Life* (1918). Zavattini's main critique was the difference in their understanding of what a story should entail and indeed its function. Camerini and other directors, Zavattini claimed, were obsessed with plot, dialogue and linear narrative. But new comedy wanted to dispense with the plot and replace it with the satire of a situation, of an environment, something his story had attempted to do.[19] This was the reason, he claimed, Camerini brought in Soldati. He was asked to rewrite the comedy into a drama and replace his abstract dialogue (harking back to the *raccontini*) with a realist equivalent along sentimental lines.

Three years later, in 1939, he followed up this analysis, in the form of an open letter addressed to Camerini in the satirical *Il Settebello*.[20] He told Camerini that it took courage to dream up the 'wrong' film (*un film sbagliato*) – as Zavattini had done for *I'll Give a Million*:

> May a plane cross the sky of the industrious Cinecittà every day and write in black smoke: COURAGE. I'm always dreaming of a film that is 'wrong' for being too brave. You know how obstinate I am; the dream could become true. [...] Listen to me: two hundred metres of film without an elephant, with nothing, a brook and a child, could be a work of art; you know that. And when you stop to daydream, as often happens, surely you can see the brook and the child in your mind's eye. Maybe life, producers, or whatever, induce you to make films with elephants. However, your nature, dear Camerini, will seek out the brook and the child in the night.[21]

4.5 Art and (film) industry

In a 1940 article in *Cinema*, 'The Best Dreams' ('I sogni migliori'), Zavattini considered the last ten years of Italian cinema which had achieved nothing more than technical perfection, using techniques to create the illusion of the real, when, in his view, the real challenge was to point the camera elsewhere. Creativity was no obstacle. The real problem was the producer's stranglehold, exerting all the decision-making power within the film industry.[22] This was due to the fact that what distinguished cinema from other forms of expression was its dependence on capital and having opted, from its inception, for commerce instead of art, exemplified by the Hollywood system, not a model that should be followed.

The only way out of such a predicament, he claimed, was to take over the means of production, by making cinema as affordable as paper, pen and ink. As for aesthetic choices, he pointed out that world cinema revolved around literary adaptations, the spectacular and the exceptional, valued above all else, at the expense of the everyday. But why draw on the imagination indirectly, through literature, when it could be accessed directly? Where to look for the new? In age-old themes of everyday life. The best dreams, he concluded, are pin sharp and devoid of any obfuscation.

Two years later, in a lecture given at a film club in Imola, Zavattini took these ideas about the nature of the film industry further, in a closer analysis of the relation between screenwriter, director, producer and film industry.[23] He began by drawing a substantial distinction between filmmakers and producers. Because only the former consider cinema an art, not the people who finance films, it is the producers who impose their will. This had been the pattern from the beginning of the short history of cinema. Its vocation had been betrayed. Thus cinema, he told his audience, is a social compromise, imposed by temporary hierarchies which contradict its destiny and real vocation. And yet, its vocation could neither be negated nor ruled out entirely. In an alternative version of cinema, the cine-camera is accessible to all. Like a pen or a paintbrush, celluloid would be as affordable as a packet of sea salt from the neighbourhood store.[24] This alternative version of cinema exists in the form of cinema's Earthly Paradise, in which what counts is a disinterested passion for cinema and where 'the cine-camera is as affordable as a bicycle and the titles of films vary, depending on the variety of our most intimate thoughts'.[25]

The Imola lecture also contains Zavattini's first formulation of the diary-film. He expanded on the ways in which the story was viewed in cinema, proposing that screenwriting could be very different from what was considered best practice in the industry. In his view, everyone has at least one story to tell which would make a film. Any news story could become the basis for a film, just as any book could provide the raw material to inspire stories. 'There's no shortage of ideas', he claimed. 'The paper that comes out at 11 o' clock is a treasure trove of stories', adding the caveat that, of course, a selection process is necessary.[26] Could the everyday become an edited film? It could, as, he added, Dziga Vertov's *Man with a Movie Camera* had already demonstrated. The main point of his lecture was that the real obstacle to a new cinema was the producer, not the filmmaker.

4.6 Magic realism in cinema: *Totò il Buono*, script, novel, film

Although the battle of wills with Camerini was lost, the screenwriter did not lose heart. Apart from attacking Camerini in the press and in public talks, Zavattini conducted his campaign for a new kind of comedy on a different terrain: first, by trying to bring his circle of comic writers from *Il Bertoldo* and *Il Settebello* into industrial cinema, by setting up a short-lived association, *Umoristi Associati*, and second, in his screenwriting, by applying the magic realism of his own fictional prose to mainstream cinema.

The most notable example is *Totò il Buono*. The first version was written in collaboration with Count Antonio De Curtis, the then up-and-coming variety comedian Totò, whose name is credited as co-author in the title, partly because Zavattini imagined him in the leading role. The script was published in *Cinema* in 1940, and countersigned by the comic, who contributed a few ideas, but later withdrew.

The first version begins with a handful of funny moments, quite typical of his *raccontini*, in which humour springs from an absurd situation reduced to a few lines. The central character is *Totò*, who embodies goodness in a fable-like time and place: the story is set in an anonymous modern city called *AAA*

(*HaHaHa*). Totò is born under a cabbage, as in Italian folklore, and lives in a place which resembles 'a strange village', with hundreds of people. It is clean and it is organized, 'but above all', 'there is', Zavattini adds, 'the kind of solidarity that comes from suffering and shared privation'. *Totò* is a misfit in the big city, where he is *incompreso*, misunderstood. However, in this strange village, he is the leader whose imagination is put to work for the benefit of the community. You can share other people's happiness, or a sunset, through a rectangular frame made of wooden poles: almost a cinematic shot in itself. Zavattini envisages a utopian village. Sometimes a villager will go missing, after being hired by the outside world to spend an hour agreeing with others. Happiness and contentment reign in this bidonville for many years, until envy and greed disrupt it from within. Gec tells the owner of the land there is crude oil on his property. The second half of the script is about attempts at repossession and attempts at resistance. Gags abound: the magnate tries to sway public opinion, by publishing the news that Totò's buckets of water have brought on a common cold to one of the policemen, who is now in bed to recover. Nonsense, magic, angels and Totò's miracles abound. Totò can make the boots the police are wearing uncomfortably tight or give them itchy feet. He can turn the shells from the guns brought out to bomb the village into popular music. The magic spell will only last twenty-four hours, but without miracles the village cannot win. More events take place until, at the last minute, Totò and his friends buy brooms, so that they can all fly off to 'that kingdom where everyone saying "good day" really mean to say good day'.

Three years later, Zavattini expanded the story into a novella by the same title. This was the literary culmination of his minimalist short stories and of his magic realism. After the war, he edited his allegorical treatment of poverty into a scenario which became the world-famous film *Miracle in Milan* (1951) directed by Vittorio De Sica.[27]

4.7 *The Children Are Watching Us*

In these years, Zavattini, Aldo De Benedetti and Alessandro de Stefani worked on the plots and dialogues of no less than a quarter of the films then produced in Italy, forging a new cinematic Italian based on the more natural-sounding language of radio and the telephone.[28] To help Vittorio De Sica, Zavattini contributed anonymously to the transitional *Teresa venerdì* (*Doctor, Beware*) (1941), rewriting the dialogue, sequence by sequence, even though the story was at loggerheads with Zavattini's blend of absurdist comedy. The film was based on a Camerini-style script about a doctor who goes to work in an orphanage, to sort out his financial problems. In this comedy of errors, De Sica, who directed the film, also played the lead role, Dr Vignali, torn between his girlfriend, played by Anna Magnani, and two other women.

The same year Zavattini presented the Imola lecture, he and De Sica embarked on an entirely new direction in *I bambini ci guardano* (*The Children Are Watching Us*) (1942). Adolfo Franci had suggested to De Sica that he make a film based on *Pricò*, a novella by Cesare Giulio Viola which dealt with the problem of adultery. The title was borrowed from a rubric Zavattini had created and edited in *Grazia*, a women's illustrated magazine, while editorial director at Mondadori publishers. *The Children Are Watching Us* is a departure from period comedy, and from Zavattini's magic realism. It was, rather, the culmination of dramatic films based on real life, no less than *Ossessione* (*Obsession*) by Luchino Visconti and his *Cinema* circle of friends.[29] Zavattini completely rewrote Viola's story. In his private diary, he remarked:

> De Sica phoned me at midnight to convey his satisfaction with my collaboration on *Pricò*. 'At first, *Pricò* was a non-entity. But today, after your intervention, it is a film I really like'.[30]

The Children Are Watching Us is the story of an adultery, of the subsequent break-up of an Italian middle-class family, the suicide of the father and the son's estrangement; a tragedy about a typical lower-middle-class Italian family, living in Rome during the Fascist era. The simple story is crafted around loss and alienation, leading to Pricò's consequential and logical refusal to live with his mother, preferring life in an orphanage. The abrupt ending of the orphanage scene, in which the child refuses to embrace his own mother and walks away down the vast emptiness of the halls and high ceilings of a religious institution, is all the more shocking, for the way it is underplayed, creating a sense of normality which increases its impact, by virtue of a total absence of sentimentality, precisely where one would expect it in the Italian cinema of the time. There is an ending, but no climax, only a hard decision made by a small child. Its plot contravenes the so-called era of 'White telephones', Italian equivalents of Hollywood films. In Viola's closing scene, the mother asks the child for forgiveness, which he grants her. Zavattini replaced it with a Modernist open ending, whereby the resolution raises further questions.

The central idea of the child's ethical gaze, the silent witness, became a recurring one in Italian Neo-realist films a few years later, in Rossellini's *Germany Year Zero* and *Europa '51*, in De Sica and Zavattini's *Bicycle Thieves*, which Zavattini's rubric by the same title in *Grazia* illustrated magazine had already framed.[31] There is no child-like confusion in the character acted by Luciano de Ambrosis's judging gaze, witnessing adultery and the dissolution of the family home. Again and again, sight, the act of seeing and sightlines stand for an allegory of adultery out of sight, as a signifier for the hypocrisy of the Fascist regime and its counterpart: the evidence in sight and 'seeing as a redemptive act', already suggested by Zavattini through the 'watching' of the title, conceived for his original rubric in *Grazia* magazine.[32] The emphasis on seeing, the child's intense gaze, brings a physicality and a materiality onto the screen, a strong sense of physical presence of *being* human as opposed to *acting* the part of a human being, which draw *The Children Are Watching Us* – and also Visconti's *Ossessione* – closer to later canonical Neo-realist films.[33]

Other aspects of *The Children Are Watching Us* are also present in Visconti's *Ossessione* (1943) and in Alessandro Blasetti's *Quattro passi fra le nuvole* (1942) (*Four Steps in the Clouds*). This latter film was scripted by Zavattini. What distinguishes these films from the mainstream regime cinema of adventure stories and comedy? First, the rejection of the Fascist family ethos of the period, through the representation of an unhappy childhood. Second, the representation of female adultery, passion and a broken marriage. Third, the representation of suicide; fourth, the family, in the face of Fascist ideals which preached procreation and motherhood, becomes a locus of destruction and disillusionment, one which offers an unflattering *pater familias* representation.[34] It is all the more extraordinary that the scenario and film were approved by the Fascist censor.

Another point is the aspiration, and partial choice, to cast non-professional actors in film roles. In *The Children Are Watching Us*, De Sica and Zavattini cast a four-year-old child, who was new to acting, as Pricò, the son. This didn't become a sine qua non feature of Neo-realism, but is, nevertheless, a recurring aesthetic choice in the films of the movement. De Sica agreed with Zavattini, stating:

> If it were possible, I'd like to take my actors from among the crowd in the street. I'd like my lead character to be that youth sitting opposite me on the tramway or that girl walking hand in hand with a child.[35]

By the autumn of 1943 after the Allied invasion of Sicily, it became clear that Italy had lost the war. The government surrendered to the Allies on 8 September. In a matter of days, the former Axis allies invaded northern and central Italy, including Rome. During the ensuing Occupation, the Germans looted the main Italian film studios, based in Cinecittà, while the Fascists of the Ministry of Popular Culture (*Minculpop*) confiscated cine-cameras and other equipment to take it north to Venice, as well as over 100 early Italian cinema film reels at the Italian film school opposite the Centro Sperimentale di Cinematografia di Roma. After the Liberation of Rome, the Allied Occupation authorities shut down Cinecittà and the national film school, the Centro Sperimentale di Cinematografia di Roma, turning Cinecittà into a prisoner of war transit camp and ammunitions depot.[36]

4.8 *La porta del cielo* (*The Door to Heaven*)

Despite this state of affairs, during the German Occupation, the Vatican commissioned Vittorio De Sica to make *La porta del cielo* (*The Door to Heaven*) (1944), mostly shot in San Bellarmino church in Rome, partly in a railway station, and partly in a basilica, San Paolo Outside the Walls. The interior Red Cross train sequences were shot in a reconstructed third-class wagon in the basement of San Bellarmino, while exterior scenes of the train were shot on location, in Trastevere railway station, which meant waiting for air raids to film when it was empty.[37] The film was funded by the Vatican, through the Centro Cattolico Cinematografico (CCC) and Orbis Film, its production house.

In November 1944, Zavattini met De Sica to discuss the film. He didn't come up with the initial idea, but, as he had already done, working on screenplays in collaboration with others at the time, he developed the material the producer Salvo d'Angelo gave De Sica, which contained two separate shooting scripts.[38] De Sica asked Zavattini to make use of them, purely as raw material for a screenplay about the Holy House of Loreto, a Catholic shrine and destination for pilgrimages.[39] *The Door to Heaven* was to be the story of a pilgrimage of sick people from different walks of life headed for the miraculous shrine of Loreto, to implore the Virgin Mary for a cure and, in the Vatican's intentions and those of Diego Fabbri, a devout Catholic screenwriter, to get it.

But Zavattini had other plans. The film gave him further scope to develop the *tranche de vie* cinematic register, in common with *The Children Are Watching Us*. Zavattini the atheist turned a script about hope and miracles into a story about everyday life, moving away from devotion as such, and turning the narrative structure of the film into a series of episodes about the characters' past, establishing for the viewer why ordinary people would wish to go on a pilgrimage. By 2 February 1944, Zavattini had finished the screenplay and filming began the following day.[40] The day before he finished the final screenplay, he narrowly escaped being sent to work in Germany as a slave for Albert Speer's *Organization Todt*.[41]

The story is simple: a Red Cross train takes its invalided passengers towards Loreto. The film investigates their lives as people, rather than their interaction as pilgrims, or their attitudes towards religious belief. They include a cross-section of contemporary society, including a paralysed businessman, a sick child, a professional pianist with a paralysed hand, an elderly house servant, seeking grace for the troubled family which was employing her, and a factory worker with an eye injury. They all get on the same train to Loreto, hoping for a miracle. But no miracle would be forthcoming. The dialogues rely on ordinary language, devoid of any grandiloquent speeches, and the camera dwells on situations, more than on plot development. In the course of the train journey, the pilgrims get to know each other and each other's plight, growing in the knowledge that they need faith to endure their fate and survive. Once again, there is no catharsis in *The Door to Heaven*. According to De Sica, the initial story climaxed in a miracle, a reward for sick pilgrims' faith. But in the definitive ending, no one is healed by God. What appears on the screen instead is a candle-lit, anonymous crowd scene procession towards the Virgin Mary's Loreto shrine, filmed in San Paolo Basilica. Thus, a story of devotion becomes a story about contemporary Italy during wartime Occupation, everyday life and suffering. For De Sica, the true miracle was the acceptance of their lot.[42] He and Zavattini preferred a realist ending.

It was, however, a godsend for actors and film crew. According to the actress María Mercader, as many as 3,000 people found shelter in San Paolo Basilica where the Loreto shrine was reconstructed and the final procession staged.[43] Mercader, who played the role of a Red Cross nurse in the film, called it 'our insurance-film', since it gave board and lodging to a troupe of 850 people, during several months of the German Occupation, which ended in July 1944, including extras and non-professional actors, working alongside established actors, such as Franco Girotti and María Mercader.[44] The filming was often interrupted by German or Fascist inspections, motivated by the suspicion that the sets were harbouring Jews or partisans. De Sica admitted that

> We were really just barely hanging on. I was afraid the ss would come and arrest all of us and send us to concentration camps, to end the farce once and for all. [...] I heard a loud explosion in the distance. I tried to figure out where it was coming from and realized it was from where we hoped, where the British and Americans were. It was the sound of their cannons. So I let out a shout that made everyone jump to their feet: 'You've done nothing for months! Shame on you! We've got to finish this film!'[45]

The Vatican, the sole funder, and the ccc, its official producer, were so disappointed with the result that, shortly after its release, the film was removed from circulation. De Sica attributed this latter-day censorship to the film's departure from standard Catholic orthodoxy.[46] In 1944, the screenwriter Ennio Flaiano remarked: '*The Door to Heaven* is the story of miracles. The first miracle, it seems to me, is the film itself, produced over seven months in the midst of incredible difficulties.'[47] Nevertheless, *The Door to Heaven* was seen by a few film critics, including Flaiano and Mario Verdone, who valued it in 1948 as a forerunner of *Sciuscià* and *Bicycle Thieves*.[48]

Post-war critique of cinema

5.1 The context

When the German Occupation in Rome was over, the Allies turned the looted and empty Cinecittà film studios into a temporary refugee housing, by order of Rear-Admiral Ellery Wheeler Stone. Stone was the Chief Commissioner of the Allied Military Commission, Italy. For the next five years, Cinecittà became a much-needed home for refugees. This meant, however, that, in addition to the lack of capital finance, Italian filmmakers also had to face the challenge of how their national cinema would survive the plans of the Film Board, which reported to the Allied Commission.[1]

A meeting took place at the new Allied Military Commission, in the Film Board's office. It was attended by representatives of film production, a representative of British interests, and one from the filmmakers and technicians. The agenda was to discuss the way forward for Italian cinema, after the defeat of Fascism.[2] Rear-Admiral Stone stated that Fascist legislation on cinema had to be overturned, adding that, because Italian cinema 'was invented by Fascism, it now had to be suppressed, including Cinecittà studios and any available equipment'. He quipped: 'There has never been an Italian film industry, nor industry producers, only speculators. Given that Italy had a rural economy, there is no need for it to have its own film industry.'[3] Fortunately, Stephen Pallos disagreed and sided with Alfredo Guarini, arguing that the challenge was to create favourable conditions in which Italian cinema could be revived.[4] Yet US economic interests were to find two allies: the Italian film industry itself, which ensured poor distribution for Italian films, so as to favour the importation of the pre-war backlog of American films, and the Right, which facilitated the glut of foreign imports.

5.2 An alternative idea of cinema: *Italia 1944*

Two films heralded a New Italian Cinema: *Rome, Open City*, a fiction film, drawing heavily on contemporary non-fictional events, and a non-fiction, *Days of Glory*, about the war and the Italian Resistance, edited by Mario Serandrei.

Both were shot in the last year of the war and both were shown at the first post-war film festival held at the Quirino Theatre, in September 1945.[5] Was it a clean break from earlier Italian cinema? It was and it wasn't. Zavattini's critique of industrial cinema did not begin after the war, and yet the war was a decisive turning point in his idea of cinema. In 1943, Zavattini was torn between comic satire and soul searching, as a closet socialist. The following year, he was involved in a tense debate which took place in Rome, in which he urged the community of filmmakers present to take responsibility for their tacit acceptance of the Fascist regime, during twenty years of dictatorship, rather than looking for scapegoats.[6]

Speaking in November 1944, as one of the founding organizers of ACCI (Italian Cinematic Cultural Association), he proposed a controversial conference: 'An accusation levelled at Italian Cinema', in which filmmakers would face up to their individual responsibilities first, to then consider and plan the future of Italian cinema: What could cinema now aspire to, emerging from the ruins of Fascism?[7] He asked himself, and the others: 'Where did we go wrong as filmmakers and as a film industry? What were we, during the Fascist dictatorship?' However, his point of view was not well received, because, in addition to a criticism of Fascism, he advocated self-criticism, aimed at Italian filmmakers and cinema itself.

His vision, of a cinema with a closer connexion to the real, a New Cinema which turned away from fiction as its mainstream form, to embrace non-fiction and engage with real events from a subjective position, dates from this period. Some of his pre-war articles had argued in favour of filming in the street, not to pave the way for Italian so-called city symphonies, but to revolutionize how mainstream cinema was created.[8] For example, Il mio paese (1940), no more than a sketch of an idea, proposed a project requiring a skeleton film crew of five, including the screenwriter, living for five months in his hometown, Luzzara, in northern Italy to film everyday life.[9] The plan to work in the physical environment extended to his ideas and influence in mass media photography. In 1947, for example, he wrote to his publisher Bompiani about the publisher's new illustrated magazine Martedì, advising him to elicit photographs from the readers, instead of relying on stock photography and film stills for the cover illustration, and to use a dozen photographers, in as many cities, for the rubric 'Things we've seen' (Cose viste), to which he suggested adding 'in Italy' to the title and extending it to cover a full-page layout: Cose viste in Italia. Cose viste was an original feature and rubric, which relied on direct observation of the environment.[10]

Parallel to the public debates was the first of a series of initiatives in the cinema aimed at a critical appraisal of the war, shifting the focus from filmmakers to ordinary people. The story Italia 1944 (published in 1948) was the earliest expression of a scenario called Italia mia. It is based on the question: 'What if?' conceiving of a performative kind of non-fiction, involving a personal interaction between film crew and filmed subjects.

What if the filmmaker creates a situation in the real world to provoke the subject? What if he relied entirely on his imagination, to suggest how the unscripted filming might unfold? Zavattini proposed filming an event in which the filmmakers would become actors themselves, placing a still functioning, battered loudspeaker and a recording of Benito Mussolini's speeches, in among the rubble, as a provocation, to engage with the people in a village by creating street theatre, in which drama would provoke a reaction among strangers, in order to question both their indifference and to elicit a reflection on contemporary history and its concomitant causes.

Italia 1944 confronts the attitudes underlying the surface of opticality, seeking out the world as it is, not as it is imagined. It envisaged in-camera montage, forcing a juxtaposition between indexical present (the bombed towns in ruins) and the unacknowledged acquiescence of Italy's indexical recent past (the delirious applauding crowds at Mussolini's Fascist rallies), in the kind of visual confrontation of sound and image which was to appear four years later in a haunting scene of Rossellini's *Germany Year Zero* (1948) set in the real Reichstag. Thus, even before the war was over, as well as carrying out his industrial cinema work as a professional screenwriter in high demand, Zavattini was also questioning mainstream cinema and its continuity. Furthermore, he was positing a discontinuity, a radical break, in the direction of a new cinema of non-fiction, with little in common with the documentary, as practised before or after the war.

The shift towards a New Cinema was also marked by a 'space of hope', at a specific historical time of insurrection, between 24 and 26 April 1945, in Genoa, Turin and Milan.[11] On the Left, the national insurrection was perceived as the beginning of a radical rupture with the past.[12] The historian Paolo Spriano wrote: 'Over the next few months the fear of imminent social revolution remained very strong in capitalist circles.'[13] However, such a perception of the imminent nature of national insurrection as a radical rupture with the past, even revolutionary, was mistaken. The radical break with the past was more apparent than real.[14]

Within a couple of years, it became clear to all that there was more continuity with the Fascist era in Italian society and political life than rupture, despite the formulation of a Constitution and a national vote which marked the end of the monarchy in Italy and granting women equal voting status.[15] This was, nevertheless, the second revolutionary moment for the Left in Italy in the twentieth century. The first was the workers' insurrectionary strikes in the north of Italy, between 1919 and 1920. It was paralleled in Germany by the Berlin Spartacist attempted revolution of 1919.

For the Italian Left, however, radical change then seemed a very real possibility. The writer Elio Vittorini, a central figure in immediate post-war Italian cultural circles, wrote about a 'new culture' in the inaugural issue of *Il Politecnico*, September 1945. His article marked a key moment at a time of crisis and new expectations of intellectuals on the Left, for the creation of a new society. New Italian Cinema, as it was first, and perhaps more accurately, called, was an integral part of the new culture. Vittorini called on Italian intellectuals to contribute their efforts to build such a new society, by means of culture, thus changing their role to become what Antonio Gramsci referred to as 'organic intellectuals'.[16] The source of Vittorini's concept was indeed Gramsci, who had theorized a 'new culture' in his *Prison Notebooks*:

> To fight for a new art would mean to fight to create new individual artists, which is absurd, for you cannot create artists artificially. One must speak of a struggle for a new culture, that is to say, for a new moral life which cannot but be intimately combined with a new intuition of life, to such an extent that it becomes a new way of feeling and perceiving reality, and, consequently, a world intimately entwined with 'potential artists' and 'potential works of art'.[17]

The 'new culture' catchphrase, common currency among Left-wing Neo-realist filmmakers in the 1940s (including Zavattini, who often uses it to situate the New Italian Cinema), was no utopian abstraction, pointing to an undefinable distant, future. Gramsci distinguished between culture, encyclopaedism and intellectualism. By 'culture' he meant the attainment of a higher awareness, with the aid of which one succeeds in understanding one's own historical value and function in everyday life. He also pointed out the need to win intellectual power or 'hegemony' as he called it, as well as economic power, to which end it would also be necessary to take an active role in culture, as well as in politics.[18] The 'new culture' phrase became a crucial signifier within the Italian post-war cultural debate. In the context of Italian cinema, it was a useful definition of cinematic Neo-realism itself, according to what film critic and screenwriter Brunello Rondi described as 'a new concept of reality, a new concept of man, of art, of how to get to know reality'.[19]

Despite its undeniable roots in the pre-war period, Neo-realism proper came into existence only *after* the opening up of cultural debates in the discursive democratic climate of the Italian Resistance, when participation in the cultural development of a new society really began. The filmmakers' participation consisted in addressing their attention to the complex dynamic of the present, understood as history in the making. The Gramscian new culture informing New Italian Cinema ruled out eternal ideas, *a priori* fixed notions and any metaphysics of reality or teleology of reality.[20] For Rossellini, writing in 1956:

> Neo-realism is above all the art of taking note (that is to say, the art of approaching an objective reality, seen as it is, unmediated by prejudice or preconceptions). Therefore, it consists in making direct contact with man.[21]

A similar intellectual climate existed in France, just after the Liberation. Maurice Merleau-Ponty published a cultural manifesto in *Les Temps Modernes*, also asserting the idea of an engaged and ethical art, in light of the experience of war and of the insights from the Resistance. In October 1945, he argued that intellectuals had to overcome the opposition between being and action, and should bridge the gap between the general public and culture, to find a way to generate political awareness.[22] He and Jean-Paul Sartre were not alone in

France. Writing in 1944, after news of Nazi extermination camps had become generally known, Henri Lefèbvre's response in *The Critique of Everyday Life* was as follows:

> We are unable to seize human facts. We fail to see them where they are, namely in humble, familiar, everyday objects: the shape of fields, of ploughs. Our search for the human takes us too far, too 'deep', we seek it in the clouds or in mysteries, whereas it is waiting for us, besieging us on all sides.[23]

Such heterodox Marxism – Sartre's, Merleau-Ponty's and Lefèbvre's – stressed a phenomenological approach to praxis: focussing critical attention on contemporary life, on what Lefèbvre called *la vie quotidienne*, 'everyday life'.

Thus in France and in Italy, there was a similar intellectual climate immediately after the war on the Left, based on the perception that a social revolution was about to happen soon.[24] The year 1945 was, from Zavattini's point of view too, a Year Zero; 'history had ousted Italians', he wrote in March 1946.[25] The war's end was an ending, the promise of a new beginning and a radical break, after twenty years of Fascist dictatorship. He understood real democracy as a practice, a process of civilization which needed to be developed day by day, in a journey of discovery, to get to know Italy as it really was after the war, and discover who the Italians really were, as concrete individuals.

In 1946, a report highlighted the extent of war damage to housing. In central Italy alone, 14.8 per cent was destroyed.[26] That same year, Zavattini wrote: 'Now the field in which we live has been cleared; the walls are gone. There isn't even a tree to distract us. [...] No longer shall we take into consideration centuries, but minutes, everyday life.'[27]

He argued that the cinema had excelled at betraying viewers through the catharsis of tears and laughter. But now, in 1946, after decades of betrayal, at long last, what could be pointed out, in the new beginning of cinema, were its shortcomings. Now was the time to do away with endings of any sort, happy or unhappy; eventually the viewers would find the key of interpretation. Why, he argued, did it make sense to advocate uncertainty? Because, certainty, in the context of post-war Italy, was suspect: 'We only fear those voices that carry too much certainty and those words that are still being used to name things with names that are [no] longer theirs.' This is the reason why doubt, not certainty, should drive the filmmaker.[28] 'Let's embrace doubt' was Zavattini's invitation to filmmakers. Time is running out, we need to act urgently, before it's too late, before the present moment is buried in books.[29] 'We're all alone among the ruins of adjectives, falling off like scabs', he wrote.[30] 'We shall be the trail blazers; the ones who stake their claim to this unknown territory.' Decades later, Béla Tarr asked the same question:

> The question really is: what is film *for*? It was a long time ago that we came to the conclusion that film is not about telling a story, its function is really something very different – so that we can get closer to people. Somehow, we can *understand* everyday life.[31]

If there could be any lingering doubts about a radical break, these were dispelled when the Left was ousted from the government coalition on 31 May 1947, by 274 votes to 231. Its expulsion marked the end of the anti-Fascist coalition.[32] What followed was strong pressure from the United States to vote for the Christian Democrats, with a view to blocking the Left's Popular Front, in exchange of material aid, through the Marshall Plan. Then, in the general election of 1948, the Christian Democrats won an absolute majority, obtaining 48.5 per cent of the votes and 305 out of 574 seats in the Chamber of Deputies.[33] Any revolutionary aims were scotched. This was the era of the new dawn of McCarthyism, spreading across Western Europe and North America. From now on, the 'new culture' had to contend with a repressive use of censorship.

5.3 Towards an ethical cinema

From the war's end in 1945 to 1954, Zavattini wrote stories for forty-seven films that went into production, and countless others which didn't.[34] But the scenarios he particularly cared about revolved around an ethics of action, in an understanding of ethics as an active principle, in response to the post-war climate and the desired radical break which almost took place, but was soon scotched after the war of Liberation. Radical change demanded follow-up, dedication, to what Zavattini and others on the Left saw as a political event.[35] For Zavattini and other socialists, between 1945 and 1947, there had been a window of opportunity for a radical change of Italian society. In the face of the event, for the philosopher Alain Badiou we are no longer individual others, distinguished by our essential differences, but the Same, insofar as the event is a shared one which requires an ethics of action.[36] Regardless of the negative outcome, of how the post-war period played out, Zavattini's ethics of action had activist connotations which he translated into a cultural politics. From his perspective, realism was to be understood as a form of honesty, requiring filmmakers to adopt an ethical stance towards the real, in fidelity to the opportunity for a radical break at war's end. As he saw it, the task ahead for filmmakers in the immediate post-war was not one of mourning, since, he claimed, no amount of mourning would suffice in the face of the enormity of suffering. Defeat could teach a lesson which victors could ignore, seduced by the promises of old myths. Taking stock of defeat meant having the freedom to dare; to dare to be honest and admit that you had betrayed your viewers, 'that cinema was the medium to do so all over the world'.[37] Such an ethical stance on cinema's destiny precedes by more than half a century Jean-Luc Godard's *Je t'accuse*. In an interview about cinema's 100-year anniversary, J. L. G. stated that cinema had failed to carry out its role, as a means of critical reflection on the real; concentrating instead on spectacle.[38] In another interview, he said:

> Motion pictures were invented to look, tell, and study things. They were mainly a scientific tool for seeing life in a different way. To be only spectacular

should be five or ten percent of cinema. All the rest should be documentary study in a broad sense, research and essays.[39]

Zavattini thought that the structure of society could be radically transformed.[40] Since the mid-1940s, he asked himself what the conditions of possibility of transcendence would be for cinema. He began to think about how cinema as an art form could go beyond the existing normative functionalism of mainstream industrial cinema and its internal structures. What intervention could take cinema from reproduction or repetition of the status quo of reality to its production? How to make the shift from the prevailing status quo, the actual, to the possible? What else could cinema be? Nor did he limit his scope to theorizing cinema on paper. As a filmmaker, a writer and a journalist, he engaged in a battle against hegemonic cinema. He took an antagonistic stance, facing his contemporaries with a choice: either transform the pre-existing structure of cinema, or allow the structure produced by past generations to self-reproduce.

5.4 Zavattini's post-war journalism

Realism for Zavattini also meant encouraging a public debate about the Italian refusal of self-criticism, regarding the defeat of Fascism and Italy's moral bankruptcy, that is to say, the need to address the lack of awareness, or even unwillingness, to ask critical questions, after the twenty-year Fascist era of collective dishonesty. He proposed the launch of a new magazine: *Il Disonesto* (*The Dishonest Person*). It didn't go ahead, but Zavattini's editorial format was later adopted and developed by the fledgling weekly *Epoca*, and with Zavattini's full cooperation. His feature, *Italia Domanda* (*Italy Wants to Know*) consisted in readers' questions, revolving around the social and political sphere. These were to be published in full, followed by the answers written by a team of writers and researchers selected by Zavattini. His other innovation was that the questions were elicited by the writers asking them in the street. The aim was to facilitate an exchange between readers and writers, people and mainstream press:

> Our publication contains a large feature entitled *Italia Domanda* precisely because we want there to be a constant flow and counter-flow between representatives of culture and the people.[41]

Commissioned writers were to pursue 'minimal documentaries about the everyday life of others', stating the time of day, and the place the notable event was witnessed and briefly narrated. His was an entirely original outlook in the immediate post-war, by comparison even with Valentino Bompiani's views. Bompiani was more interested in publishing material about political scandals. When, in 1950, Mondadori was won over by the project, he hired Zavattini as the feature editor of the fifteen-page *Italia Domanda* rubric within *Epoca*, his new illustrated magazine, an Italian *Life*, but one concerned with everyday life, following Zavattini's vision.[42] The first issue sold 300,000 copies, then stabilized at 200,000. A phenomenal success for Zavattini, which confirmed his pre-war magic touch as a media expert and innovator. His feature, *Italia Domanda*, constituted a major shift towards reader-centred, participative, journalism which influenced *Epoca*'s entire editorial slant from then on. Symptomatic, in this respect, was the cover illustration of the first issue, not the image of a star nor of a model, but a photograph of an ordinary person: a shopping assistant.[43]

Shoeshine and *Bicycle Thieves*

6.1 *Sciuscià* (*Shoeshine*)

Despite the sheer diversity of Zavattini's multiple activities at any one time, there is a common thread: the subaltern, poverty, inequality and an ethics of action. It was not so much filming out of doors and the choice of non-professional actors which typifies the New Italian Cinema. It was the formulation of a new ethics of cinema, to which Zavattini contributed by developing his theory and practice.

Sciuscià (1946) (*Shoeshine*) dealt with the war indirectly, exposing its human ruins, as opposed to the literal ruins of so-called *trauer filme*, or 'rubble film'. In this sense, the war became a spectre of absence haunting its simple story. The title, *Sciuscià*, is Pidgin English for 'shoeshine', a job taken up by many homeless or orphan children in the immediate post-war. Vittorio De Sica came up with the initial idea to make a film about them.[1] He had in mind 'a film about children who worked for a living who are aware that they shouldn't be doing what they are doing for a living'. He said so in an article for a film magazine, under the rubric: 'What film would you like to make?'[2] De Sica's account was illustrated by photographs of the children, under the title *I ragazzi* (*The Boys*), which was also a provisional title for the film. His scenario was very simple, too simple; more like a brief, informal, anecdote, documenting De Sica's encounter in Rome with real-life shoeshines, a month after the war's end. One of them was unemployed, the other was a dishwasher in a restaurant. They worked in Via Veneto. When they'd earned enough to pay for a ride, they'd go to the horse riding track for the rich and nobility in Villa Borghese. Giuseppe was twelve, his younger friend Luigi younger still. De Sica followed them, in the hope of being able to speak to them and take their photographs.[3] One was nicknamed *Scimmietta* ('Little monkey'), an orphan who slept in an elevator. The other was *Cappellone*, later arrested and detained in prison.[4] The two shoeshines spent their spare time riding a horse at the *Galoppatoio*, the public riding track on the grounds of Villa Borghese. De Sica's article contains the establishing shot for the film in a surreal juxtaposition between misery (the shoeshines) and wealth (upper-class pursuits).

Six months later, De Sica was asked by Armando William Tamburella, the producer of Alfa Cinematografica, to make a film about shoeshines, based on a very weak storyline by Cesare Giulio Viola, the author of the novel *Pricò* which Zavattini had adapted and De Sica then filmed with the title *The Children Are Watching Us*.[5] De Sica contacted Zavattini and together they went location scouting, including a visit to a minors' prison in Rome, and came into contact with the sort of people who would be represented in the film. By July 1945, they had a story and a treatment: Zavattini had turned around a nineteen-page script in forty-eight hours:[6]

> I wrote the nineteen pages with an ethical objective driving the entire film. The children's loneliness and the story of the white horse was the matrix, from the very first shot of the emotional narrative.[7]

The full screenplay took two months to write. It was co-authored by Marcello Pagliero (who had acted in *Rome, Open City*), but Pagliero soon left, to try his fortune in France, Sergio Amidei (one of the screenwriters of *Rome, Open City*), Adolfo Franci and the above-mentioned Cesare Giulio Viola. Both latter were part of De Sica's existing writing team. The screenplay for *Sciuscià* was completed by mid-September 1945, despite the rift between Zavattini and this team of writers, especially tense between Amidei and Zavattini. The orthodox Communist Amidei simply could not accept Zavattini's heterodox approach to the theme.

Filming began on 10 October and was finished on 6 January 1946. *Sciuscià* was first shown in April of that year, nearly ten months before *Paisà* was released.[8] The outdoor scenes were shot in the street, while all the indoor scenes were filmed in a makeshift studio, as was the last outdoor scene.[9] And yet, despite this, the film belongs to the canon of Neo-realism. *Shoeshine* was a huge success in the United States and in France.[10] It won an Oscar, but the film was a financial disaster in Italy, now saturated with the large pre-war backlog of Hollywood films flooding the market.

Zavattini began by coming to grips with the raw material, the shocking sight of children working, and relating to an unknown adult world outside the family, instead of going to school or playing. The act of seeing, in the sense of witnessing, had been at the heart of *The Children Are Watching Us* and features strongly once more in *Shoeshine*.[11] The viewer is reconstructed as a witness of a tragedy, mediated by drama which adds fiction to the real situation of post-war Italy. This 'ethical intention' is the added layer of the real, mediated though it is, which, as Zavattini put it, 'drives a spit', by which he meant a unifying element, through the whole scenario.[12]

The story opens with the contrast of the élite setting, the Villa Borghese riding track, and the improbable presence of two working-class children on horseback. No fiction so far. Nor was it fiction that these ragamuffins should love horse riding on a white horse. Fiction intervenes. They are saving up enough money to buy the horse. They need more and agree to become unwitting accessories to a house burglary. With the proceeds, they fulfil their dream of buying the white horse. However, they are caught and blamed for the crime, and sent to reform prison, where they grow further and further apart, as their friendship changes into rivalry and hatred, leading to the accidental death of one of them, after their release.

When De Sica was casting the characters, he discarded Scimmietta and Cappellone, the homeless boys he had interviewed, because they weren't photogenic for a film. Screen image and reality were at odds, although they really were hiring a horse for fun in their spare time. He found other faces and bodies of ordinary people, like Luciano, the four-year-old child of a Milanese factory worker, in the part of the adulterer's son in *The Children Are Watching Us*. By so doing, De Sica sought to attenuate the harshness of this reality, and make it easier for the viewer to countenance, through the screen presence of Franco Interlenghi and Rinaldo Smordoni.

In *Shoeshine*, the protagonists Pasquale and Giuseppe have no idea what is happening to them. They signify a child's uncertainty and emotional confusion. They experience reality as a game, a dream, which turns into a nightmare. In a sense, the same confusion that characterizes Zavattini's mid-1940s prose in the face of a changing world is expressed by the two shoeshines and recurs in *Bicycle Thieves* (1948) and *Umberto D.* (1952). All these characters are anti-heroes.[13]

Over and above their downfall hovers the moral bankruptcy of a situation in which children can no longer be children, but are forced by external circumstances to act like adults, while still not having reached the full maturity of an adult. By comparison, in the Naples episode of Rossellini's *Paisà* (1946), the war orphan and homeless shoeshine Pascà sets aside his childhood imagination completely, unlike his purchase, the MP called Joe, but in *Germany Year Zero* (1948), Rossellini's child character, Edmund, like Pasquale and Giuseppe, also weaves in and out of his understanding as a child and that of an adult, until the very end, when he takes full and tragic responsibility for his actions, and chooses to die by his own hand.

Indeterminacy doesn't crop up for the first time in Italian cinema with Michelangelo Antonioni's 1960s films, as Gilles Deleuze believed. It is already inscribed in the earliest Neo-realist films, complicating and problematizing the fiction/non-fiction duality. It is absent in *The Children Are Watching Us*, where there is a clear demarcation between right and wrong in Luciano's final, shocking, casting of judgement on his mother. Whereas, it features in *Sciuscià* within a verisimilitude, or better, a *mimēsis* of ambiguity, in a crossover between subjectivity and objectivity, perception and confusion, dream and reality.[14]

The film's screen-based reality is the understated real-life situation of post-war Italy in which the drama invented by Zavattini unfolds. The backdrop, unproblematic in pre-war Italian cinema, after the war's end, stands out as a new character in its own right. The very existence of a shoeshine on- and off-screen is already what Deleuze calls 'the limit-situation', its new banality being as intolerable for De Sica as for Zavattini and the viewers.[15] What is new here is not filming in the street, not montage, not camera work, not lighting, but the scandalous juxtaposition of a child protagonist and the external world, the mise-en-scène of the characters' wavering confusion, the hitherto uncharacteristic inability to act or decide.

This is achieved by turning the attention to the act of seeing, as recognizing and placing the onus on the viewer, not through identification with the characters, but through eliciting a slow, durational perception of a represented situation, no matter how invented or studio-based, for it is also suggestive of an off-screen contemporary situation which was far from fictional. Like other Neo-realist films, fiction and non-fiction blur, in an understanding of verisimilitude (Zavattini's, De Sica's or that of other Italian filmmakers) which is anything but naïve.[16] An example of this in *Shoeshine* is the white horse, which is taken for a symbol, a 'lyrical artifice', and 'a metaphor' for a child's toy, as one writer puts it, or represents the 'concrete' representation of the friendship between Pasquale and Giuseppe, as another author has argued, while at the same time being a representation of an actual horse ridden by two shoeshines in 1945.[17] Thus, in an artistic sense, the horse was a found object from everyday life, however improbable that might have seemed in the immediate post-war, which, through the artistic mediation of Neo-realism, also becomes a metaphor.[18]

The French critic André Bazin places the film's success in the context of the revolutionary nature of the Italian Liberation after Fascism.[19] This was one of the first films to put on the screen new social actors, child labour and all that this entailed, even if such harsh reality was at times mediated by melodrama, as occurs in *Rome, Open City*. However, both films were a step change, in terms of overcoming American and French aestheticism, through a kind of realism which engages with the social description of everyday life.[20] The point was that cinema's focus turned to the contemporary world, so that the treatment of reality became the theme, not just an element, instrumental to other themes.

Why is *Sciuscià* still so traumatic to watch? Partly because of the sheer physicality of the actors' screen presence, and the shock of seeing the present moment or contemporary history in the shot.[21] Unlike *Rome, Open City*, based on real events, however much retold, embellished, repurposed, by Rossellini and his screenwriters, the story in *Sciuscià* is pure invention. Yet the way the children behave on screen contributes to create the feeling of witnessing the reality of post-war Italy. All the more so because they have never acted before.

6.2 *Bicycle Thieves*

Vittorio De Sica told *La Fiera Letteraria* why he decided to make *Bicycle Thieves*:

> After *Sciuscià*, I had thirty or forty scenarios to choose from, all wonderful, bursting with events and powerful situations. But I was looking for, at least on the surface, a less extraordinary story, the kind of situation that could happen to anyone, especially to the poor, but which no newspaper would deem worthy of publishing.[22]

The film won five Italian Nastri d'Argento awards in 1949 for best film, best direction, best scenario and screenplay, photography, and sound, and the

1949 Oscar Academy Award for best foreign film; not to mention many other awards worldwide. The plot is deceptively simple: a man's bicycle is stolen. Since he depends on it for his living, he has no choice but to try and find it. His fruitless search lasts the whole length of the film. Its theft means that he will lose his job.

One day, Zavattini told De Sica: 'A book by Luigi Bartolini has just come out. Read it. We can borrow the title and the basic idea.'[23] In July 1947, Zavattini wrote to his friend Pietro Bardi:

> I suggested to De Sica that he make the whole film about the theft of a bicycle, taking the idea from *Bicycle Thieves*, by Bartolini, as I've already mentioned, but built around a different character from Bartolini. The theft of a bicycle is a huge event.[24]

The opening paragraph of his scenario, in the version published in his *Diary*, reads:

> What's a bike? In Rome there are as many bicycles as flies. Dozens and dozens are stolen every day, but no newspaper is going to publish a single line about that, not even in 6 point. Could be that the press is no longer able to establish the relative importance of events. If, for example, someone stole Antonio's bicycle, the press, in my opinion, should cover the theft with a headline splashed across four columns.[25]

De Sica wasn't convinced. Zavattini had to spell out the context for him. Here was a film that would address the relative weight given to events in the press and demonstrate how small stories are far from insignificant for the people directly involved. This was a far cry from a cinematic adaptation of a novel. Rather, Zavattini wanted to dispense altogether with Luigi Bartolini's picaresque autobiographical novel *Bicycle Thieves* (1946), which related the story of how a middle-class painter searched for his two stolen bicycles in the immediate post-war Rome, and triumphantly reclaimed them in the end.[26]

Zavattini retained only the theme (the theft of a bicycle) and the location (Rome), but replaced the plot and reversed the outcome. His would be the tragic story of an unemployed worker for whom the theft of his bike meant much more; the theft of his livelihood. It would dwell on a meandering and fruitless search across Rome in the company of his small child, and culminate in humiliation and open-ended uncertainty. But De Sica still wasn't convinced. What exactly would the film prove? Did it have a point? Zavattini replied that it presented the issues of working-class life, normally kept out of the cinema which, as he put it, was more concerned with kings and upper-class society.[27] Eventually, by 28 August 1947, De Sica had made up his mind and five months into the screenwriting, he got it. Now he could even articulate Zavattini's vision. He told a reporter:

> Why should a filmmaker look for extraordinary adventures when we can find drama in the everyday and marvel in what is generally considered banal?

If this is worthwhile for modern literature, why can't it be done in film? Start with reality and mediate it artistically. What's ridiculous is not a story of this nature, but that society turns a blind eye on social contradictions and suffering.[28]

De Sica, Zavattini and Sergio Amidei who had worked on *Rome, Open City* began to search for suitable locations in Rome.[29] Amidei was, like Zavattini himself, also a communist, but a card-carrying one, unlike Zavattini who never joined the Party. Zavattini had already mapped out the main locations in his scenario. It was now a matter of gleaning inspiration from direct contact with real people from these locations and 'shadowing' people and situations. In each, as recounted in his Cinematic Diary, the filmmakers interacted with the people they met, effectively creating the basis for scenes.

In September 1947, Zavattini, De Sica, Oreste Biancoli and Gerardo Guerrieri visited a brothel via Panico. The owner showed them round the infirmary and a few bedrooms. 'We're colleagues', she told the film director, having worked as a stage impersonator in the past.[30] She was keen to point out that she only employed married women. In one of the bedrooms, they surprised a couple.

- Open up, Anna.
- I'm busy.
- Get up and cover yourself.

Zavattini's published *Diary* homes in on such 'found' details for future artistic reference, conveying them with a hint of irony. The client, who is still putting on his braces, nods repeatedly and smiles as he recognizes De Sica. 'Pleased to meet you', he says, in what was almost a formal introduction, but in a brothel, of all places.

On 7 December 1947, De Sica, Zavattini and Andrea Lazzarini went to a soup kitchen set up in an early Christian church, *Santi Nereo e Achilleo*, where the poor were given a hot meal, a haircut, and sometimes clean clothes, but only if they arrived on time for mass, which was celebrated behind locked doors. Zavattini asked the organizers if they knew of any thieves or murderers attending. They pointed out a well-dressed man wearing dark glasses and a mac: *Cupido* was his name, a notorious child molester, who had been arrested for trying to rape a child.[31] The location visits continued well into the screenwriting. As late as February 1948, Zavattini and De Sica and others visited the home of a healer, known as *la Santona*, whose apartment wasn't far from Zavattini's home.[32] Zavattini visited *la Santona* in 1946, with a friend, Flora Volpini.[33] His second visit was different. He and the others were looking for ideas to include in the script, going as far as pretending to be genuine seekers.[34] However, faced with the healer's combination of theatrics and superstition, neither De Sica nor Zavattini nor Suso Cecchi d'Amico could help bursting out laughing in her face.[35]

These locations appear in Zavattini's original scenario, the screenplay and the film. Other locations are also envisaged in Zavattini's terse scenario: the

Fascist-era working-class housing estate in Valmelaina, Trastevere, the pawn shop, the stadium, Via del Tritone, the Traforo tunnel. Like Rossellini's Rome, *Rome, Open City*, the Rome of *Bicycle Thieves* ignores the city's layers of art and architecture, be they Baroque or Early Christian. Cinematic Rome is a modern city. The film begins in a Fascist housing estate in the district of Valmelaina, not far from Zavattini's home. Valmelaina is where the Ricci family live. Their apartment is bare. There is no running water. The women have to fetch water from a communal tap outdoors. Equally, an old indoor apartment in Trastevere (the interior of the thief's home) conveys only squalor. At one point, a Fascist bridge appears, but its function is to mark the contrast between monumental space and a small child, accentuating alienation in an anonymous city. Indeed, this could be any large city in Italy.

Lamberto Maggiorani, the man who acted the part of Antonio Ricci, worked at the Breda factory, while his fictional wife, Maria, was played by a journalist, Lianella Carrell, and Bruno, the child, by Enzo Staiola. From the very beginning, at the unemployment office, the main character, Antonio Ricci, is absent from what is happening around him. His name is called out but he is not listening. The camera follows someone else who alerts him. This is a decidedly odd and unconventional attitude. Most of the time Ricci is submissive or remissive; an ambiguous character who says very little and seems unable to cope. The situation overwhelms him; he constantly looks stunned, feverish. Words are replaced by gestures and looks between father and son, conveying doubt, uncertainty, confusion. If Ricci is despondent and devoid of any resources, his wife and son, by contrast, actively try to deal with the situation. It is his wife who decides to pawn their bed linen so as to redeem Ricci's old bicycle from the pawn shop. The child, Bruno, has a job at a petrol station. Although he is a child, his behaviour and outlook have nothing in common with Pasquale or Giuseppe in *Shoeshine*. Absolutely nothing escapes Bruno's attention. When his father is caught by the owner of another bicycle, Bruno intervenes and saves him from the owner pressing charges. Earlier, it is Bruno who calls the police when he and his father catch up with the thief.

Listed in the credits as contributors to the screenplay are Oreste Biancoli, Suso Cecchi D'Amico, Adolfo Franci, Gerardo Guerrieri and Gherardo Gerardi. Not included is Sergio Amidei, who worked on *Shoeshine* and *Bicycle Thieves*, who was as obstructive about *Bicycle Thieves* as he had been about *Shoeshine*, as De Sica soon realized.[36]

Amidei's career in the cinema had begun in the 1930s mainstream Hungarian-style Italian comedies which Zavattini had repeatedly tried to subvert, by proposing non-linear narrative writing.[37] In the 1930s, Amidei had contributed to 'the standard language of Italian cinema', precisely what Zavattini sought to undermine in *Bicycle Thieves*.[38] As late as 1 December 1947, Zavattini was still at odds with everyone in the writing group, since no one else, apart from De Sica, could understand the structure or matrix Zavattini proposed. The others considered it too fragile and openly derided it.[39] Ultimately, they didn't share his idea of cinema, underlying scenario and treatment, understandably perhaps, since it was a vision Zavattini had been developing for years.[40] They couldn't accept that a film could lack dramatic tension and traditional spectacular qualities. 'This isn't cinema', one of them remarked after reading the scenario.[41] Neither Amidei nor anyone else was convinced by the white horse of *Sciuscià*, nor could they accept that the theft of a bicycle could be the cause of so much strife, let alone understand Zavattini's open-ended outcome, but he was adamant, and, fortunately, De Sica took his side, despite the screenplay's unpopularity within the group.[42]

The bone of contention was the plot structure, which departs from traditional practice and conventional character stereotyping. Amidei and the others objected to the lack of logical sequencing in these episodes. They failed to see how each episode added a new situation, seemingly obeying a different logic and structure, producing a cumulative effect in which the character's helplessness plays out. The viewer becomes implicated, not through character identification, but through identifying with the situation.

The accusation of a weak structure presupposed the norm governing screenplays, a norm which Zavattini actively challenged in his writing practice, in line with his theorizing of the anti-narrative.[43] In 1947, he was fighting for a much looser, and very visual screenplay than usual.[44] What was at stake was, as De Sica hinted in the interview cited earlier, the introduction of a Modernist type of narrative, in which screen dialogue is reduced to a minimum, and ellipses force the viewer to play a more active role, in a vision of screenwriting as integral to directing. The way to achieve this was to fix his approach in the scenario and lock it into the screenplay, so that dialogue on the screen would be minimal and often be expressed by body language.

Screenwriting, in Zavattini's understanding and practice, breaks out of a technical form of writing, to develop into a major contribution to the film itself. As understood and practised by him, it blurs with filmmaking, instead of being a temporary, disposable form of writing, to be overridden by the production of the film. For him, screenwriting is also a form of theorizing the event, the encounter between cinema and the real. Compared to other Italian screenwriters of the time, according to Federica Villa's study of Italian screenwriting of the period, Zavattini stands out:

> He concentrates or compresses verbal language in order to intensify minimal gestures, physical movements bared in their state of becoming, never letting verbose language get in the way.[45]

Villa goes on to observe that 'moving away from the pressure of mimetic writing' leads to expressing 'possible worlds' in which what is subjective undercuts what is objective, and the real and the imaginary combine.[46] Ricci is from the outset a character who struggles with the external world which is experienced as a nightmare or a hallucination time and again, as Guglielmo Moneti has shown.[47] Ricci's onscreen ambiguity and physicality is inscribed in the screenwriting. His major trait, his indecisiveness, is conveyed by body language, not speech. And this is integral to the writing.

Zavattini's anti-narrative approach envisaged building a film around a tiny, casual event – such as the theft of a bicycle – and concentrating on developing the story around a series of apparently inconsequential episodes. For example, just before Ricci is robbed, child buskers are playing the accordion and are made to leave, a distraction from the main action. Bruno interrupts the action to pass water. Then, at one point, father and son shelter under an awning in Porta Portese together with a group of young seminarists chattering in German, until the sudden shower stops. Again, the action is suspended, when Ricci and Bruno have a bite to eat in a *trattoria*. Yet they all serve a purpose.

In defence of *Bicycle Thieves*, Zavattini was convinced that a whole epic could be written about the everyday, because, he later told an interviewer, when you take a closer look at small events, you realize that they are not small at all. Large events, by contrast, are so large in scale as to be too vague, and, therefore, devoid of any meaning.[48] But this outlook of his went against tradition. It had to be a mistake, as far as Amidei and the other writers were concerned. According to Alberto Abruzzese and Achille Pisanti, Zavattini's fragmentation of traditional cinematic narrative anticipated what was to become a recurring feature within later *Nouvelles Vagues*.[49]

Amidei was also unhappy about continuity and structure. Furthermore, in Amidei's view, the character's behaviour was improbable: any worker would have been shown solidarity in those years. Why wouldn't a communist comrade have sought help from the local party cell and found the bicycle? Amidei reached the conclusion that deep down, Ricci's individualism resembled more of the author's, Luigi Bartolini.[50] Yet Zavattini was also a communist and was well aware of the ethos of solidarity, of mutual help, among comrades. Indeed, early on in the film, that is exactly what Ricci finds in his friend. When Ricci seeks help at a local meeting in the basement of the housing block in Valmelaina, he meets Baiocco, in charge of a team of street sweepers, who show their solidarity, by trying to help Rici retrieve his bicycle.

However, Zavattini's story is allegorical Neo-realism in which, for example, extended wandering, the ambiguity of situations and of characters, and open-ended outcomes are cyphers of existence. Equally, in Rossellini's *Germany Year Zero*, Edmund's meandering through the ruins of Berlin and his suicide spell the bankruptcy of German civilization in the post-war, something which German censors understood so well that they banned the film for thirty years.

Equally, the white horse in *Shoeshine* had a real-life counterpart, documented by De Sica as well as being an underlying theme, thus becoming allegorical, as a shattered dream in the face of a harsh reality in which children are exploited. By the same token, in *Bicycle Thieves* the bicycle takes on a dual function, it represents full-time employment, success, family stability and is a pretext for an extended existential allegory of an open-ended quest for a way out of poverty, a dimension of Neo-realism and of this particular film which Amidei failed to understand.

Amidei couldn't accept that Maria, Ricci's wife, could disappear from the story, so soon after the theft.[51] He didn't think it was plausible. Zavattini fought with the others to avoid turning the story into the kind of post-romantic Edmondo De Amicis-type sentimental narrative about a family and its troubles one reads in *Cuore* (1886).[52] Amidei was adamant that the story should revolve around the traditional family structure, and around the relationship between father, mother and son. But Zavattini disagreed. Maria was superfluous after the initial sequences. Rejecting the family triangle, he argued that the film, and witnessing within the situations that come up, concerns only the father and son and emerges in their interplay, which rarely translates into spoken dialogue.

No wonder progress on the screenplay was held up for days by Amidei, who insisted that Maria's disappearance had to be justified. Most of the meetings were attended only by De Sica and Zavattini and took place in De Sica's home in the Parioli district.[53] But it was during an encounter in Amidei's home, that, in a fit of anger, Amidei lost his temper, grabbed De Sica and Zavattini by the scruff of their necks and threw them out.[54]

Amidei's departure was a godsend. Zavattini finally got his way and on 20 April 1948, the screenplay was signed off. *Bicycle Thieves* premiered on 21 November 1948 in Rome at the Barberini cinema.[55] Fellini phoned Zavattini that evening to tell him it was the best thing he'd seen from the beginning of cinema and De Sica congratulated him, saying that the film was a success precisely because they had resisted Amidei's pressure to change the film or abandon it altogether.[56]

When the lights came back on at the première in the Barberini, Sergio Amidei turned to his friends and to Maria Michi sitting next to him and said: 'I'm a fool!', a public admission that he had been mistaken.[57] He later phoned Zavattini to apologize. Yes, Zavattini had been right all along and the opening credits should say 'Story and Screenplay by Zavattini in Collaboration with De Sica', and changed it accordingly, praising his determination in refusing to change the screenplay and stating that it was Zavattini's film and that De Sica had wonderfully produced his idea, and his world.[58]

Italian critics praised De Sica, but passed under silence Zavattini's contribution. De Sica didn't help, by omitting any mention of it, as their correspondence bears out. *Sciuscià* had seen a similar standoff between director and screenwriter which was to poison their relation over the years. According to María Mercader, De Sica's second wife, 'The only person who worked on the text and screenplay up to and including its production, from the first moment the camera was rolling to the last, was Zavattini.'[59] In another interview she said:

> In *Bicycle Thieves*, there were six, seven or eight screenwriters, because that was the norm in those days. But the truth is that Zavattini was the only one who was actually writing.[60]

In a story published in the 1930s, Zavattini had imagined a father and son walking down a street and a situation similar to the scene at the end of the film, featuring the father's humiliation witnessed by his son.[61]

Unlike other screenwriters, Zavattini was directly involved in adapting the screenplay after its final version. He was also involved in casting. His was the choice for the child, Bruno, whom he picked out from the dozens of screen tests. During shooting, he got a daily report on the day's progress on the set from De Sica. They discussed over the phone whatever problems De Sica was having, and Zavattini advised him, and finally, the screenwriter was involved throughout the editing process, from beginning to end. He spent two months in the editing room, cutting sequences, down to individual frames at the moviola.[62] His involvement included working on the sound track, choosing which songs should be played by the amateur acting group in the scene set in the Valmelaina basement and, later, the scene in the *trattoria*. Zavattini had, after all, spent his formative years in Italian vaudeville, instead of attending school. The screenplay was almost entirely his work.[63] This may explain Giuseppe Marotta's response to the question: 'What do you think of *Bicycle Thieves*?' Marotta replied: 'A brilliant film by De Sica, conceived and directed by Cesare Zavattini.'[64]

6.3 André Bazin, Siegfried Kracauer and *Bicycle Thieves*

André Bazin's 1949 review essay is the most perceptive reflection on the film, for its subtlety in uncovering the film's underlying aesthetic. First of all, the critic pointed out that *Bicycle Thieves* distinguished itself from *Rome, Open City*, *Shoeshine* or Giuseppe De Santis's *Caccia tragica* (1947), by demonstrating that Neo-realism was not inexorably bound up with wartime and the immediate post-war. While the success of *Shoeshine* was partly due to the revolutionary impact of the Italian Liberation after Fascism, *Bicycle Thieves* justified and renewed the whole aesthetic on which it was based. It managed to be Neo-realist, without being either hyper-documentary or romanticized reportage.[65]

In Bazin's view, Neo-realism had been misrepresented as a series of stylistic features. Here was another film which was also filmed in the street, a film in which actors were not actors; a film about contemporary Italy; which sided with the working class; which reaffirmed the Neo-realist rejection of the extraordinary, by opting instead for filming an ordinary, everyday event, so mundane as to be of banal insignificance – a day spent in vain looking for a stolen bicycle, the prerequisite to escape unemployment. But the film's complexity was to be found elsewhere: in Zavattini's 'diabolically skilful' script.[66]

This, Bazin claimed, was the only communist film to have an aesthetic value, in addition to an implicit ideological one. A clear-cut film would have been propaganda, not a masterpiece. *Bicycle Thieves*, however, was far subtler, because there is a thesis – the desperate plight of the subaltern and a search for a bicycle which might be in vain – one that emerges directly from the situations and the characters' reactions to them, not from dialogue. Yet he argued that the seemingly objective social reality of *Bicycle Thieves* was carefully constructed. What distinguished *Bicycle Thieves* from other Neo-realist films made earlier was that it demonstrated that Neo-realism could transfer artistic 'objectivism' (*objectivisme*) of this kind from the Resistance to Revolution; a point which was lost on many critics then and now, but not on world cinema filmmakers at the time or since.[67]

Bazin observed that, unlike what happens in traditional cinema, events in *Bicycle Thieves* are not instrumental in conveying a message that feeds into the story. He considered them tightly knit anecdotes, each revealing its own phenomenological integrity.[68] They all serve a purpose. They convey, in a cinematic equivalent, the sense of the chaotic nature of everyday life, in which one receives a jumble of impressions that require one to decide, to engage, in meaning-making. This creates a sense of the inherent ambiguity of events, such that the onus is on the viewer to decide, based on subtle hints, as to which details are poignant, which are not, and what interpretation to give any one sequence. The consequence is to shift the responsibility of interpretation from the filmmaker to the viewer.[69] Thus, by writing apparently chance events into the script, Zavattini creates ambiguity and breaks away from linear narrative.

Finally, Bazin dwelled on why Neo-realist cinema chose ordinary people with no acting experience for the roles. In *Bicycle Thieves*, the father and son relationship doesn't work through shot-reverse-shot dialogue, but through Bruno's body language, his looks and gestures, his trotting alongside or behind Antonio Ricci, his father; these all serve as meaningful communication and trenchant expressions of mood which elicit the viewer's interpretation. The idea of including a second, equally important, main character, the child, was 'a stroke of genius' (*un trait de génie*).[70] Because the child is a witness. Such a simple device turns what would have been a social drama into a Greek tragedy, in which Bruno acts as chorus.[71] To employ ordinary people was not a part of a style recipe, but integral to an aesthetic which opposed the star system of Hollywood. As Bazin puts it: 'Anonymous cinema has finally established its independent aesthetic existence.'[72] Everything serves to create an impression of reality, in which stylistic distractions (including drawing attention to the camera) are kept to a minimum, to draw the eye as simply as possible to the 'cinematic' event.[73]

Bazin's essay suggests that he considered *Bicycle Thieves* a paradigm, in the sense of what the philosopher Giorgio Agamben calls 'an exemplar', containing its own aesthetic.[74] Bazin also noted that Zavattini had inscribed the aesthetic of *Bicycle Thieves* within his scenario: 'If it contains a complete system of aesthetics that is active, however invisible, in the last resort, this is dictated by the prior conception of the scenario.'[75]

Bicycle Thieves, as interpreted by Bazin, is a tragedy, but not a theatrical drama; a tragedy which overcomes the contradiction between event and spectacular action.[76]

For philosopher and film critic Siegfried Kracauer, close friend of Walter Benjamin, *Shoeshine, Rome, Open City, Bicycle Thieves, Miracle in Milan* and other Neo-realist films bring to cinematic visibility 'elements or moments of physical reality', to the point of penetrating its ephemerality. In these films, as he sees it, the street is 'that province of reality where transient life manifests itself most conspicuously'; the place of 'fleeting impressions', where 'the accidental prevails over the providential, and happenings in the nature of unexpected incidents are all but the rule'.[77] In these spaces, perception is, according to Kracauer, always already a mode of thought, particularly in *Bicycle Thieves*, occurring in what he calls 'the anteroom', the space bordering with daily life and almost part of it, where impressions form, prior to judgement.[78] The 'anteroom', already inscribed in Zavattini's scenario, is the place of undecidability, or, if you will, a preliminary stage of judgement. The problematic is poverty, not the war, nor its aftermath. And the viewer, who watches the characters watching, becomes an eyewitness herself.[79]

As Kracauer sees it, the horror of injustice is redeemed through reflection, understood as artistic mediation. He uses an analogy, the mythological figure of Perseus, who was unable to look at the Medusa in the face and could only bear to see here through her reflection on his shield. In a similar way, he argues, our witnessing as viewers is mediated.[80] A mediation of the real, *mimēsis*; not reflection theory. The much-misunderstood Kracauer of *Theory of Film* (1960) explains and defends his idea of redemption in an extraordinary sequel: *History. The Last Things Before the Last* (1969), edited by the fine philologist Paul Oskar Kristeller. Redemption, rooted in phenomenology, and nothing to do with religion, is 'to think *through* things, not above them'.[81] The potential of the cine-camera in its use in Neo-realist cinema *redeems* 'the transient phenomena of the outer world'. Redemption consists in witnessing through the act of seeing, in the anteroom of thought, before judgements and conclusions are reached. For Kracauer, such an emphasis on opticality, almost, but not quite, a form of direct experience, is already borne out by *Shoeshine*, but more so by *Bicycle Thieves*.[82]

6.4 Zavattini's qualms: *The Great Deception*

After *Bicycle Thieves* was screened and acclaimed, Zavattini dwelled on the objections made by De Sica and by others. He was left with the nagging doubt that *Bicycle Thieves* contained many stories left untold. Though the film was fictional, the story called for a genuine sense of solidarity, which explains why, no soon as he had finished writing the final screenplay, he imagined a sequel in which De Sica expressed his failure as a director in taking the themes further. He wrote *Il grande inganno* (*The Great Deception*), which proposed a personal, reflexive cinema about cinema.[83]

Zavattini could have called his scenario, *The Great Deception*, *Life after Bicycle Thieves*, since it narrates the real-life story of Lamberto Maggiorani, who played the role of Antonio Ricci. His story follows the life of Maggiorani after *Bicycle Thieves*, when he returned to his job in the factory, and was sacked, during a first wave of redundancies.

What complicates this linear narrative is that the ensuing events are seen from the point of view of the director of *Bicycle Thieves*, De Sica, who reflects on the limitations of cinema and on his own, personal, shortcomings as a director and a man who, as imagined by Zavattini, faces the plight of being Maggiorani in real life, in a story which is constantly interrupted by the free, open-ended narrative, a structure that made it possible to introduce secondary stories. Narrative is replaced by metanarrative, in the protagonist's own reflections and self-doubts, his purpose and raison d'être as a director, faced with the true, tragic, story of Maggiorani, in the aftermath of *Bicycle Thieves*.

In *The Great Deception*, fiction and reality coexist, as they tend to do in Neo-realist films which juxtapose lifeworld footage with fiction. In this case, news stories, producers, actors and directors playing themselves, that is to say, dropping their public director persona, serve to paint the contradictory picture of the film industry seen from within, begging the question of social justice and solidarity. 'It could be the film of conscience', Zavattini wrote in introducing his scenario. His scenario also brings to the fore Zavattini's Pirandellian problematic, assimilated through the mediation of his early mentor and Pirandello admirer, the judge and playwright Ugo Betti, the divide between life and art, real life and the flawed film industry. This was a preoccupation Zavattini was to develop the following year, in another scenario of his which became the film *Bellissima*, directed by Luchino Visconti.

The Great Deception, Zavattini's real-world sequel to *Bicycle Thieves*, subsumes that film's fiction into itself by turning the camera at the actors, not the characters. It reveals what goes on behind the scenes. He addresses the paradox of a society that 'cries in the picture houses for fictional heroes, but as soon as it leaves it forgets the real ones'.[84]

The confessional mode, which Zavattini had already developed in the early drafts of *First Communion*, is central to *The Great Deception*, featuring a real-life film director with qualms about his actions. He wrote a second version, in which all this has been edited out of the story. In its place, one finds a linear unfolding of events told by an anonymous narrator. The main character is now Maggiorani, not De Sica. Maggiorani's point of view replaces De Sica's and consequently, the confessional, self-doubting mode has been dropped altogether. Why utterly change the story?

Zavattini's main character, De Sica in a very unlikely confessional mode, had, in real life, objected to the idea.[85] It was too honest a representation. Yet, only two months later Zavattini went on to write the script for *Bellissima*, which developed the same theme, the divide between cinema, popular imagination and ordinary life, using imaginary characters.

The first version of *The Great Deception* is an early expression of Zavattini's explorations into personal cinema, whereas the second, watered-down version, the writer rescues De Sica from self-reflection. Zavattini told the Hungarian director: 'I wouldn't read more complex meanings into it and let me reiterate that I don't plan to include anything resembling Pirandello.'[86] Yet, Pirandello's interruptive strategies and problematics are precisely what come to mind, reading the first, reflexive and confessional version, something which Zavattini's denial only confirms.

In 1951, Zavattini returned to this problematic, in a six-minute short about *Bicycle Thieves*, directed by De Sica. It was one of a series, entitled *Ambienti e personaggi* (*Characters and Environments*), thought up and produced by Zavattini, in which Maggiorani and Enzo Stajola re-enact Ricci and Bruno. Once again, they play the scene in which Ricci returns to his Valmelaina tenement after being offered the job, the episode in the backstreets, and also the ending.[87]

Cinema as commitment

The Perugia Conference (1949)

7.1 The context: Fascist censorship revived

With the defeat of Fascism came the rejection of restrictive Fascist legislation for the film industry. It may seem to have marked the end of censorship in Italy.[1] The old law of 24 September 1923 had legalized 'preventive' censorship of all proposed films, by making the vetting of scenarios and screenplays by the Fascist Ministry of Popular Culture (MINCULPOP) compulsory.[2] The new law claimed the right to freedom to produce films.

However, a tight control over content through direct government censorship was reinstated soon after, in 1947, no sooner as the prime minister, Christian Democrat Alcide De Gasperi, had expelled the Left-wing coalition members from the government.[3] From that moment, the Christian Democrats began to take political and economic control of the Italian film industry. They proceeded to sack Umberto Barbaro, the communist director of the state-funded Rome film school, the Scuola Sperimentale di Cinema, and then dismissed his successor and former colleague, Luigi Chiarini.[4] DC minister Giulio Andreotti planned to exert total control over Italian producers, from writing scenarios, to financing, censorship and distribution. New legislation provided the legal instrument to implement his plans.[5] The New Italian Cinema was bringing underdevelopment onto the big screen and had to be suppressed.[6] Simple.

That December of 1947, *Gioventù perduta* (*Lost Youth*), by Pietro Germi, was refused its certificate for commercial distribution.[7] Thirty-five directors published an Open Letter in the press, including *L'Unità*, with the title 'The DC's political censorship is suffocating Italian cinema'. Many signed, including De Sica, Antonioni, Rossellini, Visconti, Castellani and Zampa.[8] The signatories accused the government of reviving Fascist legislation.[9] Reviving so-called preventive censorship, they claimed, was not only political, it was also ideological.[10] Andreotti's response in the Right-wing *Il Popolo* made it clear that their rebellion would have no effect whatsoever.[11] And it didn't. The minister took complete control over the economic structure of the film industry. His new legislation established a Central Office of Cinematography, reporting to an integral part of government administration, effectively reinstating, indeed increasing, political control over the film industry.[12] Once again, it became mandatory for the producer to submit screenplays of new films to this office for approval. No better man than former Fascist General Director of the Government Film Agency, Nicola De Pirro, to be in charge.[13] In the meantime, Italian distributors were consistently refusing to distribute Italian films adequately, thus blatantly disregarding their obligations. By the following year, when the Christian Democrats obtained an absolute majority, their stranglehold on the industry was guaranteed for the next decade.[14]

On 20 February 1948, the 'Movement for the Defence of Italian Cinema' organized a mass demonstration in Rome's Piazza del Popolo, organized by directors, actors and film crews. Their manifesto explained why. They objected to the dumping of old North American films onto the Italian market; they also objected to the monopoly of foreign distributors; to the stranglehold over credit; to the flaunting by Italian distributors of regulations governing foreign imports, and to censorship. They requested a law to introduce a measure of regulation within the industry, the reform of censorship, and making credit available.[15] Andreotti's response was to ignore their requests and bide his time.[16] His allies, the influential Right-wing Catholic CCC (Centro Cattolico Cinematografico) attacked the manifesto and Neo-realism itself, as a form of self-harm.[17] The Christian Democrats also put a lot of money into developing a national network of cinemas right next to parish churches, which would only show films approved by the CCC. In 1946 there were 559 in Italy, but with increased government funding the figure rose to 3,000 by 1949, and 5,449 by 1955.[18]

In September 1948, Andreotti published an official communiqué condemning films showing negative aspects of Italy.[19] Andreotti made 'preventive advice' mandatory, and extended it from initial scenario to final scenario.[20] This ongoing campaign of state censorship against the New Italian Cinema was the prelude to the Perugia film Conference, organized at the height of the Cold War.

This was the cultural and political context in which, to give it its full title, the International Conference of Cinematography was held in Perugia, from 24 to 27 September 1949.[21] Luigi Charini noted that the focus was political, not aesthetic.[22] The who's who of Italian Neo-realism was in attendance, including Vittorio De Sica, Giuseppe De Santis, Roberto Rossellini, Ludovico Visconti and Carlo Lizzani. The theme – 'Does contemporary cinema reflect the problems of modern man?' – concerned the relation between filmmaking and commitment to the social. The previous year had marked the landslide election and victory of the Christian Democrats. Meanwhile, the US senator McCarthy had begun his witch hunt. The Perugia Conference was an international event, attended by several delegates from the Eastern Soviet Bloc, as well as, among others, by the American photographer Paul Strand, who had fled McCarthyist North America to avoid persecution by moving to France, and the communist Dutch documentary filmmaker Joris Ivens.

7.2 Zavattini's inaugural paper

In his paper, 'Cinema and Modern Man', Zavattini invited delegates to look back on the history of cinema and its half-century of tears and happy endings, in the modern context of war and the very real threat of a nuclear conflict.[23]

He stated that Italian filmmakers had come to the conclusion that cinema had failed: escapism had taken precedence over critical analysis. The cinema of Méliès had prevailed over Lumière. Made-up characters in make-believe places elicited more concern from viewers – though they were total strangers – than living and breathing human beings, sitting right next to them in the theatre. Yet, what was at stake was the very destiny of cinema and its ethical purpose. The subaltern demanded solidarity, not fables, not invented stories. For as long as there was a need for a critique of injustice and of the status quo, Italian cinema and Neo-realism were duty bound to develop an ethics of truth, consolidating the relation between everyday life and artistic spectacle, by rejecting the generic synthesis of narrative storytelling, in favour of the kind of analytical scrutiny that should accompany empathy for other human beings, attended to in real-time duration.

The time would come, he claimed, when it would be possible to view the screen in the sky from anywhere in the world. Technology wasn't an obstacle, fear was. Now cinema was beginning to look promising. There was a new commitment and a budding historiography was now considering cinema as a means of cultural acquisition, bound up with contemporary life. But if the critique of society was to cease, this would spell the end of cinema and of democracy itself. The time had come for cinema to return to its origins, when everything was worthy of its attention, bypassing the plot to come to grips with empirical reality and human nature, to be found even in what appears to be banal. The ultimate spectacle would be ninety minutes in the life of a man, no shot being just a bridge to the next, but each vibrating with the intensity of a microcosm.

7.3 The Soviet realist alternative

Zavattini's paper found favour with the authoritative Marxist philosopher Galvano Della Volpe, who approved of the way the writer had framed the Conference. Yes, he agreed that this was a turning point in cinema history. An epochal reversal from filming fantasy to filming the document was underway.[24] He cited *Bicycle Thieves* as an example of what could be achieved by following an antithetical route. And yes, cinema's photographic capabilities could, and should, be adopted to address ethical, political and historical issues. Zavattini had been right to conclude that what was at stake was not a formal choice of film techniques, but a matter of substance.[25]

Cinema was indeed the most suitable expressive means to capture everyday life (*la vita reale, quotidiana*) and specific labour problems.[26] In Italian cinema, Neo-realism had demonstrated cinema's analytical capabilities, making Neo-realist filmmakers participants and sensitive observers of modernity.[27] Della Volpe defended the choice of the everyday as a focus for Neo-realism, stating that Italian cinema had to shun Benedetto Croce's and Giovanni Gentile's idealist philosophy – especially Croce's formalist distinction between poetry and non-poetry – to embrace Marx and engage with concrete phenomena in context.[28]

Umberto Barbaro, the founding director of the Italian film school, the Centro Sperimentale di Cinematografia di Roma, agreed with Zavattini that art could no longer afford to be passive towards the real world. It had an active role to play, as a tool for understanding, judging, forming and, finally, transforming society.[29] Both Della Volpe and Barbaro were heterodox Communists, like Zavattini. Their ideological views departed from the official Italian Communist Party position, but in those days, seminal theoretical texts had yet to be translated into Italian.

Carlo Lizzani, an orthodox communist, concurred that by engaging with everyday life and real situations, current cinematic realism had had the merit of exposing inequality and the contradictions and hypocrisy of society. His point was that this was no longer possible.[30] He cited two obstacles: the first was censorship. *Sciuscià, Paisà, Bicycle Thieves* and Pietro Germi's *In the Name of the Law* (1949) had all met with serious resistance from state censorship. The second was the aggressive exportation of Hollywood films flooding the Italian market at a rate of 500 films a year, in the context of a weak economy like Italy's. Lizzani's was in favour of a sort of cinematic realpolitik, choosing pragmatism over ethics.

The American screenwriter Ben Barzman was present as was the Modernist photographer and filmmaker Paul Strand. Strand firmly rejected what he called Hollywood's psychological, sensationalist realism.[31] He pointed out that Italian cinema had had the merit of rediscovering elements of silent cinema, the expressive value of objects, pantomime and straight photography.[32] But, he objected, it was inconclusive and pessimistic.[33] Besides, what about the long tradition of realist cinema in the United States?[34] He dismissed Zavattini's dichotomy, arguing that realism could take diverse forms: satire, comedy, fable, historic drama, even animation.[35] Ben Barzman spoke about Hollywood cinema, noting that American viewers spent two hundred million hours a week watching films which failed to reflect real life.[36] His objection, aimed at Lizzani, was that if Italian cinema reverted to making films in a Hollywood style, it would be fighting a losing battle.

Barzman then discussed the plight of the 'Hollywood Ten', a group of American filmmakers who were being persecuted by the Committee for Anti-American Activities, charged with working against US interests. What had they done wrong? They had tried to influence American cinema towards social concerns and to expose the most obvious contradictions within American society.[37] Barzman warned European filmmakers of the impending danger of censorship against free artistic expression and read out two letters from the Hollywood Ten who weren't able to attend the Conference.

There was also an Iron Curtain delegation, led by none other than the eminent Soviet director and film theorist Vsevolod Pudovkin, who took the opportunity to condemn Hollywood films for 'their extreme pessimism, delusion, spiritual weakness and psychic morbidity'. *Art pour l'art* had to be rejected outright and Soviet realism championed, since the purpose of cinema was didactic, to show the hero as a living example on the screen.[38] Pudovkin, and the rest of his delegation, defended Soviet socialist realism.[39] Who was the hero of our time, if not the tireless and fearless worker of real life, the hero of anti-Fascism, a character based on real life, but re-invented for the screen, embodying courage and heroism?[40] Polish film director Aleksander Ford conceded that Zavattini had a point that cinema about the everyday was more than a boring chronicle. He was, however, adamant that Soviet socialist realism avoided schematization and had the merit of guaranteeing filmmakers their artistic freedom. Hungarian critic Ferenc Hont stated that the question to ask was how to represent contemporary society effectively.[41] Antonín Martin Brousil rejected Zavattini's dialectic of documentary and fantasy; knowledge of reality is not black and white. He also claimed that Soviet socialist realism was the answer: seeking out the 'typical' within situations and treating the hero as an ordinary person who is also an extraordinary man.[42] Alberto Lattuada was unable to attend, but in his letter he argued that there was no question of choosing between Lumière and Méliès. He advocated a poetic approach as key to combining fantasy and reality, making a synthesis of fiction and non-fiction. Truth could issue forth equally from a fable as from a chronicle, as in Jonathan Swift's *Gulliver's Travels*.[43] Georges Sadoul echoed Lattuada's views.[44] The study of reality could also be served by poetry, metaphor, imagination and even dreams. There was no reason why a film shot in the studios couldn't deal with very contemporary themes.[45]

Underpinning the 'typical' hero was Georg Lukács's aesthetic, for which the imagined character should represent the 'typical' individual, placed in situations revealing the socio-historical forces at play. By comparison with particular stories of individuals, stories could attain universal resonance, by virtue of typicality which exalted the exceptional type of person embodied by the hero, by 'intensifying' the character's individuality.[46] Lukács thought that description, 'based on *ad hoc* observation', was superficial, and that it debased characters 'to the level of inanimate objects'.[47] He also shied away from the present moment, the central focus of Neo-realism, because he thought that only the past was worthy of narration.[48] What Zavattini considered an advantage – insightful phenomenological analytical description – Lukács considered a shortcoming.

Although the Dutch communist documentary filmmaker Joris Ivens spoke in favour of Soviet realism, he drew attention to critical realism within the documentary. He was speaking from experience, when he stated that it could do more than produce a mere chronicle of events.[49] As to censorship, he acknowledged that it was a problem, but one that had to be resisted. It was no mystery that capitalist societies refused to allow filmmakers to make films about social contradictions. European producers were deliberately blocking documentaries from going into production and distribution. But something could be done. He cited his documentary *Indonesia Calling* (1946), exposing Dutch arms smuggling into Java (then under Dutch colonial control). The film had been instrumental in suppressing anti-colonial resistance in Indonesia. His documentary was watched every night by 10,000 Javese.

First Communion, Miracle in Milan, Bellissima, Umberto D. and beyond

8.1 First Communion

De Sica wasn't the only director Zavattini worked with. He also wrote scenarios and screenplays for many others, including Alberto Lattuada, Pietro Germi, Marcello Pagliero, Luciano Emmer, Luigi Zampa, Renato Castellani, Claudio Gora and Gianni Franciolini.[1] Producers often asked him to fix scripts which were structurally unsound. There were two seams: run-of-the mill writing and adaptations, alongside aspirational work.

For Alessandro Blasetti, Zavattini wrote *First Communion* (1950) in 1949, and, as he often did, got it into print as soon as possible, to establish the text and his authorship, no doubt, as well as copyright his work separately.[2] Their collaboration began with *Four Steps in the Clouds* (1942) and continued with Blasetti's *A Day in the Life* (1946) and *Fabiola* (1949). *First Communion* was distributed at the end of September 1950, having won a Nastro d'Argento Award at the Venice Film Festival for best director, actor and screenplay.

The main character is hardly a Soviet-style class hero. He is Zavattini's alter ego, Carloni, a high-ranking employee whom Zavattini imagines lives in the same street and building as himself: 40 Via Merici, Rome. Carloni is a bad-tempered, self-centred, obnoxious narrator and anti-hero par excellence. In fact, the whole film revolves around Carloni who is as disagreeable as the autobiographical character and narrator of Zavattini's *Ipocrita 1943* with whom Carloni has much in common. Carloni is cast in an equally confessional mode in this fast-pace satirical comedy of a film, set between 8.00 and 10.00 am on Easter Sunday, so that screen time almost matches real time.

Shortly before the religious ceremony is due to take place in the nearby basilica, Carloni and his family are still waiting for their daughter's white dress. When it is delivered, they discover it is the wrong size. They have barely two hours to get the seamstress to make the necessary alterations. Time is against them, as are the madcap scenes that keep delaying matters. The worst thing that could ever happen, happens: Carloni gets the alterations done, but forgets about the parcel in an argument and the parcel is lost. Time is running out. Perhaps the

Cardinal will be late? When all seems lost, Carloni realizes what an unpleasant individual he actually is. His redemption is the subplot. The parcel turns up and everyone is happy, including the chastised Carloni.

In a letter dated 30 July 1962, Zavattini reminded the director, Blasetti, of the tug of war between them over the screenplay:

> The battle waged between us, during the screenwriting stage, was always fought on what the relative emphasis should be within the film.[3]

Zavattini's allusion is unclear, except to his audience of one, Blasetti. Yet Zavattini's private diary sheds light on this anodyne statement: 'I'm not going to give in. Either he accepts everything I do in the scenario as is, or I'm not letting him have the story.'[4] Still unclear: 'as is'? Thankfully, Zavattini's legal education had taught him to document meticulously all traces of his work, by systematically filing it in an unpublished archive. The unpublished production papers for *First Communion* reveal that the director and the writer were at loggerheads.[5] This only transpired towards the end of his life, mentioned in the former letter. In a marginal note in his own handwriting, Zavattini says the story began as a confession: 'The truth is that the story began as a confession and now the voice and the rest is an intrusion.' In the same working papers, appended to the screenplay, he asks: 'what is the organizing principle behind the voice?' '*Qual'è lo spiedo della voce?*'[6]

He resisted Blasetti's moralizing, which translated into pressure to include an explanatory voiceover, opting instead for a self-reflexive, confessional, inner voice, ultimately, aiming for subtlety. His notes are sometimes telegraphic, but speak volumes nonetheless:

> Voice works (or imagination) when it goes into a higher pitch, not static, not moralizing. [Then] it ruins everything. It is unbearable and destroys the pace. Everything, if clear; and here, if the voice and the imagination are at the right rhythm or not. To change the voice from how it is now would ruin the film, making it preachy, boring. *Questions*: the voice. Do we need the voice? What is its purpose? Who is it directed at? Carloni or us? Don't the events explain everything? If so, what is its purpose?[7]

These notes were written during the creative process leading to the final screenplay. In his 1962 letter, he reminds Blasetti:

> During the editing stage, I did my utmost to limit as much as possible a heavy-handed treatment, and, quite exceptionally, you allowed me to work freely on the cutting, in this sense. Right?

Even though he succeeded in avoiding didacticism, and *First Communion* ultimately followed his vision, in 1962, Zavattini was furious after reading Blasetti's recent public statements in the press:

Subtlety? What subtlety? You directors, even in exceptional cases like yours, that is, of someone who is profoundly respectful of the talent of others, go through some kind of psychological transformation, such that you have a massive memory loss, as a result of which, just before embarking on a film you want to make, with the help of thirty or forty other people, not only do you forget the person to whom you owe a specific creative debt, but you also, quite arbitrarily, contest a title which, for God's sake, could be no one else's but the undersigned, succinct and expressive as it is. And worlds apart from the kind of moralism one would find in the short stories by Canon Thouar.[8]

8.2 *Miracle in Milan*

From the very beginning, *Miracle in Milan* draws you in, like a child's game, capturing the viewer's imagination through enchantment. In the words of the French critic Claue Roy, '*Bicycle Thieves* asked the viewer to go into the streets, go to the restaurant, and into the home. *Miracle in Milan* invites you to take part in the game.'[9]

An elderly widow finds a baby under a cabbage in her vegetable patch and decides to adopt him. As a child, Totò spills milk on the floor, but instead of being reprimanded, Lolotta teaches him to see or imagine in the splashes a stream in a distant land and an excuse to play. At her deathbed, doctors come to her bedside not to confer, but to count their numbers from 1 to 100 and upwards, mumbling, in a funny parody of prayer. She dies and Totò follows her horse-drawn hearse in the company of one person: a thief who joins the cortège to dodge the law in hot pursuit, and leaves it as soon as he can.

Years go by. Totò is old enough to leave the orphanage and walks into town. On his way, a pedestrian crosses his path. Totò wishes him *good* day with all his heart. The stranger is dumbfounded by his insistence and walks away muttering to himself. Totò stops to help some workers lift tram rails. In the evening, he walks towards the neon lights outside a glitzy cinema and looks on with fascination at the wealthy crowd in furs and top hats at the exit. Meanwhile, his bag is stolen by Alfredo, a thief. Totò runs after him, but then feels sorry for him and lets him keep his suitcase. Perhaps the thief might know somewhere he can stay for the night? Yes, he is invited to the thief's lodgings. The next morning Totò wakes up. All around is a snow-covered wasteland and a bleary foggy horizon. He is not alone: dozens and dozens of tramps stretch their limbs, having all slept in cramped shelters, the less fortunate cobbled together with cardboard; while others, like Alfredo's, are made of scraps of corrugated iron.

Totò becomes one of them. Ever smiling, ever thoughtful, selfless to an extreme, he has a good word for everyone. It is only natural that he should become their leader. Every single sad and lonely individual gravitates towards a new experience outside his or her private space, to form a self-reliant community. The deserted land by the railway becomes a functional squat; a communal living space with its amenities, a statue, and public spaces (for example, the rows of seats facing the wooden frame to watch sundown, as if it were a film). The streets are given the names of multiplication tables, so that the children can learn to count – for example, STREET 8 × 9 = 72.

It is an exemplar of community life, based on solidarity, an alternative model to competitive and individualist capitalism: 'Above all', Zavattini wrote in the scenario, 'there's the kind of solidarity that springs from sharing suffering and deprivation; and intelligence has made up for the lack of means.'[10]

Endless amusing and touching gags punctuate the simple story. The tramps behave like children in a topsy-turvy world, in which magic makes it possible for a black man to be transformed into a white one, to please his white girlfriend who becomes black for the same reason; a world in which a rare ray of sunshine becomes an occasion for collective joy among the crowd of tramps chasing after it and standing in a huddle to share it. Haves and have-nots. A train slowly shunts past on the line above the field: a rich bored couple in a first-class carriage couchette look down on the spectacle of the tramps and throw an empty bottle out of the window.

When Totò meets Edvidge, their child-like love takes the shape of handstands and cartwheels of shared happiness. A tramp is so thin and hungry that his body becomes so light that a balloon lifts him off the ground and the others have to weigh him down with stones, in a borrowing from his story, *Everyone Should Have a Rocking Horse*. The scraps of metal and rubbish they collect add up to a shantytown. Through mutual assistance, they regain their dignity and somehow survive on the edge of the modern metropolis, until a loner among them called Rappi becomes so envious and bitter that he informs the landowner that crude oil is spouting from the ground where they planted a maypole to play. Later, his treachery is exposed, and a dark cloud of top hats in the sky oust him from the shantytown.

Brambi and Mobbi, two businessmen, turn up in expensive fur coats and top hats and argue over the price of the property. Theirs is a competition. Their voices, the voices of auctioneers, talking faster and faster. Soon, their bargaining voices are replaced by the sound of barking dogs. They shake hands on the deal and drive away in their shiny limos. Later, Mobbi meets the tramps:

> Here we are. Look. I can feel the cold just like you. This is because we're all equal. My nose might be slightly smaller or larger than yours, but it's still a nose. This, my friends, is the truth. A nose is a nose.

Mobbi resorts to cunning to evict them, but they defend their living space, aided by Totò's magic powers and by angelic intervention. Umbrellas appear out of nowhere to resist the police hydrants. When the troops are lined up, the commander tries to say 'charge', but instead, his manly voice hits a high soprano note and the charge becomes a laughing-stock. Time and again, they resist the police. But their eviction and arrest is only delayed. They escape, steal the dustmen's broomsticks in the square outside the Duomo cathedral in Milan, and thanks to Totò's magic powers, fly off into the sky 'to a kingdom where good day, really does mean *good* day'. In the original ending, the poor seek in vain for a place that wasn't signposted PRIVATE PROPERTY. It began with the observation: 'How large is the Earth. There's room for everybody.'

Miracle in Milan (1950) won the Palme d'Or at the Cannes Film Festival (*ex-aequo* with Steno and Mario Monicelli's *Cops and Robbers* (1951) with the duo Totò and Aldo Fabrizi in the lead roles). Jean Cocteau was the first to congratulate De Sica. One has to ask, after *Rome, Open City, Sciuscià, Bicycle Thieves* and many other Neo-realist films, how could Zavattini and De Sica switch from *Bicycle Thieves* to *Miracle in Milan*? Yet, by the same token, how could Rossellini make a film like *Francis, God's Jester* (1950) after *Germany, Year Zero*?

It helps to know that when Zavattini originally came up with the story in 1939, he envisaged an exceptional comic, Antonio de Curtis or Totò for the lead role. Indeed, the original title for *Miracle in Milan* was *Totò the Good*. Zavattini had been Totò's fan, ever since the actor had moved to Milan in the mid-1930s and spent every single night at the Trianon Theatre, in Milan, to watch Totò's variety performances.[11] Zavattini showed Totò the scenario which the comic liked so much that he even came up with a few gags himself, and agreed to sign it. This first version was published in *Cinema* in September 1940 and De Sica snapped up the story.[12] When the director agreed to go ahead with the project after the war, Totò was far from obscure, having made a name for himself in a string of film comedies, and no longer interested in the project. Consequently, Zavattini had to change the title and opted for *I poveri disturbano* (*The Poor are a Nuisance*).[13] But the Christian Democrat censors and the producers considered it too controversial. So he changed it to *Miracle in Milan*. He later remarked: 'The truth is that the poor really are considered a nuisance, and that's why they wanted to prevent us from saying so.'[14]

He asked De Sica for three million liras for scenario and screenplay, but De Sica refused, until the producer and friend Alfredo Guarini interceded on the screenwriter's behalf.[15] Once again, as was the norm at the time in the Italian film industry, several writers were called in to work on the screenplay, alongside Zavattini. As the writer Luigi Malerba says: 'In those days, not only the screenwriters signed the screenplay, but the producer, the producer's friends, the production director, even if they had no involvement in the writing.'[16] The others were indifferent to his project and proved nothing but a hindrance. They made no contribution on a screenplay which didn't make any sense to them. Yet their names were included in the credits, which gave rise to the kind of undercurrent of ill feelings about authorship, that haunted the De Sica-Zavattini partnership since *Sciuscià* and was to sour their relations from then on.[17] Eventually, De Sica publicly acknowledged that Zavattini was the author of both scenario and screenplay.[18]

In December 1948, De Sica and Zavattini went up to Milan looking for a suitable location.[19] They visited most of the working-class parts of the city, looking for ordinary people, and down and outs. They accosted all kinds of tramps and invited them for casting. De Sica was a master in directing people with no training to act. The ones he chose overcame their innate diffidence and unwillingness to conform to any social conventions and under his tutelage and encouragement, became docile actors.[20]

Eventually, they found a suitable no-man's land on the outskirts of town, a field in a far-flung neighbourhood district, called Ortica, between a train line near Lambiate station and rows and rows of tall city buildings far away in the distance, alongside Via Valvassori Peroni. As an eleven-year-old, on his way to school, the critic Lorenzo Pellizzari remembers standing in the open field, where the film troupe had built a shanty town, looking on in fascination.[21] Zavattini published an article in the Communist daily, *L'Unità*. He was happy with their choice, the place was enveloped in the city smog, and the cold. Somehow it was beautiful.[22]

> One of the most moving things I saw at Ortica, in Milan, last month was a man and a woman living under a tarpaulin full of holes about a metre and a half from the ground, two metres long, and one metre wide: the two were from Naples, displaced people, unemployed; drenched in fog and aching with pains.[23]

Zavattini took a deep breath, imbibed the fog, and on his return to 40, Via Merici, his home in Rome, he came down with a chest infection.

The first version of the screenplay was ready by March 1949 and signed by Zavattini, in collaboration with De Sica, Suso Cecchi d'Amico, Mario Chiari and Adolfo Franci.[24] The second version was begun at the end of 1949 and the film went into production in February 1950. Zavattini, ever the legal mind, published the scenario in *Il Momento* at the same time.[25] Davide Lajolo, editor–in-chief of *L'Unità* daily Communist paper, visited the set. He responded to those who criticized the special effects, the strong illumination to mimic the sun, the fake Milanese fog; the snow made from chalk; the casting of two professional actors among the tramps, stating that none of these invalidated the film's inherent realism.[26] De Sica was asked, in an interview by Radio Milano: 'Was it true that *Miracle in Milan* was declaredly anti-capitalist and polemical?'[27] It goes without saying that his answer, in the Cold War climate, had to be 'no'.

The filming was over by June 1950. De Sica asked Zavittini to help him with the editing, and to do so with the same attention to detail that he had demonstrated while editing *Bicycle Thieves* in the cutting room.[28] By 28 November, there were little more than sixty metres left to edit. All in all, Zavattini made 1,000 metres worth of cuts, the equivalent of half an hour of screen time.[29]

In Italy, Left-wing critics largely misunderstood the film: it was an escapist, evangelic fable, lacking any class consciousness.[30] This was the view of Guido Aristarco, a film critic then working for *Cinema*, but also of Luigi Chiarini, who concluded that the combination of real and fable didn't work.[31] On the Right, Gian Luigi Rondi, critic of *Il Tempo* newspaper, and a fervent Catholic, believed the film was so explicit as to be a Marxist incitement to class war, as did Catholic Dominican Father Félix Morlion.[32] These views weren't shared by all: Tullio Kezich, working for Trieste Radio, warmed to the film's authenticity, under the guise of a fable, as he told his listeners. Its dual register kept real and fable in dramatic tension.[33] In France, the filmmaker Jean Renoir appreciated the film, as did the Communist film critic Georges Sadoul who saw *Miracle in Milan* as the third part of a trilogy begun with *Sciuscià* and *Bicycle Thieves* and even better than the latter, since, in his view, the use of metaphor penetrated reality and induced solidarity in the viewer.[34]

Looking back on the, mostly, negative reception from the Left in Italy, Zavattini objected that in the original scenario, the poor don't go to Heaven, they emigrate, looking for somewhere that is not private property.[35] He went on to note that his story sought to convey 'the immense sadness of life being the way it is and not as it should be'. He also pointed out that not everyone on the Left misunderstood it: painters such as Giovanni Omiccioli, Renato Guttuso and Carlo Carrà understood it, as did many writers, including Curzio Malaparte.[36] Indeed, he added, 'fable serves to *simplify*, not *exaggerate* reality. *Miracle in Milan* is about the real world.'[37] He objected that even the Gospel is radical, pointing out that the core teaching of the Gospel, as radical as it is straightforward, is goodness:

> 'Love thy neighbour as thy self' (Matthew, 22:39). But the opposite is true in the real world, which makes the film and the Christian precept all the sadder, and, in the context of political compromise, sadder still.[38]

What context? Housing shortages, high inflation, unemployment, inadequate public transport, poor sanitation. In some places, including the capital, families were living in cramped living conditions, with adults and children sharing the same room with animals, in basements, in makeshift wooden huts and even in caves – as shown in Rossellini's Neapolitan episode of *Paisà* (1946). Shanty towns were mushrooming on the outskirts of large towns.[39] On 5 January 1949, Zavattini published an article in the Communist *L'Unità*, proposing a *Bulletin for the Poor*, in which he invited intellectuals to act as scribes for the poor, letting the general public know about their dreadful living conditions, and reporting on what they found out, in an ongoing testimonial reportage. 'The poor', Zavattini concluded, 'who constitute the overall majority of our population, are always in the right, until such a time when their needs have been addressed.'[40] At the time of the polemic over the film, in a letter to Catholic Father Morlion, Zavattini wrote:

> I have no qualms about dividing the world into two categories: rich and poor, oppressors and oppressed. [...] The Christ I seek sides with the Left. The Gospel already contains that same overwhelming power that exists in the Left of this century.[41]

Surprisingly, André Bazin, a Catholic, as well as a socialist, failed to pick up on the Christological references in *Miracle in Milan*: he considered the dove symbol only a poetic device; never once considering that there were angels, as well as magic, and that there was more to the representation of love in the film than an expression of De Sica's temperament. There was disinterested, unconditional love (αγάπη or *caritas*, Lk. 6.27-36), as opposed to brotherly love (φιλία) or sensual love. Indeed, Bazin wavers as to where to situate love and fails to define it, observing that it is better understood as a form of poetry, and comes to the conclusion that this explains the rejection of narrative logic and dramatic continuity in the film.[42] Bazin went on to give a fairly accurate definition of *caritas*, comparing and contrasting Totò to Chaplin, noting that while Chaplin's imagination and resourcefulness served his own advantage, Totò's is only and always for the benefit of others and always putting others first.[43]

Zavattini would have agreed, had the two ever had that conversation. Before the war, in his 1937 Imola lecture, Zavattini had pointed out that Chaplin's films convey individualism, not solidarity with the poor.[44] In a brief outline, published in 1940, Zavattini described a character like Totò: 'A film I'd like to make: [*Totò*] *Il Buono* in colour. A Christ-like character, very earthy, fortyish, who works miracles in technicolour.'[45] The Christ-like Totò is also reminiscent of Saint Francis of Assisi, in the way he devotes all his time to encouraging the tramps by example, and by relieving their suffering in many whimsical ways, devised by Zavattini's imagination. Poverty, in this context, regains its dignity in a thriving community of Franciscan spirituality of *ora et labora*, work and pray.

Bazin found *Miracle in Milan* perplexing. He labels it 'a poetic-realist parenthesis between *Bicycle Thieves* and *Umberto D.*' more akin to fantasy, than to realism, and nothing to do with Neo-realism.[46] Was there any connexion with *Bicycle Thieves*? There is empathy and the sheer on-screen intensity of human presence.[47] True: looks, gestures, the kind of clowning mimicry of circus acts or vaudeville Zavattini was so fond of make up for the minimal dialogue. Bazin meant actors being people, *being*, rather than (theatrical) *acting* characters on screen, as is true of Gelsomina, Fellini's lead character in *La strada* (1954).

Bazin accepted that *Miracle in Milan* conveyed the nature of contemporary Italy through social symbolism and an allegory of social alienation, but he didn't think that was enough to make it a political film.[48] He couldn't reconcile social alienation with the transformative power of the imagination, preserved from childhood. The fable element won out. He singled out the early scene, in which the elderly foster mother, Lolotta (Emma Grammatica), turns spilt milk into a stream. A small catastrophe is transfigured into a wonderful game. Likewise, in another scene, the faculty of the imagination substitutes the nightmare of childhood multiplication tables with a game.

From his remarks, it would seem that Bazin had no knowledge of the film's origin or of the source of its humour, poised between real and the magical, as Gianfranco Contini had observed in his anthology *Italie magique* (1946), based on the compressed stories Zavattini had written in the late 1920s and throughout the 1930s, epigrammatic, tightly compressed prose, with a sense of foreboding haunting the humour and the gags collected in his trilogy.

Miracle in Milan is so different from *Sciuscià*, *Bicycle Thieves* and *Umberto D.*, that it needs to be situated in its appropriate literary context. Chapters 3, 13 and 16 of his first book, *Let's Talk about Me* (1931), feature the 'World Maths Championship' which gives rise to a hilarious scene in the film. The very first line of the Preface of Zavattini's second collection, *The Poor Are Mad* (1937), begins: 'I want to teach the poor a wonderful game' and ends: 'half way through a game, a friend of mine burst into tears.'[49] In one story, the end of the film is prefigured: 'The eyes of the Lord lit up the sky and Bat saw endless flocks of birds emigrate towards warmer climes.'[50]

Yet, so much had happened in the ten years since Zavattini wrote *Totò the Good* and when he adapted it for the cinema. It was the last of many stories written in his very original prose style, employing the absurd and the fantastic with its roots in popular fairy tales, fables, nonsense literature, literary Futurism. This was combined with touches of autobiography and references to the real world which were obscured by the fable form of storytelling and by the sheer compression of his prose, with its signature gaps, ellipses and non sequiturs. Ghostly glimpses of the real world and its contradictions of class, status, injustice, rich and poor were intimately combined with the absurd and the abstract settings and characters. Sadly, from his standpoint as an atheist, if there was a God, it had to be an indifferent God.

At the 1937 Imola lecture, Zavattini had told his audience: 'When you look at what's in our *Cinémathèque*, you would conclude that we're useless at comic films and humour.'[51] His underlying bitterness and frustration, no doubt, were a reflection of his defeat, when faced with the extent to which Mario Camerini had changed his screenplay for *I'll Give a Million* (1935), into his ideal of 'Hungarian' sentimental comedy. When it came to transferring Zavattini's unique, absurdist and tragic humour to the big screen, De Sica succeeded precisely where Camerini had deliberately failed. To his credit, De Sica knew how alien Zavattini's humour was from anything that had been done in Italy until then. All the more reason for him to be very worried about the risk of taking on such a film, its gags and costly special effects required by the screenplay.[52]

After Zavattini's retrospective judgement of cinema as a whole as early as 1937, and after formulating a way forward, in his opening address at the 1949 Perugia Conference, what place could there be for a film of this kind? On one level, undoubtedly, the scenario belongs squarely among his pre-war *raccontini* short story writing, as absurdist as critical of Italian society, albeit in a veiled way. In 1943, while Zavattini had been adapting *Totò the Good* from a scenario to a children's novel, he was also writing *Riandando* (*Looking Back*), a terse, and a private account of everyday life in wartime Italy, as plain as it was shocking.[53]

The allusiveness of his 1930s story was effectively superseded by an autobiographical reportage about unmediated wartime reality. By the time he was fleshing out the scenario, to turn it into a children's novel, he was torn between these two modes of meaning-making.[54] On this level, *Totò the Good* and even the film itself should be situated in the pre-war era of his dense and enigmatic *raccontini*, or perhaps as its cinematic culmination, a decade later. Yet the fact remains that the film was made after the war, after the Liberation and, for Zavattini and others on the Left, the promise of a revolution to come, though, as it turned out, social change was soon suppressed and all their hopes with it. After visiting the Ortica set, when the filming was still underway, Zavattini's friend, writer and journalist Giuseppe Marotta, worried out loud in a published article about the transposition from fable to reality: 'Was it such a good idea to bring Zavattini's story into such an explicit and recognizable real-world environment in Milan?'[55] Marotta wondered if it would be better to stage the story in an imaginary setting, thus avoiding an inevitable clash between real and imaginary, and situating the story into the real world of poverty in 1950s Italy, of a recognizable Milan which replaced the imaginary 'Bamba' and the constructed shantytown in Ortica, itself a substitution for the village AAA (Ha, ha, ha).

This one move, and the choice of genuine tramps with two exceptions (actors Paolo Stoppa and Arturo Bragaglia), regardless of the special effects that were later added to some sequences; regardless of the comic gags, the inventive verve, somehow tipped the balance of signifiers towards the post-war and Neo-realism, understood not as film style, but as an ethics of cinema which the film industry lacked, as Zavattini had pointed out at the Perugia Conference.

When he declared that the cinema of Méliès had won and Lumière's had lost, Zavattini was referring to escapist cinema, and to cinema pursuing unfettered imagination with no ties to the real world. However, what was at stake in these years, as far as he was concerned, was cinema's destiny, its ethical, social, even political purpose. Hence, there was no contradiction. This was quite different from claiming that comedy or allegory had no future. As all his writings show, cinema required the mediation of poetry and art, no matter how close it got to non-fiction.

In these and ensuing years, Zavattini came to the conclusion that if cinema was to resist losing its social engagement, then it could embark on one of three possible directions: pursue metaphor or allegory, following the model of *Miracle in Milan*; develop durational analysis, in the wake of *Umberto D.* (its scenario was written in 1948, though it was only produced in 1952); or focus on the reconstruction of real events, as *Rome, 11 o'Clock* (1951) and *Love in the City* and particularly the episode, *The Story of Catherine* (1953) were to do. The point is that Zavattini never ruled out comedy or allegory, provided the real world was the referent. He told Giacomo Gambetti, his first biographer, that *Miracle in Milan* uses metaphor to translate into image the ideas he was expressing at the time in public.[56] Metaphor, and extended metaphor or allegory, had an advantage that had been as useful during the Fascist dictatorship as it proved to be in a country ruled by Christian Democrats:

For a very long time, for years and years, it seemed to me that fantasy had great potential and value, and that all you had to do was, as they used to say, make allusions to reality. For, although there were similarities and elements in common between fantasy and reality, they weren't so strong that you could point them out with any precision.[57]

8.3 *Rome, 11 o'Clock*

No film could be more different from *Miracle in Milan* than *Rome, 11 o'Clock*, directed by Giuseppe De Santis, and based on a contemporary news story. A single job for a typist was advertised in the paper. Ten to twenty candidates were expected to apply. In the event, nearly 300 women queued up for the interview. The stairs in the building collapsed under their weight. In that building, sited in via Savoia in Rome, there were several fatalities and many casualties. According to Giampiero Brunetta, this is the most Zavattinian of De Santis's films.[58]

In his private diary, Zavattini recounts the genesis of the scenario and screenplay.[59] De Santis confirmed that 'His participation was total, to the extent that it triggered endless lively discussions between us'.[60] One can see why. De Santis shared Carlo Lizzani's orthodox Communist vision of a popular cinema, based on Lukácsian typology, which veered away from the real into an idealism of sorts, whereas Zavattini pursued a genuinely materialist vision, based on a careful scrutiny of real-world events, and their causes, discreetly mediated through poetic rendering. De Santis was looking for a novel on screen, with a plot, twists, and dénouement. As for Zavattini, in his Modernist approach, he envisaged an allusive, anti-novel. Thus, the tensions between the two filmmakers, which De Santis hints at, were less to do with clashing personalities and more to do with clashing visions of cinema.

Before Zavattini's involvement, De Santis's initial plans to make a film about the event had got him nowhere. He soon decided to involve the screenwriter, who came up with the suggestion that they hire a press reporter to carry out background research on the real event and interview eyewitnesses and the candidates, with a view to collecting their impressions, relate to the witnesses and empathize with them, and their feelings, and look for anything that might concern the event.

Gianni Puccini suggested Elio Petri, a very young reporter working for the Communist *L'Unità*. As it happened, the previous year, in 1950, Petri had interviewed Zavattini at length, for *Filmcritica*.[61] Their meeting meant that Petri was schooled in Zavattini's ideas. The crucial insight was that personal, face-to-face contact with the Other can become an exchange, enabling a deeper contact, a participation in making meaning, through facilitating in the respondent a process of self-reflection, on condition that the filmmaker approaches the Other through empathy and respect.

As far as Zavattini was concerned, *Rome, 11 o'Clock* offered him an opportunity to visualize a fragment of *Italia mia*, his enquiry-film project. This would be a fragment of *Italia mia*, a subject's view of Italy as it is, not as one would like it to be. In this light, the film could reveal, through field research, the contradictions surrounding these fatalities and the human dimension, by giving voice to the people involved, the young unemployed typists, to present their case, talk about their lives, constraints, hardships, about what it was like to be a female working in a male environment, exploring the lives of the real people behind the names and statistics, by means of interviews and later a re-enactment, by inviting them to a casting for the film. There would be minimal intrusion and an attention to detail and accuracy in terms of social context. What he envisaged was more akin to non-fiction, than fiction. What De Santis planned as a fictive story, loosely based on real life, Zavattini planned as an ethnographic enquiry into Italian society, where under the surface of a fatality lurked social contradictions of gender inequality, which could, and should, be addressed. Hence the clash of wills in their personal correspondence.

Under Zavattini's guidance and encouragement, Petri followed the screenwriter's advice and framework: embarking on a total immersion into the reality of the street to confront the contemporary moment. As he said in the 1950 interview: 'These young people, then, should be chucked out into reality, empty handed. No prepared scripts in their pockets, no preconceived ideas about reality.' There was an agenda, a need to know, as a first step, but no script. Petri interviewed all the women, the firemen, the neighbours, the magistrates involved in the case, and anyone else who was in any way involved.

In this ethnographic approach, the results were a revelation. Petri produced an impressive sample of oral history, mistaken in film archives as the first draft of the screenplay for the film, and catalogued in this way in the Centro Sperimentale di Cinematografia di Roma archives. The Zavattini-led team discovered that women from all social classes had applied for the job, at a time when in Italy there was a growing demand for economic independence coming from women. Petri's research was shocking for how his questioning teased out from the respondents the poverty and living conditions of many of the women, the sexism they had to endure in a male-dominated office environment, their housing problems, the commuting difficulties, travelling hours to reach the centre of Rome from the *borgate* and shantytowns where most of them lived.

At a 1996 Conference, De Santis described Petri's field research as a novel, written in collaboration with the protagonists. It wasn't in the sense he intended, but it was in another sense, for it could be classed as a testimonial novel, the kind of writing that emerged in Italy in the early 1950s, most notably in Danilo Dolci's books, in which the author takes second place, to let his characters and witnesses, real people, not figments of the imagination, a chance to speak their mind.[62] The director's clash with Zavattini came down to the fact that De Santis and his writing team wanted to forge Petri's raw material into a cinematic novel, understood in the traditional sense of a fictional story. According to De Santis, Zavattini pressed him to stick to Petri's research and remain faithful to it, without going into personal stories.[63] But that is not quite so, since Petri's extensive and detailed research is about nothing but personal stories, including those gleaned from interviews with doctors and nurses, passers-by, the police and the journalists who rushed to the scene.

Zavattini's reaction was that the research was going in the right direction, but more field work was needed. For Petri's initial findings didn't reveal what it was like to be in that situation. In keeping with his theories, Zavattini wanted to get closer still to the reality of the disaster, and move away, as far as possible, from De Santis's imagined cinematic novel. Was there a way to gain access to their direct, tangible, experience? What was it like to be in their shoes? To feel the humiliation of waiting in a long queue for a typing speed test, to experience a growing apprehension, the mounting anxiety for results; what kinds of conversations were they having while they were waiting in the queue?

To address these questions, Zavattini suggested to the team that they put a similar advertisement in the Rome daily, *Il Messaggero*. Their advert would be for a real secretarial job, working for the film production team for the duration. But it would trigger a situation, simulating, by involuntary re-enactment, the original situation and then allow the filmmakers to observe the candidates and collect ideas for the screenplay. They chose a ground floor office in Via Po, in the same area.

To aid the reconstruction, each candidate would do the same typing speed test required in Via Savoia. Would the original witnesses apply? The filmmakers were counting on it. As it happened, they did, though they weren't told about the film. For their simulation, the team chose a ground floor office and seventy candidates turned up. As Zavattini had predicted, the interviews afforded screenwriters, the director and now assistant director Elio Petri an insight into the plight of the candidates. True to their plans, the successful candidate was employed for the film production job advertised.[64] In 1955, Zavattini wrote to Petri from Cuba where *Rome 11 o' Clock* was proving to be a great success and Petri published his letter as a Preface to an abridged version of his research for the film.[65] It was a mistake not to publish all the field research and what all its voices had to say about 1950s Italy, since the result would have formed a testimonial novel, on a par with Danilo Dolci's ethnographic work in the same period about a Sicilian village and its inhabitants.[66] This is what Zavattini wrote to Petri:

We met those girls who fell from the stairway after the event and listened to their stories. If we hadn't possessed a more developed socially engaged conscience, one provoked by the new events of Italian history and subsequently by cinema, we would have seen and heard far less than we did. There wouldn't have been that contact with places, with the protagonists of the news event of Via Savoia, and you wouldn't have gone to interview them, the typists, I mean; you wouldn't have produced the booklet that is about to come out in print, a document that reveals an entire outlook on life, a modern way of relating to other people.

Do you remember that morning in Via Po, when we carried out that experiment, which was called 'cruel' by respectable people, of attracting a hundred typists with an advertisement, identical to the one which caused the tragedy? A girl left the queue in a rush, and weeping, because she realized that the others were better than her, but she needed to get a job, and she was leaving with her face hidden by her hands.[67]

8.4 *Bellissima*

That same year, *Bellissima* (1951) came out. It has little, if anything, in common with *Rome, 11 o'Clock*, or with *Miracle in Milan*, yet all three films were based on Zavattini's writing. Some critics have considered *Bellissima* central to Luchino Visconti's oeuvre and marking the beginning of the end of Neo-realism, arguing that Visconti's formalist cinematography, staging and use of professional actors distanced the film from Neo-realism.[68] Is this so?

Zavattini created the scenario for Visconti's *Bellissima* between 1940 and 1942, but the film only went into production in June 1951. It was edited and cleared by state censorship by December.[69] Before his scenario was ever fleshed out by a team of other screenwriters, comprising Suso Cecchi d'Amico, the director, Visconti, and his regular assistant director, Francesco Rosi, Zavattini had written no fewer than eight versions of the story.

In Zavattini's earliest version, a widowed father wishes his young child to win a film casting competition for the main role in a film. Later, the character of the son with a speech defect becomes a stuttering daughter who has no screen presence to speak of and is offered like a lamb to slaughter, when attending her screen casting with the powerful presence of the real-world film director Alessandro Blasetti. Both imagined child characters, however, make very unlikely choices for casting and both are equally unable to satisfy their parent's ambition, hard as they try. In all the versions, there is the constant of the Neo-realist innocent eye witnessing the tawdry world of mainstream cinema.

Earlier versions and the final scenario and screenplay all feature a fixer who takes advantage of the parent's gullibility and naïve idealization of the film spectacle. In the film, this cunning character is played by Walter Chiari. Zavattini later replaced the father figure with a mother called Maddalena Cecconi, played by Anna Magnani. Maddalena almost succumbs to the fixer's bribes and to subterfuge, willing to sacrifice herself to realize her dream.

According to Lino Micciché, Visconti subverted Zavattini's scenario, transforming a linear narrative into a complex story, working on multiple levels.[70] Yet Zavattini's scenario is already complex, highlighting the behind-the-scenes production process, conflicting modes of recitation, the pulp media of popular mass-produced photo-stories and contemporary film stars, Donizetti's opera music and Howard Hawkes's *Red River* (1948), complicating the film through reflexivity and staging and dramatizing the clash of fiction and reality.[71] Zavattini's various scenarios for *Bellissima* share a critical study of popular film culture and its deluded perception of mainstream cinema, teasing out the gap between imagined lifestyles and everyday life.

It was a problem which Zavattini had already explored, thematizing the plight of the non-professional actor playing the role of Antonio Ricci, Maggiorani's character, and staging, in one of the versions, De Sica's plight as he reflects on the nature of cinema, in an unprecedented confessional mode of cinema that was ahead of its time. In the scenarios for *Bellissima*, the problem of cinema is one step removed from the story. Zavattini's scenario implicates Visconti indirectly, by introducing another famous director, Alessandro Blasetti, who plays himself in someone else's story.

The corruption and the cunning of the Dream Factory is, from the earliest draft, mediated by a child's innocent eye.[72] We judge what her gaze sees without judgement. Maddalena is taken in by the myths until the end, when she realizes their falsity, refuses to sign any legal contract and finally throws out the members of the film production unit from her tenement block, just as an earlier version featuring Fabrizio as the child's father closes the door on the allure of cinema, seeing it for what it was. What drives the structure of the story, what gives it an edge, is this ambitious parent and inadequate child dialectic, building up from situation to situation, until the decisive moment of the child's casting, replayed on the moviola, when Maddalena overhears the harsh comments about her daughter and leading to the final dramatic resolution, the cut, of the parent-shunning glamour and spectacle, alluring as they are, but also revealed to be illusory.

Zavattini's tight narrative structure is locked into his scenarios and becomes inscribed in the screenplay by others and ultimately sustains the film. He also made a decisive intervention on the treatment, in a face-to-face meeting with Visconti and the other screenwriters, whose job it was to develop his scenario. He insisted on placing the emphasis on the failed screen test, the crux of the film, avoiding distractions from unnecessary subplots, and of theatrical comedy, favoured by Suso Cecchi d'Amico and the others, to generate, instead, greater dramatic tension and a steady build-up of the situation, only resolved in the finality of Maddalena's resolve to refuse to sign the contract which confirmed her daughter Mari in the role.[73]

The changes Zavattini made in the course of writing eight versions were mostly dictated by the need to update the story, at least in relation to a changing urban Italian reality, since the 1940s. The main change was a shift of context: from the transient world of repertory theatre and travelling vaudeville, so well known to him, ever since adolescence, to the seedy side of cinema. In satirizing the workings of the film industry, Zavattini produced a critique of the spectacle, exposed its ethical shortcomings and the ways in which it was impacting on popular imagination. The child at the centre of the story was originally a boy, then recast as a little girl, but from the outset, the character is portrayed as incapable, with a speech impediment and lacking screen presence. Zavattini envisaged well-known 1930s actors Amedeo Nazzari and Vittorio De Sica, whom he intended should appear as themselves, but were replaced in his final draft with Ingrid Bergman, Roberto Rossellini and Silvana Mangano, famous for her lead role in *Riso amaro* (1949) (*Bitter Rice*).

His choice of stars changed, but not Zavattini's ironic representation of their popular perception as idealized figures. For example, Zavattini imagined a scene set in Cinecittà in which Maddalena spots the fledgling star and runs after her to get her autograph. In the scenario, Zavattini adds to the irony, by imagining a film within the film, in which director Alessandro Blasetti plays himself casting for a child actress to appear in *Prima Comunione* (1950) (*First Holy Communion*), also scripted by Zavattini, and discussed earlier.[74]

Of course, Zavattini was familiar with the production side of industrial cinema, having had ample opportunity to witness studio life, the shady world of fixers, conmen and second-rate actors, to satirize it and to imagine a scene casting situation, having also had first-hand experience himself in casting child actors.[75] Zavattini's characters in *Bellissima* stalk the spaces of the film industry's production, from editing suites to screening and casting rooms, in the genuine setting of Cinecittà. This exploration and Zavattinian shadowing of the spaces of cinematic production also enables the metaphorical exploration of the industry's mass production of stereotypes, myths and illusions, such as the Dream Factory's from-rags-to-riches allure of happiness to come.

Zavattini introduced a meta-cinematic structure which survives all subsequent variations and resists the work of subsequent screenwriters and their different ideas; indeed, it resists all the decisions made during the transposition from script to screen. Even allowing for the additions and changes, the main thrust of the story, its nub or matrix or *spiedo* never changed.[76] The mounting tension of Maddalena's blind ambition only dissolves when Zavattini subverts the happy ending stereotype, when his character refuses the studio contract, obtained against all odds.

The film's central theme was developed by Zavattini earlier than the emergence of Neo-realism itself, having been a recurring preoccupation in the stories he published in *Cinema Illustrazione* from 1930 and 1935 and in his 1940s essays published in *Cinema*. His *Chronicles from Hollywood* had widely explored the spectacle of the cinema and formed a running series of fictionalized from Our Own Correspondent-style fabricated reports, in which celebrity culture and glamour are satirized and exposed in hilarious stories, exposing an illusory belief in the false gods of Italian stardom. The very idea of cinema reflecting on itself, in other words, the imaginative exploration, through the medium of fiction, of the metalanguage of cinema, was a recurring, intertextual, investigation of Zavattini's pre-war journalism, doubtless under the influence of Pirandello's theatre and the mediation of Zavattini's Parma friend and mentor Ugo Betti, his first creative model for writing drama.

There are traces of meta-cinema even in *Bicycle Thieves*, in the sequence set up in Zavattini's script and faithfully transferred to the big screen, in the tenement basement, where Bruno witnesses the stilted rehearsals of the members of an amateur dramatics club, typical of that world and in sharp contrast to the more natural-sounding dialogue in Neo-realist films.[77]

In these post-war years, Zavattini's 1930s ironic exploration of Pirandellian problematics of illusion and reality in popular visual culture resurfaced. Several years later, he wrote:

> We must admit that cinema is a sordid affair in most cases, pointless in the extreme. Only a good film can redeem the filmmaker's soul, that is, one motivated by generosity and honesty towards mankind.[78]

8.5 *Umberto D.*

The discrepancy between writing and production seems to disrupt commonly held views about Neo-realism, mostly framed as a time-limited teleology, and complicates it. The scenario of *Umberto D.*, for example, was written in 1948 for 'the film about the man and the dog', a story which 'is no less moving than *Bicycle Thieves*, I think. It's in defence of old age pensioners.'[79] Zavattini emphasized the sadness of the scenario, 'a sadness I can hardly stand myself. Who will direct it? We'll see.'[80] The story begins:

> What is it like to be an old man? 'Old men stink', a boy once said. I fear that many people share the same view, even though they have never uttered such a cruel sentence. Am I exaggerating? I want to tell you the story of an old man and I hope that by the end you won't say I made it up. His name is Umberto D.; he is sixty with a smile on his face because he loves life so much that he struggles with the government that refuses to raise his measly pension.[81]

Umberto D. sells his watch at the soup kitchen and a few books, but it isn't enough. Then he falls ill. The only person who cares about Umberto, apart from his dog, is Maria, the housemaid. In a famous ten-minute-long scene, the length of a roll of film, Maria wakes up and makes coffee. Nothing happens, but the smallest of gestures in the kitchen. As she feels her stomach it becomes clear that she is pregnant. She burns some newspaper to get rid of the ants teeming around the sink. It's a long sequence, even in Zavattini's treatment.[82] Umberto goes to hospital where he gets better, but decides to stay as long as he can, to save money on meals. On his return to his lodgings, he discovers that his dog has been thrown out and he finds Flyke in the city dog kennels waiting his turn to be gassed. He takes Flyke home, before going to beg on the street, but a friend walks past and he pretends that he is checking to see if it's raining instead. Umberto is desperate. The only way out for Umberto D. is suicide, similar to the choice of 500 Italian pensioners who committed suicide in 1950.[83] His decision, Zavattini tells us, is motivated more by indifference than by debt.[84] Eventually, he goes to the park with his dog to throw himself in front of the train, but the dog makes him change his mind at the last minute.

   In 1948, Zavattini tells the story to De Sica who is enthusiastic, to Luciano Emmer, and to Federico Fellini.[85] Initially Zavattini imagines a triangle: an old-aged pensioner, his daughter and a dog 'he loves as much as he would a son', but then dispenses with the daughter and introduces the pensioner's landlady, based on a real story of a suicide of a pensioner caused by his landlady.[86] The character who replaces the daughter is Maria, the house servant, similar to someone Zavattini had known as a lodger, when he left Milan and moved into temporary accommodation in Rome in 1940.[87] In the story, Umberto joins other pensioners in a demonstration which is soon broken up by the police. This was no fantasy: that same year, in 1948, *Il Momento* reported such a demonstration of pensioners.[88]

Despite the success of *Miracle in Milan*, De Sica had trouble finding anyone willing to provide financial backing. When the publisher and producer Angelo Rizzoli read the script, he told De Sica: 'You must be mad!' But De Sica stood his ground, invested in the film, and Rizzoli and Guarini put up one hundred million liras.[89] While Zavattini was writing the screenplay, De Sica worked out every shot with him on paper.[90] On 15 August 1951, soon after *Umberto D.* went into production, Zavattini published the scenario, as he had done several times earlier, to stake his territory, following a practice he started in the 1930s.[91] When filming was completed, he became heavily involved in editing. In September 1952, Chaplin told De Sica he thought *Umberto D.* was even better than *Bicycle Thieves* and *Sciuscià*.[92] In December, in an interview, Zavattini told Pasquale Festa Campanile:

> Let's take any one character: Umberto D. Essentially, this is a character inspired by reality who, in other words, doesn't have an intellectual origin. But I think it is necessary to tell the story of an authentic pensioner, acted by him, not the story of Umberto D. This doesn't mean that cinema should give up on the lyric potential of developing a story.[93]

In *Umberto D.*, by comparison with *Bicycle Thieves*, there is an even stronger sense that screen time and real time coincide, though the two films are both fictions. Zavattini clarified why this is, stating that the purpose of duration is to elicit solidarity from the viewer, not to be mistaken for melodramatic sentimentalism:

> The real duration of suffering in man and its everyday reality: not a metaphysical man, but the man we meet on the corner of our street. So that the real time duration of events corresponds to a genuine contribution to our solidarity.[94]

This is borne out by the scenario and the treatment, which 'shadow' the imaginary character in his moment-to-moment actions, charting his every movement and seemingly never departing from his point of view, in what is unmistakably a phenomenological approach of seeing, sensing, walking, sitting. In an interview for *Copione* magazine, he gave a further explanation:

> In *Umberto D.*, as in the other scripts I did for Vittorio De Sica, there is a constant, the character's loneliness, or should I say characters, and the implicit or explicit demand for solidarity (not the kind of solidarity that lasts only a minute) the character makes to a world which is so indifferent towards other people's problems.[95]

The contemporary critic Degli Espinosa came to the conclusion that Zavattini had rescued the characters of *Umberto D.* and *Bicycle Thieves* from their societal invisibility, resulting from indifference.[96] *Umberto D.* and *Bicycle Thieves* tell two stories, one concerns the singularity of the protagonists, in their banal drama; the other, society. Degli Espinosa thought Zavattini's Neo-realism used the empirical datum like a painter. The 'truth' of these films, for Degli Espinosa, is down to the empathy felt by the narrator, faced with such events that have a collective dimension in common and this is what the narration conveys as empathy.[97] As Degli Espinosa saw it, reality became spiritualized through its observation.[98]

In 1952, Zavattini made an unusual move that De Sica was very unhappy about. Instead of publishing just the scenario, as he usually did, he brought out a book, which included the scenario, the treatment and the full screenplay, accompanied by a long programmatic text on the cinema.

Doubtless, auteurship was at stake: he published the documentation charting a screenwriter's contribution to films. It mattered: the scenario for *Miracle in Milan* was published in 1942 and, in a revised form, in 1951. Zavattini had already suggested to Italo Calvino, then a publisher at Einaudi, to publish a collection of his film stories. Calvino's response was enthusiastic, but the writer simply lacked the time to bring it to fruition, until 1979, when he brought out a selection, revolving around his current interests, rather than attempting to document his overall contribution.[99]

His Introduction to the *Umberto D.* book took the form of an essay, 'Some Ideas on Cinema', based on a transcription of interviews which were the outcome of several months of conversations with Michele Gandin, a documentary filmmaker and assistant editor at *Cinema Nuovo*. Zavattini covers the whole creative process of developing the idea of a film, from the initial ideas to treatment and final film script, including changes made in the course of production.

His was a challenge; a clear statement against the ephemeral nature of the script, as an unstable text, soon to be superseded by the film itself. What was exceptional for the time (and perhaps is still even today) was that his book included those ephemeral parts removed from the final product, either because they were normally changed during the editing process, or because they were superseded in production.

He was making a stand on his creative role as a film writer. Unsurprisingly, the book exacerbated the clash between De Sica the filmmaker and Zavattini the writer, highlighting, indeed celebrating the creativity of the screenwriter, by bringing to the fore his role in the entire creative process. Time and again, Zavattini was not accurately credited and De Sica tended to play down Zavattini's creative contribution in his interviews to the press.

To publish *Umberto D.* in book form was a bold move in those days for a screenwriter to confer on writing for cinema a greater aesthetic value than it had hitherto enjoyed and claiming an independent role and theoretical and ethical function for the writer, rescuing screenwriting from being considered only a technical activity. The book was important for a generation of filmmakers, including, for example, Paolo and Vittorio Taviani:

Ce petit livre nous déconcerta. C'était une oeuvre qui utilisait la page écrite, mais qui – par une sorte de transfert non cataloguable parmi les langages codifiés – appartenait d'autorité à l'univers cinématografique. Cinématografique et poétique.[100]

In January 1952, Zavattini had told De Sica in private: 'Up to now, I am only a screenwriter, not a film director. I want my due as a screenwriter.'[101] The book reflects a long polemic in private, but it also made a public declaration and theorized the aesthetic independence of the film writer vis-a-vis the director.

After *Umberto D.*, Zavattini's idea for a new cinema developed further. As far as he was concerned, *Umberto D.* was not the end or the exhaustion of an experience, but a stage in a developing a new vision of cinema, which is discussed in the next chapter. Suffice it to say, for the moment, that, as far as the screenwriter was concerned, the way forward after *Umberto D.* would be to film a genuine pensioner.[102] But even this would not suffice.

De Sica was barred from presenting *Umberto D.* as an official entry at Cannes, while a smear campaign was conducted by most of the press against the film. Zavattini attended the Cannes screening, where he faced the hostility of the Italian critics. 'I found all our enemies there', he wrote to De Sica on 23 May 1952. 'What's happening is the outcome of the battle against *Umberto D.*, the De Sica-Zavattini duo, and against Zavattini.'[103]

Far more damaging was Minister Giulio Andreotti's open letter in *Libertas*, the Christian Democrats' party daily paper, addressed to Vittorio De Sica, 'Social Ills and the Need for Redemption', 24 February 1952.[104] Its publication was timed to coincide with the release of *Umberto D.* It happened when Andreotti was still in charge of the Central Office of Cinematography, effectively vetting the little output there was of Italian film production and thus stifling and controlling the most powerful form of mass media of the era. It was a direct attack aimed at De Sica and Zavattini's latest film, *Umberto D.* and a prior warning that another film of theirs in the pipeline, *Italia mia,* would also face official opposition, should the scenario go ahead into production.[105]

Minister Andreotti accused them of a 'cinema that washes its dirty laundry in public'. He argued that

> If the world is mistakenly led to believe that the Italy of *Umberto D.* is the Italy of the mid-twentieth century, De Sica will have rendered poor service to his country which is also the nation of Don Bosco, Forlanini and of a progressive social legislation.[106]

The film's distribution and exhibition suffered very badly in Italy as a consequence. Andreotti's threat was also a deliberate warning signal for producers and the film industry to drop Neo-realism altogether, on the grounds that they were producing a negative public image of the nation. There was no public reaction from producers, for whom the message was loud and clear. Overt government opposition was bound to intimidate them and deter them from backing any more socially engaged films.

8.6 *The Overcoat*

Zavattini was also perfectly capable of writing adaptations, while arguing vigorously against literary adaptations. A case in point is *The Overcoat,* based on Nicolaj Gogol's short story about the fictional Russian public servant Akakij Akakievič. Zavattini had argued that scripts should be abolished, as he had told Elio Petri three years earlier in an interview, strongly suggesting then that the time for fiction was over, at least as far as he was concerned. And, more recently, after the release of *Umberto D.* he had complained that this film was already out of date. The way forward for Neo-realism was non-fiction, and particularly cinematic ethnography, as a model for mainstream cinema. In fairness, it is worth remembering that Zavattini didn't write *Umberto D.* in 1951 or 1952, but several years earlier. In this respect, far from being an ending, it was part of a beginning.

And what about *Miracle in Milan*? Well, it was conceived even earlier, which complicates any temptation at hard and fast classification. *Miracle in Milan* draws on Zavattini's pre-war magic realism, something it has in common with his adaptation of *The Overcoat.*

Akakievič becomes Italian and an equally unprepossessing figure, called Carmine De Carmine, who was to be brilliantly played by a good friend of Zavattini's, the comedian Renato Rascel. De Carmine is a pen pusher, a non-entity, lost in the administrative jungle of the City Corporation, which, true to magic realism, remains anonymous, and therefore abstracts from the real world, but which was actually Pavia.[107] Zavattini's adaptation and Alberto Lattuada's film reveal the same absorption of magic realism by Neo-realism, as a mode of address, if you will, which made it possible to filter the harsh realities of extreme poverty. The shield of Achilles, to reiterate Kracauer's analogy for artistic mediation of the all-too-harsh real, is, in this case, an allegorical fable, but without a trace of moralism.

Zavattini's magic realism of the 1930s and early 1940s, in which flights of fancy and gentle irony, in a combination of fact and fiction, never ignore the real world, culminates in *Miracle in Milan.* But in *The Overcoat* too, a city is suspended in the anonymity of a fable. In *Miracle in Milan,* Milan becomes the mythical Bamba; in *The Overcoat,* Gogol's Russian provincial town becomes any town whatsoever, though unmistakably Italian, as imagined by Zavattini and filmed by Lattuada. Yet both social spaces are abstractions. In both, the characters are generic, or abstracted, figures, living in an abstracted social space. The protagonist of Gogol's story, and of its Italian cinematic adaptation, is an anti-hero, the lowest of the low, whose honesty highlights the blatant corruption and empty rhetoric of public office. In both, language is subverted by absurdity, by the kind of Nonsense logic at work in Zavattini's *raccontini.* This cinematic adaptation extends Gogol's critique of authority and power to a critique of corruption and of the bombastic rhetoric of Fascism, in a re-reading of *The Overcoat* which situates it firmly in an Italian context. And yet, it is all the more powerful, the less the references are spelt out in the film, making use of subtle irony, sarcasm and black humour, framed by the distantiation effect of fable and allegory. The satire of power survives adaptation, in a narrative equivalent of Pier Paolo Pasolini's later critique simply expressed in the memorable metaphor of the *Palazzo* or the Palace, an equivalent of Parliament, seat of power and privilege. De Carmine's office is an earlier imagined microcosm and synecdoche of Pasolini's *Palazzo*.

Constantly ridiculed and humiliated by his colleagues, scheming, work-shy employees and by his boss, Carmine De Carmine's only refuge in life is his penmanship, a craft in which he excels. De Carmine becomes a mouthpiece for Gogol's critique of power, unwittingly, at the centre of hilarious situations in which the character subverts the rhetoric and duplicity of officialdom, by being himself, as when, for example, he reads out the minutes of meetings with the Secretary, but cannot help adding his own objections or mumbling asides, audible statements, highlighting, in spite of himself, the reality of intrigue and deception, but seemingly with no trace of intention. The step from the administrative machine of Imperial Russia to Fascist Italy or its continuity in the country ruled by Christian Democrats is almost imperceptible. The uncertainty of time and place made it possible to escape censorship, despite the Cold War climate.

De Carmine's worn-out, moth-eaten overcoat is a poetic cypher, chosen by Gogol, but perfectly in accord with the function of the stolen bicycle of *Bicycle Thieves*, the misplaced First Holy Communion dress of *First Communion*, or the white horse in *Sciuscià*. This is the coat of a man who doesn't belong, who is an outsider, the butt of his colleagues' jokes and of his boss's fury.

De Carmine brings to mind Chance, the odd character in *Being There* (1979), directed by Hal Ashby and based on a novel by Jerzy Kosinski. The harder De Carmine tries to please, the worse the response. Perhaps an expensive overcoat would change the way he perceives himself in terms of self-worth. It is bound to change how others perceive him. At last he can become the person he aspires to be. But no, after its theft, his illness and death, he becomes, instead, a ghost, haunting the inhabitants of the town at night, who had been so unkind to him. He takes to snatching their coats out of revenge. Finally, his former boss, the Mayor, who is in charge of the City Corporation, has an alarming face-to-face encounter with De Carmine which, true to magic realism, forces the Mayor to become a better person.

Italia mia, proposal for ethnographic cinema

9.1 Towards new ethnographic cinema

In the early 1950s, the same screenwriter and theorist who could imagine the fictional Antonio Ricci of *Bicycle Thieves*, Carloni of *First Communion* and Umberto D. of *Umberto D.* also grappled with the problem of how a New Italian Cinema might dispense with fiction altogether. He envisaged a new mainstream cinema in the form of what Thomas Waugh has called a 'committed documentary'. The voice of the all-knowing speaker would give way to the authentic voices of the people themselves, whose lived experiences would be filmed; in other words, Neo-realism, in Zavattini's vision, would develop into a new ethnographic cinema.[1] In 1951, he thought that such a cinema could speed up its production so much as to bridge the gap between filming, editing and distribution: 'The cinema must narrate that which *is happening*. The cine-camera was made to look ahead of oneself.'[2] Instead of filming fictional characters in the street, the cinema would film people being themselves.

In the spring of 1951, De Sica and Zavattini met to discuss what they would do after *Umberto D.*, before the film had gone into production. Zavattini suggested *Italia mia* (*My Italy*).[3] By September, he had copyrighted the first version of this new project.[4] What made it a departure from their earlier work was its leaning towards ethnography, which, in the course of its subsequent development over time and film projects, overturned contemporary ethnographic theory and practice, by rejecting the exoticizing and superior gaze aimed at the Other. But even in September 1951, Zavattini's plan centred on the documentary dimension of Neo-realism, aspiring to build up background research to occupy the centre screen, as he was trying to persuade Giuseppe De Santis to do with *Rome, 11 o'Clock*.

In December 1951, even before the completion of *Umberto D.*, Zavattini launched one of several related projects: *Seguendo gli uomini* (*Shadowing People*) was to include four fictional episodes to be filmed by experienced documentary filmmakers. What he had in mind was experimenting with shadowing in the real world, exclusively as a means to provide a conceptual and artistic narrative framework for a fictional film. After *Umberto D.*, this new project would inform his thinking for an alternative cinema for the rest of his life, becoming a constant preoccupation, alongside, and contradicting, his commercial screenwriting practice.

On a practical level, Zavattini came up with the framework and ostensibly limited his involvement to *Shadowing People* to overseeing the development of the project, contributing to it, through discussion and acting as a go-between with the producers of LUX film, who had shown an interest. The idea involved blending fiction with non-fiction and writing into the scenario the actual filmmakers who would take the camera for a walk in the streets of Rome. Over a period of six months, he and five documentary filmmakers and two writers were intensely involved in his project, meeting on a weekly basis.[5] But when LUX withdrew their financial commitment, the group dispersed.

There was more at stake than filming in the street. Zavattini's plan was to film the life of people in the street and to place it in its social context.[6] In his initial remarks to elucidate the conceptual basis of the project, he envisaged a roving and a reflexive camera, to film 'what is happening now: this is cinema'.[7] Exactly what he meant by this is clear from his unpublished working notes of December 1951. From January 1952, he carried out detailed and extensive research in the Rome National Library. His research shows what is left unsaid in his public statements. His notes confirm a strong interest in the everyday lives of ordinary people and where they lived, in the context of contemporary society, consistent with his pre-war experience as a journalist, working on national magazines. They also bring to light what proved to be a sustained search for specifically ethnographic material. He documented his progress and method, beginning by looking through the national press, then through regional newspapers and then articles in ethnographic journals. He was particularly interested in what he called the 'facts' by which he meant, as he noted, 'typical facts', hastening to add that these should not be confused with sensational media news, but symptomatic events, revealing events, which exposed the state of contemporary Italy.[8]

There is a political thread running through Zavattini's ethnographic research in the National Library, borne out by a quote from Gramsci he underlined in red in his notes: 'Folklore is the powerful voice of the present and its dynamism is the necessary catalyst for the future of the working class.'[9] This is consistent with how Zavattini understood folklore, not in what was at the time still the prevailing sense of the word. Indeed, he had no interest in tourist attractions, however picturesque, nor in Italian monuments, but, as he puts it in these notes, 'in the popular, in the active and reactive and resistant subaltern'.[10]

His attention was drawn to a range of issues, within a frame of reference which is, broadly speaking, political geography, such as old age in Italy; conflict over cohabitation; industrial deaths; children abandoned outside churches; unemployment; the official response to natural disasters; the lives of women; workers; internal migration; spirituality in its popular expression, or in unique manifestations; namely, Don Zeno, the visionary parish priest of Nomadelfia (the former Nazi concentration camp converted into a village for displaced people). He made a note of limit-case stories, such as that of a cave dweller who poisons herself to death with barbiturates and of Italians living in straw huts in the Po Delta valley, both symptomatic of the dearth of post-war social housing.[11] But he was also attracted by popular traditions, including the legend of the Wandering Jew and information about the Holocaust in Italy, at a time when, in post-Fascist Italy, the Holocaust was still taboo.[12]

What was the point of his research? Nothing less than a feature-length, mainstream, non-fiction, ethically responsible and ethnographic new cinema. He envisaged filming current events, as and when they occurred, whereas the fictional element of 'invented stories containing only a sense of reality' would have to be dispensed with, as he told Agostino Degli Espinosa in April 1952.[13]

The gap between life and spectacle would be reduced to a minimum, by casting events themselves as the subject. Anticipating the arguments of the Third Cinema, he argued that autonomous art had to be rejected, on the grounds of urgency. What he meant by that was that there was no time to waste. Cinema had to deal with the contradictions of Italian society and speed up the long production cycle to respond to events without delay. Consequently, the act of viewing would become interwoven with solidarity which, for the filmmaker, would involve 'meeting situations and becoming part of them', as he told another interviewer, Pasquale Festa Campanile.[14]

His outlook also opened up the possibilities of film writing. The story had to arise from the contact between the filmmaker and the event. Immediacy of production, however, had to be the outcome of patient field research, mutual participation, and attendant empathy between filmmaker and subject, an honest dialogue with the subjects and replacing 'committed' direct address with 'committed' reconstructions, or direct filming of events, as they unfold.

This aspiration for the cinema followed on from his pioneering ideas on reader participation, adopted by *Epoca* magazine. In the pages of *Epoca*, he overturned the relation between readership and content, by opening up a dialogue, so that Italian mainstream press began to find out what ordinary people thought. How? By interviewing them in the street.

Zavattini told Agostino Degli Espinosa that 'Neo-realism itself consists in the inclusion of the exigencies of everyday life within the traditional language of storytelling'.[15] But it wasn't going far enough. Times had changed. Shoeshines had disappeared. New housing was replacing some of the rubble and the public was seeking out optimism, not reality.[16] Zavattini's counterargument was that the new insights learned from the war would never be out of date.

> This sense of self-effacement and respect, as a result of being faced with the real world, would lead them to a closer analysis of the lives of others and of ordinary people.[17]

A constant preoccupation was poverty and how to deal with it. To put this in its period context, the debate over poverty in Italy came to the fore in 1948, when the Italian Communist Party campaigned for the Italian state to address poverty. The 1951 census revealed that the scope for Neo-realism as socially engaged cinema was justified by over two million registered unemployed, and a further four million 'marginally employed'. Furthermore, only a staggering 7.4 per cent of Italian homes had drinking water, an inside toilet and electricity. The statistics of Italians emigrating provided another indicator of poverty and unemployment. Between 1946 and 1957, 1,940,000 emigrated.[18] When the results of field research were made public, under the title: *A Parliamentary Report on an Enquiry about Extreme Poverty in Italy and the Means to Combat It* (1953), there was a public outcry that led to a governmental enquiry.[19] In the light of such figures, Zavattini asked his readers, what would Christ film, if he were around today? This is his answer:

> I guess that if Christ had a cine-camera to hand, he wouldn't make up parables, however marvellous these might be, but, censorship permitting, he would show us who the good and the bad are *right now*, and he would confront us with close-ups of those who make their neighbour's daily bread taste too bitter, and of their victims.[20]

9.2 Vittorio De Sica and *Italia mia*

In the spring of 1951, Zavattini presented the framework for *Italia mia* to the Swiss producer Paul Graetz. In its earliest guise, his plan was to cover the twentieth century of Italian history from 1900 up to 1950. He soon realized that it was too vast and too vague. He restricted it to the period from the Second World War until 1950.

What next? The next step was a cinema that would bridge the gap between individual and community, self and others. As he put it: 'Cinema has marched abreast with the other arts, emulating their flaws, that is, cinema has been conceived as an individual narrative, never as a collective narrative.'[21] His was also a call for a personal cinema, as the title bears out, *Italia mia*, not an impossible objective Italy, but reality seen subjectively, as a combination of a filmmaker's personal experience and the perception of a given situation.[22]

De Sica liked the idea, at least, the sketchy, incomplete, version Zavattini conveyed to him, and told him so in private.[23] In public, however, the director disparaged or seemed to misunderstand the writer, claiming that he 'would like to photograph and that is all'.[24] The two met on several occasions to discuss the project and by December 1951, they were all set to go into production, beginning with a journey across Italy in February 1952. The idea was that most of the content would result from their journey together. On 28 December 1951, they met for the last production screening of *Umberto D.*, to make the final cuts after the soundtrack had been added to the image track. That was when De Sica broke the news to him that the film they were going to make was no longer *Italia mia*, but *America mia*, since Howard Hughes had offered to pay for both their flights and stay at Hollywood, so that Zavattini could write the story and the screenplay. Apart from the short notice and the fact that the decision was made unilaterally, the whole point of *Italia mia* was that it was a personal take on the country and for this reason *My America* could never be Zavattini's America. Zavattini was denied a visa, most probably for being a known communist. De Sica wasn't. During his business trip, De Sica announced *Miracle in Chicago* which was to include an episode featuring an illiterate conscript dictating his love letter to a friend who could read and write.[25] For Zavattini, it made no sense to shift from a known entity like Italy to an unknown quantity like the United States. 'What's that *mine* got to do with it?', Zavattini asks himself, on 22 December. It wasn't only a matter of feasibility, but of personal vision. He confided his thoughts to his private diary:

> I need to have the freedom to see things from my point of view. This is where all the power of the idea lies. Besides, how will the thing pan out in practice? He will organise things with only his best interests at heart, as always. We shall see. I'll be frank. I'll say: 'Best for each of us to go his own way.'[26]

On 18 December 1951, he explained to De Sica that it would be impossible to do a film as demanding as *Italia mia*, while working in the kind of tense atmosphere that existed between them.[27] On 24 January 1952, he wrote to De Sica, to raise authorship and copyright issues, stating that *Italia mia* was a development of Neo-realism and a commitment to non-fiction.[28]

The prospected film raised yet another conflict between director and writer, which was unsurmountable, at least as far as *Italia mia* was concerned. Zavattini wanted to reject the conventional process from story to screenplay, by doing away with the screenplay and providing only an outline for a range of possible scenarios the filmmakers might encounter in the real world. It didn't help that non-fiction and investigative filmmaking were pivotal to Zavattini's proposal. De Sica was the wrong director for the job. He had always been tied down to very detailed screenplays, *Umberto D.* is a perfect example, where even the famous ten-minute scene of the maid getting up and making coffee, apparently so natural and spontaneous, had been entirely scripted, down to the tiniest detail. Their views were unreconcilable. And yet, Zavattini was unwilling to give up.

9.3 Rossellini and *Italia mia*

Enter Roberto Rossellini. When Rossellini and the producer Alfredo Guarini met Zavattini in April 1952, Rossellini told him he wanted him to be the screenwriter of his next film. Zavattini suggested *Italia mia*. At the time, Rossellini, among his many commitments, was also working on his episode for *We Women* (1953), an episode film which was based on Zavattini's loose set of scenarios, around the idea of famous actresses confiding in the viewer an episode of their real-life experience. Alfredo Guarini, Rossellini and Zavattini met again on 24 April, to discuss Rossellini's episode for *We Women*. But Rossellini wanted to talk about another project:

> I have an idea, I must produce it, I can't stop. It won't leave me alone. A journey across Italy, from the Po river to Sicily, several episodes, coming across places and characters from *Paisà*, things seen before, Saint Gennaro in Naples, etc ... We can do it together, if you like. What do you say?[29]

The idea of a journey across Italy seemed to coincide with Zavattini's *Italia mia*. They came to an agreement. Producers were interested: Guarini got involved, so did Carlo Ponti, who promised them a contract:

> Ponti, in Rossellini's presence, went as far as mentioning co-direction. I replied that there was no point in even thinking about it, given a figure like Rossellini. But I placed myself at their service, right up to the editing stage, for, if there was ever a film in which editing was both crucial and creative, this was it. As far as I'm concerned, montage is always the continuation and completion of a screenplay.[30]

In June 1952, Rossellini told a journalist:

> *Italia mia* will adopt the structure of *Paisà* and will convey an image of our nation as it is today, through a series of loosely associated episodes.

He added:

> I wanted to pick up the *Italy* theme that had already been developed in *Paisà*, though it refers to the last stages of the war. Zavattini had a similar idea: so there has been a happy meeting of minds which will now result in our cooperation.[31]

Rossellini went on to say that after *Italia mia*, in the autumn, he would make an adaptation of *Duo* (1934), the title of a novel by the French author Colette, which was to form the basis for his *Journey to Italy* (1954).

On 4 November, Zavattini and Rossellini travelled to Reggio Emilia, north of Bologna and to the village of Luzzara, Zavattini's hometown, on a journey of discovery, to find suitable locations for *Italia mia*.

In the meantime, despite all their assurances, both producers had dropped out. State censorship was most probably a deciding factor. When Umberto Del Ciglio, Andreotti's personal secretary and a member of the IFE (Italian Film Export), met Rossellini and Zavattini, in the company of Guarini, Del Ciglio happened to mention, as if by chance, that he knew about De Sica's *Italia mia* and that he and Andreotti might find funding to produce it through the Banca Nazionale del Lavoro, which financed Italian productions or through foreign capital.[32] And yet Andreotti had made his veiled threat against *Italia mia*, recommending that it be conceived as a harmless travelogue, the very type of folkloric film Zavattini was hoping to subvert with an alternative model, based on ethnography.[33]

But this turn of events didn't put Zavattini or Rossellini off. Rossellini decided to produce the film himself and planned to shoot episodes of *Italia mia* before beginning his new film, *A Journey to Italy*, and to continue to do so during that film's production. He would shoot an episode of *Italia mia*, while on location in the South. He also suggested two episodes about social contradictions in Italy, one about a village under water, Basiluzzo; another one about a swamp full of carcasses of dead animals; and yet another, about the people from Ciocaria, who spend all their time in litigation, as well as suggesting a reconstruction of a scene he had witnessed in Naples, where the everyday includes the absurd: his example being that of a pig falling from the third floor.

They embarked on a second journey to the Po Delta, where they found the man who'd acted as a floating dead corpse, at the beginning of the final episode of Rossellini's *Paisà*. On their return, Rossellini asked him to develop some ideas. Zavattini reworked the rough script he'd written for De Sica and produced a second, far more detailed, draft of *Italia mia* which he gave Rossellini on 16 December 1952. Rossellini was so keen on the project that he gave Zavattini an advance.

The year before, Florestano Vancini made a documentary about the plight of the dispossessed, living in the Po Delta: *Delta padano* (1951). *The Po Delta* exposed the predicament of 300,000 dispossessed, living in extreme poverty in bog land, on the edge of the most fertile soil in north east Italy, at the mercy of typhus and malaria, unemployment and hunger. Unsurprisingly, the documentary was denied an export visa, for having dared to present the wrong view of Italy. That it ever got made was only possible because the film industry had no role in its production, since it was funded by the trade unions.[34]

Then silence reigned. At last, Zavattini managed to make contact with Rossellini on 2 January 1953. Despite their joint press releases and a cash advance for the writing, Rossellini's other projects had to take precedence and that was that. Rossellini's *Journey to Italy* (1954) subsumed elements from *Italia mia*, such as Saint Gennaro's miracle-working episode which becomes expressive of transcendence. But the gaze over Italy was now a foreign one, in a kind of conceptual montage of opposites which is exactly the sort of dynamic Gian Piero Brunetta has pointed out, in relation to how ideas travel in cinema and how projects which we believe remained on paper didn't.[35]

Zavattini's intervention was brave: to put forward a documentary film by a high-profile director and screenwriter which had the potential of breaking out of the ghetto of Italian documentaries, in an attempt to steer the best of Italian cinema towards non-fiction filmmaking, following his ideas on how Neo-realism should realize its full potential. But Rossellini was a conservative Catholic, and no communist, not even a heterodox one like Zavattini.

9.4 *The Roof*: An episode of *Italia mia*

Did this course of events spell the end of *Italia mia*? No. Episodes, dealing with suicide, prostitution, illegitimate births and popular entertainment, crop up in several films, one being 'The Story of Catherine', in the episode film conceived by Zavattini and produced by him and others, *Love in the City* (1953). Another episode, listed in the version of *Italia mia* written for Rossellini, concerned housing shortages in Rome. This became *The Roof* (1956), directed by De Sica and based on Zavattini's research about a young couple of newly-weds, seeking affordable accommodation.

In the story, the young couple, like many other working-class Italians in the mid-1950s, resort to building their illegal, one-room, brick-and-mortar, dwelling overnight. *The Roof* wasn't the first Neo-realist film about housing; Luigi Zampa's *L'onorevole Angelina* (1947) had dealt with the historic rebellion of the residents of Pietralata against inadequate living conditions, due to the Fascist regime's failure to consider the need for transport to connect newly built peripheral districts to the city, or sanitation, or refuse collection – let alone the provision of running water (as an early scene in *Bicycle Thieves* also showed). Zampa, also a communist, like Zavattini, responded to the stir in the press about a real-life occupation in Rome. He visited Pietralata and ultimately cast some of the women who had on site, framing the real crumbling working-class suburb or *borgata*, the film was all the more shocking for being contemporary, and for showing an occupation led by a local woman, of nearby apartment blocks still under construction, after the flood of February 1947 and the failure to distribute food supplies to the area.[36] The inhabitants faced the same problems of those living in Val Melaina, the district of Rome brought to the big screen in *Bicycle Thieves*. Male film critics found the very idea of a housewife becoming a politician comic, which coloured their interpretation of the film as a comedy, despite the fact that during the Italian Resistance, many women had fought and died, alongside men, and that, in 1946, women had been given the right to vote.[37]

The Roof follows the trials and tribulation of Luisa and Natale Zambon, a young couple who found out on the grapevine that if you build a small dwelling overnight, roof included, you could claim legal ownership and get away with nothing more than a fine. It would be their last resort, since there was nothing affordable on the market. The story was inspired by Zavattini's casual acquaintance with a young couple who lived nearby. As he got to know them over time, he realized that their predicament was far from unusual, and would make a good story for a film. The real Luisa worked as a housemaid in an apartment opposite Zavattini's, and Natale was a friend of his eldest son, Arturo.[38] The two married, soon had a child, and both had jobs, but finding accommodation remained a problem. They began to look for somewhere private to stay, but they couldn't even afford the cost of a room. Eventually, they heard about this loophole in housing legislation and decided to find a suitable site, visiting places near Rome and various *borgate* or poor working-class districts on the outskirts of town. After four years working all hours and juggling several jobs, they bought a plot. Then they moved into a wooden hut, while Natale built the foundations. They were cautioned by the local police and told they had eight days to roof the building or it would be demolished. They got off lightly with a fine.

Their story, true as it was, lacked a dramatic element to make a film. But Zavattini included it as a potential episode in his revised scenario for *Italia mia*.[39] In October 1953, De Sica stepped in and by May 1954, Zavattini had produced the first draft of the scenario. But the decisive moment was when, on 24 March 1955, he interviewed a man who had built his brick hut overnight. The Zambons hadn't. This builder's account, so detailed and so full of insightful observations, gave the scenario a life of its own, combining non-fiction with fiction. That was when a good scenario began to take shape.[40] At that point, Zavattini even considered setting up a simulation, as he had already done for *Rome, 11 o'Clock*. Someone would be hired to build a brick hut under the same conditions of pressure and illegality; and would repeat the exercise, while the filmmakers informed the police, to verify exactly what would happen.

His screenwriting method consisted of a three-stage approach that matched what he had told Michele Gandin in the many interviews later edited as 'Some Ideas on Cinema'. First, a filmmaker should identify an everyday event and write down an account. Second, research it in the field. Third, a selection from the material gleaned from field research should be edited into a scenario. This crucial final stage involved selecting and collating the documentation from the research and, as always in his working practice, being prepared for any number of re-writes, in a process of constant honing and simplification.

In the event, the first scenario is an unfiltered report of what happened to the Zambon couple, based on Zavattini's preliminary interviews, and on his interviews with other witnesses. As his notes demonstrate, the first stage was deciding to make a film about the extremes to which people were willing to go. He interviewed the Zambons again and again. The second stage involved 'shadowing', which is to say carrying out extensive and detailed ethnographic field research, as his working papers demonstrate. On several occasions, he visited sites with other writers: Natalia Ginzburg, Alberto Moravia and Paola Masino.[41] To have a firm grasp of context and to help with the dialogue, he carried out further field research on shantytowns, building sites and interviews with builders, site managers, police and witnesses. These were people who'd built their own dwelling overnight, as well as getting a grasp of up-to-date housing legislation.[42] Using his previous experience as a journalist, Zavattini collected and collated information about pricing, techniques and technical terms, information gleaned from direct contact with witnesses whom he and one of his sons interviewed. The point was to come to an understanding from the perspective of the Other, the people directly involved, to find out what it was like to be in their situation and to gain an insight about the specific nature of the issues ordinary people faced; such as problems with postal delivery, refuse collection, lack of water supply, electricity, heating. The interviews built up a series of genuine biographic profiles and accounts of people's experiences, all adding to his understanding. This time there was no Elio Petri to help. Zavattini discovered that, unlike the picture he had painted in the imaginary shantytown of *Miracle in Milan*, there was no internal cohesion among neighbours living in these new shantytowns. Apart from their rivalries, they had frequent arguments over dumping refuse, for example.[43]

The comparison between working papers, scenarios and screenplay attest to Zavattini's artistic mediation. The evolving screenplay began to visualize the scenes and the sequences which dramatize the couple's experience of house-hunting and all the trials and tribulations they had to deal with. In the course of editing it, the dialogue became less literary, including snatches of 'found' material, in the form of overheard conversations. The more Zavattini whittled it down, the more essential exchanges, situations, environments and gestures emerged; thus, the paradox of *mimēsis*: genuine lifeworld material edited into film form.

However, in the end, the sharp edge is lost in the final version of the screenplay and in the film itself. The film takes on a fairy-tale air, contradicted by the real locations and the verisimilitude of the situations and dialogue. It creates an uneasy compromise between magic realism and hard-earned research and attention to detail, in real-life situations. One of Zavattini's favourite words was 'concrete', as in 'tangible'. Well, every time one might expect to get to grips with 'concrete' reality, the writing and the film shy away, drift, digress, fade.

In one sequence, a builders' lorry takes the couple past the Colosseum and up the Via dei Fori Imperiali, built to realize Mussolini's grandiose dream, to signify the legitimate continuity of empire and its related space of demagogical power.[44] By juxtaposing the ideal Fascist city with the real city of cramped living conditions and poverty, the film's social argument became all too clear. But the harsh reality of the original story is toned down. The hint at contradictions are never allowed to develop. In fairness to the film's context, and to Zavattini's predicament, the screenplay was written in a hostile, Cold War, political climate, since state censorship was still a major obstacle in 1955. As Zavattini told Michele Gandin:

> Bearing in mind the context, I'm pleased with the screenplay. My conscience is clear. However, if this were a different climate, the scenario would have emphasized individual and collective responsibility within a particular state of affairs. I have no doubt that I wittingly self-censored my work for *The Roof*.[45]

In 1955, affordable housing didn't exist. However, since *The Roof* was not a comedy, or seen to be one, unlike Zampa's *L'onorevole Angelina*, it presented a risk for producers. The project had to go through a three-step process of censorship, from approval of the story to the go-ahead for the screenplay and final permission to proceed to production, distribution and foreign sales. For this reason, after the damaging governmental attacks on *Bicycle Thieves* and

Umberto D., Zavattini and De Sica agreed to tone down Zavattini's ethnographic scenario in many ways, including the deletion of a political rally, and of the election climate in which Luisa and Natale Zambon were house-hunting.

It is important to bear in mind that the 1950s were not the 1970s. The social dimension in the real world, at the height of the Cold War, was too shocking a reality, even scandalous, as far as the Christian Democrat censors were concerned. There could be no question that the mounting political tension of the story had to be dropped or attenuated. The version of the scenario for submission to the government censor included the screenwriter's reassuring observations to show that extreme poverty was not shown, whereas new building sites would be.[46] The end result could not afford to be confrontational and some elements, deriving from Zavattini's preliminary work, could only be suggested in the film. However, in Gandin's view, *The Roof* 'for the choice of theme and the way it is developed, for the points it makes and the ethical commitment it demonstrates, is one of the bravest films of recent times'.[47] Despite its shortcomings, at the Cannes Film Festival, *The Roof* won two awards for best scenario and screenplay and *Nastro d'Argento* awards in Italy.[48]

9.5 The legacy of *Italia mia*

So much for the development of *Italia mia*. Zavattini was tough. When Rossellini and Carlo Ponti pulled out of the project altogether, he was undeterred. He archived the ideas behind the project, including the documentation, in two interviews. The two redactions of the story and the relevant correspondence are framed by the rubric: 'I film proibiti' ('Banned films'). He published the *Italia mia* scenarios, showing how it had developed from its first version to its subsequent refashioning for Rossellini. He also explained its context in an interview with Filippo M. De Sanctis of *Rassegna del Film*, who published the two scenarios and the correspondence. Doubtless, Zavattini was still aiming to attract funding, by establishing the ambitious scope of *Italia mia*, as the title of the final instalment of the interview indicated: 'How I hope to make *Italia mia*.'[49]

In 1954, Brunello Rondi, who was already working as a writer for Federico Fellini, took on the project. But nothing came of it, despite Fellini's enthusiasm.[50] However, Rossellini later adopted and adapted a similar framework to make documentaries about India for French television, *J'ai fait en beau voyage* (1957–9), and a feature-length film, *India Matri Bhumi* (1957–9).[51]

In *J'ai fait en beau voyage*, Rossellini chose to take an anthropological perspective, devoting vast amounts of time to observation in the field, as preparation for deciding what to film, breaking the media barriers between the filmmaker and the ordinary people. These Indian films fit in with the kind of research he and Zavattini had planned for *Italia mia*. Zavattini's 'Some Ideas on Cinema' seems closer to home than Alexandre Astruc's *caméra stylo*, which has been adduced as a source of Rossellini's India documentaries.[52] Even Rossellini's statement to the press fits in with Zavattini's approach:

First, I tried to observe, to make a simple reportage without any preconceived ideas, not even the intention of getting to a particular cinematic construction [...] I tried to convey my sensations as a reporter, in a poetic fashion.[53]

Vintage Zavattini. When asked whether he was going back to the beginnings of Neo-realism, Rossellini confirmed that he was, in order to 'push the documentary as far as it could go'.[54] It seems no coincidence that *India, Matri Bhumi* was to be followed by a project which Rossellini was to film and for which Zavattini had written a loose script, and namely the adaptation of the work of the visionary Brasilian nutritionist and geographer Josué De Castro, *Geopolítica da fome* (1946), *The Geopolitics of Hunger*, only just translated into Italian.[55]

But *The Geography of Hunger* didn't go ahead. According to De Castro, Rossellini exerted pressure on him to exclude Zavattini from the project, which is remarkable, given that by this time, Rossellini was closer to Zavattini, having shifted dramatically away from fiction and towards non-fiction. Be that as it may, De Castro remained adamant that Zavattini was the right person to script the documentary. Indeed, he called it a *conditio sine qua non*, having gone as far as discussing *The Geography of Hunger* with the Italian screenwriter. Zavattini obliged, by producing an outline which he sent to a British producer, Michael Altman of Co-Productions, but Altman's impossible demands over author's rights meant the project could not go ahead, despite the certainty of funding from FAO (Food and Agricultural Organization).[56] De Castro and Zavattini were so keen to collaborate that the following May, the Italian screenwriter tried his luck with another producer, Alfredo Bini. But this producer preferred to invest in an investigative documentary by Pasolini.[57] Finally, the Brazilian De Castro, or perhaps Zavattini, involved the Argentinian Fernando Birri to replace Rossellini, but still nothing came of it.[58] Yet, traces of these ideas, and of *The Geography of Hunger*, appear in an episode of a documentary produced and loosely scripted by Zavattini, *The Mysteries of Rome* (1963).

Meanwhile, Zavattini's aesthetic went abroad. As later chapters demonstrate, he transmitted his documentary and ethnographic idea of cinema to Spain, Cuba, Mexico and Argentina. *Italia mia* also materialized as a series of film-books about life in cities, towns and even humble villages. The subject matter and approach overlap with areas of enquiry listed for *Italia mia* in Zavattini's various scenarios. *Un paese* (*A village*) (1955) was the first. The second was *Napoli* (1962), commissioned by Zavattini in the 1950s.[59]

The traces and legacy of *Italia mia* mark Zavattini's parallel cinema and its equivalent in his journalism. Between November 1956 and October 1957, Zavattini interpellated magazine readers, individuals living all over Italy, whose interviews became a magazine feature, published in the Communist illustrated weekly *Vie Nuove*, entitled *Domande agli uomini* (*Questions to Men*), consisting of thirty-nine long interviews with ordinary people, of which twelve are women, twenty-seven men.[60] In 1958, he wrote the story for, and participated in, the production of *Chi legge? Viaggio lungo il Tirreno* (1962) (*Who is reading? A Journey down the Tyhrrenian Sea*) directed by writer and director Mario Soldati, a series of television documentaries, also interview-based, stemming directly from *Italia mia. Chi legge?* was also built on the participation of ordinary people and aimed to address the problem of literacy, by shadowing illiteracy across Italy. Zavattini's *I misteri di Roma* (1963) (*The Mysteries of Rome*) includes several *Italia mia* episodes, and interviews, in accordance with the initial project of the 1940s and early 1950s. Who were the interviewees? Blood donors for cash; exploited copyists; casual road construction workers. Even the feature-length free newsreel which fell within Zavattini's overall art direction, *Apollon* (1969), directed by Ugo Gregoretti, about a year-long successful occupation in Rome, is ultimately an emanation of *Italia mia*, a film which is the outcome of Zavattini's theory of shadowing, in which workers become protagonists, acting themselves and reliving and analysing their year-long, successful occupation.

Then, in the 1970s, he reworked the story of *Italia mia* for Italian television.[61] Zavattini had always valued the (unrealized) potential of television as a medium, ever since its introduction to Italy. However, from its inception, as part of Italian state monopoly, the RAI had been orientated towards a limited, escapist, spectacular format. Zavattini's work with so many young documentarians who did most of their work for television meant that, from the 1950s on, there was a steady trickle of investigative journalism by filmmakers who were directly or indirectly influenced by him.

As he saw it, like cinema, television had betrayed its potential. For the television version, he adapted his idea of a tribunal which takes intellectuals to task, including prominent filmmakers who had been part of the Neo-realist Italian New Cinema, in a dialogical film. They would challenge the state, in light of three decades of Centre Right politics and monopoly rule. There would be three episodes dealing with the facts and their interpretation.[62] The central idea was the paradox of Italian society, encompassed in the question: How did we get it so wrong? The scenario reads partly like a letter, which it was, addressed to the director Santi Colonna.

Its sense of urgency, of the need to act, to challenge the status quo in order to bring about change, also informs Zavattini's *The Truuuuth* (1982), the final version of which was also written for television. In the event, at last, the screenwriter directed a film. This is how *Italia mia* culminated in Zavattini's cinematic testament, in the one film he directed, *La veritàaaa* (*The Truuuth*). In so many ways, *La veritàaaa*, shot in 16 mm in colour and broadcast on Italian television in 1982, is *Italia mia*.[63]

Zavattini's documentary aesthetic was also key for documentary filmmakers in the 1950s, often through Zavattini's personal involvement. This is true of Ermanno Olmi, the Taviani brothers, Libero Bizzarri, Michele Gandin, Ansano Giannerelli, Alberto Grifi and many others, so that the documentary form in Italy became the new site for furthering Zavattini's Neo-realist aesthetic, given the extreme censorship in place by the early 1950s within mainstream fiction filmmaking. But this is an area which has received very little critical attention.[64] Vittorio De Seta's *Banditi a Orgosolo* ('Bandits in Orgosolo') (1961) or *San Miniato, luglio '44* (1954) ('San Miniato, July '44'), a documentary about a

German genocide, made by Paolo and Vittorio Taviani, which Zavattini worked on at the scripting stage, and which was lost in the workings of state censorship;[65] their *Un uomo da bruciare* ('A Man for Burning') (1962) made in collaboration with Valentino Orsini – at the peak of the struggle between landowners (aided by the Mafia) and farm workers – follow Zavattini's non-fiction and ethnographic, concrete, aesthetic. As does *Con il cuore fermo, Sicilia* (1965) ('With your Heart in the Right Place, Sicily'), which won the Venice Film Festival Prize for best documentary, and a *Nastro d'argento*, an essay film directed by Gianfranco Mingozzi. This medium-length film is about the experiences of ethnographer and sociologist Danilo Dolci's Sicilian experiences.

Neo-realism to come

10.1 Zavattini's 'Some Ideas on Cinema'

Parallel to the development work on *Italia mia* was its theorizing, in Zavattini's preferred mode of communication, the interview. In the months he was in close contact with Rossellini, for location scouting in the Po valley, archival papers show that, as discussed earlier, as of February 1952, Zavattini began using the National Library in Rome to carry out detailed ethnographic research for *Italia mia*. That February, he also wrote to Luigi Einaudi, a major Italian publisher, to propose a series of Neo-realist books entitled *Italia mia* which later went ahead, envisaged by Zavattini as illustrated film scenarios in book form.[1] Towards the end of February, his publisher Valentino Bompiani wrote to congratulate him on *Umberto D.*:

> It's beautiful: your film and the film both of you made, the one I like the most with its perfect 'pieces' (you say sequences). I've written to De Sica too, because the two of you really deserve a monument. Now take one more step. It's only fair that we become even more demanding towards ourselves.[2]

At the time, Bompiani didn't know that Zavattini was far more interested in what cinema could be like *after Umberto D*. The following month was when Zavattini and Michele Gandin began to record a series of interviews or 'conversations' as Gandin described them, beginning on 10 March, and record their collaborative work with several young filmmakers working with the screenwriter on developing a new script, closely related to *Italia mia*, and sharing its core methodology, *Shadowing people*. Gandin was also a film critic and an editor of *Cinema Nuovo*. The same day he and Gandin began the interviews, Zavattini visited the National Library in Rome to carry out research on ethnography as a method which could be applied to cinema. Later, Gandin collected for publication the eleven separate interviews produced over a period of five months. He limited his editorial intervention to a straightforward transcription, respecting Zavattini's express instructions not to change the linguistic register of his spoken language. These were published first as a standalone article, 'Some Ideas on Cinema', and later formed the Preface to a book containing the scenario, treatment and screenplay for the film *Umberto D.* previously discussed.[3]

From the very beginning of his activity as a screenwriter, in the early 1930s, Zavattini had made a point of publishing selected scenarios in film magazines, but he had never published a book revealing the whole process in its unfolding, from the initial idea to the final screenplay, including changes, an intervention on an entirely new scale, also serving as a textbook for aspiring screenwriters.

This section homes in on his general introduction to the book, containing the result of the interviews: 'Some Ideas on Cinema.' The first part comprises a defence of Neo-realism against its critics on both sides of the political spectrum, from fellow Communists on the Left to Catholics on the Right, while the second part goes on to frame Neo-realism as Neo-realism *to come*.

As regards the first part, he argues in favour of a cinema of the everyday and of the aesthetic value of concentrating on the contemporary moment, the central focus of Neo-realist films, rejecting the film industry's obsession with invented stories. Even when the everyday features in mainstream cinema (not only Hollywood but also European cinema) it sensationalizes it. The capitalist film industry imposed dead formulas on living 'social facts', or events. This is because it is authoritarian, in the way the creative and production cycle is organized, at the cost of a loss of spontaneity and creativity, and of reducing real-world events to feature backdrops, when they ought to be the filmmaker's main focus. The result? A watered-down version of reality. Wouldn't a direct form of cinema be preferable? Surely this is what Neo-realism had achieved, by foregrounding the expressive power of reality in cinema.

He points out three recurring criticisms levelled at Neo-realism. First, its narrow focus, centred on poverty; second, its escapism, in the sense that it offered no solutions (a criticism coming from the Left); and, third, the objection that the focus on everyday events was boring. As to the first point, Zavattini's response is that to ignore poverty as a subject means refusing to be informed; rejecting knowledge, by adopting an escapist attitude. Why would anyone want to ignore poverty? Out of fear, the root cause, in his view, since being informed would place the viewer under pressure to intervene. His conclusion was that cinema had to address poverty, and get better at doing so. As to the second objection, he made the point that filmmaking was a response to a problem, not a solution. This was as far as artists could go: making an audience feel the need to seek a solution, through empathy, by involving the viewer directly in the issue. What about the presumed banality of everyday events, and their supposed unsuitability for the cinema? He produced several arguments. Reception and quality filmmaking were significant factors. Even screenwriters were to blame, for they should also take responsibility for the lack of film culture in the public's perceptions. By not writing about the everyday, most of them were playing into the hands of the capitalist film industry and of the public. Not that he thought that situation-based, event-based filmmaking wouldn't be more demanding. But it would be worth the effort. The outcome would be far from banal, since in this kind of cinema, a durational cinema, a cinema of expanded screen time, closer to the passage of time in the real world, a new space would be created, providing a focus, and an opportunity, for in-depth analyses. Then the cinema of distraction would be replaced by the cinema of cultural value, and an ethical cinema would ensue. He noted the gap between the freedom of creative choice which characterizes literature and the lack of choice that is typical of industrial cinema. In practice, while novelists were free to tackle the everyday without attracting any criticism, screenwriters were not.

In the second part of 'Some Ideas on Cinema', Zavattini looks to the future, arguing that Neo-realism is an unfinished project, since, despite its innovations, it preferred invented stories to a documentary approach. He proposed that the cinema to come should be mainstream non-fiction. Where had Neo-realism found the story? In the street. *That* was the important event. Consequently, the following step would be event-based cinema, concerned with so-called normality or everyday life. What was generally considered empty, banal, space, could be seen differently, as worthy of scrutiny and widely shareable, due to the inter-dependence of things. Zavattini proposed that filmmakers should subvert the way cinema combined events into sequences, by taking, instead, a single event, even a single moment, and opening it up to analysis, to expose all its layers of meanings which would then form a film's substance. An ethical dimension could be found equally in a small-scale event or a large-scale event. Method was key: showing the correlation between facts or events, and how they can be traced back to a root cause. For when you scrutinize a social fact you come to realize that it is, in reality, a complex and multiple phenomenon, and far from banal. It concerns real people and this is where the ethical dimension comes in. By turning the camera on real people, the filmmaker adopts a responsible attitude to society which involves direct, social attention to what there is, in other words, attending to tangible, concrete phenomena, not to vague ideas. And the banal? Only what is irrelevant is banal. The filmmaker can avoid the banality of irrelevance by observing and conveying what we share. This is how Zavattini subverts the idea of what constitutes a spectacle. Real life can be a spectacle, when it is translated into something specific: the event.[4]

How to approach the event? A recurring metaphor used by Zavattini is *pedinamento* or 'shadowing', a concept that has already figured in this book. Shadowing extends from following a person, to tracking down reality itself. But how? He recommended that the filmmaker increase his or her engagement with the real world, by tracing the steps of reality, in a similar way that an investigative journalist follows up on a lead concerning a real-world event.[5] 'Shadowing' is a suggestive metaphor, but archival evidence mentioned earlier shows that an ethnographic outlook underpins the term which he uses for different purposes. It has generally been interpreted as a technique, but seems, rather, to be triggered by an underlying approach. At times, it is a signifier indicating both filming real people in the street, as a way of adopting a more direct approach to the real, and also adopting a well-informed, ethnographic approach to people and their social, cultural and political living context. Shadowing also signifies a listening approach attitude, to be adopted systematically towards other people, whereby those who are filmed, are filmed with respect, over time, and in their time; as Same, not Other. Shadowing produces an encounter, which requires the filmmaker to get to know the people, by becoming part of their lives for some time. In this perspective, filming in the street takes on a different significance. The street makes shadowing possible, provided theatrical constructions are replaced by genuine face-to-face encounters with real people in real environments.

Consequently, it comes as no surprise that Zavattini should consider a story which results from shadowing, preferable to a made-up story, acted out by professional actors. The preference for non-professional actors is actually a preference for ordinary people, as opposed to hero-like figures, on the grounds that heroes exclude viewers, making them feel inferior to an impossible ideal. Zavattini claims that filming real people and real situations would make viewers value themselves more, gaining a greater sense of their own self-worth, as people, and achieving a greater sense of self-awareness. Shadowing is key in this dynamic, for, by expressing an interest in people who are not assumed to be different, one conveys a sense of solidarity precisely where solidarity is lacking in society.

'Some Ideas on Cinema' also covers durational cinema, the diary-film, and the nature of the screenplay. As for durational cinema, the core concept is a theory of moments. Zavattini considers time as a succession of moments and reviews how time is represented in Neo-realist films. The moment is at the basis of the event, and of the filmmaker's approach to it. Incidentally, the philosopher and heterodox French Marxist Henri Lefèbvre, Zavattini's contemporary, developed an embryonic theory of moments, which has much in common with Zavattini's own. For Lefèbvre, the moment in time could be a decisive event, however transitory. Although it could be overlooked, it might be potentially revealing of the nature of daily existence. It might mark one of a range of possibilities; it might be potentially radical, even revolutionary, but discernible at the level of the perception of sensations.[6] Less is more than you think, applicable to time and its perception. This train of thought for Lefèbvre belonged to a phenomenological strain of thought, and in Zavattini, too, but only on an intuitive level.

For Zavattini, in the context of cinema, duration indicates a long stretch of time which includes both the work carried out before making the film and the filming itself. Moments are the minimal events which cinema should narrate, as in *Bicycle Thieves*. By dwelling in the event, Zavattini argues, the event can be explored in depth. However, the term 'duration' is as charged with meaning as the term 'shadowing'. For Zavattini, duration also means a filmmaker's attitude of patience over time, in coming to know. Patience is also a form of commitment to a socially engaged cinema. Durational cinema, as theorized by Zavattini in this text, and others, is analytical, because it gives the time to explore the event in detail, such as, for example, – his example – the ordinary event of a couple looking for somewhere to live.[7]

Zavattini says that Lefèbvre to come should not look back on the past. It should film a contemporary moment in time. His proposed structure for concentrating on the contemporary moment and real-life events is the diary form, which allows a filmmaker to engage with everyday existence. The diary is quintessentially a reflexive tool for all involved. People don't know themselves, let alone other people. It follows that, if you film ordinary people acting themselves, they will also gain an awareness of their personality and attitudes, as they appear on the screen.

Finally, he turns to screenplays. He states unequivocally that they should be abolished. He recommends instead going out and filming in the street, on the basis that the everyday is preferable to the exceptional. Cinema doesn't need a scenario. Zavattini puts it this way: 'Narrate reality as if it were a story, instead of inventing a story that is similar to reality.' Screenwriters, in his judgement, are expected to stick to the technical side of things. But writing a scenario and a screenplay should not be separated from directing the film. The roles should collapse into the figure of the director. There is no justification for having a scenario and professional actors. Neo-realism requires everyone to act themselves. Zavattini gives the example of Caterina Rigoglioso acting herself in *The Story of Catherine*, an episode of *Love in the City*, made the following year.

'Some Ideas on Cinema' has been translated into many languages including Spanish in at least two versions. In Cuba, Tomás Gutiérrez Alea translated and circulated it for study purposes among Cuban filmmakers.[8] In Spain, in 1953, the editors of *Objectivo* quoted extensively from it and made a detailed commentary. In Mexico, Pío Caro Baroja translated long sections in the spring of 1955.[9] These translations are documented, but there may well be others.

If we are to take Jacques Rancière's claim seriously that cinema belongs to what he calls the 'aesthetic regime' in which 'everything is now on the same level, the great and the small, important events and insignificant episodes ... everything is equally representable', then Zavattini's film theory, as expounded in 'Some Ideas on Cinema', marks a turning point in cinema history – long before *Cinéma Vérité*.[10] It is in this seminal text, translated into English in 1953 and anthologized for the first and only time in 1966, that the 'time-image', as Gilles Deleuze was to call it, is explored in detail.[11]

'Some Ideas on Cinema' reached out to the twenty-first century when it was cited at length by renowned Iranian filmmaker Abbas Kiarostami in *10 on Ten* (2004), a masterclass about his cinema in the form of a documentary in ten ten-minute lessons, permeated with Zavattini's theories and film practice. In the section entitled 'Subject', Kiarostami asks: 'Is cinema about story or is it about reality?' and cites Zavattini's Neo-realist aesthetic:

With its endless thirst for reality and truth, the kind of cinema I uphold never has its shortcomings of subject. As Zavattini says, the first person who passes by can be the subject of your film. The presence of millions of people with millions of problems is an unlimited source of subject matter for this kind of cinema. In my opinion, it will never come across a crisis, it will never be short of subjects.[12]

10.2 Zavattini's 'Theses on Neo-realism'

In 1953, Zavattini gave another interview, published as 'Theses on Neo-realism' (1953), which was also the outcome of verbalizing theory in the intense language and context of an interview, his preferred mode of address. It begins with a rallying cry: 'Neo-realism is our only flag.'[13] From Zavattini's perspective, the New Italian Cinema was at a juncture: either a new cinematography was going to develop out of Neo-realism taken to its extreme consequences, or mainstream cinema would prevail. He describes mainstream cinema as 'the one all of us are resisting, at least that is what *we say* we are doing'. Neo-realism, 'the most powerful appeal that exists today to turn our attention towards the real world', is worth fighting for.

The interview published as 'Theses on Neo-realism' is yet another intervention, containing a reasoned defence of the movement, in the face of 'many desertions and much disorientation', and of the wheeling and dealing of the film industry. As he saw it, Italian cinema was being hypocritical. It was also in danger of betraying its purpose through compromise, thereby becoming socially ineffective. Now was the time to regroup, consider the contribution of Neo-realism to Italian culture and plan for the future.

In 1953, the theoretical debate about Neo-realism was alive and well, but, in Zavattini's view, there was also a discrepancy between all the theorizing and heated discussions going on, as opposed to actual production. These critical exchanges had misunderstood, in his opinion, the whole point of Neo-realism. For some commentators, it was a thing of the past, for others, an impossible or utopian dream.

Responding to the former, Zavattini retorted that Neo-realism should not be confused with the tenets of nineteenth-century literature. Its scrutiny was the contemporary moment; the defining feature being 'a new attitude towards reality'. Those who believed that it was a time-bound movement were mistaken. Moreover, it should not be confused with so-called rubble films, about the immediate post-war period, since the constituent nature of Neo-realism was the discovery of current affairs. As for its connexion with the Second World War, the war had only been a catalyst, in so far as, in Italian cinema, the shocking reality of war led to shifting the focus from the scenario to everyday life. What he meant by life was a concrete reality, and especially within it, the very real contradictions in 1950s Italian society, such as displaced people who were still living in makeshift accommodation, almost ten years after the end of the war.[14]

Zavattini saw no reason why Neo-realism had to be a monolithic movement. There was room for different tendencies within it. For example, in a gesture of compromise, he conceded that historical films could coexist with a new form of cinema consisting in investigative films, which would reconstruct contemporary events with authentic characters taken from real life. The binding factor was that the different tendencies share the same unity of purpose. But there was no call for division. 'Any serious and extensive discussion should take place within

Neo-realism itself.' If they agreed to commit to a programme and direction, they would be operating within a Neo-realist framework. A critical mass of films informed by such ideas and values would have the desired effect: the relations of production would change.

Neo-realism, as he saw it, was the most powerful appeal to filmmakers to turn their attention towards the real world, an ethical act in itself. It was also ethical to strive to bring about a collective social and political conscientization. But rather than equating Neo-realism with a new ethical cinema, he saw it as a socially engaged cinema, a political cinema, and ethical as a consequence, the outcome of linking time-based events and timelessness, the particular and the universal, based on concrete experience. Filming on location facilitated what he calls 'a cinema of encounter'.

However, Neo-realist empathy and ethics should not be confused with a humanist Christian empathy, with its prayerful, if abstract, attitude of hope towards the future. By seeking instead to trace common rights back to fundamental needs, Neo-realism expressed empathy or what Zavattini called 'a sentiment of love towards life', a process of non-differentiation, in the sense that problems are shared problems. Consequently, by comparison with Christian humanism, what drove Neo-realist empathy was social urgency, a sense of emergency and responsibility which conflicted with policies aimed at not dealing with social problems. By pursuing the relation between cinema and reality and expressing an ongoing critique of society, based on a commonly held social awareness, Neo-realism, he claimed, was inherently socialist. To dissolve Neo-realism would mean giving in to a society which condones extreme poverty, exploitation and injustice.

The way forward, as far as Zavattini was concerned, was to adopt an enquiry-based approach to writing and filmmaking. This required what he calls 'cohabitation', that is to say, establishing 'meaningful relations with other people and with the real'. It would generate new relations of artistic production which wouldn't only impact on art but also on lives, by brining into existence a deeper quality of shared living among people. Few have the patience to observe and to listen. Yet, the more one deepens one's awareness of reality, the more one *analyses* people and situations, and the more the relations of coexistence become apparent. Then, the focus of attention shifts to a commonality of purpose. In other words, the concrete work in hand serves to free filmmakers from abstractions.

Zavattini drew a distinction between *analytical* narrative, proper to Neo-realism, and bourgeois *synthesis*, in a sharp distinction between materialist critical realism, concerned with concrete reality, as opposed to bourgeois idealist realism. These ideas of his could be related to psychological realism, but equally, and paradoxically, to Lukácsian Stalinist realism which, despite the use of the word 'realism', was a form of idealism, in the way it proposed to create exclusively ideal figures and situations with little or no relation to the real world.

The purpose of what Zavattini called analytical cinema was to address social issues. He argued that it was more than a purpose; it was an urgent need for cinema. But why should cinema have such a role and what made it fit for such a purpose? He though its inherent properties, and namely its indexical or photographic accuracy in conveying social facts, lend it to such an objective. Furthermore, cinema was the most powerful contemporary form of media and the most convincing. There was also its analytical capability that gave it the potential to produce concentration on an object or situation over time, in the sense of slow viewing of the same thing. By this Zavattini meant the choice and power of staying with the same subject matter when 'it requires an urgent intervention and for which the duration of our attention is always less than the necessity to really get to know it'.

Zavattini emphasized that adopting an analytical approach entailed a focus on the *particular*, in open disagreement with those such as the filmmaker and then critic Carlo Lizzani, and the other aligned PCI filmmakers and critics, who argued that such an emphasis might distort reality. In his interview response to those critics, Zavattini explained that there is a crucial distinction between the particular, understood as a concrete element of reality, and what is known as the general, which refers to an ideal or abstract, and possibly unfounded, and thus idealist, version of reality. One has to ask how exactly would the durational, or analytical, cinema he proposed and was theorizing concentrate on the particular. Quite simply, by concentrating on the small event or situation, because it is tangible, concrete, and therefore the greatest guarantee of authenticity lies in 'becoming familiar with the lives of real people and with the deeper meaning of each of their actions'. He thought that such a 'severe method', which the film industry would not allow, would serve to combat the industry's adoption of superficiality, an approach which gets in the way of the audience or the public really getting to know an issue in depth.

'Theses on Neo-realism' also contains a response to those critics who failed to see how non-fictional or documentary-based investigative cinema, of the kind Zavattini called Neo-realism, could be art. This was, quite possibly – because, in the wake of 1930s debates about art and cinema in Italian film circles, those critics equated documentary with non-art – influenced, ultimately, by the aesthetics of Benedetto Croce and, namely, his distinction between poetry and non-poetry, which has its counterpart in Clement Greenberg's view of visual art.[15]

Zavattini's objection to the accusation of naïve realism was that documentary filming can never be exclusively a mechanical process, reduced, that is, to making indexical copies of reality. For, even if it were possible to film events when they are actually taking place, it would still require 'choice and a creative act'. He unquestioningly ruled out the myth of indexical truth when he pointed out, in response to his critics:

> How can anyone possibly believe that I am talking in terms of mechanical photography? However amazing it might sound, it is impossible to capture reality automatically.

Realism, taken in Zavattini's sense, requires the mediation of the creative imagination, in his view, but in the context of the street and of the *contemporary moment*. For this is the reality the filmmaker seeks to understand. Furthermore, it is only when situations are subjected to a thorough scrutiny that their full creative potential is revealed. Producing a faithful reconstruction of events through field work, or what he called 'research', in his view, inevitably involves and requires the mediation of the imagination, provided it is 'balanced with an extensive knowledge of the event'. For only in this case can it lead to a spectacle of a very different kind, consisting in the screening of authentic 'revelations'.

10.3 Reactions to Zavattini before the Parma Conference

This polemic was of its time, for 1953 was a turning point for such debates about realism in Italian cinema, and Zavattini was undoubtedly their catalyst. This was the year of the second-most important Conference on Neo-realism to be held at the beginning of December, preceded by fierce discussions. In *Cinema Nuovo*, Guido Aristarco published an article calling for a development from Neo-realism to realism, in line with the new position upheld by the Italian Communist Party's cultural section, 'Il realismo italiano nel cinema e nella letteratura' ('Italian Realism in Cinema and Literature', a direct response to Zavattini's text 'Some Ideas on Cinema'. Zavattini's proposals also met the hostility of the authoritative Marxist film critic Umberto Barbaro, who now rejected his vision out of hand, claiming it was a form of naïve, mechanical realism, based on the indexicality of the photographic image. Barbaro's model? Russian realists who, he believed, could set an example. He thought Zavattini and Luigi Chiarini were attaching far too much importance to filming in the street and doing away with the scenario, and were wrong to allow the filmmaker to be inspired directly by empirical reality, encountered in actual everyday situations.[16]

The journalist Enzo Muzii also claimed it was high time to reconsider the aesthetics of Italian realism in cinema.[17] Muzii argued that realism should not be reduced to a formula, because it is an individual artist's response to reality and therefore neither subject matter nor theme should be codified. He claimed Zavattini was mistaken to want to limit Italian realism to what he disparagingly described as populist films in dialect and impoverished chronicles offering only a partial view of Italian society. He was also wrong to endorse a documentary bias and an essay film approach. Italian cinematic realism should develop into critical realism, combining tradition and the contemporary moment. Muzii took their side in this budding polemic, arguing that realism should not be equated with Zavattini's ideas, and, to be specific, it should not be reduced to his formula of dialect-based populism and petty chronicle of the everyday. It should, rather, embrace as a viable cinematic model, the nineteenth-century Italian historic novel, and set future realist films in the country's *Risorgimento*, the time of the struggle for national independence.

Another short piece by Muzii, in the same issue of *Emilia*, reads like a partial apology for his earlier attack on Zavattini, but also serves as a useful introduction to Zavattini's programmatic text, 'Theses on Neo-realism', published later, in November 1953, by the journal Muzii edited. As far as Muzii was concerned, now was the time for Italian realism to change direction and engage with the problems posed by nineteenth-century realist literature. Typology – as advocated by Soviet-style realism – would enable filmmakers to combine the past and present of Italian life. Films should not be exclusively about the working class. Luchino Visconti's *Senso* was still in production when Muzi wrote his article. However, Muzii was familiar with it, and saw this film still in the making, set in the nineteenth-century *Risorgimento*, the Italian struggle for national independence, as pointing the way forward.

Siding with Zavattini, critic Luigi Chiarini didn't agree with Muzii, arguing, in July 1953, that a distinguishing feature of Neo-realist cinema was precisely its documentarism, in terms of attending to the medium-specific language of cinema. Like Zavattini, he also thought that cinema should be emancipated from literature, theatre and the figurative arts, finding its inspiration directly in the real world.[18] To back up his axiom that cinema's filmic discipline-specificity is the immediate contact between the filmmaker and the reality, Chiarini cited a well-known 1930s article by Leo Longanesi: 'The thing to do is take the cine-camera into the streets, the squares, the army barracks, the stations.'[19] Chiarini proposed a sharp distinction between spectacle and film, pointing out that Neo-realism had singled out the essence of film as a 'creative elaboration of reality', an insight shared by very few filmmakers, Chiarini added, perhaps only by Zavattini and Visconti.[20] From this viewpoint, he concluded, film becomes 'an absolutely autonomous expressive form, a form emerging from the unique potential of film to "creatively elaborate on reality", in sum, a revolution'.[21]

Chiarini wasn't the only one to side with Zavattini. Earlier that same year, in February, when Agostino Degli Espinosa, a brilliant young film critic, had met Zavattini to show him a scenario of his, he was invited to join Zavattini's team of young writers and directors, for a prospective film about a strike. It was envisaged as a portrait of the event, to be told almost as it unfolded, as if it were in real time. Degli Espinosa thought that the same method could be applied to other themes, such as the life of a city, in which the gamut of feelings from joy to suffering, boredom and revolt could be situated within the collective time of work which measures the lives of individuals. Zavattini then made the point that opting for a documentary didn't necessarily exclude the mediation of poetry:[22]

You know better than I do that there are a variety of methods to carry out an investigation. They exclude neither truth nor poetry. It's always a matter of making a choice, depending on the context. And I insist on the term 'document'. I could use equally the term 'anti-spectacle', while at the same time being fully aware of the need to communicate with the greatest number of people.[23]

In his essay in *La Rivista del Cinema Italiano*, Degli Espinosa drew attention to the increasingly collective and collaborative dimension of work in modern society and its poetic aspect, consisting, he thought, in the changes which collaboration produces in human relations.[24] The collective nature of work, he stated, was challenging the family unit, conceived as a tightly knit group. He made the point that 'social space' (*spazio sociale*) was overlapping with 'physical space'.[25] He also noted a shift in interest from the novel to the chronicle, memoirs and biographies, which is certainly true of the kinds of books published by Einaudi, under Elio Vittorini's direction and later Italo Calvino's.[26] Degli Agostini stated that the distinguishing aspect of the kind of realism specific to cinematic Neo-realism was injecting realistic needs into the traditional story, which accounted for non-professional actors, real-life environments, and all the other elements characterizing the 'hunger for reality'.

Degli Agostini didn't agree that making films about invented stories with only a touch of realism was the way forward. Invention spelled a compromise with the ethical standards of realism. Narration could only be constructive and socially useful (*socialmente valido*) if it expressed the contemporary moment. He thought that cinema was well placed to do so, because the contemporary is its natural language. Therefore, he argued, cinema could only be considered ethical when it used its medium-specific language.[27]

He agreed with Zavattini that, since there is no dearth of reality, there could be no shortage of stories.[28] Neo-realism had made films about the war. However, any contemporary event, being part of a collective reality, in other words, symptomatic of it, contained concrete elements worth filming.[29] Private narratives are no longer relevant. Any hour of the day, place or person could be narrated, provided this was done in such a way as to express the inherent collective connexions.[30] Degli Espinosa called this *correlatività*, 'correlativity'. It entailed regarding human beings differently, in a concrete way, not considered as members of an anonymous crowd or an anonymous people. *Correlatività* meant no longer disregarding the singularity of each person within the collectivity.[31] Cinema would be paying an endless tribute to other people, if it followed its aspiration of narrating the whole of reality.

Was there a danger that the art of film be lost in empirical photography, as others had objected? Degli Espinosa didn't think so. Neo-realism, he observed, didn't draw directly on the apperception of raw reality, but on its collective substance (its 'correlativity', or what Merleau-Ponty has called 'coexistence'), the countless relations which link each individual to all the others. Equally, the affective dimension (passions and feelings) stems from the collective dimension of the real.[32] Degli Espinosa's conclusion was that the documentary form offered a field of observation which could inspire works of art.[33] This was entirely in keeping with Zavattini's theorization of the documentary.

Manifesto films

Love in the City and We Women

11.1 From theory to theory-in-practice: Love in the City

This period of intense theorizing led to two film projects which were so radical for De Sica that Zavattini didn't try to involve him in their gestation or production. Indeed, one of them is mentioned in his essay 'Some Ideas on Cinema'.[1]

He was referring to *The Story of Catherine* which was inspired by a news story mentioned in his public film diary, in the entry for June 1952. His reflections show that, as he saw it, this film involved an important aesthetic choice. Initially, the idea of a short film was based on the news combined with the idea of shadowing the real person involved, a nineteen-year-old Sicilian mother under prosecution for abandoning her two-year-old child outside a church. By the time Caterina Rigoglioso had changed her mind the following morning and tried to claim her son back, the clergy had called the police and the matter had gone to court.[2]

In the climate of early 1950s Italy, public opinion was scandalized. Zavattini went to the law court in the company of filmmaker Antonio Pietrangeli, to attend the hearing against Rigoglioso. Zavattini's first reaction in August 1952 was to turn the news item into a short film about a real person whom he proposed to shadow, from moment to moment, in the course of a day. As he put it in his Cinematic Diary: 'it is so clear to me that to make a film of this kind you need a new technique: I believe that it is only a matter of patience. Neo-realism is the greatest test of patience the cinema can offer.'[3] The viewer would be invited to experience, almost first hand, as an external witness, what a particular life would be like, not identifying with the character, but the situation the character is in. This way, a situation would be aligned with a person's lived experience of it. Real people would take the place of imagined characters. He developed this into what he theorized as a 'flash film' (*film lampo*): 'Films which re-enact a news story with the people involved – the most real of the real world achievable.'[4]

The film about Caterina Rigoglioso was initially envisaged as a flash film, a short. While still working on the Rossellini version of *Italia mia*, and already engaged on the shadowing project with Michele Gandin and others, in July 1952, Zavattini had met potential producers at the Astra cinema, to discuss casting the real person, Caterina Rigoglioso, for the part. A flash film was a film which could be turned around in a month, soon after the event was feasible, made on a tight budget, 'on the run', so to speak, and free from bureaucratic constraints. The stumbling block was allowing the protagonist to play herself and, inevitably, become a character in the process. However, Caterina's screen test didn't come out well. She didn't know how to move nor was she such a pleasant person. But Zavattini placed his confidence in how the real is more moving than the imagined.[5] 'Finding the protagonists in the street is not just a gag', Zavattini wrote in March 1953.[6] He went on to explain: 'The New Cinema intends to concentrate on contemporary life in its most immediate and direct aspects, the ones which concern us personally every day, every hour.'[7] He told Gandin during the interviews which appeared as 'Some Ideas on Cinema', 'The producer didn't think Caterina was "suitable for the cinema". But wasn't she Caterina'?[8] De Santis's *Rome, 11 o'Clock* was also based on a true story. The difference was that *The Story of Catherine* would not feature an actress, but the real person who was the protagonist of the story in the first place. Other Neo-realist films also featured non-professionals, but Zavattini was attempting the shift towards personal history, testimonial cinematography, and total adequation between a living person and a character.

In the spring of 1952, during the Gandin-led interviews for 'Some Ideas on Cinema', it seemed that all was lost: no *flash film*, no *Story of Catherine*. But in 1953, Zavattini succeeded in persuading a producer to accept that Rigoglioso would play herself. In the meantime, the *flash film* had become one of several episodes of a full-length documentary, relating to everyday life in Rome. All the episodes, bar one, feature real people, instead of characters portrayed by professional actors.

He thought of enlisting other Italian writers to engage in his project of bringing documentary films to the fore, and changing its public perception to one of parity with fiction, as he had argued in print. He contacted Elio Vittorini, a heterodox communist who left the Party after his line was vigorously rejected by the leader of the Party, Palmiro Togliatti. Vittorini was at the centre of the Italian cultural debate on the Left in those years, and also the editorial director of Einaudi, a major publishing house.[9] In pre-war Italy, Vittorini had taken Italian prose writing apart and problematized it in his Modernist novels *Uomini e No* and *Conversazione in Sicilia*, just as Italo Calvino or Natalia Ginzburg were doing after the war in their prose, and similarly, Franco Fortini and Vittorio Sereni in their poetry. But nothing came of it.

Zavattini's creative involvement as a writer in all the episodes of *Love in the City*, bar Federico Fellini's, was decisive. Zavattini developed the overarching framework; he was directly involved in the film's production, and invited filmmakers to collaborate on treatments and screenplays. He worked on Carlo Lizzani's episode, Michelangelo Antonioni's, Nelo Risi's (for which he was not involved in the treatment), and, for *The Story of Catherine*, he wrote the story, the treatment, the screenplay and was heavily involved in its editing).[10] Antonioni later distanced himself from the film, amid a polemic against Zavattini's film-manifesto. In response to Antonioni's public attack against the premises of the film, Zavattini defended his choices for the episode on attempted suicides, directed by Antonioni, and the episode on prostitutes, directed by Lizzani. In accordance with his theories on which direction Neo-realism was to take, as he had publicly stated, he strove to replace myth with reality, that is to say, literary nineteenth-century realist representations with 'the human face of prostitution', calling for a shared responsibility, while his vision for Antonioni's was an affirmative celebration of life. He defended his decision to allow the people directly involved to appear on the screen. 'The turning point of cinema' was 'to get closer to the real with all the freedom possible'.[11]

Love in the City is experimental in a number of ways: its structure emulates a printed magazine, the type known at the time as *rivista d'attualità*, or current affairs magazine, and this editorial framing extends to the screen titling. It explains the opening shot of what looks like a magazine Contents page which, in addition to putting forward the idea of a moving image magazine, makes explicit its critical framework. Zavattini, the former editiorial director and publishing mogul, transferred his pioneering approach to popular illustrated print media in the 1930s, to the moving image. Zavattini was also the main producer, together with Riccardo Ghione and Marco Ferreri who had already worked with him in 1951, to make several experimental newsreel-style shorts, overturning the banality of newscasts by offering the public insights about Neo-realist directors at work, entitled *Documento mensile* (*Monthly Documentary*), featuring De Sica and Lamberto Maggiorani, the lead actor in *Bicycle Thieves*, in the first short, and *Appunti di un fatto di cronaca* (1953) (*Notes on a News Story*) in the second, directed by Visconti. Incidentally, it is worth noting that the idea of a film as a series of *appunti*, personal diary-style notes or observations was something that Pasolini was to adopt and develop in the 1970s. This was the same team, consisting of Zavattini, Ferreri and Ghione, now producing *Love in the City* for a Faro film.[12]

The first eight minutes of the film, supposedly opening credits, help to understand the organizing principle and framework underpinning the documentary as a whole, for, together with the closing statement at the tail end of the film, they serve to construct the documentary form as an essay film, and suggest a statement of intent, a manifesto, Zavattini's manifesto, screened shortly before the Neo-realist Conference of Parma, held in December. A close look at those initial eight minutes of what purports to be a six-episode documentary film suggests that there are, in fact, seven episodes, the first of which, coming immediately after the opening credits, is unattributed. The first three minutes combine verbal commentary with photographs; a montage of sound and stills. *Love in the City* also closes with a final statement, drawing together the loose amalgam of episodes into a whole and restating the initial essay discourse of *Love in the City*, subtitled *The Spectator*, Issue no. 1, 'A magazine edited with film and a lens, rather than pen and paper'.

> The first issue of *The Spectator* ends here. It hasn't exhausted all the possible imaginable aspects of love in the city, but it has deliberately left out the banal. The purpose of our magazine was to seek out the more personal and authentic forms of the real, consistently with a style and purpose of a new and aware kind of cinema.

The flash film (*film lampo*), understood as a film produced over a short space of time, soon after the event, and on a tight budget, became an episode in a full-length film which took a year to get into production. However, the flash film idea lingered on in this eight-minute self-contained film-within-the-film, anonymous, and yet scripted, and directed by Zavattini himself, at least in its minimalist simplicity.

The voice-over statement, not a commentary, is accompanied by a long sequence of still photographs – not fill stills. The city in question – Rome – is not represented in its layers of history, built one on top of the other over time, like a palimpsest of scripts in an ancient manuscript. There are no Baroque façades, no Egyptian obelisks, those triumphant spoils of ancient Rome, or Renaissance domes. It is the working-class city of the periphery, amid the noisy traffic. The Rome of those eight minutes combines stone with steel. It is the Modernist city, preferred to the Catholic shrine and the Rome of the emperors. A look at the many photographs reveals high-rise apartments, some under construction, overlooking a shanty town suburb or *borgata*, factories, a demonstration, a crowd in a stadium, a sequence of images of Italian women, images containing high and low cultural connotations, ironically juxtaposed – using shot reversals – to a Hollywood star who appears in a poster, none other than Marilyn Munroe. This way, the indexical real self of women from different walks of life and occupations is contrasted with the mediatic Hollywood idealism of an escapist fantasy. Lana Turner appears in the next shot. The poster recedes, the more the close-up focusses on her stereotypical character. The voice expands on the dialectical montage, stating that love is

> Not what you often see on this same screen, played by athletic men like Kirk Douglas and seductive women like Marilyn Munroe – a manicured love, revised, improved upon, and scripted – to make you shiver with a well-calculated dose of passion.

Nothing could be further removed from 1920s *City Symphony* films. Nor is this the war-torn Rome under German Occupation of Rossellini's *Rome, Open City* or *Paisà*. Space is not an abstract construct, but public and socially divided. The words of the voice-over indicate a group editorial choice, a 'we' which refers to Zavattini, Ghione, Ferreri, but also to the directors who took part in this daring experiment, presented as an editorial team, as if they were journalists, colleagues working for the same news desk. The photographs are followed by a series of very short scenes, encapsulating a range of situations, brief moments in time, lasting no more than a minute each, each a cameo of a situation, or better, a moment in time.

It was a prototype intended to provoke a dialogue among Italian filmmakers and influence the direction of the New Italian Cinema. It drew fire. Its reception was discussed at the Parma Conference which was vigorously negative. A documentary had to know its place, which was to remain peripheral to the development of the cinema.

Three years later, mainstream contemporary cinema looked the same to Zavattini. As far as he could see, from the perspective of 1956, it was still a combination of conformism, deception and vested interests, and the media still defended a scandal-based approach to news, claiming that 'we do this because this is what the public wants'.[13] Nothing had changed.

11.2 *We Women*

Zavattini was always involved in several projects at once. The same year of *Love in the City*, he came up with *We Women*. As he often did, Zavattini adapted an earlier idea of a confessional film, which resulted in *First Communion*, to what became a companion episode film, which he produced and for which he wrote most of the scenarios, *We Women* (1953).

The two films share a preoccupation with the diary form, and a confessional, personal, mode of expression. He wrote the scenario and screenplay for *First Holy Communion* in the first person, as if he were Carloni, the main character, who, in retrospect, as a narrator, admitted what he was really like and reflected on his own shortcomings. Then Blasetti had got the wrong end of the stick, trying, but failing, to push Zavattini's characterization towards a religious-style confessional mode, supported by heavy moralizing. Zavattini had resisted and the outcome, in no small part thanks to his resistance in writing the screenplay and his involvement in the cutting room, doesn't depart from his long scenario.[14] Not only is the protagonist, as envisaged by the screenwriter, morally despicable, and therefore a Neo-realist anti-hero, he is also an anti-hero because he reflects on his behaviour, in a pioneering attempt at confessional personal cinema.

That was in 1951. *We Women* for which he planned to film real Italian women, not a character like Carloni; women being themselves and sharing their true nature and inner feelings with the audience. That was the plan. The women acting themselves would be no ordinary women, but stars, professional actresses.

His experiment consisted in showing viewers the people behind the masks played by famous actresses and seeking to match screen presence to the real-life person. *We Women* took yet another approach to the documentary, putting forward a confessional personal cinema, while also levelling an attack against the star system. Not only could mainstream cinema extend to contemporary news events, interpreted by adopting a critical point of view, it could also embrace the diary form, as Zavattini envisaged as early as July 1944:

> I was stubbornly putting into practice my plan to convert everyone to the diary form and the confessional mode in a new ethical order of cinema which I had articulated one morning in the Cinema Imperiale, as soon as the Germans had left.[15]

The reality-illusion dichotomy to be found in the scenario of *The Great Deception*, discussed earlier, about the man who played Antonio Ricci and his plight, written immediately after *Bicycle Thieves*, is also key in *Bellissima*, in which Zavattini shows his persistent curiosity about the dialectical tension between the real and the imaginary and the ways in which the illusions of ordinary people are blinded by confusing myth with the real.

Zavattini worked with several directors, including Guarini, Rossellini and Visconti, and collaborated closely with them on the scenarios and all the screenplays for *We Women*.[16] This collective effort is another foray into the documentary, whether through the reconstruction of events, or toying with the divide between fictional representation of the real and actual documentation of events. How to engage with the real, how to get closer to it, how to attend to it through the moving image?

The unattributed first episode of *We Women* is Zavattini's work. It serves as an introduction to the episodes which followed, featuring the major stars of the day in Italy: Anna Magnani, Alida Valli, Isa Miranda, Ingrid Bergman.

Zavattini's *diary* captures something of this tension and testifies to his active participation in the film.[17] Here too, he takes a reflexive, meta-filmic approach, questioning the film within the film itself, to the point of showing its workings in *Acting Contest. Four Actresses. A single Hope*. This first episode functions as an establishing shot, providing a narrative frame for the whole film. Zavattini set up a real competition for aspiring actresses, which was held at the Titanus studios where it was later re-enacted and filmed, to set up the context of the film industry spectacle, as a way in to *We Women*. *Acting Contest* does so by exploring the tense situation of a screen test, by dramatizing it, and making explicit how emotion is fabricated before the camera and then objectified. The tannoy announces the short list of successful applicants. We hear one say: 'Too good to be true. To be included in a film with la Magnani, la Bergman, la Valli, Isa Miranda ...'

Acting Contest begins with an interior scene on the landing of a wealthy apartment block, the home of the young Anna Amendola, one of the two aspiring actresses selected for the part. She has made her choice: the acting profession will have precedence over family life. The title of the film and of the episode appear on the screen, against the backdrop of Titanus film studios. Just as in *Bellissima*, there is a screen test to select two non-professional actresses for the film-within-the film. A cine-camera films the aspiring actresses, while their names are being called out. They walk up to a desk where an employee says 'yes' or 'no' to them. The successful candidates are filmed during supper. A tiny voice wishes the girls good luck; advising them to behave naturally in front of the camera which is rolling throughout the meal. At one point, two of the aspiring actresses leave the table to explore: they open a door to a room where a large screen for viewing screen tests and rushes appears in a frame within the frame, and the successful contestant looms large on the screen within the shot. The two keep staring at the screen for several seconds, before being asked to leave.

This first episode of *We Women*, like many Neo-realist films, rejects the middle-class Italian of Fascist-era films. The soundtrack conveys the rich variety of class and dialect, Venetian, Roman, Neapolitan, Milanese. When a girl is told she has been rejected, her response is in Neapolitan dialect: *Ma ccome? Vengne a Napuli son a ca da stammatina alle sei e nun me facete neanche u provinu? Io non me movo a ccà* ... 'What do you mean? I come all the way from Naples. I've been here since six this morning and you're not even going to do a screen test? I'm not budging from here!'. In 'Some Ideas on Cinema', Zavattini had defended the use of dialect as being more authentic, on the grounds that literary Italian and spoken Italian often 'don't ring true'.

A tannoy announces the winners of the contest. The voice-over of the woman who plays herself says:

> And at last it was my turn. Now everyone was staring at me; only me. But little by little, everything fell away; leaving just me and the camera. Me and the camera in which I could see the reflection of my face.

The second screen test for the shortlisted candidates shows the lighting being adjusted, the clapper board, and the reflection of the candidate in the lens, cross-cut to the camera in the centre shot. The clapper board appears on the screen, to interrupt the make-believe of viewing and punctuate the beginning of several sequences, thus breaking once again the suspension of disbelief.

This episode draws attention to the significance of acting, inviting the viewer to reflect on what it involves, highlighting the strong expectations the illusory cinema world creates, placing its whole machinery under scrutiny, and foregrounding its mise en scène. The clapper board marks the beginning of the last test. The lighting engineer adjusts the lamps, the interviewee is shot from the other end of the camera facing her, while she is answering the director's questions. Her image, surrounded by black, appears as it would through the viewfinder. Meantime, her voice picks up the story, while the scene changes to that same evening in the company of friends and again to the next morning when she gets up to go back to the film studios.

Each of the following episodes opens with shots of posters of the stars' famous films, combined with their signatures. *We Women* addresses the relation between cinema and everyday life through *mise-en abîme*. In Isa Miranda's episode, the actress's voice glides over her glamorous portrait film stills: 'It's my turn. I've been asked to talk about my life. I told this little episode to Visconti.

He liked it, so here it is.' Once her theatrical world was abruptly interrupted by a car accident and by close contact with ordinary people. A child was injured. She stopped to help and took him to hospital. For a short time, she felt what it would have been like to have a child of her own.

In the second episode, Alida Valli was getting so bored at a party that she decided to walk out and attend her housemaid's lively birthday party. Just when she was about to leave the first party, her voice marks the moment of departure with a question, a humorous intertextual reference to Zavattini's ongoing polemic that in Italian cinema there is no crisis of creativity, no shortage of new stories, by comparison with Hollywood.[18] When she gets there, she soon realizes that she cannot escape her world, because ordinary people treat her differently. They queue up to shake hands and get her autograph.

Could Neo-realism be humorous? Ingrid Bergman had asked Zavattini when she and Roberto Rossellini went to see him, to talk about what to do for their episode. She made the point that Neo-realism didn't have to be serious.[19] Ingrid Bergman's episode, directed by Rossellini, begins with a request we don't hear. It comes across as very natural. Bergman's reply: 'but I don't know what to say; I have no idea what might interest you.' She remembers a funny incident involving a neighbour's missing chicken. 'I told you! It's a silly story.'[20]

The final episode directed by Visconti features Anna Magnani arguing with a police inspector at the police station about a fine on her pet dog. Whatever its merits may be as a film, *We Women* is also a text, a polemical proposal, a manifesto.

11.3 *Stazione Termini*

During this ideological flurry of activity, Zavattini was also working on an entirely different kind of film, *Stazione Termini* or *Indiscretions of an American Wife*, which is emblematic of his ongoing predicament as a filmmaker. While he was a spokesman for the New Italian Cinema, at the same time, he was a practising screenwriter working within the film industry, having to juggle experimentation and aspirations with established film craft for his bread and butter. How could he reconcile the two extremes? He couldn't. He was attempting to redefine mainstream cinema, by steering it towards non-fiction, while also working on conventional projects, such as *Stazione Termini* or *Indiscretions of an American Wife*, a film which belongs to the kind of durational cinema enacted in *Bicycle Thieves* and *Umberto D.*, but which, in terms of content, and final outcome, in Truman Capote's rewrite, is nevertheless, to some extent at least, a throwback to Zavattini's preoccupation with adultery in *The Children Are Watching Us* (1942).

The story is quite simple: while staying in Rome to see her sister, Mary Forbes (the star Jennifer Jones and the producer's wife), an upper-class American, falls in love with an Italian American Giovanni Doria (the star Montgomery Clift), a young teacher. But her family back home in the States needs her. Her daughter has fallen ill, so she must go home. Mary is torn between passion and duty, between adultery and motherly love. She has already made up her mind. She has boarded the train in Termini railway station. Giovanni finds her and tries desperately to persuade her to stay. The film charts their moment-by-moment agonizing separation and their conflicting emotions. Duty must take precedence over passionate feelings for her Latin lover.

The background of the production is important to contextualize Zavattini's scenario and screenplay, written partly in collaboration with Truman Capote, acting on behalf of the producer David O. Selznick. Before Selznick decided to finance the film with his wife in the lead role, Zavattini's scenario had been round the houses. Rossellini, Claude Autant-Laura and Max Ophüls had all expressed an interest. Ingrid Bergman and Gerard Philipe were to act the couple, but when Selznick purchased the scenario, he was adamant that his wife, Jennifer Jones, should play the main part.

When De Sica went to Hollywood in 1952 he met Howard Hughes who was interested in producing a film directed by De Sica, on condition that they adopt customary Hollywood studio production systems. De Sica refused, so the Hughes film didn't go ahead. But then Selznick contacted the director and suggested a compromise: how about adopting the Neo-realist practice of filming in the streets, but using his own production team? De Sica agreed. Selznick's photographer was to take care of shot reversals and romantic dialogue between Montgomery Clift and Jennifer Jones, while Zavattini had to contend with imposed changes from on high, re-writes by Truman Capote, but not to Zavattini's liking. The problem was that Selznick also retained overall control on the screenplay. It was, as a result, Americanized, in the sense of minimizing the social dimension of the story. What was symptomatic was reduced to an individual case, taken out of context, thus crippling Zavattini's phenomenological method of concentrating on a particular story that expands into a general problematic. By comparison, adultery in *The Children Are Watching Us* contradicted the Fascist nuclear family rhetoric. Any such expansion is absent in *Indiscretions of an American Wife*.

The outcome was a clash between two cinema worlds and two ideas of cinema. The studio world, with its star system, its artificial sets, its lighting, its platitudes, its psychologism and individualism, opposed the Neo-realist, situation-based, often simple story, aiming at authenticity, at challenging the viewer to produce meaning by interpreting events. What was rejected was the foregrounding of the environment, filmed in the street, the everyday as inspiration, and the link between private life and public life, individual and society.

Even so, *Indiscretions of an American Wife*, at least in its Italian cut, retained its original durational, real-time pace, in which the real-world environment takes on a life of its own, duly re-enacted and staged, but nevertheless portraying the transient flow of life, so admired by Siegfried Kracauer.

The film was set in the transient nightscape of a railway station, the central station in Rome, with its vast empty spaces, beautifully rendered by the legendary director of photography G. R. Aldo.[21] The background, as in other

Italian films of the period, becomes more than a backdrop, acquiring a life of its own, suggesting transience, flux, undecidedness, bounded by its fixed Rationalist Modernist architecture, emphasizing the couple's moral constraint and the impossibility of their situation.

The film was, however, poorly received by Georges Sadoul and André Bazin in France, and by Guido Aristarco in Italy. Even De Sica felt uncomfortable about it, stating that the compromise of trying to reconcile an art film with the commercial film industry simply hadn't worked.[22] Not everyone agreed. Zavattini's former student in Parma, and film critic, Pietro Bianchi and Henri Agel appreciated the transient nightlife world the film conjured up through the moving image.[23] It was certainly De Sica's attempt at exporting Neo-realism to North America, almost completely foiled by Selznick's constant pressure to control the production during the location filming in Italy, and by the efforts to bring the star system formula into contact with everyday life. Even so, G. R. Aldo's brilliant cinematography and De Sica's choreography of the crowds milling around the station in waves and staging of Zavattini's vignettes bring the anonymous, transient, space to life, drawing the attention away from the main situation.

The Parma Conference on Neo-realism

12.1 The context

The two manifesto films and all the debates underpinning them preceded the second important conference on Neo-realism of these years, which saw Zavattini at its centre. It took place in Parma, from 3 to 5 December 1953.[1]

Only a matter of days before it was due to begin, Guido Aristarco, the editor of *Cinema Nuovo*, and a screenwriter, Renzo Renzi, were released from prison, following more than a month of detention, on the charge of offending the army in a jointly published article, a scenario for a film about the Italian occupation of Greece during the Second World War. Although it didn't dominate the conference, this shocking event placed censorship squarely on the agenda of public debate once again, as it had been at the 1949 Perugia Conference. It set the scene of the Parma Conference itself, leading to much discussion about the negative effects of official censorship, and reaching the conclusion that cinema should reaffirm its ethical origins and defend freedom of expression.[2]

The Parma Conference was attended by a large crowd and involved the participation of major Italian filmmakers, critics and journalists, and 100 speakers.[3] Vittorio De Sica opened the proceedings, claiming his unreserved support for Neo-realism, while Antonio Marchi screened his three-hour compilation of Neo-realist films. During the conference, Rome's most prominent and influential film club, the Circolo Romano del Cinema, proposed to run a week's screening of major Neo-realist films across Italy, while the *Cinema Nuovo* journalist and documentary filmmaker Michele Gandin proposed an annual prize for the best essay and series of articles on Neo-realism.[4]

12.2 Renzo Renzi and the debate about censorship

Renzo Renzi raised interesting questions, emerging from his recent direct experience of government censorship and incarceration.[5] First, he acknowledged that post-war Italian cinema had pointed the camera in a new direction and, by doing so, had looked behind the façade, beyond any unreal optimism, to express solidarity against injustice and misery. The catalyst for change had been the war and the insurrection at the war's end in cities in the north of Italy. From an artistic point of view, he argued that the war's end marked a radical change for Italian filmmaking: the rejection of empty Fascist idealist rhetoric, combined with the discovery of the scale of mass poverty.

He went on to point out that a screenplay like his was the first to question the principles justifying war, to query its presumed inevitability. It was promptly censored, because government censorship treated the war and Fascism itself a taboo topic. Renzi's proposal for a pacifist film was seen as a lack of respect for the fallen, and as contempt for the ideals of heroism and military discipline.[6] He argued that defeat should have led to public reflection and critique of the recent past. Why were Italian institutions insisting on upholding an ideology of war and heroism? Theirs was a refusal to remember and to deal with the past and stifle any attempt at memorializing it. And yet should not a real democracy be willing to challenge a hierarchical structure demanding blind faith and discipline at all costs? It was wrong to reject outright any representation of war which questioned its ideology. He told Parma delegates that it was not enough to say that the war had been a catalyst for Italian cinema. Filmmakers should question the religious mystique surrounding it and carry out an analysis of its root causes.

Censorship was also tackled by Virgilio Tosi, the active and very effective organizer of the Italian Film Clubs, the *Circoli di Cinema*, which, in hindsight, were responsible for fostering the beginnings of a film culture in Italy.[7]

Post-war Italy had faced three stages, Tosi said, going from being on bail, to being under house arrest, to cultural intimidation. In response, a producer and friend of Zavattini's, Alfredo Guarini, adopted Zavattini's analysis, making the point that the film industry, and namely the producers, distributors and picture houses, were to blame, for doing their utmost to suppress Neo-realism. They had failed, he claimed, stating that Neo-realism was still alive and relevant to contemporary Italy, motivated as it was by ethics.[8]

How do you combat censorship? By creating alternative channels of distribution. This was Ugo Casiraghi's suggestion. He was the Communist film critic of *L'Unità*, the PCI's daily newspaper. The lack of film culture in Italy didn't help matters, but this shortcoming could be tackled by the film industry, through educational campaigns to promote films 'which contribute something in terms of culture and society'.[9] What Casiraghi had in mind was nothing less than an alternative distribution circuit for a viewing public of factory workers who already received an education from within the trade unions. He argued that there was a need for low-cost, popular screenings, followed by the distribution of questionnaires to collect feedback. Carlo Lizzani pointed out that Renzi and Aristarco had been prosecuted for tackling real issues. Yet, *Rome, Open City* had already demonstrated that you cannot separate politics from the life of a society.[10]

12.3 Zavattini's paper

It is clear from Zavattini's intervention that his paper was not the first. Nevertheless, the responses to it indicate that his ideas were at the centre of the

Parma debate. As the previous chapter has shown, he had already generated a lively debate within film circles long before this conference. He had combined his film practice with cultural politics off the screen. The previous year had seen the publication of his book, containing not only the screenplay for *Umberto D.*, and all the preliminary work leading to it, but also 'Some Ideas on Cinema', a reflection on the cinema to come. In the course of the debate, Umberto Barbaro and the Communist press had defended an idealist and Soviet form of film realism and attacked him repeatedly.

By the time he stood up from his chair to speak (and left one of the sheets of paper stuck to it, he later claimed, losing the thread in his speech), he had also just made three important interventions, namely, the scenarios and most of the screenplays for two experimental films *Love in the City* and *We Women*, and, only a month before the Parma Conference, published 'Theses on Neo-realism', in effect, a position paper preparing the ground for Parma, in his typical merging of theory and practice, or *praxis*.[11] At Parma, the first point Zavattini made – Zavattini 'the accused', as Luigi Chiarini later described him – was to draw the delegates' attention away from the debated issue of censorship, to consider instead the kinds of questions he had been addressing in print in 1952 and in 1953, establishing a critical framework which could serve to give coherence and point the discussion in a constructive direction.

He began by reminding delegates that his proposals had been attacked by a number of speakers at the Parma Conference and that *Love in the City* and *We Women*, in particular, had provoked a strong backlash. Critics aligned with the Communist Party had rejected them as a combined thesis, contained in two manifesto films – a dual intervention over the nature of cinema and the direction it should take. Guido Aristarco, Edoardo Bruno and other critics, including Umberto Barbaro, strongly objected to the idea that the future of Neo-realism was news-based documentary, because, they argued, that choice reduced realism to chronicle, proposing instead critical realism, based on an unspecified notion of realistic historical fiction.[12] Gabriele Mucchi accused Zavattini of being an extremist, seeking to make the documentary mainstream, when it could do nothing more than reproduce reality. For Mucchi, it was time for a shift from realism to Verism, the label for Giovanni Verga's late-nineteenth-century realism, later also championed by *Cinema* magazine.[13]

Zavattini's response to them all was to state that the conference's real task was not to consider whether Neo-realism was over or not, but to discuss its future and natural development, since, to date, only the foundations of Neo-realism had been established. While in 'Theses on Neo-realism' Zavattini had posited the possibility of there being various currents within Neo-realism, at Parma he stated that these already existed. Now he appealed to an idea that most of the delegates shared: that in Italy the Second World War had been a catalyst for change. He reminded them that there had never been a popular consensus over going to war, in a country which was ruled by a dictatorship. The sufferings of war were the cause of the rejection of war altogether, and turning to pacifism, which had been a 'revelation'. Why hadn't other countries produced a liberation cinema, a cinema about real people, individuals, a cinema committed to pitting itself against abstract stereotypes of people? Only Italians had experienced the war as a definitive break with the past and a new beginning. By comparison, there was no such sense of destiny in other countries, only fatalism about the future.

Their insight, he continued, was the realization that 'a new horizon opened up before us, the boundless problematic of humanity, not to be taken in any abstract sense'. This had led Italian filmmakers to share a protracted collective experience, which, Zavattini suggested, was accompanied by an understanding of a new culture, a new sense of purpose, driven by social and political commitment. It required filmmakers to opt for a simple cinematic language and for the rejection of mainstream idealism as bankrupt, in light of the real world of suffering. But developing a new culture, with 'a new language', in opposition to Fascist or other forms of idealism, also required investigation, insight and reflection, regarding the real. The key was 'historical man' by which he meant not just people or individuals, divided by their separateness, but concrete citizens existing in a social context, active subjects, in the sense of possessing agency, which is to say the ability to change the situation into which they were born. Italian filmmakers had begun to point the camera towards these subjects, real people who became actors of their own stories, personal, yet relatable to shared existence.

> War has made it possible for some to perceive clearly the new panorama of interrelated being, entirely extraordinary, entirely marvellous, and not in a fairy tale sense. While others, without the excitement of make believe, are unable to relate to their equals.

Zavattini asked his audience this question: How do you make this happen? His answer was cohabitation, a complex concept, combining participation and solidarity, and an attitude of empathy towards the Other. He went on to explain the nature of cohabitation further. It was more than simply becoming acquainted with another person. Rather, it consisted in a deeper level of familiarity, which could be attained through 'tangible' relations, extended over time. Akin to investigative journalism, the kind of in-depth research he advocated was cinematic. It involved multidimensional research, which he described as 'poetic' research, but also personal, and 'subjective'. He explained that 'by poetic, I mean total, aimed at expressing as many dimensions of the reality under investigation as possible'.

His mention of intellectuals in relation to a 'new' culture was a reference to the Marxist concept of the Gramscian organic intellectual; simply put, in Zavattini's context, it signifies a profile of a socially and politically engaged filmmaker who may or may not be a party member (he wasn't), but seeks to effect change, through organizing and working closely within situations, instead of remaining aloof in an ivory tower, and claiming aesthetic autonomy.[14] This provides the context for what he went on to say. He argued that intellectuals, including filmmakers, needed to develop a new practice, in a concrete way, one built on empathy and solidarity and only by doing so, through a face-to-face encounter, could they renew culture. Film art would be made possible by a combination of experimental social and artistic investigation. He conceded that his theory and practice of coexistence or cohabitation had met with rejection from some quarters. There were critics who objected that, at best, it was anecdotal (they called it *bozzettismo*, a penchant for cute populist cameos), and that finding more of such material for inclusion in a film couldn't be classed as research, being, in their opinion, nothing more than a collection of 'mere details, lacking any internal cohesion and divorced from the broader societal context'.

He put this question to the delegates: What could they agree on? What did they all have in common? His replay was the now, the contemporary moment, which they shared, over and above any aesthetic considerations of cinema. Neo-realism, by comparison with other national cinematographies, 'came into close proximity with reality' and this was its foundation. Such an attention, of course, presupposed 'adopting a particular attitude towards life', in other words, a commitment, that is, 'an authentic ability to engage with reality and participate in contemporary social events'.

But he didn't stop at participation in a generic sense of the term. The kind of commitment he proposed required what he termed 'participative presence', whereby artistic intuition takes the concrete object as its focus. On a practical level, it involved shadowing people, in all the senses Zavattini had already espoused in previous texts, discussed in the previous chapter of this book.

Commitment and shadowing extend to solidarity, actively contributing to combating suffering. Commitment also requires a sense of urgency. Again, he emphasized that he wasn't talking in the abstract, but about the plight of concrete people and their tangible suffering. This had been and, Zavattini proposed, could continue to be, the subject-object of the Neo-realist gaze, a knowing, active, committed and empathetic gaze. A gaze which rested on one of the strengths of Neo-realism, namely, its ethical foundation, which gave the movement the confidence to choose any subject matter whatsoever, any person or object of scrutiny, any particular theme, and proceeding to show how it formed part of a broader context. Which is why it didn't make sense to think in terms of a narrow or broad theme. What mattered was the point of view and exploring and expressing in a suitable language the uniqueness and multiple nature of each person.[15] So much for the accusation of *bozzettismo* and *crepuscolarismo*, reducing a story to mundane events. These terms expressed a critique, levelled before and after the war, at documentary forms of cinematic realism, referred to also as 'intimist', 'crepuscolarist' or 'naturalist'.

Zavattini's was no unrealistic, utopian vision, given that the medium itself lent itself to making such a proposal feasible, unique as it was in making it possible to gain unexpected insights. He made the proviso that it was a medium which could convey the real directly, though not exclusively through its mechanical attributes. He opposed the search for the symbolic (the type) with a search for the original, rooted as it is in the real, phenomenological world. But most importantly, he didn't equate the cinematic original with a copy of reality. To aim for a reconstruction of an event, of a situation was not the same as aiming to create a copy, since the reconstruction always involves the mediation of artistic practice. This was his response to the accusation levelled at him of advocating naïve realism.

His proposal for change championed anti-spectacular cinema and opposed mainstream Italian film industry. He was aware of that. But then, he continued to argue, capital also sought a compromise, reducing cinema to a pleasure-based event, limiting its scope to entertainment. Equally, Neo-realism was at odds with the ruling government's values, and worse still, perceived as a threat. He told the other delegates that they should not be intimidated but press on with themes of social inclusion. To those who objected that this cinema was not a watchable show, he responded that it was a different kind of spectacle.

It was important to keep trying, accepting that experimentation, however much it might result in imperfect cinema, given the commercial and production pressures, was key to developing a film culture, through an ongoing dialogue with viewers. One way to do so was to think in terms of the diary form, eliciting a creative contribution from ordinary people, something he had already experimented with. He stated that what he had learned from his efforts developing a diary project could also be applied equally to cinema and working with non-professional actors, as a means for them to learn more reflexively, through acting and the medium of cinema, about themselves, in a process of self-emancipation and personal growth.

In the last part of his paper, Zavattini abandoned the theoretical level of the debate to make a robust reference to recent and current research on inequality in Italy. This line of argument was also a rejection of Soviet idealism masquerading as realism. Realism entailed turning cinema's attention to the social. An ethical imperative, surely. Especially in the light of the most recent research on poverty in Italy which should not and could not be ignored. Indeed, there was an urgency for cinema to remain committed, in light of undeniable 'social facts'.

He then cited the latest volume of government-sponsored research on poverty, *Proceedings of the Parliamentary Enquiry on Poverty in Italy and the Means to Fight It.*[16] He contended that in this context, art and cinema had everything to do with what he described as 'the "objective" immensity of facts we should be familiar with, both as men and as citizens'. As far as he was concerned, the social dimension was central to a Neo-realist perspective. Filmmakers, then, should be carrying out enough research to be in possession of

> An interpretative frame of reference of social reality in its environmental and institutional dimensions, capable of being enlivened by the language of statistics, interpreted in sociological terms.

This was the scale of the problematic they all faced, an entirely different proposition, not to be confused with making shots and editing them in sequence, the technical dimension. Consequently, he argued, the way forward for filmmakers was embedding or coexisting with what they wish to get to know, through a spirit of enquiry.

12.4 Neo-realism or Neo-realisms?

One of several negative reactions to Zavattini's paper came from Filippo Sacchi, film critic at *Epoca* magazine, who informed him that

> Art does not equate with a photographic representation of reality, but a recreation of it, which affords it a more durable representation and places it into the realms of history. The enduring moment of art consists in a free and personal reconstruction of the social fact.[17]

The fact is that neither Sacchi nor most of the others present were willing to consider his proposals seriously. Sacchi's objection shows that he had chosen to ignore Zavattini's stance, and that the writer had already demonstrated that he was no naïve realist, but had already made the distinction between mechanical medium-specificity and artistic, cinematic, intervention.

Carlo Lizzani, who had recently directed one of the episodes of *Love in the City*, conceded that there had been no significant social improvement in Italy since the immediate post-war years, which meant that those critics who continued to identify Neo-realism with the immediate post-war period were mistaken. Not even the founding of a Republic in 1946 had produced any radical change in certain strata of Italian society. He felt he could support Zavattini's ideas for the future of Italian cinema, expressed in his 'Theses on Neo-realism', but only if they be rooted in Italian society and its politics, in which case, they could provide a means to tackle the contemporary social dimension. That was as far as he was prepared to go.

This sounds like an endorsement. But, in reality, Lizzani's contribution to Parma was an endorsement of socialist, or better, Soviet, cinematic realism. He went on to argue that the ultimate aim was now to make films that apply the theory of the typical to Italian reality. Lizzani argued that Lukács had established the correct paradigm to follow. Consequently, the future of Italian cinema should go beyond filming the social fact. Why? Because he and other orthodox party colleagues now had a new argument, provided by Georg Lukács, two of whose works had been translated into Italian.[18] But there was nothing 'new' about 1930s Soviet realism. Lizzani's objection was based on a different conception of realism, in which current affairs could only serve as a point of departure. Armando Borrelli had already made the same point back in January 1953, in an intense broadside at the screenwriter and theorist.

> It seems to us that, if we stop short at Zavattini's limits and do not go beyond them, we risk holding back Italian cinema from creating genuine

realism, the kind that has been made by Soviet films, which are generally recognized as representative of a great school.[19]

And now, in the Parma Conference, Lizzani was conceding that Italian cinema was indeed at a crossroad: either it was prepared to change, or it would face involution.[20] Lizzani's notion of change, however, was diametrically opposed to Zavattini's. Lizzani dismissed the Catholic Gian Luigi Rondi's denials of a common programme, retorting that filmmakers were far from being isolated individuals who were divorced from society. Lizzani also rejected the fatalist view expressed by Fernaldo Di Giammatteo, who argued that Italian cinema was currently in a state of involution. Lizzani's 'third way' was to advocate that Italian filmmakers should no longer focus on social class, but on the typical, the only 'genuine', 'advanced' realism acceptable.

He went further, announcing that the time had come to abandon the term 'Neo-realism' altogether. He argued that while it was true to say that Neo-realism had been a turning point for Italian cinema, there was now room for several kinds of realism, an exception made for what he called 'intimism', 'crepuscolarism' and 'naturalism', all epithets he applied to Zavattini who had nothing to do with realism.[21] 'Crepuscolarism'? This was a watchword, in circulation at the time in the debate about realism; 'naturalism' was a scholarly reference to Lukács's writings on Zola and Flaubert, mentioned earlier.[22]

Lizzani's stance was in perfect alignment with party headquarters, as its cultural weekly *Rinascita* had made very clear at the beginning of the year, when Borrelli had accused Italian filmmakers of not going far enough in their engagement with reality.[23] Borrelli had claimed that they lacked an ideologically informed understanding. Why didn't they apply the kind of realism theorized by Lukács, based on the type? After all, since the form of realism recommended by Lukács was the only valid realism, surely contemporary events could only serve no more than as an initial idea.[24] Writing in January 1953, Borrelli had gone on to dismiss Zavattini's proposals whose only merit was to have pointed the camera towards what Gramsci calls the 'national-popular' and represented the subaltern's suffering and inequality. Even so, only 'great' realism, he claimed, could expose root causes.[25] Borrelli had also shunned the documentary, for conveying a merely uncritical view of reality, due to the failure to distinguish between what was of primary and of secondary importance, and most importantly, of singling out the 'typical' from what was not.[26] He agreed with Guido Aristarco that what was lacking was '*critical* realism'.[27] Needless to say, both Aristarco and Borrelli equated critical realism with the typical.

12.5 The Catholic stance at the Parma Conference

The Communists called the Catholics 'a small clerical platoon'.[28] The Catholics didn't agree with Zavattini, nor with Lizzani, whose views, they well knew, were aligned with the PCI. In response to complaints about government censorship being a major problem for Italian cinema, Vito Pandolfi observed that the decline of Italian cinema was caused by a general lack of creativity. He was not alone among Catholic film critics.[29] In response to Zavattini's proposals, Pandolfi stated that they had to be dismissed outright. At best, they formed a personal poetic. Pandolfi's coup de grace was that, even if it had proved possible to turn Zavattini's private vision into cinema, Zavattini had no merit whatsoever. Any merit was entirely due to De Sica's interpretation.

Sante Uccelli caused an uproar between Catholics and Communists, by defending Zavattini from both the Communists and from fellow Catholic film critics. Uccelli was the National Secretary of the Italian Cineforum. He accused Lizzani of betraying a bias and offering only a partial analysis. Whereas, he, Uccelli, claimed that Neo-realism constituted a new attitude towards the real world, based on the dialectics of research, carried out at a horizontal level of world and society, but also on a vertical level, intended as both theological and religious. The two levels intersected in the human being, the 'foundation of our theocentric humanism'.[30] Uccelli clearly thought there was something to be gained by endorsing Zavattini's vision. Uccelli shared with Giancarlo Vigorelli, Valmarana and Gian Luigi Rondi the view that the only valid form of Neo-realism was Catholic, compounding humanism with Christian *caritas*, but not in any concrete sense of the word.[31]

Giancarlo Vigorelli pitted Marxist theory against Christian belief and Marxist aesthetics against his Christian realist aesthetics.[32] Long last, he claimed, the Marxist monopoly over Neo-realism had lost its grip on the movement.[33] Neo-realism was something more than an artistic tendency; a social, political and ethical protest which, he believed, had sometimes succeeded in conveying a religious message, through realism instead of through symbolism. Vigorelli's 'second way' negated the 'first way', and namely, Soviet realism, which he condemned as pure propaganda.[34] For Vigorelli, Neo-realism was a form of realism, modelled on Alessandro Manzoni's Christian realist novel, *The Betrothed*, written in the nineteenth century, displacing Verga, the writer who had been the inspiration for Visconti and the pre-war *Cinema* circle, to which Luchino Visconti, Giuseppe De Santis, Antonello Trombadori and Mario Alicata had belonged. The *Cinema* circle edited the publication in its last years and launched a debate about realism, favouring Giovanni Verga's nineteenth-century model, known as Verism.[35] That debate had been sparked off by an article published in 1941 in *Cinema*, co-authored by De Santis and Alicata.[36]

The Catholic critic Gian Luigi Rondi denied there was any such thing as a group. Only individual authors existed in cinema, and consequently there could be neither evolution nor involution. He went on to claim that, since there was no Italian cinema, there could be no general crisis of Italian cinema. There could only be a crisis of individual filmmakers.[37] Once again, an argument resting on aesthetic value.

Zavattini had hoped that the conference would help to regroup. But he was wrong. There was the new orthodox position, adopted by the Communists, then the heterodox Marxist view, adopted by Zavattini, and the Catholics were split between those who rejected Neo-realism, and those who made a claim to a spiritual Neo-realism. The conference proceedings or final statement was a disappointment. It only went this far:

> Italian cinema owed its success to Neo-realism which should be safeguarded from the dangers that have weakened it. The aesthetic of Neo-realism should have a wider diffusion and upcoming government legislation should both value and promote new Italian film culture.[38]

This was a lame statement, barely able to affirm 'the positive value of Neo-realism, the basis for Italy's cinema' and could make only a veiled reference to censorship: 'the need to defend it from all kinds of dangers and the cause of its weakening.' The most it could do was request better legislation:

> A plea to government to bear in mind the cultural dimension of cinema, in future legislation regarding the Italian film industry, and in particular the cultural value of Neo-realism.[39]

12.6 Reporting the Parma Conference in the press

And after the Parma Conference? In his *Cinema Nuovo* editorial, 'More than a flag', Guido Aristarco, who had published Renzi's scenario and was also punished with incarceration, echoed a phrase in Zavattini's essay 'Theses on Neo-realism': 'Neo-realism is our flag.'.[40] Aristarco agreed with Zavattini that Neo-realism was not a thing of the past, to be relegated within the immediate post-war climate and, therefore, no longer relevant in 1953. For there was no cultural or social issue which could not be translated into the artistic form of Neo-realism, and, as the invitation and call for papers for the Parma Conference had stated: 'Neo-realism is a work in progress.'[41] Aristarco also endorsed the call for the defence of realism and Neo-realism, asking producers, distributors, filmmakers and film clubs, and the public, to support the best of Italian cinema. Censorship was at the centre of his editorial, thus effectively sidestepping Zavattini's proposals. Neo-realism was under siege, as was the freedom of expression for which it stood.

Elsewhere in *Cinema Nuovo*, Livio Zanetti, who covered the magazine's commentary on the Parma Conference, sought to isolate Zavattini from the debate. Zanetti recognized that Zavattini was a 'key figure' in recent Italian cinema, in view of his theorizing and film practice, and highlighted the screenwriter's proposal to lead Neo-realism further down the path of the documentary. He conceded that Zavattini's ideas had been a focus for the debate at the Parma Conference. He thought that Zavattini's attempts at creating a place in the mainstream film industry for research-based documentary cinema were laudable, and recalled Zavattini's experimental *Documento mensile* (1951), featuring Visconti and De Sica, and produced by Zavattini, Marco Ferreri and Riccardo Ghione. However, as far as Zanetti was concerned, Zavattini's poetic was personal, and in no way to be confused with an aesthetic. Zanetti objected to Zavattini's film reportage approach, which had resulted earlier that year in *Love in the City* and the personal diary-film *We Women*, accusing him of 'extreme empiricism' and of adopting nineteenth-century literary *tranche de vie* approaches to art uncritically.[42]

His next move was to suggest that Zavattini and his work could cause a 'contagion', especially among young filmmakers. For if Zavattini's theses only amounted to a personal poetic, geared to the development of his own work alone, then they could not be generalized, something Zavattini had been trying to do for several years. To the extent that Zavattini's efforts were successful among young newcomers to the film industry, the 'Zavattini effect' was tantamount to a 'contagion' (*contagio*).[43] Zanetti agreed with Lizzani that the alternative typological approach was the most convincing, despite its rejection of field research. He dismissed Zavattini's theory of shadowing as no more than a distinction between the dimension of fantasy and of the document, and hardly original.[44] His conclusion was that Zavattini was nothing but a dreamer, deluded by such grandiose utopian pretensions; a total put-down.

Luigi Chiarini published four of the most representative conference papers in *La Rivista del Cinema Italiano*, lashing out against the Christian Democrats' 'lies' in his editorial. Chiarini listed instances of censorship which had targeted Neo-realist films and cited the notorious article by Minister Giulio Andreotti who had accused the film *Umberto D.* of giving Italy a poor public image. Chiarini made the crucial point that only films which carried social content had been targeted.[45] He also noted the contradictions in applying censorship. It was no accident that since 1948, government censorship had blocked filmmakers such as Luchino Visconti, Peppe De Santis and Luigi Zampa from having control over the means of production. Why was it that saucy films had no problem in attracting the 8 per cent state-funding subsidy? Why was it that *Il cammino della speranza* finally received the state subsidy only after a public outcry, following a press campaign?[46]

Chiarini's further response appeared in the introduction to his book, published soon after the Parma Conference, *Il film nella battaglia delle idee* (1954), which contains his defence of Neo-realism as the best expression of Italian cinema.

He posed filmmakers and critics this question: How do you go on changing Italian cinema for the better, given the total control exerted by the state? There could be no doubt that cinema was moving in the direction of gross spectacle. But the responsibility for this lay with censorship and with hostile mainstream criticism, which abetted state censorship as necessary.

It was a rallying cry to Italian culture to fight a campaign to defend its art cinema, whose fate was, he argued, in the hands of the public. Filmmakers could help the public discriminate between good and bad cinema, through a process of education, and specifically, by acquiring a film culture.

Neo-realism had had to contend with accusations of moral pessimism, with claims that it was degrading to Italy's international image, or that it was part of a communist plot. As a result, producers had gradually stopped providing financial backing to Neo-realist films or even to films which were even mildly allusive to contemporary Italy.[47] *Anni facili* (1953) was the last Neo-realist risk a producer was prepared to take. In the event, it was still subjected to heavy cuts. Government censorship ensured that a certain Italy – those parts of the country which only attract attention when a calamity occurs, that appear in a few documentaries about the Po Delta, Campania and Calabria, in sum, the Italy of poverty – would not be visible to Italians.[48]

The Catholic stance at the Parma Conference emerged more clearly from reports in the Catholic press, which show that there was a split among Catholic critics. There were out and out detractors and there were those arguing for a Christianized form of Neo-realism. On 20 January 1954, *L'Osservatore Romano*, the Christian Democrats' official party daily, dismissed the Parma Conference findings out of hand, denying any detrimental influence of government censorship or political interference with Italian cinema.[49] Emilio Lonero claimed that the conference had failed to define Neo-realism; not even the main theorist of the movement, Cesare Zavattini, had succeeded in defining it. Zavattini's paper, in Loner's view, only complicated matters. He noted that Zavattini's practical intervention as director of *Love in the City* had generated a very strong negative reaction among delegates. Zavattini's poetics of the Other, considered as a neighbour, and an object of interest and empathy, had been received as nothing more than empty rhetoric.

Bianco & Nero, the prestigious state-owned journal of the Centro Sperimentale di Cinematografia di Roma, opted not to report on the event. Instead, it published a single article putting across a Catholic response by Gian Luigi Rondi.[50] This critic agreed with Lonero that the speakers at the conference had been unable to come up with a satisfying definition of Neo-realism. Gian Luigi Rondi rejected the idea that it was an aesthetic movement, considering it instead only a period of film history, beginning with Visconti's film *Ossessione* (1940) and De Robertis's *Uomini sul fondo* (1943), developed by Rossellini's *Rome, Open City* (1945), and still active in certain works of cinematic poetry in 1953. The themes had been a response to the impact of the war and were the expression of Christian *caritas*, combined with a sense of solidarity between man and man, the only element Neo-realist films had in common. He argued that reality could only be approached from a Christian point of view, because only a Christian understanding of reality could produce works of art, since it alone offered a total comprehension of it.[51] He condemned the Italian Marxist approach, because it adopted Soviet realism, a watered-down version of reality which was far from being realist, since filmmakers who were not Christian in their outlook – by which he meant the Communists – could be neither poets nor realists.[52] Zavattini's poetic of the neighbour, or filming through coexistence with the subject who is being filmed, had to be dismissed and replaced with an 'evangelical love which allows us to see the suffering image of Christ even in our enemy'.[53] Rondi also rejected outright Zavattini's championing of a documentary approach to everyday life as non-poetry, by which he meant unartistic, a reference to philosopher Benedetto Croce's idealist aesthetics.[54]

The Catholic Varese Conference
on Neo-realism

13.1 Varese: Phenomenology and Neo-realism

A year later, the Catholics organized the Varese Conference (9–12 September 1954), a counter-conference, as its title makes clear: 'International Meeting on Cinema.' The proposed theme was: 'Does Neo-realism have a Future? Is the crisis due to exhaustion or to a lack of depth?' Zavattini could not, or, most probably, was unwilling to attend. However, he sent a telegram that the organizers decided not to read out aloud:

> I hope the Conference will show concrete solidarity towards Italian cinema, on the basis of its cultural and political prestige to request from those responsible for censorship a broader view and to request them not to pursue a biased interpretation of freedom.[1]

Varese was an important event.[2] At the quality end of the spectrum there was a philosophical defence of Zavattini's durational and personal Neo-realism, in a detailed phenomenological interpretation by Amédée Ayfré, later upheld by Brunello Rondi, brother of the influential Catholic critic. Its title suggested another attack against Neo-realism, which is hardly surprising, given the support and physical presence of members of the Christian Democrat government, and surprisingly, perhaps, of Federico Fellini.[3] After all, these were the very same people responsible for the policies damaging Italian cinema and establishing a successful stranglehold over creation, production and distribution of all Italian cinema, which is why it is understandable that Zavattini boycotted it.

According to Lino Del Fra, a documentary filmmaker who was covering the conference on behalf of *Cinema Nuovo*, there was no attempt at placing the Neo-realist film movement in its broader cultural context or within contemporary Italian society. Instead, the Christian Democrats, including Onorevole Ponti and the minister responsible for cinema, Onorevole Giuseppe Ermini (Andreotti's replacement), concentrated on discussing aesthetics in 1930s-era discussions with the philosophers in attendance, on whether or not cinema was to be considered an art form.

The conference was split in two. The more open-minded academic side had positive things to say about Neo-realism. It was represented by the Dominican Thomist Father Morlion, professor at the Pro Deo University, accompanied by some of his colleagues. Morlion's bland defence of Neo-realist filmmakers was based on the idea that their work was inspired by Catholic sentiments and that Neo-realists were citizens of a Catholic country. Then there were the hard liners, the members of the CCC (the Catholic Cinema Circles).

Among these detractors, Ghelli and Lunders denied outright that Neo-realism was a tendency in cinema, restating the Catholic objection at Parma that there could only be individual works of art. Gian Luigi Rondi, the president of the CCC, repeated that Neo-realism was over. It had ended with Renato Castellani's *Due soldi di speranza* (1952). In his view, only Rossellini had expressed Christian revelation. By comparison, Visconti, Zavattini and De Sica were not Neo-realists, because they had failed to draw inspiration from the divine and were out of step with the times.

Taddei objected that 'the Church had never given signs of rejecting Neo-realism'. Some of the delegates hoped that there would be a shift away from materialist issues, relating to 'the stomach, the home, or relations of social coexistence'. The existentialist Gabriel Marcel thought that magical realism was the one aesthetically valid form of realism, but instead of singling out *Miracle in Milan* for its magical realism, for how the event can be combined with the imagination, Marcel commended *Pane, Amore e Fantasia*.[4] He admired 'its virginity, which creates the illusion, or at least the awareness, of a certain original human presence'.[5] Marcel told the delegates that he also appreciated Fellini's *La strada*, for how the characters were enveloped in magic and the dream world, but Marcel chose to ignore the core aspects of Neo-realism: contemporary history and social analysis. Much harsher criticism came from Castelli-Gattinara, who dismissed Neo-realism altogether, for doing away with the religious dimension of the three theological virtues, faith, hope and charity, and replacing them with secular solidarity and hope.[6]

Had the Varese Conference ended at that point, it would have amply fulfilled the organizers' views: Neo-realism had never existed. Even if it had, it was now over. But there were two major surprises in store for delegates: Amédée Ayfré's unconditional support of Neo-realism, and an out and out attack on censorship from José André Lacour, a Belgian screenwriter and playwright, a writer who was living in France, and stood up to give an unreserved defence of Neo-realism. Lacour distributed his paper to all those present and then told the hostile and embarrassed crowd:

Censorship is destroying cinema. You can't say anything anymore. Soon the only choice directors will have is between silence and prison. Everyone obeys the official state of affairs. Worse still: in the end we won't even realize it. We'll castrate ourselves. It will seem natural to prostrate before the taboo of government, family, and old maids.[7]

At this point, someone described as the 'Defender of Censorship' sprang to the defence of government and the institution of the family.[8] But Lacour was not put off:

> The phenomenological description of contemporary man had such a good start. But now it is about to end. At the very point in which the truth was beginning to be heard. It ends just when some directors really wanted to say something important. It would be mistaken to suppose that Neo-realism is retreating because the public is bored with it. The reason is that directors will soon have no choice but silence and prison. Which topics should contemporary films cover? Surely those that move and excite the public? Colonialism, sexuality, the police, strikes, brainwashing; unexamined, still existing to this day, to our shame. Have you ever seen a film about the 500,000 tragedies of 50,000 North Africans living in France? Or a film about oil in the Middle East, that is more than an excuse for a show in technicolour? We'll end up thinking it is natural that we no longer talk about anything and that we prefer to ignore whatever burns, bleeds, hurts or might hurt. Cinema will have no future, for as long as the problem of national censorships is not resolved.[9]

As soon as the direction Lacour was taking became clear, the organizers confiscated his mimeographed handouts. Yet somehow, the *Cinema Nuovo* reporter taking notes managed to keep his copy and was able to publish his speech verbatim.

But the main contribution to the public debate on Neo-realism came in the form of a carefully argued analysis, based on phenomenology by Abbot Amédée Ayfré. His defence of Neo-realism is worth recounting in detail, first, because it is a vigorous riposte to the objections levelled at Zavattini before, during and after the Parma Conference, and second, because Ayfré's analysis cannot be confused with the petty polemics of the CCC and of other Catholic film critics present at Varese. He raised the stakes and took Zavattini's side in an argued, cogent and vigorous philosophical defence, which also contained an intelligent rebuttal of Soviet realism.

Ayfré's paper revisited the main points of an article he had published two years earlier, in *Bianco & Nero*, in which he had tried to situate the practice of realism within the history of cinema. At one extreme, there was Dziga Vertov's documentary *Man with a Movie Camera* (1929).[10] Undoubtedly, the Russian had filmed genuine people, taken from real life, filmed in the street, and, moreover, he hadn't worked from a script.[11] But Vertov had achieved nothing more than *naturalism*. To go further, to film what Ayfré called 'the event in conscience' would require a reconstruction, which is precisely what French realism, or what Ayfré termed *verism*, had achieved.[12] However, *verism* imposed preconceived ideas on the real, an approach it shared with the third kind of realism: Soviet realism.[13] But these kinds of realism had failed to revolutionize vision, by prejudging experience.[14] By comparison, Neo-realism showed the event, instead of turning it into a story. There is no real beginning, middle and ending; only blocks of reality.[15] For example, if the last sequence of Rossellini's *Germany Year Zero* was something entirely different, this wasn't achieved through dialogue. It was so, because the characters 'existed on the screen', especially in the last long sequence of the film, achieved through the characters' 'existential attitude', not something conveyed through the child's acting, but by his 'being there'.[16] The child is a concrete, embodied sign, not an empty symbol.[17]

Ayfré cited the philosophy of Edmund Husserl and his pupil Martin Heidegger for the concept of things manifesting themselves to the human being, considered a co-witness to concrete human events.[18] Likewise, *Bicycle Thieves* presented the phenomenon in all its dimensions, creating a world in which beings *exist*, before assuming a societal, symbolic or even metaphysical role, achieving 'an impression of reality'.[19] Thus Neo-realism of this kind was what Ayfré called 'phenomenological realism', because it proceeded by *phenomenological description*.[20] Robert Bresson also employed non-professional actors. Yet Bresson's aims were antithetical to Rossellini's or De Sica's. Bresson moulded his actors or 'models', to fulfil his own abstract and formalist vision.[21] Neo-realist films challenge the passive spectacle of cinema, because of the effort of interpretation they require from the viewers.[22] But eliciting interpretation was a Modernist trait, shared with Modernist literature. In the Neo-realist approach, viewers are allowed the space and the freedom to interpret reality as it is presented on the screen, because the filmmaker refuses to interpret reality for them.[23] The phenomenological realist is opposed to a drama developing a conceptual thesis or an emotional theme of some kind or other, in which all the elements serve to illustrate the theme or thesis.[24] By deliberately not infusing the event with ideas and passions of any kind, including religious ones, phenomenological realism was refusing to intervene.[25]

Ayfré's paper reads like an out and out defence of Zavattini's Neo-realist aesthetic, embracing the screenwriter's emphasis on the everyday, and, on the closer scrutiny, afforded to events, no matter how apparently insignificant. More than a defence of Neo-realism, his is a glowing celebration of the film movement, entirely at odds with what any of the other Catholic delegates were saying. At Varese, Ayfré singled out the achievement of Neo-realism, distinguishing it from other forms of realism. The world, as it appears in the films of Rossellini, Lattuada, De Sica and Zavattini, is viewed subjectively, by a specific character with a singular conscience. Their films shared a cinematic aesthetic, phenomenological realism'.[26] Neo-realist cinema thus adopted a concrete description of the real, in which there is no attempt to psychologize or to moralize, but only to witness physical reality and human interactions in the way they appear. This explains the attention for even the slightest gesture, attitude or behaviour, details once deemed too insignificant or off the point for cinematic purposes. Such dwelling on detail could not but affect the very structure of Neo-realist films, a structure which resembles the fragmentary structure of contemporary Modernist literature.[27]

What is only hinted at in Bazin's film criticism on Neo-realism is spelled out by Ayfré. Neo-realist film phenomenology describes reality as it is, not as the filmmaker would like it to be. An encounter with reality replaces the construction of reality.[28] Its film style is elliptical, which explains why, by comparison with other kinds of cinema, so many Neo-realist films seem to be poorly structured. Taking a phenomenological approach can show how Neo-realist films work. If they seem poorly structured, it is because they follow a different organizing principle: the reason they do not conform to the established structure of cinema – based as it is on the Hegelian model of thesis, antithesis and synthesis or, to put it in other terms, dramatic plot resolution in three stages – is because 'reality is messier than that'.[29]

In Neo-realist films, he argued, the tidy three-part structure is defied by how time functions in these films, by duration. By comparison with the presentation of time in classical cinema, artificial and compressed, Neo-realist films are built on an entirely different concept of time: situations play out and time itself becomes a concrete element.

He told the delegates: 'We are no longer in the realm of doing, but of being; revelation replaces demonstration.'[30] By that he meant 'the revelation of the real', not the exposual of a preconceived thesis. Consequently, instead of a direct message, Neo-realist films contained an element of ambiguity. After watching a Neo-realist film, the viewer could be left wondering what to think, just as in real life. In this way, the mystery of being, its ontological mystery, was foregrounded.

Finally, Ayfré tackled the relation between phenomenological realism and the Christian supernatural. Because it is phenomenological, Neo-realism is averse to conveying a message or a thesis. Consequently, it cannot be a vehicle for Christian apologetics or abstract theology. However, because the Christian supernatural is transcendent, it incorporates all dimensions, including concrete reality, in which Christian grace reveals itself through human gestures or words, in other words, through concrete signs. Neo-realist cinema respects the mystery of being and therefore interpretation is required.[31]

Although Ayfré names Edmund Husserl and Martin Heidegger, with the concept of lifeworld or *lebensweldt* in mind – Zavattini's everyday – Ayfré's explication and phenomenological analysis departs from both their accounts of phenomenology. It is closer to Maurice Merleau-Ponty's *Sense and Non-sense* (1947), which includes an essay devoted to film and phenomenology: 'Le Cinéma et la Nouvelle Psychologie' in which Merleau-Ponty considers film in the same durational terms as Ayfré; that is, as a new reality, 'not as a sum total of images but a temporal *gestalt*'.[32] Merleau-Ponty insists on the centrality of the temporal structure, as well as on the physicality of the body and its gaze.[33] 'They directly present to us', Merleau-Ponty writes, 'that special way of being in the world, of dealing with things and other people, which we can see in the sign language of gesture and gaze and which clearly defines each person we know.'[34] In the same essay, Merleau-Ponty also evokes 'the surprise of the self in the world', in 'describing the mingling of consciousness with the world, its involvement in a body, and its coexistence with others'.[35]

Paradoxically, given its premise, at the Varese Conference, Neo-realism could not have received a more effective and eloquent defence than Ayfré's nor a more strident denunciation of the effects of the Christian Democrats' censorship of Italian cinema. The conference, reported entirely in negative terms by *Cinema Nuovo*, and by Luigi Chiarini, was clearly misunderstood by the Left, yet it succeeded, despite the organizers' plans, in pinpointing three key aspects of a debate the conference had no intention of pursuing: censorship, context and aesthetic value.

13.2 Varese: Brunello Rondi's critical response

Brunello Rondi, Gian Luigi's brother, didn't speak at the Varese Conference. Perhaps he wasn't present, which is unlikely, since his brother was in attendance and gave a paper, as was Fellini, for whom Brunello was working as a screenwriter, for Fellini's *La strada*. Then again, had Brunello spoken in public, he would have expressed views directly in conflict with his brother's and sided with the French philosopher Ayfré. But respond he did, a year later, very discreetly, when he published a systematic book-length contribution, in response to Varese, part rebuttal and part constructive proposal. By then, he had begun his artistic collaboration with Fellini, the only Neo-realist filmmaker present at the conference. Indeed, Brunello Rondi's collaboration as co-scriptwriter was to last until Fellini's death.[36]

In his book, Brunello Rondi systematically refuted most of what was said at Varese, so he must have been present. Yet, he said nothing about censorship, despite the fact that censorship remained a key obstacle to the New Cinema in a battle which Neo-realism had undeniably lost and which Giulio Andreotti had won.

Brunello's criticism and interpretation in no way avowed the apologetic Catholic Neo-realism of Gabriel Marcel nor the simplistic approach adopted by Father Morlion, let alone the equally aggressive stance of his brother Gian Luigi and the other members of the CCC who had spoken up at Varese. Indeed, he rejected the claims made by Ghelli and Lunders that there could only be individual works of art, each to be appraised on artistic merit, and dismissed the idea that Neo-realism did not exist. If, he rebutted, one applied the same argument to Impressionism or Romanticism, in which the works of very different individual artists were recognizable, despite the differences in style, as belonging to a movement, the assertion makes no sense at all.[37] Brunello also denied that a film such as *Pane, Amore e fantasia* was a promising development in Italian cinema: all responses to points made by other delegates present at Varese.

Thus, his was a belated response both to Varese, and to the Parma Conference. In the place of ruins, he built a monument to Neo-realism as an aesthetic. Read in conjunction with Ayfré's and Zavattini's theories, his book was, and remains, a useful guide to durational cinema which reads like a treatise on Neo-realism as a living entity, not a polemical tract. Brunello disagreed with his brother's controversial assertion that Visconti, Zavattini and De Sica could not be classed as Neo-realists, because their inspiration was neither drawn from the divine nor in step with the times. Nor did he share his brother's view that Renato Castellani's *Due soldi di speranza* (1952) marked the end of Neo-realism. Though neither Zavattini nor Ayfré are ever mentioned, Brunello agreed with both: Neo-realism was not time-bound.

Unlike the PCI-aligned Communist critics, and in disagreement with his brother Gian Luigi and everyone else at Varese – bar Ayfré – Brunello Rondi carried out a careful contextualization of Neo-realism, in historical, critical, theoretical and philosophical terms. He considered Neo-realism a paradigmatic event, nothing less than a rediscovery of cinema and more an experimental cinema than a definitive set style. Each single work was open and experimental in nature, and its full potential unrealized. Italian cinema was unlike other national cinemas. With the exception of the works by Pietro Germi, Giuseppe De Santis or Carlo Lizzani, for whom plot and narrative exposition remained central, each Neo-realist film contains a world, hinted at, more than revealed, in its entirety.

Rondi followed Zavattini and Ayfré in refusing to accept the view of those critics who believed that Neo-realism was limited to the immediate post-war. They failed to understand the ways in which it expressed a new philosophy of existence and relation, which was not time-bound. Furthermore, Neo-realism embodied a new ethics and a new Modernist form of narration. His claim that 'Neo-realism belongs within the most advanced European literary, cultural and philosophical dialogue' echoes Ayfré's Varese paper and, indeed, his earlier article in *Bianco & Nero*.[38] Rondi went on to state that Neo-realism 'is closer to T.S. Eliot's Modernism than to nineteenth-century realism or Verga's Verism'.[39] Rondi also discredited the evolutionist approach, put forward by the *Cinema* circle, which stressed a continuity between Neo-realist traits in pre-war and post-war Italian cinema. Rondi's objection was that such criticism – sidestepping any polemical reference to Lizzani or Barbaro, both obvious referents – erred in considering the defining factor of contemporary Neo-realism its undeniable historic roots. Rondi's rebuttal was that a careful study of the major Neo-realist films reveals that its major concerns are contemporary, thus rejecting any form of idealism, be it Marxist or Christian.[40] His line of interpretation is also antithetical to Crocean idealism.

Brunello Rondi cuts a unique figure among Italian film critics for the weight he afforded Ayfré's phenomenological interpretation and André Bazin's observations. Rondi considered the durational aspect as the defining aspect of Neo-realism, which he calls 'a new cinema of duration', and furthermore, 'a new cinema of the encounter', including parallel encounters, corresponding to an existential awareness, on the one hand, and to a historic awareness, on the other hand.[41] Such an awareness comes about with 'the discovery of a social perspective'.[42] As for durational narrative, Rondi attributed to Zavattini the merit of excelling in creating a new 'cinematic time'.[43] But Zavattini's intervention was not limited to adopting the different representation or presentation of time in Italian cinema. Rondi also suggested that Neo-realism sought to bridge the gap between the screen world and the world of the everyday and hinted at Zavattini's *Italia mia* project and the ideas inspiring it:

> There's a strong desire today within Neo-realist cinema for its characters to meet their equals, almost following the pace of an analytical stroll or a precious pilgrimage [...] a dream for the cine-camera to go on a *Tour of Italy*.[44]

Unlike his brother, Brunello sided with Zavattini in his conviction that, having discovered its strengths as a philosophical cinema, Neo-realism should continue to develop, rejecting nineteenth-century humanism in favour of a twentieth-century narrative humanism.[45] What would that look like? A correlative of the Modernist anti-novel, based on seemingly monotonous everyday life, as a source of inspiration, and on the minute fragment, as a basis for an anti-epic narration.[46] Pure Zavattini, in theory and in practice, up to, but no further than, *Umberto D.* For it was Zavattini who theorized a diary-based cinema, a personal cinema, an anti-epic cinema and a cinema of encounter. Far from being a post-mortem, Rondi's Varese rebuttal looked to the future, with the work of Fellini in mind, as the future potential embodiment of Neo-realism.[47]

One may wonder if Zavattini was familiar with Brunello Rondi's work. He was. Zavattini had read a draft version of Rondi's book and Rondi had also been within his sphere of cultural influence.

13.3 Varese: Zavattini's response

Although he didn't attend, Zavattini made a response to what he saw as the main issue raised by the Varese Conference and namely the conflict between an idealist and a materialist cinema. The Catholics posited a new version of Neo-realism, having rejected contemporary cinematic Neo-realism. In its place they proposed a Catholic Neo-realism, denoted by transcendence, by faith, hope and charity. Actually, the conference had been more nuanced than he thought, since it had included a third way, Ayfré's phenomenological realism which, unlike the orthodox Communist or Catholic approaches, did not reduce cinema to conveying a message, and was closest to Siegfried Kracauer's, also phenomenological, mentioned earlier.

Zavattini produced two separate arguments. His first, accepted that Neo-realism was essentially materialist, which of course raised the problem for the Catholics as to how a religion could be reconciled with a materialist cinema.[48] They had accused Neo-realism of base materialism (not, one might add, materialism in a strictly philosophical sense) in dualist fashion to transcendence.[49] The polemic, as they framed it, consisted in an unreconcilable difference, in a dogmatic position, which forced them to reject the film movement as it was. But, Zavattini argued, there was a flaw in their logic, given that Neo-realism also contained a strong ethical dimension, which was also of the order of transcendence. Unless, that is, Catholics had a unique claim to transcendence and, consequently, the concept of transcendence belonged exclusively to Catholics by definition; unless they could conceive of no higher ethical principle to aspire to other than a God. He argued that Neo-realism also belonged to an ethical dimension, for suggesting a transcendence of the material conditions of life, through faith and hope and actions which would make this possible. The first step to transcending it was presenting the actual state of a situation. Zavattini contended that if one understood Catholic transcendence as a progressive human change of self in a journey of self-improvement, likewise, there could be other such journeys towards ethical principles which don't equate with a God. But surely God is democratic. If so, aspirations such as desiring sameness among human beings who appear different and such as seeking to find a way to coexist, or, if you like, cohabit, must surely be acceptable to a democratic God.

His second point introduced the concept of positive action within a given situation. If for Catholics, transcendence was curtailed to a general principle, was there no possibility of intervening, of taking the step from reflection to action? To put this in other terms, was human agency excluded? Or must we believe that transcendence can be equated with intolerance?

Zavattini's position was essentially historical materialist (as opposed to idealist), and eminently reconcilable with Ayfré's phenomenological interpretation which could see transcendence in Neo-realism just as it was, with no need to change it.

Zavattini and cinematic ethnography

Un paese

14.1 *Un paese*, an episode of *Italia mia*

The reason *Italia mia* ran aground in January 1953 was Rossellini's change of heart. He claimed that he had to concentrate on *Duo*, based on the novel published in 1936 by Colette, later renamed *Journey to Italy* (1953). But the two filmmakers had irreconcilable views. Even so, Rossellini's film borrows something from Zavattini's *Italia mia* project, the idea of a journey of discovery of a culture and a people, now seen through the eyes of a foreigner, played by his wife Ingrid Bergman.

Zavattini often saw his ideas developing into different projects, even running concurrently. In this case, a year earlier, in February 1952, Zavattini had approached the publisher Giulio Einaudi to suggest a book series – 'Neo-realist books' – to run alongside *Italia mia*, and form a printed photographic equivalent.[1] He eventually proposed Rossellini as the author of an *Italia mia* book on Rome, the playwright Eduardo De Filippo for one on Naples, and Luchino Visconti for one about Milan. The *Italia mia* book series was to follow a research method which would make them Neo-realist books.

Zavattini wrote to Einaudi specifying social categories connected with a choice of cities: Mario Soldati would cover rail workers; Alberto Lattuada, the peasants of the Po valley; Luigi Chiarini, bricklayers; Michelangelo Antonioni would explore Termini railway station in Rome; Piero Nelli would do Sundays for Italians; Giuseppe De Santis, love in Italy; and Luciano Emmer, whom he'd also worked with on *Una domenica d'agosto* (1950), in which a story is compressed within the time frame of a single day, the theme of the village.[2]

Zavattini acted in the role of publisher, and commissioning editor, bringing to bear all his pre-war experience as editorial director. The first of these projects to come to fruition was *Un paese* (1955) (*Un paese. Portrait of an Italian Village*).[3] The photo-book was intended as a prototype for the *Italia mia* series and had the full backing of his publisher who also approved the whole series.[4]

Virgilio Tosi, who ran the Italian film club association, spoke English and acted as an intermediary, arranged for Paul Strand and Zavattini to meet in the summer of 1952 and, later that year, Strand invited Zavattini to collaborate on a book about an Italian village.[5] Strand was an American filmmaker and famous Modernist photographer foreigner, whom Zavattini had already met at the Perugia Conference of 1949. Strand had spoken as a Left-wing documentary filmmaker who filmed *The Plow That Broke the Plains* about the Dust Bowl and the deterioration from rich grassland to windswept desert, and *This Native Land*, about civil rights violations all over the United States. At Perugia, Strand had distinguished between two forms of realism: the realism of Hollywood and his form of realism which was no different from Neo-realism, in his view.

Since the 1920s, Strand had wanted to make a book about a village, not a collection of portraits, but a portrait of a village, inspired by reading Edgar Lee Masters's *Spoon River Anthology*. He had already made *Time in New England* (1950), followed by *La France de Profil* (1952), intended as a portrait of rural France. This latter was made after Strand had been forced to emigrate from the United States at the height of the McCarthy witch hunts.

Neither book worked out, in terms of integrating text and image.[6] Looking at the illustrated pages of *Time in New England*, the reader is none the wiser about the inhabitants of New England, since Nancy Newhall's selection of writings tells us only about American writers interested in the topic. As for *La France de Profil*, Claude Roy's creative text, poetic though it is, ignores the real people in Strand's photographs.[7]

Strand went to Zavattini's hometown, Luzzara, on 7 December 1952 to begin to work on the project.[8] In March 1953 the two met in Rome to organize a trip back to Luzzara together. Zavattini carried out interviews with local people and went back on 30 December to follow up on the research carried out by Valentino Lusetti, a local farmer. Zavattini conducted eighteen interviews and collected these and all the other interviews and background information and combined it with his own research to produce the text to go with Strand's photographs, taken with an old large format camera. Finally, in March 1954, Zavattini visited Luzzara again to instruct the local primary school teacher to give his twenty-three pupils a diary as an assignment, covering the period from 20 to 23 March. Excerpts from these make up the closing pages of the book.[9] Zavattini was not new to collecting and publishing interviews within a framework of his own making. In 1949, he had elicited a diary from several children who lived in his street and published a selection of them as 'The Children of Via Merici with whom I'd like to make a film'.[10]

Would the book reflect the Neo-realist approach? Or at least Zavattini's ethnographic direction? In October 1953, Zavattini was recommending, to Giulio Einaudi, the publisher, that the series name *Italia mia* should appear on it.[11] But by January 1954, he had to inform Einaudi that Strand was adamant that no reference should appear on the cover.[12] Finally, when in the autumn of 1955 *Un paese. Portrait of an Italian Village* went to press, the series title *Italia mia* is indeed absent from the cover, but it is embedded in the narrative of the book's genesis, inscribed in Zavattini's introduction. Strand ensured that the book would be a deluxe production, large format, comprising black-and-white photographs and text on glossy art paper, having insisted on the quality of paper stock, on the quality of printing, and being involved in all stages of production.

14.2 *Un paese* and photography history

Un paese. Portrait of an Italian Village follows a typical text-plus-captions format, the norm in the photojournalism of *Life*, *Fortune* or *Picture Post* of the day.[13] Yet the captions are entirely overshadowed by the bold images with an abundance of dramatic black blocks. In each portrait, an unfathomable stare confronts the viewer. It could easily be mistaken for the protracted gaze of silent witnesses of early photography, which relied on large format cameras perched on a tripod and long exposures. That was the context of Strand's early photographs published in *Camera Work*, with the exception of candid camera photographs, taken in the street.[14]

Edward Steichen's *The Family of Man* (1955) exhibition at the Museum of Modern Art was based on the idea that we are all equal. Steichen had carried out a selection from no fewer than two million photographs, organized by theme and accompanied by captions, and said:

It was conceived as a mirror of the universal elements and emotions in the everydayness of life – as a mirror of the essential oneness of mankind throughout the world.[15]

Un paese. Portrait of an Italian Village takes a completely different approach; unlike Margaret Bourke-White's photographs for *Fortune* magazine: *You have Seen Their Faces* (1937), where she used artificial lighting for her carefully arranged subjects, aided by composition and framing – all to achieve a more dramatic effect.[16] *Un paese* departs from Dorothea Lange's less theatrical images, but theatrical nonetheless, such as the contrived and carefully orchestrated setup of 'Plantation Owner and His Field hands Near Clarkesville, Mississippi 1936'.[17] The book also has nothing in common with Henri Cartier-Bresson's *Paris Match* feature, shot during his trip to Moscow in 1954 (also published in 1955). Cartier-Bresson had no contact with the people he photographed nor wanted any.[18]

What sets *Un paese* apart from *The Family of Man*, or any other books or features within photojournalism, is the idea that, while we might all be the same, the material circumstances of our lives can be very different.

Un paese shares its ethical approach in being concerned about the subjects in the photographs with a very different book, namely, James Agee and Walker Evans's *Let Us Now Praise Famous Men* (1936). It is equally discrete, equally untheatrical and equally unobtrusive. James Agee and Walker Evans went to Alabama to write about the experience of living for a month with poor sharecroppers. Agee's article was supposed to provide 'a photographic and verbal record of the daily living and environment of an average white family of tenant farmers'.[19] But 'Three Tenant Families' ran to eighty pages and, unsurprisingly, was turned down by *Fortune*.[20] So then Agee expanded his essay into a 400-page narrative, prefaced by thirty photographs by Walker Evans, and published it in book form in 1941. The book was an extraordinary achievement at the time, but one which was met with indifference.[21]

Witnessing poverty at first hand provoked Agee's awe and sense of connectedness to the three families whom he saw as invested with dignity and even holiness.[22] His account also conveys the experience of breaking the barrier between self and other to write a documentary record while questioning his ability to do so. His writing is a reflection on what he personally experienced. Ultimately, Agee's writing is about relating to other people's lives. He chose to narrate his growing empathy for the ordinary people in the photographs and the epiphany he experienced while in Hale County, Alabama. And yet, his genuine empathy and soul-searching became a 400-page monologue about witnessing and feeling the anguish of poverty, a book about his empathy, his feelings, not about the people he and Walker had met.

14.3   Zavattini's dialogical approach

There is no such photographic monologism in *Un paese. Portrait of an Italian Village*. Zavattini's dialogical approach provides a democratic space for the polyphony of voices belonging to the people and their silent portraits.[23]

Virgilio Tosi has already noted the dialectical relation between text and images.[24] There is certainly a clash between what people look like in the book, and namely, mute photographic monoliths, and the dynamism conveyed by what they have to say. In the images, they are being made to keep still, unsmiling and silent, while through their words, their being there, their physical presence, becomes a social being, conveyed through verbal communication of people relating to other people, who belong to the same community. The text, discrete as it is, in a small point size, is at loggerheads with the imposed silent gaze and isolation of the contemplative icon, which seems to constitute Strand's ideal of portrait photography.

In fact, there is a clash in the adoption in all but name of the aesthetic developed for *Italia mia*, such that the community's voice breaks the barrier of the silent icons, thanks to the sensitive and unobtrusive editing of interviews with the people in the photographs. The careful selection and combination of text articulates the voices of the people in the shots. The spoken language of the interviews is translated into a written form which does not betray the interviewees. Zavattini had told his publisher:

I'll be the secret director of what will come out of the mouths of those people, but I have such confidence in the things others are ready to say that in the end, I'll only be a coordinator, the person making the selection and the very idea of making any contaminating interventions appalls me. It seems a rather unusual formula, despite the very common external appearance of interviews. I'd like the words, the stories and confessions of the inhabitants whom we meet either in the street or in their own homes or even at the bar, during long or short interviews, whether they are difficult or easy, to elicit reality in its most concrete form.[25]

When, on 28 December 1952, Strand recommended extending the area from the narrow focus of a village (which he found flat and architecturally uninspiring) to the surrounding environs, Zavattini's response was to insist on the village. But he had a contribution to make to the direction the photography would take in the book. For, on 18 September 1953, Zavattini wrote to say that he liked the photographs, but thought that the book needed new ones to convey collective life, showing people in a situation, in the village square, dancing, shooting, cycling, working or simply walking under the street arcades.[26]

Zavattini thus extended his involvement to that of a project editor, or commissioning editor, with a say on the content of the choice of photographs. The extra photographs he proposed served to link the typical Strand still-life iconic, if mute, portraits, to a way of life, the activity along the river, showing people at work and in an old people's home (Strand resorted to candid camera shots for the latter, as he had done on several occasions throughout his career).[27] What was at stake here was an aesthetic the two didn't share; namely, the aesthetic of *Italia mia*, of human beings considered as social beings. This explains why Zavattini asked his contacts in Luzzara for the results of the recent elections and for local reactions to the results, and why he needed data about income and people's diet by class and so on.[28] Consequently, there are two totally antithetical kinds of photographs and layouts.

The understated part of the book, appearing in small type in the layouts of the book, combines lively voices of individuals telling their story: the blacksmith and the part-time maid stare out of blocks of black background, but their static, silent gaze is contradicted by what they have to say. She describes her job and her exploitation, while he tells of the shrinking trade in making horseshoes. A set of photographs present a story of absence: desolate sand banks in the Po and empty bicycle saddles in the wood relate to the story of Paolina, a young suicide who drowned, and bicycles stacked against the birch trees, relate to an anonymous voice of a labourer lamenting the scarcity of work and the need to leave.[29] On the facing left-hand page, there is nothing but white space.

Strand's austere approach to portraiture (the dignified ordinary person often portrayed holding or next to his or her tools or his or her workshop on the facing page) resembles August Sander's *People of the Twentieth Century* (1928), for example the 'Pastry Cook', a full frontal portrait of a cook in his apron posing next to the range and a pot. Similarly, Strand's three-quarters shot of the village postwoman in her overalls, Renza Grisanti, is looking out at the viewer with her daughter, Riga Compagnoni, leaning against her, and looking away, in a moment of protracted stillness. But her photographic representation conflicts with her memory, now collective memory. For her interview concerns the war and the Reggio massacre, in which her husband was executed by the Fascists, after 1943, the year Italy signed an armistice with the Allies and the peninsula was immediately occupied by Italy's former allies.[30] Renza Grisanti's most private and painful recollection, equally part of the collective memory of the village, removes the photographic barrier of isolated portraits, bringing the village to life through memory.

All this was not enough. To make the village come to life required a different approach altogether; Zavattini's. The second half of the book follows the static image and dynamic words model, enveloping the village into a staccato collection of silent and severe looking presences, while the first half follows Zavattini's art direction, for example, an image of a couple of male villagers standing and chatting, facing elderly seated villagers doing the same on a street corner outside a bar or the weavers looking away (but overshadowed by the product of their work, the huge stacks of straw hats on the facing page) or the unlikely portrait of absorption of the men with their backs turned, gazing at something we can't see. What we can see is a partly torn poster of *Gone with the Wind* (*Via col vento*) and election posters: 'For Peace and for Italy Vote for this Symbol': PCI (*Partito Comunista Italiano*).[31] People are absorbed and self-contained in the aerial shot of crowds in the street on market day. They don't look at the camera. They lack the stiffness of Strand's large format Deardorff posed pictures, in a throwback to early-twentieth-century pictorialism.[32] These images attenuate the rigidity of the rest of the long-exposure studio portraits. This was how Zavattini influenced Strand to make photographs closer to the documentary tradition than to the art photography Strand had always pursued.[33]

Un paese. Portrait of an Italian Village stands out as unique in Strand's later career. Its contribution to the history of photography and to the history of film, as will become apparent in the chapter about the documentary in Argentina, is primarily due to its dialogical nature.[34] *Un paese* is not a book of photographs accompanied by text or captions; it consists of *two portraits* of the village, one silent and one verbal and, far from being complementary, they clash. The voices break out of the silence of their iconic, austere and dignified image and subvert it.

14.4 *Un paese* magazine preview

There was another, earlier, version of the project, which appeared in February 1955, when twenty-five of the photographs, accompanied by the voices of the people portrayed in them, appeared in *Cinema Nuovo*, as part of a series entitled 'The photo-documentaries of *Cinema Nuovo*'.[35] In this context, the project featured as a photo-documentary, entitled 'Twenty-five people by Zavattini and Strand' ('25 persone di Zavattini e Strand'), a storyboard for a film, and a model of practice for a whole series of illustrated shooting scripts, for what Zavattini and Guido Aristarco, the editor of *Cinema Nuovo* and foreign correspondent of Jonas Mekas's *Film Culture*, hoped would become a new crop of Neo-realist films. Strand managed to wipe off *Italia mia* from the cover, but the Einaudi press release promoting the book clearly stated the following:

> This volume is the first in the series *Italia mia* directed by Zavattini and inaugurates a new type of book, born from the encounter with cinema, a synthesis of film and book which aims to present in photographic and written testimonial pages the experience of this new contact with the real brought about by cinema, Italian cinema in particular, in the last few years.[36]

Cinema Nuovo had published the previous year the photographs of another famous American photographer, none other than Walker Evans; an article by Elio Vittorini in which the writer recounts his experience as an editor of publishing the literary anthology of American writers, *Americana*, in 1941, which contained a section of photographs by Lewis Hine, Alfred Steiglitz and many images by Walker Evans. Vittorini considers the potential of photography as a juxtaposition in the relationships created by sequencing images, to narrate a story.[37] But in the article itself Evans's photographs are a separate entity.

By comparison, *Un paese. Portrait of an Italian Village* offered *Cinema Nuovo* a new editorial direction in producing photo-documentaries which doubled up as illustrated film scenarios. *Un paese* also heralds a new model for visualizing fragments of *Italia mia*, each a story for a film. These fragments appeared as photo-documentaries about Naples, Rome, as well as remote villages further South, in Lucania and Sicily. Guido Aristarco's editorial objective was to visualize real-life stories of this kind, following Zavattini's idea of non-fiction cinema, for the benefit of potential producers. All the photo-documentaries published by *Cinema Nuovo* in 1955 were collected in a book with an Introduction by Zavattini, in which he said photography was so important for education that it needed to become a mainstream subject in the schools. What he didn't do, though, was provide a rationale for the photo-documentaries included in the collection. The rationale can be found elsewhere, in among the photo-documentaries, in the form of a commentary to one of the features by assistant editor Michele Gandin, which is worth citing in full:

> It isn't true that Neo-realism has exhausted itself. It isn't true that Italian reality no longer offers themes as powerful and enticing as those from the immediate post-war period. To claim this is tantamount to claiming that Italy is dead, and Italians are dead. On the contrary, it is true, instead, and stands to reason, that the themes have changed because reality has changed. Ten years don't go by in vain. However, you need only view this reality with the very same ethical commitment, the same freedom, the same love, the same expectation of truth of those days, because it offers us stories which are equally human and equally dramatic. Take this one, for example. It's all true and all documented. Such a film wouldn't cost more than fifty million. Are we going to find a producer willing to make it?[38]

In the 1970s, Antonin Brousil, the director of the Prague School of Cinema and a film critic, in a poll for a selection of the best documentary films in the history of cinema, voted for *Un paese*, which he described as a 'film on paper'.[39] This connexion between Neo-realism and documentary evidence, based on eye-witness accounts and contemporary oral history, is the outcome of Zavattini's developing idea of cinema in the early 1950s.

Gandin's statement appears in the 1955 June issue of *Cinema Nuovo*, introducing a specifically ethnographic reportage, the idea for a film, illustrated by the photographer Enzo Sellerio; 'Borgo di Dio' ('Borough of God'), like *Un paese*, is also about a remote village, but situated at the other end of the peninsula, in Sicily and the text is also the result of one-to-one interviews with the villagers. The interviewer was none other than Danilo Dolci, an Italian ethnographer who had moved from northern Italy to Trappeto, a village near Palermo, to live there permanently and devote his life to improving the lives of its inhabitants through education, improved sanitation, campaigning and testimonial writing. Like *Un paese* in its *Cinema Nuovo* feature, 'Borgo di Dio' served as a preview to a book and a proposal for a film which was never made. But the book, published that very year, became a milestone in Italian ethnography, *Ladri di Partinico* (1955), 'The Thieves of Partinico', entirely based on interviews with the villagers themselves, as Zavattini had been doing for *Un paese*, since the project's inception, in 1953.[40]

A full-page image of a mother and an undernourished child is one of the images of the photo-documentary 'Borgo di Dio'. The caption reads as follows:

> A mother from Trappeto with her child: he is six months' old and weighs 2.7 kilogrammes. In Danilo Dolci's book, as in the film proposal by the authors of this photo-documentary, no one is trying to 'insult Italy', but only to signal a desperate situation. Since, as Danilo Dolci has written, 'we must work fast and efficiently, because people are dying!'[41]

The defensive comment harks back to Giulio Andreotti's 1952 article about Zavattini and De Sica's film *Umberto D.* which he had criticized (as an emblem of Neo-realism) for exporting a damaging image of Italy's poverty. The other captions to 'Borgo di Dio' follow Zavattini's lead. They convey researched facts and villagers' own insights sparingly and effectively. They are testimonial captions, unlike, by comparison, the words accompanying the images in the other photo-documentaries, which gloss over the images, providing a generic non-inclusive, non-participatory, comment.

14.5 *Un paese* and the ethnographic impulse

Such a testimonial dimension was central to Danilo Dolci's ethnography and is shared by Zavattini's main preoccupation with witnessing and participation in *Un paese*. In Dolci's words: 'The aim wasn't to examine or judge, but to try and listen, sitting around a large table, to each person's news and opinions, one by one, to understand one another.'[42] Dolci's ethnographic writing was going in the same direction as Zavattini's cinematic shadowing and coexistence. Indeed, the same ethnographic impulse represents a significant aspect of Zavattini's idea of cinema, and his major contribution to the book he made in collaboration with Strand.

Dolci's and Zavattini's militant ethnography was before its time, in that it involved fieldwork which demanded a new attitude of listening and personal contact with the subject, not something that could be improvised on a photo shoot or result from setting up a Deardorff camera on a tripod in a remote village of non-English speakers. Like Zavattini, Dolci also adopted the diary form to communicate in public and report the results of his field research, in the book mentioned earlier, *Banditi a Partinico* (1955).[43] Dolci had trained as an architect who then worked in the village of *Nomadelfia*, at Fossoli, one of several former Nazi concentration camps in Italy. Then he moved to the remote village of Trappeto, in Sicily to work among the poor. His activity transformed the village, by forming a community, by providing education, housing and new infrastructure, in an ongoing struggle to improve living conditions, while at the same time carrying out and managing field research to document the situation. One of Zavattini's mottos was *conoscere per provvedere*, 'to come to know in order to effect positive change', a fair description of Dolci's approach too.

What distinguishes Dolci's books, *Banditi a Partinico*, 'Thieves in Partinico', and *Inchiesta a Palermo (1956) 'Palermo Inquest'*, is that they are not *about* a subject – the unemployed – but about making a space for them. The former is a testimonial choral voice of a selection of 500 people Dolci interviewed, between the ages of 18 and 50. They are allowed to speak for themselves, recognized as witnesses who talk about their lives and experiences. Both books are crowded with voices saying what they do, think and feel.

That same year, in the same run of photo-documentaries, *Cinema Nuovo* published the work of ethnographer, Ernesto de Martino, *Narrare la Lucania* ('Narrating Lucania'), a region of southern Italy, illustrated with the photographs taken by Zavattini's eldest son, Arturo.[44] This was a small selection from hundreds of photographs Arturo took in the village of Tricarico in 1952, for De Martino.[45] Therefore, 'Narrating Lucania', a quintessentially ethnographic project, photographed by Zavattini's eldest son, dates from before *Cinema Nuovo* was ever founded. This begs the question as to Zavattini's connexion with the rise of new ethnography in Italian culture.

Italian post-war ethnography is coeval with literary and cinematic Neo-realism, dating from when, in 1949, in the pages of the Italian Communist magazine *Società*, De Martino argued that it was crucial to document everyday reality of life in the South, including its customs.[46] He was adopting Antonio Gramsci's outlook, as set out in *The Southern Question*.[47]

Gramsci had made the distinction between *national* and *popular*, noting how detached professional intellectuals were from other Italians.[48] Folklore, as Gramsci called popular culture in all its forms, had only been understood in terms of the picturesque, when in actuality it encapsulates a world view.[49] This broader, or philosophical, sense of folklore, formed a set of values for Gramsci. He regarded them an expression of 'common sense', which he opposed to 'good sense'. Good sense, in his terms, means an outlook informed by a political and social awareness identified with historical materialism.[50] The point is that De Martino applied Gramsci's recommendation that folklore should be made an object of study.[51]

In December 1952, Italian ethnography and Italian filmmaking came into direct contact, when De Martino published an article in a magazine outside his disciplinary boundaries, *Filmcritica*, connecting ethnography to filmmaking, 'Realismo e folclore nel cinema italiano' ('Realism and folklore in Italian Cinema').[52] He urged Italian filmmakers to participate in 'the cultural unification of the Italian nation', encouraging them to take popular culture seriously.[53] In particular, he suggested that filmmakers should turn their attention to filming southern Italy, its people and its customs.

It was key to bringing about ethnographic films about the world of peasants and also informs Vittorio De Seta's extraordinary non-fiction films. De Seta was a self-taught filmmaker and a man of independent means; a Sicilian landowner, who took De Martino's advice published in 1952. He made the first of a series of ten related films in 1954 (all ten were recently screened in the Museum of Modern Art of New York).[54] In his seminal article, De Martino expressed his support for Italian Neo-realism, citing Zavattini as a key figure. He referred to what he calls the 'half-fable' *Miracle in Milan* and to the 'apparent' chronicle of *Bicycle Thieves* and to *Rome, 11 o'Clock*, which, however diverse they might appear in their approach, De Martino argued, shared one important aspect: they included the world of the subaltern in ways that succeeded in avoiding propaganda.[55] Arturo Zavattini was unable to confirm any direct contact between De Martino and his father, Cesare Zavattini, however, while Zavattini was working on *Italia mia* with Rossellini, Zavattini wrote in his Cinematic Diary that he and Rossellini had had a meeting with a couple of ethnographers, one of whom had played them recordings of Lucan mourners and a folk song:[56]

> During these meetings, in accordance with Rossellini's prior arrangements, we received advice from a couple of experts in Italian matters from, that is, an ethnographic perspective. There was the extraordinary evening when a famous scholar let us hear some records reproducing the choruses of professional funeral mourners in Lucania and a certain song accompanying a dance.[57]

Hence, while Arturo Zavattini never met De Martino in person, his father did meet this ethnographer, and acted as a go-between for De Martino's first ethnographic expedition, lasting three or four weeks. But why was Arturo sent to photograph Tricarco? Why Tricarico, of all places? Because that is where Rocco Scotellaro, the poet and author of *Contadini del sud*, had written *Canzone della Rabata*, in collaboration with the farm workers from Tricarico.

Scotellaro was an intermediary who knew how to convey popular discourse. Tricarico was also attracting poets, such as Leonardo Sinisgalli and Carlo Levi, as well as international researchers like the anthropologist Friedrich Friedmann, a practitioner of pragmatist applied anthropology, the North American historian George Peck and the famous documentary photographer Henri Cartier-Bresson.[58]

Arturo Zavattini's photographs are exceptional for documenting the cultural context, the locations and the village's way of life.[59] He produced 'the first sample of mature ethnographic photography in Italy, marking a new season for social sciences in Italy'.[60] Today, Italian ethnographers point out that it is this dimension of *Un paese* which makes the book stand out from other photographic books, combining text and image.[61] In this and other projects which are the legacy of *Italia mia*, or indeed, its extension, Zavattini carried out systematic observation, fieldwork, direct, on-site, documentation, the use of cultural guides and double-checking evidence with local inhabitants.[62]

Just to place Zavattini's cultural intervention in context, *Un paese* anticipates by decades the work by Sandro Portelli on the town of Terni, in *Biografia di una città* (1985) and the 1970s dialogue leading up to it, between historians of oral culture and anthropologists.[63] Zavattini's hybrid methodology for *Un paese* and other projects, such as *Rome, 11 o'Clock*, noted even by an outsider, none other than Ernesto de Martino himself, and *The Roof*, meets the standards of contemporary ethnographic practice, which expects the 'observing subject' to be directly and personally involved, not going as far as claiming any measure of objectivity, but openly acknowledging and valuing a *subjective* viewpoint, combining description with observation from the writer's declared perspective.[64]

Zavattini's transmission of Neo-realism to Spain

15.1 Cinema and Spain

Critics have openly recognized that Neo-realism was the catalyst and the point of departure for a radical renewal of Spanish cinema, providing filmmakers with a model of practice, to concentrate on 'the problems which arise from everyday life', as Marsha Kinder points out.[1] It was. But Zavattini's personal contribution seems to have been overlooked.[2]

Zavattini visited Spain on four occasions: the first, as part of the Italian delegation at the Second Italian Film Week in Madrid in 1953, the second, in 1954, to work on a scenario with Luis Berlanga and Ricardo Muñoz Suay, after the two filmmakers had visited him in Rome to collaborate on a separate scenario; the third, in 1966, in Barcelona for an exhibition, and the fourth in Madrid, in 1977.

Zavattini couldn't attend the First Italian Film Week in 1951, against a backdrop of Spain's dictatorship, which did its utmost to deprive the country of its history. During the first decade of dictatorship from 1939 to 1949, Spanish feature films, produced by *Cifesa* (Conpañía Industrial Film Español), provided only escapist entertainment and ignored the tensions of contemporary Spanish society. Yet these were the years known as 'the years of hunger', of rationing, black racketeering, shortages of fuel and electricity.[3] Cultural repression, political repression, in the face of poverty, and economic crises.[4] What did *Cifesa* and the censored national film industry have to offer? Nothing better than folkloric spectacles, religious dramas and historical epics, according to one historian.[5] The only aspects of contemporary Spain that were allowed to be shown were the regime's triumphs: new roads, new reservoirs and the spectacle of sports, conveyed in state monopoly newsreels, the *Noticiarios y Documentales*, commonly known as NO-DO. Precious little could be shown and said.[6] Fascist Spain and Italy had in common the practice of so-called Final Censorship. In Spain, viewing and vetting of finished films before their exhibition began in 1937.[7] It ensured that preventive censorship at the early stages of vetting the stories was followed up during production. Francoist cultural hegemony also extended to education, in which school textbooks imparted a re-writing of history.[8] The regime's beliefs were summed up in the slogan: 'One blood, One ideal.'[9]

The year 1951 was the year José María García Escudero was appointed minister for cinema. He made the surprising decision to deny state funding to *Alba de América* (1951), directed by Juan de Oruña, a major production by *Cifesa*. Instead, he chose to fund *Surcos* (1951) (*Furrows*), by José Antonio Nieves Conde. *Surcos* had the merit of bringing poverty in contemporary Spain to the screen, as well as the mass exodus from the country to the city, and post-war black marketeering. But Minister García Escudero's choice caused an outcry. He was sacked, and his decision was overturned, in favour of *Alba de América*. *Surcos*, his choice, was banned by the Spanish Board of Classification.[10]

However, during his brief term of office, García Escudero also authorized the First Italian Film Week.[11] This, the first showcase of Italian cinema, was held in Madrid, from 14 to 21 November 1951, with the collaboration of Giuseppe Cardillo, a left-leaning assistant director of the Italian Cultural Institute. The only Italian filmmakers present were De Sica and Renato Castellani. The rest of the delegation comprised officials.[12] Zavattini was absent, but perhaps *Miracle in Milan*, which was screened, spoke for itself.[13]

15.2 Zavattini at the Second Italian Film Week

More influential than the First Italian Film Week was the Second Film Week, which ran from 2 to 9 March 1953. It was also organized by Giuseppe Cardillo. Indeed, the second season of Italian Neo-realist screenings has been memorialized by Spanish film historians as 'a mythic reference point' for Spanish cinema.[14] In addition to the films, there was a seminar on Italian cinema. The works included a larger selection of Neo-realist films, three based on scenarios by Zavattini (*Umberto D.*, *Bellissima* and *The Overcoat*).[15] Short films were screened behind closed doors, in the Italian Cultural Institute, as were Roberto Rossellini's *Rome, Open City*, *Paisà* and Visconti's *Ossessione*. This time, the Italian delegation was much larger, including Arciboldo Valignani, secretary of ANICA, the Italian association of producers, Emmanuele Cossuto and other officials, such as Nicola De Pirro, the all-powerful general director of Theatrical Spectacle for the State, Minister Giulio Andreotti, and the film critic Lo Duca, a name that crops up again in those years, in Cuba.[16] For a Spanish eyewitness this was

> The moment of discovery of a new cinema which they had only read about in Italian and French film journals, practically impossible to get hold of and the confirmation of a cinema that was miles apart from the attributes of Francoist cinema. For the first time, we saw *Umberto D.*, *Bellissima*, *Il cappotto*, *Processo alla città*, *Due soldi di speranza*. And, behind the closed

doors of the Italian Institute, and only for the benefit of friends of Professor Cardillo, we were blown away by *Rome, Open City, Ossessione*, and *Paisà*.[17]

'We were fascinated', was Luis Berlanga's response to coming into contact with Italian Neo-realism at that Second Italian Film Week.[18] Another Spanish filmmaker, the communist Juan Antonio Bardem put it like this: 'It was a window open to Europe.'[19] Bardem also claimed that it was 'the most decisive event of his formative years as a filmmaker'.[20] Speaking in the presence of Zavattini and Georges Sadoul, Bardem could not have been more scathing about the state of Spanish cinema: 'Current Spanish cinema is politically useless, socially false, intellectually debased, aesthetically meaningless, and industrially infirm.'[21] Another eyewitness, a very young Carlos Saura, attended the screenings, and later remembered:

Neo-realism came as a shock. The Italian Cultural Institute brought a week of Italian Neo-realist cinema and they invited members to screenings. It was a fantastic experience. I will never be able to thank them enough for that. And it was then that we started to formulate the problem for ourselves, Bardem and Berlanga, naturally, before the rest of us: a cinema within the terms of Spanish underdevelopment; that is to say, with more of a basis in realism and a cinema of a very modest production scale.[22]

Although there had been much talk about Neo-realism in the film clubs and at the Spanish film school, the IIEC (*Instituto de Investigaciones y Experiencias Cinematográficas*), the first national Spanish film school, it was only during the Second Italian Film Week that the audience really got an idea of what it was, based on their direct experience of watching the films. Its reaction was very warm at the filmmakers' presentations before the screenings. Marcelo Arroita Jaúregui, writing for *El Correo literario*, said:

Cesare Zavattini was the key figure of the Film Week and attracted the most extraordinary, emotional and compelling ovation at the Film Week at the Rialto, standing on the stage at the Rialto the day *Umberto D.* was screened.[23]

This was the Spanish public's first encounter with Zavattini, although two of his books, *I poveri sono matti* and *Io sono il diavolo* had been published in José Jan Janés's *Antología de humoristas italianos contemporáneos* (1943), the same year Zavattini's scenario for *Una famiglia impossibile* was published and made into a film. Furthermore, *Four Steps in the Clouds* had been screened in Spain in 1948. Then in 1952, the Catholic *Revista internacional de cine* published a sequence from the screenplay of Pabst's *La voce del silenzio*, adapted by Zavattini.[24] And finally, in 1953, *Revista Española*, an important literary magazine, published the story of *Totò il Buono*.[25]

Zavattini began his journey to Spain on 3 March 1953 'in the middle of the night', at 3.30 am and checked in to the Hotel Palace.[26] As always, he kept a private diary wherever he went, but the only time Franco is mentioned in this one is to quote him as saying that to live is to await death. To which Zavattini's very private response was: 'I want to die, but make the Revolution before that.'[27]

At the Rialto, the first film to be shown during the Second Italian Film Week was *Bicycle Thieves* in the presence of Zavattini, Alberto Lattuada and his wife, the actress Carla del Poggio, Luciano Emmer, Luigi Zampa and De Sica, all of whom Zavattini had worked for.[28] In his handwritten diary, De Sica's name appears as a one-line pencil remark.[29] Zavattini scribbled a note about the two of them waiting in the wings for a signal to go on stage at the Rialto cinema.[30] De Sica received a resounding applause. He smiled and smiled, Zavattini remembered, but, Zavattini wryly noted, he had to take a break from smiling so much and for so long, before smiling again. The Festival also screened *Miracle in Milan*, Visconti's *Bellissima* (1951), Pietro Germi's *Il cammino della speranza* (1950) Michelangelo Antonioni's *Cronaca di un amore* (1950) and Fellini's and Lattuada's *Luci del varietà* (1952).

The audience at the Rialto included young members of IIEC, and Bardem and Berlanga, who had trained there. These filmmakers had collaborated on *Esa pareja feliz* (*The Happy Couple*) (1951), produced with the help of the film school, which provided the film crew. But it was withheld from distribution for two years. *Esa pareja feliz* is a parody, ridiculing social life under Franco's Fascist regime and caricaturing the kind of official cinema churned out by Cifesa.[31] For their next film, *Good morning, Mister Marshall!* (1952), they turned to an independent company, UNINCI.[32] This was an umbrella company, in which Ricardo Muñoz Suay, Berlanga, Bardem and, later on, Luis Buñuel, Rafael Azcona and Carlos Saura had a stake. UNINCI also had the backing of the clandestine Spanish Communist Party, which included among its members Bardem and Muñoz Suay.[33]

After watching *Il cammino della speranza* (*The Path of Hope*), Zavattini, the film critic Paulino Garagorri and a few others, stood on the pavement in the Gran Vía of Madrid, to observe the public's reactions as they left the cinema.[34] These were the same people who were to become the mouthpiece of Zavattini's ideas and of the Neo-realist movement in Spain: Bardem, Berlanga, Muñoz Suay, Eduardo Ducay and Paulino Garagorri himself.[35] Ducay wrote that they were most interested in what Neo-realism had achieved and what they could learn from it, and also absorb and adapt it to their Spanish context.[36]

Who were they? Muñoz Suay, the leader of the Communist Youth during the Civil War, was imprisoned from 1945 until 1948. He later worked in collaboration with Bardem and Berlanga on *Welcome, Mr. Marshall!* (1952) and *Death of a Cyclist* (1955) and held regular meetings in his Madrid home, where Holocaust survivor and communist militant Jorge Semprún would lead discussions on Marxist thought.[37] Muñoz Suay was a key clandestine cultural organizer of the Spanish Communist Party (the PCE or *Partido Comunista*

Español), responsible for promoting cultural dissidence within the universities, together with Enrique Múgica, both under Semprún's guidance.[38]

Ricardo Muñoz Suay and Eduardo Ducay met Zavattini for the first time when they interviewed him at length for the film feature section in the arts magazine *Indice*, edited by Muñoz Suay.[39] Muñoz Suay asked him about the nature of artistic collaboration between a director and a screenwriter: 'Who's who in the creation of a film?' Zavattini replied: 'It would be ideal if the director were also the screenwriter. I think the best films are a single effort.'[40] 'Will there be a Spanish cinema?' Zavattini answered: 'If Italians were to make cinema in Spain, they would do so from an Italian perspective. You have to do it. You should do *España mía*.'[41]

Muñoz Suay invited Zavattini and other members of the Italian delegation to watch *Good morning, Mr. Marshall!*, which he and Berlanga were about to send to Cannes. Zavattini's response was that 'It could open a new path for Spanish cinema'.[42] After the screening and the positive reception, Muñoz Suay suggested to Zavattini and Berlanga that the three of them make a film in collaboration.[43]

15.3 Mingling with Spanish critics and directors

The hosts arranged the usual kinds of activities lined up for such occasions: a tour to admire the grandeur of old Madrid, seeing the sights, trips to Toledo, Segovia and El Escorial, accompanied by the architectural historian Fernando Chueca Goitia as a guide; a bullfight at the Plaza de Vista Alegre, but no attempt was made to have any genuine cultural exchange.[44] Zavattini wasn't impressed. When they were taken to the Escorial, his reaction was that the place was 'like a tomb'. He was more attracted by what was going on off the tourist trail; by the sight of nuns with such broad head gear that the filmmakers had to step aside to let them pass; by the sight of a peasant who was so pregnant that she had to support herself with her hands; by the villages on the outskirts of Madrid, such as Illianas, with its single-storey houses. Wherever they went in the capital, the only thing that really attracted Zavattini's attention was the coming and going of all kinds of people to the coffee bar, their interactions and body language. He told his hosts that when he was a child, his father ran a bar which was where he woke up to other people's problems.[45] The bullfight in Plaza de Vista Alegre horrified the actress Carla del Poggio, and Luigi Zampa couldn't get over the fact that children were allowed to watch such a gruelling show. What struck Zavattini was that the public showed empathy for a wounded picador, but not for the bull's silent torment. When the show was over, they went to see the pens and the slaughterhouse, where the six bulls were chopped up into cuts of meat. Zavattini heard voices, each asking for a particular cut, while the workers were relaying what was going on in the corrida.[46]

Garagorri's impression was that it was all a mystery to the Italians. At two in the morning, Zavattini took him by the arm and, as they walked by his hotel, he told him about his future projects, above all the investigative films in the pipeline, with which Zavattini intended to break the stereotypes of mainstream cinema. Zavattini was amazed by how much the Spanish knew about Italian cinema. He wrote in his Cinematic Diary: 'They knew everything. They were saying that the good things they knew, they'd learned from the Italians.'[47]

When the Italian delegation was taken to Toledo, to visit the town's Baroque cathedral, Zavattini listened to Fernando Chueca Goitia's efforts to expound its artistic virtues, telling them all about the façade and its dome, glistening with gold. But he later noted: 'All you could hear standing near the altar was that it was gold, gold, gold. Then they stretch out their hands.'[48] No, the Toledo that awoke his interest was elsewhere, in the town's *lebensweld*, its lifeworld, in the deserted streets, except for the blind selling daily lottery tickets.

Toledo's life and soul appeared to him in sudden flashes, Zavattinian moments, shots of films never made, such as the joyful instance when he heard the sounds of hundreds of children spilling out from the school at recreation, and into the street to play football with the priests. At last, the gloomy mood of the Escorial was dispelled.[49] Or when they crossed paths with a procession going down a steep hill and straying this way and that. It was a small cortège of ten people following a child's coffin, carried by four pallbearers, all children, three of them wearing red, and somewhat distracted by the sights of the city, as if they had never seen Toledo before. The following year, he was to devote the final episode of *L'oro di Napoli* (1954) to a child's funeral. Screened two years after the release of *Umberto D.*, *Il funeralino* has no story to speak of, just a funeral procession of children and a mother walking behind a shining black hearse, drawn by four horses in the streets of Naples, in a minutely observed moment of everyday life. Perhaps the sight reminded him of the funeral procession that followed the hearse of Maria Serafina, his sister, who died when she was only a few months old.[50] Or the funeral he refused to attend, his brother's. But when *Gold of Naples* was shown abroad, *Il funeralino*, the last, most poignant episode of all, was censored, even though it was the film's conclusion, ending the noise of Naples in silence.

Zavattini found the sights of Spain boring. He said so himself, stating that the real sights were hidden from view, like the impoverished Madrid he sought out.[51] The screenwriter preferred simply *being* in among ordinary people and getting to know them, with no hurry or particular destination in mind. He explained to Garagorri that he was unable to write, unless he had a personal connexion with the people he was describing. 'I'm no intellectual, you know. What I love most is what's alive before me and what promises a better future.'[52] After the Italians left, Garagorri thought over the experience: Zavattini had taught them that you could be an important figure in the cinema – such as Zavattini himself – while at the same time being kind, unaffected and constantly connected.[53] They were impressed.

15.4 Zavattini and the launch of *Objectivo*

As a result of the direct contact with Zavattini, the problematic of developing a Spanish Neo-realism began in earnest, leading to passionate debates among

Marxists belonging to the clandestine Communist Party. Zavattini's visit to Spain had a galvanizing effect on the young Spanish filmmakers. Ricardo Muñoz Suay wrote to tell him that he had their unconditional support: 'We know what you represent in today's world.'[54]

An immediate knock-on effect of Zavattini's visit was that Muñoz Suay, Paulino Gargorri, Ducay and Bardem launched a new film magazine, in May 1953. They were familiar with, and admired, Luigi Chiarini's *La Rivista del Cinema* and Guido Aristarco's *Cinema Nuovo*, for being the best published in Italy, though they also read *Bianco & Nero*. Indeed, Muñoz Suay even put himself forward as a Spanish correspondent of *Cinema Nuovo*, since his views, he assured Zavattini, 'totally coincide with the ideology of *Cinema Nuovo*'. Thus, it does not come as a surprise that their initial choice for a title for the new magazine was *Cinema Nuevo*. But Spanish censorship scotched that.[55] So they settled for *Objectivo*. Ricardo Muñoz Suay told Zavattini in a letter that

> The first issue will be almost exclusively dedicated to Zavattini. We're going to include various articles by all of us about you. But we'd like to open the issue with an article of yours. You are free to write whatever you like. It could be a message to young Spanish filmmakers, or a defence of freedom of expression in cinema, or something about your work. Do whatever you like.[56]

True to their word, the launch issue of *Objectivo* devoted no fewer than eighteen pages to Cesare Zavattini.[57] By then, Muñoz Suay had already written a review article, probably in *Arte y Letras*, about *Umberto D*.[58] His *Objectivo* piece is a detailed review of Zavattini's book, the film, including the screenplay, the treatment and the Preface containing 'Some Ideas on Cinema'. Muñoz Suay admired the book's unusual nature, because it made explicit the full production process, from conception to final amended shooting script. This, Muñoz Suay, observed, had made it possible for him to work backwards, tracing *Umberto D*. to its initial idea, expressed in Zavattini's short scenario, and to follow its development into a treatment and a screenplay, documenting how the film had emerged from scratch, including even the changes made to it during the production process, and the cuts, and compare the writing process to De Sica's film.[59]

Muñoz Suay's in-depth, quite scholarly study is an indication of another route of the transmission of ideas of Italian Neo-realism to Spain. Muñoz Suay admitted that Zavattini, with whom he would remain friends, as their correspondence shows, was what Esteve Riambau has very recently called 'the most genuine importer into Spain of the aesthetic and political model' of Neo-realism.[60] The point is that he and the rest of the group of Spanish dissident filmmakers opted for a model of practice which, as their contributions make clear, they both understood and were willing to adopt. Theirs was a choice in favour of Italian Neo-realism which implied a rejection of Soviet socialist realism, the Lukácsian realism which Lizzani and the other card-carrying Party members, praising and idealizing the worker hero, were championing at the Parma Conference, inconceivable, in any case, during Franco's Fascist dictatorship.

The second issue of *Objectivo* of January 1954 published a story from Zavattini's collection *Ipocrita 1943*, 'Cine en casa'.[61] This excerpt introduced Spanish filmmakers to Zavattini's very Modernist diaristic mode of writing – personal, political and ahead of its times. What is striking about all the *Objectivo* articles is how well informed the Spanish dissident filmmakers were about Italian film culture, film criticism and lesser-known Neo-realist films, some of which had not even been distributed in Spain.

Muñoz Suay appreciated the value and critical potential of Zavattini's focus on the everyday. He understood that *Miracle in Milan* was less of a departure from Neo-realism than a departure from the investigative strand of Neo-realism. In *Miracle in Milan*, he noted a tension between fairy-tale fiction and the reality of non-fiction, in what he dubs 'Nothing less than a new form of cinematic expression'.[62] One finds here the kind of analysis that thinks in terms of a movement, defined by several strands of Neo-realism, with an eye to weighing up what was most suitable for a Spanish audience, given the Spanish political context.

Critics were wrong, Muñoz Suay claimed: *Bicycle Thieves* did not spell the exhaustion of Neo-realism. And Zavattini had proved them wrong a second time, with *Umberto D.* in which, Muñoz Suay stated, as Zavattini had told the French critic André Bazin, he wanted to create a cinematic spectacle lasting ninety minutes about a man, in which nothing happens. Muñoz Suay rated *Umberto D.* as the highest point of synthesis of Zavattini's work up to the time of writing. In the film, Muñoz Suay noted the search for the banal and the durational element, above all, pointing out the difference between psychological realism (which he refers to as 'traditional realism') and Zavattini's Neo-realism, in which each moment of a character's situation is analytically observed and broken down.[63]

Muñoz Suay, unlike most Italian film critics of the time, was able to appreciate the phenomenological import of Zavattini's film practice, as theorized in the Preface of Zavattini's book and as it played out in the films themselves: 'to see objects in themselves, not the concept of objects in themselves' (*'ver le cosas en sí, yi no el concepto de las cosas en sí'*).[64] That meant, as the French phenomenologist Merleau-Ponty had argued throughout his *Phenomenology of Perception* (1945), embarking on a direct analysis of empirical reality, not filtered by *a priori* concepts, but carried out through direct, empirical experience. This practice becomes, to pick up Muñoz Suay's commentary again, an ongoing, daily perception of things (*'ver cotidianamente'*). Far from being an expression of exhaustion of Neo-realism, Muñoz Suay concluded, *Umberto D.* was the highest, most complete, the most daring and the most Modernist expression of Zavattini's intentions for a Neo-realist film practice.[65]

> To reduce things to a minimum, people's lives, to tell the story of how tonsillitis develops in a character, to narrate almost in the style of a Joyce, doesn't this endanger the very essence of cinema?[66]

With the full documentation afforded by Zavattini's book, Muñoz Suay carried out a meticulous study, comparing the screenwriter's contribution to the director's. To what point did the text match the film? His conclusion was that the film was contained *almost in its entirety* in the screenplay for *Umberto D.*, which De Sica then 'fabricated' into a film. To prove his point, he compared text and screen version of the pioneering slow cinema scene of the young housemaid, in which every single movement of her awakening is traced moment by moment in real time. He realized the function of so much minute detail: to provide an analytical observation of the character and her predicament (an unwanted pregnancy, a disaster in the early 1950s, as recent tragic revelations after the event have amply documented).[67] His conclusion was that, even if, for the sake of argument, the film were screened in separate fragments, it would still work, since there were several self-contained films within *Umberto D.*

Juan Bardem's article in the inaugural issue of *Objectivo* was a survey of the latest edition of the Cannes Film Festival of that year, in which Italy's entries were *Stazione Termini (Indiscretion of an American Wife)* (1953), discussed earlier, *La provinciale, (The Wayward Life)*, a drama by Mario Soldati, starring Italian star Gina Lollobrigida and *Magia Verde (Green Magic)* (1952), a nature documentary about an expedition by the director, Gian Gaspare Napolitano, the cameraman, Craveri, the screenwriter, Bonzi and one other crew member, across the Mato Grosso forests, in Paraguay, the Amazon jungle, as far as Bolivia.[68] Judging from these entries, he concluded in his article that Italian cinema was in a state of disorientation, not only because the three films clearly suggested three separate directions but also because they had little in common with Neo-realism, the Italian school that had flourished since 1945.[69]

Was the selection of films a matter of pure chance? He suspected that it wasn't. He surmised that it was a telling sign of disaggregation. It was, he stated, the result of a parting of ways between contemporary Italian everyday life and Italian cinema which, based on his direct contact with Italian filmmakers visiting Spain, he put down to ever more effective censorship. The 'asphyxiation of the real', as he put it, was crushing a new film style, a new and consolidated movement, and forcing different directions for the future of Italian cinema.[70]

But Bardem seems more interested in what the new Italian cinema had achieved. In his understanding, it is 'a cinema in which *what* is being narrated (*lo que se cuenta*) is given more importance than *how* it is narrated (*cómo se cuenta)*' with content prevailing over form.[71] 'What drives the film style which is extremely direct, restrained, and concise, are the themes', he pointed out. His article about the 1953 edition of the Cannes Film Festival reveals Bardem's admiration for Neo-realism and what the new Italian cinema had achieved, on the one hand, and frustration at its forced repression, on the other hand. 'For the first time, after many years, the viewer gets to grips with the truth', he remarked with underlying regret.[72] Was there an alternative? Yes, indeed: 'Zavattinismo.' This is how Bardem put it:

> The hope, the secret weapon, new formula and saving grace could be Zavattini or rather, 'Zavattinism'. Though Zavattini's focus is fixed on

these 'moments' of his. Zavattini purifies his role as honest observer, and his dramatic world is concentrated on the 'fragment of everyday life'. As far as Zavattini is concerned, each fragment of human life provides enough dramatic substance to be spectacular. The most recent and most pure example of the everyday life fragment approach is *Umberto D*. The film *Stazione Termini* could have also been an example of it, had it not been adulterated at the outset through an important concession to the Hollywood star system.[73]

In the same issue, Paulino Garagorri reflected on the recent years of Italian film production:

It is the most interesting and influential of all. Its exemplarity is based on a new discovery of the expressive and aesthetic qualities of the natural image of things and people, a source of inspiration of the most pure and dynamic cinema of all time. Neo-realist filmmakers are a group of men among whom what stands out particularly is the contribution of screenwriters, and among these, Cesare Zavattini especially emerges.[74]

Muñoz Suay sent Zavattini the first issue of *Objectivo* on 6 July 1953, and invited him to contribute an article to the second. He also asked him if he would speak to Don Joaquín Reig, the producer of *Good morning, Mr. Marshall!*, in Rome at the time. Could Zavattini suggest to Reig an idea for a film, based on three or four episodes about contemporary Spain, written by Zavattini and directed by young Spanish filmmakers Berlanga, Maesso, and Muñoz Suay?[75]

This version of events contradicts José Enrique Monterde's account. The Spanish film historian claims that the idea of making a film in collaboration arose after Zavattini visited the IIEC, where he watched Luis García Berlanga's *¡Bienvenido, Mr. Marshall!*[76] Muñoz Suay and Berlanga sent their proposal for a film to Zavattini who replied on 14 July 1953, saying: 'I'm enthusiastic about the idea of writing a script with your collaboration and I really hope the project will go ahead.'[77] But a year later, since they still hadn't signed a contract, Zavattini wrote to Muñoz Suay to try and get the project off the ground.[78]

The same launch issue of *Objectivo* carried an eleven-page article by Ducay, 'La obra de Zavattini (Notas para una interpretación)' ('The Work of Zavattini: Notes towards an Interpretation'), which perfectly complemented Muñoz Suay's study.[79] Ducay agreed with Zavattini on the ways in which a screenwriter whose activity was usually subsumed into the film itself can be an author in his own right. Ducay traced back to the 1940s scripts mixing satire with comedy, to express solidarity with the working class. He was struck by Zavattini's approach, and how he had worked in conditions which were similar to Spain's, under a dictatorship, making a social critique, when freedom of speech was denied by the Fascist regime, by using his particular brand of humour, poised between the unreal and the irrational, and informed by satire.

Ducay's well-informed introduction to the films Zavattini had scripted drew attention to their recurring themes: poverty, solidarity and the contemporary. After the war 'The cine-camera seeks the documentary even in fiction films' and 'The image is populated by ideas, criticism, complaints, through the expression of emotion'. He stated that 'Zavattini educates the sensibility for a new cinema in a whole generation, through his decisive emphasis on aspects of real life, with its problems, and its contemporary themes'.[80]

Ducay also cited Zavattini's 'Some Ideas on Cinema' on escapism as a betrayal of the mission of the Cinema. Ducay observed that in the films scripted by Zavattini the war is only present obliquely. Whereas after *Germany, Year Zero*, in his view, Rossellini was going into decline, *Bicycle Thieves* was proof that De Sica and Zavattini were not. *Bicycle Thieves* was an analysis of consequences, a story built on a minimal fact, an event, a slice of everyday life. Spectacular reality was shunned in favour of 'social curiosity' and Zavattini's call for 'social attention', so lacking in contemporary society, is brought to bear on the minimal event, as if under a powerful microscope. It was Zavattini's merit to have forced the director to adopt a documentary approach, to place the camera in the midst of fragments of reality. Unlike French and Italian Left-wing critics, the Spanish communist Ducay thought that *Bicycle Thieves* was concerned with the theme of solidarity and brought to the fore the anti-hero.[81]

Then, in January 1954, Muñoz Suay got in touch again:

> Your struggle and that of your collaborators to fight for 'Neo-realism' is our very same struggle, our very same objective. [...] Like you, we would also wish to see in realism an almost biological necessity for cinema, ours and that of contemporary man and time. This is the reason why your name is so closely linked to *Objectivo* and to our group. This is the reason why Berlanga, Bardem, Garagorri, Ducay and I consider you not only a teacher, but the leader of all our cinematic endeavours.[82]

The main purpose of Muñoz Suay's letter was to insist that they wanted to collaborate with Zavattini: 'I myself, and all of us, would very much like to work with you, in close collaboration. It would be not only an honour but the dearest ambition of our cinematic work.'[83] They had a date in mind: June or July of 1954, and wanted Zavattini to write the scenario for the film, with their collaboration. Muñoz Suay asked Zavattini whether he would prefer to work from a plot to be written by the two Spaniards and asked him whether, perhaps, he already had an idea, they could discuss and develop. Muñoz Suay explained to the Italian writer that 'to co-author a scenario with Zavattini would be my greatest dream'. He went on to tell him that 'It would be the timeliest and most effective help you could give for the resurgence of our cinema. It would be a way of giving us new weapons to fight, from within our horse of Troy, for the benefit of a worthy, realist, truthful cinema.' It would be a way of giving us new weapons to fight, from within our horse of Troy, for the benefit of a worthy, realist, truthful cinema.'[84]

Then in the month of April 1954, a Spanish producer involved with Berlanga and Muñoz Suay went to see Zavattini in Rome. On 23 April Zavattini sent them a telegram: 'I'm waiting for you. Regards. Zavattini.'

15.5 The collaborative scenario: *Film Festival*

Luis Berlanga and Ricardo Muñoz Suay travelled to Rome on 26 May 1954 to work with Zavattini.[85] Berlanga suggested writing a film script about a film festival. But what he had in mind was an entertaining, relaxing, spectacle of a film. Zavattini agreed in principle to the idea of a film festival, but suggested a peace festival, by which he meant an anti-war film.

In the context of the times, when the world lived under the constant threat of an atomic war, during what was known as the Cold War, a film of this kind was in keeping with Left-wing anti-war campaigns developed later on, towards the end of the 1950s, with the Aldermaston March in Britain and other such demonstrations of dissent elsewhere.[86] Several years later, in 1963, Zavattini was to produce and write the script for an anti-war documentary in Italy which went into production as the little-known *Newsreel for Peace* (*Cinegiornale della pace*).

'When the three of us began to collaborate in Rome' – Muñoz Suay remembered – 'it was clear that Zavattini was the leader and we the disciples.'[87] However, from the very beginning, Berlanga wasn't entirely happy about the political direction this scenario was taking, and showed signs of disagreement. They stayed in Rome for a month and a half, meeting in Zavattini's home. Muñoz Suay took photographs of the screenwriter, and painted a written portrait of him: 'working in full flow, raising or lowering your voice, depending on the scene you were creating.'[88]

After their return to Spain, Berlanga put together an outline treatment and sent it to Zavattini, who corrected it and returned it to him. He met again with Muñoz Suay and Berlanga and the three of them set to work on *Festival de cine*.[89] They proposed three possible titles for the scenario: *Festival de las estellas*, *Gran Festival* and simply *Festival de cine*. After Berlanga and Muñoz Suay left, Zavattini worked on the scenario. But Berlanga didn't like its pacifism. To him, it sounded like a one-sided public commitment at the height of the Cold War. In the proposed ending, violence breaks out among the film festival delegates, and a mushroom appears on the last frame captioned 'End of the world and end of the film'. Muñoz Suay came to the conclusion that what put off the producers was the prospect of a high-budget film, containing four or five episodes within it. He compares *Film Festival* to a Russian doll.[90]

It must have been great fun writing this fierce satire about cinema.[91] 'Ladies and Gentlemen', *Festival de cine* begins. The voice is the narrator's who sets the scene of an international film festival, describing the air of expectation and hypocrisy of those present. He begins by evoking the history of silent cinema from 1895 until the invention of sound. He describes the emotional shock of the first audience, faced with the Lumiérès Brothers's single-shot sequence of a train coming into a station and of their other films recounting how early cinema fascinated audiences with galloping horses across prairies and with all that followed in escapist cinema: '*Es la época de la despreocupación*', as he puts it, 'It's the era of entertainment.' Cinema benefitted from technology to seek an amazing reconstruction of life, including the recording of sound. Would cinema now make films about peace in the new Cold War climate?

In the film-within-the film, the fictional festival organizers thought it would. In the story, the Festival brings together filmmakers from all over the world. Some of the films screened are no more than an amusing sketch, others longer and more complex. After each screening, the narrator conveys the audience's responses, ironically implying, through amusing observations about their behaviour, that peace, or the lack of it, exists at different levels. The irony is that, naturally, all the members of the jury defend their country's entry. The stories, in this realist frame, are fables, mildly reminiscent of the light touch of *Miracle in Milan*, yet the moral of each tale is anti-war. *Festival de cine* ends with the imaginary dimension of the fable merging with the realist dimension of the narrative frame: when jurors finally return to decide the winner of the competition, they hear the sound of gunfire and can hardly see for all the smoke billowing across the festival hall. While the fighting continues among the delegates from different countries, the image of an atomic mushroom looms large on the silver screen, to the tune of happy music leading to the closing credits. In Zavattini's description of the scenario:

> Filmmakers from the world all turned up with their films about world peace. The sky was full of doves. Even when you took your hat off, doves flew out. But it all went to pot. They'd written good stories about solidarity, but the ending was bleak: a terrible row which led to war. The last shot showed an atomic mushroom and the words: END OF THE WORLD AND END OF THE FILM. That conclusion seemed such a cynical and desperate ending that we were alarmed and interrupted the work which had fascinated us in so many ways.[92]

What he meant by 'interrupted' was not putting any more effort into the scenario. They were, however, pleased enough to publish it in Spain several months later, on 10 December 1954. The cover of the *Film Festival* booklet bears three different titles, possibly intended as alternatives: *Film Festival, The Grand Festival* and *Festival of the Stars*.[93] Indeed, almost a year later, in October 1955, Zavattini told Berlanga: 'It [*Festival de cine*] would have made a good film, if we hadn't had reservations about political issues.'[94] Zavattini agreed to meet up again with them in Rome, to replace *Film Festival* with a fresh project, along the lines of *Italia mia*.[95] They'd write stories about contemporary Spain, emerging from a field trip across Spain.

15.6 *España mía*

So it was that, at the end of July 1954, Zavattini, Berlanga, Muñoz Suay and assistant director and production designer Francisco Canet embarked on a journey across Spain in a car 'to see, before beginning to write', as Zavattini later explained.[96] Muñoz Suay wrote:

> From 31 July to 23 August 1954, Zavattini, Berlanga and I travelled some 6,000 kilometres on Spanish highways and byways with the idea of writing scenarios about events taking place in Spain, but which hadn't been invented.[97]

Muñoz Suay was amazed by Zavattini's ability to recreate and invent whenever he was faced with an unfolding, real-life experience. For him, the journey became an initiation. Muñoz Suay's existing vision of Spain, which the Spaniard later admitted had been too schematic, hadn't allowed him to appreciate at the time the human landscape in the deeper Spain around him.

The journey enacted their new plan, which entailed writing stories about contemporary Spain; stories that would emerge from being observers in the field in different parts of the country, not the folkloric Spain of NO-DO newsreels, but a Spain that was being kept hidden from the general public. The plan was to get into the places and towns off the beaten tracks, in keeping with the idea of *Italia mia*. Theirs would be an ethnographic journey through the heart of Spain, conceived as *España mía*.

For Muñoz Suay, the journey became an initiation. Thanks to Zavattini they were discovering empathy and a sense of coexistence (Muñoz Suay called it 'compenetration') with the lives of ordinary people whom they met in their own land; stopping along the way when a man or a woman attracted Zavattini's attention. They would be walking along a footpath, or down the main road, in a city or a village, and then, at his insistence, they would change the itinerary, to visit a place they had chanced upon. It was this approach that led to their exploration of Andalusia, Extremadura, Castille, Catalonia, Galicia, Aragón and Valencia. As Muñoz Suay wrote in his memoir, 'His *Italia mia* (*My Italy*) was becoming *España nuestra* (*Our Spain*).'

In the course of a month and a half of travelling, they visited Cuenca, Teruel, Alcañiz, Los Monegros, Barcelona, the eastern coast, the Mancha, Abila, Zamora, Lugo, Vigo, Salamanca, Valladolid and Madrid. In the second part of their trip, they went to Córdoba, Ecija, Albarracín, Seville and Libro (Tenuel), Tendilla (Guadalajara), Cañete and Villanueva de la Jaca (Cuenca).[98] The first issue of the successor to *Objectivo*, *Cinema Universitario*, included an account of this trip, written by Muñoz Suay, and accompanied by his photographs.[99] When they eventually published the stories, Muñoz Suay sent Zavattini a copy, writing in the covering letter: 'I'm very keen and very happy to be sending you in a few days' time the first volume of *España mía*.'[100]

In Tendilla, Guadalajara, they spoke to an old woman by a church with a Gothic portal. She was eighty-five and very talkative. She had survived several wars and remembered watching columns of exhausted soldiers marching where she and the filmmakers stood, asking for water. They were covered in dust and sweat. Zavattini asked her if she was familiar with the cinema. Only a week earlier, she'd seen her first film which, she explained, was made by a local film enthusiast.[101] In Cañete, near Cuenca there was a man standing by the road. They were shocked by the remoteness of the place and his work. He was ladling water with a primitive wooden tool.

The schoolteacher from the village told them the man they saw on the outskirts of the village was seventy. He had moved into common land belonging to the village and had gone to live on it with his wife. He lived there almost in total silence, together with his wife and son, who was once a factory worker in Barcelona, and whose son and wife had died. Whenever a villager going hunting walked past 'his' land, the old man would offer some grapes.[102]

Zavattini was struck by the remoteness of some of the places they visited. In Alcañiz, a petrol attendant kept repeating the word 'sequia', drought. The man told the filmmakers:

When it rains, Monegros is the best grain harvest in Spain. Even if you piss on this land, grass will grow, so good is the earth. But when there's drought, people go to Zaragoza or Barcelona, carrying only their bare essentials. Then profiteers come and charge 30 or 50 cients for just one litre.

Muñoz Suay was amazed by this hidden Spain and surprised at witnessing the primitive conditions in which people lived, in lands with no drinking water, in a landscape he described as 'the sea's empty bowl'. In a place called Caspe, a village containing only a couple of huts, José Ignacio told them his wife had to walk to Bujaraloz to give birth. Zavattini asked her: 'What season of the year do you like best?' Her husband replied: 'Summer and autumn. We poor have no coat. And in summer you don't need one. You can go around naked.' Zavattini then asked: 'Don't you get bored by all this loneliness?'[103]

The four filmmakers got as far as the outskirts of *Las Hurdes*, the very same village Luis Buñel had filmed for a documentary, back in the 1930s.[104] Berlanga had read an article about the place with the title: 'Las Hurdes is a social evil in the heart of Spain.' It described an otherworldly place in Martilandrán and La Fragosa, in a region called Estremadura. The article reported that in a village, Nuñmoral, a group of students, who were members of the Falange, and a priest came across a child who had never laughed in his life. One of the students spent a week trying to make him laugh and eventually succeeded.

In his public Cinematic Diary, Zavattini wrote: 'I said: it's a film.'[105] Everyone agreed with him. So they set off for Las Hurdes, but were forced to stop on the way at Casar de Palomeros, on the edge of a place a priest once refused to go to, scared or shocked by the inbred community that lived there. On their return to Madrid, they tracked down all but one of the students and spent hours interviewing them about their experience. The students gave the filmmakers Arizcún's address. He was the one who had made Jesusín laugh. They couldn't speak to him because he'd gone back home, in the Canary Islands. But they sent him a telegram and a few days later, on 27 August 1954, Arizcún wrote Berlanga a long letter which Zavattini published in his diary.

Arizcún wrote that the group leader was called Captain Reyna. When they reached the village, late one evening, they could hear shuffling noises and see shadows of people, half-lit by lanterns. They discovered that the children were unable to sing and didn't know any songs. The group handed out sweets to all of them, and everyone, except for one child, accepted them. The child was Jesusín. The students were aware of how Las Hurdes was perceived by the Spanish media who would make the village idiots Crescenzio and Juanito pose for portrait photographs and dispense small gifts to the children. Arizcún thought Jesusín's refusal was a deeper rejection of a patronizing, superior society. He picked up the barefooted child on his shoulders and took him to his home, an empty house. The villagers told him that the mother was working in the fields and the father was working in Castille. But eventually someone told him the truth: Jesusín's mother was a prostitute and his father a beggar and a drunk, who would sometimes show up. During the week, the students set up their temporary cinema and showed *Popeye* cartoons to children who had never watched a film in their lives. The children laughed and cried, as they contemplated a different world from their own. One student was so amazed at the response, he was sorry they didn't have a camera to film it. Jesusín and his mother were near the screen and the child was enthralled by what he saw. The child was always solemn, sad. But before the group left, he laughed when a sudden gust of wind blew Arizcún's hat off.

This letter was the basis for their scenario which took the story in a very different direction from the article, expressing solidarity towards poverty, isolation and accompanying alienation, sentiments which were also conveyed by Arizcún's letter to Berlanga. The scenario slows down events to such a point that everything seems to happen in a time warp, giving a sense of what it is like to travel across hard terrain, across a dusty landscape with no one in sight, except herds of sheep and swine in walled off pens. The seven students and the priest, replacing the Falange Captain Reyna in the scenario, had a purpose: to bring the cinema to a remote community. The narrator is one of the students, seven boys and three girls, and a Catholic priest.

They reach the silent, remote village of Nuñmoral that looks deserted. When some villagers finally make an appearance, they shy away from the newcomers. The story proceeds at a very slow pace. You can almost see the shots. The old man staring, silent and motionless. Houses with no chimney, because the villagers believe smoke is good for their chestnuts, even though it means breathing in smoke into their lungs. The extreme poverty, the dullness of minds, their clothes. When someone finally shows the students the way to the primary school, the priest tells the nun in charge that they have come to bring the cinema to the village.

Children and mute villagers watch as the volunteers set up the big screen, driving wooden posts into the ground. They watch a documentary about the wonders of nature in distant lands. Then Chaplin's silent *Easy Street* (1917) looms large above them. One of the students notices that all the children are laughing except Jesusín. He tries to befriend him, clowning and making funny faces, but Jesusín remains solemn and detached. The story follows the two, describing their relationship moment by moment. It is deeply Neo-realist and Zavattinian in the way it establishes and builds up the situation, gradually gathering emotional power by staying within it, and adding observational details. Its intensity allows no diversion. Nothing whatever distracts from the seemingly impossible relation between the student and the child from elsewhere. You see it from the young man's point of view, not the child's. It all hinges on the clash of an encounter and the gulf between their two worlds and of course begs the question as to how such a world could still exist in the mid-twentieth century and, more importantly, why nothing had been done about it. Of course, it also stood for something else. To break the isolation within such an extraordinary situation was a transcendence of material conditions. Art as cinema could foster a will to fight back.

As the credits of the title of the printed booklet *Cinco Historias de España* indicates, Zavattini and the Spaniards wrote all the scenarios in collaboration, a method Zavattini was accustomed to and which was also a characteristic of post-war Italian cinema practice. The narrator's voice in the opening paragraph of the first scenario, *The Shepherd*, introduces all five stories, weaving in a declaration of intent: he claims that reality and not fantasy suggested the stories narrated and that these are about ordinary people, the working class and that this is the first of the stories, indicating that from the outset, the filmmakers were planning an episode film to go into production in 1955.[106] So it would seem that *Cinco Historias de España* is indeed yet another incarnation of *Italia mia*.

The last story, *Emigrantes (Emigrants)*, opens in a bustling marketplace in the village of Lugo in Galizia a place where people dance the Muñerva to the sound of Galician bagpipes. A family spends all their savings to buy a sewing machine. It's an investment. It will be a source of employment when they emigrate to Uruguay. They belong. Everyone knows them at the market. It is a very simple story with hardly any plot to speak of, more of a protracted situation, minutely observed. The family gets on a slow train, leaving the past behind. The daughter sees Antonio her boyfriend, a construction worker who is working on the roadside and rushes up to keep up with the train. He calls out to her, hanging on to the side for a while. Then he decides to borrow a bicycle from a workmate and cycles 100 kilometres to meet her at the port to say goodbye. One is left with a sense of longing, of the strong feeling between the two young lovers and a sense of separation and loss which resonates as the loss of emigration.

All five stories are credited to the three filmmakers. However, Zavattini's sensibility, outlook and type of detailed observation is apparent everywhere in the writing. The plan was to develop a treatment for a full-length feature film of five episodes, as the narrator writing on behalf of the team indicates in the introductory paragraph to the first story.

After his return to Italy in September 1954, Zavattini told Berlanga he hoped that they would make the film based on the five stories.[107] In the event, they only got as far as publishing the scenarios of *Five Spanish Stories*, in April 1955.[108] Zavattini wrote to Berlanga several times, but to no avail. He encouraged him to carry the project forward into production by no later than the summer months. He estimated that the treatment wouldn't take more than ten days or so.[109]

Muñoz Suay later wrote an account of their 6,000-kilometre journey across Spain, as, Muñoz Suay decided, the most effective way to convey to Spanish filmmakers Zavattini's approach to Neo-realism. The purpose of the journey and the thinking behind it were[110]

> To write about events taking place in Spain, but which hadn't been invented beforehand. We wanted to write them, after seeing or hearing them. And this is how the scenario came about, which we are completing and hoping will be made into a film. Travelling across Spain with Zavattini, was, on many occasions, the equivalent of meeting an unknown Spain, even to ourselves.[111]

Muñoz Suay made two crucial observations which put across Zavattini's ethnographic and participative approaches to documentary, reflecting an evolving form of Neo-realism, in which the principle of coexistence was key: 'Neo-realism is a conscious participant of reality. It adopts the point of view before it. The artist has to observe reality by co-existing with it.'[112] 'Collecting witnesses, co-habiting with the humble, and with the rich, touching reality ourselves, we are doing Neo-realism.'[113] He equated this stage of Neo-realism with a cinematic ethnography, built on notes, observations, conversations and oral testimonies.

15.7 The new *Cinema Universitario*

A new film magazine appeared in Spain in March 1955. Its inaugural issue carried the weight of all the experience of *Objectivo*, which was due to be closed down by government censorship later that year. They shared some of the writers, indeed the founding editors of *Objectivo* C. Pascual said: 'We cannot speak objectively about *Objectivo*. For us it's the magazine of passion.'[114]

The first issue of the student magazine contained an endorsement of Neo-realism by the prestigious existentialist philosopher Jean-Paul Sartre, who defended Neo-realism from accusations of pessimism and emphasized how it revealed the real conditions of Europe, pointing out its extraordinary power of persuasion.[115] The first issue also included an interview about Italian Neo-realism with the writer Azorín, who objected: 'What need is there for art to deal with the repulsive? And where is the aristocracy and the middle-class in

Italian Neo-realism?'[116] Basilio Martín Patino, the editor, invited the reader to consider whether the project of a new Spanish cinema that was realist would be nothing more than second-hand Neo-realism.[117] The answer to this question, he pointed out, could be found elsewhere in the first issue, and also in the manifesto for a new Spanish cinema, included in the issue. He stated that the main issue was to work towards cinematic realism, in the tradition of Spain's literature and art. And anyway, what was the alternative? Current Spanish cinema looked professional, from a technical point of view, but, he concluded, all that glitters is not gold.

In the same launch issue, Joaquín de Prada applied concepts from Zavattini's 'Some Ideas on Cinema' which Ricardo Muñoz Suay had previously discussed in the inaugural issue of *Objectivo*. De Prada explained that Zavattini's form of Neo-realism 'had evolved towards the documentary', with *Love in the City* and *We Women*, and cited him as saying: 'It's not a question of making things seem real, but of giving real things their whole expressive value.'[118] And 'Cristo proibido', another article, by Patino, cited Zavattini verbatim: 'If I weren't worried of committing the sin of vain glory, I'd say that Christ wielding a cine-camera wouldn't be making parables.'[119] This was as powerful a critique of Catholicism for Catholic Spain as it had been in devout Italy.

One of the Spanish filmmakers, *Objectivo*'s editor, Eduardo Ducay, put Zavattini's ethnographic approach into practice in December 1954, in collaboration with the photographer, Juan Julio Baena. Ducay had met Zavattini in 1953, and had been one of his Spanish hosts during that first visit to Spain. Ducay had also written an essay about him in the first issue of *Objectivo*.

Ducay now wrote for *Cinema Universitario* where he described his field research: 'Fotodocumentales I: Objectivo Sanabria' is entirely in keeping with Zavattini's ethnographic research towards an *España mía*, described by Muñoz Suay in the previous article, and with some of the photo-documentaries *Cinema Nuovo* was to publish in the course of the year, all photo-reportage reports, doubling up as scenarios for potential films.[120]

Ducay, Baena and Carlos Saura, following Zavattini's lead, also discovered unknown parts of Spain; Saura photographed them, and they spoke to the local people, just as Ducay himself had witnessed Zavattini doing during their 1953 excursions. The Spanish ethnographic travelogue 'Objectivo Sanabria' was intended as a first step towards a documentary film, as Ducay pointed out. Eventually, it became *Carta de Sanabria* (1956), an eighteen-minute documentary filmed in 35 mm in Zamora, at the same locations featured in the article. The photography was by Carlos Saura; the cinematography was by Juan Julio Baena and the script by Ducay. It was produced by UNINCI. *Carta de Sanabria* follows Zavattini's artistic direction, enacting in this way an episode of *España mía*.[121]

This vigorous and varied endorsement of Italian Neo-realism in the first issue of *Cinema Universitario* was accompanied by a manifesto in support of a new cinema and a call for papers for a proposed Conference. The manifesto was signed by none other than the three founding editors of *Objectivo* – namely, Eduardo Ducay, Juan Antonio Bardem and Paulino Garagorri – and by Basilio

Martín Patino, as well as by the new editors of *Cinema Universitario*, showing just how close the links were between the two magazines.

The call for papers was published within a section entitled: 'Boletín de las Primeras Conversaciones Cinematográficas Nacionales.'[122] Clearly, the *Objectivo* editorial team, members of the student union, and of film clubs, had been working very closely long before the 'Conversations' film Conference and long before the launch of the new film magazine, in March.

As Bardem explained, the manifesto called for an urgent and timely debate on the state of Spanish cinema, in order to change it. For, he argued, while other cinemas were focussing on everyday reality, Spanish cinema continued to dwell on topics which had nothing to do with contemporary society.[123] This was the reason why they were launching an appeal to students, writers, journalists and critics, to discuss and analyse the problems of Spanish cinema in the National Film 'Conversations' forum, as a first step towards radical change. They suggested a radical break, a new beginning, as the final sentence in the manifesto made clear: 'Spanish cinema is dead. Long live Spanish cinema!'[124] A statement with a 1960s ring to it, but made a decade earlier. In a separate article on Spanish documentary in this same issue, Joaquín de Prada pointed out that

> Spain has no cinema and as a consequence (or cause), neither does it have a documentary tradition. Spain, as a tangible entity, practically doesn't exist. Its geography doesn't exist; its climate doesn't exist; nor do its local antagonisms exist. Tangible Spain is our failure. The failure of all of us, the Spain of documentary. I might add that I'm talking about those aspects of Spain which raise questions.[125]

15.8 The 'Salamanca National Film Conversations'

This is the context of the 'Conversations', held two months later, which were then renamed the First National Film Congress. It took place at Salamanca University, on 14–15 May 1955. It was officially sanctioned by the Directorate General of University Teaching, Cinematography and Theatre of the University of Salamanca and organized by *Cine Club Universitario* and the SEU, the Students Union.[126] The main organizers of the 'Conversations' were Basilio Martín Patino, the leading figure in *Cinema Universitario*, who also ran the Salamanca Students Film Club, which he himself had founded, José Maria Prada and Muñoz Suay, not a signatory of the manifesto, but an influential member of the *Objectivo* editorial team, who had collaborated with Zavattini in Rome and in Spain with Zavattini and Berlanga, and was, like Zavattini, a communist.[127] Patino was to become a leading director during the so-called transition period from 1950s to 1960s Spanish cinema. Years later, he summed up his position in an interview:

I at least never believed in new cinema as opposed to old cinema, but rather in free cinema and regulated cinema, in lucid cinema and opportunistic cinema; one exploits the audience, the other speaks to it sincerely, from deeper roots.[128]

The event was supported by the former minister for Cinema, García Escudero, by students from IIEC, by university lecturers, several film directors, and film and cultural magazines: *Otro Cine, Signo, Ateneo, Alcalá, Índice, Insula* and, of course, *Objectivo*, all signatories in support of the event. Of these, *Objectivo* was soon to be banned. Since well over a hundred organizations adhered to the project, as the initial response shows in the long list of signatories of forty-six associations and a further sixty-two names, in all probability, many more must have participated.

The screenings at the 'Conversations' brought theory and practice together, following the *Cinema Nuovo* editorial method and, crucially, Zavattini's transmission of ideas. Marsha Kinder claims that Neo-realism was the vehicle to express these ideas and generate an influence, and concludes that the Salamanca Conference was 'an event that helped to establish Neo-realism as the primary aesthetic model for the first phase of the New Spanish cinema'.[129]

But it is important to bear in mind also that the Salamanca event was a culmination of debates, created by *Objectivo* and the fledgling *Cinema Universitario*, which picked up where *Objectivo* had left off. And furthermore, that both were, to a great extent, the outcome of the reception, discussion and assimilation of Zavattini's theories and film practice.[130] One of the merits of both *Objectivo* and *Cinema Universitario* was to have transmitted Zavattini's ideas and critique of mainstream cinema and the film industry to Spanish filmmakers.[131] The reason the event was called the *Conversaciones nacionales*, the 'National Conversations', was that they had organized a National Symposium, centred around debate.[132] In their open forum, the participants with strong vested interests in the future of Spanish cinema discussed politics and, for the first time during the Francoist regime, reflected on what they considered the depressing reality of Spanish cinema as it was. Neo-realism was indeed upheld as the way forward, two years after the Parma Conference of Neo-Realism. Needless to say, all the *Objectivo* editors were well informed of all the discussion that had taken place in Italy, thanks to the detailed reporting in *Cinema Nuovo*, the film magazine the *Objectivo* team had wanted to emulate and Guido Aristarco himself who accepted their invitation to attend the Symposium, as a guest of honour.

Actually, it was Joaquín de Prada who prepared the ground, in the launch issue of *Cinema Universitario*, in his article entitled: 'El cine y la España tangible (Notas para una Escuela Española de Documental.'

If the Spanish newsreel production house, NO-DO, were re-organized, de Prada argued, it could produce effective and relevant filmmaking in documentary cinema, moving from 'anthropocentrism' to 'ontocentrism', the primacy of being, of 'things that just are, things which speak and the author, writer or director listens to them, collects them', in accordance with Zavattini's Neo-realist documentary, and clearly picking up on the phenomenological and existential strain in the Italian debate discussed earlier.[133] Azorín was out of date, old fashioned and foreign to young filmmakers' interests. So it won't come as a surprise that de Prada cited Zavattini's 'Some Ideas on Cinema': 'Cinema should not be concerned with the past. It has to accept. TODAY, TODAY.'[134] And quoted Zavattini a second time:

> The necessity to know our country and the absolute faith in meeting it will be effective for the creation of our national and human consciousness.[135]

In what reads like a Modernist manifesto, conveying the thrust of Zavattini's 'Some Ideas on Cinema', Julio Bardem focussed the minds of the 100 or so delegates by describing the status quo of Spanish cinema, when he stated: 'Spanish cinema is politically ineffective, socially false, intellectually abject, aesthetically nonexistent and commercially crippled.'[136] Speaking on behalf of both *Objectivo*, *Cinema Universitario*, and with the authority of all the manifesto signatories, he also said:

> The importance of cinematic art in the social life of our country gives us no choice. For Spanish youth who want to get closer to cinema there's only one resort: to begin.[137]

He set out the situation very clearly:

> Spanish cinema continues to be a cinema of painted dolls. The problem with Spanish cinema is that it has no problems. It is not a witness of our times, which our times demand from any artistic endeavour.[138]

The message is a clear, uncompromising statement about what cinema, and specifically Spanish cinema, should be: political, in tune with the social, thought-provoking, challenging the audience in its aesthetics. It should take issue with the tradition of Spanish films, and should be sufficiently funded.

In a long, manifesto-style intervention, Bardem argued that cinema occupied a privileged position in modern society, owing to its power and reach as a mass medium. He declared that this had to be Year Zero for Spanish filmmakers, a turning point. Time to rethink cinema, after half a century of escapism, as its main pursuit. Echoes of Zavattini's retrospective view at the first half of a century of cinema history? For Bardem, the time had come to give weight and legitimacy to political commitment to a new cinema, a contemporary cinema; one which pointed the lens on modern society and the 'social facts' which could become scenarios to replace the provincial and triumphalist Francoist cinema. *Triunfalismo* was a key word at the time, meaning an outlook which ignored and thus denied 'social facts', such as endemic poverty under Franco, the imposition of Castilian Spanish, celebration of an ideal language in an ideal nation, policed over by Fascist ideology and its state enforcers.[139]

Therefore, the job at hand entailed radically rethinking cinema. Why? Because Spanish cinema, as it stood, presented an unproblematic view of society. This was a problem, if bearing witness to one's times is deemed essential. Its lack of substance made it 'a hollow body', an empty shell, characterized by the representation of stereotypes.[140] 'We must make it "new" in respect to the problems of our day, which are also new ... . Spanish cinema is dead. Long live Spanish cinema.'[141]

Bardem stated in no uncertain terms that the Spanish state had a problematic attitude towards cinema, creating dualities where there should be none and making an enemy of cinema. Indeed, it constituted a serious obstacle to the development of a new, national, cinema. He dismissed its haphazard rules of censorship, since the application of censorship was a moveable feast, which left filmmakers in a position of having to carry out their own preventive censorship. He called for clearly specified written guidelines and made a plea for the abolition of censorship, in respect of film clubs.[142]

Unsurprisingly, following Joaquín de Prada's call for a Spanish documentary in the launch issue of *Cinema Universitario*, the need for a new Spanish documentary was also raised at the 'Conversations' forum by Muñoz Suay.[143] He argued that one of the reasons for the crisis of the Spanish cinema was the inexistence of a documentary movement. Apart from its technical use as a training ground for film crews working on fiction films, the documentary served to return reality to national screens.[144] Among the final resolutions of the 'Conversations' which met with unanimous approval by the delegates, one stated that

> Documentary cinema should acquire a national character, making films with a social function and which reflect on the situation of Spanish society, its ideas, conflicts and reality in the contemporary moment.[145]

After Bardem's inaugural speech at the Conference, *Death of a Cyclist* was screened. The film had just been exhibited at Cannes, where it had won the Cannes International Critics' Prize. At the Conference, Barlanga and Bardem's *Good morning, Mister Marshall!* was also shown.[146] The canonical Italian Neo-realist film, *Bicycle Thieves*, was also screened, but blemished by the Spanish censors who had tampered with the film, adding an ending to the open-ended story, with the inclusion of text stating a happy ending, to close the narrative.[147]

These Spanish films mark the two directions Neo-realism was taking in its transmission and transformation into new Spanish cinema. *Death of a Cyclist* shows clearly to what extent Julio Bardem had moved away from Luis Berlanga. His film takes a cue from Zavattini's theory on reducing a plot to a situation, to an event, and then letting the cine-camera and the researcher linger within the situation, to explore and analyse its causes and context. Characteristically based on an actual event, a hit-and-run accident, reported in the news, half of Bardem's film was filmed in the street. A worker is killed on his way to work. In the wake of *Rome, 11 o'Clock*, Bardem also proceeds, in unmistakeably

Zavattinian fashion, from the news item, the 'social fact' to the lives of the people, an adulterous upper-class couple, who caused the accident, developing the raw material into a drama exposing the social injustice of the times.

Bardem, a member of the editorial team which had founded *Objectivo*, directly modelled on Aristarco's Italian *Cinema Nuovo* – to the point that they had even intended to call it *Cinema Nuevo* – emulating the *Cinema Nuovo* editorial approach, but distanced himself from the views of its editor, Guido Aristarco. At the time, Aristarco was arguing in favour of a new teleology, one which saw Neo-realism only as a step in the direction of Soviet-style realism, rather than as an alternative to it. By comparison, Bardem and the other Spaniards sided with Zavattini. Bardem brought to bear Zavattini's argument in favour of the use value of cinema, and its ultimate social purpose – Neo-realist witnessing – but never championed the socialist hero, or Lukács's didactic typology, proposed by Aristarco. In a short piece written the following year and published in *Cinema Universitario*, Bardem made this clear:

> Using light, images and sound to show the reality of our context, here and now. To be a witness to our human moment. Then, in my opinion, cinema will be above all, a witness, or it will be nothing. To direct the viewing public towards the best cinema, not the most commercial, this seems an important task for cinema. This direction should entail, above all else, a turn towards reality, realism in the context of cinema.[148]

Muñoz Suay referred back to Zavattini, that at the Conference they had talked a great deal about him and his type of Neo-realism, and was hoping to send the Italian writer a report specifically dedicated to Neo-realism.[149] But Muñoz Suay forgot to mention that *Bicycle Thieves* had been screened.[150] In more ways than one, Zavattini was there, Muñoz Suay told him. After all, what were these 'Conversations', if not an echo of the debates that took place at the Conference on Neo-realism in Italy at Parma, on very specific themes?[151]

Just as at the Parma Neo-realist Conference in Italy eighteen months earlier, regime censorship came to the fore during the week. In Fascist Spain too, as in democratic Italy, filmmakers had to submit their shooting scripts to a government-appointed panel, which had the power to adjudicate as to whether a script could be allowed to be made into a film. And even when the finished film made it into production, in Spain too, it was still required to be submitted for final approval, risking further cuts, sometimes confiscation, or, at the very least, a poor rating which would bar it from any public funding.[152]

15.9 After Salamanca

The Salamanca National Conference provoked a strong negative reaction among Right-wing circles which accused the delegates of being politically biased; worse, communists.[153] Predictably, the Francoist regime was unhappy with the conclusions of the Salamanca 'Conversations'. The denunciation of state censorship in the public arena echoed the Parma Conference on Neo-realism and reported in detail in *Cinema Nuovo*. The Parma Conference itself had served as a model of practice to be emulated by Salamanca. The Spaniards had read about the heated debates between Catholics, Marxists and Zavattini, a non-aligned communist, as to which type of realism to aim for and the Conference's condemnation of political state censorship, as reported in *Cinema Nuovo*.[154] Surprise, surprise, after its pivotal role in organizing an oppositional film Conference, *Objectivo* was banned.[155] But not before it published in-depth discussions of Italian Neo-realist films, emphasizing the need for a national cinema based on realism and human values.

However, *Cinema Universitario* picked up where *Objectivo* left off. It took over the mission of being the mouthpiece for cinematic Spanish Neo-realism. Two of the *Objectivo* editors were on its editorial board, and Berlanga also sometimes contributed articles.[156] Surprisingly, given that *Objectivo* had been banned altogether, *Cinema Universitario* also published articles by Zavattini, Aristarco and Jean-Paul Sartre, the documentarian filmmaker Joris Ivens and the film critic Georges Sadoul, all communists.

In the second issue, of December 1955, Juan García Atienza published a piece drawing on the concept of *España mía*, based on the ethnographic project *Italia mia*, to suggest there was a collective responsibility to make films about Las Hurdes, Los Monegros, Sanabria, the same places which had featured in Muñoz Suay's and Ducay's reportage, both of which had appeared in the inaugural issue.[157] What would it take for Spanish filmmakers to make films that weren't escapist? Atienza asked his readers. Adopting Zavattini's shadowing yet again, he made the point that filmmakers had the responsibility, the obligation – as he put it – to see, get to know and 'compenetrate' or coexist in these places and among these people, be they in remote villages or in the towns nearby. No impersonal portrait would do. Spanish cinema lacked a social conscience, he added, preferring to avoid issues, instead of dealing with them. Spanish cinema didn't exist. It wasn't cinema at all. It vegetated, avoiding the present altogether, looking back to the falseness of a legendary past with no real substance. To show, to document, to witness, that would be the shape of the much-needed critical new cinema.

Two tendencies within Spanish Neo-realism emerged: a socialist one and a populist one. The former General Director of Cinema under Franco, José García Escudero, returned to office in 1962.[158] In his view, a new cinema could help reinvigorate the image of Fascism through populism, as he argued in his book *Cine social* (1958).[159] Escudero's book appropriated the arguments of the Left to serve a Right-wing Fascist and Catholic perspective, just as Italian Fascism had done in the 1920s.[160] A co-option of this nature, however, was an exception in Spain, since the aesthetic of considering cinema not an end in itself, but a means to an end, was generally adopted to resist the Fascist regime and adapted, using irony and sarcasm, to continue to resist it.[161] In Spain, Neo-realism needed to adapt in order to resist the Fascist regime, and it did so in two ways: either by employing various kinds of humour, irony and satire or by tackling problems in an oblique mode of address, following Zavattini's theories of the everyday and his vision for a political and ethical cinema. This was what Bardem was to attempt, after he and Berlanga had parted company. The third way, which consisted in expressing an open denunciation of poverty, met with more resistance, except in independent documentary filmmaking.

The impact of Neo-realist ideas was to upstage Hollywood conventions in Juan Antonio Bardem's *Muerte de un ciclista* (*Death of a Cyclist*, 1955) with its debunking of traditional Spanish values, and Bardem's *Calle mayor* (*Main Street*) (1956) awarded the Venice Film Festival International Critics' Prize the following year. Based on a play, *Calle major* provides a rich portrait of provincial life, without excluding all the repressions and restrictions of 1950s Spain. The main character, a spinster, whose life is at a standstill with no foreseeable way of escape, becomes the victim of a prank by young men. It won Bardem another International Critics' Award at Cannes, in the face of censorship at home, which, predictably enough, accused him of presenting a negative image of Spain abroad.[162]

In 1956, Berlanga published a long article in *Cinema Universitario*, recounting a very detailed history of Neo-realism going back to the pre-war period of the early 1940s and its development, but also the challenges of government censorship it faced after the war. Berlanga noted that Zavattini's documentary of Neo-realism, in *Love in the City*, now had to contend with the lightweight entertainment of 'La Lollo', the pinup star Gina Lollobrigida.[163]

In 1957, an issue of *Cinema Universitario* published a new text by Zavattini entitled 'Neo-realism is not dead'.[164] The Italian screenwriter argued that if we understand Neo-realism as a cinema of political commitment and an ethical cinema, then Neo-realism is always relevant, for no period in history is devoid of problems. The task in hand is to identify them and express them through the cinematic medium. There was a growing awareness that cinema doesn't only mean spectacle and entertainment. In the meantime, what have its enemies put in its place? Nothing at all, he concluded.

Two years earlier, Marco Ferreri, who had worked closely with Zavattini in the early 1950s, moved to Spain. Ferreri, alongside, Riccardo Ghione, and together with Zavattini, had produced the Zavattinian Neo-realist *Love in The City* (1953), and the two documentary shorts that had preceded it in 1951 and 1952. Then Ferreri decided to emigrate. He got a job as a salesman for Totalscope, a lens manufacture.[165] In Spain he met the screenwriter Rafael Azcona, just when Luis Berlanga met Azcona. Both began to work with him. Ferreri's three Spanish films, *El pisito* (1958) ('The Little Apartment'), *Los chies* (1959) ('The Boys') and *El cochito* (1960) ('The Wheelchair'), were all co-scripted by Azcona, and adopt Berlanga's approach, replacing Berlanga's gentle parody of Spanish society with harsh satire.[166] It is a quintessentially Spanish form of black humour, known as *esperpento*, which brings out the grotesque, ridiculous and absurd aspects of life.[167]

To complete this reconstruction of transmission to Spain, it is necessary to mention the early work of Carlos Saura, who also belongs within the same oppositional cinema of Berlanga, Bardem, Muñoz Suay and Ferreri, with its roots in Neo-realism, and particularly Zavattini's line within it, which had no truck with Soviet realism.

Saura's *Los gofos* ('The Hooligans') is set in the *chabolas*, the shanty towns of working-class districts.[168] *Los golfos* is a Spanish Neo-realist film. According to Peter Besas, it was the first time a Spanish filmmaker had used reportage and filmed ordinary people in Spain.[169] However, unlike Berlanga, Ferreri or Azcona, Saura doesn't resort to picaresque Spanish humour, to *esperpento*, to sarcasm, not even to parody. *Los golfos* is Neo-realist for its social commitment, for its anti-heroes (young layabouts living on theft), for adopting the model of the open-ended story and the rejection of tight plots, for taking a Zavattinian oblique approach to tackle social issues, for preferring a looser style to stage acting, and for filming in the context of everyday life, combining the non-fiction of the street with the fiction of the story. His low-budget film casts ordinary people instead of professional actors.[170]

Los golfos had problems with the censors, of course, in keeping with the context of the Fascist Spain of that era. Berlanga once estimated that 80 per cent of his projects had been banned.[171] Although the censors had vetted the script at the outset, they stopped *Los golfos* from going into general release four times. When Saura applied for general release, after managing to get the film to Cannes, he was told: 'Dirty clothes should be washed at home', the same words levelled at Bardem's film, and used by Giulio Andreotti in Italy, to attack Zavattini and De Sica's *Umberto D*.[172]

In Spain, Zavattini's legacy of social and political commitment was also conveyed by filmmaker Mario Camus who stated: 'I belong to a generation who believed in revolution', and cited Zavattini: 'What we [are] attempt[ing] is to move man to take an interest in the world around him and particularly in what is happening today or in an immediate yesterday.' 'The result for me', Camus added, 'was *Los farsantes* [1963] and *Young Sánchez* [1963].'[173] Even after the advent of the New Wave, Patino, in his compilation film *Canciones para después de una guerra* (1971) ('Songs for after a War'), included a tribute to Zavattini, a scene from *Bicycle Thieves* (1948), the one in which Antonio is putting up a poster of Rita Hayworth in *Gilda*.

Transmission of Neo-realism to Cuba

16.1 Zavattini in Latin America

Since the early 1950s, Zavattini took to travelling abroad, giving conferences while visiting many countries, including the then Soviet Union, and other countries within the Soviet Bloc, as well as North Africa (in 1968, for a conference on documentary filmmaking to outline an independent political cinema in 1967, which he had theorized, initiated and developed in Italy, and namely, the Free Newsreels, both films and grassroots movement), eventually to the United States, as well as closer to home, to countries in Western Europe. Of course, a detailed reconstruction of all these travels would not be feasible.

However, after the reconstruction of his activities in Spain, it makes sense to consider Zavattini's relation to Latin America, not least because he visited this part of the world at least nine times, travelling to Cuba, Mexico, Venezuela, Argentina and Brazil. The focus in this, and the two following chapters, however, is on Mexico and Cuba, two countries where he worked and taught at length, followed by a chapter dedicated to his relation with Argentinian cinema. Wherever he went he was offered an opportunity for listening and learning, and for a personal transmission of a critical Neo-realism, *in fieri*, as theorized and practised by him, as committed and popular cinema, a topic which has to date attracted little or no attention among English-language film historians. This chapter concentrates on Zavattini's interventions in Cuba.[1]

16.2 Zavattini in Cuba

Zavattini's first 1953 Cuban visit marked the first of several face-to-face contacts with the pioneers of the New Cuban Cinema and a direct transmission of contemporary Italian film theory and practice to Cuba from the major theorist of Neo-realism. This trip was sponsored by the recently set up UNITALIA (The National Union for the Diffusion of Italian Film Abroad). Alberto Lattuada and the actress Marisa Belli were also with him. This was not the first time that he and Lattuada had represented the New Italian Cinema abroad.

The most significant event during his brief visit was the Havana Conference, organized by the cultural society Nuestro Tiempo.[2] It took place soon after his arrival on 5 December 1953.[3] Zavattini and Lattuada were the guest speakers. The screenwriter and director were involved in a *cabildo apierto*, an open question and answer discussion, quite unusual at the time. A close friend of Fidel Castro attended, Alfredo Guevara, who was then a Professor of History of Culture, at the National University of Havana. Guevara had no doubt that Zavattini, as he remembered many years later, had opened up a new, ethical, dimension of cinema which had political potential, one concerned not with man in the abstract, but with real-life people and their contemporary society.[4] There were also Tomás Gutiérrez Alea and Julio García Espinosa, recently back from Rome, where the two had attended the Centro Sperimentale di Cinematografia di Roma, a prestigious film school which had also attracted other Latin Americans, and namely, Gabriel García Márquez, Óscar Torres, Fernando Birri and Néstor Almendros.[5]

José Massip, a lecturer in film history and film aesthetics, was also present. A couple of years earlier, he had set up a debating section within Nuestro Tiempo, to help establish a national Cuban cinematography which broke away from Hollywood, Mexican and Argentinean cinema. Most of the members, including Massip and Alfredo Guevara, were communists, covertly fighting the dictatorship of General Fulgencio y Zaldívar Batista. The Cuban Conference took place immediately after the Italian Conference on Neo-realism in Parma which ended on 5 December, the same day Zavattini touched down at Havana airport.[6]

Zavattini was amazed at what the Cuban club members knew.[7] He had no inkling that, although Cuba had no cinema of its own, it did have a thriving film culture, albeit restricted to the members of its many film clubs, supported by José Manuel Valdés Rodríguez, the director of the Department of Cinema at the National University of Havana. The university boasted its own well-stocked film library, thanks to the Museum of Modern Art of New York and the Paris-based *Cinéthèque française*, so that staff and members of the university film club could access the latest European film journals, including *Cinema Nuovo* and *Cahiers du cinéma*.

Hence, his surprise when he was asked about Parma, where he had cited the recent findings of the 'Popular Survey on Poverty and Exploitation in the South', to associate the reality of extreme poverty in Italy to the realism of Neo-realism, which he had declared 'an unfinished project'.[8] Poverty was also a main concern in Cuba, since, although the country was no longer under direct foreign rule, it was a neocolonial state, in the thrall of the West, which quarried its raw materials at low cost, in time-honoured fashion. The 1953 Cuban census showed that almost half the population lived in shacks, overcrowded *bohíos*. There was no water, no electricity, no toilet, and 23.6 per cent of the population was illiterate. The average salary was less than US$6 a week.[9]

Zavattini told the Cubans that 'any cinema that seeks to address the contemporary world's serious problems is Neo-realist'. 'At this stage', he added,

'Neo-realism has become the conscience of cinema.'[10] The practice of Neo-realism required the filmmaker to go beyond the appearance of reality. Alfredo Guevara was to remember Zavattini's words for the rest of his life and recount his experience in a book containing correspondence with Zavattini and some of his writings, as they appeared in Cuba in the 1950s, in *Ese diamantino corazón de la verdad* (2002).

> Neo-realism seeks, it finds, it aims to hunt down reality, reveal or unveil it, go beyond the surface, going deeper, down to the raw matter hidden within it. To effect change, Neo-realism would need to adopt a range of forms and methods, some newly devised, put them into practice, sometimes discard them, in constant, ongoing research.[11]

Zavattini advocated a socially engaged cinema, on the grounds that witnessing and publishing the facts would not be enough; Cuban cinema should also push for positive action. He repeated what he had said and written before: 'To know, in order to act.'[12] He drew the distinction between observing reality and intervening, conceiving of Neo-realism as a *critical* realism. 'Neo-realism, I might add, should not limit itself to observation, but extend to action. To look and to act. This is the problematic.' The aim of Neo-realism was to nurture social awareness in the audience and the willingness 'to fight in society'. He stressed that the person who is observing and intervening is, after all, a member of society: 'Someone who lives a concrete life, in a concrete society with problems which need to be resolved in a concrete way.'[13] There was a recurring misunderstanding which had to be dispelled, and namely, that the scope of Neo-realism was restricted, humanist, and tantamount to a generic universalizing. No. The aim was to come to grips with actual human beings, inhabiting a specific world, which we can come to know.[14] Any analysis of the real world must begin by recognizing that the world is divided by social and political inequality. Conscience, in his sense, meant developing a critical attitude, leading to commitment and action. His materialist realism is in line with Marx's materialist philosophy, pitted against Hegel's idealism, which is hardly concerned with the concrete man.[15] Massip later wrote to Zavattini to tell him:

> After your departure, we never stopped fighting as strenuously as we could for Neo-realism; especially for our own Neo-realist cinema. I want you to know that your brief stay in Cuba was inspirational for our work.[16]

16.3 The Cubans opt for Neo-realism

After his departure, some of the Nuestro Tiempo Film Club members began to send him long letters in which they openly requested his help to develop a New Cuban Cinema, based on Neo-realist principles. Moreover, immediately after his departure, Massip published a paper on realism he had written for a talk and, in February 1954, Guevara published his personal account of the Havana Conference.[17]

Then, in May of that year, Julio García Espinosa read out to the Nuestro Tiempo members: 'El Neorrealismo y el Cine Cubano', a more than competent interpretation of Neo-realism, containing a lucid analysis which faced the Cubans with a choice. Espinosa dismissed Soviet realism, be it Zhdanov's variety or Lukács's. Somehow, against all odds, despite its contemporary, real-world themes, Neo-realism had proved a success abroad. The commentators who had reduced it to a series of technical choices were wrong. They had missed the point. Neo-realism was the way forward.[18]

They also organized a series of screenings of Neo-realist films at Nuestro Tiempo, while asking Zavattini for, and obtaining, further seminal texts about the movement, for them to study and circulate among cinéphiles in Cuba. In 1954, Zavattini acted as a go-between with the editor of *Cinema Nuovo*, Guido Aristarco, who agreed that Alfredo Guevara could collaborate on Zavattini's Neo-realist Bulletin.[19]

The Cubans put theory into practice, making what they themselves described as a Neo-realist film, an experimental documentary, a re-enactment of the everyday life of exploited Cuban charcoal workers, who spent their lives toiling in the swamps, just south of Havana. The result was 'a modest documentary of obvious Zavattinian inspiration', Massip later acknowledged.[20] The framework was Zavattini's, as set out in the texts he sent them about *Italia mia* which they had used as a guide.[21] The film, *El Mégano* (1955) attempted to put Zavattini's ideas in practice, having nothing to do with the pioneers of documentary, the great Robert Flaherty or John Grierson. Instead, it hinged on Zavattini's concept of 'shadowing' the real, to identify situations and social actors, and engaging with them through coexistence.[22]

Zavattini was able to return briefly to Cuba in 1955, thanks to Manuel Barbachano Ponce, an independent Mexican producer whose livelihood depended on making documentary newsreels and TV commercials. Barbachano Ponce contracted him to write several scenarios, including some in collaboration with the Nuestro Tempo circle. Zavattini came up with several ideas; one revolved around music, *Cuba Baila*; another was about what was called 'dead time' in Cuba; that is to say the time of unemployment between harvests in a *monocultivo* or single-crop sugar cane economy, which was seasonal.[23] The third, modelled on Zavattini's *Italia mia*, was *Cuba mía*. *El Mégano* fitted into the overall framework of *Italia mia*. Alfredo Guevara, Massip, Gutiérrez Alea, García Espinosa and others were involved in all three. Of these, in addition to *El Mégano*, only *Cuba Baila* went into production after the Cuban Revolution and was a great success.

Zavattini met some of the Cubans again in Mexico in 1957 where he was working on several projects for Barbachano Ponce. Then, in December 1959, the writer returned to Cuba for a prolonged stay which lasted until the end of February 1960. On 2 January 1960, immediately after the news of the victory of the Revolution, Zavattini wrote to Alfredo Guevara, who was still in Mexico, working for the Mexican producer, expressing his unconditional support. He told Guevara that cinema was the ideal medium to get to know and show others Cuba's problems.[24]

After Alfredo Guevara returned from exile to Cuba, he was soon appointed director of ICAIC (*Instituto Cubano de Arte y Industria Cinematográfica*). Zavattini immediately advised Guevara on 2 January 1959, the day after the victory of the *Rebeldes* against Batista and long before ICAIC had been formed, to get documentary footage of the Revolution in the provinces, and do so without delay, for later use.[25] The Cubans from the Nuestro Tiempo film club then founded *Cine Rebelde*, borrowing the name from *Radio Rebelde*, the Cuban clandestine broadcasting station. Then, in May 1959, Gutiérrez Alea filmed *Esta tierra nuestra*, a documentary which clearly illustrates the new legislation on redistribution of land in Cuba, which had been drafted the year before, while the fighting was still on, and García Espinosa made *La Vivienda*, a documentary explaining the Revolution's new housing legislation.[26]

Small wonder, then, that Fernando Bernal, Guevara's Economic Consultant at the newly formed ICAIC, should write to Zavattini on 29 May 1959, requesting his advice on 'production, distribution, and funding' and asking him to act as a go-between with experts in the film industry on setting up a fledgling industry.[27] As well as asking Zavattini to contribute stories and screenplays, Bernal requested him to act as an adviser on content, and to train an ICAIC team of writers. At the time, the only experienced writers in Cuba were the ones Zavattini himself had trained, including the exile Spaniard García Ascot, with whom Zavattini worked on his Mexican projects which are covered in a separate chapter.

16.4 Zavattini and Cuban cinema during the Revolution

As soon as Zavattini arrived in Havana, on 11 December 1959 he set to work, setting up an ICAIC film seminar, an intense teaching event and screenwriting workshop, to discuss and select prospective films for ICAIC and the New Cuban Cinema. Predictably, the Cuban organization's plan was to narrate revolutionary events, in the form of a straightforward linear reconstruction of key moments. Zavattini argued against this, claiming that it would be more beneficial to find a way to avoid a mechanical replication of events. They should avoid naïve realism. He used shock tactics with the fledgling ICAIC writers in his seminar.[28] He told them: 'Screenwriting is the easiest thing in the world'; that 'there is no such thing as technique'.[29] He challenged them. What were they afraid of? 'By the time I leave Cuba, you'll know all I know. Really, from a technical point of view, I don't know anything. Nor do I understand why some youngsters are scared of the techniques involved in screenwriting.'[30] He was, of course, questioning the mystique surrounding the craft, as he had done before in Italy, and he was emphasizing what screenwriting meant, within Cuba's new political and social situation, and namely, the need for their political commitment. He argued that if the Revolution was the most relevant subject matter, it followed that it should take precedence over artistic autonomy.

Zavattini was not the only important figure from the West to work in Cuba. Towards the end of 1960 and in 1961, the critic Georges Sadoul and the communist documentary filmmaker Joris Ivens also spent time in Cuba.[31] Ivens was also an official, invited, guest. Unsurprisingly, given their similar political orientation, Ivens repeated Zavattini's advice: let the Revolution guide you:

> If you allow me to give young Cuban filmmakers some advice, I'd say this is the best lesson in cinematography for you. Forget technical and stylistic issues. These will be resolved in good time. The main thing is to allow life into your studios, so that you don't become film camera bureaucrats.[32]

As for Zavattini, he used his seminar to discuss with the participants all the proposed projects presented to him earlier by correspondence with ICAIC. He instigated field research to find out what had changed in Cuba, since his earlier visits, before attempting to document the Revolution, by interviewing its witnesses. The next step was to decide what to communicate to the public about this new revolutionary reality and how to put such a powerful mass medium as cinema to effective use. Manuel Octavio Gómez, who wrote the story entitled *La prensa amarilla (The Reactionary Press)*, made the point that

> To walk anywhere with Cesare becomes an experience that takes you by surprise. The everyday takes on a new meaning. Minimal events, in his gaze, take on such proportions as to fill an entire film.[33]

Zavattini taught his seminar students that before they attempted to document events and reconstruct them, it would be necessary first to understand what had changed in Cuba, if anything had, and in what way. But this would only be possible by getting in touch with the witnesses themselves.

On 15 January 1960, Zavattini held a conference at ICAIC, presided over by Alfredo Guevara. Hours beforehand, Zavattini was interviewed by Cuban television. This was his opportunity to set the agenda for the ICAIC Conference. He began by citing Cuban national hero and poet José Martí, to define their legacy of 'an aesthetic concerned with the relation between politics and art', which meant political commitment. Zavattini pointedly asked: 'What else should cinema be concerned with, when everything is being transformed and renewed?'[34] He added that, after the Revolution, Martí's aesthetic 'should be the aesthetic of Cuba and of its cinematography', in which 'the highest goal equates ethics with aesthetics'.[35]

Zavattini reiterated the ideas he had put forward to the Nuestro Tiempo circle in 1953 and also during his brief, if intense, visit to Cuba in 1955. The biggest obstacle the ICAIC faced was a resistance coming from within, and namely, seeking to defend art for art's sake. He warned delegates that opting for political cinema did not mean opting for propaganda, as one of his students,

Hosé Hernández, had insisted it should, during his seminar.[36] Was the Revolution not part and parcel of contemporary, everyday life in Cuba? Then the question was, how do you go about filming the Revolution? His answer was that you seek out the personal dimension in each event, including the Agrarian Reform.[37]

Why the Agrarian Reform? Because, in the contemporary context, the Agrarian Reform was so crucial a revolutionary intervention that only when it was carried out would the historic remit of the 26 July Movement be fully realized, when, he added, citing Ernesto Che Guevara: 'not a single landless *campesino* exists nor a land could be found that is idle.'[38] As far as Zavattini was concerned, the establishing shot for the New Cuban Cinema was the Revolution itself; as he put it: 'Today, we already have the shot.'[39]

After five weeks of discussion over which ideas to develop and why, Zavattini and the seminar students went into production mode, developing his scenario and treatment for *El Joven Rebelde* (1961) (*The Young Revolutionary*), a film written by Zavattini and directed by García Espinosa. Zavattini also contributed to an episode film, *Historias de la revolución* (1961) filmed by another former Nuestro Tiempo member, Tomás Gutiérrez Alea. He also supervised the writing of the three episodes of *Cuba 58* (1962) with García Ascot, episodes which told stories in an oblique way, thus avoiding the direct address of propaganda.[40]

The seminar also developed a scenario based on an idea for a satire about the local dictator Trujillo, *The Little Dictator*. His advice was to replace Trujillo with the Cuban dictator, Batista. As a result, a vague idea became a substantial treatment which adopts the dictator's point of view, and shows, among other things, the inner workings of the mass media, based on Zavattini's prior publishing and film experience.[41] This latter project, unfortunately, never went any further, possibly because the Cubans realized that Zavattini's deconstruction and ridiculing of media propaganda and its crafty manipulations might well backfire. After all, even Fidel posed among the sugar cane fields, smiling as he wields his machete across swathes of cane, just like the Batista caricature in the treatment.

On 24 February 1960, Zavattini held his last seminar session, a showdown orchestrated by Zavattini himself, following a plan he had discussed in private with Alfredo Guevara, to confront the internal ideological split at ICAIC caused by Guillermo Cabrera Infante and Néstor Almendros, and probably a few others. On that occasion, Zavattini presented his outline for another film, *Colour versus Colour (Abstract Painter versus Figurative Painter), a Drama on Canvas*.[42] Two artists, one, a figurative artist, the other, a non-figurative artist, are holed up in a farmhouse, in hiding during the days of the war of Liberation. Their confinement gives rise to discussions about commitment and doubt. This scenario was Zavattini's solution for turning the autonomy argument on its head, by proposing a story for a film which would incorporate operative, constructive doubt. For, artistic autonomy at all times was the root cause of the split within Zavattini's seminar.

On the eve of his departure, he was interviewed by Héctor García Mesa and Eduardo Manet, co-editors of the inaugural issue of *Cine cubano* and members of what they described as 'The Zavattini Seminar'.[43] The long section devoted to the Italian theorist and screenwriter included a tribute, in the form of testimonials written by seminar participants. The editors officially acknowledged Zavattini's transmission of knowledge, effected through what they called 'Socratic' teaching, working collaboratively with the ICAIC Seminar.[44] But most of the space dedicated to Zavattini was for a long interview with Zavattini, titled 'Towards a Debate with those against Commitment'. The Italian film writer demarcated three factions: the Zavattinians, the *Nouvelle Vague* fans and the hard liners, who argued in favour of political propaganda, applied to feature filmmaking.[45]

Zavattini's contribution deserves close analysis, for many reasons. He had faced, from the outset, a lively debate concerning the nature and the legitimacy of political commitment within his seminar, a problematic which came to a head, as we will see in more detail later, the following year, almost a year after his departure, in January 1961, when the short *Pasado Meridiano*, or P.M., screened on television as part of the cultural programme hour by *Lunes de Revolución*, sparked a major controversy.[46]

During his long stint working in Cuba, Zavattini took the objections expressed by Néstor Almendros and Guillermo Infante Cabrera very seriously.[47] He brought up the matter on 15 January, at the ICAIC Conference, and further external evidence of the controversy appears in a letter from Almendros, in which the Cuban writer objected that politically engaged filmmaking would transform the relation between art and society into one between art and communism. In another letter, Almendros repeated his question during the seminar: 'What stories should we write in two years' time?'[48] Almendros argued that the Muse would be betrayed, if they relinquished their autonomy, in other words, poetry and commitment were incompatible. As far as he was concerned, the themes were as ephemeral as the Revolution itself. Furthermore, a year into the Revolution, 'The game has gone on for too long.'[49] Almendros and Cabrera questioned the ICAIC and Zavattini selection. The themes were 'ugly'. They cited as their preferred alternative source of inspiration and model of practice the works of Jack Kerouac and Eugène Ionesco. Zavattini responded with several counter objections.

Faced with reality, however confusing and uncertain it might seem, filmmakers had to make choices. Inevitably, they involved ethics. How could the subject matter be considered ephemeral? The Cuban Revolution wasn't. It was an exceptional event, a break with the past and a catalyst which redeemed national dignity, after colonial and post-colonial rule. It was ongoing. They had to achieve full literacy and the distribution of land to the dispossessed. Zavattini told them: 'We can see that in a small corner of the world someone is really doing something; words and actions are being made to coincide.'[50] If anything, ICAIC risked *not being revolutionary enough*, he stated. Yet, the problematic of art and commitment was topical, because the Cuban Revolution was topical, with repercussions stretching beyond national borders and raising the issue of freedom throughout Latin America.[51] Moreover, to opt for *art pour l'art* exposed a lack of courage, in the face of contemporary reality, a reality and a historical moment which could not be ignored.

And yet this is precisely what Zavattini's opponents within his seminar wanted to do, to seek refuge in their ivory towers.[52] He also made the point that if the impact of the Cuban Revolution led to forming a general outlook and psychology, it followed that cinema too would need to encompass that.[53] In any case, the collective resonance of the issues neither excluded nor contradicted poetry, for there is no opposition between commitment and poetry, since poetry is not in opposition to the real.[54]

Did he think another approach was viable, in these circumstances? Their appeal to Ionesco and Kerouac, examples of an alternative model, certainly deserved a detailed response. These writers were negationist, therefore not relevant within the Cuban context, where what was required was an affirmation of a new reality, a New Cinema capable of spreading a sense of hope, kindled in Cuba by the Revolution, right across the globe.

Zavattini elaborated. Ionesco and Kerouac had had the merit of exposing the disintegration of a capitalist society (in Ionesco's counter-myth, represented as dysfunctional and a source of alienation). However, their critiques, whether of the American Dream or of post-war French colonialism, were irrelevant, except in a European or North American context, which celebrated the diversity of a subculture.[55] Alienation or Beat Generation aesthetics, as a response to Capitalism, were inappropriate within the new Cuban revolutionary context.[56] Not that negation wasn't appropriate for the First World. But, within the Cuban context, the affirmation of a different model of society was an appropriate response. Furthermore, adopting negation as *modus operandi* in the face of the Revolution was tantamount to censorship. It meant that you had no faith in an alternative to the mainstream, hegemonic, capitalist myth. And besides, the victory of the Revolution was itself a negation of a system of values and therefore an affirmation of their opposite. He concluded his rebuttal, arguing that affirmation of this new reality by the New Cuban Cinema was the right choice.[57]

The final part of 'Towards a Debate with those against Commitment' dealt with what to do next, encapsulated in this question: how do you go about shaping a new revolutionary cinema of commitment?

He was not alone in his defence of commitment. Others would follow his lead. Soon Jean-Paul Sartre, during his stay in Cuba in 1960, in the company of Simone De Beauvoir, would also defend political commitment in cinema, and their position was echoed by Joris Ivens.[58] Just before he left, Zavattini argued that the New Cinema would be an affirmation of the new revolutionary reality, drawing on what was going on, since Cuban cinema belonged to a special time, the time of Revolution. The relevance of Neo-realism in this context was to think in terms of a cinema open to the relation between individual and collective, to the pressing needs of the contemporary and historic moment. Neo-realism had worked:

The lesson of Neo-realism is of a cinema which is consistent with reality, a cinema which is a social medium. And in Cuba today, there's a Neo-realist situation, in so far as the relation between individual and society is being brought to an extreme, to a deeper stage.[59]

Neo-realism had produced consequences, acting as the conscience of cinema and as a means of social communication.[60] Neo-realism meant interpreting, taking on a critical and analytical stance, not limiting oneself to illustrate social facts. It contained a subjective and personal point of view, inviting the question: 'Who is looking?' It would opt for what Zavattini called 'indirect speech' (anticipating by several years Pier Paolo Pasolini's idea regarding the cinema of poetry).[61] Zavattini didn't elaborate on this point, but it seems connected to the principle of creating distance from the event. He envisaged a cinema which could deal with any subject matter and could be satire, comedy, drama, science fiction or a romantic film. Because you can 'somehow give a voice to this big event which concerns six million people and interests many millions more'. Its narrative would be 'detached', adopting an aesthetic filter to create distance between the raw events of the Revolution and the Cuban public: 'Narrate them in such a way that they appear as distant as possible.'[62] 'How? Through language.'[63]

The New Cuban Cinema would avoid propaganda, which meant discarding Stalinist realism. Was there a socialist alternative? He thought there was. Realism could be committed, socialist, without being Zhdanovist. Hence, its form of realism would have to be concrete, as he had originally suggested to Cubans in 1953. The problem was generic idealism, regardless of whence it came. He opposed 'a world that settles for words', and 'an indeterminate socialism'. Realism, as he understood it, meant translating the real into the language of cinema, which of course, inevitably raised the problem of representation. He thought that a direct (by which he meant indexical) representation of events should be discarded, since it would be no better than 'a repetition', a replication of events. So, for example, *The Attack against the Moncada Barracks* should *suggest* what caused the attack.[64] The reason why 'pure' representation should be avoided was because it would only be a 'repetition', which only goes as far as a faithful replication of social facts. He clarified his point:

> It isn't a question of accepting the story the way a printer does who transcribes on his posters that which the client demands, but of getting to the bottom, as far as possible, of the meaning of these events.[65]

In his work as a consultant, Zavattini had opposed from the outset, even before setting foot again in Cuba in 1959, the linear reconstruction of events put forward by Jomí García Ascot, Alfredo Guevara and Tomás Gutiérrez Alea, preferring a personal and subjective narrative, diary-based, the kind which emerges later on in Cuban cinema in *Memorias de subdesarrollo* (1968) by Tomás Gutiérrez Alea, and can be found eight years before, in Zavattini's rough outlines for scenarios, entitled *Las Muchachas Rebeldes* or *¿Quien es?*, after his encounters with strangers and 'shadowing' people in Cuba. Even *Revolución en Cuba*, another outline of his, envisaged as a documentary reportage, was subjective, adopting the point of view of a foreigner, but built on prior field research. This was how New Cuban Cinema could eschew political propaganda, opting instead for a personal approach, that is, making films about personally witnessed social facts, 'The way I saw them', as he put it.[66] He invited Cubans to ask themselves: 'Who is looking?'[67] Ultimately, the objective was to 'give a voice to this big event which concerns six million people and many more million'.[68] 'Our ambition' he went on to say, 'is a cinema that takes this message everywhere, but it should do so by filtering the real, using film language to create distance between event and narrative.'[69]

Zavattini brought to Cuba his recent work and experiments towards a new framework for films, organized around the principle of a private, personal, diary, as his scenario, entitled *Diary of a Woman*, dated 8 June 1959 demonstrates. It was set on the day Mussolini had appeared at his balcony of Piazza Venezia in Rome, to announce that Italy was siding with Nazi Germany and declaring war against Britain and the United States. The story combines a personal life and perspective and a big event, of historical proportions. The social dimension was kept in the background: 'the small story against the background of the great story', as De Sica described it a few years later.[70] Subsequently, Zavattini reworked his idea in the 1960s and 1970s. *Diary of a Woman* reflected his continued interest in experimenting with the diary and the confessional mode, later resulting in *Diary of a Man* and *The Guinea Pig*, part of the same proposal of subjective cinema.

Zavattini's defence of a politically, and poetically, engaged cinema anticipated by several years Julio García Espinosa's famous Latin American Manifesto: 'Towards an Imperfect Cinema' (1973). García Espinosa argued that Latin American cinema needed to be 'imperfect'.[71] For only in an ideal world would it have the luxury of being disinterested or autonomous from society.[72] Once again, materialist realism, the 'concrete' world, was key. García Espinosa's conclusion was that filmmakers had to deal with problems with society in their work, which is why the New Cinema was inevitably imperfect.[73]

Zavattini had to return home, in order to meet his deadline for an adaptation of *Two Women* (*La ciociara*). He left only a matter of days before the arrival of Jean-Paul Sartre and Simone De Beauvoir. Yet in Rome he carried on working on the screenplay for *El Joven Rebelde* and immediately began to set up an Italy–Cuba organization to help with counter-information about the Revolution and to enlist support and funding.

In 1961, *Pasado Meridiano* or *P.M.*, the fifteen-minute film, directed by Sabá Cabrera Infante, Guillermo Cabrera Infante's twin sister, and by Orlando Jímenez Leal, was censored by the ICAIC. In the uncertain Cold War climate, Alfredo Guevara's ICAIC, tasked with granting public release to films, objected that this short depicted the same kind of people on the margins of society (unemployed black and mulatto *Habaneros*) as Lionel Rogosin's *On the Bowery* (1956).

True, but where are the signs of the desperation of New York slums in *P.M.*?[74] Instead, *Pasado Meridiano* features upbeat Afro-Cuban music and people simply having fun; similar to Karel Reisz and Tony Richardson's *Momma Don't*

Allow (1956). On the contrary, in Cuba, Néstor Almendros, now the *Bohemia* magazine film critic, thought the film was experimental and poetic.[75] He was right, it was. In the event, Almendros, the Cabreras and *Lunes de Revolución* were outraged. The contentious issue was discussed in a series of meetings at the highest level.[76] Alfredo Guevara accused them of ideological confusion; they were trying to spread bourgeois existentialism, a point that Zavattini had amply discussed the previous year.[77] This school of thought, quite fashionable in the West at the time, mostly thanks to the novels of Jean-Paul Sartre and Albert Camus, claimed that because man is alienated by living in an alienated world, communication is impossible which, in the Cuban context, was incompatible with the idea that social relations are possible and indeed necessary to effect change, let alone a revolution.

That critical, tense, 1963, Julio García Espinosa sided with the ICAIC and Fidel's 'Palabras a los Intelectuales' ('Words for the Intellectuals'), stating in *Cine cubano* that filmmakers had an obligation to find a direct connexion with reality as their first priority – which is just what Zavattini had recommended.[78]

In 1963, Zavattini invited the ICAIC to contribute to the *Cinegiornale della pace* (*The Newsreel for Peace*), a collaborative documentary protesting against the Cold War, and in 1968 to the *Cinegiornali liberi* (*Free Newsreels*). Why did the Cubans not follow his lead? One explanation is that in Cuba, newsreels served as one-directional, overt, political propaganda. Amazing as the Cuban *Noticiarios* were, Zavattini's grassroots intervention in Italy was implementing a different model of practice, a counter-cinema, aiming to replace the *auteur* in fiction film with a collaborative, grassroots vision of committed cinema, letting ordinary people take over the means and relations of production. But evidently that was going too far.

By 1977, New Cuban Cinema was history. In Italy, film critic and historian Lino Miccichè curated a Festival of Cuban cinema at which he made no mention of Zavattini's work in Cuba, neither of his teaching and advisory role, nor his visits, nor the part Zavattini played in the transmission of Neo-realist theory and practice to Latin America, and specifically to Cuba.[79]

Zavattini wrote to him to complain, reminding the Italian film critic of his involvement, from its very inception, in teaching, writing, creating frameworks and influencing the Cuban outlook on and off the screen, shaping screenplays and animating theoretical debates.[80] What was at stake was not an oversight, but the omission of a chapter of Cuban and Latin American film history, concerning the transmission of Neo-realism and its development, and Zavattini's role, from 1953 to 1961, several years before the Latin American *Tercer Cine* movement which, incidentally, cited in its 1968 manifesto Zavattini's grassroots *Cinegiornali liberi*, as a model of counter-cinema practice to be emulated.[81] Twenty years later, Miccichè was prepared to admit that 1960s New World Cinema owed most of its formal practice and theoretical underpinning to Neo-realism, acknowledging that it had been used as a model by underdeveloped countries, including Cuba.[82]

Transmission of Neo-realism to Mexico

17.1 Zavattini's first trip to Mexico

Immediately after his brief stay in Cuba, in 1953, Zavattini flew over to nearby Mexico. The Parma Conference on Neo-realism had clashed with the Italian Film Week in Cuba, which was a part of an Italian tour of several Latin American capital cities organized by UNITALIA.[1]

In Mexico, when, on 9 December, Zavattini, his friend the director Alberto Lattuada and the actress Marisa Belli were faced with an audience of 2,500 people, the writer told the crowd:

> Neo-realists take the same view of their films as Diego Rivera of his *murales*. When people see their stories told on the walls, he hopes they will grow in their awareness of who they are.[2]

He received 'a standing ovation, one of the greatest a filmmaker has ever received at any time', according to the reporter Octavio Alba, writing for *Cine mundial*.[3]

He appeared on television, gave radio talks and interviews to the press. He met the Modernist painter Rufino Tamayo, the muralists Alfaro Siqueiros and Diego Rivera, and the actress Dolores del Río. But no matter where he went, the Mexican film industry doggedly chose to ignore him.[4] Siqueiros had recently published *Siqueiros, por la vía de una pintura neorrealista o realista social en México* (1951), claiming an allegiance with Neo-realism, on the grounds that cinematic Italian Neo-realism equated with Mexican muralist paintings.[5] From the very outset, Zavattini's plan was the transmission of Neo-realism, as he said in an interview given on 10 December, the day after his arrival, going so far as to encourage *Cine mundial* to translate and publish his 'Some ideas on Cinema'.[6] He told the Italian-born Amadeo Recanati that he was in Mexico for two reasons: first, to share his personal ideas about cinema and, second, to talk about the past and current success of New Italian Cinema.[7] This is what he actually said, on 11 December:

I consider Neo-realism the conscience of world cinema. It is cinema as a creative medium, faced with itself and its destiny. I'm convinced that, without Neo-realism, the cinema could easily perish. Entire civilizations have become extinct, and therefore it is absurd to assume that cinema should be immortal. Neo-realism is the new lymph that will save the cinema from extinction.

Given that it is a modern medium of expression and the most suitable for the Neo-realist idea to manifest, it will survive, just as the observation of life, moment by moment, is inexhaustible. I don't look down on, for example, historical films, because you can interpret on-going problems using historical events of a social and human nature. But I do think that the priority is to concentrate on contemporary issues, issues of the moment, this moment, the passing moment.[8]

He defended the need for socially engaged cinema, citing the painter Diego Rivera, whom he had met two days earlier. Neo-realist cinema proposed stories drawing on real-life events, as inexhaustible a source as the script they can inspire. On this common ground, he thought the movement could develop, and sustain any number of tendencies.[9]

Francisco Pina of *Novedades* greeted him as *Cesare Zavattini, precursor del Neorrealismo*.[10] Pina realized that Zavattini's film aesthetic was continually developing and drew a distinction between the kind of *mimēsis* which expects to simply capture objective reality as opposed to the Italian screenwriter's kind, which consisted in seeking to interpret it. Zavattini told Pina:

Now I'm interested in the drama of things actually taking place, not of things thought up earlier. It is necessary to transform reality into poetry, exercising our poetic abilities on the spot, turning our backs on our office and walking, I mean physically walking, among other people to observe and understand them.[11]

Zavattini also met the film critic Pío Caro Baroja, whose tangible response to the Italian filmmaker's film theory was a book on Italian Neo-realism, *El Neorrealismo cinematografico italiano, Prólogo y notas de Cesare Zavattini* (1955), which includes long sections of Zavattini's 'Some Ideas on Cinema', passages from other writings by Zavattini, and a Prologue and Epilogue, penned by Zavattini himself.[12] After Zavattini left, Pío Caro Baroja wrote to Zavattini, telling him that the battle for Neo-realism was also a Mexican battle. He then began to write a book about Neo-realism.[13]

Baroja's book endorses Zavattini's strand of Neo-realism. In the chapter 'The Theory of Neo-realist Cinema', he observes that Zavattini's central role in the movement consisted in the practice of theorizing cinema through scripts and articles, while making it at the same time. This is a pretty good description of what authentic praxis consists in. Baroja agreed that the way filmmakers should face reality was by analysing it, including its minute details and events, however insignificant they might seem. Didactic fables should be discarded, to fix the gaze on everyday life and narrate it in a direct way. Film work should include empathy towards other people and relating to the social, by addressing problems which society fails to resolve, and finally, like the Cubans before him, Baroja also concluded that it was a mistake to equate Neo-realism with its technical choices.[14] In his Epilogue to Baroja's book, Zavattini noted that in Mexico

> A cinema of presence can develop over and above a cinema of absence. A cinema of presence would be a Neo-realist cinema, as opposed to a conformist cinema.[15]

17.2 Zavattini's second journey to Mexico

The former Mexican museum curator Fernando Gamboa was instrumental in arranging Zavattini's second trip to Mexico in 1955. He had first met Zavattini in 1951 at the Venice Biennale, when he was touring an exhibition of Mexican muralist art which he had curated. Four years later, Gamboa told the producer Manolo Barbachano Ponce, that if his production house Teleproducciones really wanted to make a New Mexican Cinema, as Barbachano had claimed it did, then help from abroad was needed, and Zavattini was the right man to make it happen.[16]

So it was that Barbachano Ponce commissioned Zavattini to write several film scripts, and subsidized his second trip to Mexico, in 1955. Once again, Zavattini was greeted by an enthusiastic response. He received an important Mexican cultural endorsement of Italian Neo-realism, in the form of a manifesto proposing a Mexican form of Neo-realism, written by Gamboa himself and published in *Novedades*.[17] Gamboa boldly mapped the realist future of Mexican cinema, based on a Mexican version of Neo-realism, just as Julio García Espinosa had done the year before in Cuba, in his essay 'El Neorrealismo y el cine cubano' (1954).

Gamboa claimed that Latin American cinema was at a crossroads: it could go on making irrelevant and repetitive commercial films of the worst kind, or it could opt for a New Cinema. He consequently discarded the kind of realism to be found in Hollywood products. If the Italians had done it, so could the Cubans and the Mexicans. Gamboa argued that North American realism represented only the external appearance of reality and unreal, false situations. He argued that it had its own agenda: namely, to persuade the public that we live in the best of worlds. Although French psychological realism was better – he cited Jean Renoir – it remained within the confines of interpersonal relationships and of the drama of the individual. Its limitation was that the social dimension of reality was reduced to a backdrop. Was another option possible? He said there was; a version of realism that was poised between document and poetry, between analysis and emotion.

Zavattini's 1955 visit coincided with the release of the first attempt at Neo-realism in Mexican cinema, at least, of its first version. *Raíces* ('Roots') dealt with contemporary Mexican themes. It was an adaptation of four short stories by Francisco Rojas.[18] *Raíces* was, Pío Caro Baroja wrote, 'the first step towards Mexican Neo-realism'.[19] Its director, Benito Alazraki Algranti, was a former lecturer in philosophy at Mexico City's Universidad Autónoma, who had directed sixteen documentaries for Producciones Barbachano Ponce.

Baroja considered *Raíces* a celebration of the dignity and unique identity of the Mexican *Indios*, victims of racism by city dwellers, which they were. It shows poverty and violence in Latin America, and used actors taken from the streets, who lived where it was filmed. However, he later changed his mind, coming to the conclusion that *Raíces* expressed a defeatist acceptance of suffering, as opposed to the New Italian School's outright condemnation of it.[20] Zavattini had seen the first version, comprising three episodes, during his first short visit in 1953, and now suggested cuts to the production house. He also became friends with Benito Algranti Alazraki.[21] Zavattini even went as far as personally contacting the organizers of the Locarno Film Festival, in order to get *Raíces* into their selection.[22]

When he saw it again in Rome in its definitive version, he was still supportive, though less than enthusiastic. He conceded it 'a useful film, a film with potential, containing at least some suggestions for a New Mexican Cinema'.[23] But the Mexican public, according to the producer Manuel Barbachano Ponce, detested it: 'Dreadful! In this *thing*, you see nothing but *indios*; not a single famous actor; no well-known director. Appalling!'[24]

Cine mundial announced that Benito Alazraki and Zavattini would be making a film in collaboration.[25] Zavattini had high hopes, as he wrote to Caro Baroja:

> Right now, the Neo-realist lesson is being absorbed beyond Italian borders. Now it needs to be developed aggressively. Over here, there is a danger of giving in, that is, of not reacting vigorously against licit and illicit manoeuvres by those who would want to cancel the traces of ten long years of work in which many Italians have taken part.[26]

The Mexican film industry, however, ignored him once again, despite the warm welcome by the Mexican media, the press, film critics and television. For example, on 28 June there was a round-table discussion on Neo-realism and the rebirth of Mexican cinema, with Zavattini presiding. Not a single writer, actor or producer invited him to their studios. According to Emilio García Riera, 'it was really scandalous and shameful'.[27] Speaking on behalf of the film industry, the Mexican screenwriter and director Adolfo Fernandez Bustamante wrote that 'Mexicans know suffering only too well. What they want is to have fun'.[28]

Nevertheless, Zavattini's second visit achieved five objectives: further dissemination of Neo-realist film theory, direct contact with the Mexican film club circuit, and, at his behest, the formation and launch of a club federation, the *Federación Mexicana de Cine Clubs*; ethnographic field research over two months of travel across the width and breadth of Mexico, and, finally the creation of several film scripts.

As mentioned earlier, Zavattini was contracted to work for Producciones Barbachano Ponce. He was to write three stories, two about Mexico, and one about Cuba.[29] Later, Gamboa and Zavattini met in Rome and agreed that Zavattini would write *México mío*, a Mexican version of *Italia mia*, the proposed feature-length documentary, originally planned for De Sica, then adapted for Roberto Rossellini which informed a number of his other projects, such as the manifesto-film *Love in the City* (1953), the photo-documentaries for *Cinema Nuovo* (1953–5), the feature film *Il tetto*, *The Roof* (1955) and the book *Un paese* (1955). Zavattini's other story for the Mexicans was a whimsical adaptation, *El Anellito magico* (*The Small Magic Ring*), based on *Diamo a tutti un cavallo a dondolo* (*Everyone Should Have a Rocking Horse*), to be turned into a satirical comedy on Mexican society, using magic realism in the way *Miracle in Milan* had done.

Zavattini's plan for *México mío* was to reject conventional tourist-style travelogues in favour of an investigative documentary. The other scenarios would tackle Mexican social problems, such as the problematic of fighting the expropriation of common land, drought or health. There would be a Cuban film too, about racial conflict, but without a trace of exoticism. Zavattini told Barbachano that to come up with *México mío*, he had to get to know the country first.[30]

This explains why he spent most of his time in Mexico in 1955 on field trips, in the company of Gamboa. The former curator was, naturally, keen to show the Italian Mexican tourist attractions: including the museums, the churches, cathedrals, skyscrapers, *fiestas* and spectacular natural wonders.

But the Italian screenwriter was particularly interested in economic and social production, preferring to meet ordinary people, especially while they were at work. 'My method', Zavattini wrote, 'was to get Mexicans to talk.'[31] The highlight of their field trips, as far as he was concerned, was piecing together a Mexican oral history of the 1938 expulsion of the multinationals. All you had to do was ask. He had countless conversations with people about the Mexican Revolution, but the real revolution, he concluded, took place in 1938.

Zavattini lost his patience, and subverted Gamboa's exotic sightseeing trips, to engage in a cinematic form of investigative, ethnographic research, which he had perfected earlier in Italy. His main interest was labour, oil fields and the extraction of crude oil, to understand the 1938 event, when British, North American and Dutch oil companies were ousted from Mexico, in a second, defiant, revolution.[32]

By the end of his second Mexico trip, Zavattini came up with three stories: *La Carrera Panamericana* (a Mexican version of *Italia mia*, later called *México mío*, a documentary that eschewed the exotic to present the everyday lives of Mexicans without idealizing them); *The Small Magic Ring*; the adaptation of *Everyone Should Have a Rocking Horse*, intended as a satirical comedy on Mexican society, and *El Petróleo* ('Crude Oil'), also called *El Año Maravelloso* ('The Marvellous Year').[33]

17.3 Zavattini's Mexican scenarios

As for *El Anellito magico*, it was doomed from the beginning, since Teleproducciones had no idea how to develop Zavattini's story into a screenplay. After all, magic realism was hardly their speciality, since Teleproducciones made almost exclusively newsreels and commercials, not whimsical social critique and any form of irony escaped them; nor were they able to implement his suggestions. So they pressurized him to develop the story, expecting him to produce a full screenplay. They plundered *Miracle in Milan* for gags, but Zavattini vetoed such additions. When the satirical bite underlying Zavattini's comic plot was cast aside and the Mexicans reduced the story to gags and laughter, inevitably, the result was more akin to a poor caricature of the great P. G. Woodhouse, without his lightness of touch. They expected realism, yet they couldn't understand magical realism. For example, at one point, they made the objection that balloons wouldn't be able to carry the weight of a worker.[34] After his return to Italy, the Mexicans sent him a version of the scenario, which bore no sign of social criticism or humour. In June 1956, Barbachano and his associate, the documentary film editor Carlos Velo, met Zavattini in Rome. Six months later, Barbachano wrote to tell him that they had just finished casting for actors.[35] Then the project disappeared into thin air and magic realism with it.

Zavattini's cinema always took place off the screen as well as on it, and his interventions in Mexico were no exception. A case in point was his conference in Mexico City, at the end of his 1955 trip, when he also animated a debate at *Cine Club Progreso*. In the first, Carlos Velo later remembered as if it were happening in the present:

> Zavattini abandons the lectern and begins to talk with everyone. He knows how to ask, he knows how to listen and say so many things.[36]

Velo was hinting at something premeditated, an approach adopted by Zavattini for the event. For, the conference was run as a question and answer session. His interviewer was Juan Miguel de Mora, a filmmaker and a journalist who had made two films *Naskará*, shot in Guatemala and shown at Cannes in 1953, and *Festín para la muerte*, filmed in Venezuela in 1954.[37] To prove that there was no shortage of inspiration for films, Zavattini picked up *Novedades* and read out the headlines, while giving a running commentary.[38]

He prospected an ethical cinema, a cinema on the move, ready to emigrate. Since it is 'only a direct and immediate acknowledgement of life itself, and therefore, of its human and social problems, there is no reason it cannot be exported'.[39] 'Neo-realism', he told his audience 'is an unfinished project. Neo-realism is the cinema, as a form of expression, faced with itself and its destiny', with a prophetic ring which brings to mind Jean-Luc Godard's *Historie(s) du Cinema* (1998).[40]

Zavattini extended the scope of ethics to politics, claiming that its role was not limited to supporting a sense of civic participation in the public sphere. Its purpose was also to continue the interrupted Mexican Revolution. This would be a cinema in which attractions would serve a social dialectic.[41] What mattered was *how* you tackled your subject. The situation in Mexico was just waiting to be told. In Italy, Neo-realists were called the Antichrists. He turned the definition on its head:

> We are *Antichrists*, whenever we decide *against* action; every time we block our ears, not to hear the accusation that we are accomplices, levelled at us by daily events. Would this cinema cut out the imagination?

He added:

> Imagination must be nourished by reality: by an investigative approach. When we speak of a documentary spirit, this doesn't mean passive reproduction, but making choices, within the broadest possible panorama, about what, from the point of view of our role as citizens, we consider a necessary object of investigation. To do so, you need to establish a relationship between what I call 'cohabitation' and what is going on. Easy to say, but hard to do.[42]

Finally, he departed from the conventions of public speaking by opening up to the floor and asking those present what kind of film they would like to see. Vincente Vila who was there reported that 'Proposals popped up like new grass after a good rain'.[43] Juvenile delinquency, Mexican workers (known as *braceros*) crossing the border with North America; the *Otomí* ethnic tribe; Mexican women – they had just been given the vote – politics; drought; child mortality; the housing shortage.[44]

At Cine Club Progreso, Zavattini discovered that the club's statute claimed the film club was fighting for 'the development of an authentic Mexican cinema'.[45] He told the organizers, Pío Caro Baroja and Francisco Pina, to establish a Federation of Mexican Film Clubs. The *Federación Mexicana de Cine Clubs* was launched almost immediately.[46] To help develop a film culture, he also proposed a professional film club, along the lines of the Circolo Romano del Cinema.[47] Years later, in 1961, these same organizers launched the short-lived *Grupo Nuevo Cine* and the film journal *Nuevo Cine*, modelled on the Italian Neo-realist *Cinema Nuovo*.

As for *El Año Maravelloso*, the story inspired by Zavattini's field research across Mexico in 1955, the producer let him know in January 1957 that they weren't satisfied with the well-developed fictional story, against the backdrop of the famous 1938 expropriation of the multinationals.[48] So a second round of field research on the oil fields was carried out in February and March 1957, involving more interviews with eye witnesses and technicians, following Zavattini's advice.[49]

The amazing story of collective rebellion was, of course, problematic from the outset, and fraught with objections from Producciones Barbachano Ponce. Zavattini made a clever move when he proposed Mario Moreno, a popular, much beloved Mexican, known as *Cantinflas*, for the lead role, to displace the actor's usual hilarious underdog character, to cast him instead as a Cervantes-style picaresque figure, able to rise above his situation and conquer his own independence. Hadn't Roberto Rossellini done so, in casting the Italian vaudeville comedian Aldo Fabrizi, for the tragic figure of Don Pietro, in *Rome, Open City*?[50] Alfredo Guevara, who had escaped from Cuba due to Batista's regime, was working for Producciones Barbachano in 1957. Guevara thought that *Cantinflas* would have transformed the film 'taking on an exceptional ethical weight'.[51] However, the fact of the matter is that nothing Zavattini ever suggested to the Mexicans was acceptable, which makes one wonder why that was.

The root of Zavattini's difficulties was that *El Petróleo*, also called *El Año Maravelloso*, indeed any of his projects, apart from the doomed magical realist *El Anellito*, which Zavattini refused to turn into a *Miracle in Milan* Mark 2, sought to address Mexican reality head on, dealing with what Zavattini called 'the facts', by which he meant social facts, singled out for being symptomatic of a more complex situation. The 'facts' were that, according to the 1950 census, 60 per cent of fifty-two million Mexican homes contained only a single room, 25 per cent comprised two rooms. Most homes were wooden huts (70 per cent) and only 18 per cent brick dwellings. A mere 17 per cent had running water. In 1955, 89 per cent of Mexican families earned less than 600 *pesos* a month, equal to US$69. In 1956, it emerged that the majority of the population, that is, 60 per cent, was undernourished and had housing problems; that 40 per cent were illiterate and 46 per cent didn't go to school.[52] This was also Alfredo Guevara's explanation. Barbachano and his team were simply unable to accept Zavattini's effective political critique. Privately, in his field diary, Zavattini wrote that the rejection of *El Petróleo* was a rejection of a provocation that went beyond the limits of acceptance for Producciones Barbachano Ponce.[53]

An early version of *México mío* revolved around the international road rally on its new Pan American motorway.[54] An establishing shot of road and racing cars, followed by a brilliant shot reversal, montage as reality of opposites, a close-up of spectators, whose individual lives were to be shadowed by the filmmaker. To be specific, he planned to film fifty 'moments' in their lives, in order to paint an authentic portrait of contemporary Mexico. There would be dance, song and everyday life, *braceros* leaving to cross the border, oil workers and ordinary people. The road would be a metaphor for the journey of discovery, not of folklore, but of exploitation, conflict, illiteracy. When the Pan Americana rally was scrapped, this version of the scenario was no longer topical, and was cancelled, as a result.

During that second visit to Mexico in 1955, Zavattini also wrote the story for a project that wasn't included as part of his contract, *¡Torero!* a documentary about the life of Luis Procuna, directed by Carlos Velo.[55] Velo himself, in private, thanked Zavattini for his help, for reducing to a minimum the 'Voice of God' approach (which characterized Grierson-style documentaries of that era), to allow diegetic sound to tell the story.[56] There is also strong internal evidence as to the Italian screenwriter's direct creative involvement: the life of the torero was compressed to a single day, typical Zavattini format. *¡Torero!* didn't use professional actors and thrives on Zavattinian-style detailed observation of everyday life. Procuna is the real Procuna, but so are all the other characters, including his wife and four children. Significantly, Procuna the bullfighter is no hero. This man would be considered, in today's terms, a celebrity, but also a normal person who is allowed to be afraid, like everyone else. But this was an alien concept in the context of the macho Mexican culture of the period. Furthermore, Procuna relates his personal story, his weaknesses, and becomes an anti-hero, showing his vulnerability, his fear of death, dreading to face the corrida after the death of another bullfighter and his own illness. Even when certain scenes are accompanied by commentary, the voice-over is always Procuna's personal, reflective, spoken diary and first-person account. The many stories within the story, or 'moments', form *cuentecitos* (little stories), no different from Zavattini's micro-events. And finally, the life is a life behind the scenes, a life shadowed by the camera, yet another Zavattinian recurring theme.

When the film was screened in Spain, it attracted the attention of Juan García Atienza, a Spanish film critic, very familiar with Zavattini's film theory and his experiments, being an associate of Muñoz Suay and Eduardo Ducay.[57] It was Juan García Atienza who spotted how different *¡Torero!* was from the rest of Carlos Velo's work. García Atienza recognized how the film was built on the principle of shadowing a person. He also noted the fact that the protagonist is portrayed as an anti-hero, hardly typical of Mexican cinema.[58]

There were simply too many coincidences for him not to identify Zavattini's direct involvement and influence. Carlos Velo had taken an ordinary event and analysed it, concentrating on the fears and hopes and difficulties of one man, no different, in his shortcomings and normality from the rest of us, despite his fame. García Atienza claimed that what made *¡Torero!* one of the best contemporary documentaries was Zavattini's vision of everyday reality. Velo had come very near to the screenwriter's vision of 'integral' or 'total' Neo-realism, finding dramatic interest in everyday events, no matter how seemingly insignificant.[59]

How strange that Velo could work from Zavattini's *¡Torero!* scenario, but reject his ideas for *México mío*.[60] *México mío* was also supposed to consist in a series of episodes, containing moments of Mexican everyday life, including an episode about bullfighting which may have been the source of inspiration for *¡Torero!*

The Mexicans also found it problematic that the film was to be the outcome of popular participation, triggered by interpellation of ordinary people contacted through a national competition to discover what people thought and which aspects of their country they felt were significant. They wanted a script. Teleproducciones had paid for a scenario, but what they really wanted was a fully developed screenplay written by the famous Italian screenwriter. But Zavattini resisted. In the event, there was no competition, no participation, other than what Zavattini himself instigated in his various contacts with individuals and groups.

The writing for *México mío* began during the last days of Zavattini's stay in Mexico in 1955 and continued during his 1957 trip and by correspondence and a few meetings with the Mexicans in Rome. Then, in 1959, the project was quietly shelved. The correspondence and production papers show that, as far as Teleproducciones Barchano Ponce were concerned, Mexico deserved an exotic celebration. Whereas Zavattini's Mexico was centred on ordinary people and their lives.

Zavattini met constant opposition from Carlos Velo, the front man, and the producer's brother, Miguel Barbachano.[61] For example, when Zavattini visualized shots to help Velo plan out the film, the best Velo could do was produce descriptive lists of potential locations.[62] Velo eventually wrote what he imagined was a screenplay, and called it that. Zavattini found a tactful way to let him know that it was didactic and excessively informative.[63] Worse still, the Mexicans replaced the same idea of a day in the life of the Mexican people with a weekend, a clever move to herald all the European connotations of leisure time.[64] Finally, to add insult to injury, *México mío* was to depend heavily on a magniloquent 'Voice of God' celebratory commentary, extolling the country's folkloric and natural wonders.

But wasn't the whole point of a *personal* emphasis conveyed in the very title, *My Mexico*? What was at stake was a clash between two conflicting approaches to the country. One was Mexican, but middle class and elitist, celebrating Mexican art and natural beauty, but denying its twentieth-century history, the other analytical, reflective, observational; based on ethnographic-style field research and personal, to the point of being disarming, surprising, innovative, truly revolutionary.

Zavattini asked Velo: 'How many spectacles, however grandiose and beautiful, can one show?'[65] Could you make a film which is nothing but a compilation of beautiful sequences, devoid of a story of real people?[66] The Velo-Barbachano team systematically swopped any situations Zavattini suggested with Velo's dizzying array of location shots, long descriptive sequences, all devoid of any meaning.[67] Even in the few instances Velo's screenplay allowed the voice of real people to be heard, they were limited to symbolic remarks.[68] Finally, Zavattini's damning point was that if one took away the superficial commentary, its emptiness would become blatantly obvious.[69]

In desperation, perhaps, Zavattini offered two more stories, one about Mexican *machismo*, the other about Mexican *braceros*.[70] One of them was based on a true story Laura Alazraki, the wife of the director of *Raíces* ('Roots'), discussed earlier, had related to Zavattini in 1955, in which a couple gets married, but on their first night the husband goes out on the town with his friends. When he returns home at dawn, he discovers that his bride has committed suicide.[71] The point was that the groom wanted to state his independence and dominance over his wife, and impose double standards, in true *macho* fashion.[72] A good story, a true story, but too close to the bone for the Mexicans. Zavattini refused to compromise and that was that.

But years later, he returned to Mexico for one last time, for a field trip, while writing a scenario and full adaptation for a film based on a novel by an anthropologist, Oscar Lewis (1914–1970). Lewis had spent thirty summers of annual leave from his university post, conducting ethnographic research in Mexico. It resulted in *Life in a Mexican Village* (1951), followed by *The Children of Sánchez, Autobiography of a Mexican Family* (1961), based on voice recordings of Mexicans living in extreme poverty. The central figure in *The Children of Sánchez* is an authoritarian father who lives in a cramped room together with his many children who, in the recordings, complain about their father and childhood and their father equally complains about them.[73]

Lewis presented *The Children of Sánchez* as if it were a novel, to be read as a literary prose, although it is, in actual fact, a compilation of field research. His book is more interesting as a testimonial literature – if repetitive – than as a pioneering work of *community anthropology*, espousing a controversial theory of 'the culture of poverty', a bleak cul de sac for the have-nots.[74]

Zavattini did what he could for the director Hall Bartlett, given that the screenwriter's reaction to the book was as follows:

> You find yourself in a circle of Hell, a place of endless shouting, weeping, insults, cries of newborn babies, funeral lamentations, maledictions, prayers.[75]

True to his practice, Zavattini visited Mexico City with Bartlett and Anthony Quinn, the Mexican-born Zampanò character in Federico Fellini's *La strada* (1954). Quinn played the father, Jesús Sánchez. Zavattini spent two days talking to Consuelo, the daughter. To his horror, he discovered that most of the family were still living in the same room they had shared for over twenty years.[76] He completed the screenplay by 27 March 1972.[77] After its production was blocked, at last, in 1976, CONACINE, the Mexican state production house, allowed Hall to shoot the interior scenes in their Churubuseo Studios and to film the street scenes.[78] Then it was banned again for years, by government censorship in a nation where democracy consisted in a single party, the PRI (*Partido Revolucionario Institucional*) running the country, from the glorious days of the Mexican Revolution until the year 2000.

17.4 Zavattini's Contribution to Mexican cinema

Zavattini's wrote the scenario for *¡Torero!*, a confessional and personal documentary, a diary-film which was entirely alien to Mexican documentary as it then was, the documentaries produced by Manuel Barbachano Ponce's Teleproducciones. Zavattini was also instrumental in the foundation of the Mexican Federation of Film Clubs in 1955. During his third visit in 1957, he worked with a team of promising young Mexican writers whom Carlos Velo later admitted had been greatly influenced by Zavattini, including people who later became major Mexican authors, such as Carlos Fuentes, Elena Poniatowska,

Gastón García Cantú, Juan de la Cabada and Pepe Revueltas. They had all participated in Zavattini's weekend meetings at Barbachano Ponce's residence.

Carlos Fuentes in *La región más transparente* (1958) was the first to convey in Mexican literature an open critique of Mexico, as he did again in *La muerte de Artemio Cruz* (1962). Zavattini's *raccontini* approach is evident in Cristina Pacheco's novels, which convey through dialogue, the voice and the point of view of working-class women. Poniatowska, considered 'the most significant writer of narrative documentary', according to Velo, also adopted Zavattini's *raccontini* framework and style.[79] She also adopted his aesthetic of urgency. After working with him, she abandoned celebrity interviews for a radical literary ethnography or *testimonio*, in which the subaltern becomes a witness. For example, in *Hasta no verte, Jesús mío* (1969) the protagonist, a washerwoman, tells the story of her experience of the Mexican Revolution and of its aftermath, in the spoken language of the Mexico City working class.[80] While her famous *La noche de Tlatlolco* (1971) was a collection of oral histories of the massacre of students at *Tlatlolco* in 1968, in Mexico, it was Zavattini who pioneered the *testimonio* during his fieldwork for *México mío* and disseminated his ideas through teaching Barbachano Ponce's team of aspiring screenwriters. Poniatowska also absorbed Zavattini's aesthetic of the event, tempered by a poetic version of documentary cinema, to show how historic events are experienced and become personal experience.

After his 1955 departure, apart from the impressive press coverage, only one experimental film, based on Zavattini's ideas, appeared. It was screened on *Canal 4* television.[81] It didn't emanate from Teleproducciones and was most probably made by a group of Mexican enthusiasts who were reported in the press for their plan to make a 16-mm Neo-realist film.[82]

Zavattini also influenced Jaime García Ascot, who resigned from Barbachano Producciones and left Mexico in 1959 to work in Cuba from December 1959 until the first two months of 1960. In Cuba, García Ascot wrote and directed two episodes of *Cuba 58*, following Zavattini's teachings and advice. The next year, García Ascot returned to Mexico, where he formed the *Grupo Nuevo Cine*, together with Carlos Fuentes, Pío Caro Baroja, Francisco Pina and Gabriel García Márquez, all of whom knew Zavattini and, bar the Colombian Márquez, had collaborated with him. García Márquez, who had studied film and screenwriting in Italy, at the Centro Sperimentale di Cinematografia di Roma, and once visited him in his home, in the early 1950s, remembered:[83]

> Cesare Zavattini, our teacher of storyline and screenplay, one of the great names in the history of cinema and the only one who spent time with us students out of class hours. He sought to teach us another perception of life, as well as his craft.[84]

This was the group that published a manifesto and brought out a film journal. Their attempt to launch Mexican New Cinema also shows clear signs of Zavattini's influence.[85] Francisco Pina of *Novedades* had met Zavattini in 1953.

He also organized an important meeting with Zavattini in *Cine Club Progreso*, a club which had fought to establish New Mexican Cinema in 1955, following Zavattini's encouragement. Pío Caro Baroja was the author of the seminal book on Neo-realism published in Mexico, and co-organizer at *Cine Club Progreso*. It was Zavattini who had suggested to them a New Cinema, in Mexico, in the first place, theorized it, and persuaded them to set up the *Federación Mexicana de Cine Clubs*, along the lines of the Circolo Romano del Cinema, thus laying the foundations for fostering and developing film culture in Mexico.[86]

Their print manifesto was accompanied by a film manifesto, written by García Ascot, directed by him and acted by his wife, playing herself in a Zavattinian diary-film: *En el balcón vacío* (1961). The film claimed the validity of a cinema of poetry, putting forward a personal form of documentary, deeply influenced by Zavattini.

En el balcón vacío, like *¡Torero!*, also available online, is a diary-film. García Ascot's wife narrates her personal story of emigration to Mexico from post–Civil War Spain, creating a powerful and intimate self-portrait, along the lines of *¡Torero!* in which, incidentally, García Ascot was also closely involved. It should not come as a surprise, then, that Barbachano Ponce presided over preliminary meetings of the *Grupo Nuevo Cine*, but refused to take on the production of their films.[87] Regrettably, this brave attempt to break through the climate of indifference and of a stifling Mexican industrial closed shop failed miserably.

Transmission to Argentina

18.1 Another transmission route

The case of Argentina is very different. Zavattini only visited Argentina in 1961. In Argentina, the transmission of Neo-realism took a different route, through a personal contact between an Argentinian filmmaker, Fernando Birri, and Zavattini himself. Their unpublished correspondence and Birri's own archive of his activities *La Escuela Documental de Santa Fe* (1964) in the 1950s prove the close connexion between Birri and Zavattini, whom Birri considered not only the father of Neo-realism but also, like Gabriel García Márquez, also his personal, inspirational, teacher. Fer Birri too had studied at the Centro Sperimentale di Cinematografia di Roma.

Birri's extremely long and detailed letters to Zavattini demonstrate to what point Birri assimilated and transmitted to Argentina a particular idea of cinema, a new paradigm, based on a stronger emphasis on the documentary that Zavattini had been advocating in those years in Latin America and Europe. Transmission is directly evidenced in Argentinian photo-documentaries, and later in film documentaries, drawing directly on the framework of Zavattini and Paul Strand's photo-book *Un paese*, discussed in an earlier chapter, and on Birri's direct experience of filmmaking in 1950s Italy, while working on De Sica's *The Roof*, and on his assimilation and deep understanding of Zavattini's *Story of Catherine*, in *Love in the City*.[1]

The earliest concrete proof of a direct connexion between Zavattini and Birri, generally credited as the father of Latin American cinema, dates from 21 May 1955, when Birri congratulated the screenwriter for being awarded the Lenin World Peace Prize (jointly with filmmaker Joris Ivens), but they had already met. Birri later remembered a screening and walking over to speak to Za, as he was usually called.[2]

Birri went to study in Rome in 1950, after discarding IDHEC (Institut des Hautes Études Cinématographiques) in Paris, in favour of the Rome Centro Sperimentale di Cinematografia di Roma, since, in Birri's opinion, as he told Julianne Burton many years later, the New Italian Cinema was 'conquering the cinemas of all over the world'.[3] In 1955, Birri acted in *Gli Sbandati* (1955), the first feature by Citto Maselli, a close friend of Zavattini's and the director of *The Story of Catherine*. After making *The Story of Catherine*, Maselli would often go round to Zavattini's home, at the end of the day for a chat.[4] *Gli Sbandati* brought up the taboo subject of Fascism within the Italian middle class, a film which saw Zavattini's close involvement.[5]

Birri was particularly interested in Zavattini's work, singling out *Love in the City* (1953) as the key Neo-realist film which, he claimed, was 'the most advanced film within the contemporary Neo-realist school of cinematography'.[6] He considered Zavattini 'The leader of the artistic revolution and its major exponent'.[7] That same year, Birri asked Zavattini to put in a good word with Vittorio De Sica, so that he could be given a job in the production of *The Roof* (1956). He then introduced himself to De Sica during the castings at Titanus studios, on 26 September 1955, shortly before the film went into production in October, and, thanks to Zavattini, he was hired as an assistant on the set.[8]

18.2 Birri disseminates Neo-realism in Argentina

The Roof was wrapped up at the end of the Perón dictatorship, during what was called the *Revolución Libertadora*.[9] And Birri returned to Argentina, on 6 April 1956, the day before the end of shooting.[10] On 5 April, he wrote to Zavattini telling him that '*The Roof* is, by far the most useful, clearest demonstration of all I think cinema needs to say'.[11] He considered the film a model of practice: 'Based on this model, and following your teachings, I shall begin my professional life in Argentina.'[12]

Birri was optimistic about the situation in Argentina. As far as he could tell, it could only improve, after a period when the film industry had suffered 'rigid protectionism, leaving us with no legal regulation', as he explained to Zavattini.[13] In Buenos Aires, out of 400 foreign films in circulation, more than half were North American, but only 20 were Italian.[14]

After his departure, the first time Birri met Zavattini again in person was in 1958 and in Rome. However, before and after that date, Birri kept up an intense correspondence with him, asking the Italian screenwriter for advice and sending very long reports on his efforts to promote Neo-realism in Argentina; particularly Zavattini's *in fieri* version, as evidenced in *Love in the City* (1953) and *The Roof* (1953).

From the day he returned to Argentina in 1956, Birri put all his energy into becoming the country's one-man ambassador for Neo-realism, combining a series of articles about the movement with numerous talks given in film clubs. These were the only cultural spaces receptive to the New Cinema. Birri even asked Zavattini to use his influence with the editor of *Cinema Nuovo*, Guido Aristarco, so that he would be tasked with setting up an Argentinian editorial desk and, in that capacity, be commissioned to write a regular column for Zavattini's *Neo-realist Bulletin* (*Bolletino del Neo-realismo*), a four-page insert.[15] Birri also organized frequent screenings of Neo-realist films, prefaced by his introductory talks, as, for example, in 1957, when he went to La Plata to talk about Neo-realism before showing *Sotto il sole di Roma*.[16] Wherever he went as the ambassador, everyone wanted to know 'what made Neo-realism possible?'[17]

> I've given talks in those film clubs before screening Neo-realist films, among such people, in bars, at home, in the University, talking in the street all night long until dawn. They wanted to know absolutely everything and in detail. Is it true that Rossellini writes his dialogues on little bits of paper? Is it true that Zavattini doesn't have a car?[18]

They also asked if it was true the actors were working class and not professionals. Moreover, Birri appeared on radio broadcasts, discussing Neo-realism, and he was asked the same question again and again. His public was curious to know the following:

> 'How could people act who had no experience of acting?' 'How was it possible to make a film with such a simple storyline?' 'How was the screenplay written?'[19] 'Do film crews really have an emotional stake in their work?' 'Was it true that the first Neo-realist films were made with only a couple of nails, a hammer and a lot of good will?'[20]

Birri's stock answer was that there was no secret formula, only conviction and the effort filmmakers made to increase awareness of social reality.[21]

In his new role as a go-between, Birri gave special importance to writing articles and giving talks about *The Roof*, as one would expect, given his direct involvement in its production. The kudos of working with De Sica was pivotal in raising his profile in the Argentinian film milieu, as was his personal contact with Zavattini. Soon after his arrival, Birri was appointed the arts editor of *Lyra*, the Argentinian magazine with the biggest circulation in the country, founded in the 1940s.[22] Birri's main focus in writing about Neo-realism in *Lyra* was to prove that here was an international, alternative cinema which could be imported into Argentina.[23]

His campaign to gain a professional profile in Argentina, based on his participation in the making of *The Roof*, began almost immediately. Birri invited Zavattini to write a Preface to the first of a series of articles on Neo-realism and *The Roof*. One month after his return, in May 1956, he asked De Sica to include his name in the credits of *The Roof*, a validation, which, he claimed, would give his voice more authority.[24] He argued that it would also serve Zavattini's international plans, enabling Birri to be the voice of Neo-realism in Argentina, which he called 'the future battlefield for a new Neo-realist front'.[25]

'I kept faith with the intellectual and ethical responsibilities I acquired in Italy from the school of Neo-realism', he assured Zavattini.[26] That was, he argued, only his part of the bargain. So now he expected validation from the Italian Neo-realists. Birri was invited to present *The Roof* at a first, restricted, screening at the

Italian Embassy in Buenos Aires and hence at the public première, organized by the film clubs.[27] But on the eve of the screening, his presentation was cancelled, because the letter from Zavattini or De Sica confirming his contribution to *The Roof* still had not arrived. Birri then faced growing scepticism and complained to Zavattini that now he was being called a cheat in public. In March 1957, he told Zavattini: 'At this stage of our cinema, the screening of *The Roof* will be like casting a seed in fertile land. It will serve to guide us, to give more substance to concepts and discussions of a certain kind through sight and sound.'[28] But matters only got worse when the Argentinian copy of *The Roof* was screened, and there was no sign of his name in the credits. He'd failed to have his name added. All he could do was request a testimonial letter.[29] At last, in May 1957, much to his relief, two testimonials arrived, one from Zavattini and the other from De Sica, confirming his involvement on the set.[30] Just how important this must have been is made clear by the fact that in August 1957 not only did he publish the letters in translation in a local, Santa Fe daily, but he went to the trouble of also including photographic reproductions of the Italian originals.[31] He was vindicated.

> As far as the loving respect with which I intervened in *The Roof* is concerned, in assisting the production, day in, day out, no one can deny it any longer, after your letters. Those who are feeling put out by the campaign for *a healthy national, realist, and critical cinema*, and continue to do so will be seriously deterred.[32] Whereas the others who, as I said to you, are supporting the idea we are defending together, this group of young promoters of a new Argentinian cinematography, have breathed a sigh of relief. [...] All the things I was saying on the radio, in the press, in the coffee bars, about you and about Italian Neo-realism and about the living, vivifying, lesson coming from contemporary Italy, was all true.[33]

If it is undeniable that by 1957, Neo-realism as a historic movement had been defeated in Italy, Birri made it clear that it was a contemporary model for Argentinian cinema. In Buenos Aires alone, three films scripted by Zavattini were screened the same week of July 1957 (*Bellissima*, *Teresa venerdì* and *Miracle in Milan*). This latter film was screened in five cinemas in the capital and many more on the outskirts of town.[34] In the meantime, Birri wrote a screenplay for a feature film about a pregnant girl working in a slaughterhouse where forty cows were slaughtered every hour. It owed much to Zavattini's investigative method of working, writing fiction based on 'very extensive field research'.[35]

18.3 Adopting the Neo-realist photo-documentary

In addition to promoting Neo-realism, shortly after his return to Argentina, Birri approached the Universidad Nacional del Litoral at Santa Fe, his hometown. At the time, it was already a popular university, established in the early twentieth century which offered extramural courses to working people, night classes, essentially, and awarding degrees. His father had graduated there and Fernando Birri had also been awarded a degree in Jurisprudence in the 1940s, before travelling to Europe and choosing to study film in Italy. Birri met the director of the Department of Social Sciences, Ángela Romera Vera, who invited him to run an evening class on filmmaking.[36] He assumed that no more than twenty students would enrol. One can only imagine his surprise when 135 appeared. This was the first of many more courses in film which he organized. To structure the course, he followed the same curriculum established by the former director of the Centro Sperimentale di Cinematografia di Roma, Luigi Chiarini, and even adopting Chiarini's textbook. It seems more than just a coincidence that the book was translated in Buenos Aires that same year, as *El cine en el problema del arte*.[37]

As for his workshops and practicals, he got his students to research and produce photo-documentaries, which, by Birri's own admission, closely followed the Zavattini model of *Italia mia-Un paese*, in the form in which it had appeared in *Cinema Nuovo*. He recognized this when he reported to Zavattini that his students were developing along the lines he and other Neo-realists had established, in the battle for Neo-realism in Italy.[38]

On his first evening, Birri began his class using a battered old projector to show two of the *Cinema Nuovo* photo-documentaries, *Un paese* and 'I bambini di Napoli' ('The Children of Naples').[39] The slide show included a translation of the words into Spanish. In the context of a new course, his was an excellent choice to garner support from the university and particularly the Sociology department, which employed him. There was total silence in the auditorium and later much excitement and many questions. The students talked until 1.00 am the next morning. As he told Zavattini, he saw his task as assimilating the Neo-realist lesson, not imitating it.[40]

Because Litoral University had no equipment they could borrow, the students enlisted the help of the Santa Fe Photo Club and used their cameras and the Club's technical know-how to 'rediscover their own town', as he put it, concentrating on photographing the poor districts on its outskirts.[41] A week later, Birri projected the students' photo-documentaries. 'However incomplete, however imperfect the results, nevertheless, they work', Birri reported back to Zavattini. These photo-documentaries were so well received by his Sociology department that they were published three days later by the university.[42] A paragraph from his pamphlet *Los fotodocumentales* (1956) reads like the opening words of the opening sequence of *Love in the City*:

These are the men, the women, the children, the squares, the narrow lanes, the roads, the carts, the fires, the markets, bridges, islands, labour, miseries, contradictions, whom we are submitting to your attention today.[43]

Thus shadowing and cohabitation, Zavattini's ethnographic approach to photography and cinematography, was introduced to Argentina. Integral to it was the personal film diary, expounded in the Italian writer's cinematic public diary. 'People can write their own daily biography', Birri, directly inspired by his mentor, explained in the pamphlet. 'This way, we can come to know the Argentinian man through his problems, his suffering and his hopes.'[44]

Under the auspices of the Sociology department, Birri's students wrote texts for their photo-documentary assignments, based on their interviews with the people they had shadowed in their cinematic fieldwork. Visualizing their ethnographic methodology, and using photography to document ordinary people's present and past, which was then all compacted on a page and edited in a comprehensible narrative, was the perfect vehicle for what the department was about, and for the working model which Birri could present, promote and disseminate. The first viewing public of the *fotodocumentales* was, as one might have guessed, made up of faculty and namely, the members of the Sociology department of the university.

But Birri also planned to use the photo-documentary format or *fotodocumental*, as a feasibility study to seek funding for a film. Not unlike Zavattini and the Italian Neo-realists, he too had to defend his choice of pointing the camera at extreme poverty, as a way of documenting contemporary Argentina. Ethnographic field research served 'to show a section of the social composition of contemporary Argentinian life'.[45] Not that the faculty members in the Department of Social Sciences needed convincing.

> When you make such a commitment, you discover a human continent which has been entirely ignored by politics which busies itself with government programmes and official directives. A colourless human multitude which lives in conditions that far outreach poverty, terribly deprived from anything resembling social solidarity.[46]

The loose structure of evening classes were soon given an administrative shape, for the sake of continuity. They became the *Escuela Documental de Santa Fe*. The *fotodocumentales* were intended and planned as a first stage towards filmmaking, just as Michele Gandin had explained to the readers of *Cinema Nuovo* in presenting a photo-documentary about Danilo Dolci's ethnographic work. Birri followed suit, the following year. The Argentine *fotodocumentales* also consisted of notebooks, containing stories, photographs, locations and portraits for potential casting.[47]

Birri was very skilled at promoting these ideas outside the university too, within specialized film circles, using the student projects as his vehicle. In January 1958, he and his students organized the first *fotodocumentales* exhibition.[48] It wasn't long before he was invited to the SODRE (Society of Radio-Electric Transmissions) *Festival Internacional de Cine Documental y Experimental* in Montevideo. SODRE, which brought together the best in experimental art and theatre.[49] And it was at the 1958 edition of this Festival that PRIDAL (*Productores y Realizadores Independientes de America Latina*) was formed, with the participation of Nelson Pereira dos Santos from Brazil, Patricio Kaulen from Bolivia and the Argentinians Leopoldo Torre Nilsson and Simon

Feldman.[50] The 1958 SODRE Festival attracted the best of experimental cinema: among the screening were Brazilian Nelson Pereira dos Santos's Neo-realist *Rio Zona Norte* (1957), similar to his earlier *Rio Cuarenta Grados* (1955), and Alberto Miller's *Cantegriles* (1958), the first New Cinema film from Uruguay, an eight-minute documentary short film, showing two clashing and contemporary realities: a shanty town and the Cantegril Country Club, at Punta del Este.[51]

18.4 Photo-documentary as script: *Tire dié*

The most famous photo-documentary was their first, *Tire dié* ('Throw me a Dime'), about children begging along a train line, at exactly the point where the train had to slow down to walking pace to cross a bridge, adjacent to a cluster of makeshift shacks. The captions in the text are inclusive, letting the children tell their own stories and placing them in a social context. Here was a 'social fact', pinpointed by ethnographic field research, following the photographs-plus-extended-captions format of *Un paese*.

Some of the same students, and new cohorts, then developed the photographic scenario into a filmed documentary. They produced and filmed it themselves, working in the evenings, from 1956 to 1958, and in all seasons. Birri's role was limited to coordinating and recording their work in progress, using the students' field notes, extracts of which he later published in *La Escuela Documental de Santa Fe* (1964). There were as many scripts as there were stories being told to the students, during their trips to the shanty towns. They always filmed on location and later responded among themselves in fervent discussions about the work, the problems they faced and technical issues.[52] The first stage of editing *Tire dié* was done in Buenos Aires, combining footage from the different lines of enquiry the students had pursued.[53]

In addition to contributing a framework and theoretical underpinning to the *Escuela Documental*, Zavattini had a decisive role to play in the final editing of the film. On 29 June 1959, Birri took a copy to Rome for a private screening for Zavattini. The first version was exactly fifty-nine minutes long. Birri was defensive about this first version, reminding the Italian screenwriter of the technical and organizational challenges and of the didactic context of the film's making. He then took note of absolutely everything Zavattini had to say.[54]

It is important to bear in mind that Zavattini's professional activities extended to mercilessly editing the footage of some of the most important films he worked on, such as *Sciuscià*, *Bicycle Thieves*, *Umberto D.* and Blasetti's *First Communion*. On this occasion, he carried out what can only be described as a verbal montage or post-production edit. In practice, he whittled the film down to thirty-three minutes and suggested removing all the repetitions. As a result, there would be only one scene – the last – featuring the train crossing the bridge. This scene would consequently have more resonance. He also advised Birri to pare down the lengthy interviews, and finally, to cluster them at the beginning of the film. A year later, the final material edit of the film was completed. On 27 July 1960, Birri confirmed to Zavattini that he had carried out point by point all the suggestions the Italian screenwriter had made.[55]

At the time, Birri was willing to recognize Zavattini's legacy and direct influence, including his involvement in *Tire dié*, telling him that the film would serve to show that Neo-realist ethics had survived the passage of time and stating that

> *Tire dié* was directly connected (*se vincula directamente*) to *Un paese* and the *Cinema Nuovo* photo-documentaries, which sought to develop the Neo-realist experience, at a time when it was no longer possible to do so.[56]

Roberto Raschella, a discerning Argentinian critic, and foreign correspondent for *Cinema Nuovo*, considered *Tire dié* on a par artistically with documentaries by Joris Ivens and Robert Flaherty, but insisted that the theory underpinning *Tire dié*, its conceptual framework, owed these pioneers nothing, but everything to Zavattini.[57] As for John Grierson, the other giant of documentary, he is never mentioned. He wrote that *Tire dié* was obviously linked to the photo-documentary *Un paese* (1955) and to *Italia mia*, the basis for *Un paese*, but also to Zavattini's film manifesto *La Storia di Caterina* ('The Story of Catherine') in *Love in the City*.[58] Raschella concluded that *Tire dié* adopted Zavattini's rejection of a dramatic, comic or tragic narrative structure of reality, preferring 'a reduction of reality'. In the course of the transmission from the European continent to Latin America, Raschella added that 'the old wine of reality is new to Argentinian cinema'.[59]

18.5 Critical and popular Neo-realism: Birri's *Los Inundados*

The students' field research at the Escuela Documental led to the feature film *Los Inundados* (1961) (*The Flooded*), produced using the university's resources, and justified by its dual purpose, artistic and pedagogical. The film was also based on a photo-documentary *Los Inundados* (*The Flooded*) (1958), then developed into *La Inundación en Santa Fe* (1959), a ten-minute 35mm documentary.[60] This fieldwork was the basis which Birri combined with an episodic narrative structure and storyline inspired by a short story about flooding in Santa Fe, by Miguel Ángel Correa (1881–1943), known by the pseudonym Mateo Booz.[61] He tried to get Zavattini to vet his screenplay before the film went into production, but couldn't. *Los Inundados* shared with *Tire dié* some of the actors, none of whom were professionals, a student film crew, serving as assistants to a professional crew, and 3,500 *Santafesinos* living locally.

The film centres on one of the families displaced by flooding. The family winds up on a goods train, travelling from one end of the line to the other, on account of bad paperwork. Birri's Neo-realist gaze also dramatizes how to con the locals when they seek political support before the local elections, using the promise to address the flooding problem as a lever to get elected. It shows how Argentinian media represents homeless families as hopeless cases, and as an unruly, potentially dangerous, crowd, deservedly living in poverty. *Los Inundados* is undoubtedly antithetical to Torre Nielsson's elitist art films, but the film went down well with the Argentinian popular audience.[62]

The film's Neo-realist matrix was soon noticed by Italian filmmaker Elio Petri, who viewed it at the Mar del Plata Film Festival in 1962, and *Cine cubano* also picked up on it in 1963, as the title of their article suggests: 'Neorrealismo argentino: *Los Inundados*.'[63] Birri considered *Los Inundados* 'the film-manifesto of our movement, under the banner of a national, realist, critical and popular cinema'.[64] Though in cinema history it was overshadowed by *Tire dié*.

Birri kept most, if not all, of the files, papers, documents, relating to his teaching, at the Universidad Popular de Santa Fe, and collected them for publication, by the university, in a print run of 500 copies, with the title *La Escuela Documental de Santa Fe* (1964). Not a moment too soon! The growing political instability, and threat of an impending military coup, made him decide to leave Argentina. The coup took place soon after he left the country to find initial refuge in Brazil. Again and again, his book openly acknowledges Zavattini's direct influence, direct transmission and legacy. But he chose not to include any of this history from the interviews given in English many years later, even when pressed.

The correspondence between Birri and Zavattini, always prompted by Birri, lasted until the early 1980s, when the Argentinian filmmaker asked his permission to waive his author's rights so that he could make an adaptation of Zavattini's *Io sono il diavolo* (*I am the Devil*), containing some of his *raccontini*, his minimalist stories, dating from the 1930s to the early 1940s.[65] Birri got as far as an adaptation, written in collaboration with Luciano Valletta, and even as far as a pre-treatment.[66] It was too late, perhaps. Zavattini had mostly lost interest in the cinema, after writing and directing *La veritàaaa* (*The Truuuuth*).

Years after Zavattini's death, Birri worked on what he described as the 'Dossier Projecto Cesare Zavattini' or 'El Projecto Za', which materialized as a collaborative film, *Za2005*, a compilation of excerpts of Latin American films, including *Tire dié, Los Inundados* and *Memorias de subdesarollo* – a posthumous tribute to Zavattini and an acknowledgement of his cinematic legacy.[67]

Experimenting with non-fiction
in the 1960s

19.1 *Censorship 1960*

In 1960, Zavattini left Cuba with a heavy heart. There was still so much to do. His screenplay for the feature film *El Joven Rebelde* for ICAIC could be done remotely, and by correspondence. Even so, it meant abandoning the field work, the teaching, and developing other Cuban projects, to go back to work on an adaptation of a novel, *La ciociara*, by Alberto Moravia, into the feature film *Two Women* (1960).

In Cuba, Zavattini had given as much as he had gained from the experience of teaching, writing and listening, and getting to grips with the purpose of cinema in an exceptional, revolutionary, context. But he now had to attend to the bread and butter side of his work and *Two Women* was one of several literary adaptations he did at the time. In the event, although he complained about *Two Women*, in his correspondence, *Two Women* won an Oscar and was one of four top box-office films in 1960, despite its ugly theme, rape in German-occupied Italy during the latter years of the Second World War, and mostly thanks to the lead actress, Sofia Loren.[1]

Another bread and butter job was his contribution to the screenplay for Carlo Lizzani's *L'oro di Roma* (1960) ('The Gold of Rome'), about the German persecution and spoliation of the Jews of Rome in 1943. He wasn't interested in either of these adaptations. Nor was he that keen on reworking an old scenario of his for the film *Il giudizio universale* (1961) (*The Last Judgement*). It had nothing to do with Zavattini's current plans, after working in Cuba. *The Last Judgement*, also directed by De Sica, is based on his scenario and screenplay and shares the same vein of magic realism as *Miracle in Milan*, but that was then. He had written the scenario years before, and magic realism was no longer appropriate, as far as he was concerned.

At this point, in the 1960s, what was a matter of 'urgency', and what inspired him the most, was the 'social fact'. So he somehow had to juggle *We Women* for De Sica, with setting up an Italia-Cuba Association at the same time, and lobbying for it too, while also finishing off the ICAIC feature *El Joven Rebelde*, and working on an entirely different scenario, *Censorship 1960*, in which he argued for the need for immediate action, and, exceptionally, using cinema as agitprop and included a proposal for counter-cinema.

After all, he had just witnessed the Cuban Revolution, and, moreover, had directed discussions at the new Cuban ICAIC, where he had defended the role of oblique political cinema, be it fiction or non-fiction, and had led discussions on art and autonomy versus art and commitment.

What prompted Zavattini to write *Censorship 1960*, planned as a twenty-minute, medium-length film, was yet another attack against the freedom of artistic expression. This was the 'social fact' that demanded a response from Italian filmmakers, in his view. Needless to say, with the passage of time, the Italian political climate of 1960 has largely been forgotten. However, it is worth remembering that that year Fellini's *La dolce vita* was censored, and Visconti's film *Rocco and his Brothers* was also banned, as well as *Arialda* (1960), by Giovanni Testori, a play directed by Visconti.

There were several other victims of the Centre Right's hold on Italian cinema, and the quite sudden increase of censorship. *Censorship 1960* mattered to him enough to include it in his first anthology of his scenarios, published in 1979. After all, his own work was censored several times and, for example, the bite of *The Roof* was attenuated by censorship and even self-censorship. Over the years, Zavattini had devoted what time he could spare to fighting official film censorship in Italy, by founding and building up professional associations to combat it. The scenario opens with this consideration:

> This idea came from the need to create an object, let's call it that, which, in no uncertain terms, would serve as focus for a freer cinematography and which would combat the worst overt or covert cases of today's censorship. For years, filmmakers have been fighting against today's system of censorship, but have never reached breaking point. The system is a political system, in so far as it represents a specific interpretation of national life as it is deemed that it should be, in accordance with the views and the practical interests of the dominant class and dominant party.[2]

And continues:

> The purpose of this documentary is to respond to the need for a text in which all the members of Italian culture, filmmakers included, can recognize the contingent state of contemporary Italian cinema, while also using it as a common point of departure to put up a fight and reinstate the freedom of expression.

19.2 A film adaptation and a television documentary

Of course, no producer came forward to back *Censorship 1960*. However, the following year Zavattini adapted *Le italiane e l'amore* (1961) ('Italian Women and Love'), featuring the correspondence from the Letters page of a popular weekly illustrated magazine, *Vie Nuove*. This project was also closer to his interests and was initiated even before he went to Cuba, as was another project, for television, made in collaboration with Mario Soldati, the investigative television series *Chi legge? Viaggio lungo il Tirreno* (1960) ('Who can read? A journey down the Tyrrhenian coast'). Both went into production. The eight-episode television series was investigative journalism, stretching from end to end of the Italian peninsula, to establish the scale of literacy in Italy and how Italians of different social classes related to the written word. 'Who can read?' is yet another fragment of *Italia mia*.[3]

Developing a culture of asking people for their opinion, based on investigative journalism into personal life and its links with society, was something that Zavattini had pioneered before and after the war. It was he who had created a public forum in the popular press for reader participation in the 1940s and earlier still, at a time when the very idea of interpellating ordinary people and publishing their views in the wide circulation popular press of the time was unheard of. Before going back to Cuba for the last time, he launched a column in the Communist *Vie Nuove*, which ran from 1956 to 1957, 'Domande agli uomini' ('Questions for Men'), collecting interviews with ordinary people who set their own agendas in their responses to a set questionnaire.[4] His was the editorial strategy behind it, acting as its editor, and supervising the work of his two interviewers.[5] *Vie Nuove* was also publishing agony aunt personal letters, addressed to a journalist Gabriella Parca, who collected and edited her letters column and published it in book form, with a Preface by Zavattini. This book, *Le italiane si confessano* ('Confessions of Italian Women'), soon became a bestseller, for exposing the problems faced by young Italian women in 1950s Italy.[6] The content of the letters is personal, intimate and confessional. The confessional mode of address was something Zavattini had theorized, along with the diary form, and both had found their expression in *Vie Nuove*, a favourite stomping ground for Zavattini. He adopted this framework to make a film, drawing on the *Vie Nuove* agony aunt correspondence, to engage eleven film directors to make as many episodes.[7] Yet another experiment, turning real-world problems into cinematic stories. But Zavattini was critical of the result. In the shift from genuine testimonial accounts to a cinematic reconstruction of events, the documentary edge was mostly lost.

19.3 *The Mysteries of Rome*

Zavattini decided to do away with stories altogether for his next related project, *The Mysteries of Rome*. It would develop the ethnographic-cum-reportage seam he'd established in *Italia mia* and its offshoots: the film-book *Un paese, Portrait of an Italian Village*, and the experimental manifesto-film *Love in the City*. Initially, Carlo Ponti offered to finance *The Mysteries of Rome* in July 1961. But the producer insisted that Zavattini work from a written screenplay, for at least four of the proposed episodes. He also demanded a reconstruction of events.[8]

As a compromise, in September, Zavattini submitted no fewer than fifteen ideas, to give Ponti something specific, as to what he was trying to do.[9] He planned to approach the city with 'the freedom of a diary', he told Ponti.[10] This was exactly the opposite of what Ponti wanted to hear. Again, as he had done in Mexico with Carlos Velo and their producer Manolo Barbachano, Zavattini had to insist on an open-ended documentary, based on the idea that what could be determined by research would have to stand the test of the face-to-face encounter between filmmaker, subject and situation, refusing re-enactments and refusing to substitute ordinary people with actors.

When Ponti changed his mind, Zavattini didn't give up. His old friend, the producer Alfredo Guarini stepped in, offering to act as an intermediary with Titanus.[11] Nothing came of it, or of Fellini's interest, as happened to all the projects filmmakers submitted to Fellini's CineRiz production company. At last, in March 1962, the producer Achille Pazzi, who had financed Antonioni's *Il Grido* (1957) (*The Outcry*), stepped in.[12] The following month, Zavattini's team of young filmmakers, who had worked in television and cinema, began shadowing the city, looking for 'social facts', symptomatic stories which would never make the headlines. The film was shot between June and August 1962.[13] By the end of December 1962, Zavattini had finished editing the film.[14]

The Mysteries of Rome begins with an aerial view of the city from a helicopter.[15] Its route maps a city which appears strangely devoid of monuments. Instead, you see the boundaries between middle- and working-class areas, two coexisting realities, as you do, if fleetingly, in *The Roof*: shanty towns and middle-class districts. Cinematic space develops outwards into a mosaic structure, by accretion, replacing the abstract, aerial city with the city understood as lived space. The film ventures into the lived spaces of children playing football in an orphanage, mutilated by wartime bombs. It leads the way to the sounds and fears of giving birth; to a doctor visiting a poor household; to the notorious building in Via Tasso, remembered as the former Gestapo headquarters in occupied Rome, accompanied by a discreet voice-over, recalling how neighbours remembered the sounds of torture leaking out of the holes in the walls. We listen to blood donors selling their blood for cash, to exploited copyists; to casual road construction workers waiting to be hired on the street corner and showing the interviewer their injuries, caused by lack of health and safety measures on site. We get a glimpse of the developing world, through photos of destitution at the United Nations' offices in Rome.

Taken as a whole, these sorties into the everyday produce a network of interrelated spaces of the lived city which populate the mapping of spaces made by the opening aerial sequence. The closing aerial shot produces a cinematic allegory, by travelling over the same spaces. A final voice-over singles out each one with the word 'here' (*qui*). Here is another lived space, though obscured by distance.

The Mysteries of Rome seeks to uncover, in the public and private space, what is invisible to civil society, to create a Cinematic Diary of a city.[16] One might assume that, since the city in question was the Eternal City, the documentary would dwell on the city's ancient history, its Republican, then Imperial, and later Papal splendour. But no; the viewer is denied any panoramic views of Rome's monuments over layers of time. Nor does *The Mysteries of Rome* have much in common with pre-war documentary films about cities, known as City Symphonies, after *Berlin. A City Symphony* (1929), because it prefers to tackle the city's contradictions and collective memory, to 'break the barriers of conformism', instead of perpetuating the stereotypes and the folklore of mainstream representations of urban space, as Zavattini told an interviewer.[17]

It might be tempting to relate *The Mysteries of Rome* to *Chronicle of a Summer* (1960), Jean Rouch's and Edgar Morin's manifesto for *cinema verité* or Chris Marker's rejoinder, *Le Joli Mai* (1962), but *The Mysteries of Rome* belongs to an earlier, pioneering ethnographic debate and related discoveries, closer to Ernesto de Martino's empirical research, based on Gramsci's sociopolitical outlook. Its genealogy is to be traced right back to *Italia mia*, originally envisaged by Zavattini as early as 1944.

19.4 Zavattini and ethnographer Josué de Castro

In relation to *The Mysteries of Rome*, Zavattini referenced in passing the Brazilian medical doctor and ethnographer Josué de Castro and his groundbreaking *Geography of Hunger*, first published in Brazil in 1946. Zavattini had met De Castro in person in 1961, after corresponding with him in 1960, for a documentary version of his book. His mapping technique (showing where exactly hunger is to be found and what kind of hunger it is, to produce 'a map of misery') confirmed his own *Italia mia* cinematic ethnographic approach. Furthermore, De Castro's analysis and proposal for radical change was well known within Italian Left-wing circles, ever since it was translated into Italian in 1954. De Castro applied human geography, but turned it on its head, replacing conventional descriptive methods with interpretative social science, to consider human poverty and distress, thus moving away from contemporary geographical studies of human accomplishment. Everything about the man appealed to Zavattini's experimental intervention. His research geared towards 'a reckoning', demonstrating how colonialism had produced the universal hunger of starvation, the outcome of natural catastrophe, but especially 'hidden hunger' or malnutrition.[18] What was also appealing to Zavattini was that De Castro hadn't written just a history of hunger, a feat in itself, but a geography about the present, a study of living reality; an analysis of 'social facts'.

The Mysteries of Rome, as far as Zavattini's plans went, at least, would apply to Rome De Castro's approach to urban space, applying the same extraordinary geopolitical mapping De Castro had used to chart the extent and causes of world hunger.[19] Zavattini also planned, and therefore, in accordance to his usual practice, theorized, a concrete, empirical project, drawing on his personal territorial and social knowledge of the city, combined with preliminary research, based on the press, magazines and fieldwork. This enabled him to develop a cognitive map of the city, linking known activities to specific places, one which did not coincide with existing media stereotypes. De Castro's influence is also directly visible in the above-mentioned episode, linking the Italian capital to Europe and the majority world. The Food and Agricultural Organization offices appear on the screen, while someone explains the nature of the problem, leafing through photographs of malnutrition and starvation. Just as de Castro's mapping highlights the conflicts and contradictions concerning 'hidden hunger' or malnutrition, Zavattini's mapping of *The Mysteries of Rome* highlights the 'contradictions' of urban space, not during the immediate post-war period, but during the emerging economic boom of the beginning of the 1960s.[20]

19.5 Mapping the city

Mapping the city meant building on the realization that the city is a divided urban space in which, as Zavattini told an interviewer, *anomie*, beliefs, cynicism and faith, poverty and wealth coexist.[21] His intervention sought to break 'the barriers of conformism' and challenge the stereotypes and folklore of mainstream representations of urban space.[22] Rome was a dialectical space. *The Mysteries of Rome* would be a constant tension towards the discovery of the city's contradictions or 'secrets'.[23] For example, was Catholicism the only form of spirituality in town? *The Mysteries of Rome* investigated minority forms of worship. Lori Mazzetti, British Free Cinema pioneer and co-signatory of the Free Cinema Manifesto, interviewed people attending a Pentecostal meeting at Quadraro, while her colleagues interviewed a spiritual healer.[24] Paolo Nuzzi investigated illegal abortions and the plight of couples unfamiliar with birth control methods, and the root cause, poverty.[25] Luigi di Gianni interviewed the women who worked at the same shore of the Tiber as the prostitute Filomena Porcari, murdered two years earlier.[26]

Zavattini wanted to interview Pasolini and get him to speak openly about homosexuality. Needless to say, this was a taboo subject for Italian society in 1962.[27] The interview didn't go ahead, but Zavattini's suggestion fed into Pasolini's *Comizi d'amore* (1964) 'Love Meetings', which adopted Zavattini's investigative approach for a gentle set of interviews, mostly about male sexuality, conducted with strangers, young Italians Pasolini had approached in different parts of Italy, adopting and adapting Zavattini's *Italia mia*'s investigative and ethnographic shadowing and journey structure.

Just as he had done with *Love in the City*, Zavattini treated *The Mysteries of Rome* as if it were a single-issue magazine.[28] His was the approach of a former editorial director who had run newsrooms in 1930s Milan and who had initiated and overseen collaborative projects, before and after the war. For *The Mysteries of Rome*, he set up a main desk in the production house, so that the fifteen young filmmakers, many of whom were already working for Italian state television, acted as if they were reporters gathering news to fit into allocated pages. The production house doubled up as a safe haven, available to all the filmmakers at any time of the day or night.[29] Indeed, the film would be 'of the order of the newspaper', Zavattini said.[30] His reporter-filmmakers would be reconciling *immediatezza*, or immediacy, with *giudizio critico*, critical judgement, and would work from the particular or empirical phenomenon, to suggest the general.[31] They formed separate film crews and worked on the preliminary field research with Zavattini, feeding them into the masterplan.[32]

The early planning stages became a teaching experience for the documentary filmmakers involved in the project, no different in this respect from the workshops the screenwriter had run in Mexico and in Cuba. Once again, Zavattini taught the importance of approaching filmed subjects with empathy and respect, questioning from the very outset any filmmaker's attitude and intentions in approaching new situations. Once again, he demanded from each of his collaborators a sense of solidarity and patience, the willingness to engage in private conversations, and to accept no for an answer.[33]

This is what it meant to make contact with the Other. It was vital to treat people as intelligent subjects worthy of respect. It was preferable to interview people on camera, whenever possible.[34] He told his team that they were to discriminate between surface appearance and the underlying city, hidden from view, but a repository of lives, memory and experience.

In this respect, Zavattini was providing an alternative to the superficial approach adopted by newsreels and state television, which had been introduced only six years earlier on a single channel, RAI 1, under the tight control of the Christian Democrats. Because the powerful new medium had the potential of reaching into people's homes, it was a new challenge for the government, which consequently favoured escapist programming – game shows like *Lascia or raddoppia*, satirized by the semiotician and media expert Umberto Eco at the time, comedies and showgirls, interspersed with government bulletins which were masquerading as news. From Zavattini's viewpoint, making such choices had to be opposed for two reasons: on the one hand, it would only favour the process of forgetting contemporary history, namely the trauma of war and Fascism; on the other hand, the problems of contemporary society would be ignored. *The Mysteries of Rome* would inevitably face obstruction from public institutions who were reluctant to being transparent within the social sphere.[35] And it did on several occasions.

Zavattini argued that beyond Rome's picturesque appearance and its representations was the unknown modern city. To discover it would take *conoscenza* or knowledge – by which Zavattini meant research – and *convivenza*, coexistence, the outcome of shadowing, or *pedinamento*, an operative metaphor for a cinema of encounter, of patience, of staying with the scene, as willing participants relating with the people they were filming, of listening to the other and treating her as the same; a cinema of discovery. He welcomed the element of chance, *il caso*, or the unexpected, as an integral part of the artistic process.[36] In the event, circumstances made *pedinamento* far from easy. They often met with reticence from officials, as Zavattini had anticipated, but also from the people living in poverty.

In his scenario for this experimental documentary, Zavattini elicits a sense of physical presence, of being there, through a phenomenological feel for the city, for its sights and sounds. The scenario conjures them up in such surprising detail as to suggest that the written guidelines are more than guidelines. In more ways than one, it was Zavattini who directed *The Mysteries of Rome*.[37] His was the idea and most of the research. It was he who shaped the sequencing of episodes and even decided which cuts to make during the editing, for which he was solely responsible. This was also the view of Ansano Giannarelli, the closest of the documentary filmmakers to Zavattini, who spent long, late-night, preparatory sessions held in the writer's home. Zavattini himself was directing the film, by acting out proposed scenes. And ten years earlier, Luigi Chiarini's prefatory note to Zavattini's scenario and screenplay for *Umberto D.* had already made the point that the screenwriter's involvement in filmmaking extended to shaping the films he worked on, to the point of being an unacknowledged director.[38]

While it is true to say that there was no screenplay, his practice was to dictate the first draft of his screenplays. In this case, it wasn't typed up, but for Giannarelli the sessions were so detailed as to constitute a virtual form of directing by proxy, so that the filmmakers working in the field were acting vicariously on his behalf, more in the capacity of cameramen than directors.[39]

One example Giannarelli remembered was the night Zavattini imagined, acted out and provided the voice-over, for a single long take about the Gestapo headquarters in Rome. It was so vivid as to make those present feel that Zavattini himself was filming it there and then. His scenario visualizes close-ups of fleeting anonymous faces, taxi drivers watching the rich strutting down the wealthy Via Veneto at night; describing with words the sounds of children coming out of school, the sight and visual impact of the city as it shifts from day to spectral night, in the course of its compressed twenty-four-hour time frame.[40]

The scenario frequently makes appeal to the sense of hearing; Zavattini's virtual, or verbalized, image is often accompanied by virtual sound: he describes the clanging of milk crates when they are loaded onto lorries or the deafening noise of a jet landing at Fiumicino airport; he recalls the insults hurled across the notorious Cenci restaurant; all functioning as sonic shocks between adjoining shot sequences, already imagined.[41] Sometimes his spatial practice is to point to symbolic space, one devoid of accompanying dialogue or interviews: for example, the law courts are presented in writing visually, as a combination of huge empty halls and small figures.[42] The scenario is also very visual: again and again, he conjures up visions, rather than dialogues. For example, internal official spaces featuring dramatic differences in scale, high ceilings and long hallways dwarfing ghostly barristers draped in black gowns. These are already intercut (on paper) with scenes taking place outside the building, signifying the shift from abstract impression to concrete situation. His writing shows how the bureaucracy of public administration can become a shot of rows and rows of 'silent' archives, followed by one of interminable clusters of rubber stamps in the Ministry of Foreign Affairs where 1,000 candidates take an exam for only 10 jobs.[43] All this on paper.

19.6 From non-fiction to fiction: *Assault on Television*

Coordinating *The Mysteries of Rome* and directing it by proxy, while facing constant harassment from the police and the authorities to prevent the film from going ahead, must have been a frustrating experience. Zavattini sought refuge in fiction, as a means to critique Italian media, and particularly state-owned Italian television, as promising a medium as it was disappointing showing few signs in the early 1960s of fulfilling its potential. The outcome was the fictional *Assalto alla TV* (*Assault on Television*).[44]

A bit of context. The same year, ever the attentive cultural observer, Zavattini had spoken about television, but not to rule it out, as, ever since the 1930s, he had championed visual culture, as a key expression of popular culture. In 1961, he was interviewed by the Communist daily *L'Unità*, in a topical public debate about the growing phenomenon of television.

Yes, television had been a disappointment. In the eight years since its launch, it had been a source of misinformation and a pernicious influence on public opinion, with an ever-growing body of viewers of mostly, with few exceptions, game shows and appealing to the lowest common denominator of taste in entertainment-based programming. He questioned the choices made by its managers and pointed the finger at the ivory tower of the Italian intellectual class, which looked down on what they considered low culture, popular culture and, therefore, not worthy of critical attention, in a form of misplaced elitism.

And yet, Zavattini could see that its potential was there for the taking. Together with Mario Soldati, in 1958 he had created a television series about literacy in Italy, *Chi legge? Viaggio lungo il Tirreno*, or *Who reads? Voyage along the Tyrrhenian Sea*, filming his journey up and down the Italian peninsula in the company of Soldati, and engaging with members of the public from all walks of life, whom they interview. *Chi legge?* was successful, useful and thought-provoking.

For Zavattini the main questions to ask were: Could television improve? Could it become useful? Could it add something valuable to Italian culture and current affairs? He thought so, as did Umberto Eco, who also didn't deny, in his 'Appunti sulla televisione' ('Notes on Television') the hypnotic effect of television. Eco also valued its potential, as a site for experimentation, and for the benefits of bringing the visual into the homes of ordinary people.[45]

For Zavattini, television was a wasted opportunity, because, with a few exceptions, it limited its scope to song contests, sport, newscasts, based on government propaganda and highly successful shows like the pioneering quiz show *Lascia e raddoppia* (*Double or Quits?*). The show was launched in 1955, only a year after television was introduced to Italy, presented by Mike Bongiorno, and, as one historian puts it, 'Italy was hooked'.[46]

But, as a former pre-war media mogul of Italian mass publishing, Zavattini could see that the general trend was not an inevitability; television was, after all, just a medium of communication. So it all depended on how it was used. Really, as far as Zavattini was concerned, television was a promising site for change within the public sphere, towards a greater sense of responsibility, citizenship and social conscientization, produced by widening participation to public discourse.

Now, what he omitted in his interview was that power was a deciding factor, the issue of who controls the mass medium; as decisive an issue for television as it was in the film industry: the means and relations of production, yet again. This explains the content of his story about television. Zavattini imagined that a disaffected candidate for a television reporter job had taken over the means of production, in order to give ordinary people a say, an open mic to broadcast their opinions on what was wrong with the invisible city, beneath the city of appearances. He must have thought that shadowing could also be fictional, and undoubtedly fiction afforded more control and fewer headaches than the endless problems of *The Mysteries of Rome*. His expectations were dashed, when the levers of power in the public sphere materialized in vetoes, not to mention interruptions, and even arrests during the film's production cycle. Furthermore, the documentary never got as far as mainstream distribution. Only a handful of critics were able to watch it, at its single matinée screening. *The Mysteries of Rome* reminded him that the very existence of free cinema or free television hinged on who owned the means of production. But Zavattini never gave up. For the time being, he resorted to fiction, to target Italian television. *Assault on Television* also represents a further stage of critical reflection. Zavattini's new scenario marks a shift, however temporary it was. Why bother making ethnographic films in Italy about the city to expose its flaws, unless filmmakers could take over the means of production which would guarantee the free circulation of ideas and an unbiased documentation of social facts?

This is why, in the first draft of *Assault on Television*, Zavattini imagines that his fictional hero, Enzo, wants to make contact with ordinary people, to find out what they really think about major social and political events which, according to Zavattini, are always present in the background of our lives. This character is a modern-day Don Quixote with an impossible mission, competing for a job at RAI-TV (the national television monopoly). He is turned away, after challenging his interviewers for the choices they make as programmers. During a visit to a primary school, Enzo tells the children their history books are full of lies and that the school fails to teach the meaning of freedom and democracy. But the only reaction to this quest for truth in the public is fear and embarrassment, no different from the non-fiction responses At long last, the police arrest him, after chasing him from the beginning. The police inspector asks him what it is he wants to achieve. 'A radical change of regime and of government', he replies: 'I'm left wing.'

Twenty years before independent television stations were established in Italy, Zavattini imagined Enzo stealing a TV news camera from the national broadcasting news crew, to broadcast the views of ordinary people, in search of their truth, as opposed to the truth of the media. It must have been great fun to write. Little did he realize that twenty years later, it would become a one-hour-long film, which would be broadcast on television.

By 1963, he made the scenario more abstract, and, as the new title *Don Quixote '63* suggests, his protagonist Enzo (standing in for Zavattini) has become Don Quixote, whom nobody heeds. Zavattini imagines an assault on state television, led by the imaginary knight who, in Miguel Cervantes's invention, fought against windmills, mistaken for the enemy, in an analogy expressing the imbalance between reality and lofty ideals.

As always in Zavattini's film practice, taken as a whole, writing was a way of theorizing, testing ideas to see where they would go. In the meantime, what seemed feasible to him now seemed improbable. Perhaps there was more to the problem of truth and agency than broadcasting social facts.

He looked for ways to create distance between the scenario and the urgency of current events, to make space for critical reflection, which is why, for the third version, he envisaged a storyteller as the main character. Then he shelved the scenario until 1968, when he invited Ugo Gregoretti to direct the film, now envisaged as a musical.[47] No better man than Enzo Jannacci, the professional and very popular folk singer, whose songs encompassed social critique so effortlessly.

Two years earlier, Pasolini's film *Hawks and Sparrows* (1966) had employed allegory to create distance, and used his own recognizable northern voice, animated by a crow who argues with the comedian Totò, to put across Pasolini's damning views about Italian society. Totò voiced opinions of the typical Italian corrupt Everyman, affected by *qualunquismo* or the lack of social consciousness, combined with apolitical populism; Ninetto Davoli, a boy from the slums, represented innocence. Then Jannacci and Gregoretti fell through, and for several years the scenario was shelved, but, as often happened to Zavattini, never forgotten.

19.7 From fiction to personal film: *The Guinea Pig*

At the very same time as seeking to critique the powerful grip over television by the state, using fiction, Zavattini was involved in the non-fictional *The Mysteries of Rome*. In a series of interviews about the documentary, Zavattini changes the subject entirely. He and one of his sons were also working on a personal film, *The Guinea Pig*, a behind-the-scenes film about an Italian celebrity whose life is bankrupt and the reasons why that is so. An introspective film, a confessional film.

It was typical of him, to be launching one project, while working on another, each quite different from the other. The screenwriter had been given a rare opportunity to shadow the life of a famous celebrity and film actor, and carry out an in-depth, testimonial, research on his life, after Maurizio Arena had fallen out of favour with the film industry. Here, at last, was a chance to expose the failings of the industry, and yet again, as his story for *Bellissima* had done so well, critique the myths of cinema, in the words of a witness and a victim, another Lamberto Maggiorani.

Another notable feature was the plan to replace the classic three-part dramatic structure with an on-screen, autobiographic diary of the main character, a real person reflecting on his life and actions, far more extensive and ambitious in scope than the idea of actresses being themselves in *We Women*. Zavattini's son, Marco Zavattini and Dino B. Partesano, the young director, spent weeks and months shadowing Maurizio Arena, interviewing him and sharing his everyday life, and get him to tell his own story in his own words, to produce a personal film diary. Then Arena pulled out, before they went ahead with filming him in 16 mm. The first film of this kind would have to wait for one of Zavattini's followers and admirers, the young Alberto Grifi, who was to make *Anna* ten years later. *Anna* was a personal film and a dialogical film, with Zavattini's *pedinamento* or shadowing functioning as its operating principle, in which the distance between camera lens and subject is utterly broken down.

19.8 More field research: *Why?*

Alberto Grifi and his friend Giorgio Maulini, both aspiring filmmakers at the time, went to visit Zavattini at his home in Via Merici, in January 1963, hoping that he would finance a film they wanted to make. He didn't. But he gave them a challenging alternative: to collaborate on his next project, entitled *Why?*

What Zavattini had in mind was a collaborative and investigative documentary, which would be the outcome of interviews with young people about their relation to the older generation. The war's end had offered Italians an opportunity to establish a new society, after twenty years of Fascist dictatorship, but they simply hadn't taken it. Time for the next generation to challenge their parents.[48]

Why? fell through. However, Grifi and Massimo Sarchielli went on to make their experimental *Why? – Anna* (1971–2) – based on extensive interviews with a sixteen-year-old pregnant girl, a drug user and a casual acquaintance whom the two met in Piazza Navona, in Rome. They filmed eleven hours of cheap, quarter-inch video tape in Sarchielli's flat, then edited it and transferred four and a half hours onto 16-mm film and screened it in Berlin and Venice to great acclaim.[49]

Grifi acknowledged Zavattini's legacy again and again. On one occasion he wrote:

Everyone was saying it: 'You need to go and see Zavattini!' He was the A&E of Italian cinema! Political conscientization! So, I became a habitual visitor to his open house. 'The cinema is capable of changing life with

courage, with impassioned struggle, because it is life we have to build.'
That was the sentence, almost a rallying cry, that the Grand Old Man kept
repeating obsessively, springing up and down on the divan and disturbing
the neighbours. It was a kind of warning for me, a forewarning as harsh as
truth. So much so, that it was only years later and in the nick of time that I
understood certain fundamental truths, things they never dream of teaching
in film schools ...[50]

19.9 *The Newsreel for Peace*

Zavattini's experimental and collaborative *Why?* film project failed to attract
the funding it needed, but another ambitious enterprise did. *The Newsreel
for Peace* (*Cinegiornale della pace*) received financial support from the Italian
Communist Party, thanks to the mediation of the critic Mino Argentieri, in
charge of the party's film section, and due to the writer's closer ties to a party
that had changed its tune towards him. Zavattini regularly published articles in
their women's magazine *Vie Nuove* and was always in touch with the younger
generation of party members.

The title suggests a documentary about a range of issues, all relating to peace,
bearing in mind that Zavattini, along with Joris Ivens, had been awarded the
Lenin World Peace Prize in 1955, and that in the 1950s and 1960s 'peace' was
a key word for the Left's international campaign for nuclear disarmament,
in the threatening atmosphere of Cold War politics. The word 'peace' was a
signifier and constant reminder of the tense climate of fear which the Cold War
engendered.[51]

During his recent long stay in Cuba, the filmmakers Zavattini worked with
had suggested to him the idea of an alternative, anti-war newsreel. When he got
back from Cuba, he found the time to work on a print project, a fortnightly
publication providing up-to-date news and opinion columns about peace. *Il
Giornale della pace* (*The Journal for Peace*) received the support of prestigious
contributors: Elio Vittorini, Italo Calvino, Pier Paolo Pasolini and Mario Soldati.
Zavattini hoped it would signal a sense of urgency to the general public, in
addressing the issue and would bring to the table organic Left-wing intellectuals,
especially Aldo Capitini, who had been a champion of unilateral disarmament
since the early 1950s and was an admirer of Mahatma Gandhi.

Zavattini would be the editor-in-chief and his writers would be Vittorini,
Pasolini, Moravia, Bassani and others. At last, they would generate a new
debate about politics and the relation with subjective everyday life. As always
for Zavattini, there had to be an alternative to party political propaganda for an
urgent intervention addressing fear with reason and research. *The Journal for
Peace* didn't go ahead, but it led to a new opportunity, a film. He retained the
framework of an analytical discussion but transferred it to a different medium.[52]

The plan was that *The Newsreel for Peace* would advocate genuine freedom of speech in Italy, just as *The Mysteries of Rome* had done, albeit to a non-existent audience, by researching and bringing on to the big screen the contradictions of a city.

How he could possibly have imagined that Visconti, Fellini or Antonioni, or Nanni Loy, for that matter, would be keen on his project remains a mystery. Loy wasn't interested, Fellini said he couldn't understand what Zavattini had in mind, Antonioni could – after all, his first film had been a documentary. But Antonioni wrote a lofty letter, saying that his vision took him in another direction. Visconti also declined. Zavattini didn't realize to what extent they all thought in terms of an *auteurist* cinema, a cinema not predicated on cooperation, let alone participation, as their stance over the protest at the Venice Film Festival in 1968 later made clear.[53]

The Newsreel for Peace was not originally intended as a collaborative project among professionals, but that is how it turned out.[54] At first, Zavattini launched an appeal published in the Communist weekly *Rinascita* on 9 June 1962, addressed to anyone who owned an 8- or 16-mm camera. His idea was revolutionary, because it envisaged a grassroots cinematic practice. He then set up a committee tasked with selecting the general public's entries, footage or photography. However, the responses were disappointing: the respondents supported the project but had neither the know-how nor the equipment to collaborate. The organizing committee received poems, photographs, but very little footage. As a result, *The Newsreel of Peace* became something else; a documentary made by young professional filmmakers (some of whom had already collaborated with Zavattini on the film *The Mysteries of Rome*).[55]

Why call it a newsreel? In the United States, newsreels harked back to the preachy voice-overs of pre-war *The March of Time*. The mainstream narrative of newsreels drew its certainties from an assumed all-encompassing technological progress, a teleological view of life, harshly contradicted by the camps and two world wars, though it was. They still offered cinema audiences a mixed diet of sports events, shots of dignitaries, heads of state shaking hands on diplomatic missions while getting on or getting off a plane, and usually tailing off with show business gossip and images of glamorous film stars appearing at gala events. They were funded directly by the government, due to their potential for influencing public opinion. And news was reduced to triviality. Zavattini's collaborative *The Little Dictator*, a spoof written in collaboration with young Cuban writers in 1960, is proof of how familiar he was with newsreels and how well he could parody them.[56] Newscasts on Italian television newscasts were no better. Newsreels migrated to television, at the expense of genuine news analysis, and of the public's need for accurate information. Everything could be turned into an uninterruptible show: gala nights, shocking crimes, fashion parades, music and sport, indiscretions about Hollywood stars, princesses and heads of state, the pope and the scandals of the day, as Guy Debord was to show.

Zavattini's *The Newsreel for Peace* sought to replace the mediatic spectacle with an alternative model, providing critical analysis through open and uncensored debate, just as Guy Debord's book, *The Society of the Spectacle*

(1967), based on the work of the French Situationists, to which group Debord belonged, attacked the trivialization of the media in aphorisms which explained how cinema, television and newsreels flattened out everything into meaninglessness, to form a mediatic hell. As Debord put it: 'The spectacle is not a collection of images; it is a social relation between people that is mediated by images.'[57] For Zavattini, the root cause was power and power was down to who owned the means of production and who controlled the relations of production.

The Newsreel for Peace is a collaborative essay film, tackling racism, the nuclear race, the threat of total destruction and collective fear. There is a feature about rearmament and the spread of nuclear weapons to France and West Germany. The interviews include a conversation with French existentialist philosopher Jean-Paul Sartre, another with the American Left-wing documentary filmmaker Lionel Rogosin who had recently made *The Bowery* (1959). It also includes what was still a taboo subject in France, and namely, torture by the French colonizers during the Algerian war of independence that had only just been won by the Algerians. Another very sensitive subject was the existence of US nuclear installations in Italy. There were also interviews with Italian prominent intellectuals, the Altamura Peace March, an extraordinary event at the time, all the more so because it took place in the industrially underdeveloped Deep South of Italy. To cover the topic of peace, in Zavattini's materialist terms, meant bringing to the fore Italian current affairs, systematically sidestepped by official media, radio and the single RAI state television channel.

The Newsreel for Peace features interviews with ordinary people, two very touching interviews, one with a teacher and students, who knew Gianni Ardizzone, a student who was shot dead by the police during a peace march about Cuba, the other with a survivor of a Nazi wartime massacre. There are interviews about Marzabotto, the scene of a war crime. What is so striking about them is the silence, the hesitations and the gaps of emotion, which Zavattini didn't cut in the editing suite. Each one of the three survivors and eyewitnesses interviewed reaches the point where he or she is lost for words in talking about his or her experience during the massacre, in which a whole town was executed, mostly women and children, entire families, by the German army in retreat.

The Marzabotto episode, swept under the carpet for fifteen years, and filmed on the spot, was an early attempt at memorialization in Italian cinema. The events are brought back to light in the very place where the massacre happened. A child surviving under stacks of dead bodies, a husband pointing to the spot where his wife's shoe was the first clue as to her whereabouts. No voice-over, no imposed 'reflexive' presence of a filmmaker, as Zavattini lets the survivors take over the screen. Memorializing wartime massacres in the early 1960s was also a sharp political statement, since no Italian de-Nazification or de-Fascistization programme ever took place in Italy. In the 1950s, Fascism and even the Italian Resistance were a taboo subject.[58]

His scenario for *The Newsreel for Peace* reads like the contents of a cultural magazine on topical issues, conceived by a journalist combining publishing know-how with filmmaking experience. It also materializes Zavattini's ideas of how cinema could diversify alongside spectacle, to become, at least in part, attentive to world events.[59] In this sense, it is an experiment and an Italian proposal for cinema to break out of traditional documentary to become a visual essay.

On balance, *The Newsreel for Peace* was a response to a cinema trapped by an industrial framework and a lack of vision willing only to accommodate and reward individualism and *auteurism*, in the final analysis, and contribute to develop the spectacle further, out of touch with the needs of the social, as Zavattini was to write in 1967.[60] It was an experiment in changing production methods, proposing as an alternative a 'model combining an individual and collective approach, geared to investigating a topic, as a preliminary stage to identify what action would be required', using the organizational structure of the Communist weekly *Rinascita*.

In retrospect, this proved to be a haphazard. The plan was that the film would be the first instalment of many investigative reportages highlighting social needs.[61] But *Rinascita* couldn't stretch its resources that far. Although his scenario allowed for a range of topics – from the personal dimension to the collective, both social and political – the filmmakers, who stepped in to make up for the lack of grassroots contributions, had, he thought, given in to the pressure from the Communist Party to generate propaganda.

Despite all the time, effort and experimentation, the film was screened only once in May 1963. No one saw it. What was gained by working on the film was, for Zavattini, putting to the test an idea to later revisit it, rethink the theory behind it, which was his usual a posteriori approach: rethink, regroup and come up with a better plan.

For the party, it was an early attempt at making political cinema, which might prove far more effective than propaganda. But it took several years for the lessons of linking alternative production to alternative distribution and screening to be learned.

Zavattini never gave up. The more you shadow him, the more this much, at least, emerges. Three years later, in 1966, he contributed to a new documentary film magazine, *Cinema Documentario*. Those directly involved a key figure in Italian film club circles, Virgilio Tosi, documentary filmmakers Libero Bizzarri, Gianfranco Mingozzi and Michele Gandin, and the film critic Lino Miccichè, founder of the Pesaro Film Festival, and another screenwriter, Renzo Renzi.

His appeal simply had not worked. Home-movie enthusiasts did not contribute to *The Newsreel for Peace*. *Rinascita* readers who wanted to contribute didn't have an 8-mm camera, let alone the more expensive 16 mm. As often with Zavattini the filmmaker-cum-theorist, he thought about the problem. Yes, the film industry itself, and its illusions, contributed to a specific idea of what cinema was and what it could or could not do. But what about the audience? What was needed was a shift of focus which would come about with the advent of a film culture in Italy. How? Through education. The cine-camera should be introduced into the school curriculum, as a medium to create visual essays. This was not the first time he had thought about making the association between the audience and formal education. In 1955, he had already suggested that still cameras should be introduced into schools, in his introduction to the photo-stories published by *Cinema Nuovo*.

Film culture was one problem; another could be summed up in this question. Why this indifference to current affairs in the general public? And home-movie makers? If he had had any illusions, and he did, when calling for footage from them to make *The Newsreel for Peace*, he had soon lost it. As he puts it:

> They have no intention of sidestepping mainstream cinema's limitations and corruption. Having broken out of cinematic illiteracy, they continue to expect others to explore the world and then tell them about it.[62]

But something could be done. Whatever the current situation, in future, home-movie makers could become budding documentarians, especially if home-movie making were to change into something far more interesting than the moving image equivalent of holiday snaps or birthday parties. They could become personal, introspective. What was, or might have seemed, utopian in 1966, is no longer so. Thirty years later, the BBC elicited home movies, now called videos, from their audience. They were to send them in, and a generous selection would be broadcast. In the intervening three decades, video-cameras had been invented, editing simplified, and were now a domestic object. Consequently, amateur filmmakers responded, and in great numbers, and some of what they sent were personal, first-person narratives. What had changed in the intervening years was the development of a film culture. Zavattini's provocative article refers to the first-person narrative, not understood as a narcissistic exercise, but as a means of gaining insight about oneself. This development could only come about if a film culture were fostered.

Jacques Rancière framed as what art and aesthetics does: 'a redistribution of the sensible.'[63] Seeing, seeing differently, seeing oneself differently, as through a self-reflective lens of the personal camera, is already a political action and one which resists what Zavattini in his article calls 'integration', doubtless, in the wake of Umberto Eco's essay collected in *Apocalittici e integrati* (1964), in which Eco uses the word 'integrated' to define a conformist, someone no longer capable of independent thought or opinion.

Several years later, Pier Paolo Pasolini wrote about 'homologation' which was the Marxist principle of a general public which had become a victim of a 'culture industry', following Theodor Adorno's and Max Horkheimer's *The Dialectic of Enlightenment* (1944). In a chapter about culture as an industry, seen as integral to capitalist command structure, Adorno and Horkheimer speak of the 'coercive nature of society alienated from itself', which had control over the individual self, in which broadcasting was a one-way street, and the consequences of television would be 'quite enormous', and ready-made clichés would be the rule.[64] Zavattini makes a reference to a 'one-dimensional man', which originates in Herbert Marcuse's *One-Dimensional Man: Studies in the Ideology of Advanced Industrial Society* (1964), which came out in Italian translation in 1964, adding a Freudian element to an analysis of modern alienation.[65]

Zavattini and the 1968 Venice Film Festival

20.1 Preparing the ground for debate

As early as 1956, Zavattini had organized the Economic Cinema Conference, on the economics of industrial cinema, which brought to the table producers and filmmakers, having already pointed out the limitations of the film industry in the early 1940s. But before discussing this important, but mostly forgotten, antecedent of conscientization among Italian filmmakers, some context might be helpful.

Zavattini's behind-the-scenes involvement in the institutional transformation of Italian cinema began much earlier, in 1944. And earlier still, in the 1930s, he had raised questions about power and decision-making, and the relations of production, within the film industry. After the war, Zavattini was instrumental in instigating the first Italian association, to provide a meeting place for its members and the opportunity to watch new and old films, and equally instrumental in replacing it with the more ambitious Circolo Romano del Cinema, the CRC, the Roman Centre for filmmakers, not a union, as such, but a less informal association which was to become a key reference point for Italian filmmakers.

It was set up when filmmakers and others in the film industry rallied round to form a united front, in defence of the artistic quality of cinema, and against governmental censorship, in response to what had happened in 1947, when the Left was excluded from the government coalition, and the Christian Democrat Party took direct control of monitoring the Italian cinema industry, reinstating the tried and tested procedures existing during the Fascist dictatorship.

In 1956, at Zavattini's behest, the role of the filmmakers' association was expanded. The 1956 agenda for Italian filmmakers was the future of Italian cinema and the reform of the film industry. Zavattini worked towards creating a constructive dialogue between different parts of the film industry, traditionally (and still today) operating in isolation, in an attempt to steer it towards quality and ethical conscience, by facilitating an exchange of views among producers, distributors and filmmakers, screenwriters and directors. Their discussions found a focus in Zavattini's proposal for an Economic Cinema Conference. Its purpose was to question and openly discuss the future of Italian cinema with the main players within the industry and also question the balance of power, by attempting to give the makers more say in determining its prospects, and more control over the relations and means of production.

The situation of Italian cinema was critical, under threat from the dumping of product by the North American film industry and from the distributors' tight control of cinemas. At a two-day seminar held on 30–31 October 1956, in preparation for the conference itself, he launched a rallying cry to filmmakers, an appeal to do their utmost to take a firm stand on the value of quality. At that seminar, Zavattini succeeded in bringing to the table members of various constituencies within the Italian film industry, ANICA, *Associazione Nazionale Autori del Cinema* (ANAC), AGIS and SIAE, in addition to the new Italian Film Circle. That meeting discussed, among other topics, the weight of Hollywood imports on the Italian market, the impact of censorship, co-productions, and US investment in Italian films. It was a heated debate with clear lines of demarcation, vested interests and no final agreement.

From 16 and 17 November 1956 until February 1957, the group met several times, finally presenting its findings at the Economic Conference itself, held on 31 March 1957. Zavattini succeeded in bringing together representatives from the different sectors of cinema, with a view to finding a common consensus to propose a new legislation. However, a telling sign was that the producers, distributors and exhibitors insisted on not including the unions in the discussions. They listened to what Zavattini and the other filmmakers had to say about producing a cinema of quality, and the need for their cooperation to develop a new cinema. Their side argued that the crisis of Italian cinema could not be attributed to structural causes, in opposition to Zavattini's side, comprising all the members of the new Italian Film Circle.[1]

His was a bold attempt to bring the parties into dialogue, more than ten years before the protest of 1968 in France and Italy led filmmakers to raise questions once again about film festivals and power. In terms of Zavattini's interventions, such initiatives demonstrate that he was pursuing a vision of what cinema could be, while being fully aware of the complex interplay of influencing factors within the film industry. He was successful in creating a dialogue with the producers, but nothing came of it. Nevertheless, as far as the screenwriter and theorist was concerned, it led him to think seriously about alternative production and funding, more along the lines of a counter-cinema. He began to envisage a participative new cinema, ideas which drove the Venice Film Festival protest, led by him, with strong support from ANAC and the Committee of the *Cinegiornali liberi* or Free Newsreels, of which he was chairman and central organizer, in 1968.

After the Economic Conference on Cinema, more and more filmmakers joined the ANAC, an existing film industry association, which was to have a leading role in representing their interests, by creating and disseminating debates over a range of issues, including the function and purpose of film festivals. Eventually, this led to existing ones being critiqued (notably, the Venice Film Festival), and new ones being formed, the Levante Film Festival, the Porretta Terme Film Festival, at Zavattini's behest, and the Pesaro Festival of Free Cinema, an offspring of Porretta Terme and charged with continuing its legacy.

Zavattini applied the lessons learned from the Economic Conference on Cinema to developing an alternative. Both non-fiction films, conceived and produced by Zavattini, *The Free Newsreel for Peace* and *The Mysteries of Rome*, can be traced back further than his Cuba interventions, to the Economic Conference's sobering lessons. As was always the case with Zavattini, his theory spiralled through practice and back through reflection on practice.

20.2 Dealing with censorship

In 1960 – the year Zavattini was directly involved in developing the New Cuban Cinema after the Cuban Revolution, and after his interventions at the ICAIC, when he defended the role of oblique political cinema, be it fiction or non-fiction, and had led discussions on art and autonomy versus art and commitment, apart from working on the adaptation for De Sica's *We Women* – he wrote a scenario containing a proposal for counter-cinema, and in the face of a sudden growth of censorship, he began to argue for the need for immediate action among filmmakers, and went as far as using cinema as an agitprop.

Why? Because that year, there was a sudden swing to the Right, when the Christian Democrats, in power since 1947, sought support to prop up their government by forming a coalition with the Fascist Movimento Sociale Italiano (MSI), which led to riots in June in Genoa, where the neo-Fascist MSI planned to hold its annual Congress that lasted several days. This choice of venue was intended as a provocation, since Genoa had been active in the wartime Resistance and was still proudly anti-Fascist.

This confrontation led to a new wave of militant anti-Fascism across Italy, with demonstrations taking place in several towns, met by police retaliation, using live ammunition against the crowds, in Sicily and Reggio Emilia, and causing several deaths.[2] In the midst of growing pressure for social and political renewal, as the country moved away from the Centre-Right, the Tambroni coalition government fell. However, central control over the media remained non-negotiable.

This was the tense political context for Zavattini's initiative, to do something, 'to act', as he puts it and, finally, to work towards Antonio Gramsci's idea of a *nuova cultura* (new culture). Hence, that year was a turning point for Zavattini who responded vigorously to a new wave of official, governmental censorship. *Arialda* (1960), by Giovanni Testori, a play directed by Luchino Visconti, was censored for obscenity as well as Visconti's *Rocco and his Brothers* (1960). Emilio Lonero, the Catholic director of the Centro Cattolico di Cinematografia, appointed in 1960 as the new director of the Venice Film Festival was held responsible for vetoing Visconti's *Rocco and his Brothers* and Fellini's *La dolce vita* in March, causing a strong reaction.

Zavattini made a public appeal for the defence of free speech in an interview with Tommaso Chiaretti, 'An Act of Courage', for *Mondo Nuovo* published at the end of the year.[3] Yes, films were currently being censored, but they had attracted funding and gone into production. But in the current climate, other projects would never get that far, films about directly political themes regarding contemporary Italy, such as the general elections, and interpellating ordinary people to speak out, to express their opinions in public. Censorship at every turn would make sure of it. Worse still, the gravity of the current situation was clear from the fact that censorship was so engrained that filmmakers themselves never even imagined making such films. But he argued that socially engaged cinema was even more necessary in the face of the opposition it met, at every level. To overthrow it would bring the struggle against censorship to a more incisive level, and to a broader scale. He called for action. His analysis was that censorship was more than a question of legislation, it was a cypher of a state of affairs going back to the war, and the pseudo-democratic regime that followed. Democracy, looking back fifteen years, had not spelt an entirely new, and different way of life, by comparison with the Fascist dictatorship.

The new wave of censorship in 1960 prompted Zavattini to write *Censorship 1960*, for a short, non-fiction film, for which, needless to say, he could find no producer, precisely because of the theme. In 1979, he still deemed it viable for inclusion in the first anthology of his scenarios, published that year. He had several ideas for *Censorship 1960*, not entirely discounting the possible mediation of fiction. The objective would be out and out propaganda, a call to action addressed to the general public, for solidarity and to produce a film which would reach the hearts and minds of as many people as possible. The film would dig deeper, to establish the root causes of persistent censorship of the arts and make the connexion between the Establishment, culture and democracy, and the suppression of the budding new culture of post-war Italy, of its home-grown cultural revolution.

To this end, he considered a series of short interviews, an author's monologue, the headlines in the daily press, or a phone call to the government office responsible for censorship, or powerful ecclesiastical figures who also wielded power on what could or could not be allowed to pass, or forays into past, or looking ahead to what the future might have in store for freedom of expression. Alternatively, he thought about focussing on the contradictions of a big city, or filming live a discussion among a group of filmmakers and playwrights in a room.

20.3 *Rinascita* round-table discussion

Zavattini was increasingly looking for ways to develop his model of investigative documentary outside mainstream production channels which had ostracized him. An unlikely ally, in the early 1960s, was the Italian Communist Party now more sympathetic than it had been in the Stalinist years. Back then, his film theory had been severely attacked by party film critics, as earlier chapters have shown. The PCI had rejected his focus on everyday life and the potential for emancipation it enclosed. Then, the party had belittled his work, just as it had crushed Elio Vittorini's *Il Politecnico* Left-wing cultural magazine. Zavattini's ideas were deemed no better than a chronicle or a description. In sum, the party had accused Zavattini of being unable to see the bigger picture, the vision of history in the making, which a shining new realism, Stalinist realism, would be able to convey.

However, by the 1960s, Lukács was no longer the dominant influence. Now the party had its own production house for documentaries, Unitelefilm, and a younger generation of film critics, who doubled up as party activists, became involved. This made it possible for Zavattini to shift his Cinematic Diary from *Cinema Nuovo*, now a monthly publication, to the weekly Communist cultural magazine *Rinascita*, and strengthen his ties with influential party intellectuals, such as, for example, Antonello Trombadori, or the young Mino Argentieri.

In 1965, *Rinascita* hosted a panel discussion about budding new legislation for the Italian film industry. Zavattini was invited. A new law, concerning Italian cinema, proposed by the socialist Achille Corona, then minister of Tourism and Spectacle, was passed on 5 June 1965.[4] This was the first official acknowledgement that cinema was not confined to its industrial activity, a crucial premise for a promising new direction in Italian arts management and funding, which Zavattini's Economic Conference had tried to establish in 1957. But even now, in 1965, the new law was nothing more than a token gesture. It brought about no changes.

The round-table discussion took place only a month later, in July 1965. The theme for the debate was Italian culture during the years of the Resistance. It was organized by *Rinascita*, and promised to be yet another celebration of the Italian Resistance and a validation of the Communist Party. But Zavattini railroaded this agenda, to focus on the new legislation and seek to thrash out a platform for action and pressure for change, hopefully driven by the Communist Party. The other participants were painters, the Communist Party members Renato Guttuso and Carlo Levi, respectively, a famous figurative painter and a novelist and the Communist Member of Parliament Mario Alicata, who was also the editor-in-chief of *L'Unità*, the Communist Party daily, previously an active member of the pre-war *Cinema* editorial group which also included Giuseppe De Santis, Luchino Visconti and Carlo Lizzani.

Zavattini succeeded in his intent. What was the current status and fate of Italian cinema? He asked the others. He was not concerned with the quality of specific films or of a range of films, but with the political, emancipatory potential of cinema and the need for socially engaged cinema, the same problematic he had defended in Cuba and in Mexico.

He expressed his dissatisfaction about mainstream cinema: 'We are stuck with an elitist cinema, bolstered by its myth of being a separate caste, even when it comes to the more commercial films.'[5] Italian cinema had had two major insights after the war; first, that cinema could attend to contemporary history; second, it had demonstrated that the industrial system of production could be subverted:

What was impressive was how it [*Rome, Open City*] conveyed the hope of transforming spatially and temporally a film's production, so that it would no longer have to be submitted to an American-style conveyor belt system, which meant that anything was now possible and that, consequently, it would be feasible for new films to free themselves from all the restrictions that had relegated cinema to a hobby. This is how it was then understood and how many still view it today, a chamber cinema, as they've called it, a place you go to when you want to take time off. Well, that glimmer of possibility has been snuffed out.[6]

He put it to the other participants that the problem was power, hegemony over Italian cinema, and that the challenge they faced was what to do about it. He wanted to mobilize the party, to get it on his side for a major cultural battle. But, truth be told, in 1965, he was speaking to deaf ears, even though *Rinascita* had helped him organize, produce and fund *The Free Newsreel for Peace*. Somehow, against all odds, he had managed to produce *The Mysteries of Rome*, highlighting the city's deeply divided nature, its contradictions and demystifying the tourist layers of public perception. Undeterred, Zavattini was adamant that something could be done and that he would do what he could to subvert it, by setting up alternative production channels, and build a genuine grassroots network.

20.4 *Sequences from a Cinematic Life* and Free Newsreels Collective

In April 1967, Zavattini made a selection from almost three decades of published Cinematic Diary entries, accompanied by some other diary-based texts and called the book *Straparole*, literally, 'Glut of Words', which was translated into English as *Sequences from a Cinematic Life* (1971), long out of print.[7]

In a brief prefatory note, Zavattini reviewed the years of 'projects, fixed ideas, proposals, interviews, speeches, even theoretical statements – and all on the cinema', summing up his interventions for change. What was originally time-bound occasional writing, chronicle even, in 1967 read as history, conveyed in a tightly edited and layered text, combined with other texts, including a subjective diary, embedded scenarios, conference papers and enticing accounts of his journeys to Cuba and Mexico. *Straparole* brings to life over two decades of struggle and testifies to Zavattini's ongoing, uncompromising polemic with the film industry and with his peers. One benefit of this retrospective gaze meant reliving Italian film history in the making:[8]

> Oh, they were good times, though! It was a constant demonstration. There was the presumption one could change the world or the government, with a dozen films, and slogans uttered with the searing force of a flying bullet: Neo-realism is the conscience of cinema; cinema is either useful or it isn't

cinema; engage with what's happening, not with what has happened already; aim to know, in order to take action; reject a film history which refuses a dialogue with cultural history; [...] move away from your desk [...]; make the crucial difference between cinema and film; [...] [make] a film a day; [make] flash films.[9]

The publication of *Straparole* preceded by only a few months the nationwide campaign Zavattini launched to circumvent the Italian film industry. While in 1967, the first of two waves of student and worker protests were taking place, escalating as far as occupations of university campuses stretching from Turin to Florence, from Lecce in Puglia to Messina in Sicily; the élite of Italian cinema remained aloof. These events spelled the emergence of grassroots politics, but no concomitant change of perspective was forthcoming in Italian cinema circles.

In the summer of 1967, Zavattini attracted several disaffected filmmakers, including Bernardo Bertolucci, the Taviani brothers, Marco Bellocchio and many others. They met in Reggio in Emilia where they established, under his lead, an activist film collective; not a film club or circle, but a political film collective, calling themselves the Free Newsreels Collective. They held a meeting to discuss the status of industrial cinema in Italy, following on from Zavattini's work with the Communist Party: 'There can be no *pax cinematographica*', Zavattini told them.

Consequently, the way forward was to give back to cinema its revolutionary function which would require filmmakers to work outside conventional channels and set up a network of film circles and independent filmmaking, waging a guerrilla war on industrial cinema with 16- or even 8-mm cameras for a low-cost cinema, made by the many for the many.[10]

By March of 1968, when the second wave of student protests began in Rome, spreading all the way down to Sicily, the Free Newsreels Collective had consolidated their activities, and developed a far-reaching network, with centres in many Italian cities. These met regularly and developed an analysis and activity which was to make them a political referent and a strong influence in shaping the debate over Italian cinema and table this debate at the Venice Film Festival.

The quality and scope of the Free Newsreels debate is significant, for it was not limited to a concern over the limitations of the Festival system. It also encompassed the purpose of cinema and considered alternatives to current practice. Where did politics figure in cinema? Was it limited to political content? The Free Newsreels Collective and ensuing movement were asking these kinds of questions long before the Cannes Film Festival was occupied in 1968.

20.5 The 1968 Cannes Film Festival

When, in February 1968, Henri Langlois, the director of the *Cinémathèque Française*, was sacked by the minister of Culture, François Mauriac, French filmmakers protested, until Langlois was reinstated in April 1968. They also called for reform of the French film industry.[11] This was followed by the resignation of four jury members, which, in turn, led to the cancellation of the Cannes Film Festival competition.

After the occupation of the Sorbonne campus and of the entire university of Paris on 13 May, filmmakers decided to boycott screenings at Cannes, in solidarity with students and workers. A general strike was declared, and millions joined the protest. On 17 May, filmmakers set up the *General Estates of French Cinema* (*Etats Généraux du Cinéma*) to which 1,500 filmmakers adhered. They wanted to 'transform the system, the state of affairs in which the cinema of France has been so self-enclosed, so cut off from any social or political reality'.[12] The *Etats Généraux* seemed mostly concerned with the closed shop within the French film industry. Nevertheless, they did support collective filmmaking and made *Le Joli mois de mai* and *Ce n'est qu'un début*.[13] The following year, Jacques Doniol-Valcroze and a few other filmmakers organized a supplementary programme at Cannes.[14]

But the French 1968 protest didn't stretch as far as showing any solidarity for Italian filmmakers at the Venice Film Festival, later that year. In theory, the French movement supported the protest planned by the Italian Association of Filmmakers, but in practice, when its representatives Citto Maselli and Marco Bellocchio went to Paris, the French refused to support the Italian struggle, especially Jean-Luc Godard, François Truffaut and the rest of the *Cahiers du cinéma* circle, which was close to Rossellini, who was one of the 105 veteran filmmakers who were adamant politics should be kept out of Italian cinema.[15]

20.6 Venice Film Festival 1968

In Italy, dissent over the function and purpose of film festivals dates from much earlier, at least from the 1957 Economic Conference of Cinema and the foundation of ANAC, and of the new Italian film festivals which ventured to make up for the deficiencies of the Venice Film Festival. These tended, however, to shy away from tackling the problems for which they had originally been set up. The Festival of Porretta Terme was established by Zavattini, among others, to provide a new model of film festival, open to independent filmmaking, which led to the founding of the Pesaro Film Free Cinema Festival in 1965. Despite these initiatives, the Venice Film Festival remained unchanged.

Not that everyone agreed with Zavattini. A sizeable number of members within ANAC didn't think that anything should change. Eventually, there was a split which came to a head at the 1968 Venice Film Festival, driven by Zavattini's new grassroots cinema movement of Free Newsreels the *Cinegiornali liberi*, and a focussed agenda. But the protest at the Venice Film Festival of 1968 had another, specific, precedent. In 1960, there had been a call to boycott the Venice Biennale. The four shortlisted candidates, Luchino Visconti, Antonio Pietrangeli, Florestano Vancini and Citto Maselli, had refused to attend screenings.[16] But now the political climate was no longer dominated by the Right. In Italy, organized student political protests against the Establishment began in 1967.[17]

In June 1968, the Pesaro Film Festival became the cultural target for the Student Movement, aided by the film journal *Ombre Rosse*.[18] But the ensuing occupation had nothing to do with cinema. Its target was the Centre-Left coalition in Pesaro. They wanted to drive a wedge between the Student Movement and its main rival, the Italian Communist Party, which was a member of the coalition. Pesaro was only a pretext. On this and later occasions, the Student Movement failed to see the revolutionary potential of a focussed attack against the media and specifically against the Italian film industry's control over production, financing and organization. It is ironic that, of all the parties, their main foe was not the capitalist state, but the PCI, the only party giving emerging filmmakers some opportunities, and actively supporting the new and alternative Italian documentary.[19] The editors of *Ombre Rosse* joined the protest, purporting to represent the views of the Student Movement in relation to the Festival, by questioning the feasibility of using cinema for protest within a capitalist bourgeois society.[20] They flatly denied that documentary films could help build political awareness, by eliciting debate and by disseminating news.

What happened in Venice, by comparison with Cannes or Pesaro, was informed by Zavattini's endeavours to address the root cause, the closed shop of Italian film industry and its elitism, something he had already attempted to do, broaching the subject before, during and after the Economic Conference on Cinema. It was Zavattini who brought to the table this advanced debate, one that he himself had instigated, within Italian film circles and now to Venice.[21]

A month before Langlois's reinstatement, on 6 March 1968, 105 members left the Italian filmmakers' association to form the ANAC (*Associazione Autori Cinematografici Italiani*), led by Nanni Loy.[22] Their departure is indicative of the tense political cultural climate and the pressure to reform the film industry from within. Zavattini described the split as 'historic'.[23] He was right. Italian filmmakers divided into two opposing factions: one was represented by Zavattini and a younger generation of filmmakers, the other, by the old guard, including the pioneers of Neo-realism, Roberto Rossellini, Federico Fellini, Luchino Visconti and Michelangelo Antonioni. Why did the latter resign? Because they didn't want cinema to change. Cultural and political issues had to be kept out. Their approach to the film industry was corporativist.

Those who didn't leave began to question the state of cinema. They included Zavattini, Pasolini, Vittorio De Seta, Citto Maselli, Gillo Pontecorvo, the Taviani brothers, Liliana Cavani, Bernardo Bertolucci, Marco Ferreri and Marco Bellocchio. All these filmmakers were involved, at least at the outset, with Zavattini's Free Newsreels. They included Silvano Agosti, and, perhaps surprisingly, even Carlo Lizzani, the former defender of Soviet typology.[24] Those who remained issued this statement:

> The ANAC Assembly has accepted the resignations of some of its members and the fact that a group of them has formed a new association. Their

association's programme is based on two points: placing the emphasis on the category's economic interests and defending Italian cinema. But which Italian cinema? And is it still possible to defend *all* Italian cinema?[25]

The spokesman for ANAC in this instance was Zavattini himself, who accused of corporativism the 105 signatories who had resigned.

20.7 'Is cinema over?' Free Newsreels historic debate

Sometime between the second half of April and early May 1968, a key debate about cinema took place in Zavattini's home. Participants included, among others, Marco Bellocchio, Liliana Cavani, Michele Gandin, founder members of the Free Newsreels Collective and Movement.[26] Their agenda was to discuss the future of Italian cinema and question the very aesthetic of cinema. Before the meeting, the decision was made to film the discussion.[27] The subtitle was: Is cinema over?[28]

Zavattini set the tone of the discussion in very broad terms, then remained uncharacteristically silent for the entire duration of the discussion. He went straight to the point, making the distinction between, on the one hand, what he called 'militant cinema', 'a cinema of counter-information' and, on the other hand, 'a cinema of self-management' or autonomous cinema, achieved by taking over the means of production.

His position was revolutionary, and clearly the real way forward, since, as Paolo Bertetto argues, to advocate the rejection of the means of production was more significant than to press for the aesthetic quality of individual films.[29]

Zavattini added:

> I have no confidence in modern cinema, because it is useless and has become a mediation that distances you from the real world. Is this the end of cinema as we know it?[30]

In the ensuing debate, two rival groups vied for supremacy. One was the Free Newsreels Collective, launched in August 1967, the other, the Student Newsreels Collective (*Cinegiornali del Movimento Studentesco*), which came into existence on 2 February 1968 on the initiative of the filmmaker Silvano Agosti.[31]

At this filmed meeting in Zavattini's home, the documentary filmmaker Giuseppe Ferrara remarked that a plain recording of events would fall short of cinema's potential scope. Pier Giorgio Murgia stated the obvious: the kind of cinema they were discussing was a cinema of commitment. And then each participant in the lively discussion tried to define what that might entail. 'A cinema of action, more than of thought', noted Zavattini. A cinema which, in Gianni Toti's view, would challenge passive consumption with action. But how?

The Free Newsreels Collective had been discussing this question since that summer of 1967, reaching the conclusion that, if it was going to be a revolutionary practice, new cinema had to give ordinary people a camera which they could use as a means for discussion and political critique. The very act of supplying cameras would enable them to learn their way experientially to political action, according to Zavattini. 'The camera', Liliana Cavani said at the meeting, 'would become a vehicle for a shared language.' The end result would be Free Newsreels, made by people who were normally passive viewers. Elda Tattoli, also present at that foundational meeting in Reggio, said that you don't have to be a professional to express your personal experience within a situation, when you film it.

The potential of filmmaking was to grow a collective political awareness. Ferrara made the point that 'this kind of cinema would be an alternative to the system in which we are subalterns'. He also thought that people would discover their personal route to political action and become co-authors and accomplices in changing cinema. Thus, the Free Newsreels would lead to a new cinema practice across a network of film centres in which political activity would come first, cinema second. Then an alternative distribution network would also have to be set up, so that films could be screened widely, as Gianni Toti explained. In sum, the gist of their interventions reiterated the main points of their 1967 meeting.

Silvano Agosti, the leader of the Student Newsreels Collective who had recently edited his film about the student protest at Rome University, complained that the main problem was a general lack of political awareness, which was why 'The camera should be used to film situations you have set up to trigger protest against institutions'. Bellocchio and Samperi concurred that newsreels could only be used to document what was going on in a revolutionary situation, such as in Rome in early 1968, not to filter the real through a personal cinematic vision. Bellocchio said he sympathized with the students who refused to mediate reality photographically, because they preferred to get directly involved in street protest. He couldn't see how giving ordinary people a camera could be considered revolutionary. The most they could do was to shoot film as if they were journalists recording events and produce poor-quality reportage.[32] Samperi concurred. With a cine-camera in hand, ordinary people were bound to replicate the cinema they knew. Besides, he thought that the only events worth filming were marches and occupations.

20.8 *Venice is a farce*: The Free Newsreels boycott

By the autumn of 1968, when political activity reached its apex in the factories, Agosti's Student Newsreel Collective folded, while the Free Newsreels Collective went from strength to strength.[33]

On 17 June 1968, the new ANAC Statute was ratified. Members agreed to help cinema express itself freely and fight all the forces preventing it; to defend their artistic freedom from censorship; to establish the conditions for a new industrial organization favourable to free cinema; to create incentives for a cinema of protest and research-based documentary and, finally, to defend authors' rights.[34]

Leading up to the Venice Film Festival, two eminent filmmakers resigned from the Venice jury: the editor of *Film Culture*, Jonas Mekas, and the former British Free Cinema signatory, the filmmaker Edgar Reitz.[35] On 3 July, ANAC stated that, with the help of artists, intellectuals, the unions and the Student Movement, they would prevent it from running, and boycott Venice altogether, because Venice, as it stood, was a farce.[36] ANAC's line, which coincided with Zavattini's, attracted the support of the film clubs' association (FICC) of the nationwide cultural association ARCI, but not that of CUC, representing the Student Movement (Centri Universitari Cinematografici). The CUC only went as far as calling for a generic debate about what a new Venice Film Festival might be like, but saying nothing about joining the boycott.[37] Then, on 15 August, Pier Paolo Pasolini took sides in his article 'Why I'm Going to Venice', addressed to a hostile public opinion which was being kept in the dark by the mainstream media. He stated:

> I agree with Argentieri and, consequently, with ANAC and the whole movement of dissent concerning the protest over the Venice Film Festival and what it represents: it is a question of the most elementary democratic rights, and to come out in support is the least that can be done. I shall accept the invitation, however, and shall send my film [*Teorema*] to Venice.[38]

In the face of media mystification or spin, Pasolini's article painstakingly explained the reasons for launching a protest. The Venice Festival was still governed by antiquated Fascist-era legislation, which it was high time to abolish. Management from above needed to be replaced by self-management (*autogestione*). Filmmaking should not be subject to financial speculation. There should be a space for oppositional cinema, and cultural infrastructures needed renewal. However, Pasolini conceded that, until such changes took place, he and other filmmakers would continue to make use of the existing system, while fighting to change it. But he saw no point in blocking screenings in protest.[39] His letter hinted at the *Free Newsreels*. Pasolini argued that there was no longer any need to defend the Italian cinema industry which was producing 250 films a year nor any reason to worry about censorship that was relenting.

On 19 August, Zavattini wrote to the Festival Director Luigi Chiarini:

> In three or four days' time, I'll be coming to Venice. [...] I am mobilized by ANAC, you are against ANAC and ANAC is against Venice. It's quite possible we shall clash on the steps of the Cinema Pavilion. [...]
>
> I am looking forward to going to Venice. I think that a protest against Venice makes sense, in so far as it coincides with, and expresses solidarity for, other struggles; some of them only recently over, others yet to take place.[40]

[...] Opposing Venice is no childish, pointless rebellion, but the outcome of demands which [...] current events, in the face of the blatant urgency that defines the moment we are living, have rescued from a certain lethargy.[41]

Zavattini explained the Free Newsreels platform: the real challenge was posed by the fundamental structure of the film industry which relied on government financing to support only one kind of cinema, at the cost of excluding '*another cinema*' drawn towards experimentation. In doing so, however, it ran the risk of irrelevance, because what was going on in the world was being ignored.[42] *So it was necessary* to '*create the conditions and the means to make a* different *cinema possible, one with a permanent sense of civic responsibility*'.[43] Commenting on the recent split among filmmakers into two: ANAC and AACI, Zavattini commented that

> Our friends are closing ranks, to form a separate caste, but this is no time to do so; it is the time to open the door to all those who are making cinema. Auteurs include anyone trying to cut a path through the forest of myths and rituals, to widen as much as possible the space for truth, with the blows of a cine-camera, even just a humble 8mm.[44]

In response, AACI explicitly rejected the Venice boycott. Rossellini and its president, the filmmaker Pietro Germi, said as much.[45] Germi wrote to Chiarini to express AACI's support, accusing Zavattini's side of an irresponsible, chaotic, pseudo-protest.[46] The experimental director Carmelo Bene declared that he would stand by Chiarini and go to Venice, siding with AACI. He remarked that 'The youngsters of ANAC are trying to peddle their mediocrity for culture'. Bene added that Fascism had done something positive for culture, whereas these young filmmakers had achieved nothing at all.[47] Within a week from the call for a boycott, over eighty Italian filmmakers supported the protest.[48] Just before the Festival was about to open, Pasolini reached an agreement with the ANAC Committee. There would be no outright boycott, nor any further personal attacks against its director. Instead, they would press for reform, aimed at a renewal of the structures of Italian cinema.[49] Bernardo Bertolucci, among others, who had initially supported the launch of the Free Newsreels, now sided with Pasolini.

On 24 August, the ANAC Steering Committee opted for a peaceful occupation and planned to run the Venice Festival independently. At their General Assembly, Zavattini explained the reasons for occupying the Venice Festival:

> The protesters have rejected the culture of film festivals, be they mainstream or marginal, for sharing a restrictive idea of cinema that stifles anyone who wants to use cinema as means for struggle at the heart of real events. These festivals are organised for the media, to create the illusion of a widespread film culture, when, all things considered, festivals have become the false consciousness of cinema.[50]

Sadly, given all his efforts to effect change in the 1950s, now Chiarini was to interpret this protest as a personal attack. ANAC were criticizing his Festival, Italian cinema and his person. Eventually, he resigned. Then the Steering Committee and the mayor of Venice reached the agreement to the effect that the authorities would deal exclusively with administrative matters, while the cultural organization would be run by ANAC filmmakers, who would also oversee the implementation of new regulations. In this way, self-management (*autogestione*) would become a reality.[51] This was, doubtless, a victory, albeit a short-lived one.

Meantime, Ugo Pirro, writing in the Free Newsreels Bulletin, was adamant that the real problem was the economic structures of Italian cinema. Radical reform, he argued, was far from a utopian dream, even though filmmakers were an integral part of the system they wanted to change. He summed up ANAC arguments, borrowing Zavattini's ideas. How could you achieve a cinema '*of the many for the many*' when the Festival calendar was so out of touch with the real world?[52] Outside, the crowd was chanting: '*Free festival, festival run by authors!*' While Ferreri egged them on: '*Louder! Louder! Speak up! Louder!*' Then came the announcement that '*the Festival has been temporarily cancelled, for reasons beyond our control*'.[53]

The journalists sided with the ANAC assembly. The overwhelming majority voted in favour. In the evening, the occupation was evacuated when Zavattini refused to leave the hall on his own two feet. So the authorities carried him out in his chair. Then Marco Ferreri was assaulted by the local Fascists, a threat Zavattini and Mino Argentieri managed to avoid by hiding behind a bush.

Pasolini's press articles published on 26, 27 August, and on 3 September, countered the media's trivializing of events.[54] Pasolini insisted that the protest was *not* essentially cultural nor was it about ousting the director. It was unequivocally political.[55] The protest was about a redistribution of power from the central government to filmmakers and critics, and it was legal, well within the parameters of the Italian Constitution. To put this differently, ANAC's action was a *political* bid for democratic power, rather than an action limited to the cultural dimension. Pasolini argued that what was at stake was '*an entirely new form of direct democracy for Italy and perhaps even for Europe*'.[56]

Bellocchio, who had also taken part in Zavattini's *Free Newsreels* collaborative project and assisted in filmmaking, changed his mind shortly before the Festival, siding with the Student Movement, and accusing ANAC of being *reformist*, before setting off to Anacapri for his summer holidays.[57] Later, *Ombre Rosse* condemned the protest, having boycotted it all along:

Filmmakers are notable for their corporativist initiatives and absence of ideas. It was a rear-guard battle and, what is more, based on contradictory and wrong objectives. As for the overall aims of ANAC – and namely, state-financed bodies, art films, a parallel circuit of distribution – their deluded ideas, their corporativism (creating a happy island in a crappy world), and their inability to engage with the general public, whereas, an art circuit could possibly lead to slightly larger audiences; but it could only serve to broaden the split between 'experts' and the masses. Moreover, it wouldn't even begin to address how to reach the masses, instead of just the bourgeois élites.[58]

In retrospect, the protest at the Venice Film Festival was an important event because Zavattini and the other ANAC filmmakers dared to challenge the film industry itself, which was a far more advanced position politically, compared to the generic calls for reforming cinema in France.[59]

In October of that year, ANAC confirmed their support for Zavattini's Free Newsreels and several filmmakers became directly involved. They agreed on a common goal, based on two points: to interrupt the film industry's stranglehold on the cinema and a commitment to support the Free Newsreels.[60] Years later, in reference to the Venice '68 Film Festival, the influential critic Lino Miccichè acknowledged that ANAC had shown '*the highest level of critical consciousness demonstrated by Italian filmmakers collectively since Neo-realism*'.[61] Miccichè's book was published in 1995, the same year of Lars Von Trier's *Dogme 95* Vow of Chastity Manifesto appeared, which came nowhere near making such revolutionary demands and was later considered something of a joke, even by the people directly involved.[62]

Zavattini's Free Newsreels

21.1 Theorizing guerrilla filmmaking

As for the Free Newsreels Collective, circles mushroomed in different cities across the country, and their discussions about democratizing the cinema began long before the 1968 Venice Film Festival. Forming this collective was only the last stage of many years of Zavattini's work, beyond or outside the confines of the frame or screen; dating from the Economic Conference of Cinema of 1957.

The Free Newsreels were a grassroots organization run by filmmakers. They began to meet regularly and plan. It was born as a collaborative project, driven by imagining and theorizing guerrilla filmmaking, as an alternative and autonomous practice. In August 1967, Zavattini described what were to become the Free Newsreels: a cinema made by non-cinema groups, 'a cinema that would be so low cost', he wrote, 'that, by comparison, contemporary low budget films are capitalist – a cinema, above all, by the many for the many; a mini-newsreel in 16 mm'.[1] In an earlier text, 'Four Questions to Filmmakers', Zavattini defined cinema as 'a camera and an individual who needs to free himself or herself of any inferiority complexes towards mainstream cinema'.[2]

I'm convinced that you can only work outside mainstream cinema, let's call it that. Or, at least, *also* outside it. [...] I don't see with these short-sighted eyes of mine any other way for anyone wanting to restore to cinema its revolutionary and determining function which lasted a day, but demonstrated it was in the real.[3]

He set out a more focussed idea of what he had in mind:[4]

Free newsreels are cinema to be made totally outside cinema's usual channels. By now, cinema has institutionalised a certain type of closure, a certain kind of creative works. [...] We don't believe it is possible – actually, we totally exclude it – to carry out a renewal of cinema within the confines of contemporary cinema.[5]

He envisaged a kind of territorial occupation of neighbourhood space, by projecting 8- or 16-mm free newsreels in among families and neighbours, creating what he called a 'guerrilla cinema', in the sense of finding an alternative way of developing a critical awareness among ordinary people. Theirs would not be a cinema of storytelling. Zavattini was in contact with a producer, Unitelefilm, the Italian Communist Party's filmmaking unit which specialized in documentaries. They soon provided their full support, to the point that they financed four of the Free Newsreels. In one text, addressed to the Unitelefilm director and to one of its filmmakers, Riccardo Napolitano, Zavattini pointed out that this type of cinema emerged outside traditional, elitist, channels. The norm was that cinema consisted in a relationship between filmmakers and the public; a cinema established 'by the few for the many'. The alternative he and the others involved, envisaged, would be 'a cinema of many for the many'.[6] By comparison, not even *Cinéma Verité* could be described as oppositional, as Zavattini put it:

> That was a flash in the pan which, more than the creation of a different kind of film to explore different areas of reality, held out the promise of a rejection of the institutionalization of contemporary cinema. What happened was that even *Cinéma Vérité* was re-absorbed, so that its films only appear to be different, but, are ultimately indistinguishable.[7]

Zavattini's analysis was based on an understanding that the Italian cinema industry resisted autonomies of practice, despite the *auteurist* art cinema of filmmakers like Bellocchio, Pasolini or Antonioni. Zavattini had placed his hopes on television, but, apart from some pioneering investigative programmes, overall, it had proved resistant to change. Although cameras were getting cheaper, there was still a chasm between the medium's potential and the use to which it was put.

A film festival such as Pesaro, itself the beneficiary and heir to Porretta Film Festival, still had a role to play, but the concept of cinematic freedom, bandied about at the Pesaro Free Cinema Festival, was deceptive. In an article published in the Free Newsreels October 1970 Bulletin, Zavattini was willing to acknowledge Pesaro's merits in screening international experimental cinema. But it was not enough: that Festival limited any dialogue with the public to 'debates with auteurs'. Ultimately, it reaffirmed the division of labour and cultural elitism congenial to the Establishment. He pointedly asked:

> Could, or would, Pesaro be willing to support a cinema which was not institutionalized, not industrial, not profit-based, but genuinely democratic, with a horizontal hierarchy of production, distribution and screening? [...]
>
> Let's take a look at what has been achieved and what remains to be done in cinema; not just in terms of screenings, but also of planning. Let's make the link between the internationalism of a battle against imperialism (only some of the Pesaro films shown to date fit that bill anyway) with a no less urgent battle against home grown capitalism.[8]

The answer to his question was, of course, that no, Pesaro couldn't and wouldn't. Sure enough, when the Free Newsreels Collective showed one of their experimental films at the 1969 Pesaro Festival, the reception was hostile.[9] Without a doubt, militant film criticism appreciated cutting-edge linguistic experimentalism, Brechtian interruptions of cinematic practices, anti-narrative strategies, as well as political content and themes – such as Costa Gavras's *Z* (1969), based on Jorge Semprún's screenplay. But it failed to engage with the root of the problem, the means and relations of production, the real terrain of struggle with the institution of cinema.

For Zavattini and for the Free Newsreels organization, what was ultimately at stake was not reform, but a revolutionary approach to cinema, centred on power, on the ownership of the means and relations of production, and postulating 'a cinema now', a 'cinema by everyone for everyone' and 'a cinema together', all slogans formulated by Zavattini and circulated in print in the Free Newsreels bulletins. As Citto Maselli acknowledged, Zavattini was the 'spiritual father of a line that sought to create favourable conditions for a cinema with ethical, social and political themes at its heart'.[10]

21.2 Free Newsreels at AID Algiers

The visibility of the Free Newsreels was not limited to Italy. They became internationally known, when Zavattini presented their work at the Association of Documentary Filmmakers meeting in Algeria in 1968, as he was to tell delegates in Pesaro in 1970.[11] This landmark event was organized by Gian Vittorio Baldi, the director of one of the episodes of Zavattini's collaborative *Italian Women and Love*, and, that same year, 1968, of the experimental *Fuoco!*

Perhaps this explains how Fernando Solanas and Octavio Getino, the authors of the Third Cinema Manifesto, already knew about the Free Newsreels, and cited them as a glowing example of genuine militant cinema in their manifesto, while cinema critics – unlike Zavattini, Solanas or Getino – failed to appreciate how cinema could make an effective, directly political, intervention, as a politics of cinema (rather than being only a cinema about politics) and see that *Apollon* had achieved just that.[12]

Zavattini, along with some of the Italian filmmakers who had worked with him on his documentaries, Lori Mazzetti, Nelo Risi, Ansano Giannarelli, was among the invited participants at the 1968 Annual General Conference of the International Association of Documentarists (AID), held that year in Algiers (25 February–1 March 1968). Other delegates included the pioneers of twentieth-century documentary, Joris Ivens, Georges Franju, Agnés Varda and Jean Rouch.[13] According to Ansano Giannarelli, Alberto Cavalcanti, Fernando Birri and Jonas Mekas were also in attendance.[14]

At the end of the conference, Zavattini was appointed one of the new vice presidents of AID. Ansano Giannarelli gave a presentation on non-fiction film in Italy, while Zavattini presented the Free Newsreels at a special screening event, and other films separately. The day after the conference ended, on 2 March 1968, the daily *El Moujahid* published an article reporting that Zavattini saw the *Cinegiornali liberi* as 'The solution to the problems raised by the evolution of the documentary form and a kind of future for cinema, one that tends towards the creation of a universal political awareness'.[15]

In his talk, Zavattini suggested that there could be African Free Newsreels too. This struck the filmmaker Sarah Maldoror, considered the matriarch of African cinema, who had lived in Algiers since 1963. Zavattini's was a 'brilliant presentation', as she said in her letter to him. She agreed with him: 'I consider the Free Newsreels model the key to African cinema of tomorrow.'[16] She went on to say: 'I continue to think that the future of cinema will develop thanks to you.'[17] In June of that year, Zavattini published an excerpt of her letter in the first issue of the *Cinegiornali liberi*.[18] The following year, she directed *Monamgabée* (1969), shot in Algeria and based on a short story by Luandino Vieira, 'The Complete Fact of Lucas Matesso'. One would expect *Monamgabée* to bear some resemblance to *The Battle of Algiers* (1966), the full-length feature Sarah Maldoror helped Gillo Pontecorvo make, as one of his assistant directors.

Her fifteen-minute short is political (against Portuguese colonization), in a different way, bearing the signs of Zavattini's influence, not directly of the Free Newsreels, but in terms of the choice of theme, technical choices and its obliqueness, closer to what Zavattini had suggested to the Cuban ICAIC filmmakers in 1959 and 1960. Its minimalism almost does away entirely with plot, in favour of an abstracting durational pace and use of sound.[19] But one must consider also his influence, wherever he went, be it Algeria, Senegal, Egypt, Russia, France, Czech Republic, Poland or elsewhere in the many trips this book has not researched, in terms of an example of commitment to a new ethical and, indeed, political cinema.

As Zavattini had explained early on, in the foundational meeting at his home that year, the crucial problematic of cinema in 1968 wasn't counter-information but self-management. This was the Gramscian problematic of cultural hegemony, related to the cinema. How do you intervene? How do you open up spaces for alternative filmmaking which is not elitist? Of course, Zavattini's burning questions, regarding guerrilla filmmaking, were more urgent and of greater interest to the Developing World in its politics of liberation from colonialism, than to most filmmakers in the West.

21.3 Applying the shadowing model: *Apollon*

Today, of some thirty-five Free Newsreels produced, fifteen have survived the passage of time and have been restored.[20] Free Newsreels could be long or short; they could be made in collaboration or not; about a single theme or not; non-fiction, lyrical or diaries. Their defining feature was that they were critical, explorative and connected with ordinary shared spaces: 'They could be shown in a room, a coffee bar, a small square, any wall will do to screen what you've done.'[21] Marco Bellocchio contributed to the *Cinegiornale Libero di Roma no. 1* (1968) ('The Rome Free Newsreel'), an experimental documentary film, close to Situationist *détournement*, turning institutional messages upside down.

'The Rome Free Newsreel' consists of nine shorts, of which the most striking is Elda Tattoli's *Appunto* ('Notes'), a feminist statement using archival images of women of the past who fought to establish their authority. Her montage is followed by a memorable face-to-face confrontation between a man and a woman, over the relations between the sexes. Somehow, it hasn't dated. *In una clinica psichiatrica di Roma si ascoltano le elezioni* ('A Rome Psychiatric Clinic follows the Election Results') uses displacement to generate a sense of estrangement, by concentrating on an unusual type of viewer doing something 'normal', while *Cinegiornale Libero di Torino N. 1. Scioperi unitari alla Fiat* (1968) ('Turin Free Newsreel No. 1. Combined strikes at Fiat') demonstrated that it was possible to do a flash film after all. It was shot in the morning outside the Fiat factory gates and screened to workers the same evening in the open, outside the factory. It put into practice what the slogan *Cinema subito* ('Instant Cinema') meant: speeding up the industrial process to serve the present moment, while also turning a film into a practical and effective tool for political militancy.[22]

Cinegiornale libero No. 5. Battipaglia (Free Newsreel no. 5, Battipaglia) (1969) shadowed a demonstration in the streets, after a factory closure and the loss of jobs in one of the poorest regions of Italy. During the protest, the police used live ammunition and killed two people. In the self-reflexive documentary *Battipaglia: Autoanalisi di una rivolta* (1970) ('Battipaglia. Self-analysis of a Revolt'), filmed a year later, many of those who took part in the street protest and their families are filmed as viewers during the screening of *Battipaglia*. You see their expressions, hear their voices and their reasons which, in conventional newsreels or television, the media and its controllers had consistently ignored. Shot reversals alternate documentary footage and interviews with their close-ups. In the ensuing discussion, a sharp collective analysis of the event connects the protest to the lack of investment and forced emigration due to local unemployment: issues which the media had consistently failed to cover.

Vajont: 2000 death sentences (1970) (*Vajont: 2000 condanne*) takes a discreet and unspectacular approach to address tragedy and suffering. The collapse of the Vajont dam, a sad chapter of Italian history and miscarriage of justice in 1963, due to poor engineering, caused 2,000 deaths and wiped out a village. A sea of crosses marks the place where the village of Longarone once stood. Such events tended to be reported as the work of fate, catastrophes, denying witnesses airtime to have their say. But these particular witnesses have their say in the film, in early 1970, shortly after the news of the acquittal of those responsible for negligence in building the dam.

Ugo Gregoretti took over from Zavattini as president of ANAC during the Venice '68 protest and later joined the Free Newsreels movement in November 1968.[23] He became a member of the new Rome-based Free Newsreels Collective, which was planning to make a film about workers' struggles, in one of the factories in Rome or its environs. It went ahead when they made the Free Newsreel no. 2 (*Cinegiornale libero n. 2*).[24] The fledgling, Rome-based, Free Newsreels Collective was considering several possibilities, when it was contacted in December, by the print workers of the Apollon Occupation Committee, to discuss the feasibility of making a film, celebrating their year-long, successful struggle. They wanted to inspire workers involved in other factory occupations and thought that media exposure might help them win. It was quite a story. They had occupied their printworks in Rome the year before, and their occupation had lasted more than a year, and was still holding out against management.

Over a period of time, two workers had convinced the workforce to strike in June 1967, because the new management was winding down operations, with a view to sell the site and cash in its spiralling real estate value. All their jobs were at stake, so when negotiations failed, they occupied. They had gradually grown in political awareness and taught themselves through trial and error how to organize, through the direct experience of negotiation and having to contend with management's ploys. How they coped with the difficult learning process and kept going against the odds was the story to tell. The workers' motive was to share their experience.

At that first meeting, the workers told the Free Newsreels group that several activists from the Student Movement had already been to visit the site and meet them. Others on the Left had come and gone, including filmmakers. Other filmmakers had invited them to make a film, but the workers refused. The problem was that they all shared the same response: telling the workers what they should do. But none of these people had any experience of unions or strikes, let alone occupations. What the workers actually needed was for someone to come and film the story of what they were going through and how they had faced, and continued to face, the day-to-day challenges of running a long-term occupation and had succeeded in holding out for twelve months already. The result was the collaborative *Apollon. Cinegiornale libero n.2. Una fabbrica occupata* (1969) ('Apollon. Free Newsreel 2. An Occupied Factory').

In December 1968, Zavattini got technical support from Unitelefilm, the PCI's filmmaking unit, for the use of cameras and other equipment and, with an eye to distribution, from the party's cultural association, ARCI, to sideline the problems he had faced in earlier experimental projects and, for once, ensure that the people who mattered most could view *Apollon*.[25] The Communist Party also provided finance to produce the film. It had changed its tune. In the current political climate, it saw the potential of the Free Newsreels and was willing to endorse them, and indeed began to emulate their media model by launching its own *Terzo Canale* (Third Channel).[26]

Unlike the previous visitors, the Free Newsreels Collective listened – and shadowed them, to the point of coexistence. What kind of film did they want to make? Who was it aimed at? What type of film language did they envisage? Would it be a strictly political analysis or were they aiming to also move an audience, even entertain? To address such questions and translate them into film production, the Free Newsreels Collective formed an Apollon Steering Committee that developed the overall plan of action and shaped the Free Newsreel *Apollon*, as an exemplary model of cinematic practice.[27]

Through frequent late-night conversations, filmmakers and workers discussed, imagined, and finally wrote the film together, based on their ideas and a lot of preliminary research. It became clear over time that their film would be a diary of their occupation, in the mould of Zavattini's diary-film, a popular film that would attract a larger audience and solidarity from other factories, and also encourage other workers by example. 'We've gotta make 'em laugh, make 'em weep, make 'em furious', the workers told them.[28]

Their political experience was proof positive of how to go about organizing, providing other workers with a practical and visual document of activist, practical know-how. So closely involved in all the decisions were the workers that, in effect, they became co-directors, as well as organizing the film's distribution, promotion, presentation and far-flung screenings, which they attended and indeed presented.

Apollon charts how the relationship between political avant-garde in the factory and the other workers gradually developed over time long before and during their occupation, showing just how fast political awareness can grow in the midst of political conflict, when faced with tangible political issues, such as diplomacy, negotiation, internal conflicts and even spying. It reconstructs the sort of story that can only be reconstructed. The actors act themselves, all genuine Apollon workers, act out the story of how the struggle had escalated, leading up to the occupation, and how they had created an internal network of organization, so advanced that it included a self-sufficient and self-funded food cooperative.

By February 1969, the film was completed, and its first screening took place in the factory, during the workers' assembly. In March, the workers were reinstated, and their battle won. Then the film's distribution began, preceded by a press conference. In the context of militant cinema of the time and its aims, by comparison with the French *Cinétracts*, *Apollon* was screened 1,200 times in front of 240,000 viewers, in secondary schools, universities, union and ARCI cultural circles, but the most effective site of distribution were other factories dotted around the country for which *Apollon* was a testimony to a victorious struggle against all odds and a publicity coup for the PCI ahead of the autumn contractual bargaining. It was also exported to Switzerland, Germany, the United States, and bought by Swedish and Finnish television.[29]

After the Venice protest was over, Gregoretti claimed total authorship over *Apollon* in 1969, and caused a split, barely a month after the film had been completed, as a debate held in Rome on 18 March 1969, documents very blatantly.[30] Gregoretti the *auteur* pitted himself against the structure that had made the film's production and funding a reality. For Gregoretti, the film was a showcase, for the PCI and for its cultural milieu, of what he could do. Zavattini said very little at that meeting, while Gregoretti launched into a lengthy complaint about having to make do with a *cinema della fretta* (a rushed cinema), and blaming the film's artistic ensuing shortcomings on the Free Newsreels Collective, while at the same time claiming ownership. Gregoretti, followed by the other members of the Rome Apollon Collective, dissociated themselves from the Free Newsreels and made *Contratto* (*Contract*).

Whereas, for the Free Newsreels Collective it was a crippling moment. The Free Newsreels had taken over the means and relations of production, but they were hijacked by Gregoretti's *auteurism*, an underlying contradiction: it was now *his* film. The Free Newsreels group lost its momentum, but it managed to keep going until 1971. While Gregoretti was invited by the unions to make a film in the same Zavattinian model of practice, *Contratto* (*Contract*) was also a great success. *Contratto* shadows the real, entirely dependent on the same form of Zavattinian documentary, a rallying cry in time for the impending salary negotiations in autumn.

The fact remains that, unlike most political cinema, *Apollon* did more than relate a success story of a year-long occupation, begun on 4 June 1967.[31] Not only was it participative, ethnographic in Zavattini's *Italia mia* mode of enquiry, it was also an example of political expanded cinema, understood as an off-screen social practice, and generating new social space, integral to filmmaking, as film screenings and ensuing discussions, *Apollon* proved to be an effective means of training for documenting labour struggles at the height of the so-called Hot Autumn, explaining how to organize and run an occupation, fund it, promote it, feed it and win it.

21.4 Grassroots, not counter-information

Zavattini's initiative of collaborative Free Newsreels, both in the sense of an idea of cinema and of an activist movement, with centres for their creation and production stretching to different towns dotted around Italy, is a little-known, but extraordinary, attempt, by one of the fathers of Neo-realism to open up and transform the nature of cinema towards a socialized practice, proving itself to be more effective than Italian student militant cinema.

The Free Newsreels produced an ongoing debate about the nature of cinema among a network of new film circles and over a four-year period discussed the notion of what a total reversal of mainstream cinema could be like. Having gained the support of ANAC, in advance of the Venice '68 Film Festival, the Free Newsreels group was instrumental in setting the terms of the debate, and steering negotiations, not only towards reform but also reimagining the purpose of film festivals altogether. It didn't happen, but they tried, and their reasons are still valid in the twenty-first century, and is a pioneering example of guerrilla filmmaking, an entirely unique form of political cinema.

Zavattini's original plan was to involve ordinary people using amateur Super 8 cameras, just as he had hoped to do with *The Newsreel for Peace*. Again, he underestimated the gap between the established practice of using the moving image only to make home movies to record family events and the high level of film culture the kind of project he envisaged would require. That said, in challenging the elitist foundations of the film industry itself, the Free Newsreels were no less experimental than the experimental cinema of, say, Carmelo Bene, Alberto Grifi or Mario Schifano.[32]

In 2001, at the notorious G8 meeting in Genoa, there were more than 1,000 digital cameras, up to perhaps 5,000, according to some. The smaller estimate and an hour of footage from each would translate into 1,000 hours of footage from a single event.[33] From this point of view, Zavattini's proposal of owning the means of production (cameras, cheap or free editing suites, uploading onto free sites) begins to sound less utopian.

The Truuuuth

Zavattini's testament?

22.1 After the Free Newsreels

In the 1970s Zavattini returned to radio, having been an occasional broadcaster in the 1930s and after the war. He had his own chat show, running from 1976 to 1977, *Voi ed io* ('You and I') and published a fragmentary, minimal, personal diary, that lingered on social mores, not cinema, in the Communist daily *Paese Sera*.

These were the years when his painting became more and more iconic, making enigmatic self-portraits in which silence and abstract space prevails. The writer had always mixed with artists, ever since his Parma days, and had steadily built up a collection of tiny works he commissioned from many artists over decades. His 8 × 10 private gallery included works by Renato Guttuso, Giorgio De Chirico, his brother Alberto Savinio, Morandi and members of the Roman School of painting. His book *Ligabue* (1967), a long poem about a self-taught artist and recluse, was rescripted for a three-episode television biopic, then shortened for cinema and won a prize at the Montreal Film Festival of 1978. Zavattini also made a television programme with Luciano Emmer on Van Gogh: *Cesare Zavattini e 'Il Campo di grano dei corvi' di Van Gogh* (1972). He had always admired the painter and indeed in the 1950s he had travelled to Holland to carry out research for a scenario, but the film never materialized.

He kept up his writing and publishing in the 1960s and 1970s. *Straparole* (1967) contained a sizeable anthology of his Cinematic Diary as well as some literary texts. He made forays into experimental writing with anti-narrative, aphoristic prose *Non libro più disco* (1970) (*Non-Book plus Disk*), not to mention a collection of his poems in dialect, *Stricarmi di parole* (1973), which attracted Pasolini's unreserved admiration. In literary circles, dialect, as a legitimate form of artistic expression, was appreciated. In 1946, Pasolini had published a collection of poems in Friulan dialect, and Carlo Emilio Gadda published a detective story which is literature at its finest, *Quer Fattaccio Brutto de Via Merulana* also came out in 1946 in *Letteratura*, then in book form in 1957.

Zavattini also brought out new editions of his pre-war prose, collected a selection of his pre-war articles as *Al macero* (1975) (*Pulped*). In 1976, he and an Italian photographer, Gianni Berengo Gardin, produced a new *Un paese*, entitled *Un paese vent'anni dopo* (*Un paese twenty years later*). It had very little in common with the earlier book. How had village life changed? That was the emphasis; no longer was he concerned with collective memory, but with social change, in the wake of the 1960s.

He was in the thick of organizing the Free Newsreels, when his *Non libro più disco* ('Non-Book plus Record') came out. It included a recording of his voice reading a paragraph from the book, followed by a protracted shout of protest against society and its predicaments, worthy of George Maciunas's art movement *Fluxus*. Their manifesto stated they wanted to 'purge the world of its sickness'. Maciunas, and his pupil and follower, Fluxist Nam June Paik, would have approved of the double-page spread in Zavattini's book in which a page of typescript page is reproduced in landscape format, and is almost entirely blotted out by black ink, or of the following spread, partly covered in red ink. He would have appreciated the words in 60-point Sans Serif Bold type. He would have smiled at the line drawings surrounded by reflections in bubbles, at black or red ink blots spattered crossed the page, at text forming crosses and columns, harking back to early Modernist experiments of avant-garde typography and poetry. Marinetti's Futurist *parole in libertà*, or 'free-style words', have returned as entire blocks of type, in different sizes. Shapes on the page, call them Constructivist or De Stijl. But the content is also striking, personal and political, a mixture of fiery invective, 'social facts' raising questions about Italian society. Zavattini rattles the reader out of indifference, striking similes, what might seem at first glance like Futurist Nonsense.[1] As Italian experimental writing goes, compared to the work of the *Gruppo '63*, his prose is still readable and would reward critical attention.[2]

In 1976, he published the book *La notte che ho dato uno schiaffo a Mussolini* (*The Night I gave Mussolini a Slap*), also experimental, quite short, but with a postscript many times its length, containing his thoughts on the inadequacy of Italian society, life, customs, and reflections on time and change, picking up the doubt-ridden persona of his *Hypocrite '43*, in Zavattini's diary-style voice, adapted to carry philosophical reflections, weaponized against capitalist society, its contradictions and injustice, and hypocrisies, couched in a disarming first-person narrative.

In 1979, as a last and decisive intervention to develop the documentary and memorialize its history, Zavattini founded the *Archivio Audiovisivo del Movimento Operaio* (the Audiovisual Archive of the Working Class), aimed at preserving documentaries and establishing a permanent archive of papers relating to Italian society, social facts, workers' struggles. He became its first president and was directly involved in establishing its goals and methods of working, alongside Paola Scarnati.[3] In his inaugural address, he said that the Archive should serve the present:

The Historic Archive of the Working Class is an archive of the present, more than of the past, and its documentas will not be stacked on the shelves for ever, but are rather, charged with a vibrant impatience to engage in the contemporary dialectic of democratic struggles, contributing to the foundations of a less constrained civic education.

Today, we all know less than we should know, and what we do know, we half-know. And that is not the worst of it. We even say less than the little we know. [...] Although the flow of news is increasing exponentially, and more and more channels are stacking up, equally, the more the container grows in size, the less it contains, to the point of gradually becoming an empty shell.[4]

22.2 Re-imagining *Quixote '63*

Clearly, there was no let-up for Zavattini in the 1970s. He worked on several projects simultaneously. While he had shelved *Quixote '63*, he had not forgotten its potential, and was still unwilling to throw in the towel. After all, the story could be brought up to date, refer to more recent events and symptomatic events, so as to convey rebellion against stifling Italian society with its stranglehold on the media, and now it could also benefit from his recent experimental literary writing, in a kind of internal intertextuality. The character Enzo, his modern Don Quixote, now called Antonio, could voice the doubts and uncertainty which characterize the long commentary in *The Night I gave Mussolini a Slap* (1976). The more he revised the scenario, the more it grew offshoots of hundreds and hundreds of pages of notes, comments and reflections, far too extensive to converge into a definitive screenplay.

A film about social facts and the urgency of their dissemination was gradually turning into a film about societal indifference, hypocrisy and inaction, an invective in prose, though in a different medium. The problem he faced was that the revised script contained too many aphorisms, asides and tirades about society, to make a film. Too bitter; it wouldn't work. So he decided to borrow the anti-narrative structure from his literary experimentation, using fragments of dialogue to suggest, rather than explicate. That didn't work either. Then he wrote a series of long monologues directed at his imagined interlocutors, each emerging from a different door, one of twenty doors placed in a semicircle within a large empty hall. Each character (including the Catholic Pope) would attract a vitriolic invective, in a catastrophic vision of history, offended by attacks against human dignity, by an endless series of crimes against humanity, by interminable, unbearable suffering met with total indifference. He vented his contempt for intellectuals berating their failures, their unwillingness to shoulder their responsibility to defend the basic principles that ought to govern civil society. The complicity and reprehensible action of government, the alienation of mind from the body, of society from nature, and the gap between actions and beliefs were to blame.

Then he edited out all this excess detail. Still, the script was overpowered by all his recent literary experiments. So he imagined a new situation. A paradox: his lead character was too sane not to be considered insane. In the final redaction he placed his main character, Antonio, in a mental asylum, and staged his escape which led to the interaction with different characters in new situations. No trace of the tirades, replaced by the protagonist's irony and his clowning body language, suggesting, more than stating, partly reminiscent of Chaplinesque or Buster Keaton silent film era miming. Zavattini imagined a reckless race against time in Rome, harking back to his earliest scripts about a man on the run and a chase (*La fuga*, 'The Escape'). For this 1978 version, Zavattini imagined that

> The protagonist wants to change the world in an hour and a half, in order to find out the truth, with the police at his heels. In a combination of bravado and critique, he is adamant that if, for once in our lives, we all said what we actually think – something that primordial, historic and contingent causes prevent us from doing – we would save body and soul, and become immortal.[5]

Now it fell to his protagonist to perform dissent, instead of making speeches about it. Wit and everyday language would avert rhetorical temptations, just as contemporary stand-up comedians, such as Lenny Bruce, were able to crack jokes about serious issues. What better choice than Roberto Benigni, then an up-and-coming stand-up comedian, combining comedy with short social satire? On stage and on television, Benigni's invented character conveyed a naïve persona, intelligent, yet armed with a child-like innocence, which suited very well Benigni's comic persona, in the face of intrigues. The two worked on the script for months before Benigni decided to pull out. Zavattini wrote to him on 19 January 1979 to say that he considered *La veritàaaa* his testament, not the film before the last film, but his final film.[6] However, Benigni didn't exit the scene empty-handed. He borrowed Zavattini's idea of a confrontation between Pope and Everyman to make the television satire *Il Pap'Occhio* (*The Mess*), a play on words in Italian, since the first part of the word cyphers the Catholic Pope. Undoubtedly, Benigni would have made an excellent contribution to the script and delivered an exacting interpretation. His loss threatened to put a stop to the project. Zavattini responded by deciding to go it alone and play Antonio, as well as direct the film.[7]

Zavattini added a few vowels to the word 'truth' in Italian, used for the title, *La veritàaaa*, to signify a calling out, a refrain, a need for something absent, and a gap between words and their objects, and most importantly, between social facts and inaction. Antonio would set out to discover the truth about contemporary society, as Zavattini explained in December 1980:

> The need, taken to its extreme urgent and necessary limits, to get to know, in the midst of a confusing and contradictory (and irresponsible) situation as ours in contemporary Italy, a little more than is already known, to be in a position to say that one has come close or at least made a public effort, to get to know the 'mythical' truth.[8]

22.3 *The Truuuuth*: The story

In the grounds of the asylum, Antonio, an inmate and the main character in the film, remarks on the news in the paper. The Cold War seems far from over. Reagan's Star Wars project is exacerbating the conflict of the superpowers, while massacres are taking place in many parts of the world, including Lebanon. Headlines appear in the frame as material evidence, indexical traces of the real world; documents of war in different countries. Later on, all the wars since 1945 are listed, and Antonio mentions in passing the two-day agony of Alfredino, the child who fell into a well and was filmed in real time until the end. The nation was moved and for once, as far as Zavattini was concerned, television did its job, covering the 'social fact' as it was unfolding. Antonio condemns the Red Brigades as 'dictators' for carrying out acts of terrorism with no popular mandate to do so. There is even an ironic reference to a recent Italian scandal involving Italian masonry, hinting at unfounded theories about the hypothetical involvement of Italian and foreign secret services being the mandates of the Moro kidnap and assassination.

While Antonio is commenting on current events, protesters chant and march for peace outside the asylum walls. No, chanting isn't enough, Antonio exclaims. What is the problem? To find out, he decides to escape. With a prodigious leap he clears the perimeter walls in search of 'the truth' and joins a tour to the catacombs where he interrupts the tour guide to say what nobody wants to hear. But doesn't quite say it, barely hinting at what earlier versions of the script had spelt out in hundreds of pages of detail. His acolytes follow him to Piazza Venezia, where he commands their attention from the same balcony where Mussolini had once thrilled acquiescent, adoring, Italian masses with his theatrical speeches. It is eerie to watch the way Antonio looks down on the crowds from on high; the way the scene is shot, the way it is lit; Zavattini's histrionic stance and his baldness cannot but lead one to make the association between the dictator and Antonio. The intertextual reference confirms this: 'Italians!' Antonio booms. But he fails to inspire patriotic emotions, succeeding in undermining his own authority instead, through a parody of authoritarian rhetoric. He is going to tell Italians the truth they don't want to hear: they are 'dickheads', hastening to add that he is no exception. The speech is about the gap between values and hypocrisy surrounding them. He encourages his audience to purge themselves, by vomiting the words that don't mean what they stand for. Everyone does as he suggests, and the flow of vomit comprises words, concepts and betrayed values.

In the third scene, Antonio breaks into the state television studios to set up a free television channel, 'The Channel of Freedom'. People of all ages and walks of life queue up to be interviewed and say what they think: the truth, their truth. In a sense, it hardly matters what they have to say, for they are finally allowed to speak their minds. A procession of ordinary, the many extras Zavattini coached and cajoled to do more than take on walk-on parts, pick up the mike. At last they are given a voice. Antonio interviews Garibaldi, a national hero whose epic battles belong to the history of Italian independence from Austro-Hungarian rule. Garibaldi represents the paradigm of probity. Is this what Italy has come to? Had I known? What captures the imagination is the cinematic image; the faces of these people; their diversity; their sheer numbers; queuing up to speak and be heard. This, the pace of editing, and the visual pressure and chaos, resonates more than their lines of dialogue. Then it is Antonio's turn to be interviewed by a journalist, accompanied by a cameraman using videotape and a photographer. Again, the questions seem less important than the shot of Zavattini's physical presence with the crew.

Antonio makes his way to a large screen displaying archival footage of bombing. He tries to prevent a bomb from exploding by rewinding the footage. Officials from the television studios beat him up for encouraging people to take control of public space in his 'Television Channel of Truth'. The bomb whistles, falls on target and explodes. The explosion includes an interior scene of smoke and a woman with a dead child. Antonio and another person look into the television screen and he speaks to the woman inside the frame. A child's limb has somehow fallen through the screen beyond the threshold between real situation and the space where news is edited and broadcast. He picks it up, promising her to show it to the pope, who will doubtless understand her plight and can surely be persuaded to do something about the war.

It is getting dark. Antonio goes to St. Peter's Square, to call on the pope at his balcony. Despite the mastiffs and Swiss guards, Antonio is undeterred. He openly confronts the pope with the light of logic (just as in the *Divine Comedy* Virgil uses logic to enlighten Dante's confusion in his downward journey of discovery, flawed as it is). Faced with the material evidence of suffering, the pope's response is limited to sentimental pieties. 'Rest your head on my shoulder', he suggests. 'No, you rest your head on mine', Antonio responds, 'I am just as old, if not older than you'. The most elevated thing the pope can do is hide in a tree, before he is led away in a procession. Then the police inspector and the asylum male nurse arrest Antonio. (There are traces of Zavattini's 'Little Dictator', the hilarious parody of Batista, the Cuban dictator.)

As the film draws to a close, the character removes his costume to reveal Zavattini the writer and filmmaker, changing into the red lumberjack's checked shirt, black beret and thick rimmed spectacles handed to him from the edge of the frame, which he often wore in later life. The end dovetails into a 'Postscript' in which Zavattini at eighty takes centre stage, looking smaller than his raging character. By now, everything worth saying has been said. Perhaps it is no more than a pretext for the cine-camera to make its appearance again, in a series of shot reversals of the camera and Zavattini, now filmed within the film as himself, taking us back to Pirandello and the Italian version of Brecht's *verfremdungseffekt*, or distancing from the suspension of disbelief of the theatrical or cinematic spectacle. Only the cameraman is brightly lit, the lens of his camera caught in a big close-up as it zooms. Filmed in the act of filming.

The truth? What truth? There is no such thing, some will say. He meant, of course, the undeniable reality of suffering and the unreality of ignoring it. Why couldn't the world be different? After all, hadn't this been Elio Vittorini's question in the immediate post-war, in his landmark article 'Una nuova cultura' ('A new culture') for *Il Politecnico* of September 1945? Vittorini's wake-up call to Italian intellectuals to get involved, to take social responsibility:

> Man has suffered in society, man suffers. And what does culture do for the man who suffers? It tries to console him. [...] Could we ever have a culture which is capable of protecting man from suffering, instead of limiting itself to consoling him? A culture which prevents, warns off, helps to eliminate exploitation and slavery, and triumph over material needs, this is what the old culture in its entirety needs to become.[9]

22.4 *The Truuuuth*: The context

Almost fifty years on, nothing had changed. Zavattini had made the same point in 1965, at the *Rinascita* magazine round table, in Reggio at the foundational meeting to set up the Free Newsreels in the summer of 1967, and on many other occasions. *The Truuuuth* is firmly rooted in its social and political context. The film was made for television and screened, only a few years after Pier Paolo Pasolini's political and social opinion columns were published in *Il Corriere della Sera*, entitled *Lutheran Letters*, followed by a second series, his *Corsair Writings*. Pasolini resorted to the opinion column to convey his reflections and invectives about the state of Italian society. In those years, committed writers resorted to satire, irony, paradox and the Apocalypse. Pasolini's last film, *Salò*, 'The 120 Days of Sodoma' (1975) and Marco Ferreri's *La grande abbuffata* (1973), ('La Gran Bouffe') were both apocalyptic, in the wake of 1968 and the defeat of a generation.

By contrast with the apocalyptic vein, present in Italian Left-wing of 1970s and 1980s culture, condemning the society of the spectacle and low-culture television as its worst offender, Zavattini's *La veritàaaaa!* calls for a permanent revolution, and does so on Italian RAI TV.

His quixotic clowning and playing a character close to himself to discuss matters of public concern in familiar language was later appropriated by Nanni Moretti, whose humorous and ironic *Dear Diary* (1993) sees him as a commentator and principal actor in a contemporary journey through his hometown Rome.

The Truuuuth is like a set of Chinese boxes within boxes within boxes, rather like Zavattini's life. On 8 September 1982, the year it was screened, it is interesting to see how a contemporary, Mario Verdone, saw the film. Verdone was a film critic and director of the Centro Sperimentale di Cinematografia di Roma. He wrote to Zavattini about *The Truuuuth*, in a letter which has only recently surfaced. In Verdone's view, the film draws attention to thought as an activity, as reflective conscience, as a constant redefining of our lives, giving it its meaning.[10] Peace stands out for Verdone; not so much the problem of world peace, in vague terms; rather, the viewer's active response to the challenge of bringing it about. He singles out the way the film draws attention to madness, to signify freedom of thought. Verdone does not elaborate, but it seems he means thinking beyond, or outside, conventional thinking, which normative thought the French describe as *la penseé unique*. Verdone objects to how, in his opinion, Zavattini let off the Red Brigades too lightly, nor does he appreciate the staged exchange between Antonio and the pope, which is not surprising, considering that Verdone was a practising Catholic.

But these objections do not deter him from valuing how the film conveys ideas through monologue, word, not dialogue, image, theatrical monologue, press reports, literary prose, all brought together into a single multidisciplinary combination. Could such a film be considered a film in its own right? It could. A 'total' film, he calls it, which suggests Richard Wagner's *Gesamtkunstwerk*, but also the later theatre work of Antonin Artaud, of Eugenio Barba, or of Peter Brooke. Verdone also picks up on Zavattini's use of Futurist *parole in libertà*, the programmatic use of nonsense in Filippo Marinetti's avant-garde poetry, and the affinity with Eugène Ionesco's experimental television film *La vase* (1971), made up exclusively of images. This is *cinéma réalité*, not *cinéma vérité*, a performative essay, in which the actor acts and exists as a performing self, as it were, an intermediary of thought, a film of a very different kind which, Verdone concludes, should become part of the canon of experimental films.

The distortion of the word 'truth', by extending the vowel ('a' in Italian) into a long sound, conjures up a voice calling out to others, a search for something absent, for a truth to come, or the hidden truth which needs to be sought out, uncovered, by deconstructing and problematizing packaged truths. Consequently, seeking the truth is more than a rhetorical ploy or a literary fantasy. *The Truuuuth* employs the imagination to engage with the real, just as some of his other works had done, namely, *Miracle in Milan*, originally a fable, and 'The Day of Judgement' (1961) resorting to the apocalyptic idea of the end of the world as a frame for creating extreme situations. The *Don Quixote* frame was to serve a similar purpose. Zavattini's film about establishing the truth or uncovering the truth, as his documentary reportage had striven to do, tables the urgent need to abolish hypocrisy, corruption and double standards, through black humour, irony, monologues, dialogues, sarcasm, fast-paced delivery, clowning, pace and strong physical presence of Zavattini himself. In real life, from the 1970s on, Zavattini was often on radio, as raconteur, essayist and commentator on social and political affairs, always the agent provocateur, like his alter-ego, his character Antonio, the mental patient who escapes from the asylum, the court jester, the Shakespearian fool, the outsider. *The Truuuuth* is his last word as a filmmaker, finding yet another vehicle to convey that open-ended challenge to consensus and indifference.

22.5 Aldo Moro

One has to resist the temptation to close with *The Truuuuth*, as the title of the chapter indicates. However, following Zavattini's endings, such as the one in this film, the first directed by him, we will finish with a postscript or two.

Zavattini's mention of the Red Brigades and Mario Verdone's understandable critique point to the historical climate of those last years of Zavattini's life and his remarkable commitment. He wasn't winding down. For, while he was re-writing *The Truuuuth* for the umpteenth time – there are literally thousands and thousands of pages of different versions in the Rome AAMOD archives and in the Zavattini Archive in Reggio – he received a request from a producer, Lazar Wechsler, only days after Moro's assassination, to write a documentary about the Moro kidnapping and murder and get it filmed.[11] Zavattini set to work, while he was still toiling over *The Truuuuth*, but working in two very different modes, as he had always done since the war. *Aldo Moro: Before, During, After* was to film the director and the writer in discussion, while sifting through the recent footage about the case, from television footage, state-run national television, private companies, radio broadcasts, books, press, photography, and discussing all the raw material, to offer a reflective critique of the events and, above all, their causes.

The kidnap and assassination of the Italian prime minister Aldo Moro, by the Red Brigades, was their worst and most traumatic act of terrorism. Moro's escort of five men was shot dead and the prime minister was held in captivity for fifty-five days and sentenced to death by a puppet tribunal, while the nation – indeed, the entire world – looked on in horror. The Christian Democrats and the Communist Party refused to negotiate Moro's release, unlike the Socialist Party and others who tried to mediate. The president was shot dead in an underground car park and photographed in the boot of a car, symbolically parked between the party headquarters of the Christian Democrats and the Communists, as if they were to blame. His state funeral was on 9 May 1978.[12]

Zavattini's understanding of the Moro Affair was far more complex than Verdone might have imagined, as Zavattini's scenario clearly indicates.[13] In a tour de force, he was aided by Enzo Muzii, the filmmaker who was going to shoot the film and who collaborated on the script. They seek the root cause of terrorism, arguing that it feeds on the shortcomings of Capitalism, but at no point do they condone such an act of violence.

Zavattini's stance was original at the time. The PCI, the Italian Communist Party, and the PSI too were mistaken. There had been no infiltration by foreign secret services into Italian society. They were also wrong to think that Italian terrorism and, particularly, the Red Brigades had nothing to do with the social and political context in Italy, and, moreover, nothing to do with Italy's far Left.

Conversely, the screenwriter argued, while their actions should not be condoned in any way, one could not ignore the social, political and economic context of the country with all its unresolved contradictions, left to fester since the end of the Second World War. His approach was historical materialist, worthy of the best Marxist tradition, of a man who had always voted for the PCI, ever since 1946, while keeping his distance, and maintaining his own critical position on many issues, never joining the party. His stance on the Moro kidnap and assassination was unusual, perhaps even unique, at the time. For Zavattini, especially, the unfinished business of 1945, the shift from Fascism to real democracy, was at least partly to blame. There was no conspiracy, but a great deal of unfinished business.

22.6 *Telesubito*

The year after *The Truuuuth* was shown on RAI national television, in 1983, Zavattini was approached by Alessandro Carri to ask him to develop the scope of an existing television station, *Telesubito*.[14] They met several times that year, and the following year, to discuss setting up a different kind of television with a view to producing a model of democratic practice. They understood one another. Carri was also acutely aware of the problem of inane media in Italy, being directly involved in parliamentary commissions.[15]

In Italy, there were hundreds of private channels, mostly vehicles of repetitive, poor-quality commercials. Financial vested interests meant that very few had any real visibility, in terms of viewers, notably, the escapist *Canale 5*, Berlusconi's channel, *Italia 1* and *Rete 4*, at the expense of most of the other inadequately funded and very amateurish channels.

NTV was formed in Bologna, financed by a cooperative, based on popular shareholding. When Zavattini was contacted, NTV had followed the trend, imitating what other channels were doing, having inherited from national broadcasting the mixture of entertainment and generic newscasts. Could Zavattini help develop a genuine alternative, based on his media theories on the unrealized potential of television, a 'new television'?

His response was that it was high time for a radical critique of both public and private broadcasting. There had to be a cheaper, more effective, approach. Here was an opportunity to resist viewer manipulation, and have no truck with the illusionist deformation of the real and perpetrating television mythologies.

His fictional television film *The Truuuuth* addressed radical change in an original way. It could also be addressed by using non-fiction differently, as the Free Newsreels had attempted to do.

Telesubito would combine facts with analysis and reflection, on a twenty-four-hour basis, adopting the point of view of ordinary people, not of the élite, and deconstructing content to break down mediatic mythologies, and make connexions between one event and another, instead of broadcasting issues in isolation from the broader context. The new television he had in mind would cease to be dependent on advertising and on a sales orientation, which only contributed to mass consumerism. It would be grassroot television. Participation would take the shape of non-professional presenters, interviewers, witnesses, engaged in discussion, following on from the suggestions his fictional television film *The Truuuuth*. The name *Telesubito*, *ImmediateTV*, reflected the need for immediacy, between identifying a social fact and broadcasting its analysis, addressing the gap he saw both in his critique of mainstream cinema, and of national and private television broadcasting. Other names he used were *Telepace* and *Televerità PeaceTV* and *TruthTV*, to repurpose the medium and make it people-friendly and emancipatory.

As he had done on numerous occasions in the past, he critiqued the gap between knowledge and action, knowing and taking appropriate steps, instead of putting issues and their resolution on the long finger, so to speak, including environmental issues of desertification, pollution, alternative forms of renewable energy, problems which were only beginning to be part of discourse in the 1980s, although Rachel Carson's early warning, *Silent Spring* (1962) had become a classic by then.[16] *Subito* meant now, immediately, instead of *mañana*, postponement, the norm. Internal opposition to Zavattini's plan and analysis and, fierce external competition, above all, led to the sale of NTV to TV7. He was eighty-two when NTV folded, but continued to believe until the end that art and visual culture could make a change. 'I have no interest in my posthumous existence', *Non mi interesso postumo*, were not his last words, when he passed away into posterity in 1987.

22.7 Postscript: *Ligabue*

Many of Zavattini's later texts tail off in a postscript. The most striking is probably the postscript of *The Night I gave Mussolini a Slap* (1976), in which the text is relatively short, by comparison, a freewheeling, experimental, prose, a stream-of-consciousness bricolage of thoughts, arguments and rebellion against conformism. In the years Zavattini was experimenting with prose and writing the screenplay for *The Truuuuth* (also followed by a postscript), the writer was also working on a television adaptation of his prose poem, *Toni Ligabue* (1967).

In 1956, he had met a strange man called Ligabue (1899–1965) or Antonio Ligabue or Toni. He was struck by Ligabue's paintings and by the man who painted them, who had impressed him more than he could say. But Zavattini did say, in a long poem he published in 1967, which was reprinted in 1974, and, again, many years later. Ligabue's work could be considered Outsider Art, *Art Brut*, or *arte naïf*, in Italian and Ligabue, an Italian Douanier Rousseau (1844–1910), or Henri Rousseau. The point is that Zavattini was also a painter, and had painted since the 1930s. Even his first book, *Parliamo tanto di me* (1931), contained a few of his drawings. Zavattini had also frequented painters, beginning in his years as a law undergraduate in Parma, but he had never belonged to any specific group, such as, say, the *Scuola romana*, active before and after the Second World War, or the loose group formed around *Arte informale*, Italian post-war abstraction. Like Ligabue, Zavattini was also self-taught. Zavattini's abstract self-portraits remind me of the work of Jean Fautrier or of Jacques Dubuffet. To some, his simplicity of means recalls the watercolours of Paul Klee, most of which are very small, but no less significant than the colossal works by American Abstract Expressionists. But perhaps a better comparison could be made with the strange semi-abstract paintings by Osvaldo Licini. All this to point out that meeting Ligabue in person struck more than one chord for Zavattini. There was Ligabue the renowned painter, but there was also Ligabue the stranger, the misfit, with whom, according to some, Zavattini identified.[17] Perhaps, to a limited extent, at least.

Ligabue was born in Switzerland, but spent almost his entire life in Reggio in Emilia where Zavattini was born. They met in person on three occasions, but, as Zavattini admits in his prose poem, *Ligabue*, he couldn't bear to shake hands with him. He paints a moving portrait of a man whom everyone shunned, disgusting to the touch, a bachelor who stank, who neither washed nor changed his clothes, who was fabled to have slept in cemeteries, who lived in the woods for many years, who ran after elderly hotel chambermaids, could not play a game of cards, who eventually earned enough from his paintings to own nine motorbikes, which he caressed with a soft cloth, and roared like a lion when he was painting a lion. These and many more such anecdotes all read as fiction, but they are not.

In the first thirty lines, the reader learns all the basic facts, name, place of birth, death, where Ligabue went as a ten-year old after his mother's death, the orphanage, his suffering, his loneliness, madness, and the lack of any understanding, let alone kindness from the villagers of Gualtieri, the small village near Luzzara, where Zavattini was born, and which became Ligabue's adoptive home for the rest of his life. The poem reads like a monologue, a series of guilty musings, almost private. Zavattini looks on and into a life from the outside, stating facts, but suggesting thoughts to accompany them. It is intensely visual, cinematic.

Small wonder then, that the prose poem became the basis for a scenario for a three-episode television film, *Ligabue* (1977), directed by Salvatore Nocita, from a screenplay written by Zavattini with the assistance of Arnaldo Bagnasco. *Ligabue* won two prizes at the Festival of Montreal. Both the poem and the TV film apply Zavattini's ethnographic fieldwork to map the figure of Ligabue, combining anecdotes with interviews, recordings and footage, collected in Ligabue's village, Gualtieri. The film relates the life of an unhappy man who was treated like a village idiot, though he was more eccentric than mad. The prose poem and the film implicate the viewer in Zavattini's cinematic, empathetic, gaze, at a wretched man who happened to be a famous painter; a person who was, more importantly, at least as Zavattini saw him, an outcast from an ignorant society. Zavattini, the poet, Giovanni Raboni argues, was an outsider himself, and perhaps best placed to appreciate the work of Ligabue.[18]

Notes

Introduction

1 Stefania Parigi, *Fisiologia dell'immagine. Il pensiero di Cesare Zavattini*, Turin: Lindau, 2006.
2 Aldo Bernardini and Jean A. Gili (eds), *Ciao Zavattini, hommage à Cesare Zavattini*, Paris and Bologna: Editions du Centre Pompidou, 1991. Paolo Nuzzi (ed.), *Cesare Zavattini: Una vita in mostra*, Bologna: Edizioni Bora, 1997. Volume One deals with literature, Zavattini's thought, his pre-war work in writing comics, his screenwriting, work for television and cinema, while Volume Two, edited by Renato Barilli, contains a catalogue of his paintings, from 1938 to 1988, prefaced by an essay by the art critic Renato Barilli, entitled 'Nostra pittura quotidiana'.
3 Orio Caldiron, 'Introduzione', in Zavattini, *Uomo, vieni fuori! Soggetti per il cinema editi e inediti*, edited by Orio Caldiron. Rome: Bulzoni, 2006.
4 Parigi, *Fisiologia dell'immagine*.
5 In Italian, the word 'Neo-realismo' mostly appears in print entirely in lower case, consistently with usage, and without a hyphen. However, in the past some critics have written 'Neo-realismo' or 'Neorealismo'. In English, it usually appears as Neorealism. For several reasons, 'Neo-realism' is the preferred form in this *Intellectual Biography*.
6 Judith Butler, *Frames of War: When Is Life Grievable?* London and New York: Verso, 2010, 8.
7 Trinh T. Minh-ha, *Framer Framed*, New York: Routledge, 1992.
8 Francesco Casetti, *La Galassia Lumière. Sette parole chiave per il cinema che viene*, Milan: Bompiani, 2015.
9 Cesare Zavattini, *Selected Writings*, 2 vols, edited and translated by David Brancaleone, New York: Bloomsbury Academic, 2021.
10 These issues are explored in David Brancaleone, 'Framing the Real: Zavattini and Neo-realist Cinematic Space as Practice', *Architecture, Media, Politics, Society*, in Proceedings of 'The Mediated City' Conference, London, Ravensbourne, 1–3 April 2014, http://architecturemps.com. The question of realism and ethical responsibility emerged at the turn of this century and was addressed in a magisterial discussion by Georges Didi-Huberman, *Images in Spite of All*, Chicago: Chicago University Press, 2007. The philosophical confusion among post-modernists or post-structuralists, as they sometimes prefer to be called, regarding realism has, over several decades, centred on an emphasis on adequation as the central criterion, Neo-realism included. In this book, realism is not understood in terms of the extent to which films succeed or fail to mirror reality or create an illusion of it. For, as Stephen Halliwell's *The Aesthetics of Mimesis* demonstrates, there has always been more to *mimēsis* than the anti-realist turn since the 1960s, understood. Bazin, Zavattini and also Kracauer, make this amply clear in many statements. Cf. Stephen Halliwell, *The Aesthetics of Mimesis: Ancient Texts and Modern Problems*, Princeton and Oxford: Princeton University Press, 2002.

11 Colin MacCabe, 'Bazin as Modernist', in Dudley Andrew and Hervé Joubert-Laurencin (eds), *Opening Bazin: Postwar Film Theory and Its Afterlife*, Oxford: Oxford University Press, 2011, 66. Cf. Antonio Vitti (ed.), *Ripensare il neorealismo: cinema, letteratura, mondo*, Pesaro: Metauro, 2008. This at the very least suggested it was time to rethink the movement, while Geoffrey Newell-Smith's *Making Waves*, published the same year, distinguishes between the first new wave and the subsequent new waves, which latter are considered heavily indebted to Neo-realism in adopting some of its main tenets, and his crucial essay of 2012, 'From Realism to Neo-realism', in Lúcia Nagib, Chris Perriam and Rajinder Dudrah (eds), *Theorizing World Cinema*, London and New York: I.B. Tauris, 2012, 147–59 which sides with the filmmaker who can be considered the first theorist of Neo-realism, Cesare Zavattini. Nowell-Smith overturns existing orthodoxies and reductive approaches that reduce it to a recipe, dictated by external circumstances (location shooting, non-professional actors, loose plot and so on). An early appreciation in anglophone literature can be found in Siegfried Kracauer, *Theory of Film. The Redemption of Physical Reality*. Princeton: Princeton University Press [1960] with an Introduction by Miriam Bratu Hansen, 1997. The philosophical underpinning can be found in his posthumous *History. The Last Things Before the Last*, Princeton: Markus Wiener Publishers [1969] with a Preface by Paul Oskar Kristeller, 2014.

12 Thomas S. Kuhn, *The Structure of Scientific Revolutions*, Chicago: Chicago University Press, 1962.

13 Ansano Giannarelli, *Zavattini Sottotraccia*, edited by Ansano Giannarelli and Aurora Palandrani, Rome: Archivio Audiovisivo Del Movimento Operaio and Edizioni Effigi, 2009, 87.

14 Gian Piero Brunetta, *L'isola che non c'è. Viaggi nel cinema italiano che non vedremo mai*, Bologna: Cineteca di Bologna, 2015, 16. On *Italia mia*, in the same volume, Cf. Brunetta, 'La Sicilia di De Santis e Visconti e le mille e una Italia di Zavattini', 147–61.

15 Brunetta, *L'isola che non c'è*. 13.

16 Zavattini, 'Il Neorealismo continua', in Mino Argentieri (ed.), *Neorealismo ecc.*, Milan: Bompiani, 1979, 92–4.

17 Michael Baxendall, *Painting and Experience in Fifteenth Century Italy: A Primer in the Social History of Pictorial Style*, Oxford: Oxford University Press, 1990, 37–40. Naturally, Baxendall's category and argument refers to the period understanding of paintings, dependant on what was known at the time by painters, patrons and theorists such as Leon Battista Alberti. However, the same approach has been adopted to justify a reconstruction of early 1950s understanding within a set cultural milieu shared by Italian filmmakers and critics of the time.

18 Vitti, *Ripensare il neorealismo*.

19 Laura Ruberto and Kristin Wilson (eds), *Italian Neorealism and Global Cinema*, Detroit: Wayne State University, 2007.

20 Geoffrey Newell-Smith, *Making Waves, New Wave cinemas of the 1960s*, London and New York: Bloomsbury, 2013 and *ibidem*, 'From Realism to Neo-realism', 147–59.

21 David Brancaleone, *Zavattini, il Neo-realismo e il Nuovo Cinema Latino-americano*, Parma: Diabasis, 2019.

Chapter 1

1 Zavattini's reminiscences are drawn from interviews with Giacomo Gambetti, in Gambetti, *Zavattini mago e tecnico*, Rome: Ente dello Spettacolo, 1988; from Zavattini, *Io. Un'autobiografia*, edited by Paolo Nuzzi, Turin: Einaudi, 2002; and a long article originally published as Zavattini, 'Luzzara', *Primato*, 1 February 1942, now in *Le voglie letterarie*, in Silvana Cirillo (ed.), Zavattini, *Opere 1931-1986*, Milan: Bompiani, 1991, 988.

2 Zavattini, 'Io sono di Luzzara', in Paolo Nuzzi (ed.), *Io. Un'autobiografia*, Turin: Einaudi, 2002, 3.

3 Zavattini, *ibidem*, 4, 11.

4 Zavattini, in Gambetti, *Zavattini mago e tecnico*, 73–133.

5 Zavattini, 'Bergamo era tutta luce', in Nuzzi (ed.), *Io. Un'autobiografia*, 13.

6 In Giovanni Pascoli's 'La madre', from *Poemi conviviali* (1904).

7 Giovanni Pascoli, *Canti di Castelvecchio*, Bologna: Zanichelli, 1907.

8 Zavattini, 'Bergamo era tutta luce', 15.

9 Zavattini, *ibidem*, 15.

10 Zavattini, *ibidem*, 17.

11 Zavattini, 'Di colpo sulla luna', in Nuzzi (ed.), *Io. Un'autobiografia*, 18.

12 Zavattini, *ibidem*, 21.

13 Zavattini, 'Occhio per occhio', *Primato*, 1 June 1942, in *Le voglie letterarie*, 1011.

14 Sergio Corazzini, 'Desolation of the Poor Sentimental Poet', from his *Piccolo libro inutile*, in Pier Vincenzo Mengaldo (ed.), *Poeti italiani del Novecento*, Milan: Arnoldo Mondadori Editore, 1990, 36.

15 Zavattini, 'Occhio per occhio', 1011. Zavattini was unfamiliar with Papini's cultural activities in the first two decades of the twentieth century. Papini co-founded with Giuseppe Prezzolini several important literary reviews, *Il Leonardo*, *Lacerba* and *La Voce*, which broadened the scope of Italian literary discourse towards Russia, France, Germany and the United States. For years, Papini was a voluntarist, indebted to William James's pragmatist philosophy of 'The Will to Believe' (1896).

16 Cesare Zavattini, Letter to Giovanni Papini, 28 August 1937, in Cesare Zavattini, *Una, cento, mille, lettere*, edited by Silvana Cirillo, Milan: Bompiani, 1988, 46.

17 Giovanni Papini, *Un uomo finito* in *Opere. Dal Leonardo al Futurismo*, edited by Luigi Baldacci, Milan: Arnoldo Mondadori Editore 1977, 208. To ensure his readers picked up the scholarly reference, Papini added: 'in the book of memory' ('*nel libro della memoria*') which is the incipit of Dante's *La Vita Nuova*, and chapters later, he used the phrase: 'in the genuine new life' ('*in vera vita nova*'). Papini, *Un uomo finito*, 363.

18 Dante's *La Vita Nuova* is a book of poems woven into a narrative which includes their gloss in prose, a formal combination reminiscent of Boethius's *Consolation of Philosophy*. *La Vita Nuova* begins: 'In that part of the book of my memory, which was preceded by very little reading, there is a rubric that states: *Incipit vita nova*. Below that rubric, I find words written down which it is my intention to interpret in this little book; if not all of them, at least their gist.' Dante Alighieri, *La Vita Nuova*, edited by Domenico De Robertis, Milan and Naples: Ricciardi Editore, 1980, 27.

19 Papini, *Un uomo finito*, 377.

20 In 1912–13 Papini was a Futurist and still an atheist, as he keeps reminding
    the reader in his confessional book. Later, he converted to Catholicism. In his
    1932 edition of *Un uomo finito*, and in later ones, Papini deleted the passages
    in which he states that he is an atheist. Cf. Luigi Baldacci, 'Note ai testi', in
    Giovanni Papini, *Opere. Dal Leonardo al Futurismo*, 760–3. Papini later
    became a Fascist, befriending Benito Mussolini, at the time of his apology of
    Fascism, entitled *Italia mia* (1939). Cf. Giuseppe Nicoletti, 'Cronologia', in
    Giovanni Papini, *Opere. Dal Leonardo al Futurismo*, XLIV.

21 Papini, *Un uomo finito*, 140–3.

22 Papini, *ibidem*, 327.

23 Papini, *ibidem*, 200.

24 Papini, *ibidem*, 213.

25 Papini, *ibidem*, 326.

26 Papini, *ibidem*, 373.

27 Walter Mauro, 'Reale e "surreale" di Zavattini', in Gianni Grana (ed.),
    *Novecento. I contemporanei. Gli scrittori e la cultura letteraria nella società
    italiana*, Vol. 6, Milan: Marzorati Editore, 5435–40.

28 Ugo Betti, 'La padrona', in *Teatro completo*, Bologna: Cappelli Editore, 1971,
    25.

29 Cf. Gino Saviotti, Letter to Zavattini, 6 December 1973, ACZ Corr. S169/7,
    unpublished.

30 'A G. S. nella cui casa feci l'università'. Cited in Gino Saviotti, Letter to
    Zavattini, 6 December 1973, ACZ Corr. S169/7, unpublished. Zavattini,
    Letter to Gino Saviotti, 14 November 1973, ACZ Corr. S169/9, unpublished.
    Zavattini expressed his gratitude to Betti for his role in his informal education
    as a writer.

31 Zavattini, Letter to Gino Saviotti, 14 November 1973, ACZ Corr. S169/9,
    unpublished.

32 Cf. Stanley G. Payne, *A History of Fascism 1914-1945*, London: University
    College London Press, 1995, 107. Martin Clark, *Modern Italy 1871-1995*, 2nd
    edn, London and New York: Longman, 1996, 150–3.

33 Gianfranco Buiani, 'L'Italia di Oltretorrente. La battaglia di Parma', *Cinema
    Nuovo*, III, no. 48 (10 December 1954): 377–82. See also, Margherita
    Becchetti, 'Parma e l'Oltretorrente tra biennio rosso e biennio nero', *Centro
    Studi Movimenti Parma*, http://www.csmovimenti.org/agosto-1922-barricate/,
    accessed 27 March 2018.

34 Zavattini, 'Pirandello a Parma', *Primato*, 15 November 1941, now in *Le voglie
    letterarie*, 974.

35 Cristina Scarpa, 'Sebastiano Timpanaro snr', in Giorgio Inglese, Luigi Trento
    and Paolo Procaccioli (eds), *Letteratura italiana. Gli autori*, Vol. 2, Turin:
    Einaudi, 1990, 1718. Timpanaro was an uncompromising intellectual and an
    important figure in Zavattini's youth, acting as one of his informal teachers
    in the Parma years. Their mutual friendship is proven by the tone and content
    of Timpanaro's letters. In a letter Timpanaro uses the very familiar *tu* form of
    address and his salutation reads: *con affetto il tuo Seba, affectionately your
    Seba*[stiano]. Especially at the time, when the *voi* form was being encouraged,
    tu was reserved for close friends and family. These letters are undated;
    however, there is internal evidence in one in which Timpanaro mentions

L'Italia Letteraria, which indicates a *post quem* date of 1930, when the review changed its name from *La Fiera Letteraria*. Timpanaro's anti-Fascism is clear from the tone of the letter, for, in the second decade of Fascist dictatorship, he discusses in considerable detail a book by the philosopher Benedetto Croce about the Italian nineteenth-century *Risorgimento*, and liberalism. This is hardly surprising, given his contacts with Piero Gobetti. Sebastiano Timpanaro Senior, Letter to Zavattini, ACZ Corr. T122/2 (post-1930), unpublished and Timpanaro, Letter to Zavattini, ACZ Corr. T122/3, (pre-1943), unpublished.

36 David Ward, *Piero Gobetti's New World: Antifascism, Liberalism, Writing*, Toronto, Buffalo and London: University of Toronto, 2010.

37 Ward, *ibidem*, 27.

38 Ward, *ibidem*, 20.

39 Ward, *ibidem*, 26.

40 Ward, *ibidem*, 21.

41 Mario Isnenghi, 'Piero Gobetti', in Armando Balduina, Manlio Pastore Stocchi and Marco Pecoraro (eds), *Dizionario Critico della Letteratura Italiana*, Vol. 2, Turin: UTET, 1974, 236.

42 Zavattini in Gambetti, *Zavattini mago e tecnico*, 110.

43 Zavattini, 'Pirandello a Parma', 974.

44 Guido Conti, 'Il giovane Zavattini', in Zavattini, *Dite la vostra. Scritti giovanili*, edited by Guido Conti, Parma: Guanda, 2002, 14.

45 Zavattini, 'Con il Maria Luigia sulla spiaggia della Marca Polita', *La Gazzetta di Parma*, 19 August 1926, now in Zavattini, *Dite la vostra. Scritti giovanili*, 145–8.

46 Zavattini, 'Pirandello a Parma', 973–5. For the virtual literary circle, cf. Guido Conti, 'Un'amicizia lunga una vita', in Bertolucci and Zavattini, *Un'amicizia lunga una vita. Carteggio 1929-1984*, edited by Guido Conti and Manuela Cacchioli, Parma: Monte Università Parma, 2004, 20.

47 Gualtiero De Santi, *Ritratto di Zavattini scrittore*, Reggio Emilia: Aliberti Editore, 2002, 20–1.

48 Conti, 'Il giovane Zavattini', 37.

49 Conti, 'Un'amicizia lunga una vita', 20.

50 Zavattini, *La Gazzetta di Parma*, 15 March 1927. The full review in Conti, 'Un'amicizia lunga una vita', 58–9.

51 Zavattini, 'Holliwood', *La Gazzetta di Parma*, 4 March 1928, now in Zavattini, *Cronache da Hollywood*, edited by Giovanni Negri with a Preface by Attilio Bertolucci, Rome: Lucarini, 1991, 3–4.

52 Jean Baudrillard, 'Simulacra and Simulations', in Jean Baudrillard, *Selected Writings*, edited by Mark Poster, Stanford: Stanford University Press, 1988, 166–84.

53 Zavattini, 'Holliwood', 3–4.

54 Zavattini, Letter to Attilio Bertolucci, August 1931, in Bertolucci and Zavattini, *Un'amicizia lunga una vita*, 147.

55 Zavattini, 'Rodenstack & Co.', in *L'Illustrazione*, 2 March 1930, Zavattini, *Dite la vostra. Scritti giovanili*, 504–5.

56 Bertolucci and Zavattini, *Un'amicizia lunga una vita*, 23.

57 Zavattini to Ugo Betti, cited in Bertolucci and Zavattini, *Un'amicizia lunga una vita*, 61.

58 Zavattini, 'Corriera di Parma', in *La Fiera Letteraria*, 18 May 1930, in Bertolucci and Zavattini, *Un'amicizia lunga una vita*, 59–60.

59 On 1920s Parma, as a late and fertile Futurist cultural milieu for Zavattini, cf. Conti, 'Il giovane Zavattini', 11–140.
60 Zavattini, 'Cena con Montale', *Primato*, 15 December 1941, now in *Le voglie letterarie*, 979–98, 979.
61 Zavattini, Letter to Enrico Falqui, 23 November 1929, ACZ Corr. F512/36. Unpublished.
62 Zavattini, 'Le recensioni', *Primato*, 15 June 1942, now in *Le voglie letterarie*, 1015.
63 Gieppi was the author.
64 Zavattini, *La Fiera Letteraria*, in *Dite la vostra. Scritti giovanili*, 320–90.
65 Zavattini, '*Gli Indifferenti* di Moravia', *La Fiera Letteraria*, 7 July 1929, in Zavattini, *Dite la vostra. Scritti giovanili*, 356–8.
66 Zavattini, 'Le recensioni', 1015.
67 It appeared in print on 21 July 1929. Zavattini, Letter to Enrico Falqui, 10 July 1929, ACZ Corr. F51230. Unpublished.
68 Zavattini, 'Le recensioni', 1015.
69 Eugenio Montale, *Ossi di Seppia*, Turin: Gobetti Editore, 1925.
70 Guido Conti, in Bertolucci and Zavattini, *Un'amicizia lunga una vita*, 88.
71 Zavattini, Letter to Alessandro Minardi, 1 August 1929, ACZ Corr. M829/71. Unpublished.
72 Elio Vittorini, 'Le Giubbe Rosse', in Valentino Bompiani and Cesare Zavattini (eds), *Almanacco Letterario Bompiani 1932*, Milan: Bompiani, 1931, 24–6.
73 Vittorini, *ibidem*, 24–6. This description relies on Vittorini's memoir in the Bompiani Almanac. His article was written at the behest of Zavattini who edited the Almanac alongside Valentino Bompiani.
74 A partial list of those attending reads like a Who's Who of the best of twentieth-century Italian literature. It includes novelists and short story writers, Elio Vittorini, Vasco Pratolini and Carlo Emilio Gadda; critics, Sergio Solmi, Gianfranco Contini and Giacomo De Benedetti; poets, Umberto Saba, Eugenio Montale, Giuseppe Ungaretti, Salvatore Quasimodo, Sandro Penna.
75 Roberto Farinacci was a Fascist leader. Cesare De Michelis, 'Solaria', in Armando Balduina, Manlio Pastore Stocchi and Marco Pecoraro (eds), *Dizionario Critico della Letteratura Italiana*, Vol. 3, Turin: UTET, 1974, 408–10.
76 Vittorini, 'Della mia vita fino ad oggi (1949)', in *Diario in pubblico*, Milan: Bompiani, 1991, 192–3. By then, Papini had abandoned American philosophical pragmatism, had converted to Catholicism and had forged links with the Fascist dictatorship.
77 Zavattini, 'Cena con Montale', 979–81; 979.
78 Zavattini, Letter to Bertolucci, prior to 31 October 1929, in Bertolucci and Zavattini, *Un'amicizia lunga una vita*, 90.
79 *Ibidem*, 90.
80 Zavattini, Letter to Bertolucci and Alessandro Minardi, 16 December 1929, in Bertolucci and Zavattini, *Un'amicizia lunga una vita*, 107.
81 Zavattini, 'Cena con Montale', 979–81; 980.
82 Zavattini, 'Soldatissimo', in Nuzzi (ed.), *Io. Un'autobiografia*, 45.
83 Letter to Bertolucci, prior to 31 October 1929, in Bertolucci and Zavattini, *Un'amicizia lunga una vita*, 90. The stories appeared in *Solaria*, no. 12, IV, 1929, cf. Guido Conti, in Bertolucci and Zavattini, *Un'amicizia lunga una vita*,

93. The three stories were first published in *Tevere*, 11 December 1929, now in Zavattini, *Dite la vostra. Scritti giovanili*, 460–2.
84 Raffaele Crovi, 'Il mio Zavattini', in Pierluigi Ercole (ed.), *Diviso in due. Cesare Zavattini: cinema e cultura popolare*, Reggio Emilia: Edizioni Diabasis, 1999, 171–3; 173. Crovi was referring to: Elio Vittorini, 'Oggi, "Great Attraction!"', *Il Bargello*, 27 September 1931.
85 'Timpanaro è entrato nella Sancta Rosa'. ['Timpanaro has been welcomed into the Sancta Rosa']. Cf. Zavattini, Letter to Alessandro Minardi, Attilio Bertolucci and Pietro Bianchi, 4 November 1929, in Bertolucci and Zavattini, *Un'amicizia lunga una vita*, 94–5. Sebastiano Timpanaro Senior, 'C.Z. Parliamo tanto di me', *Solaria*, September 1931. Rafaello Franchi, 'Un umorista', *Il Lavoro*, Genoa, 28 April 1931.
86 Zavattini, 'Cena con Montale', 979–98, 980.

Chapter 2

1 De Santi, *Ritratto di Zavattini scrittore*, 68.
2 Zavattini, Letter to Attilio Bertolucci, post 23 March 1930, in Bertolucci and Zavattini, *Un'amicizia lunga una vita*, 117.
3 Zavattini, 'Le recensioni', 1014.
4 De Santi, *Ritratto di Zavattini scrittore*, 72.
5 Zavattini, 'Le recensioni', 1016.
6 Attilio Bertolucci's brother. Cf. Zavattini, Letter to Alessandro Minardi, 17 February 1930, ACZ. Corr. M890/135. Unpublished.
7 Zavattini, 'Diviso in due', *Primato*, 1 March 1942, now in *Le voglie letterarie*, 994.
8 Zavattini, *ibidem*, 994. For the date of employment, cf. Zavattini, Letter to Alessandro Minardi, Bertolucci and Pietro Bianchi, 18 October 1930 in Bertolucci and Zavattini, *Un'amicizia lunga una vita*, 123.
9 Zavattini, 'Diviso in due', 993.
10 Zavattini, Letter to Falqui, ACZ Corr. 512/59, 22 January 1931. Unpublished.
11 Zavattini, 'Luzzara', 988.
12 Valentino Bompiani, *Via privata*, Milan: Mondadori, 1973, 78.
13 Zavattini, 'Diviso in due', 994.
14 Valentino Bompiani, Letter to Zavattini, Milan 27 July 1934, in Zavattini, *Cinquant'anni e più. Carteggio con Valentino Bompiani*, edited by Valentina Fortichiari, in Zavattini, *Opere. Lettere*, Milan: Bompiani 2005, 611–13.
15 Zavattini, Letter to Falqui, ACZ Corr. F512/59, 22 January 1931. Unpublished.
16 Zavattini, Letter to Falqui, November 1931, ACZ Corr. F512/74. Unpublished.
17 Valentino Bompiani and Cesare Zavattini (eds), *Almanacco Letterario Bompiani 1932*, Milan: Bompiani, 1931.
18 Zavattini, Letter to Falqui, early 1932, ACZ Corr. F512/88. Unpublished.
19 Zavattini, Letter to Falqui, *ibidem*.
20 Zavattini, Letter to Falqui, 9 October 1933, ACZ Corr. F512/99. Unpublished.
21 Zavattini in Gambetti, *Zavattini mago e tecnico*, 96.
22 Zavattini, Letter to Minardi, ACZ Corr. M890/167, 1931. Unpublished.
23 Zavattini, Letter to Falqui, October 1931, ACZ Corr. F512/70. Unpublished.

24 Zavattini, 'Il matrimonio di Gatto', *Primato*, 15 January 1942, now in *Le voglie letterarie*, 986.

25 Zavattini, 'Diviso in due', 995.

26 Carlo Melograni, *Architettura italiana sotto il fascismo. L'orgoglio della modestia contro la retorica monumentale 1926-1945*, Turin: Bollati Boringhieri, 2008, 46.

27 Melograni, *ibidem*, 300.

28 Melograni, *ibidem*, 300.

29 Melograni, *ibidem*, 301–2.

30 Lorenzo Pellizzari, 'Za soggettista e sceneggiatore', in Paolo Nuzzi (ed.), *Cesare Zavattini. Una vita in mostra*, 159.

31 Zavattini, 'Diviso in due', 994.

32 Zavattini, 'Recentissime', *Cinema Illustrazione*, no. 25, 21 June 1933, cited in Giuliana Muscio, 'Zavattini e Hollywood: tra mito e divulgazione', in Ercole (ed.), *Diviso in due*, 135.

33 Zavattini, 'Erich Von Stroheim è sempre quello', *Cinema Illustrazione*, 14 December 1932 in *Cronache da Hollywood*, 123.

34 Zavattini, 'Tutta la storia e i pettegolezzi di Hollywood in quattro camere', *Cinema Illustrazione*, 14 June 1933 in *Cronache da Hollywood*, 147–8.

35 Zavattini, 'Rottami', *Cinema Illustrazione*, no. 2 1933, in Giuliana Muscio, 'Zavattini e Hollywood: tra mito e divulgazione', in Ercole (ed.), *Diviso in due*, 137.

36 Zavattini, 'Bisogna vivere, dice Wynne Gibson, per essere artiste', *Cinema Illustrazione*, 6 June 1933 in *Cronache da Hollywood*, 145–6.

37 Zavattini, 'La beneficiata dei direttori', *Cinema Illustrazione*, 31 May 1933 in *Cronache da Hollywood*, 143–4.

38 Zavattini, *ibidem*, 143–4.

39 'Un terribile articolo sincero fa cambiare parere a Joan', 5 July 1933, cited in Giuliana Muscio, 'Zavattini e Hollywood: tra mito e divulgazione', in Ercole (ed.), *Diviso in due*, 145.

40 Anthony Verna, *Biblioteca di Rivista di Studi Italiani*, XXXIII, no. 2, December 2015, 256. Cf. Enrico Bernard, 'La narrativa di Bernari tra cinema e fotografia', *Rivista di Studi Italiani*, XXI, no. 2, December 2013, 52–88.

41 Zavattini contributed articles to *Marc'Aurelio* since its launch in 1931.

42 Michela Carpi, *Cesare Zavattini Direttore Editoriale*, Reggio Emilia: Biblioteca Panizzi and Archivio Zavattini and Aliberti Editore, 2002, 85.

43 Zavattini, Letter to Cesare De Michelis, Luzzara, 19 August 1967 in Zavattini, *Una, cento, mille, lettere*, 479.

44 *Le Grandi Firme* was a fortnightly magazine, edited by Dino Segre, whose nom de plume was 'Pittigrilli'.

45 Zavattini, 'Diviso in due', 995.

46 Zavattini, 'Commendatore', *Primato*, 15 March 1942, in *Le voglie letterarie*, 997–9.

47 Gian Franco Venè, *La Satira politica*, Milan: SugarCo, 1976, 19. Gianni Bono, 'Marc'Aurelio', in *Guida al fumetto italiano*, Milan: Epierre, 2003, 1251–2. The others were Furio Scarpelli, Agenore Incrocci (who signed himself 'Age', as part of the Age and Scarpelli duo of screenwriters) and Stefano Vanzina (who signed himself 'Steno'), Vittorio Metz and Ruggero Maccari.

48 A small selection are collected in Zavattini, 'Cinquanta righe', in *Al macero.*
    1927-1940, now in Zavattini, *Opere 1931-1986*, edited by Silvana Cirillo,
    Milan: Bompiani, 1988, 1235-48.
49 These suggestions are mentioned in Zavattini's correspondence with one of the
    co-editors of *Marc'Aurelio*, De Bellis. Cf. Zavattini, Letter to Vito De Bellis,
    4 August 1937 in Zavattini, *Una, cento, mille, lettere*, 354.
50 Zavattini, Letter to Vito De Bellis, 4 August 1937 in Zavattini, *Una, cento,*
    mille, lettere, 351-5.
51 Zavattini, Letter to Vito De Bellis, 19 November 1937, Zavattini, *Una, cento,*
    mille, lettere, 355-6.
52 Nerbini published the adventures of Flash Gordon in the serial comic
    L'avventuroso, as 'Gordon Flasce', Carpi, *Cesare Zavattini Direttore*
    Editoriale, 30.
53 Zavattini, 'Montecavo', *Primato*, 15 May 1942, in *Le voglie letterarie*, 1010.
54 Zavattini, *ibidem*, 1010.
55 Zavattini in Gambetti, *Zavattini, mago e tecnico*, 105-6. Oscar Cosulich,
    'Za soggettista di fumetti', in *Cesare Zavattini, una vita in mostra*, Bologna:
    Bora, 1997. S. Micheli, 'Zavattini e i fumetti', in G. Moneti (ed.), *Lessico*
    zavattiniano. Parole e idee su cinema e dintorni, Venice: Marsilio, 1992, 92-7.
56 Cirillo, 'Cronologia', in Zavattini, *Una, cento, mille, lettere*, xxv.
57 Carpi, *Cesare Zavattini Direttore Editoriale*, 64.
58 Zavattini, *Il Settebello*, no. 236, 14 May 1938, cited in Carpi, *Cesare Zavattini*
    Direttore Editoriale, 74.
59 Carpi, *Cesare Zavattini Direttore Editoriale*, 72.
60 Zavattini, Letter to Vito De Bellis, 4 August 1937 in Zavattini, *Una, cento,*
    mille, lettere, 354-6. At the same time, the managing director of Disney-
    Mondadori, Cesare Civita, who was to become a lifelong friend of Zavattini's,
    went into exile for the same reason and later helped Saul Steinberg establish
    himself in New York.
61 Carpi, *Cesare Zavattini Direttore Editoriale*, 86.
62 Parigi, *Fisiologia dell'immagine*, 246.
63 Zavattini, in Gambetti, *Zavattini, mago e tecnico*, 214-16.
64 Carpi, *Cesare Zavattini Direttore Editoriale*, 78.
65 Arnoldo Mondadori, Letter to E. M. Gray, 25 July 1939, cited in Carpi, *Cesare*
    Zavattini Direttore Editoriale, 78.
66 Carpi, *Cesare Zavattini Direttore Editoriale*, 121.
67 Carpi, *ibidem*, 125-6.
68 Carpi, *ibidem*, 124.
69 Carpi, *ibidem*, 128.
70 Zavattini in Gambetti, *Zavattini, mago e tecnico*, 106.

Chapter 3

1 Zavattini, Letter to Alessandro Minardi, 4 October 1930, ACZ. Corr.
   M890/140. Unpublished. Campanile, as Umberto Eco has shown, displaces
   language, adopting the exacting logic of Nonsense, in order to generate
   humour. There's no mention of Zavattini in Eco's essay, but Eco's analysis

confirms Zavattini's view that Campanile, in seeking out the absurd, the extravagant, ridicules rhetorical pomposity, and creates a sense of estrangement, by taking such a close look at common places as to entice the reader to question them. Umberto Eco, 'Campanile: il comico come straniamento', in *Tra menzogna e ironia*, Milan: Bompiani, 1998, 53–97 and Eco, 'Ma cosa è questo campanile?' in Eco, *Sugli specchi e altri saggi. Il segno, la rappresentazione, l'illusione, l'immagine*, Milan: Bompiani, 2015 [1985], 366–78. Given its prominence in the period between the wars, it does seem odd that Eco makes no mention of Zavattini's humour, which also hinges on estrangement, exploiting the potential of language to represent the impossible in correct syntax, in its Futurist moments, taking a leaf out of Aldo Palazzeschi's Futurist poetry, in what can be described as a verbal equivalent of M. C. Escher's architectural drawings of stairways, visualizing the impossible and making it sound possible.

2 Zavattini, in *Io. Un'autobiografia*, 58.
3 Zavattini, 'Le Ore', in Zavattini, *I poveri sono matti*, in Zavattini, *Opere 1931-1986*, 82–4.
4 Zavattini, 'Fra quattro minuti', *ibidem*, 102.
5 Zavattini, 'Lo stabilimento', *ibidem*, 127–8.
6 Simon Critchley, *On Humour*, London and New York: Routledge, 2002, 10–11.
7 Giovanni Papini, Letter to Zavattini, 23 August 1937, in Silvana Cirillo (ed.), *Una, cento, mille, lettere*, in Zavattini, *Opere. Lettere*, Milan: Bompiani, 2002, 73–4.
8 Zavattini, 'Imola, autunno 1942', in *Cinema*, reprinted in Giacomo Gambetti, *Cesare Zavattini: cinema e vita*, Bologna: Bora, 1996, 98–104; 98.
9 Pietro Pancrazi, 'Io sono il diavolo', *Corriere della Sera*, 27 February 1942. Ferrante Azzali, Lorenzo Bocchi, and Luigi Bruno, cited in De Santi, *Ritratto di Zavattini scrittore*, 418–19.
10 'La corriera di Man', in Zavattini, *Io sono il diavolo*, in Zavattini, *Opere 1931-1986*, 140–1.
11 'Fegato', in Zavattini, *I poveri sono matti*, 209–10.
12 'Allegria', in Zavattini, *ibidem*, 205–6.
13 'Un fatto di cronaca', in Zavattini, *ibidem*, 195–6.
14 'Tram', in Zavattini, *I poveri sono matti*, 166–7.
15 Critchley, *On Humour*, 79–91.
16 The philosopher Simon Critchley speaks of 'the background meanings implicit in a culture', in our lifeworld structures, which, thanks to humour, can be taken out of the habitual context in which we experience them. Critchley, *On Humour*, 90.
17 The concept of lifeworld, or *lebenswelt*, first emerges in Edmund Husserl's *The Crisis of European Sciences and Transcendental Phenomenology: An Introduction to Phenomenological Philosophy*. Evanston: Northwestern University Press, 1989, 108–9. It was adopted by Maurice Merleau-Ponty's phenomenology and later by Jürgen Habermas. Its genealogy, in respect of humour, has been traced back to the Earl of Shaftesbury for whom it involves the practice of sceptical reason 'to question everything'. Critchley, *On Humour*, 80–3.
18 Croce's critique dismissed humour and Pirandello's essay on humour as futile, on the grounds that humour only works on a case-by-case basis, thus making

it impossible to generalize what humour might be. It is clear that Pirandello's theory of humour is anti-idealist, which goes some way to explaining Croce's bullying riposte in his review, his outright dismissal of Pirandello's book, based on only two points: first, that Pirandello is out of his depth, and, therefore, lacks the authority to carry out such a discussion, and second, that humour cannot be classified, since it takes on different forms, depending on the author. Such an endeavour, for Croce, is 'a pointless hunt for the ineffable'. Cf. Benedetto Croce, 'L'umorismo di Luigi Pirandello', *La Critica*, VII, 20 May 1909, 219–23 now in Pirandello, *Saggi e Interventi*, edited by Ferdinando Taviani, Milan: Arnoldo Mondadori, 2006, 1571–2.

19 Luigi Pirandello, *L'umorismo*, in Pirandello, *Saggi e Interventi*, 775–948. His two-part treatise was first published in 1909, then reprinted in 1920.
20 Pirandello, *L'umorismo*, 945, 947.
21 Pirandello, *ibidem*, 947.
22 Pirandello, *ibidem*, 930.
23 Pirandello, *ibidem*, 1576.
24 Umberto Eco, 'Pirandello ridens', in Eco, *Sugli specchi e altri saggi*, 358.
25 Eco, *ibidem*, 360.
26 Eco, *ibidem*, 360.
27 Jerry Palmer, *Taking Humour Seriously*, London and New York: Routledge, 1994, 93.
28 Aristotle, *Rhetorica*, translated by W. Rhys Roberts, in Jonathan Barnes (ed.), *The Works of Aristotle*, Princeton: Princeton University Press, 1984 cited in Palmer, *Taking Humour Seriously*, 94, 96.
29 Critchley, *On Humour*, 10. Zavattini, *Io. Un'autobiografia*, 59 and Zavattini, cited in Conti, 'Il giovane Zavattini', 137. Conti's research into the cultural background of Parma in the 1920s convincingly shows that Futurism lingered in Parma, extending its cultural influence long after 1918, and that Surrealism was alien to Zavattini's concerns and literary taste. Zavattini himself explains in an interview in the above cited *Dite la vostra*, that his personal dislike of the novel as a literary form had much to do with how his prose style developed and his choice of short, fragmentary prose, in preference to extended narrative. Cf. Zavattini, cited in *Dite la vostra*, footnote 132, 137.
30 Zavattini, cited in Luigi Malerba, 'Introduction', in Zavattini, *Opere 1931-1985*, edited by Silvana Cirillo, Milan: Bompiani, 1991, xv.
31 Gualtiero De Santi, 'Gabriel García Márquez in Za's fantastic Mirror', in Alberto Ferraboschi (ed.), *Zavattini Beyond Borders*, Reggio Emilia: Corsiero Editore, 2019, 201–12. The Latin American writer met Zavattini in the 1950s, on various occasions, and visited him once in his home. Cf. Letter to Gabriel García Márquez, 12 December 1982, ACZ, Corr. M 295/1. Gabriel García Márquez went to Rome to study cinema and screenwriting. Zavattini was the only person who met with him and other students outside class. He also said that the Italian screenwriter taught a different perception of life, as well as the trade of screenwriting. Cf. Gabriel García Márquez, in De Santi, *ibidem*, 210.
32 Gabriel García Márquez, cited in Gerald Martin, *Vita di Gabriel García Márquez*, Milan: Mondadori, 2013, 597.
33 Gabriel García Márquez, cited in Martin, *ibidem*, 202.
34 Gianfranco Contini, *Italie magique. Contes suréels modernes*, translated by H. Breuleux, Paris: Aux Portes de France, 1946. Gianfranco Contini,

'Postfazione', in *Italia magica. Racconti surreali novecenteschi scelti e presentati da Gianfranco Contini*, Turin: Einaudi, 1988, 248–9. Beatrice Sica, 'Massimo Bontempelli e *l'Italie magique* di Gianfranco Contini', *Bollettino '900*, nos. 1–2, June–December, 2010, http://www3.unibo.it/boll900/numeri /2010-i/, accessed 10 August 2020. This section benefits from Beatrice Sica's excellent contextualization of Contini's book. The film historian Gian Piero Brunetta links Zavattini to Palazzeschi the Futurist and author of *Perelà* and *Piramide*, Brunetta cited in Zavattini, in Silvana Cirillo (ed.), *Zavattini parla di Zavattini*, Rome: Bulzoni, 2003, 82.

35 The authors are in the order in which they appear: Aldo Palazzeschi, Antonio Baldini, Nicola Lisi, Cesare Zavattini, Enrico Moravich, Alberto Moravia, Tommaso Landolfi and Massimo Bontempelli. Contini excluded all but Moravia and Palazzeschi from his canonical book. Cf. G. Contini, *Letteratura dell'Italia unita 1861-1968*, Florence: Sansoni, 1968. In *Italia magica*, 5, Contini claims that Palazzeschi is one of the few prose writers of his generation whose work was on a European level. Contini borrowed the 'magic realism' framework from Bontempelli. Contini's selection of three stories by Zavattini are *Italia magica*, 149–56: 'Al caffè', 'Racconto di Natale', 'Dal medico', 'Ballo a A …', all four from *Io sono il diavolo* (1941).

36 Massimo Bontempelli, 'Il nostro pudore', in Bontempelli, *Il neosofista e altri scritti. 1920-1922*, Milan: Mondadori, 1929. Bontempelli points to a tendency already established by the *Crepuscolari* poets Sergio Corazzini and Guido Gozzano and the former Futurist Aldo Palazzeschi. Cf. Beatrice Sica, 'Massimo Bontempelli e *l'Italie magique* di Gianfranco Contini'.

37 Fulvia Airoldi Namer, *Massimo Bontempelli*, Milan: Mursia, 1979, 81.

38 Bontempelli, *Mia vita, morte, miracoli*, Milan: Bompiani, 1938, 921, cited in Namer, *Massimo Bontempelli*, 84.

39 Gianfranco Contini, *Altri esercizî*, Turin: Einaudi, 1978, 259–60.

40 Contini, *ibidem*, 259–60.

41 Bontempelli is a key figure in this pre-war tendency, as Beatrice Sica has shown. Yet Contini, she points out, minimizes Bontempelli's role, by affording him only a few pages in the anthology, and, by comparison, dedicating a third of the book to Palazzeschi. Italian 'magical realism', as defined by *Italie magique*, had nothing to do with French Surrealism as it is borne out by the fact that when the book was published in Italian, in the 1980s, Contini's 'Postfazione' made no mention of possible connexions with Surrealism in Italy, such as most blatantly, Alberto Savinio, the one Italian writer who was directly involved in French Surrealism, alongside his brother, the painter Giorgio De Chirico.

42 Contini, *Altri esercizî*, 406–7. Contini draws a distinction between the existential realism of Calvino's *Racconti* (1949), such as 'Ultimo viene il corvo', from the fable-like tone of *Il Visconte dimezzato* (1952), or the world of the worker 'Marcovaldo', in *I nostri antenati*.

43 Calvino, Letter to Eugenio Scalfari, 21 December 1942, in Calvino, *Lettere. 1945–85*, edited by Luca Baranelli, Turin: Einaudi, 2000, 104. Calvino, Letter to Luigi Baldacci, 15 January 1968, Calvino, *Lettere*, 982.

44 Calvino, Letter to Eugenio Scalfari, 1943, in Calvino, *Lettere*, 127.

45 Letter to Luigi Baldacci, 15 January 1968, in Calvino, *Lettere*, 982.

46 Luca Baranelli and Ernesto Ferrero (eds), *Album Calvino*, Milan: Arnoldo Mondadori, 1995, 48. Calvino contributed a few cartoons to *Il Bertoldo* with the pseudonymn Jago in 1940.

47 Italo Calvino, 'Ricordo di Vittorio Metz', in Mario Basenghi (ed.), *Saggi. 1945-1985*, Vol. 2, Milan: Arnoldo Mondadori, 1995, 2900–4.

48 Italo Calvino, 'Raccontini giovanili', in Mario Berenghi and Bruno Falcetto (eds), *Romanzi e racconti*, Vol. 3, Milan: Arnoldo Mondadori, 1994, 764–830.

49 Calvino, 'Il funerale', in Calvino, 'Raccontini giovanili', 816–17. The funeral procession follows a horse-drawn hearse, proceeding initially at a slow mournful pace, but then the horses begin to trot, worse still, break into a gallop, while the mourners desperately try to keep up. The story is that simple.

50 Zavattini, *Diario di cinema e di vita* (a collection of articles published in periodicals between 1940 and 1967, and collected in *Straparole*), in Zavattini, *Opere 1931-1986*, 397–651. A new edition of the Cinematic Diary appeared separately in 1979, alongside a separate volume entitled *Neorealismo ecc.*

51 Zavattini, *Ipocrita 1943*, in Zavattini, *Opere 1931-1986*, 275–310. Parts were published in 1944 and 1945, the rest only in 1955.

52 Zavattini, *Ipocrita 1943*, in Zavattini, *Opere 1931-1986*, 277.

53 Zavattini, *ibidem*, 282–3.

54 Zavattini, *ibidem*, 286.

55 Zavattini, interviewed by Silvana Cirillo, in Cirillo (ed.), *Zavattini parla di Zavattini*, 94–5.

56 Zavattini, *Riandando* (included in *Straparole*), in Zavattini, *Opere 1931-1986*, 653–723.

57 Cesare Zavattini, *Sequences from a Cinematic Life*, translated by William Weaver, New York: Prentice Hall, 1971.

58 Zavattini, *Diario cinematografico*, edited by Valentina Fortichiari, Milan: Bompiani, 1979, 62.

59 Zavattini, *ibidem*, 160.

60 Valentina Fortichiari, 'Introduzione', in Cesare Zavattini, *Diario cinematografico*, edited by Valentina Fortichiari, Milan: Bompiani, 1979, 7.

Chapter 4

1 Zavattini, interviewed by Francesco Savio, in Savio, *Cinecittà Anni Trenta: Parlano 116 Protagonisti Del Secondo Cinema Italiano (1930-1943)*, Vol. 3 (NAZ-ZAZ), Rome: Bulzoni, 1155–6.

2 Zavattini to Alessandro Minardi, 12 February 1933, ACZ. Corr. M890/179. Unpublished.

3 Pellizzari, 'Za soggettista e sceneggiatore', 157.

4 Pellizzari, *ibidem*, 157.

5 Zavattini, *Io. Un'autobiografia*, 80. *Quadrivio*, II, 43, 19 August 1934. Then in Zavattini, *Uomo, vieni fuori!*, 5–29. Raffaele Masto, 'I dolori di un giovane soggettista. Colloquio con Zavattini', *Cinema*, I, 4, 25 August 1936 now in *Cinema 1936-1943. Prima del neorealismo*, edited by Orio Caldiron, Rome: Scuola Nazionale di Cinema 2002, 33–4.

6 Zavattini, *Io. Un'autobiografia*, 80.

7 Zavattini, in Masto, 'I dolori di un giovane soggettista', 2002, 33.

8 Zavattini, Letter to Bompiani, Milan August 1935, in Zavattini, *Lettere. Cinquant'anni e più*, edited by Valentina Fortichiari, Milan: Bompiani, 2005, 65–6.

9 Pellizzari, 'Za soggettista e sceneggiatore', 159.

10 Zavattini, 'Imola, autunno 1942', 95–104.

11 Zavattini, 'Charlot, Imola, 24 April 1937', in Gambetti, *Cesare Zavattini: cinema e vita*, 86–94; 90.

12 Zavattini, in Gambetti, *Zavattini mago e tecnico*, 126–7.

13 Zavattini, *Basta coi soggetti!*, edited by Roberta Mazzoni, Milan: Bompiani, 1979, 307. Pellizzari, 'Za soggettista e sceneggiatore', 159.

14 Gambetti, *Zavattini mago e tecnico*, 127. Gualtiero De Santi, *Ritratto di Zavattini scrittore*, Reggio Emilia: Imprimitur, 2014 e Parigi, *Fisiologia dell'immagine*, 167.

15 Masto, 'I dolori di un giovane soggettista', 33–4.

16 Zavattini, in Masto, *ibidem*, 33.

17 Zavattini, in Masto, *ibidem*, 33–4.

18 Zavattini, in Masto, *ibidem*, 34.

19 Zavattini, in Masto, *ibidem*, 34.

20 Zavattini, 'A Mario Camerini', originally published in *Il Settebello*, 1938–9, in Zavattini, *Neorealismo ecc.*, edited by Mino Argentieri, Milan: Bompiani, 1979, 32–3.

21 The letter is reprinted in Zavattini, *Neorealismo ecc.*, 32.

22 Zavattini, 'I sogni migliori', *Cinema*, v, no. 92, 25 April 1940, 252–3, now in Caldiron (ed.), *Cinema 1936-1943*, 158–9.

23 Zavattini, 'Imola, autunno 1942', 95–104.

24 Zavattini used a pen metaphor to indicate cinematic creativity and authorial independence in 1942, several years earlier than Alexandre Astruc's *caméra stylo*. Cf. Alexandre Astruc, 'Du stylo à la caméra et de la caméra au stylo', *L'Écran Français*, 144, 30 March 1948.

25 Zavattini, 'Imola, autunno 1942', 96.

26 Zavattini, *ibidem*, 97.

27 The script was soon published. Cf. Zavattini, 'Totò il Buono', *Cinema*, v, no. 102, 25 September 1940.

28 Gian Piero Brunetta, *The History of Italian Cinema, A Guide to Italian Film from Its Origin to the Twenty-First Century*, Princeton and Oxford: Princeton University Press, 2009, 84–5.

29 Zavattini, in Gambetti, *Zavattini mago e tecnico*, 128. The film drew on French cinema, Renoir, and American film, but it was also the outcome of theorizing about Italian naturalism called *verismo*, in the work of Giovanni Verga.

30 Zavattini, private diary entry, 17 July 1942, in Nuzzi (ed.), Zavattini, *Io. Un'autobiografia*, 119.

31 After rewriting the play, sequence by sequence, of *Teresa Venerdì* (1941) (cf. Gualtiero De Santi, *Vittorio De Sica*, Milan: Il Castoro-La Nuova Italia, 2003, 30–1) and before writing the screenplay for *La porta del cielo* (1944), Zavattini worked on many films. *I sette peccati* (1942), dir. Laszlo Kish; *Avanti c'è posto* (1942), dir. Mario Bonnard; *Don Cesare di Bazan* (1942), dir. Riccardo Freda; *Quattro passi fra le nuvole* (1942), dir. Alessandro Balsetti; *Quarta pagina* (1942), dir. Nicola Manzari; *C'è sempre un ma!* (1943), dir. Luigi Zampa; Gian Burrasca (1943), dir. Sergio Tofano; *Il biricchino di papà* (1943), dir. Raffaello Matarazzo; *I nostri sogni* (1943), dir. Vittorio Cottafavi; *L'Ippocampo* (1943), dir. Gianpaolo Rosmino; *Silenzio si gira! Musica per tutti* (1943), dir. Carlo Campogalliani; *Pireutas juveniles* (1944), dir. Giancarlo Cappelli and Salvio Valenti; *I bambini ci guardano* (1944), dir. Vittorio De Sica.

32 Karl Schoonover, *Brutal Vision: The Neorealist Body in Postwar Italian Cinema*, Minneapolis and London: Minnesota University Press, 2012, 153. Schoonover quite rightly emphasizes physical perception.

33 The philosopher Stanley Cavell has written about this kind of screen ontology in *The World Viewed: Reflections on the Ontology of Film*, Cambridge, MA and London: Harvard University Press, 1979, 181. It does not only apply to Neo-realist films but is also a predominant feature of them.

34 Jean A. Gili, 'La naissance d'un cineaste', in Orio Caldiron (ed.), *Vittorio De Sica*, Rome: Bianco & Nero, 1975, 50–65. Stefania Parigi, *Neorealismo. Il nuovo cinema del dopoguerra*, Venice: Marsilio, 2012, 38.

35 Vittorio De Sica, 'Volti nuovi nel cinema', in *Cinema italiano* xx, Rome: Edizioni di Documento, 1942, 39.

36 Noa Steimatsky, 'The Cinecittà Refugee Camp (1944-1950)', *October*, 128, Spring, 2009, 23–50; 31. Alfredo Baldi, 'Un anarchico al csc', *Bianco & Nero*, nos. 588–9, May–December 2017, 126–35; 130.

37 De Santi, *Vittorio De Sica*, 46.

38 One was by Piero Bargellini and Esodo Pratelli. Cf. Zavattini in Maria Mercader, in Paolo Nuzzi and Ottavio Iemma (eds), *De Sica e Zavattini. Parliamo tanto di noi*, Rome: Editori Riuniti, 1997, 66.

39 Carlo Musso, Diego Fabbri, Adolfo Franci and Vittorio De Sica were some of the other credited screenwriters. Cf. Aldo Bernardini and Jean A. Gili (eds), 'Filmographie', in *Cesare Zavattini*, Bologna and Paris: Centre Georges Pompidou and Regione Emilia-Romagna, 1990, 201.

40 Zavattini to Bompiani, 2 February 1944, in Zavattini, *Cinquant'anni e più*, 718.

41 Zavattini to Bompiani, *ibidem*, 717.

42 Vittorio De Sica, *Tempo Illustrato*, Milan, 16 December 1954, now in Nuzzi and Iemma (eds), *De Sica e Zavattini*, 70.

43 Mercader, in Nuzzi and Iemma (eds), *De Sica e Zavattini*, 66.

44 Mercader, *ibidem*, 66.

45 Vittorio De Sica, interviewed by Armando Stefani, 'Per salvarmi dalle ss girai un Kolossal', T7, 6 July 1969, in *Il cinema ritrovato*, Cineteca di Bologna, http://www.cinetecadibologna.it/evp_tenerezza_ironia_desica/programmazione/app_5057/from_2013-07-02/h_1130, accessed 7 August 2018.

46 Vittorio De Sica, *La Porta del Cielo. Memorie 1901-1952*, Cava de' Tirreni: Avagliano Editore, 2004, 88.

47 Ennio Flaiano, *La porta del cielo*, *Domenica*, no. 18, 6 May 1945, now in *Lettere d'amore al cinema*, Milan: Rizzoli, 1978 and in Nuzzi and Iemma, *De Sica e Zavattini*, 70–1.

48 Mario Verdone, 'De Sica "ladro onorario". Dalle biciclette ai clowns', *Il Progresso d'Italia*, 20 December 1948, now in Gualtiero De Santi (ed.), *Ladri di biciclette. Nuove ricerche e un'antologia della critica (1948-1949)*, Atripalda: Quaderni di Cinemasud, 2009, 139–41.

Chapter 5

1 Lorenzo Quaglietti, *Storia economico-politica del cinema italiano 1945-1980*, Rome: Editori Riuniti, 1980, 37–8.

2 Pilade Levi, an Italian American in US Army uniform and later General
   Manager of Paramount in Rome, Stephen Pallos, formerly filmmaker
   Alexander Korda's assistant and representing British film industry interests at
   that meeting, Italian producer Alfredo Guarini, and Alfredo Proja, an Italian
   producer. Quaglietti, *Storia economico-politica del cinema italiano*, 37.

3 Quaglietti, *Storia economico-politica del cinema italiano*, 38. The reason for
   this was that the Allied Psychological Warfare Branch, PWB or, in full, the
   Political Warfare Executive Subcommission, then in charge of film distribution,
   in addition to its main war propaganda activities, served the interests of
   Hollywood studios, which were keen to resume their exportation of films to
   Italy, earlier banned, by the Fascist regime.

4 Pallos represented the British component of PWB (Allied Psychological Warfare
   Subcommission) and was also on the Allied Film Board.

5 Also shown were Serghei Eisenstein's *Ivan the Terrible* (1944) and Marcel
   Carné's *Les Enfants du Paradis* (1945). David Forgacs, *Rome Open City*,
   London: British Film Institute, 2000, 18. *Days of Glory* is virtually unknown
   outside Italy, as well as being almost invisible in Italy. Recently its restored
   version has been made available on the web. It is the first documentary about
   the Italian Resistance, shot and filmed in the last months of the war and
   completed immediately after Germany's surrender. According to Ansano
   Giannarelli, an expert on Italian documentary history, filmmaker and former
   director of the Archivio Audiovisivo del Movimento Operaio, which restored
   it, this film is highly significant for two reasons. First, it contains exceptional
   documents about contemporary Italy during the last year of the Second World
   War, concerning the struggle by the Italian Resistance against the Germans who
   occupied the country after the Armistice of 8 September 1943. Second, because
   major Italian filmmakers were involved in filming and making it: Giuseppe
   De Santis, Marcello Pagliero, Umberto Barbaro, filmmaker and critic, and
   Luchino Visconti. Some of the sequences are filmed in synchronized sound
   and on location. Cf. Ansano Giannarelli, 'Un documento della nostra storia
   civile e cinematografica', in Mario Serandrei, *Giorni di gloria*, edited by Laura
   Gaiardoni, Rome: Bianco & Nero, Scuola Nazionale di Cinema and Editrice il
   Castoro, 1998, 17–18.

6 Cf. Valentina Fortichiari, in Zavattini, *Diario cinematografico*, 1979, 431.

7 Zavattini, 'L'Associazione culturale cinematografica italiana', a paper given
   at the first assembly of the first Italian professional filmmakers' association,
   published in Zavattini, in *Neorealismo ecc.*, 49–52.

8 There is a link: just as in the assembly, Zavattini proposed to stage a public
   (cultural) prosecution of filmmakers, including himself, in the script, the
   screenwriter imagined a trial scene provoked by the film crew which would
   accuse Italian families of indifference, and put himself forward as a public
   prosecutor, whose bona fide legitimacy was due to a willingness to admit his
   own shortcomings during the regime.

9 Zavattini, 'Quadernetto di note', *Cinema*, no. 90, 25 March 1940, then in
   Neorealismo ecc., 1979, 35–6.

10 Zavattini to Bompiani, 19 November 1947, in *Una, cento, mille, lettere*, 122–3.

11 On the spaces of hope, cf. David Harvey, *Spaces of Hope*, Edinburgh:
   Edinburgh University Press, 2000. Harvey uses the figure of the architect as an
   analogy to imagine the construction of a space of hope. Cf. *Spaces of Hope*,

201. Paul Ginsborg, *A History of Contemporary Italy: Society and Politics 1943-1988*, London: Penguin, 1990, 66–8.

12 Ginsborg, *ibidem*, 66–8.

13 Ginsborg, *ibidem*, 68.

14 Ginsborg, *ibidem*, 71.

15 Ginsborg, *ibidem*, 71.

16 Elio Vittorini, 'Una Nuova Cultura', *Il Politecnico*, no. 1, 29 September 1945, 1. Antonio Gramsci, *Quaderni del Carcere*, Vol. III, edited by Valentino Gerratana, Turin: Einaudi, 1977, Notebook 12, §1, §2, §3; 1513–51. The issue is dealt with in many other sections of the *Prison Notebooks*. Antonio Gramsci, 'The Intellectuals', in Antonio Gramsci, *Selections from the Prison Notebooks*, edited and translated by Geoffrey Nowell-Smith and Quintin Hoare, London: Lawrence and Wishart, 2007, 9 and David Forgacs (ed.), *An Antonio Gramsci Reader: Selected Writings, 1916-1935*, New York: Schocken Books, 1988, 300–22.

17 Gramsci, *Letteratura e vita nazionale*, Rome: Editori Riuniti, 1971, 24. (Selection from Prison Notebook VI). My translation. Cf. Forgacs, *An Antonio Gramsci Reader*, 395.

18 Gramsci, in Forgacs, *ibidem*, 57 and 70.

19 Brunello Rondi, *Il Neorealismo italiano*, Milan: Guanda, 1956, 108.

20 Rondi, *ibidem*, 118.

21 Rossellini, 'Prefazione', in Rondi, *Il Neorealismo italiano*, 9.

22 Maurice Merleau-Ponty, 'La guerre a eu lieu', *Les Temps Modernes*, October 1945, reprinted in Merleau-Ponty, *Sens et non-sens*, Paris: Nagel, 1948, 151. *Temps Modernes* was founded by Jean-Paul Sartre, Maurice Merleau-Ponty and Simone De Beauvoir. *Les Temps Modernes*, like *Il Politecnico*, also practised a multidisciplinary methodology. Both publications were seeking to convey a critical and militant view of the world, which wasn't in tune with the conventional Left in either country, be it the line of the PCF, in France or of the PCI in Italy. Jean-Paul Sartre, 'La Nationalisation de la littérature' (1945), in *Situations* II, Paris: Gallimard 1948, 40–1.

23 Henri Lefèbvre, *Critique of Everyday Life Volume 1: Introduction*, translated by John Moore, London and New York: Verso, 1991, 132.

24 Ginsborg, *A History of Contemporary Italy*, 68.

25 Cesare Zavattini, 'I pesci rossi e il disonesto', in *Cinelandia*, Rome, March 1946, no. 8, 3, later in Zavattini, *Neorealismo ecc.*, 55–8.

26 Ugo Torricelli, 'Italia, case distrutte', *Domus*, no. 212, August 1946, 30–1.

27 Zavattini, 'I pesci rossi e il disonesto', 55–8.

28 Zavattini, *ibidem*, 58.

29 Zavattini, *ibidem*, 55.

30 Zavattini, *ibidem*, 55.

31 Béla Tarr, interviewed by Jonathan Romney at the British Film Institute, 2001, DVD Special Features, *Werckmeister Harmonies*, *Damnation*, Artificial Eye.

32 Ginsborg, *A History of Contemporary Italy*, 112.

33 Ginsborg, *ibidem*, 141.

34 Pellizzari, 'Za soggettista e sceneggiatore', 157–69; 157.

35 This is the opposite of the ethics of incommunicability developed by Emmanuel Lévinas in *Totality and Infinity* (1960), except in so far as at the centre of his philosophy of the Other is a philosophy which takes the relationship with others, or more precisely, 'The Other', into consideration. Cf. Emmanuel

Lévinas, *Totality and Infinity: An Essay on Exteriority*, translated by Alphonso Lingis, Pittsburgh: Duquesne University Press, 1998. Alain Badiou, 'Does the Other Exist?' in *Ethics: An Essay on the Understanding of Evil*, translated and introduced by Peter Hallward, London and New York: Verso, 2012, 27. To Lévinas's philosophy, more recently, Alain Badiou made two objections. The first is that the Other presupposes the underlying Alterity of the Godhead and it is therefore a theology more than a philosophy as such, and second, that even if we can accept essential difference, there comes a time when, from an ethical standpoint, we are the Same.

36 Badiou, *Ethics*, 41. Badiou's ethics, which stems from the experience of a crucial moment in history, is an activist ethics: its categorical imperative is that once we recognize the event for what it is, the onus is on us to take part in the emancipatory project and act on the insights gained. See especially, 'Ethics as a Figure of Nihilsm', 30–9 for a reversal of Lévinas's position and 'The Ethic of Truths', 40–57 for his version of ethics. I am indebted to film historian Lúcia Nagrib who made this comparison, between Lévinas's and Badiou's opposite approach to ethics and the Other. Cf. Lúcia Nagrib, *World Cinema and the Ethics of Realism*, London and New York: Continuum, 2011, 32–3.

37 Zavattini, 'I pesci rossi e il disonesto', in *Neorealismo ecc.*, 56.

38 Jean-Luc Godard, *Due o tre cose che so su di me. Scritti e conversazioni sul cinema*, edited by Orazio Leogrande, Rome: Minimum fax, 2007, 244–5.

39 Godard cited in David Sterritt (ed.), *Jean-Luc Godard: Interviews*, Jackson: University of Mississippi, 1998, 176.

40 In *Histoire(s) du cinéma* (1998), Godard notes cinema's lack of social and political responsibility after the war: 'the obligation to resist, there's one film that did it knowingly – *Rome, Open City* – and after that it vanished. Nothing forced Roberto to make that film.' Jean-Luc Godard and Youssef Ishaghpour, *Cinema: The Archaeology of Film and the Memory of a Century*, Oxford and New York: Berg, 2005, 94.

41 Zavattini to Bompiani, 21 April 1947 in Zavattini, *Cinquant'anni e più*, 172.

42 Carpi, *Cesare Zavattini Direttore Editoriale*, 162.

43 Carpi, *ibidem*, 165.

Chapter 6

1 Vittorio De Sica, 'Sciuscià, Giò?', *Film d'oggi*, 1, no. 3, June, 1945, 4–5.

2 De Sica, 'Gli anni più belli della mia vita', *Tempo*, XVI, no. 50, 16 December 1954, 18–22.

3 De Sica, 'Sciuscià, Giò?', 4–5.

4 De Sica, 'Gli anni più belli della mia vita', 18–22.

5 Zavattii, Letter to Giuseppe Marotta, 10 May 1946, in Silvana Cirillo (ed.), *Una, cento, mille, lettere*, in Zavattini, *Opere. Lettere*, 136–7. Vittorio De Sica, *Tempo Illustrato*, 16 December 1954.

6 Zavattini, in Nuzzi and Iemma (eds) *De Sica e Zavattini*, 77.

7 Zavattini, *ibidem*, 77.

8 Aldo Bernardini, 'Filmografia', in Caldiron (ed.), *Vittorio De Sica*, 318.

9 Adolfo Franci, in Nuzzi and Iemma (eds) *De Sica e Zavattini*, 78.

10 De Sica, 'Gli anni più belli della mia vita', 18–22.

11 Cf. These pages build on Karl Schoonover's very perceptive discussion in *Brutal Vision*, 149–57.
12 Zavattini, Letter to Giuseppe Marotta, 10 May 1946, in Cirillo (ed.), *Una, cento, mille, lettere*, 136–7.
13 Guglielmo Moneti, '*Sciuscià* (e dintorni): Cesare Zavattini e la scrittura della realtà', in *Neorealismo fra tradizione e rivoluzione. Visconti, De Sica e Zavattini. Verso nuove esperienze cinematografiche della realtà*, Siena: Nuova immagine editrice, 1999, 65–7.
14 Gilles Deleuze, 'Beyond the Movement-Image', in *Cinema 2, the Time-Image*, translated by Hugh Tomlinson and Robert Gaeta, London and New York: Bloomsbury, 2013, 1–24.
15 Deleuze, *ibidem*, 18.
16 Torunn Haaland, *Italian Neorealist Cinema*, Edinburgh: Edinburgh University Press, 2014, 123–4. This is more than suggested in Haaland's book, echoing much of the literature in English. Integral to Zavattini's theories and Neo-realist poetic *tout court*, is a far subtler understanding of realism, whereby verisimilitude or *mimēsis*, in the classic sense, always demands artistic mediation. This is borne out by the formerly misunderstood André Bazin and still largely misunderstood Siegfried Kracauer and many of Zavattini's interviews and writings. Colin McCabe's chapter in *Opening Bazin* is just one among recent changes of heart in this respect. Cf, McCabe, 'Bazin as Modernist', 66–76. For Kracauer's critical *fortuna* since the bad old days, cf. Miriam Bratu Hansen, 'Introduction', in Siegfried Kracauer, *Theory of Film: The Redemption of Physical Reality*, Princeton: Princeton University Press, 1997, vii–xlv. Hansen recognized the coexistence of indexicality and iconicity in Kracauer's *ibidem*, xxi. After Gertrud Koch reframed Kracauer's thought. cf. Gertrud Koch, '"Not Yet Accepted Anywhere": Exile, Memory, and Image in Kracauer's Conception of History', translated by Jeremy Gaines, *New German Critique* 54, Autumn 1991, 95–109. At last, Devin Orgeron, in 'Visual Media and the Tyranny of the Real', in Robert Kolker (ed.), *The Oxford Handbook of Film and Media Studies*, Oxford: Oxford University Press, 2008, 83–113; 85, contextualized Kracauer's thought, based on Koch and Hansen's work in German archives, defending Kracauer and Bazin for concentrating on the photo-mechanical nature of the cinematic medium, while showing that they fully appreciated artistic mediation. Redemption, in the context of Kracauer's 'Photography' (1927) essay, points to the ethical element, choice, in a transformative approach to society.
17 Moneti, '"*Sciuscià* (e dintorni)"', 72. Giuseppe Ferrara, *Il nuovo cinema italiano*, Florence: Le Monnier, 1957, 229–30.
18 However 'anti-realistic' a dimension it might seem to represent, as Haaland believes (cf. *Italian Neorealist Cinema*, 126), Zavattini's written drama is Neo-realist, as opposed to realistic. Even *Italia mia*, Zavattini's later project, leaning heavily towards non-fiction, envisaged artistic mediation, in shots, montage and adaptation of the real.
19 André Bazin, 'Voleur de bicyclette', *L'Esprit*, 18, no. 161, November 1949, 820–32, now in Bazin, *Qu'est-ce que le cinéma*, Paris: Les Éditions du Cerf, 2013, 295–309; 297.
20 Bazin, 'Le réalisme cinématographique et l'école italienne de la Libération', *L'Esprit*, no. 141, 1, January 1948, 58–83, now in Bazin, *Qu'est-ce que le cinéma*, 257–85.

21 Luca Pes, 'Storia critica nel film', in Roberto Mordacci (ed.), *Come fare filosofia con i film*, Rome: Carrocci Editore, 2017, 69–85. As Pes points out, the atmosphere of an entire era can be evoked by a film. The force of impact of such evocation is integral to the shock of *Sciuscià* for its contemporary viewers and equally today, heightened by the clash of childhood imaginary with an unwanted, lived, real, played out by the characters, but also felt as genuine by viewers of the banal spectacle. There is also a poignancy in details such as the Fascist Roman salute by the reform warden in post-war Italy, and the remark that in 1936 there was less crime. Microcosm points ironically to a macrocosm in an offhand remark.

22 Vittorio De Sica, 'Abbiamo domandato a Vittorio De Sica perché fa un film dal *Ladro di biciclette*', *La Fiera Letteraria*, 3, no. 5, 6 February 1948, now in Caldiron, *Vittorio De Sica*, 258.

23 De Sica, 'Gli anni più belli della mia vita'.

24 Zavattini, Letter to Pietro Bardi, July 1947, in Cirillo, *Una, cento, mille, lettere*, 155.

25 Zavattini, 'Ladri di biciclette, 20 aprile 1948', in *Diario cinematografico*, edited by Valentina Fortichiari, in Zavattini, *Opere. Cinema*, Milan: Bompiani, 2002, 77.

26 Luigi Bartolini, *Ladri di biciclette*, Rome: Polin, 1946.

27 Zavattini, *Io. Un'autobiografia*, 151.

28 De Sica, 'Abbiamo domandato a Vittorio De Sica perché fa un film dal *Ladro di biciclette*', 258.

29 Zavattini, *Io. Un'autobiografia*, 151.

30 Zavattini, 'via Panico, settembre 1947', in *Diario cinematografico*, *Zavattini. Opere*, 70–1.

31 Zavattini, 'La messa dei poveri, 7 dicembre 1947', in *Diario cinematografico*, *Zavattini. Opere*, 71–3.

32 Zavattini, 'Ladri di biciclette, 20 aprile 1948', in *Diario cinematografico*, edited by Valentina Fortichiari, in Zavattini, *Opere. Cinema*, Milan: Bompiani, 2002, 77.

33 Zavattini, in Gambetti, *Zavattini mago e tecnico*, 86.

34 Zavattini, *Io. Un'autobiografia*, 152.

35 Zavattini, 'La Santona, 12 febbraio 1948', 'La Santona, 13 febbraio 1948', in *Diario cinematografico*, *Zavattini. Opere*, 74–7.

36 Zavattini, *Io. Un'autobiografia*, 151–2.

37 Federica Villa, *Botteghe di scrittura per il cinema italiano*, Rome: Biblioteca di Bianco & Nero, 2002, 30.

38 Gian Piero Brunetta, 'La commedia e il lavoro di bottega', in Sandro Bernardi (ed.), *Si fa per ridere ... ma è una cosa seria*, Florence: La Casa Usher, 1985, 60.

39 De Sica, cited in Zavattini, Letter to Giuseppe Marotta, 26 January 1949, in Cirillo, *Una, cento, mille, lettere*, 179.

40 Zavattini, Letter to De Sica, 20 January 1950 in in Cirillo, *Una, cento, mille, lettere*, 198.

41 De Sica, 'Perché avremmo dovuto separarci?', in Zavattini, 'Diario', *Cinema Nuovo*, II, no. 16, 1 August 1953, 70, now in Caldiron, *Vittorio De Sica*, 272–4.

42 Zavattini, *Neorealismo ecc.*, edited by Mino Argentieri, Milan: Bompiani, 1979, 383–4. Zavattini was interviewed by Lorenzo Pellizzari in March 1962. This text and the Appendix it appeared in was omitted from the 2002 edition of *Neorealismo ecc.* Cf. Zavattini, *Opere. Cinema*, 2002. De Sica, 'Perché avremmo dovuto separarci?', 273.

43 He developed his ideas in a series of interviews which were edited and
    published as 'Some Ideas on Cinema' (1952). The original version appeared in
    a film journal. Cf. Zavattini, 'Alcune idee sul cinema', *La Rivista del Cinema
    Italiano*, 1, no. 2, December 1952, 5–19. It was then included in a book in
    which Zavattini presented the whole process of writing for cinema, from
    scenario to screenplay, including additional and final corrections. Cf. Zavattini,
    Umberto D. Dal soggetto alla sceneggiatura: Precedono alcune idee sul cinema,
    Milan: Fratelli Bocca, 1953, 5–19. The text was translated into English and
    abridged by Pier Luigi Lanza with the title: Zavattini, 'Some Ideas on Cinema',
    Sight and Sound, October 1953, 64–9 and later reprinted in the anthology: *Film:
    A Montage of Theories*, edited by Richard Dyer MacCann, New York: Dutton,
    1966, 216–28. A new translation and critical edition is now available in Cesare
    Zavattini, *Selected Writings*, 2 vols, edited and translated by David Brancaleone,
    Vol. 2, New York: Bloomsbury Academic, 2021.
44 Zavattini, *Io. Un'autobiografia*, 157.
45 Villa, *Botteghe di scrittura per il cinema italiano*, 45.
46 Villa, *ibidem*, 45.
47 Guglielmo Moneti, '*Ladri di biciclette*: le visioni lungo la strada', in Moneti,
    Neorealismo fra tradizione e rivoluzione, Siena: Nuova immagine editrice,
    1999, 93–138.
48 Zavattini, *Neorealismo ecc.*, 383. He explained this to Lorenzo Pellizzari in 1962.
49 Alberto Abruzzese and Achille Pisanti, 'Cinema e letteratura', in *Letteratura
    italiana*, Vol. 2, Produzione e consumo, Turin: Einaudi, 828–9.
50 Sergio Amidei, in Franca Faldini and Goffredo Fofi (eds), *L'avventurosa
    storia del cinema italiano raccontata dai suoi protagonisti 1935-1959*, Milan:
    Feltrinelli, 1981, 135.
51 Ugo Pirro, *Celluloide*, Milan: Rizzoli, 1983, 127.
52 Edmondo De Amicis, *Cuore*, Milan: Treves, 1886.
53 Emi De Sica, cited in Nuzzi and Iemma (eds), *De Sica e Zavattini*, 1997, 99.
54 Pirro, *Celluloide*, 127.
55 Zavattini, *Io. Un'autobiografia*, 154. This first screening was organized by the
    Circolo Romano del Cinema.
56 Zavattini, *ibidem*, 155.
57 Pirro, *Celluloide*, 127.
58 Zavattini, *Io. Un'autobiografia*, 156.
59 María Mercader, cited in Nuzzi and Iemma (eds), *De Sica e Zavattini*, 1997, 96–7.
60 María Mercader, in Pina Bisceglie et al. (eds), *La città del cinema. Produzione e
    lavoro nel cinema italiano, 1930-1970*, Rome: Napoleone, 1979, 203–5.
61 Zavattini, 'La voce *Strade*', in Gustavo Marchesi and Giovanni Negri (eds),
    Al macero 1927-1940, now in Zavattini, *Opere 1931-1986*, edited by Silvana
    Cirillo, Milan: Bompiani, 1988, 1084–5.
62 Zavattini, cited in Nuzzi and Iemma (eds), *De Sica e Zavattini*, 1997, 110.
    Zavattini, Private diary, October 1950, in Zavattini, *Io. Un'autobiografia*, 166.
    Gambetti, *Zavattini mago e tecnico*, 158.
63 Zavattini, *Io. Un'autobiografia*, 156. Zavattini, *Opere. Lettere*, 173–86; 192–9.
64 Giuseppe Marotta, in *Bis*, 6 January, 1949, cited in Nuzzi and Iemma (eds),
    De Sica e Zavattini, 1997, 126.
65 Bazin, 'Voleur de bicyclette', 295–309; 297.
66 Bazin, *ibidem*, 298.

67 Bazin, *ibidem*, 302. Note the choice of word: objectivism, not objectivity, indicating that in Neo-realism objectivity is a desired effect, an aesthetic construction, not a given. For example, in Calcutta, Satyajit Ray's *Apu* trilogy.

68 Bazin, *ibidem*, 299.

69 Bazin, *ibidem*, 300.

70 Bazin, *ibidem*, 302.

71 Bazin was not aware that the idea dated back to Zavattini's 1930s stories, in which ethical witnessing was already suggested, however succinctly.

72 Bazin, *ibidem*, 305.

73 Bazin, *ibidem*, 307.

74 Giorgio Agamben, 'Che cos'è un paradigma?' in *Signatura rerum. Sul metodo*, Turin: Bollati Boringhieri, 2008, 11–34. Agamben maps the term backwards from Alfred Kuhn's *The Structure of Scientific Revolutions* (1962) and Michel Foucault's *Les Mots et le choses* (1974) through to Aristotle and Plato: as matrix, set of ideas based on underlying unacknowledged rules, *dispositif* or discursive regimes of thought at a given time, to book, as exemplar (to which one can add film), to sensitive *analogon* (Plato) and the dialectic itself, as an operating principle and a paradigmatic method. This is what Bazin achieves, seeing further than the stylistics approach to Neo-realism, to identify its underlying principles, as a multiplicity of an aesthetic, mediating the real with the imaginary.

75 Bazin, 'Voleur de bicyclette', 307.

76 Bazin, *ibidem*, 309. Bazin opposes action, proper to theatrical cinema and Hollywood, but not only, also to pre-war French realist cinema, and event 'événement'. Gilles Deleuze was to further explicate this in *Cinema 2*. Cf. Gilles Deleuze, *Cinema 2*, 1–24; 25–43; 82–101; 131–42; 154–5; 277–80. His examples are mostly French, given that he knew this cinema well, but are equally valid for Neo-realism which he knew less well. See also, Deleuze, *Cinema 1, The Movement Image*, translated by Hugh Tomlinson and Barbara Habberjam, London and New York: Continuum, 2012, 209–19.

77 Siegfried Kracauer, *Theory of Film: The Redemption of Physical Reality*. Princeton: Princeton University Press (1960) with an Introduction by Miriam Bratu Hansen, 1997, 255, 62.

78 Kracauer, *Theory of Film*, 308–11. Kracauer, *History: The Last Things Before the Last*, Princeton: Markus Wiener Publishers, 2014 [1969] with a Preface by Paul Oskar Kristeller, 211–17.

79 A recent re-evaluation and defence of Kracauer's interpretation of the ethics of witnessing in Georges Didi-Huberman, *Images in Spite of All: Four Photographs from Auschwitz*, translated by Shane B. Lillis, Chicago and London: The University of Chicago Press, 2008, 172–8.

80 Kracauer, *Theory of Film*, 305–6.

81 Kracauer, *History: The Last Things Before the Last*, 192. In 1960, Kracauer states that memorialization or, as he puts it, 'redeeming from oblivion', is the benefit of such an approach. 'The Found Story and The Episode' which was to become a chapter of Kracauer's *Theory of Film*, was first published in *Film Culture* 2, no.1, 1956, 1–5 and translated into Italian and published by *Cinema Nuovo* that same year. The Zavattinian thrust of Kracauer's argument, to be found not only in this excerpt, but also recognizable as a recurring feature of Kracauer's book, has not been picked up by Johannes von Moltke's *The Curious Humanist. Siegfried Kracauer in America*, Oakland, California: University of California Press, 2016 or in von Moltke and Kristy Rawson (eds), *Siegfried*

Kracauer's American Writings. Essays on Film and Popular Culture, Berkeley, Los Angeles, London: University of California Press, 2012. As for Miriam Bratu Hansen, cf. Hansen, *Cinema and Experience. Siegfried Kracauer, Walter Benjamin, and Theodor W. Adorno*, Berkeley, Los Angeles, London: University of California Press, 2012, she drew attention to the themes linking the post-war book to its first sketchy draft, written in Marseilles in 1940, but did not consider what Kracauer's repeated references to Neo-realist films might mean.

82 Kracauer, *History: The Last Things Before the Last*, 192.

83 '*Il grande inganno*. Idea per un film di Cesare Zavattini', *L'Unità*, 8 January 1950, 2, and Genoa edition, 11 January 1950, 2. *Tu Maggiorani* was recently published in Zavattini, *Tu, Maggiorani*, in Caldiron (ed.), *Uomo vieni fuori*, 138–46. A typescript with corrections of the first draft of the scenario *Il grande inganno* (*The Great Deception*), is in the Zavattini Archive, with a double title: 'Tu Maggiorani', '*Il grande inganno*', ACZ, Sog. NR 29/2, fols 26–30. The Zavattini Archive contains three copies of the scenario in all. One with author corrections (fols 1–9) (Zavattini's signature appears on each page, indicating that this is a legal SIAE copy). The first draft appears on fols 26–29. There are also two articles which consist in the two editions of the final version of *Il grande inganno*, *The Great Deception*. The first version, submitted for copyright, contains Zavattini's signature on each page. This text was published by Orio Caldiron. However, the earlier version, revised by the author Zavattini, is the one published in two almost identical articles: '*Il grande inganno*. Idea per un film di Cesare Zavattini', in *L'Unità*, 8 January 1950, 2, and 11 January 1950. These are two regional editions.

84 Zavattini, Letter to Radványi, 9 March 1950, *Uomo vieni fuori*, 146.

85 Zavattini suggests as much indirectly in a letter to the Hungarian director Géza Radványi, who was lined up to direct the film. Cf. Letter to Géza von Radváni, 9 March 1950, Zavattini, Letter to Géza Radványi, 9 March 1950, ACZ Corr. R24/2. Unpublished.

86 Zavattini, *ibidem*, 145.

87 De Santi, *Vittorio De Sica*, 69. It formed part of a project initiated by Zavattini, *Documento Mensile, 1 (Monthly Document, no. 1)* an artistic newsreel produced by Riccardo Ghione. Stefania Parigi, in a private communication, told the author that a copy of the film is in France.

Chapter 7

1 5 October 1945, Mino Argentieri, *La censura nel cinema italiano*, Rome: Editori Riuniti, 1974, 66.

2 Law no. 2387, cited in Quaglietti, *Storia economico-politica del cinema italiano*, 52.

3 Ginsborg, *A History of Contemporary Italy*, 112.

4 Quaglietti, *Storia economico-politica del cinema italiano*, 50.

5 Quaglietti, *ibidem*, 52.

6 Alberto Abruzzese and Giorgio Fabre, 'L'industria culturale tra cinema e televisione', in di Monte and Fago et al. (eds), *La città del cinema*, 25–36 and Quaglietti, *Storia economico-politica del cinema italiano*. The Catholic-financed film *Cielo sulla palude* (1949), by Augusto Genina (the story of a rape victim who was beatified by the Vatican), was an exception.

7 Virgilio Tosi, _Quando il cinema era un circolo. La stagione d'oro dei cineclub (1945-1956)_, Venice: Fondazione Scuola Nazionale di Cinema and Marsilio, 1999, 55.

8 Quaglietti, _Storia economico-politica del cinema italiano_, 53–4. Camerini, Mattòli, Alessandrini, Guarini, Franciolini, Mastrocinque, Malasomma, Bragaglia, Matarazzo, Francisci, Comencini, Ferroni, Bianchi, Gambino, Campogalliani, Marcellini, Ballerini, Morelli, Pozzetti, Cottafavi, Vassallo, Benedetti, Bologna, Antonioni, Fellini, Blasetti, Soldati, Camerini, De Sica, Lattuada, Germi, Rossellini, Vergano, Visconti, Barbaro, Chiarini, De Robertis, Fasano, Elletto.

9 Quaglietti, _Storia economico-politica del cinema italiano_, 53–4.

10 Argentieri, _La censura nel cinema italiano_, 71. Article 2 of law no. 379 of 16 May 1947.

11 Giulio Andreotti, 'Paure di registi', _Il Popolo_, 14 December 1947, 1.

12 Argentieri, _La censura nel cinema italiano_, 68. It is also true to say that, despite restrictive legislation, in pre-war Italy, _The Children Are Watching_ and _Obsession_ were not censored. It is quite possible that both would have been, had they been proposed for production after the DC took control of the film industry from 1947 onwards.

13 Tosi, _Quando il cinema era un circolo_, 57.

14 Ginsborg, _A History of Contemporary Italy_, 141.

15 Tosi, _Quando il cinema era un circolo_, 56.

16 Argentieri, _La censura nel cinema italiano_, 73.

17 Tosi, _Quando il cinema era un circolo_, 105. The CCC was a very influential body which influenced a large proportion of the public, by imparting its advice to Catholic audiences as to what was suitable for viewing.

18 Tosi, _ibidem_, 103.

19 Argentieri, _La censura nel cinema italiano_, 76.

20 Law no. 958, of 1 January 1950, cited in Quaglietti, _Storia economico-politica del cinema italiano_, 65.

21 The following filmmakers and writers formed the organizing committee: Alessandro Blasetti, Mario Camerini, Renato Castellani, Giuseppe De Santis, Vittorio De Sica, Pietro Germi, Alberto Lattuada, Antonio Pietrangeli, Roberto Rossellini, Mario Soldati, Luchino Visconti, Luigi Zampa, Zavattini, Corrado Alvaro and Alberto Moravia. The Proceedings were published by Barbaro, who stated that the conference was organized by Left-wing filmmakers. Cf. Umberto Barbaro (ed.), 'Prefazione', in _Il cinema e l'uomo moderno_. Atti del Convegno Internazionale di Cinematografia (Perugia 24–27 Settembre), Milan: Le Edizioni Sociali, 1950, 11.

22 Luigi Chiarini, 'Due congressi', _Bianco & Nero_, October 1949, 3–6.

23 Zavattini, 'Il cinema e l'uomo moderno', in Zavattini, _Neorealismo ecc._, 61–5. A shorter version was published in _Straparole_: 'Inutile, 1949', then in _Diario cinematografico_, 75–6.

24 Galvano Della Volpe, Perugia Conference Paper, in Barbaro, _Il cinema e l'uomo moderno_, 87–91.

25 Della Volpe, _ibidem_, 90.

26 Della Volpe, _ibidem_, 90.

27 Della Volpe, _ibidem_, 91.

28 Barbaro, _ibidem_, 49–56.

29 Barbaro, Perugia Conference paper, 56.

30 Carlo Lizzani, Perugia Conference Paper, 119–26. Surprisingly, given the historic importance of this event in the history of Neo-realism, neither Lizzani's own contribution to this conference, nor to the Parma Conference of 1953, is included in his book, which he edited himself. Cf. Carlo Lizzani, *Attraverso il novecento*, Turin: Bianco & Nero and Lindau, 1998.

31 Strand, Perugia Conference Paper, 173.

32 Strand, *ibidem*, 179.

33 Strand, *ibidem*, 178.

34 Strand, *ibidem*, 174.

35 Strand, *ibidem*, 175.

36 Ben Barzman, Perugia Conference paper, 57–64.

37 Director Edward Dmytryk, screenwriters Albert Maltz, Dalton Trumbo, Samuel Ornitz, Herbert Biberman, Ring Lardner, writers John Howard Lawson, Alvah Bessie, Lester Cole and the producer Adrian Scott.

38 Vsevolod Pudovkin, Perugia Conference Paper, 137–52. Régine Robin, *Socialist Realism: An Impossible Aesthetic*, Stanford: Stanford University Press, 1992.

39 M. Papava, Perugia Conference Paper, 127–36.

40 Boris Cirkov, Perugia Conference Paper, 79–86.

41 Alexander Ford, Perugia Conference Paper, 105–10.

42 A. M. Brousil, Perugia Conference Paper, 68–78; 73, 75.

43 Alberto Lattuada, in Barbaro, *Il cinema e l'uomo moderno*, 93–7.

44 Georges Sadoul, Perugia Conference paper, 153–70, 168.

45 Sadoul, Perugia Conference Paper, 169.

46 Georg Lukács, 'The Intellectual Physiognomy in Characterization', in Lukács, *Writer and Critic and Other Essays*, edited and translated by Arthur Kahn, London: Merlin Press, 1970, 149–88, 154.

47 Lukács, 'Narrate or Describe?' in Lukács, *Writer and Critic and Other Essays*, 133, 139.

48 Lukács, *ibidem*, 41.

49 Joris Ivens, Perugia Conference Paper, 111–18.

Chapter 8

1 Alberto Lattuada, *La freccia nel fianco* (1945), Pietro Germi, *Il testimone* (1946), Marcello Pagliero, *Roma città libera* (1946), Luciano Emmer, *Domenica d'agosto* (1950), Luigi Zampa, *È più facile che un cammello …* (1950), Renato Castellani, *È primavera* (1950), Claudio Gora, *Il cielo è rosso* (1950), Gianni Franciolini, *Buongiorno elefante!* (1952).

2 *Prima Comunione*. Cf. Orio Caldiron, *Cinema 1936-1943*, Rome: Fondazione Scuola Nazionale di Cinema, 125. Zavattini, 'Bellissima', *Cinema*, 2, no. 25, 30 October 1949.

3 Zavattini, Letter to Alessandro Blasetti, 30 July 1962, in Zavattini, *Una, cento, mille, lettere*, 234.

4 Zavattini, *Io. Un'autobiografia*, 160–1.

5 The unpublished typescript with handwritten annotations by Zavattini. Cf. *Prima Comunione*, Screenplay, ACZ, Sog. R 45.

6 Zavattini, *Prima Comunione*, ACZ, Sog. R 45/3, fol. 59.

7 Zavattini, *ibidem*, fol. 63.

8 Pietro Thouar, *Racconti per giovinetti*, Florence: Bemporad, 1890. Pietro Thouar (1809–61) was an educator and writer from Florence who wrote moralizing, quite boring, educational books for children. But he was married, not a prelate, not a canon.

9 Claude Roy, 'Réflexions sur *Miracle à Milan*', *Cahiers du cinéma*, no. 7, December 1951, 35.

10 Zavattini, *Totò il Buono* (1940), in Caldiron (ed.), *Uomo vieni Fuori!*, 75. Author's translation, 75.

11 Silvana Cirillo, *Za l'immortale. Centodieci anni di Cesare Zavattini*, Rome: Ponte Sisto, 2013, 45.

12 'Totò il Buono', *Cinema*, v, no. 102, 25 September 1940. Then in Zavattini, *Uomo, vieni fuori!*, 80. The novel first appeared in weekly instalments in *Tempo* in 1942, and in book form the following year. Cf. also Gualtiero De Santi, *Ritratto di Zavattini scrittore*, Reggio Emilia: Aliberti editore, 2006, 159–73.

13 Zavattini, *Io. Un'autobiografia*, 165.

14 Zavattini, *ibidem*, 165. *Vie Nuove*, 26 March 1950, cited in Nuzzi and Iemma (eds), *De Sica e Zavattini*, 144.

15 Zavattini, Letter to De Sica, 20 January 1950, in Zavattini, *Opere. Lettere*, 2002, 193.

16 Malerba, 'Prefazione. Un mestiere zoppo', Zavattini, *Umberto D.*, in Zavattini, *Dal soggetto alla sceneggiatura. Come si scrive un capolavoro*, edited by Guido Conti, Parma: Monte Università Parma, 2005, vii.

17 Zavattini, Letter to De Sica, 20 January 1950, in Zavattini, *Opere. Lettere*, 196. De Sica, Letter to Zavattini, 31 January 1950, in Nuzzi and Iemma, *De Sica e Zavattini*, 153.

18 De Sica, cited in Nuzzi and Iemma (eds), *De Sica e Zavattini*, 169.

19 Zavattini, *Io. Un'autobiografia*, 166.

20 De Sica, in Caldiron (ed.), *Vittorio De Sica*, 262.

21 María Mercader, cited in Nuzzi and Iemma (eds), *De Sica e Zavattini*, 155. Lorenzo Pellizzari, in conversation with the author, Milan, 2015. The conversation was filmed and recorded.

22 Zavattini, *Unità*, 5 January 1949.

23 Zavattini, *ibidem*.

24 Parigi, *Fisiologia dell'immagine*, 254.

25 Zavattini, 'Totò il Buono', *Il Momento*, 23 February 1950.

26 Davide Lajolo, cited in Nuzzi and Iemma (eds), *De Sica e Zavattini*, 162.

27 De Sica, Radio Milano interview, cited in *ibidem*, 158.

28 Zavattini, 'October 1950', Private Diary, cited in *Io. Un'autobiografia*, 166. Zavattini, Letter to Bompiani, 12 November 1950, in Zavattini, *Opere. Lettere*, 840.

29 Zavattini, '27 November 1950', Private Diary, cited in *Io. Un'autobiografia*, 166.

30 Zavattini, in Gambetti, *Zavattini mago e tecnico*, 161, 164.

31 Luigi Chiarini, 'Impossibilità di sintesi tra realtà e favola', *Cinema*, no. 62, 15 May 1951.

32 Guido Aristarco, 'Miracolo a Milano', *Cinema*, no. 57, 1 March 1951. Gian Luigi Rondi, cited in Davide Lajolo, cited in Nuzzi and Iemma (eds), *De Sica e Zavattini*, 171–4.

33 Tullio Kezich, Radio Trieste broadcast, 5 March 1951, cited in Nuzzi and Iemma (eds), *De Sica e Zavattini*, 179.

34 Georges Sadoul, cited in Nuzzi and Iemma (eds), *De Sica e Zavattini*, 182. De Sica, in Caldiron (eds), *Vittorio De Sica*, 282.
35 Zavattini, *Io. Un'autobiografia*, 168.
36 Zavattini, 'Miracolo a Milano', *La Voce Repubblicana*, 7 July 1951.
37 Gambetti, *Zavattini mago e tecnico*, 161.
38 Zavattini, *Io. Un'autobiografia*, 167.
39 Official report, dated 30 June 1949, cited in Consuelo Balduini, *Miracoli e boom. L'Italia dal dopoguerra al boom economico nell'opera di Cesare Zavattini*, Reggio Emilia: Aliberti Editore and Archivio Zavattini-Biblioteca Panizzi, 2013, 92.
40 Zavattini, *Unità*, 5 January 1949.
41 Zavattini, Letter to Father A. Félix Morlion, 29 November, 1949, in Zavattini, *Opere. Lettere*, 190–1.
42 André Bazin, 'Vittorio De Sica: metteur en scène', in *Qu'est-ce que le cinéma?*, 321, 324.
43 Bazin, *ibidem*, 311–29, 324.
44 Zavattini, 'Charlot, Imola, 24 April 1937', 88.
45 Zavattini, 'Quadernetto di note, 25 March 1940', *Cinema*, no. 90, 25 March 1940, now in Zavattini, *Diario cinematografico*, *Opere. Cinema*, 2002, 31.
46 Bazin, 'Une grande œuvre: *Umberto D.*', *ibidem*, 331–5; 332. Bazin, 'En Italie', in Bazin et al., *Cinéma 53 à travers le monde*, Paris: Les Éditions du Cerf, 1954, 85.
47 Bazin, 'Vittorio De Sica: metteur en scène', 322–3.
48 Bazin, *ibidem*, 323.
49 Zavattini, *I poveri sono matti*, in Zavattini, *Opere 1931-1986*, 69–70. The game in question was pretending to one's own family to be someone else, raising the question of harbouring different identities or personae, depending on the social context. Placing the absurd in the form of a game at the very beginning coloured the whole book, distancing it from the funnier first collection *Let's Talk All about Me*.
50 Zavattini, 'Una domenica di maggio', in *I poveri sono matti*, in Zavattini, *Opere 1931-1986*, 114–18.
51 Zavattini, 'Charlot, Imola, 24 April 1937', 86–94; 89.
52 Zavattini, in Gambetti, *Zavattini mago e tecnico*, 186.
53 Zavattini, *Riandando* (included in *Straparole*), in Zavattini, *Opere 1931-1986*, 653–723.
54 Zavattini, cited in Gambetti (ed.), *Cesare Zavattini: cinema e vita*, Vol. 1, 1996, 27.
55 Giuseppe Marotta, cited in Nuzzi and Iemma (eds), *De Sica e Zavattini*, 160.
56 Zavattini, in Gambetti, *Zavattini mago e tecnico*, 177.
57 Zavattini, cited in Gambetti, *Cesare Zavattini: cinema e vita*, Vol. 1, 1996, 24.
58 Gian Piero Brunetta, *Il cinema neorealista italiano. Da 'Roma città aperta' a 'I soliti ignoti'*, Rome and Bari: Editori Laterza, 2009, 97.
59 Zavattini, *Io. Un'autobiografia*, 172–3.
60 Giuseppe De Santis, 'Zavattini nel cinema italiano prima e dopo il 1940', in Giacomo Gambetti (ed.), *Cesare Zavattini: Cinema e vita. Atti del Convegno di Studi*, Bologna: Edizioni Bora, 1997, 33. The following reconstruction is based on De Santi's reminiscences published at the 1996 Conference cited above.
61 'Basta coi soggetti', in Zavattini, *Neorealismo ecc.*, 70–3.

62 Danilo Dolci trained as an architect, but then became an ethnographer
    through practice, working first at Fossoli, a former Nazi concentration camp,
    which a Catholic priest, Don Zeno, turned into the community and village
    of *Nomadelfia*. Dolci then moved to a small village in Sicily, where he lived
    and worked among the poor, and where he combined his efforts in education,
    building new housing and infrastructure, to improve living conditions, with
    field research, translated into pioneering testimonial literature, especially
    Banditi a Partinico (1955), 'Thieves in Partinico' and *Inchiesta a Palermo*
    (1956).

63 Giuseppe De Santis, 'Vi racconto come andò con *Roma, ore 11*', *Cinema
    Nuovo*, no. 282, April 1983, 32–5.

64 De Santis, 'Zavattini nel cinema italiano prima e dopo il 1940', 23–36; 34.

65 Zavattini, 'Lettera da Cuba', in Elio Petri, *Roma, ore 11*, Edizioni Avanti!,
    1956, 13–15. The letter was sent after 5 September 1955, during Zavattini's
    second trip to Cuba. The letter was first published in *La Risaia*, 23 March
    1956, then in the book, and again *Roma, ore 11*, in: Cesare Zavattini,
    Gli altri. Interventi, occasioni, incontri, edited by Pierluigi Raffaelli,
    Milan: Bompiani, 1986, 20–2 and again in Zavattini, *Opere 1931–1986*,
    Introduction by Luigi Malerba, edited by Silvano Cirillo, Milan: Bompiani,
    1991, 1633–5.

66 *Roma, ore 11*, ACZ, Sog. R46/4, Copia C. Sceneggiatura, fol. 1. Soggetto
    e sceneggiatura: G. De Santis, B. Franchina, R. Sonego, C. Zavattini, fol.
    12: whole page deleted in pencil. Fols 124. 125: pencil corrections, cuts,
    accompanied by explanations, all in Zavattini's hand. *Roma, ore 11*, ACZ,
    Sog. R47, Sceneggiatura (copia). In bound copy on 54 v. drawing in pencil
    relating to the point in the story when the stairs fall, on fol. 55 r. *Roma, ore
    11*, ACZ, Sog. R47, U7/3 Documentazione. Interviews with the typists. 64 fols;
    fol. 64, interview with the first journalist on the scene.

67 Zavattini, 'Lettera da Cuba', 13–15. Author's translation available in
    Zavattini, *Selected Writings*, Vol. 2.

68 Lino Micciché, *Visconti e il neorealismo. Ossessione, La terra trema* e
    Bellissima, Venice: Marsilio, 1990.

69 Nicola Dusi, 'Scritture a confronto: *Bellissima* tra differenza e ripetizione, a
    partire da Zavattini', in Dusi and Lorenza Di Francesco (eds), *Bellissima tra
    scrittura e metacinema*, Parma: Diabasis, 2017, 110.

70 Micciché, *Visconti e il neorealismo*, 196–7; 200; 208–9. According to Stefania
    Parigi, reflexivity emerges in Zavattini's writing as early as the late 1920s. Cf.
    Parigi, *Fisiologia dell'immagine*, 170.

71 Dusi, 'Scritture a confronto: *Bellissima* tra differenza e ripetizione, a partire
    da Zavattini', 123.

72 Silvia Pagni, '*Bellissima*: sceneggiature a confronto', in Dusi and Di Francesco
    (eds), *Bellissima tra scrittura e metacinema*, 99.

73 Pio Baldelli, *I film di Luchino Visconti*, Manduria: Lacaita, 1965, 102, cited
    in Dusi, 'Scritture a confronto: *Bellissima* tra differenza e ripetizione, a partire
    da Zavattini', 136.

74 Zavattini wrote *Prima Comunione* for Blasetti in 1949. He published it in
    Cinema, 2, no. 25, 30 October 1949.

75 Cristina Jandelli, 'Cerchiamo un bambino distinto. La genesi di *Bellissima*',
    in Dusi and Di Francesco (eds), *Bellissima tra scrittura e metacinema*, 85.

The clash between the two worlds (of illusion and everyday life) were also explored by Fellini's *Lo sceicco bianco* (1952), (*The White Sheik*), in *We Women* (1953), produced and conceived by Zavattini and Antonioni's *La signora senza camelie* (1953) (*The Lady without Camelias*).

76 Jandelli, 'Cerchiamo un bambino distinto. La genesi di *Bellissima*', 89.

77 Jandelli, *ibidem*, 88.

78 Zavattini, 'Il progetto del film', in Francesco Bolzoni, 'Zavattini e il film inchiesta', in *I misteri di Roma*, Rome: Cappelli Editore, 1962, 13–32; 21.

79 Zavattini, Letter (undated) to Alessandro Minardi, in Zavattini, *Opere. Lettere*, 2002, 166.

80 Zavattini, '18 December 1948', Private diary, in *Io. Un'autobiografia*, 161.

81 Zavattini, *Umberto D.*, 28.

82 The treatment appears in translation, in the companion volume to this one. Cf. This translation appears in the companion volume, Zavattini, *Selected Writings*, Vol. 1.

83 Balduini, *Miracoli e boom*, 114.

84 Zavattini, *Umberto D.*, 66.

85 Zavattini, '18 December 1948', 161.

86 Zavattini, *Umberto D.*, 217–30. Zavattini, 'La genesi della storia di Umberto D.', *Cinemundus*, XXX, 13, 15 December 1951, cited in Zavattini, *Uomo, vieni fuori!*, 111.

87 Zavattini, 'La genesi della storia di Umberto D.', 111.

88 *Il Momento*, 16 October 1948, cited in Balduini, *Miracoli e boom*, 112.

89 Maria Mercader, in Nuzzi and Iemma (eds), *De Sica e Zavattini*, 190.

90 Mercader, *ibidem*, 190.

91 A translation of the story appears in the companion volume, Zavattini, *Selected Writings*, Vol. 1. Originally published as: Zavattini, '*Umberto D.*', *Teatro Scenario*, IV, 15–16, 15 August 1951, then reprinted in Zavattini, *Umberto D., dal soggetto alla sceneggiatura: Precedono alcune idee sul cinema* and now in Zavattini, *Dal soggetto alla sceneggiatura. Come si scrive un capolavoro*, 27–33.

92 Zavattini, *Io. Un'autobiografia*, 190.

93 Zavattini, interview with Pasquale Festa Campanile, 'Il cinema, Zavattini e la realtà', *La Fiera Letteraria*, no. 47, 9 December 1951 in Zavattini, *Neorealismo ecc.*, 1979, 83.

94 Zavattini, 'Cinema italiano domani', in Alessandro Blasetti and Gian Luigi Rondi (eds), *Cinema italiano oggi*, Rome: Bestetti, 1950, in *Neorealismo ecc.*, 1979, 76.

95 Cesare Zavattini and Vittorio De Sica, 'Regista e soggettista di fronte al personaggio', *Copione*, no. 1, 1 January 1952, 7.

96 Degli Espinosa, *Rivista del Cinema Italiano*, I–II, nos. 1–2, January–February 1953, 14. The first part of his article is based on notes given to or recorded by Degli Espinosa at Zavattini's home. The article is very close to the text of the notes. These were subsequently published by Mino Argentieri in *Neorealismo ecc.* (1979).

97 Espinosa, *Rivista del Cinema Italiano*, I–II, nos. 1–2, 17.

98 Espinosa, *ibidem*, 17.

99 Italo Calvino, Letter to Zavattini, 11 December 1951, in Calvino, *Lettere*, 330.

100 Paolo and Vittorio Taviani, in Aldo Bernardini and Jean A. Gili (eds), *Cesare Zavattini*, Paris and Reggio Emilia: Centre Pompidou and Regione Emilia-Romagna, 1990, 158–9. 'This little book took us by surprise. Here is a work that uses the written word, but which, for some kind of displacement that is hard to pin down with codified language, both cinematic and poetic, belongs entirely to the universe of cinema.'

101 Zavattini, Letter to De Sica, Rome 24 January 1952, *Una, cento, mille, lettere*, 172–4.

102 Zavattini, *Neorealismo ecc.*, 83.

103 Nuzzi and Iemma, *De Sica e Zavattini*, 244.

104 Giulio Andreotti, 'Lettera aperta a Vittorio De Sica', in *Libertas*, cited in Quaglietti, *Storia economico-politica del cinema italiano*, 84. Tosi, *Quando il cinema era un circolo*, 173–4.

105 The editor of *Cinema Nuovo* responded. Cf. Guido Aristarco, 'Ottimismo e pessimismo', *Cinema Nuovo*, no. 3, 15 January 1953, 39.

106 Giulio Andreotti, 'Piaghe sociali e necessità di redenzione', *Libertas*, 7, 28 February 1952.

107 An essay by Mino Argentieri has proved very useful. Argentieri, 'Uno dalle mezze maniche da Pietroburgo a Pavia', in Lino Miccichè (ed.), *Il cappotto di Alberto Lattuada. La storia, lo stile, il senso*, Turin: Lindau, 1995, 57–68.

Chapter 9

1 Thomas Waugh, 'Introduction: Why Documentary Filmmakers Keep Trying to Change the World', *or* 'Why People Changing the World Keep Making Documentaries', in Thomas Waugh (ed.), *Show Us Life: Toward a History and Aesthetics of Committed Documentary*, Metuchen, NJ: Scarecrow Press, 1984, xi–xxvii.

2 Zavattini interviewed by Pasquale Festa Campanile, 'Il cinema, Zavattini e la realtà', 81–5.

3 Zavattini, 'Come non ho fatto *Italia mia*', *La Rassegna del film*, 2, no. 12, March 1953, 21.

4 Zavattini, *ibidem*, 21.

5 Both worked in the cinema industry, the poet Attilio Bertolucci and the novelist Giorgio Bassani.

6 As often happened in Zavattini's writing, an idea would drift from one project to another changing its name and developing further. This was, for example, how an episode about illegal house construction found its way into the *Italia mia* version Rossellini planned to film and produce in mid-1952. Zavattini included it in the scenario for Rossellini on 16 November 1952. However, Rossellini abandoned *Italia mia*, but the episode became a full-blown feature: film *The Roof* (1956).

7 Zavattini, 'Ciò che sta acadendo: questo è il cinema', Zavattini interviewed by Pasquale Festa Campanile, *Il Momento*, Saturday, 8 December 1951, 3.

8 Zavattini, 'Lavoro in biblioteca', Saturday 22–Monday 25 January 1952, ACZ, TV2 Televisione, *Italia mia* 1, fols 77–81.

9 Zavattini, *ibidem*, 10 May 1952, ACZ, TV2 Televisione, *Italia mia* 1, fol. 15.

10 Zavattini, *ibidem*, Saturday 22–Monday 25 January 1952, ACZ, TV2 Televisione, *Italia mia* 1, fol. 78.

11 Zavattini, 'Lavoro in biblioteca', Saturday 22–Monday 25 January 1952, fol. 80.

12 Zavattini, *ibidem*, 10–12 May 1952, ACZ, TV2 Televisione, *Italia mia* 1, fols 18–28. My thanks to Giorgio Boccolari for information about cultural attitudes about the Holocaust in post-war Italy.

13 Zavattini to Agostino Degli Espinosa, 18 April 1952, in Zavattini, *Neorealismo ecc.*, 1979, 84–5.

14 Zavattini interviewed by Campanile, 'Il cinema, Zavattini e la realtà', 81–5.

15 Zavattini, Letter to Degli Espinosa, 18 April 1952, in Zavattini, *Neorealismo ecc.*, 1979, 84–5. The text was published in *Paese Sera*, according to Enzo Muzii, 'Il cinema e la realtà, Zavattini. Tesi sul Neorealismo', *Emilia*, no. 17, November 1953, 219.

16 Zavattini, 'Il Neorealismo continua', 92–4. A note by Zavattini states that the article was written in June 1952. Mino Argentieri has pointed out that an article by the same title was published in the daily paper *La Gazzetta di Modena*, on 18 May 1953, based on the bibliography in Sandro Petraglia and Stefano Rulli, *Il Neorealismo e la critica. Materiali per una bibliografia*, Pesaro: Mostra del Nuovo Cinema, 1974. Cf. Argentieri in Zavattini, *Neorealismo ecc.*, 1979, 94.

17 Zavattini, 'Il Neorealismo continua', 92–4. A note by Zavattini states that the article was written in June 1952. Mino Argentieri has pointed out that an article by the same title, and thus, most likely one and the same, was published in the daily paper *La Gazzetta di Modena* (18 May 1953), based on the bibliography in Petraglia and Rulli, *Il Neorealismo e la critica*, 94.

18 Ginsborg, *A History of Contemporary Italy*, 187, 201, 211.

19 Lorenzo Piersantelli, 'Un'inchiesta sulla miseria in Italia', https://lpiersa ntelli.wordpress.com/2013/02/21/uninchiesta-sulla-miseria-in-italia/. Following Piersantelli's door-to-door field research, in 1951, the government commissioned independent research which was concluded in 1954. Camera dei Deputati, *Atti della Commissione parlamentare, di inchiesta sulla miseria in Italia e sui mezzi per combatterla*, Rome: Camera dei Deputati, 1953. Now in Archivio Storico della Camera dei Deputati, http://archivio.camera.it/patrimoni o/archivi_del_periodo_repubblicano_1948_2008/. A documentary was made in 1953, directed by Giorgio Ferroni and produced by the Istituto Luce. http://sen ato.archivioluce.it/senato-luce/scheda/video/IL3000088346/1/Inchiesta-parla mentare-sulla-miseria-in-Italia.html, accessed 7 July 2017. From Zavattini's point of view, the documentary is very interesting, because it visualizes the kind of image of Italy he had in mind. With one significant difference, namely, that whereas the voiceover speaks on behalf of the people in the frame, he wanted to allow their voices to tell their own story which he did in the fragments of *Italia mia* that made it on screen, developed as films in their own right.

20 Zavattini, 'Il Neorealismo continua', 92–4.

21 Zavattini to Degli Espinosa, 18 April 1952, in Zavattini, *Neorealismo ecc.*, 1979, 84–5.

22 On the concept of the subjective element in Zavattini, cf. Laura Rascaroli, *The Personal Camera: Subjective Cinema and the Essay Film*, London and New York: Wallflower Press, 2009, 111–13.

23 Zavattini, *Io. Un'autobiografia*, 177–89.

24 De Sica, interview by Tommaso Chiaretti, *L'Unità*, 22 January 1952, in Nuzzi and Iemma (eds), *De Sica e Zavattini*, 1997, 212–13.

25 Francesco Bolzoni, 'Zavattini e il film inchiesta', in *I misteri di Roma*, Rome: Cappelli Editore, 1962, 35–153, 45.

26 Zavattini, *Io. Un'autobiografia*, 2002, 178–89.

27 Zavattini to De Sica, Rome 18 December 1951, Nuzzi and Iemma (eds), *De Sica e Zavattini*, 1997, 206–7.

28 Zavattini to De Sica, Rome 24 January 1952, in Zavattini, *Una, cento, mille, lettere*, edited by Silvana Cirillo, Milan: Bompiani, 1988, 172–4.

29 'sketch' in English in the Italian sentence. Zavattini, *Io. Un'autobiografia*, 2002, 180.

30 Zavattini, *Io. Un'autobiografia*, 177–83.

31 Rossellini, 'Rossellini e il Neo-realismo', in *Il Giornale di Vicenza*, 5 June 1952.

32 Zavattini, Private diary, *Io. Un'autobiografia*, 182.

33 Argentieri, *La censura nel cinema italiano*, 86.

34 *Delta padano* (1951) by Florestano Vancini, https://www.youtube.com/watch?v=I9-xNrN9ERI, accessed 6 July 2017.

35 Brunetta, *L'isola che non c'è*.

36 She also obtained improved transport and services.

37 In 1951, nearly 7 per cent of Italians were homeless, and an additional 22 per cent lived without adequate sanitation, according to Peter Rowe. Peter G. Rowe, *Civic Realism*, Cambridge, MA: MIT Press, 1997, 107.

38 Zavattini, 'Diario', *Cinema Nuovo*, no. 8, 1 April 1953, cited in Michele Gandin (ed.), *Il tetto di Vittorio De Sica. Dal soggetto al film*, Bologna: Cappelli Editore, 1956, 29.

39 Zavattini, 'Come spero di fare *Italia mia*', *Rassegna del film*, 2, no. 13, April 1953, 21–9.

40 Zavattini's detailed notes were published in Gandin, *Il tetto di Vittorio De Sica*, 60–1.

41 Paola Masino, author of *Nascita e morte di una massaia* (1945).

42 Gandin, *Il tetto di Vittorio De Sica*, 17.

43 Zavattini, in Gandin, *Il tetto di Vittorio De Sica*, 58.

44 Cf. Mark Shiel's excellent historical reconstruction of Mussolini's building programme in the above-mentioned Shiel, *Italian Neorealism: Rebuilding the Cinematic City*, London: Wallflower Press, 2006 and *ibidem*, 'Cinema and the City in History and in Theory', in *Cinema and The City: Film and Urban Societies in a Global Context*, Oxford and Malden, MA: Blackwell, 2001.

45 Zavattini, in Gandin, *Il tetto di Vittorio De Sica*, 20.

46 Gandin, *ibidem*, 21.

47 Gandin, *ibidem*, 21. A study of *The Roof* appears in Schoonover's *The Neorealist Body in Postwar Italian Cinema*, 172–83. Schoonover highlights what he takes to be 'the exploitation of the poor for the sake of spectacle', ibidem, 179. The passage refers to the end of the film, when the police come to check on the completed dwelling, the couple have a child with them who is embraced, as if theirs, but borrowed from a neighbour. Judging from Gandin's archival documentation, however, what might have seemed a screenwriter's failing was in fact a common ploy. That the employment of ordinary people as actors was exploitative is a moot point. The same accusation has often been made before with respect to documentary photography; notably, by John Berger and Susan Sontag.

48 Orio Caldiron in Zavattini, *Uomo, vieni fuori!*, 216.
49 Zavattini, 'Come non ho fatto *Italia mia*', 21–8. Zavattini, 'Come spero di fare *Italia mia*', 21–9.
50 Brunello Rondi, Letter to Zavattini (undated, but marked as 1954), ACZ R/330.6. Unpublished.
51 Luca Caminati, *Roberto Rossellini documentarista. Una cultura della realtà*, Rome: Carocci Editore, 2012. Cf. Interviews with Rossellini, 'Intervista con i *Cahiers du cinéma*', edited by Fereydoun Hoveyda and Jacques Rivette and 'Uomini drappeggiati e uomini cuciti', edited by François Tranchant and Jean-Marie Vérité, in Roberto Rossellini, *Il mio metodo. Scritti e interviste*, edited by Adriano Aprà, Venice: Marisilio, 2006, 169–90.
52 Cf. Caminati, *Roberto Rossellini documentarista*, 55. Astruc, 'Du stylo à la caméra et de la caméra au stylo'. The pen metaphor, as Laura Rascaroli has pointed out, had already been used by Zavattini in an essay published in *Cinema*, 92, 25 April 1940, now in Zavattini, *Neorealismo ecc.*, 37–40. Cf. Rascaroli, *The Personal Camera*, 194.
53 Rossellini, 'Intervista con i *Cahiers du cinéma*', 169.
54 Rossellini, *ibidem*, 177.
55 Adriano Aprà, 'Rossellini documentarista?', in Caminati, *Roberto Rossellini documentarista*, 131. Josué de Castro, *Geografia della fame*, Bari: Leonardo Da Vinci, 1954. Cf. Josué de Castro, Letter to Michael Altman, Co-Productions, 14 June 1960, ACZ D 133/1. Cf. Josué de Castro, Letter to Zavattini, 23 May 1961, ACZ D 133/3. De Castro to Zavattini, 22 May 1961, ACZ D133/2. Both unpublished.
56 Josué de Castro, Letter to Michael Altman, Co-Productions, 14 June 1960, ACZ D 133/1. Unpublished. No sign of Zavattini's letter to Altman, at least, not in the Reggio Zavattini Archive.
57 De Castro, Letter to Zavattini, 23 May 1961, ACZ D 133/3. Unpublished.
58 De Castro, Letter to Zavattini, 22 May 1961, ACZ D 133/2. Unpublished.
59 Herbert List and Vittorio De Sica, *Napoli*, Hamburg: Sigbert Mohn Verlag, 1962. Vittorio De Sica and Herbert List, *Napoli e i suoi personaggi*, Milan: Rizzoli, 1968. Alberto Ferraboschi, 'Il cinema diventa libro: il progetto di *Italia mia* e *Un paese*', in Alberto Ferraboschi and Laura Gasparini (eds), *Paul Strand e Cesare Zavattini. Un paese. La storia e l'eredità*, Milan: Silvana Editoriale, 2017, 36–51.
60 Renzo Martinelli (ed.), *Domande agli uomini di Cesare Zavattini*, Florence: Le Lettere, 2007.
61 Zavattini, *Italia mia*, in Zavattini, *Basta coi soggetti!*, 173–87.
62 Cf. Zavattini, 'Italia mia', in *Neorealismo ecc.*, 1979, 178.
63 Zavattini, *La veritàaaa*, edited by Maurizio Grande, Milan: Bompiani, 1983.
64 Michele Guerra, *Gli ultimi fuochi. Cinema italiano e mondo contadino dal fascismo agli anni Settanta*, Rome: Bulzoni Editore, 2010, 169.
65 Paolo and Vittorio Taviani, in Bernardini and Gili (eds), *Cesare Zavattini*, 158–9.

Chapter 10

1 Zavattini, 'Come spero di fare *Italia mia*', 23.
2 Valentino Bompiani to Zavattini, 26 February 1952, in Zavattini, *Cinquant'anni e più*, 848.

3 'Alcune idee sul cinema', in Zavattini, *Dal soggetto alla sceneggiatura. Come si scrive un capolavoro: Umberto D.* Preface by Luigi Malerba and Epilogue by Gualtiero De Santi, footnote 1, 4. This version, originally published in *La Rivista del cinema*, Rome and Milan: Fratelli Bocca Editore, no. 3, 1, January 1954, contains a preface which explains that Gandin edited the text, based on Zavattini's statements during face-to-face meetings. Only the typescript specifies the dates. In all, there were eleven meetings, beginning on 10 March 1952 and ending on 3 May 1952. These subheadings are replaced by a line space in Zavattini, *Dal soggetto alla sceneggiatura. Come si scrive un capolavoro: Umberto D.*, but have been reinstated for this edition.

4 The art critic Renato Barilli has written about the concept of the event in relation to Zavattini. Cf. Renato Barilli, 'evento', in Moneti (ed.), *Lessico zavattiniano*, 78–85. It is clear from 'Some Ideas on Cinema' that the indexical aspect of the event is not the only one, as far as Zavattini is concerned. This puts paid to notions of a supposed naïve realism in Zavattini whose understanding of *mimēsis* exceeds and complicates such notions.

5 The dictionary of Zavattini's concepts *Lessico zavattiniano* has no entry for shadowing, though the category is discussed by its contributors, though it recurs in Zavattini's writings and has generally been understood in a diminutive, almost literal sense exclusively. And yet, the concept of the event and of current affairs is central for Zavattini and shadowing the event and the people associated with it, or producing it, is integral to it.

6 Henri Lefèbvre, *The Production of Space*, translated by Donald Nicholson-Smith, Oxford: Blackwell, 2004, 417, 424.

7 By the time he was interviewed by Gandin, in 1952, Zavattini had already included this episode in *Italia mia*, later developed in *The Roof* (1956), the feature film based on investigative research carried out by Zavattini.

8 Gutiérrez Alea to Zavattini, 27 May 1956, ACZ Corr. A 101/2. Unpublished. Typescript is in Italian.

9 Pío Caro Baroja, *El Neorrealismo cinematografico italiano, Prólogo y notas de Cesare Zavattini*, Mexico City: Editorial Almeda, 1955.

10 Jacques Rancière, *The Future of the Image*, translated by Gregory Elliot, London and New York: Verso, 2007, 120, 122.

11 The original version of this text appeared in a film journal as Zavattini, 'Alcune idee sul cinema', *La Rivista del Cinema Italiano*, 5–19. It was included in a book by Zavattini which presented to the reader the whole process of writing for cinema, from scenario to screenplay, even including additional and final corrections. Cf. Zavattini, *Umberto D. Dal soggetto alla sceneggiatura: Precedono alcune idee sul cinema*, 5–19. The text was translated into English and abridged by Pier Luigi Lanza with the title: Zavattini, 'Some Ideas on Cinema', 64–9 and later reprinted in the anthology: *Film: A Montage of Theories*, edited by Dyer MacCann, 216–28. Zavattini, *Selected Writings*, Vol. 2, includes the full, unabridged text, in a new critical edition in English.

12 There are several texts in which Zavattini discusses the supposed shortage of scenarios. As early as 1942 or 1943, Zavattini in 'The Importance of Scenarios' (*L'importanza dei soggetti*) states: 'I dare say that there is no such thing as a good or a bad story, just as there is no sunset which contains in itself the virtues of a good painting.' Zavattini, 'L'importanza dei soggetti', in *Neorealismo ecc.*, 48 and 'Basta coi soggetti', 70–3; 71.

13 A few paragraphs of 'Some Theses on Neo-realism' were translated by David Overbey, totalling some 940 words out of nearly 4,000 words. Overbey translated the title as 'A Thesis on Neorealism'. However, Enzo Muzii, the editor and journalist who interviewed Zavattini, called it 'Theses on Neo-realism', ('Tesi sul Neorealismo'). In Italian, *tesi* can be singular or plural. That the plural is intended is clear from Enzo Muzii's introduction to 'Tesi sul Neorealismo', *Emilia*, no. 17, November 1953, 219. The unabridged edition appears for the first time in Zavattini, *Selected Writings*, Vol. 2.

14 The reference is to the housing emergency in Naples in the 1950s, of which a prime example was the 'Granili', a building complex in Naples, a huge rat-infested, stinking building which had once housed a military barracks during the Bourbons' rule. The building epitomized the housing shortage emergency of the 1950s, since after 1945, it became a refuge for displaced persons or evacuees and was still populated by homeless DPS. Cf. Zavattini, *Diario cinematografico*, '19 November 1953', *Cinema Nuovo*, no. 24, 1 December 1953, then in *Diario cinematografico*, in Zavattini, *Opere. Cinema*, 2002, 171–80. In his published film diary, Zavattini mentions the (then) recently published book about Naples by Anna Maria Ortese, *Il mare non bagna Napoli*, Turin: Einaudi, 1953 in which a woman tells Ortese, who was visiting one of the tenements: 'This is no home, madam, as you can see, it's where the oppressed live. Wherever you go, the walls wail.' ('Questa non è una casa, signora, vedete, questo è un luogo di afflitti. Dove passate, i muri si lamentano.')

15 Benedetto Croce, *Poesia e non poesia; note sulla letteratura europea del secolo decimonono*, Bari: Laterza, 1923. Clement Greenberg, 'Avant-garde and Kitsch' (1939), in *Art and Culture*, Boston: Beacon Press, 1961, 3–21, 9. The cinema was included in Greenberg's list of what he called *kitsch*, an equivalent of sorts of Croce's *non-poesia*, together with comics, magazine covers, popular music and theatre, to Greenberg writing in 1939, all 'simulacra of genuine culture'; but of great interest to Zavattini, who considered them part of Modernism, and who pioneered Italian visual culture accordingly, ever since the late 1920s.

16 Umberto Barbaro, 'Il cinema di fronte alla realtà', in *Rivista del Cinema*, II, no. 6, June 1953, 6–33.

17 Enzo Muzii, 'Realismo adulto', *Emilia*, July 1953.

18 Luigi Chiarini, 'Discorso sul neorealismo', *Bianco & Nero*, XII, no. 7, July 1951, 3–28 picks up from where he left off in 'Spettacolo e film', II, no. 2, *Belfagor*, 31 March 1952 and reprinted it under the title Chiarini, 'Miscellanea', in *La Rivista del Cinema*, II, no. 6, June 1953, 76–88, 83.

19 Chiarini, 'Miscellanea', 83.

20 Chiarini, *ibidem*, 84–5.

21 Chiarini, *ibidem*, 87.

22 Agostino Degli Espinosa, *La Rivista del Cinema Italiano*, I–II, nos. 1–2, January–February 1953, 6–17, 6.

23 Zavattini, cited in Degli Espinosa, *La Rivista del Cinema Italiano*, 6.

24 Degli Espinosa, *La Rivista del Cinema Italiano*, 10.

25 Degli Espinosa, *ibidem*, 11.

26 Degli Espinosa, *ibidem*, 12.

27 Degli Espinosa, *ibidem*, 12.

28 Degli Espinosa, *ibidem*, 12.

29 Degli Espinosa, *ibidem*, 13.

30 Degli Espinosa, *ibidem*, 12.
31 Degli Espinosa, *ibidem*, 12.
32 Degli Espinosa, *ibidem*, 15.
33 Degli Espinosa, *ibidem*, 17.

Chapter 11

1   Zavattini, 'Alcune idee sul cinema', in Zavattini, *Dal soggetto alla sceneggiatura. Come si scrive un capolavoro: Umberto D.*, 21.
2   Zavattini, 'Ferragosto 1952', *Diario cinematografico*, 82.
3   Zavattini, *ibidem*, 82.
4   Zavattini, '26 gennaio 1953', *Cinema Nuovo*, no. 6, 1 March 1953, *Diario cinematografico*, 1979, 85. Zavattini, 'Le battone. 15 febbraio 1953', *Cinema Nuovo*, no. 5, 15 February 1953, *Diario cinematografico*, 1979, 86–8. Regarding the first episode of *We Women*, Zavattini, '25 giugno 1953', *Cinema Nuovo*, no. 19, 15 September 1953, *Diario cinematografico*, 1979, 105–6. Zavattini, 'Caterina. 27 giugno 1953', *Cinema Nuovo*, *Diario cinematografico*, 1979, 106–7. Zavattini, 'Appunti senza data, 28 luglio 1953', *Cinema Nuovo*, no. 17, 15 August 1953, *Diario cinematografico*, 1979, 112–13. Zavattini published extracts of Antonioni's letter about his episode for *Love in the City*, Zavattini, '15 dicembre 1953', *Cinema Nuovo*, no. 25, 15 December 1953, *Diario cinematografico*, 1979, 128–9. The first episode of *We Women*, Zavattini, 'Dicembre 1953', *Cinema Nuovo*, no. 31, 15 March 1954, *Diario cinematografico*, 1979, 129–31.
5   Zavattini, 7 July 1952, in Private diary, in *Io. Un'autobiografia*, 191–2.
6   Zavattini, '30 marzo. Festival', in *Diario cinematografico*, 1979, 108.
7   Zavattini, *ibidem*, 108.
8   Zavattini, 'Alcune idee sul cinema', 21.
9   Zavattini, 30 April 1953 diary entry, in Zavattini, *Neorealismo ecc.*, 101.
10 Michela Carpi, 'Filmografia e bibliografia', in Cesare Zavattini, *Dal Soggetto alla Sceneggiatura. Come Si Scrive un capolavoro: Umberto D.*, Parma: Monte Università Parma Editore, 2005, 217–30 and specifically 237.
11 Zavattini published extracts of a letter by Antonioni taking issue with Zavattini about the premises for his episode for *Love in the City* in *Cinema Nuovo* no. 31, 15 March 1954, claiming the impossibility of such a project.
12 *Love in the City* (1953). Episodes: Carlo Lizzani, *L'amore che si paga*; Dino Risi, *Paradiso per tre ore*; Michelangelo Antonioni, *Tentato suicidio*, Federico Fellini, *Un'agenzia matrimoniale*, Francesco (Citto) Maselli and Zavattini, *Storia di Caterina*; Alberto Lattuada, *Gli italiani che si voltano*.
13 Zavattini, '1956', in *Neorealismo ecc.*, 108.
14 The translation into English of *First Communion* is included in *Selected Writings*, Vol. 1.
15 Zavattini, Private diary, in *Io. Un'autobiografia*, 170–1.
16 Carpi, 'Filmografia e bibliografia', 237.
17 Zavattini, 'Undated Notes – 28 July 1953' [diary entry], in *Diario cinematografico*, edited by Valentina Fortichiari, Milan: Bompiani, 1979, 111–16.
18 Zavattini, 'Some Ideas on Cinema', 6. Author's translation.

19 Zavattini, 'Undated Notes – 28 July 1953', 113.
20 Zavattini, *ibidem*, 113.
21 De Santi, *Vittorio De Sica*, 87–93.
22 De Sica, cited in De Santi, *ibidem*, 87.
23 Henri Agel, *Vittorio De Sica*, Paris: Éditions Universitaires, 1955. Guido
    Aristarco, 'Il mestiere del critico', *Cinema Nuovo*, no. 9, 15 April 1953.
    Umberto Barbaro, 'I film. *Stazione Termini*', in *La Rivista del Cinema Italiano*,
    no. 6, June 1953. André Bazin, *Vittorio De Sica*, Parma: Guanda, 1953. Pietro
    Bianchi, *Maestri del cinema*, Milan: Garzanti, 1972.

Chapter 12

1 The conference was Zavattini's own initiative. It was presided over by the
   producer Alfredo Guarini, the directors Antonio Marchi and Citto Maselli, and
   organized by, among others, Pietro Barilla, Virginio Marchi and Luigi Malerba.
   Many filmmakers and critics took part: the directors, screenwriters and
   representatives of the film clubs; directors Michelangelo Antonioni, Vittorio
   De Sica, Federico Fellini, Carlo Lizzani, Pietro Germi, Luciano Emmer, Piero
   Nelli, Nelo Risi, Marco Ferreri, Virgilio Tosi of the Italian Federation of Film
   Clubs; the producers Alfredo Guarini, Marco Ferreri and Riccardo Ghione,
   the writers Giorgio Bassani, Carlo Bernari, the screenwriters Sergio Amidei,
   Suso Cecchi d'Amico, Attilio Bertolucci, Renzo Renzi and Luigi Chiarini, the
   editor of *La Rivista del Cinema Italiano*, the publisher Ugo Guanda, the film
   critics Filippo Sacchi, the journalist Piero Gadda Conti, the theatre critic and
   director Vito Pandolfi, writing for *La Rivista del Cinema Italiano*, Giancarlo
   Vigorelli and Gian Luigi Rondi, film critics writing for the Catholic *La Rivista
   del Cinematografo*, Mario Gromo, film critic for the daily *La Stampa*, Ugo
   Casiraghi, film critic for the Communist daily *L'Unità*, Gabriella Smith, film
   critic for the Communist daily *Paese Sera*, Arturo Lanocita, critic for the *Nuovo
   Corriere della Sera*, Livio Zanetti, writing for *Cinema Nuovo* and the *Cinema
   Nuovo* journalist and photographer, Benedetto Benedetti. Cf. Argentieri,
   Neorealismo ecc, 131. Argentieri's list does not include the Catholic critics,
   whose names are added in this reconstruction.
2 Luigi Chiarini, 'Importanza di un convegno', *Rivista del Cinema italiano*, III,
   no. 3, March 1954, 5.
3 Giancarlo Vigorelli, 'Fine di un monopolio', *La Rivista del Cinematografo*,
   February 1954, cited in Sergio Trasatti (ed.), *I cattolici e il Neorealismo*, Rome:
   Ente dello Spettacolo, 1989, 99–108.
4 Benedetto Benedetti, 'Sviluppi del Convegno', *Cinema Nuovo*, no. 26,
   31 December 1953, 398.
5 Renzo Renzi, 'Il neorealismo nei film di guerra', *La Rivista del Cinema Italiano*,
   no. 3, March 1954, 34–9.
6 Renzi cited typical war films which met with approval: *Carica eroica*, *Penne
   nere*, *I sette dell'Orsa Maggiore*, *La pattuglia dell'Amba Alagi*.
7 Virgilio Tosi, 'Realismo e libertà', cited in Emilio Lonero, 'Note sul Convegno
   di Parma', *Rivista del Cinematografo*, XXVII, no. 1, January, 8.
8 Alfredo Guarini, cited in Lonero, *ibidem*, 8.

9   Ugo Casiraghi, 'Il pubblico e la critica', cited in Lonero, *ibidem*, 8.

10 The idea became *Mediterraneo* (1991), directed by Gabriele Salvatores.

11 The following papers were published in *La Rivista del Cinema Italiano*, no.
    3, March 1954: Cesare Zavattini, 'Il neorealismo secondo me', Carlo Lizzani,
    'Neorealismo e realtà italiana', Renzi, 'Il neorealismo nei film di guerra', Vito
    Pandolfi, 'Gli sceneggiatori del neorealismo'. Among the other papers were
    Giancarlo Vigorelli, 'La seconda strada della cultura italiana', *Bianco & Nero*,
    xiv, no. 12, December 1953, Pietro Bianchi, 'Realtà e poesia', Virgilio Tosi,
    'La censura cinematografica e il neorealismo', Ugo Casiraghi, 'Neorealismo
    e rapporto con il pubblico', Fulvio Jacchia, 'Il cinema americano in Italia',
    Alfredo Guarini, 'Problemi della produzione'. Cf. Argentieri, *Neorealismo ecc.*,
    1979, 131–2.

12 Guido Aristarco, *Cinema Nuovo*, no. 27, January 1954. Edoardo Bruno, *Film
    Critica*, no. 32, 1954.

13 Gabriele Mucchi, *Cinema Nuovo*, no. 30, March 1954.

14 Ten years later, in an interview about this period, Zavattini mentioned
    Gramsci's concept of *nuova cultura*. Zavattini, 'Un atto di coraggio, interview
    with Tommaso Chiaretti', *Mondo Nuovo*, 11 December 1960, later in
    Neorealismo ecc., 1979, 224–9. Gramsci, 'The Intellectuals', 9 and Forgacs,
    An Antonio Gramsci Reader, 300–22.

15 His reasoned position was entirely at loggerheads with orthodox Italian
    Marxists at the conference and their leaning towards Lukácsian aesthetics of
    the type.

16 Piersantelli, 'Un'inchiesta sulla miseria in Italia'. The Parliamentary Enquiry
    began in 1950 and was completed in 1954. Camera dei deputati, *Atti della
    Commissione*. Available online: Archivio Storico della Camera dei Deputati,
    http://archivio.camera.it/patrimonio/archivi_del_periodo_repubblicano_1948_
    2008/. Also available online is a documentary directed by Giorgio Ferroni and
    produced by the Istituto Luce: Istituto Luce_Inchiesta sulla Miseria_Parte 1:
    https://www.youtube.com/watch?v=IkbApjfd9fc.

17 Filippo Sacchi, cited Lonero, 'Note sul Convegno di Parma', 8.

18 Georg Lukács, *Saggi sul realismo*, Turin: Einaudi, 1950 and Georg Lukács,
    Il marxismo e la critica letteraria, Turin: Einaudi, 1953.

19 Armando Borrelli, 'Naturalismo e realismo nel cinema italiano', *Rinascita*, x,
    no. 1, January 1953, 41–4; 44.

20 Lizzani, 'Neorealismo e realtà italiana', 30–3. The reference to
    'crepuscolarismo' ('twilight-ism') and 'intimismo' ('intimism') is to a literary
    movement which influenced 1930s Italian cinema. The main figures were Guido
    Gozzano, Sergio Corazzini and Aldo Palazzeschi. In the face of reality, the
    crepuscolari dwelled on a sense of disillusion for the present and nostalgia for
    the past, personal perception and experience. In film criticism, *crepuscolarismo*
    became shorthand for a quick put-down.

21 Lizzani, 'Neorealismo e realtà italiana', 30–3.

22 It had been used two years earlier by two writers, Giacinto Spagnoletti and
    Enrico Emanuelli, in a collection of radio interviews edited by the Catholic
    writer and critic Carlo Bo, in which Italian writers were asked to comment on
    Neo-realism in the arts. Emanuelli remarked that 'De Sica is going down the
    road of poetic crepuscolarism'. Cf. Carlo Bo (ed.), *Inchiesta sul Neorealismo*,

Turin: Edizioni Radio Italiana, 1951, 71. Giacinto Spagnoletti, in Bo, *Inchiesta sul Neorealismo*, 73.

23 Borrelli, 'Naturalismo e realismo nel cinema italiano', 41–4.

24 Borrelli, *ibidem*, 44.

25 Borrelli, 'Alcuni aspetti teorici del neorealismo', *Rivista del Cinema Italiano*, II, no. 6, June 1953, 41–2.

26 Borrelli, *ibidem*, 34–42, 43. The dualist distinction between typical and non-typical is perhaps not so far removed from Croce's opposition of the poetic and the non-poetic.

27 Borrelli, *ibidem*, 35.

28 Lonero, 'Note sul Convegno di Parma', 7.

29 Pandolfi, 'Gli sceneggiatori del neorealismo', 40–5.

30 Sante Uccelli, cited in Lonero, 'Note sul Convegno di Parma', 8.

31 Vigorelli, 'Fine di un monopolio', 105.

32 Little did Vigorelli know that the Marxist Gramsci had devoted many pages of his *Prison Notebooks* to a study of Manzoni which showed that Manzoni was far from being a realist in his characterization of class. Gramsci, *Letteratura e vita nazionale*, 99–104. (Selections from Notebooks VI, VII and VIII.).

33 Vigorelli, 'La seconda strada della cultura italiana', 35–47.

34 Vigorelli, *ibidem*, 39, 47.

35 Vigorelli, 'Fine di un monopolio', 104.

36 Mario Alicata and Giuseppe De Santis, 'Verità e poesia: Verga e il cinema italiano', *Cinema*, 127, 1941, 216–17, followed by Alicata and De Santis, 'Ancora di Verga e del cinema italiano', *Cinema*, 130, 314–15.

37 Alberto Lattuada was unable to attend, but sent a letter of support to the conference, in which he stated that the defining characteristic of Neo-realism was its 'human qualities'. Neo-realism could only be defined by negation: conformist, religious, racist, nationalist, Fascist, propagandist. An ethical attitude also distinguished it, which was why it had been censored and had attracted Giulio Andreotti's 'dirty laundry' jibe. Lattuada reiterated the point he had made at the Perugia Conference of 1949: that even if you resort to fantasy, as Georges Méliès had done, you can still be considered a realist. He concluded that the way forward was to develop a film culture in Italy and for filmmakers to stick together. Alberto Lattuada, 'Una lettera', *La Rivista del Cinema Italiano*, no. 3, March 1954, 46–7.

38 Findings summary based on Statement approved by the conference and cited by Mino Argentieri, in Zavattini, *Neorealismo ecc.*, 2002, 768–9.

39 Findings summary, 768–9.

40 Guido Aristarco, 'Più che una bandiera', *Cinema Nuovo*, no. 26, December 1953, 391. Livio Zanetti, 'Crescere è difficile', *ibidem*, 392.

41 Aristarco, 'Più che una bandiera', 391. Zanetti, 'Crescere è difficile', 392.

42 Zanetti, *ibidem*, 395.

43 Zanetti, *ibidem*, 395.

44 Zanetti, *ibidem*, 395.

45 Chiarini mentioned the campaigns directed by the Right-wing daily *Il Tempo* against Neo-realism from *Miracle in Milan* to *Anni facili*, films which had not only been criticized, but heavily censored, and pointed out that the Catholic *Quotidiano* had complained about the success in Britain of 'communist

films' praising 'bicycle thieves and rags'. Luigi Chiarini, 'I film, la politica e la censura', *La Rivista del Cinema Italiano*, no. 3, March 1954, 48–52.

46 In his book *Il film nella battaglia delle idee* (1954) which came out around the same time as the issue about the Parma Conference, Chiarini was able to devote more space to a discussion about the resistance against government censorship. Cf. Luigi Chiarini, *Il film nella battaglia delle idee*, Milan: Fratelli Bocca Editori, 1954.

47 Chiarini, *ibidem*, 12.

48 Chiarini, *ibidem*, 9–29.

49 Lonero, 'Note sul Convegno di Parma', 7.

50 Gian Luigi Rondi, 'Neorealismo, arte cristiana', *La Rivista del Cinematografo*, no. 1, 1954, 95–7.

51 Rondi, *ibidem*, 96.

52 Rondi, *ibidem*, 97.

53 G. L. Rondi, cited in Lonero, 'Note sul Convegno di Parma', 8.

54 Croce, *Poesia e non poesia*.

Chapter 13

1 Argentieri, *Neorealismo ecc.*, 163.

2 Official proceedings were never published. This reconstruction is based on a detailed account by Lino Del Fra, a documentarist: 'Battezzata a Varese la poetica dei teologi', *Cinema Nuovo*, 44, 10 October 1954, 211–13; 211 and references in other texts. The major contribution made by the Varese Conference was philosophical, not theological (despite Del Fra's misleading title), namely, in the intervention by Amédée Ayfré who related phenomenology to cinema in detail.

3 The other two film directors in attendance were Claudio Gora and Antonio Ciampi. Some Catholic philosophers attended, including the genuine phenomenologist Amédée Ayfré and the self-proclaimed existentialist Gabriel Marcel; the Dominican Father Felix Morlion, who taught cinema in Italy, Father Nazzareno Taddei, the philosopher Guido Tagliabue Morpurgo, who rejected Benedetto Croce's idealism, in favour of existentialism, and was the author of *Le strutture del trascendentale. Piccola inchiesta sul pensiero critico, dialettico, esistenziale* (1951) and the film and theatre critic Nicola Ciarletta. The Left, Zavattini included, were blind to the phenomenological interpretation, which they probably confused with *crepuscolarismo*.

4 Gabriel Marcel, cited in Del Fra, 'Battezzata a Varese la poetica dei teologi', 212.

5 Marcel, cited in Del Fra, 'Battezzata a Varese la poetica dei teologi', 212.

6 Del Fra, *ibidem*, 212.

7 Del Fra, *ibidem*, 213.

8 Del Fra, *ibidem*, 213.

9 José André Lacour, 'Il silenzio o la prigione', *Cinema Nuovo*, 44, 10 October 1954, 213.

10 Amédée Ayfré, 'Cinema e realtà', *Bianco & Nero*, no. 1, January 1952, 6–21.

11 Ayfré, *ibidem*, 6.

12 Ayfré, *ibidem*, 7.
13 Ayfré, *ibidem*, 8. Ayfré also mentions Carné-Prévert's *poetic realism*, a variant of psychological realism.
14 Ayfré, *ibidem*, 9.
15 Ayfré, *ibidem*, 13.
16 Ayfré, *ibidem*, 11.
17 Ayfré, *ibidem*, 12.
18 Ayfré, *ibidem*, 12.
19 Ayfré, *ibidem*, 15.
20 Ayfré, *ibidem*, 12–13.
21 Ayfré, *ibidem*, 16.
22 Ayfré, *ibidem*, 16.
23 Ayfré, *ibidem*, 18.
24 Ayfré, *ibidem*, 17.
25 Ayfré, *ibidem*, 17.
26 Ayfré, *La Rivista del Cinematografo*, no. 11, November 1954, in Trasatti (ed.), *I cattolici e il Neorealismo*, 119.
27 Ayfré, *ibidem*, 117.
28 Ayfré, *ibidem*, 109–21; 116.
29 Ayfré, *ibidem*, 116.
30 Ayfré, *ibidem*, 117.
31 Ayfré, *ibidem*, 120.
32 Jean-Paul Sartre, *L'Être et le néant*, Paris: Éditions Gallimard, 1943.
33 Maurice Merleau-Ponty, 'The Film and the New Psychology', in *Sense and Non-Sense*, translated, with a Preface, by Hubert L. Dreyfus and Patricia Allen Dreyfus, Evanston: Northwestern University Press, 1966, 48–59; 54, 57; Merleau-Ponty, *Sens et non-sense*. Maurice Merleau-Ponty, *Phénoménologie de la perception*, Paris: Gallimard, 1945.
34 Merleau-Ponty, 'The Film and the New Psychology', 58.
35 Merleau-Ponty, *ibidem*, 58.
36 Brunello co-scripted Fellini's *Prova d'Orchestra* (1979) and *La voce della luna* (1990).
37 Rondi, *Il Neorealismo italiano*, 129.
38 Rondi, *ibidem*, 73.
39 Rondi, *ibidem*, 72.
40 Rondi, *ibidem*, 113–14.
41 Rondi, *ibidem*, 78.
42 Rondi, *ibidem*, 75.
43 Rondi, *ibidem*, 77.
44 Rondi, *ibidem*, 76.
45 Rondi, *ibidem*, 81–6.
46 Rondi, *ibidem*, 87–9.
47 Rondi, *ibidem*, 133–8.
48 Zavattini, 'Terrestrialità del Neo-realismo', in *Neorealismo ecc.*, 162–3. According to Mino Argentieri, the text was either a draft for an interview or a questionnaire. He conjectures it was written around 1954. Given that it discusses the Varese Conference that took place in September 1954, it is *post quem*.

49 Zavattini calls it 'terrestriality', though the word 'materialism' was current in the debates to which he was referring, possibly to cast off the negative connotations of materialism.

Chapter 14

1 Elena Gualtieri, *Paul Strand Cesare Zavattini. Lettere e immagini*, Bologna: Comune di Reggio Emilia-Biblioteca Panizzi and Fondazione Un Paese and Edizioni Bora, 2005, 13. Cf. Letter to Giulio Einaudi, 28 February 1952.

2 Letter to Giulio Einaudi, 13 June 1952.

3 *Italia mia* was to have several lives. One episode about housing became the feature film *The Roof* (1956) (*Il tetto*). The idea of a journey of discovery, involving interviews with ordinary people, became a television documentary directed by Mario Soldati, *Chi legge? Viaggio lungo il Tirreno* (1960) for which Zavattini wrote both storyline and screenplay.

4 Of the many projects proposed, three materialized and went as far as commissioned photography and layout, two of which were published. The second one was *Napoli* (1962) by Vittorio De Sica, only published in Italy in 1968, the third, *Italians in New York*, by George N. Fenin, the New York correspondent for *Cinema Nuovo*, who was to become one of the editors of Jonas Mekas's *Film Culture*, went as far as commissioned photographs and layouts. Cf. Ferraboschi, 'Il cinema diventa libro: il progetto di *Italia mia* e *Un paese*', 36–51. List and De Sica, *Napoli*. De Sica and List, *Napoli e i suoi personaggi*, 1968.

5 Gualtieri, *Paul Strand Cesare Zavattini*, 45.

6 Paul Strand in Michael E. Hoffman (ed.), *Paul Strand: Sixty Years of Photographs. Profile by Calvin Tomkins. Excerpts from Correspondence, Interviews and Other Documents*, New York: Aperture, 1976, 30 and Gualtieri, *Paul Strand Cesare Zavattini*, 45.

7 Calvin Tomkins in Hoffman, *Paul Strand: Sixty Years of Photographs*, 31.

8 Gualtieri, *Paul Strand Cesare Zavattini*, 15.

9 Gualtieri, *ibidem*, 25.

10 Zavattini, 'Altra gente in Via Merici', *Bis*, no. 8, 4 May 1948, in Zavattini, *Diario cinematografico*, 1979, 58–63.

11 Zavattini to Giulio Einaudi, 30 October 1953, in Zavattini, *Una, cento, mille, lettere*, 411–13. The editorial deletions have been restored by consulting the typescript in the archive. Zavattini to Giulio Einaudi, 30 October 1953, ACZ E87/113.

12 Zavattini to Einaudi, 18 January 1954, Gualtieri, *Paul Strand Cesare Zavattini*, 27.

13 Since the 1920s photojournalism had done this with brilliant results. W. Eugene Smith's 'An Accident Interrupts His Leisure', for *Life* is organized around a situation and the main protagonist. W. Eugene Smith, such as 'An Accident Interrupts His Leisure', *Life*, 20 September 1948, 118–19.

14 Alfred Stieglitz, *Camera Work: The Complete Photographs 1903-1917*, Cologne: Taschen, 2008.

15 Edward Steichen, *The Family of Man*, catalogue, New York: The Museum of Modern Art, 1983 (1955), 3.

16 Margaret Bourke-White, *You Have Seen Their Faces*, New York: Viking, 1937. Sharon Corwin, 'Constructed Documentary', in Sharon Corwin, Jessica May and Terri Weissman, *American Modern Documentary Photography by Abbott, Evans, and Bourke-White*, Berkeley, Los Angeles and London: University of California, 2011, 108–32. Margaret Bourke-White, 'At the Time of the Louisville Flood', 1937 in William S. Johnson, Mark Rice and Carla Williams, *Photography from 1839 to Today, George Eastman House, Rochester N. Y.*, Cologne: Taschen, 2000, 592.

17 Dorothea Lange, 'Plantation Owner and His Field Hands Near Clarkesville, Mississippi 1936', in Johnson, Rice and Williams, *Photography from 1839 to Today*, 602.

18 Henri Cartier-Bresson, 'The People of Russia', *Paris Match*, 29 February and 5 February 1955, in Mary Panzer, *Things as They Are: Photojournalism in Context since 1955*, London: Chris Boot and World Press Photo, 2005, 38–43. The English title is a blanket term as given in Panzer (2005) to denote several features for *Paris Match* in French with French headlines, 'Un dimanche au stade', 'Dans le rues de Moscou' and so on.

19 James Agee and Walker Evans, *Let Us Now Praise Famous Men*, London: Violette Editions, 1988, 9.

20 Belinda Rathbone, *Walker Evans: A Biography*, London: Thames and Hudson, 1995, 144.

21 James Agee and Walker Evans, *Let Us Now Praise Famous Men*, Boston: Houghton Mifflin, 1941. The original assignment was turned down by *Fortune* in 1936, but was published in book form in 1941. Agee and Evans, *Let Us Now Praise Famous Men*, 1941. In the second edition of 1960, the photographs are twice as many.

22 A detailed study of the language and other features by Victor A. Kramer, among Kramer's many other achievements in his monograph, shows how Agee used various rhetorical strategies to convey religious or mystical undertones to his experience, investing or seeing holiness in the tenant farmers. Victor A. Kramer, *A Consciousness of Technique in 'Let Us Now Praise Famous Men'*, New York: Whitston Publishing Company, 2001, 112–19.

23 For Bakhtin, dialogism takes place in literature, and particularly in the novel form which is taken as a privileged site. In this book, though, prose is compressed into very short stories, a Modernist fragment which nevertheless has its roots in the real.

24 Virgilio Tosi, 'Postfazione', in Gualtieri, *Paul Strand Cesare Zavattini*, 257–61.

25 Zavattini explained to his publisher the purpose of the writing: 'The text in the book will comprise my Preface of ten pages or so and then about fifty *statements* (or confessions) made by people from my town which are a kind of very succinct autobiographies, as I explained to you some time ago. Taken as a whole, their combination should convey a feel for the town's identity, but in no sense do I mean folkloric.' Zavattini, Letter to Giulio Einaudi, 30 October 1953, in Zavattini, *Una, cento, mille, lettere*, 411. Letter to Paul Strand, 23 January 1953, in Gualtieri, *Paul Strand Cesare Zavattini*, 64. In the same letter to Strand, Zavattini states: 'Clearly, as far as I am concerned, while Luzzara is indeed my home town, I consider it just like any other town in the

world; the fact that I was born there provides me with a more precise insight, but also one that is more heart felt and certainly an authentic tone.' Gualtieri, *Paul Strand Cesare Zavattini*, 65.

26 Zavattini to Strand, 18 April 1953, cited in Gualtieri, *Paul Strand Cesare Zavattini*, 22.

27 Strand to Zavattini, 28 December 1952, cited in Gualtieri, *Paul Strand Cesare Zavattini*, 62.

28 Gualtieri, *Paul Strand Cesare Zavattini*, 22, 25.

29 Strand and Zavattini, *Un paese*, Milan: Scheiwiller, 1974, 18–19.

30 Strand and Zavattini, *ibidem*, 96–7.

31 Strand and Zavattini, *ibidem*, 36.

32 Strand and Zavattini, *ibidem*, 34–5.

33 Gualtieri, *Paul Strand Cesare Zavattini*, 23, 27.

34 Julia Kristeva, 'Word, Dialogue and Novel', in Toril Moi (ed.), *The Kristeva Reader*, Oxford: Basil Blackwell, 1986, 34–61; 47.

35 Zavattini and Paul Strand, 'I fotodocumentari di *Cinema Nuovo*. 25 persone di Zavattini e Strand', *Cinema Nuovo*, 4, no. 53, 25 February 1955, 137–44.

36 'Zavattini e Visconti presentano *Italia mia*', *Notiziario Einaudi*, March 1955, cited in Ferraboschi, 'Il cinema diventa libro: il progetto di *Italia mia* e *Un paese*', 44.

37 Elio Vittorini, 'La foto strizza l'occhio alla pagina', *Cinema Nuovo*, III, no. 33, 15 April 1954, 200–2.

38 Michele Gandin (commentary) Enzo Sellerio (photographs) 'Borgo di Dio', in Guido Aristarco (ed.), *I fotodocumentari di Cinema Nuovo*, Milan: Cinema Nuovo, 1955, 458–64.

39 Tosi, 'Postfazione', 260.

40 Zavattini and Strand, 'I fotodocumentari di *Cinema Nuovo*. 25 persone di Zavattini e Strand', 137–44. Then in Aristarco, *I fotodocumentari di Cinema Nuovo*. Ernesto de Martino, 'Narrare la Lucania', *Cinema Nuovo*, no. 59, 1955, 377–84. Cf. Francesco Faeta and Giacomo Daniele Fragapane (eds), *AZ. Arturo Zavattini fotografo. Viaggi e cinema 1950-1960*, Rome: Contrasto, 2015, 26.

41 *Ibidem*, 461.

42 Danilo Dolci, *Inchiesta a Palermo*, Palermo: Sellerio, 2013, [1956], 23.

43 'Diario per gli amici' ('Diary for my friends'), in Danilo Dolci, *Banditi a Partinico*, Palermo: Sellerio, 2013, [1955].

44 De Martino, 'Narrare la Lucania', 377–84.

45 Cf. Faeta and Daniele Fragapane, *AZ. Arturo Zavattini fotografo. Viaggi e cinema 1950-1960*, 26. Arturo Zavattini confirmed it in 2016, in an email to the author. Arturo never met the ethnographer in person, confirming that the go-between was his father.

46 Ernesto de Martino, 'Intorno a una storia del mondo popolare subalterno', *Società*, v, no. 3, September 1949, 411–35.

47 Faeta makes the point that in a file in the De Martino archive in Rome there de Martino's notes on Gramsci. Francesco Faeta, 'Il sonno sotto le stelle: Arturo Zavattini, Ernesto De Martino, "Un paese lontano"', in Francesco Faeta (ed.), *Fotografi e fotografie: Uno sguardo antropologico*, Milano: Franco Angeli, 2006, 121.

48 *Ibidem*, 185.

49 Gramsci, *Letteratura e vita nazionale*, 267 (Selection from Prison Notebook VI).
50 *Ibidem*, 268.
51 *Ibidem*, 274.
52 Ernesto de Martino, 'Realismo e folclore nel cinema italiano', *Filmcritica*, no. 19, December 1952.
53 De Martino, *ibidem*, 185.
54 Guerra, *Gli ultimi fuochi*, 169; 171.
55 De Martino, 'Realismo e folclore nel cinema italiano', 183.
56 Zavattini, 'Come non ho fatto *Italia mia*', 21–8; 27.
57 Zavattini, *ibidem*, 21–9; 29. De Martino was the ethnographer who researched the region of Lucania, its rituals and popular songs.
58 Faeta, 'Il sonno sotto le stelle', 113–39 and Cesare Colombo (ed.), *Lo sguardo critico: Cultura e fotografia in Italia 1943–1968*, Turin: Agorá, 2003. Maria Antonella Pelizzari, '*Un Paese* (1955) and the Challenge of Mass Culture', *Études photographiques*, 30, 2012, http://etudesphotographiques.revues.org/3483, accessed 9 December 2015. Faeta, 'Il sonno sotto le stelle', 116, 123.
59 Faeta, 'Il sonno sotto le stelle', 113, 125.
60 *Ibidem*, 125. C. Gallini, cited in Faeta, 'Il sonno sotto le stelle', 115. His photographs were published first in the Communist daily newspaper *Paese Sera*, then in the Communist weekly magazines *Vie Nuove* and *Noi donne* in 1952 and finally in *Cinema Nuovo* in 1955, as part of the photo-documentaries.
61 Franco Ferrarotti, *Mass media e società di massa*, Bari: Laterza, 1992. Pietro Clemente, 'I paesi di Qualcuno', in Ercole (ed.), *Diviso in due*, 61. Faeta, 'Il sonno sotto le stelle', 113–39. Zavattini's outlook differs from Carlo Levi's archaic outlook in his novel *Cristo si è fermato a Eboli* (1945) which is later to be found in Pier Paolo Pasolini's nostalgia for a pre-industrial society, but has an affinity with Ernesto de Martino's ideas and even more with Danilo Dolci's. Clemente, *ibidem*, 66.
62 Faeta, *ibidem*, 129.
63 Clemente, *ibidem*, 59; 63. Alessandro Portelli, *Biografia di una città. Storia e racconto: Terni 1830-1985*, Turin: Einaudi, 1985.
64 Clemente, *ibidem*, 61.

Chapter 15

1 Marsha Kinder, *Blood Cinema: The Reconstruction of National Identity in Spain*, Berkeley and London: University of California Press, 1993, 28.
2 Ricardo Muñoz Suay, 'Za e la Spagna', 1994, ACZ Carte rosse 125, fols 1–9; fol. 1r. Unpublished.
3 John Hopewell, *Out of the Past: Spanish Cinema after Franco*, London: British Film Institute, 1986, 39.
4 Helen Graham, 'Pop Culture in the "Years of Hunger"', in Jo Labanyi (ed.), *Spanish Cultural Studies: An Introduction*, Oxford: Oxford University Press, 1995, 238.
5 Graham, *ibidem*, 237.
6 Sheelagh Ellwood, 'The Moving Image of the Franco Regime: Noticiarios y Documentales, 1943-1975', in Labanyi (ed.), *Spanish Cultural Studies*, 201–3;

201. Founded in 1942, under the aegis of the Falange Español Tradicionalista, the general secretariat of the Francoist Single Party.

7   Hopewell, *Out of the Past*, 37.

8   Graham, 'Pop Culture in the "Years of Hunger"', 237.

9   Peter Evans, 'Cifesa: Cinema and Authoritarian Aesthetics', in Labanyi (ed.), *Spanish Cultural Studies*, 215.

10 Kinder, *Blood Cinema*, 29.

11 Jo Labanyi, 'Censorship, or the Fear of Mass Culture', in Labanyi (ed.), *Spanish Cultural Studies*, 211.

12 Muñoz Suay, 'Za e la Spagna', 1994, ACZ Carte rosse 125, fol. 3r.

13 Also shown was Renato Castellani's *È primavera*, based on a scenario by Zavattini.

14 José Enrique Monterde, 'Continuismo y Disidencia', in Román Gubern, José Enrique Monterde, Pérez Peruchia, Esteve Riambau and Casimiro Torreiro, *Historia del Cine Español*, Madrid: Catedra, 1995, 239–93; 280.

15 There were also Luigi Zampa's *L'onorevole Angelina* (1949) and *Processo alla città* (1952), *Due soldi di speranza* (1952) by Castellani, *Il cammino della speranza* by Pietro Germi, and *Gli uomini non guardano il cielo* (1952), by Umberto Scarpelli.

16 José Enrique Monterde, 'Zavattini en España', in *Ciao Za*, Valencia: Filmoteca del la Generalitat, 1991, 11.

17 Muñoz Suay, 'Za e la Spagna', 1994, ACZ Carte rosse 125, fol. 3r.

18 Berlanga, cited in Hopewell, *Out of the Past*, 51. Berlanga, *Cahiers du cinema*, no. 94, April 1959, 6.

19 Bardem, cited in Hopewell, *Out of the Past*, 51.

20 Peter Besas, *Behind the Spanish Lens: Spanish Cinema under Fascism and Democracy*, Denver: Arden Press, 1985, 34.

21 'El cine español actual es: políticamente ineficaz, socialmente falso, intelectualmente ínfimo, estéticamente milo, e industrialmente raquítico.' Bardem cited in Gubern et al., *Historia del Cine Español*, 283.

22 Marvin D'Lugo, *The Films of Carlos Saura*, Princeton: Princeton University Press, 1991, 35.

23 Monterde, 'Zavattini en España', 13.

24 Muñoz Suay, 'Za e la Spagna', 1994, ACZ Carte rosse 125, fol. 7r.

25 Muñoz Suay, *ibidem*, fol. 7r. Translated by Rafael Sánchez Ferlosio, author of the novel *El Jarama*. Two short stories (*Un juego divertido* and *Cuento de Navidad*) of Zavattini's were published in *Antologia de humoristas italianos contemporáneos*, edited by José Janés in 1943, extracts from *I poveri sono matti* and *Io sono il diavolo*. Zavattini, 'Totó el Bueno', in *Revista Española* of May–June 1953. A summary of the scenario came out in *Objectivo*. *Cine en casa*, an extract from *Ipocrita 1943*, also appeared in *Objectivo*, no. 2, January 1954. '*La voz del silencio*' (scenario) appeared in *Revista Internacional del Cine*, no. 5 October 1952.

26 Zavattini, 'Spagna, 9 marzo 1953', *Cinema Nuovo*, no. 9, 15 April 1953, *Diario cinematografico*, 1979, 94–6. Zavattini, 'Viaggio in Spagna', unpublished notebook, fols 62–8; fol. 62r.

27 Zavattini, 'Viaggio in Spagna', unpublished notebook, ACZ, fol. 62r.

28 Kinder, *Blood Cinema*, 451. Gubern et al., *Historia del Cine Español*, 280. Zavattini, 'Spagna, 9 marzo 1953', *Diario cinematografico*, 1979, 95.

29 Zavattini, 'Viaggio in Spagna', unpublished notebook, ACZ, fols 62–8; fol. 67v.
30 Zavattini, *ibidem*, fol. 67v.
31 Rob Stone, *Spanish Cinema*, Harlow: Pearson Longman, 2002, 5.
32 Hopewell, *Out of the Past*, 250. Later, Buñuel, Rafael Azcona and Carlos Saura would also become shareholders.
33 Hopewell, *Out of the Past*, 250.
34 Paulino Garagorri, 'Cesare Zavattini (Apuntes)', *Objectivo. Revista del Cinema*, no. 1, June 1953, 7–8; 7. Garagorri states that he read Zavattini's account in his diary about his first trip to Spain. 'Cesare Zavattini (Apuntes)', 8.
35 Garagorri, 'Cesare Zavattini (Apuntes)', 7–8. Ricardo Muñoz Suay also published a spate of articles about Zavattini, Muñoz Suay, 'Neorrealismo en el Palace', *Indice de Arte y Letras*, 1953; Muñoz Suay, 'En busca del tiempo vulgar', *Objectivo. Revista del Cinema*, no. 1, June 1953. 'El caballo de Troya: Zavattini y el Neorrealismo', *Objectivo*, no. 4; 'Un material neorrealista', *Cine Universitario*, no. 1; 'Más notas sobre Zavattini', *Cine Universitario*, no. 2; Muñoz Suay, 'Una patética confesión *zavattiniana*', *Cinema Universitario* (Salamanca), no. 2, October–November–December, 1955. 'Carnet de notas Carta de Zavattini', *Cine Universitario*, no. 3.
36 Eduardo Ducay, 'La obra de Zavattini (Notas para una interpretación)', *Objectivo. Revista del Cinema*, no. 1, June 1953, 9–19; 9. Ducay cites French and Italian film magazines *La Revue du Cinéma*, *Cinema Nuovo*, *La Rivista del Cinema* and *Bianco & Nero*. Ducay was both a filmmaker (he began making documentaries in 1951) and a critic.
37 Esteve Riambau, 'The Clandestine Militant Who Would Be Minister: Semprún and Cinema', in O. Ferrán and Gina Herrmann (eds), *A Critical Companion to Jorge Semprín. Buchenwald Before and After*, New York: Palgrave Macmillan, 2014, 71.
38 Labanyi, 'Literary Experiment and Cultural Cannibalization', in Labanyi (ed.), *Spanish Cultural Studies*, 295; Barry Jordan, 'The Emergence of a Dissident Intelligentsia', in *ibidem*, 245–55; 248.
39 Muñoz Suay, 'Neorrealismo en el Palace'. Muñoz Suay, 'Za e la Spagna', 1994, ACZ Carte rosse 125, fol. 3v.
40 Muñoz Suay, 'En busca del tiempo vulgar', 23.
41 Muñoz Suay, 'Za e la Spagna', fol. 4r.
42 Muñoz Suay, *ibidem*, fol. 4r.
43 Muñoz Suay, *ibidem*, fol. 4r.
44 Monterde, 'Zavattini en España', 13.
45 Garagorri, 'Cesare Zavattini (Apuntes)', 7.
46 Zavattini, 'Spagna, 9 marzo 1953', 94. Garagorri, 'Cesare Zavattini (Apuntes)', 8.
47 Zavattini, *ibidem*, 95.
48 Zavattini, *ibidem*, 94.
49 Zavattini, *ibidem*, 94.
50 Zavattini, 'Io sono di Luzzara', in *Io. Un'Autobiografia*, 8.
51 Zavattini, 'Spagna, 9 marzo 1953', 96.
52 Garagorri, 'Cesare Zavattini (Apuntes)', 8.
53 Garagorri, *ibidem*.

54 Muñoz Suay, Letter to Zavattini, 1 May 1953, ACZ, Corr. M850/4.
55 Muñoz Suay, *ibidem*.
56 Muñoz Suay, *ibidem*.
57 Kinder, *Blood Cinema*, 26. Garagorri, 'Cesare Zavattini (Apuntes)', 7–8. Ducay, 'La obra de Zavattini (Notas para una interpretación)', 9–19; Muñoz Suay, 'En busca del tiempo vulgar', 20–4. In actual fact, in the following issue, there was another short article by Muñoz Suay and a short scenario by Zavattini which has never been translated into Italian. Ricardo Muñoz Suay, '*Sobre* Umberto D.', *Objectivo*, no. 2, February 1954, 6. Cesare Zavattini, 'Cine en casa', *Objectivo*, no. 2, February 1954, 5–6. Giovanni Calendoli, 'Neorrealismo: 1955', *Objectivo*, no. 9, September–October 1955, 18–24; J. G. Atienza, 'Conversaciones con Giuseppe De Santis', *Objectivo*, no. 9, September–October 1955, 25–31. J. G. Atienza, 'Te querre siempre. Remedios para familias mal avenidas', *Objectivo*, no. 9, September–October 1955, 39–41. Muñoz Suay to Zavattini, 18 April 1953, ACZ, Corr. M850/3. On letter-headed paper: 'Indice de Arte y Letras.'
58 Muñoz Suay doesn't say where it was published, but, given that he was the editor of *Indice de Arte y Letras*, it is very likely that his review of *Umberto D.* appeared in that publication.
59 Zavattini, *Umberto D. Dal soggetto alla sceneggiatura: Precedono alcune idee sul cinema*, 1953.
60 Riambau, 'The Clandestine Militant Who Would Be Minister: Semprún and Cinema', 71–88; 71.
61 Zavattini, *Ipocrita 1943*, in Zavattini, *Opere 1931-1986*, 278–310.
62 Muñoz Suay, 'En busca del tiempo vulgar', 20.
63 Muñoz Suay, *ibidem*, 21.
64 Garagorri, 'Cesare Zavattini (Apuntes)', 7–8; 7.
65 Muñoz Suay, 'En busca del tiempo vulgar', 21.
66 Muñoz Suay, *ibidem*, 21.
67 Muñoz Suay, *ibidem*, 22. He reprints the scene in its original Italian version taken from the published book.
68 It won the Silver Bear at the Berlin Film Festival that year and was nominated for the *Palme d'Or*.
69 Juan Antonio Bardem, 'Cannes, 1953', *Objectivo*, no. 1, June 1953, 29–34.
70 Bardem, *ibidem*, 29.
71 Bardem, *ibidem*, 29.
72 Bardem, *ibidem*, 30.
73 Bardem, *ibidem*, 30.
74 Garagorri, 'Cesare Zavattini (Apuntes)', 7–8; 7.
75 Muñoz Suay, Letter to Zavattini, 6 July 1953, ACZ, Corr. M850/5. Unpublished.
76 Monterde, 'Zavattini en España', 17.
77 Muñoz Suay, 'Za e la Spagna', fol. 4r.
78 Muñoz Suay, *ibidem*, fol. 4r.
79 Ducay, 'La obra de Zavattini. (Notas para una interpretación)', 9–19.
80 Ducay, *ibidem*, 14.
81 On the figure of the anti-hero, Ducay cites Lorenzo Quaglietti's 'L'eroe positivo', *Bianco & Nero*, December 1949.

82 Muñoz Suay, Letter to Zavattini, 17 January 1954, ACZ, Corr. M 850/7. Unpublished.

83 Muñoz Suay, *ibidem.*

84 Muñoz Suay, *ibidem.*

85 Muñoz Suay, *ibidem.*

86 Muñoz Suay, 'Za e la Spagna', 1994, ACZ Cart. rosse 125, fol. 4r.

87 Monterde, 'Zavattini en España', 17.

88 Muñoz Suay, 'Za e la Spagna'.

89 Suay, 'na patética confesión *zavattiniana*'.

90 Zavattini, 'Cannes. 7 maggio 1958', *Diario cinematografico*, 1979, 284.

91 Muñoz Suay, 'Za e la Spagna', fol. 4v.

92 Cesare Zavattini, Luis García Berlanga, Ricardo Muñoz Suay, 'Festival de cine' 1954, ACZ, Sog. NR 13/3 and published as *Festival de cine*, Madrid: Graficas Cine, 1954 (dated 11 December 1954). They also wrote five stories altogether in collaboration. There was enough material for a full-length feature film of five episodes which were never made. Cesare Zavattini, Luis García Berlanga and Ricardo Muñoz Suay, *Cinco Historias de España y Festival de Cine*, Madrid: Graficas Cine, 1955 (dated 15 April). Cf. Cesare Zavattini, Luis García Berlanga and Ricardo Muñoz Suay, *Cinco Historias de España y Festival de Cine*, Valencia: Filmteca, 1991.

93 In his published diary, writing about Cannes in 1958, and how film festivals might be helpful in changing attitudes towards the cinema, by making a call for films on contemporary society, needs and contradictions of everyday life, Zavattini remembered that project. Cf. Zavattini, 'Cannes, 7 maggio 1958', *Diario cinematografico*, 284.

94 Cesare Zavattini, Luis García Berlanga, Ricardo Muñoz Suay, 'Festival de cine' 1954, ACZ, Sog. NR 13/3, published as privately printed booklet, *Festival de cine*, Madrid: Graficas Cine, 1954 (dated 11 December 1954).

95 Zavattini to Berlanga, 10 October 1955, ACZ, CE 749/16. Undated and unpublished typescript letter.

96 Muñoz Suay, 'Za e la Spagna', fol. 4v.

97 Zavattini, 'Roma, 6 marzo 1955', *Diario cinematografico*, 173–6.

98 Muñoz Suay, 'Una patética confesión *zavattiniana*'.

99 Monterde, 'Zavattini en España', 14.

100 Muñoz Suay, 'Un material neorrealista', *Cinema Universitario*, no. 1, January–February–March, 1955, 19–25.

101 Muñoz Suay to Zavattini, 24 May 1955, ACZ, Corr. M850/8. Unpublished.

102 Muñoz Suay, 'Un material neorrealista', 19–25; 20.

103 Muñoz Suay, *ibidem*, 21.

104 Muñoz Suay, *ibidem*, 23.

105 Luis Buñuel, *Las Hurdes* (*Land Without Bread*) (1932). Zavattini, 'Roma, 6 marzo 1955', 174.

106 Zavattini, 'Roma, 6 marzo 1955', 174.

107 The opening paragraph of Zavattini's *Soldier and Servant* contains a reference to 1955. Zavattini, 'Soldado y Criada (1954)', in Zavattini, *Uomo, vieni fuori!*, 351.

108 Zavattini, Letter to Berlanga, ACZ, 749/11. Undated and unpublished typescript. Zavattini, Letter to Berlanga, 6 September 1954, ACZ Corr. 749/12. Typescript. Unpublished letter in which Zavattini offers some reflections

on the writing process. He makes it clear that it was done in collaboration, under Zavattini's overall guidance. Zavattini notes that despite the many disagreements between Luis Berlanga and Ricardo Muñoz Suay, the two share values and spontaneity.

109 Zavattini, Berlanga and Muñoz Suay, *Cinco Historias de España*, 1955 (dated 15 April). A Spanish film club published the five stories together with *Festival de cine*, the first scenario the three worked on. Cf. Zavattini, Berlanga and Muñoz Suay, *Cinco Historias de España y Festival de Cine*, 1991. This is confirmed by internal evidence, and by the correspondence between Berlanga and Zavattini.

110 Zavattini, Letter to Berlanga, 9 September 1955, ACZ Corr. 749/13. Typescript. Unpublished letter.

111 Muñoz Suay, 'Un material neorrealista', 19–25.

112 Muñoz Suay, *ibidem*, 19.

113 Muñoz Suay, *ibidem*, 19.

114 Muñoz Suay, *ibidem*, 19.

115 C. Pascual, 'Tres revistas españolas de cíne', *Cinema Universitario*, no. 1, January–February–March 1955, 64.

116 Jean-Paul Sartre, 'El neorrealismo no es pesimista', *Cinema Universitario*, no. 1, January–February–March 1955, 47.

117 Basilio Martín Patino, [Editorial], *Cinema Universitario*, no. 1, January–February–March 1955, 2.

118 Basilio Martín Patino, 'Nuestro cine', *ibidem*, 4.

119 Joaquín de Prada, 'El cine y la España tangible', in *ibidem*, 12.

120 Basilio Martín Patino, 'Cristo proibido', in *ibidem*, 2.

121 Eduardo Ducay and Juan Julio Baena, 'Fotodocumentales I: Objectivo Sanabria', in *ibidem*, 31–5.

122 Marisol López, 'Sanabria tiene carta: el rodaje de Ducay y Saura', *La Opinión de Zamora*, 18 November 2016.

123 Cf. *Cinema Universitario*, no. 1, *ibidem*, 85–6. The manifesto and article are signed by three of the founding editors of *Objectivo* (Juan Antonio Bardem, Paulino Garagorri and Eduardo Ducay), as well as by: Basilio Martín Patino, Marcelo Arroita-Jáuregua, Joaquín de Prada, José Maria Pérez Lozano and Manuel Rabanal Taylor.

124 Bardem et al., 'Boletín de las Primeras Conversaciones Cinematográficas Nacionales', *ibidem*, 85–6.

125 Bardem et al., *ibidem*, 85–6.

126 de Prada, 'El cine y la España tangible', 9–15.

127 Besas, *Behind the Spanish Lens*, 1985, 40.

128 Besas, *ibidem*, 103. Patino would go on to make the important *Canciones para después de una guerra* (1970) ('Songs for after the War'), made in what was still a repressive cultural and political climate. It is an archival composite film which reconstructs Spanish Fascism through its visual culture and period newsreels, which the filmmaker managed to smuggle into Spain from Portugal, exposing through documentation the real Spain of the Franco regime. Besas, *Behind the Spanish Lens*, 1985, 107.

129 Besas, *ibidem*, 106.

130 Kinder, *Blood Cinema*, 27.

131 Monterde, 'Zavattini en España', 11.

132 Juan Francisco Cerón Gómez, 'El cine de Juan Antonio Bardem y la censura franquista (1951-1963): las contradicciones de la represión cinematográfica', *Imafronte*, no. 14, 1999, University of Murcia, 28.

133 Besas, *Behind the Spanish Lens*, 39.

134 de Prada, 'El cine y la España tangible', 9–15, 11.

135 de Prada, *ibidem*, 13. The manifesto became Bardem's speech at the Conference itself. The issue of Spanish documentary was also discussed, because it appeared in the Conclusions. None of the sources consulted, including the commentary in the following issue of *Cinema Universitario*, discuss the detail of the Conclusions, but they do mention resolutions on censorship and documentary. Therefore, de Prada's article discussion paper, 'El cine y la España tangible', is considered the source for the Conversations, just as the manifesto was used for Bardem's speech.

136 de Prada, 'El cine y la España tangible', 14.

137 Bardem, cited in Besas, *Behind the Spanish Lens*, 1985, 40.

138 Bardem et al., 'Boletín de las Primeras Conversaciones Cinematográficas Nacionales', 85–6.

139 Bardem et al., *ibidem*, 85–6.

140 Besas, *Behind the Spanish Lens*, 1985, 75.

141 Bardem, cited in Besas, *Behind the Spanish Lens*, 1985, 41.

142 Bardem, *ibidem*, 41.

143 Bardem, *ibidem*, 41.

144 Muñoz Suay, 'Cine documental', *Cinema Universitario*, no. 3, May 1956, 37.

145 Muñoz Suay, *ibidem*, 37.

146 Muñoz Suay, *ibidem*, 37.

147 Stone, *Spanish Cinema*, 5, 47.

148 Stone, *ibidem*, 5, 47.

149 Bardem, '¿Para qué sirve un film?', *Cinema Universitario*, no. 4, December, 1956, 24–5.

150 Muñoz Suay, Letter to Zavattini, 24 May 1955, ACZ, Corr. M 850/8. Unpublished.

151 Stone, *Spanish Cinema*, 47.

152 Muñoz Suay, 'Za e la Spagna', fol. 7v.

153 Stone, *Spanish Cinema*, 5, 37.

154 Bardem, cited in Besas, *Behind the Spanish Lens*, 1985, 42.

155 Cerón Gómez, 'El cine de Juan Antonio Bardem y la censura franquista (1951-1963)', 28.

156 Kinder, *Blood Cinema*, 26.

157 José Enrique Monterde, '*Cinema Universitario*', in José Luis Borau (ed.), *Diccionario del cine español*, Madrid: Alianza-Academia de las Artes y las Ciencias Cinematográficas de España-Fundación Autor, 1998, 227–8.

158 Juan García Atienza, 'Notas hacia la definición de un realismo cinematográfico español', *Cinema Universitario*, no. 2, October–November–December 1955, 41–4.

159 Besas, *Behind the Spanish Lens*, 1985, 42.

160 José García Escudero, *Cine Social*, Madrid: Primera, 1958.

161 Kinder, *Blood Cinema*, 31.

162 This state of affairs has led some to conclude that Spanish Neo-realism was a co-opted cinema under Fascism, arguing that it could be also used by the

Right. In theory, it could have been. In practice, it was not. Cf. Ian Aitken, *European Film Theory and Cinema: A Critical Introduction*, Edinburgh: Edinburgh University Press, 2001, 248–9.

163 Besas, *Behind the Spanish Lens*, 1985, 42.
164 Luis García Berlanga, 'Cine italiano', *Cinema Universitario*, no. 3, May 1956, 28–35.
165 Muñoz Suay, 'Za e la Spagna', fol. 7r. The Spanish title is not a direct translation of any single text by Zavattini. It is dated 'Rome, December 1957'. The text was published as Zavattini, 'El neorrealismo no ha muerto', *Cinema Universitario*, no. 6, December 1957, 31–3.
166 Hopewell, *Out of the Past*, 58.
167 Besas, *Behind the Spanish Lens*, 1985, 47.
168 Hopewell, *Out of the Past*, 59.
169 Hopewell, *ibidem*, 45.
170 Besas, *ibidem*, 118.
171 Stone, *Spanish Cinema*, 59, 63.
172 Labanyi, 'Censorship, or the Fear of Mass Culture', 207–14, 210.
173 Besas, *Behind the Spanish Lens*, 1985, 48.
174 Hopewell, *Out of the Past*, 51.

Chapter 16

1 This and the following two chapters draw on Brancaleone, *Zavattini, il Neo-realismo, e il Nuovo Cinema Latino-americano* (2 vols, Vol. 1 print, Vol. 2 online). The author would especially like to thank Arturo Zavattini and the staff at the Zavattini Archive in Reggio Emilia, particularly the former head archivist Giorgio Boccolari and Roberta Ferri, in charge of the Zavattini Archive, for making it possible to research that book.

2 Fornarina Fornaris, *Ecu Red*, http://www.ecured.cu/index.php/Nuestro _Tiempo_%28Revista%29, accessed 14 December 2015. Fornarina Fornaris was one of the founders of Nuestro Tiempo, and one of the main contributors to its magazine *Nuestro Tiempo*. http://www.cubaliteraria.com//monografia/ sociedad_nuestro_tiempo/revista.html, accessed 14 December 2015.

3 'Conferencia de Cesare Zavattini y Alberto Lattuada (se produjo sobre la base de preguntas y respuestas, dirigidas indistintamente a uno o al otro)', Biblioteca Panizzi of Reggio Emilia, Archivio Cesare Zavattini, E 3/2. fols 9–19. Unpublished. An Italian edition appears in Volume 2 of the above cited *Zavattini, il Neo-realismo, e il Nuovo Cinema Latino-americano*, which comprises a selection of correspondence and papers, mostly hitherto unpublished. Guevara took notes at the conference which he later published in the film club bulletin (Alfredo Guevara, 'Zavattini y Lattuada en Nuestro Tiempo', Havana: *Boletín de Cine Nuestro Tiempo*, no. 5, February 1954, 6, 7, 11), after sending a copy to Zavattini for approval. José Massip, 'El major camino del cine: El realismo', *Nuestro Tiempo*, no. 4, Havana, January 1954.
    Cf. 'Cuba 1953. 31 December 1953', in *Cinema Nuovo*, no. 27, 15 January 1954, then in *Diario cinematografico*, in Cesare Zavattini, *Opere. Cinema. Diario cinematografico*, edited by Valentina Fortichiari and *Neorealismo*

ecc., edited by Mino Argentieri, Milan: Bompiani, 2002, 186–90. Zavattini's published film diary corroborates the account set out in this typescript. It provides a clear summary of the question and answer session. Alfredo Guevara, future director of ICAIC (*Instituto Cubano de Arte y Industria Cinematográfica*) does not identify himself as author of the transcript and commentary, but the covering letter in the Zavattini Archive confirms his identity. Alfredo Guevara to Zavattini, 5 February 1954, in Alfredo and Cesare Zavattini, *Ese diamantino corazón de la verdad*, Madrid: Iberautor Promociones Culturales, 2002, 15–17.

4 Alfredo Guevara, 'Del Neo-realismo, del compromiso', in Guevara and Zavattini, *Ese diamantino corazón de la verdad*, 265.

5 Letter from Guevara to Zavattini, 10 June 1954, ACZ Corr. G 583, fol. 2. Unpublished.

6 José Massip to Zavattini, 26 April 1955, ACZ Corr. M 369/1. Unpublished.

7 Guevara, 'Conferencia de Zavattini e Lattuada', ACZ E 3/2. Unpublished.

8 Piersantelli, 'Un'inchiesta sulla miseria in Italia'. Camera dei deputati, *Atti della Commissione*. Cf. Archivio Storico della Camera dei Deputati, https://archivi o.camera.it/inventari/scheda/commissione-sulla-miseria-italia-e-sui-mezzi-c ombatterla-1951-1954/CD300003060/istituto-nazionale-previdenza-e-credi to-comunicazioni.html, accessed 10 August 2020.

   Giorgio Ferroni directed a documentary at the time that was produced and funded by the Istituto Luce. (Istituto Luce_Inchiesta sulla Miseria _ Parte 1: https://www.youtube.com/watch?v=IkbApjfd9fc, accessed 21 March 2013).

9 Leo Huberman and Paul Sweezy, *Cuba: Anatomy of a Revolution*, New York: Monthly Review Press, 1961, 3.

10 Zavattini, 'Cuba 1953', 187.

11 Zavattini, cited by Alfredo Guevara in Guevara, 'Discurso pronunciado por el cro. Alfredo Guevara con motivo del inicio de la Semana de Cine Italiano en Cuba el 16 de diciembre 1976. Estreno pelicula Amarcord', ACZ E 3/2, 2. Unpublished.

12 Cf. Guevara, 'Conferencia de Cesare Zavattini e Alberto Lattuada', ACZ E 3/2. Unpublished.

13 Cf. Guevara, *ibidem*.

14 Cf. Guevara, *ibidem*.

15 Karl Marx, *Economic and Philosophic Manuscripts of 1844* in Marx, *Writings of the Young Marx on Philosophy and Society*, translated and edited by Loyd D. Easton and Kurt H. Guddat, New York: Anchor Books, 1967, 282–337, especially 315 and ff.

16 Massip to Zavattini, 26 April 1955, ACZ Corr. M 369/1. Unpublished.

17 Guevara, 'Zavattini y Lattuada en Nuestro Tiempo', 6, 7, 11. Massip, 'El major camino del cine: El realismo'.

18 Julio García Espinosa, '"El Neorrealismo y el Cine Cubano', Conferencia celebrada en la Asociación cultural Nuestro Tiempo', La Habana, Mayo 13 de 1954, ACZ E 3/1, fols 27–46. Unpublished.

19 Zavattini to Guevara, 6 March 1954 in Alfredo Guevara and Cesare Zavattini, *Ese diamantino corazón de la verdad*, 18. Guido Aristarco to Alfredo Guevara, 2 June 1954, in Guevara and Zavattini, *Ese diamantino corazón de la verdad*, 23.

20 Massip, 'Cronaca cubana', *Bianco & Nero*, LX, no. 6, November–December 1999, 51.
21 Gutiérrez Alea to Zavattini, 20 April 1955, ACZ Corr. A 101/1. Handwritten in Italian. Unpublished.
22 The medium-length film is viewable online. For the concept of 'shadowing', cf. Giorgio Tinazzi, 'Cinema del pedinamento', in Nuzzi (ed.), *Cesare Zavattini. Una vita in mostra*, 193–6; 194.
23 Fernando Gamboa to Zavattini, 17 November 1954, in Gabriel Rodríguez Álvarez (ed.), *Cartas a México. Correspondencia de Cesare Zavattini 1954-1988*, Mexico City: Universidad Nacional Autónoma de México, 2007, 45.
24 Zavattini to Guevara, 2 January 1959, ACZ E 2/4. Unpublished.
25 *Ibidem.*
26 Julianne Burton, 'Revolutionary Cuban Cinema', *Jump Cut*, no. 19, December 1978, 17–20.
27 Fernando Bernal to Zavattini, 29 May 1959, ACZ E 2/7, fol. 46. Unpublished.
28 The typescript transcription is not dated, however, given the introductory and generic nature of the talk and the reference to 'the weeks ahead', there can be little doubt it was written very soon after his arrival in Cuba on 11 December 1959. This text from the ICAIC archive was first published in an Italian translation by Stefania Parigi in *Bianco & Nero*, where Parigi states that it is the transcription of a talk given by Zavattini. Cf. Stefania Parigi, 'L'Officina cubana', *Bianco & Nero*, LX, no. 6, November–December 1999, 102–3.
29 Zavattini, 'Come si scrive una sceneggiatura', *Bianco & Nero*, LX, no. 6, November–December 1999, 102–3; 102. Eventually, he conceded that 'technique is a matter of time, experience and application', *ibidem*, 103.
30 *Ibidem*, 102.
31 Hosé Hernández, Letter to Zavattini, 4 June 1960, ACZ E 2/7, fols 28–32. Unpublished.
32 Joris Ivens, 'Joris Ivens en Cuba', *Cine cubano*, no. 3, November 1960, 22.
33 Manuel Octavio Gómez, 'Jovenes cineastas opinan sobre Zavattini', *Cine cubano*, no. 1, 1960, 43.
34 Zavattini, Official speech at ICAIC, ACZ E 3/2, fols 2–8.
35 Zavattini, *ibidem*, fols 2–8.
36 Hosé Hernández to Zavattini, 4 June 1960, ACZ E 2/7, fols 28–32. Unpublished.
37 Zavattini, 'Cuba 1960', *Paese Sera*, 18 April 1960.
38 Ernesto Che Guevara, cited in Zavattini, 'Cuba 1960', *Paese Sera*, Saturday 23 April 1960.
39 Zavattini, Official speech at ICAIC, ACZ E 3/2, fols 2–8.
40 The director of photography was Otello Martelli and one of the cameramen was Zavattini's son, Arturo. Cf. David Brancaleone, *Zavattini, il Neo-realismo e il Nuovo Cinema Latino-americano*.
41 This treatment appears in English, in a new translation from the original typescript in *Cesare Zavattini: Selected Writings*, edited and translated by David Brancaleone, New York: Bloomsbury Academic, Vol. 1, 2021.
42 'Color contra Color', Soggettini cubani, ACZ Sog. NR 27/6, fol. 19.
43 "Héctor García Mesa and Eduardo Manet (eds), 'Un'intervista con Zavattini', *Cine cubano*, no. 1, 1960.
44 Massip, *Cine cubano*, no. 1, 1960 and Massip, 'Cronaca cubana', 54.

45 Hosé Hernández, Letter to Zavattini, 4 June 1960, ACZ E 2/7, fols 28–32. Unpublished.

46 Robert E. Quirk, *Fidel Castro*, New York and London: W.W. Norton and Company, 1993, 381.

47 Zavattini mentioned their opposition to Valentino Bompiani, telling him about their fear of confusing art with propaganda, a legitimate fear which Zavattini was keen to address head on. Cf. Zavattini, Letter to Valentino Bompiani, *Cinquant'anni e più ... Lettere 1933-1989*, edited by Valentina Fortichiari, Milan: Bompiani, 315–23.

48 Néstor Almendros to Zavattini, 1 March 1960, ACZ E 2/7 fol. 40. Unpublished, in Italian.

49 Zavattini, 'Per una discussione con i "non impegnati"', in *Bianco & Nero*, LX, no. 6, November–December 1999, 104–14; 105.

50 *Ibidem*, 106.

51 *Ibidem*, 106.

52 *Ibidem*, 105.

53 *Ibidem*, 106.

54 *Ibidem*, 106.

55 *Ibidem*, 105.

56 *Ibidem*, 105.

57 *Ibidem*, 112.

58 *Ibidem*, 106.

59 *Ibidem*, 109.

60 *Ibidem*, 112. Cf. Hosé Hernández to Zavattini, 4 June 1960, ACZ E 2/7, fols 28–32. Unpublished.

61 *Ibidem*, 106.

62 *Ibidem*, 106.

63 *Ibidem*, 106, 109.

64 *Ibidem*, 109.

65 *Ibidem*, 105.

66 On first-person, subjective cinema, cf. Rascaroli, *The Personal Camera*, 111–13, in which the author argues that Zavattini had a pioneering role in the history of cinema.

67 'Per una discussione con i "non impegnati"', 106.

68 *Ibidem*, 112.

69 *Ibidem*, 109.

70 Vittorio De Sica interviewed by Giulio Mazzocchi, 'Domande a Vittorio De Sica per *Un mondo nuovo*', *L'Europa letteraria*, VI, no. 42, May 1965, cited in Zavattini, *Uomo, vieni fuori!*, 321.

71 Julio García Espinosa, 'Por un cine imperfecto', Caracas: Rociante-Fondo Editorial Salvador de la Plaza, 1973, English translation: 'Towards an Imperfect Cinema', in Michael T. Martin, *New Latin American Cinema. Vol. 1. Theory, Practices and Transcontinental Articulations*, Detroit: Wayne State University, 1997, 197.

72 Kant is in the background, having drawn the distinction between mechanical art and art as an aesthetic endeavour. While the first is functional, aimed at a practical end, the exclusive purpose of the second is to engender pleasure and beauty, which are both disinterested aesthetic feelings. Cf. Immanuel Kant, *Critique of Judgement*, translated by W. S. Pluhar, Indianapolis: Hackett, 1982.

73   Julio García Espinosa, 'Towards an Imperfect Cinema', in Martin, *New Latin American Cinema*, 197.

74   The short is viewable online.

75   Hugh Thomas, *The Cuban Revolution*, London: Weidenfeld and Nicolson, 1986, 564.

76   Quirk, *Fidel Castro*, 1993, 382.

77   Quirk, *ibidem*, 383.

78   Julio García Espinosa, 'En Cuba el cine busca al público', *Cine cubano*, no. 13, August–September 1963, 13–20. Fidel Castro, 'Palabras a los intelectuales', in *Política cultural de la revolución cubana: documentos*, Havana: Editorial de Cinecias, 1977, 74–5.

79   Lino Miccichè, 'Introduzione al cinema cubano', press cutting in ACZ E 4/1.

80   Zavattini to Miccichè, 2 November 1977, in Zavattini, *Una, cento, mille, lettere*, 329–30.

81   Octavio Getino and Fernando Solanas, 'Vers un troisième cinéma', *Tricontinental*, no. 3, Paris, October 1969, 89–113, 343. English translation, cf. Octavio Getino and Fernando Solanas, 'Towards a Third Cinema: Notes and Experiences for the Development of a Cinema of Liberation in the Third World', in Martin, *New Latin American Cinema*, 37. The author is grateful to Laura Rascaroli for pointing this out.

82   Lino Miccichè, 'Sul neorealismo oggi', in Giorgio Tinazzi and Bruno Torri (eds), *Patrie visioni. Saggi sul cinema italiano 1930-1980*, Pesaro: Marsilio, 2010, 97–113; 103–5.

Chapter 17

1   'Cesare Zavattini racconta: è sempre valida la lezione Neo-realista', *Il Momento*, 24 December 1953.

2   Zavattini, 'Messico. 13 dicembre 1956', in Zavattini, *Diario cinematografico*, 1979, 226–38. '...lui spera che il suo popolo, a vedersi raccontato sui muri, prenda più coscienza di sé'. Zavattini, 'Messico. 13 dicembre 1956', *Cinema Nuovo*, no. 97, 31 December 1956; no. 98, 15 January 1957; no. 99, 1 February 1957; no. 100, 15 February 1957, now in *Diario cinematografico*, in *Zavattini cinema*, 2002, 332.

3   Octavio Alba, 'Hoy llega a México el famoso Zavattini quien realizarà dos películas con Alazraki y Velo', *Cine mundial*, Mexico City, 24 June 1955, 9.

4   Zavattini to Diego Rivera, 16 January 1954, in *Cartas a México*, 37.

5   David Alfaro Siqueiros, *Siqueiros, por la vía de una pintura neorrealista o realista social en México*, Mexico City: Instituto Nacional de Bellas Artes, 1951.

6   Interview with Zavattini, *Cine mundial*, no. 295, 11 December 1953. In English, the new, critical edition in translation, cf. Brancaleone, *Cesare Zavattini. Selected Writings*, forthcoming, 2020.

7   Amadeo Recanati, Letter to Zavattini, 9 January 1954, in *Cartas a México*, 35.

8   Interview with Zavattini, *Cine mundial*, no. 295, 11 December 1953.

9   *Ibidem*.

10 Francisco Pina, 'Cesare Zavattini, precursor del Neorrealismo', in 'México en la Cultura', in *Novedades*, Mexico City, February, 1954, 4–8; 5.

11 *Ibidem*, 5.

12 'Alcune idee sul cinema' was translated into Spanish and published in *Cine cubano*, according to Alfredo Guevara. He reprinted 'La dimensión moral del neo-realismo', in Guevara and Zavattini, *Ese Guevara e Zavattini, Ese diamantino corazón corazón de la verdad*, 267–84. Caro Baroja, *El Neorrealismo cinematografico italiano*, 188–90; 193–5; 199–201; 243–4; 247. In December 1954, Zavattini gave him permission to publish extracts. Zavattini to Pina, 22 December 1954, ACZ Corr. P 424/5. Unpublished.

13 Pío Caro to Zavattini, 13 February 1954, in *Cartas a México*, 39.

14 *Ibidem*, 177–8.

15 Zavattini, 'Epilogo', in Caro Baroja, *El Neorrealismo cinematografico italiano*, 273–5.

16 Gamboa, in Tarcísio Gustavo Chárraga and Elvia Vera Soriano, *Cesare Zavattini en México, Cesare Zavattini en México (Un documento para la historia del cine nacional)*, Mexico City: Universidad Nacional Autónoma de México, 1985, 113.

17 Raquel Tibol, a young critic, interviewed Gamboa. However, Gamboa's text reads as a finished article written by Gamboa himself. Raquel Tibol, 'De los muros a las pantallas o Fernando Gamboa frente al cine y dentro del el', in 'México en la cultura', *Novedades*, Mexico City, 26 June 1955, 4.

18 *Cartas a México*, 20. Pío Caro Baroja later collaborated on Zavattini's *El Anillo mágico* with Jomí García Ascot and writer Fernando Benítez on the scenario for *El Petróleo*, and with Carlos Velo for Zavattini's *Carretera Panamericana* and with Fernando Gamboa and Carlos Velo on *México mío*. Cf. *Cartas a México*, 21.

19 Caro Baroja, *El Neorrealismo cinematografico italiano*, 160.

20 Caro Baroja, '*Raíces* in *El Neorrealismo cinematografico italiano*', 160.

21 Zavattini to Benito Alazraki, 25 May 1954, *Cartas a México*, 40.

22 *Ibidem*, 40.

23 Zavattini, in Caro Baroja, '*Raíces* in *El Neorrealismo cinematografico italiano*', 163.

24 Manuel Barbachano, in Chárraga and Soriano, *Cesare Zavattini en México*, 126.

25 Alba, 'Hoy llega a México el famoso Zavattini quien realizarà dos películas con Alazraki y Velo', 9.

26 Zavattini, cited in Caro Baroja, *El Neorrealismo cinematografico italiano*, 163–4.

27 Emilio García Riera, *Historia documental del cine mexicano*, Mexico City: Era, 1974, 19, in Chárraga and Soriano, *Cesare Zavattini en México*, 37.

28 Adolfo Fernandez Bustamante, 'Punto y Raya', *Hoy*, Mexico City, 6 July 1955, 31–2.

29 Gamboa to Zavattini, 14 March 1955, in *Cartas a México*, 55–6.

30 Zavattini, cited by Barbachano, in Chárraga and Soriano, *Cesare Zavattini en México*, 129.

31 Zavattini, 'La terra e la luna', *Il Contemporaneo*, 24 September 1955, 1.

32 *Ibidem*, fol. 14.

33 *Ibidem*, fol. 18.

34   Jaime Ascot, '*L'Anello. Seconda continuità provvisionale. Osservazioni*', ACZ
     Za Sog. NR 8/5, fols 38–9, Unpublished manuscript, 1957.

35   Barbachano to Zavattini, 18 January 1957, in *Cartas a México*, 115.

36   Carlos Velo, in Chárraga and Soriano, *Cesare Zavattini en México*, 134–5.
     Alvaro Beltrani, 'No lo extrañe a Zavattini qe lo espere un mitotini', 'Flecha
     Neorrealista', *Novedades*, 21 August 1955.

37   Beltrani, 'No lo extrañe a Zavattini qe lo espere un mitotini', 'Flecha
     Neorrealista'. Zavattini to Alvaro Beltrani, 16 September 1955, ACZ E/72,
     fol. 18. Unpublished. Anon., 'Entrevista publica con Zavattini en la Sala
     Manuel M. Ponce', *Novedades*, Mexico City, 22 August 1955.

38   Zavattini, 'La terra e la luna'.

39   'Projecto de cuestionario para entrevista publica al Sr. Cesare Zavattini', ACZ
     E 7/1, fol. 12. Unpublished.

40   *Ibidem*, fol. 12.

41   Zavattini, 'La terra e la luna'.

42   Zavattini, 'Appunti per la conversazione del 24/8 Mexico D.F.', ACZ E 7/1,
     fols 1–12. Fol. 12: 'Projecto de cuestionario per entrevista publica'.

43   Vicente Vila, 'Zavattini y el público', 'Cambio de rollo', *Diario Cine Mundial*,
     29 August 1955, 6.

44   Later, in an article for an Italian Communist weekly, *Il Contemporaneo*,
     Zavattini observed that 'the Mexicans themselves identified the real themes
     of their lives and history. This allowed me to understand their level of social
     awareness and their way of looking and criticizing this reality of theirs.'
     Zavattini, 'La terra e la luna', 1.

45   Zavattini to Felipe Carrera, 29 January 1956, ACZ E/72, fol. 52. Spanish
     translation in *Cartas a México*, 221; 222. Carrera was a Venezuelan refugee
     Zavattini met during the debate on Neo-realism.

46   Carl T. Mora, *Mexican Cinema: Reflections of a Society*, Jefferson: McFarland
     and Company, 2005, 104. Mora fails to attribute the initiative to Zavattini or
     to anyone else.

47   Zavattini to Felipe Carrera, 29 January 1956, ACZ E/72, fol. 52. Zavattini
     to Francisco Pina and Pío Caro Baroja, 27 December 1955, in *Cartas a
     México*, 97.

48   Zavattini to Gamboa and Teleproducciones, 28 November 1955, in *Cartas
     a México*, 94. Barbachano to Zavattini, 18 January 1957, in *Cartas a
     México*, 115. Velo to Zavattini, 7 November 1955, in *Cartas a México*,
     88.

49   Barbachano to Zavattini, 18 January 1957, in *Cartas a México*, 115.

50   Nelli, Interview with Zavattini, *Arte del Cinema*, 3 October 1957, ACZ E 7/4,
     fol. 5.

51   Alfredo Guevara, 'Ese poeta que andaba por el mundo', in Guevara and
     Zavattini, *Ese diamantino corazón de la verdad*, 287–96.

52   Lewis, 'Introduction', *The Children of Sanchez: Autobiography of a Mexican
     Family*, New York: Vintage Books, 1961, xxix–xxx.

53   Zavattini, (Notebook), 'Appunti e materiale vario raccolto durante il soggiorno
     messicano, 1955-1957', ACZ E 6/2, fol. 36v. Unpublished.

54   Zavattini, 'La terra e la luna', 1.

55   José Massip, 'Cronaca cubana', *Bianco & Nero*, LX, no. 6, November–
     December 1999, 51.

56 Gamboa to Zavattini, 14 October 1955, in *Cartas a México*, 78.

57 Juan García Atienza, 'Notas hacia la definición de un realismo cinematográfico español', 41–4.

58 García Atienza, 'En busca del neorrealismo integral. Carlos Velo y ¡*Torero!*', *Cinema Universitario*, no. 4, December 1956, 20–2.

59 Atienza, *ibidem*, 22–3.

60 What purports to be a Mexican version of *Italia mia*, published in 2006, is actually a script that in no way coincides with the project. *México mío* in Cesare Zavattini, *Uomo vieni fuori!*, 357–63. Cf. Zavattini to Manuel Barbachano, 16 March 1958, in Zavattini, *Una, cento, mille, lettere*, 420, which includes the story. A new version of the scenario of *México mío* has recently been published in Brancaleone, *Zavattini, il Neo-realismo, e il Nuovo Cinema Latino-americano*, Vol. 2.

61 Zavattini, 'Appunti e materiale vario raccolto durante il soggiorno messicano, 1955-1957', ACZ E 6/2, fol. 237. Unpublished.

62 *Ibidem*, fol. 228.

63 Zavattini, 'Prime reazioni', ACZ Sog. NR 20/3, fol. 262. Tarcísio Gustavo Chárraga and Elvia Vera Soriano included a copy in their unndergraduate dissertation, *Cesare Zavattini en México (Un documento para la historia del cine nacional)*, Città del Messico: Universidad Nacional Autónoma de México, 1985. In 2006, they published 'La presencia del Neorrealismo en América Latina: Cesare Zavattini en México', *Quaderni del CSCI. Rivista annuale di cinema italiano*, Madrid: Istituto Italiano di Cultura di Barcellona, 129–40. Their account is limited to the 1955 visit and consists in a biography of Zavattini and interviews with the Producciones' staff and directors.

64 *Ibidem*, fol. 256.

65 *Ibidem*, fol. 262.

66 *Ibidem*, fol. 262.

67 *Ibidem*, fol. 268.

68 *Ibidem*, fol. 263.

69 *Ibidem*, fol. 268.

70 Zavattini, 'Mexico mio', in Caldiron (ed.), *Uomo, vieni fuori*, 357–61. The letter was first published in Zavattini, *Una, cento, mille, lettere*, 416–20 and later translated into Spanish. Cf. *Cartas a México*, 122–5.

71 Zavattini to Manuel Barbachano, 16 March 1958, in Zavattini, *Una, cento, mille, lettere*, 420.

72 Zavattini, Notebooks concerning Mexican journeys, 'Primo taccuino. Dalla mia partenza da Roma al 4/7/55', ACZ E 6/1, fol. 32r. Zavattini, 'Appunti per la conferenza sul Messico', ACZ E 63, fols 1–53.

73 Argentina Brunetti, 'Con Cesare Zavattini. Ricognizione in Messico per *I figli di Sanchez*', *Il Progresso Italo-americano*, Sunday 9 January 1972.

74 Oscar Lewis, 'Culture of Poverty', in Daniel P. Moynihan, *On Understanding Poverty: Perspectives from the Social Sciences*, New York: Basic Books 1969, 187–220.

75 *Ibidem*.

76 Zavattini to Bartlett, 29 June 1977, ACZ Corr. Bartlett 611, fol. 6a. 29 June 1977.

77 Zavattini to Argentina Brunetti, 27 March 1972, ACZ Corr. 69/3, fol. 5. Unpublished manuscript.

78 *Ibidem*, fols 7–8.
79 Gerald Martin, 'Latin American Narrative since c. 1920', in Leslie Bethell (ed.), *The Cambridge History of Latin America, Vol. x. Latin America since 1930: Ideas, Culture and Society*, Cambridge: Cambridge University Press, 1995, 129–222. Velo, in Chárraga and Soriano, *Cesare Zavattini en México*, 157.
80 *Ibidem*, p. 202; Robert M. Buffington, 'Poniatowska, Elena', in *Mexico: An Encyclopedia of Contemporary Literature and History*, Oxford Santa Barbara and Denver: ABC Clio, 2004, 399–400.
81 Recanati to Zavattini, 21 November 1955, in *Cartas a México*, 91.
82 Recanati to Zavattini, 14 October 1955, ACZ Corr. Recanati R113/1. Unpublished letter. In Italian, with handwritten signature.
83 De Santi, 'Gabriel García Márquez in Za's fantastic Mirror', 201–12. The Latin American writer met Zavattini in the 1950s, and visited him once in his home. Cf. Letter to Gabriel García Márquez, 12 December 1982, ACZ, Corr. M 295/1. Gabriel García Márquez went to Rome to study cinema and screenwriting. Zavattini was the only person who met with him and other students outside class. García Márquez also acknowledged that the Italian screenwriter taught a different perception of life, as well as the trade of screenwriting. Cf. Gabriel García Márquez, 'Zavattini? Mai sentito', *Cine cubano*, no. 155, November 2002, 32–3.
84 Márquez, ibidem, 32–3.
85 Ernesto R. Acevedo-Muñoz, *Buñuel and Mexico: The Crisis of National Cinema*, Berkeley, Los Angeles and London: University of California Press, 2003, 149.
86 Mora, *Mexican Cinema: Reflections of a Society*, 104. Mora fails to attribute the initiative to Zavattini or to others.
87 Emilio García Riera, *Historia documental del cine mexicano 1961-1963*, Conaculta: Imcine, Universidad de Guadalajara, 1994, 7. Cf. Aranzubia Asier, 'Nuevo Cine (1961-1962) y el nacimiento de la cultura cinematográfica mexicana moderna', *Dimensió antropológica*, 52, May–August, 2011, 101–21.

Chapter 18

1 Birri has gone down in film history as a pioneer and his cultural politics have been framed accordingly. In 1984, during the Fifth International Festival of New Cinema in Havana, he rightly claimed a foundational role in the birth of New Latin American cinema. Cf. Fernando Birri, 'For a Nationalist, Realist, Critical and Popular Cinema', in Martin, *New Latin American Cinema*, 95–8. Originally in *Screen*, 26, nos. 3–4, 1985, 89–91. How did the change come about? He stated that it was the outcome of historic necessity (filmmakers had become politically aware) and 'it was in the air', because the cinema of the time had ignored the social in Latin America. No mention of Zavattini in two important interviews in English, today's lingua franca. Cf. Birri in Julianne Burton (ed.), 'Fernando Birri, The Roots of Documentary Realism', in *Cinema and Social Change in Latin America. Conversations with Filmmakers*, Austin: University of Texas, 1986, 4; 1–12. The earlier Italian version was Julianne Burton, 'Fernando

Birri: Pioniere e Pellegrino', in Lino Miccichè (ed.), *Fernando Birri e La Escuela Documental*, Pesaro: XVII Mostra Internazionale del Nuovo Cinema, June 1981. The later English version cut Birri's comments on *Los Inundados*.

2   Birri, Letter to Zavattini, 21 May 1955, ACZ 901/2. In Italian. Unpublished.

3   Birri in Burton, 'Fernando Birri, The Roots of Documentary Realism', 4. The interview was translated into Italian in Burton, 'Fernando Birri: Pioniere e Pellegrino'. The English version excludes a section where Birri discusses *Los Inundados*.

4   Maselli, in (filmed) conversation with the author, in the summer of 2015.

5   Birri in Burton, 'Fernando Birri, The Roots of Documentary Realism', 3.

6   *Ibidem.*

7   *Ibidem.*

8   Zavattini to Gamboa, 31 May 1955 and 16 September 1955, in *Cartas a México*, 65, 69. He also told the author as much at the end of two filmed and recorded interviews in his home in July 2015.

9   Thomas E. Skidmore and Peter H. Smith, *Modern Latin America*, Oxford and New York: Oxford University Press 1997, 92.

10   Gandin (ed.), *Il tetto di Vittorio De Sica*, 257.

11   Birri, Letter to Zavattini, 4 April 1956, ACZ 901/3. Unpublished.

12   *Ibidem.*

13   Birri, Letter to Zavattini, 24 July 1956, ACZ 901/5. In Italian. Unpublished.

14   Birri, Letter to Zavattini, 27 July 1957, ACZ 901/9. Unpublished.

15   Birri, Letter to Zavattini, 24 July 1956, ACZ 901/5. In Italian. Unpublished.

16   *Ibidem.*

17   Birri, Letter to Zavattini, 9 March 1957, ACZ 901/6. Unpublished.

18   *Ibidem.*

19   *Ibidem.*

20   *Ibidem.*

21   *Ibidem.*

22   *Ibidem.* Birri, Letter to Zavattini, 4 April 1956, ACZ 901/3. In Italian. Unpublished.

23   Birri, Letter to Zavattini, 30 March 1957, ACZ 901/7. On letter-headed paper: 'Universidad Nacional del Litoral. Instituto Social. Instituto de Cinematografia'. In Italian. Unpublished.

24   Birri, Letter to Zavattini (and De Sica), 19 May 1956, ACZ 901/4. Unpublished.

25   *Ibidem.*

26   *Ibidem.*

27   *Ibidem.*

28   Birri, Letter to Zavattini, 9 March 1957, ACZ 901/6. On letter-headed paper: 'Universidad Nacional del Litoral. Instituto Social. Instituto de Cinematografia'. In Italian. Unpublished.

29   *Ibidem.*

30   Zavattini, Letter to Birri, 10 May 1957, ACZ 901/25. Unpublished.

31   Birri, 'Fernando Birri y "El Techo" de De Sica', *El Hogar*, no. 2491, Buenos Aires, 30 August 1957, 85. Birri gave me copies of transcripts of these letters accompanied by accurate references at the end of our second interview at his home in Piazza Bologna, in Rome, in July 2015.

32   Italics added. The phrase became a sign of Birri's manifesto.

33 Birri, Letter to Zavattini, 27 July 1957, ACZ 901/9. In Italian, unpublished.
34 *Ibidem.*
35 *Ibidem.*
36 Fernando Birri, *Fotodocumentales* (1956), in *La Escuela documental de Santa Fe*, Santa Fe, Argentina: Editorial Documento del Instituto de Cinematografía de la Universidad Nacional del Litoral, 2008, 33–8.
37 Luigi Chiarini, *El cine en el problema del arte*, Traducción de Elsa Martina, Buenos Aires: Ediciones Losange, 1956, and Chiarini, *Il film nei problemi dell'arte*, Rome: Edizioni Ateneo, 1949.
38 Birri, Letter to Zavattini, 17 February 1958, ACZ 901/10. In Spanish. Unpublished.
39 Zavattini and Strand, '25 persone di Zavattini e Strand', 137–44. Chiara Samugheo (photography) and Domenico Rea (commentary), 'I bambini di Napoli', *Cinema Nuovo*, IV, no. 63, 25 July 1955, 57–64.
40 Birri, Letter to Zavattini, 9 March 1957, ACZ 901/6, (unpublished) and Zavattini, Letter to Birri, 10 May 1957, ACZ 901/25. Unpublished.
41 *Ibidem.*
42 *Ibidem.*
43 Birri, *Fotodocumentales* (1956) later collected in *La Escuela Documental*, 33–8.
44 Birri, *Fotodocumentalales*, Santa Fe, Argentina: Instituto de Cinematografia de la UNL-Instituto Social, 1956, cited in *La Escuela Documental*, 33–8.
45 Birri, *La Escuela Documental*, 40–1.
46 *Ibidem.*
47 Birri, *Fotodocumentalales*, 33–8.
48 *Ibidem*, 33.
49 *Ibidem*, 17.
50 Ana Maria López, 'An "Other" History: The New Latin American Cinema', in Martin, *New Latin American Cinema*, 135–56; 136.
51 *Ibidem*, 18.
52 *Ibidem*, 73.
53 *Ibidem*, 72.
54 Birri, Letter to Zavattini, 22 June 1959, ACZ 901/11. Unpublished.
55 Birri to Zavattini, 27 July 1960, ACZ 901/14. Unpublished.
56 *Ibidem.*
57 Roberto Raschella, 'Una fecha', Buenos Aires, 31 October 1958; Raschella, '*Tire dié*', *Tiempo de cine*, no. 3. Buenos Aires, October 1960, then in Birri, *La Escuela Documental*, 59–62. Zavattini, 'Alcune idee sul cinema', *Neorealismo ecc.*, 2002, 718–36. Raschella also cites Lino Del Fra, whom Birri never mentions in his collected articles in *La Escuela Documental*. Del Fra was, as mentioned earlier, also a documentary filmmaker. He was also, together with his wife Cecilia Mangini, part of a circle of documentarians close to Zavattini which included Michele Gandin, Luigi Di Gianni, Gianfranco Mingozzi, Citto Maselli and Elio Petri.
58 Raschella in Birri, *La Escuela Documental*, 60.
59 *Ibidem*, 61.
60 Birri, *La Escuela Documental*, 138.
61 Mateo Booz, *Santa Fe. Mi país*, Santa Fe: Castellví, 1953. *La Escuela Documental*, 162.

62 Voice-over commentary at the beginning of *Los Inundados*.
63 Manuel Horacio Giménez, 'Apuntes del diario de filmación', in Mario Rodríguez Alemán, 'Neorrealismo argentino. Los Inundados', *Cine cubano*, no. 11, Havana, June 1963, and collected in Birri's, *La Escuela Documental*, 163–4.
64 Birri, *La Escuela Documental*, 155.
65 Birri, Letter to Zavattini, 3 May 1981, ACZ 901/19. Postcard. Unpublished.
66 'Texto entrevista F.B. para film Zavattini, *Páramo de Mérida*', John Hay Library, Brown University Library, Birri, FE2, Box 18, Folder 13; '*Io sono il diavolo*-Zavattini, Pre-trattamento', Fernando Birri y Luciano Valletta, John Hay Library, Brown University Library, Box 47, Folder 3, Birri, FE2; *Io sono il diavolo. Dal libro di Cesare Zavattini*, 'Guion o pre-guion de Fernando Birri e Luciano Valletta', John Hay Library, Brown University Library, Box 18, Folder 6, Birri, FE2 [undated, but probably 1982, on the basis of correspondence with Birri in the Zavattini Archive of Reggio Emilia; 'Dossier Projecto Cesare Zavattini', John Hay Library, Brown University Library, Box 18, Folder 3–4, FE1, 2005. [This is ZA2005, a homage to Zavattini signed by Latin American filmmakers, including Birri and Espinosa.] 'El Projecto Za', John Hay Library, Brown University Library, FE1, BOX 62, FOLDER 2, 1984. Also, 'Evviva Zá. Texto definitivo', John Hay Library, Brown University Library, FE1, BOX 28, FOLDER 2, 1982. With the exception of *Io sono il diavolo*, all these projects were intended as homages to Zavattini.
67 At the end of a second film interview with the author, in 2015, Birri produced a copy of ZA2005 as a gift, together with copies of *Los Inundados* and *Tire dié*, with English subtitles.

Chapter 19

1 The other winners were Fellini's *La dolce vita*, Visconti's *Rocco e i suoi fratelli* (1960) (*Rocco and His Brothers*), and Luigi Comencini's *Tutti a casa* (*Everybody Go Home*) (1960).
2 Zavattini, *Basta coi soggetti!*, 148–51 and 313–16.
3 Giannarelli (ed.), *Zavattini Sottotraccia*, 58.
4 Martinelli (ed.), *Domande agli uomini di Cesare Zavattini*, 6. A much earlier version pioneered by Zavattini in 1947 was 'Italia domanda' ('Italy wants to Know'), which gave the fledgling weekly illustrated magazine *Epoca* a decisive edge over the competition. In Zavattini's proposals to the publisher, Luigi Einaudi, the whole magazine was to be built around readers' questions, using investigative journalism that was as innovative as it was participative. When the first issue of *Epoca* came out in 1950, Zavattini's organizing principle for the publication was reduced to a regular column. However, it was his column that sold the copies and spelled the weekly magazine's success.
5 Piero Anchisi and Lucio Battistrada. Cf. Martinelli (ed.), *Domande agli uomini*, 7. The questions, as the editor Martinelli rightly observes, are typical of Zavattini's approach. The interviewers treated interviewees as equals, as social agents, empowered citizens, to discuss the private and public dimensions of their lives, their views on society, politics, history and constitute valuable fragments of an unwritten people's history, from 1930s to 1950s Italy.

6   Giannarelli (ed.), *Zavattini Sottotraccia*, 63–8. Gabriella Parca (ed.), *Le italiane si confessano*, Florence: Parenti Editore, 1959. The third edition, published by Feltrinelli in 1964, included two Prefaces, the original one by Zavattini and a second one by Pier Paolo Pasolini, who followed the development of diary, notebook and confessional documentary, in *Vie Nuove* and soon began to experiment himself.

7   Directors included Lorenza Mazzetti, one of the three signatories of the pioneering British Free Cinema Manifesto and director of the Neo-realist film *Together* (1956), Marco Ferreri, Citto Maselli and Gian Vittorio Baldi, best known as an Italian experimental filmmaker in later years.

8   Bolzoni, 'Zavattini e il film inchiesta', 62. The directors were Libero Bizzarri, Mario Carbone, Angelo d'Alessandro, Lino Del Fra, Luigi di Gianni, Giuseppe Ferrara, Ansano Giannarelli, Giuio Macchi, Lorenza Mazetti, Enzo Muzii, Piero Nelli, Paolo Nuzzi, Dino B. Partesano, Massimo Mida, Giovanni Vento and Gianni Bisiach. One of Zavattini's sons, Marco Zavattini, was involved in art direction. Several film critics were also involved, including Lino Miccichè, Callisto Cosulich and Mino Argentieri.

9   Bolzoni, *ibidem*, 62.
10 Bolzoni, *ibidem*, 62.
11 Bolzoni, *ibidem*, 62.
12 Bolzoni, *ibidem*, 63.
13 Bolzoni, *ibidem*, 134.
14 Bolzoni, *ibidem*, 146.
15 Bolzoni, *ibidem*, 35–153; 142.
16 Bolzoni, *ibidem*, 14.
17 Bolzoni, *ibidem*, 14–15.
18 Josué de Castro, *The Geography of Hunger*, Boston: Little, Brown and Company, 1952, 23.
19 Cf. Francisco de Assis Guedes de Vasconcelos, 'Josué de Castro e *Geografia da Fome no Brasil*', *Cadernos de Saúde Pública*, 24, no. 11, Rio de Janeiro, November 2008, https://www.scribd.com/document/417962678/Josue-de-Cast ro-e-a-Geografia-Da-Fome-No-Brasil, accessed 10 August 2020.
20 There are also other lived spaces, in the brief episodes including ones about Catholicism and alternative forms of Christianity. But most of the film is about the contradictions of the city.
21 Bolzoni, *ibidem*, 13.
22 Bolzoni, *ibidem*, 14–15.
23 Bolzoni, *ibidem*, 13.
24 Bolzoni, *ibidem*, 101.
25 Bolzoni, *ibidem*, 103–4.
26 Bolzoni, *ibidem*, 110.
27 Bolzoni, *ibidem*, 15.
28 Bolzoni, *ibidem*, 54.
29 Zavattini, 'Il progetto del film', 13–32; 30.
30 Bolzoni, *ibidem*, 66.
31 Bolzoni, *ibidem*, 66.
32 Bolzoni, *ibidem*, 14.
33 Bolzoni, *ibidem*, 68.
34 Bolzoni, *ibidem*, 21.

35 Zavattini, 'Il progetto del film', 13–32; 30.

36 Bolzoni, *ibidem*, 15.

37 Bolzoni, *ibidem*, 140. In one of several testimonies, Ansano Giannarelli, one of the filmmakers involved and a key figure in coordinating production, agreed. Cf. Ansano Giannarelli, 'Il lungo cammino dell'inchiesta filmica', in Antonio Medici (ed.), *Schermi di guerra. Le responsabilità della comunicazione audiovisiva*, Annali 6, 2003, Archivio Audiovisivo del Movimento Operaio, Rome: Ediesse, 2004, 29–54.

38 Luigi Chiarini, 'Avvertenza', in Cesare Zavattini, 'Some Ideas on Cinema', in Cesare Zavattini, *Dal Soggetto alla Sceneggiatura. Come si scrive un capolavoro: Umberto D.*, 1–3.

39 Ansano Giannarelli, 'Zavattini e l'esordio sul set', in Gambetti (ed.), *Cesare Zavattini: cinema e vita*, 122.

40 Bolzoni, *ibidem*, 27.

41 Bolzoni, *ibidem*, 19; 25.

42 Bolzoni, *ibidem*, 18.

43 Bolzoni, *ibidem*, 19.

44 Zavattini, *Basta coi soggetti!*, 322.

45 Zavattini, *L'Unità*, 6 May 1961, in *Neorealismo ecc.*, 1979, 173–4. Umberto Eco, 'Appunti sulla televisione' (1961), later, published in Eco, *Apocalittici e integrati*, Milan: Bompiani, 1964, 317–57. Eco concluded his scholarly article, stating that the rise and success of television had the potential of developing a complementary new culture, within a broadly televisual society which was here to stay, alongside the existing, traditional, book-based high culture and society. In the 1970s, Pier Paolo Pasolini expressed a more pessimistic view, no different, in his stance, from Guy Debord. Both Debord and, later, Pasolini highlighted its mesmerizing effects on the viewing public, which, by the early 1970s, had contributed to create, in Pasolini's view, a homogenized capitalist society, effecting an anthropological change which could not be reversed.

46 John Foot, *The Archipelago: Italy since 1945*, London and New York: Bloomsbury Publishing, 2018, 116. Eco later published an article about Mike Bongiorno, 'Fenomenologia di Mike Bongiorno', in *Diario minimo*, Milan: Mondadori, 1963, 30–6.

47 Zavattini, *ibidem*, 322.

48 The other filmmakers taking part were Francesco Aluffi, Roberto Capanna, Giorgio Maulini, Umberto Monaci, Pier Luigi Murgia, Andrea Ranieri, Vittorio Armentano and Marcello Bollero. The script was published in 1979 and re-issued on the centenary of Zavattini's birth, in 2002.

49 Adriano Aprà, 'Itinerario personale nel documentario italiano', in Lino Miccichè (ed.), *Studi su dodici sguardi d'autore in cortometraggio*, Turin: Associazione Philip Morris and Progetto Cinema and Lindau, 1995, 281–95.

50 Alberto Grifi, cited in Sirio Luginbühl and Raffaele Perrotta, *Lo schermo negato. Cronache del cinema non ufficiale*, Brescia: Shakespeare, 1976, 68–73.

51 Zavattini, 'Prima reazione all'invito di Piovene', in *Neorealismo ecc.*, 1979, 205–11.

52 Zavattini, 'La pace, la pace, la pace', *Rinascita*, 9 June 1962, in Zavattini, *Diario cinematografico*, 320–3. Zavattini, 'Il Cinegiornale della pace', *Rinascita*, 1 October 1962, in Zavattini, *Neorealismo ecc.*, 236–40.

53 Zavattini, speaking to Gianni Melli in an interview published by *La Fiera Letteraria*, 6 May 1962, now in Zavattini, *Neorealismo ecc.*, 221–3.

54 'Zavattini, "Il cinegiornale della pace"', in Zavattini, *Neorealismo ecc.*, 236–41.

55 The correspondence is kept in the AAMOD archive.

56 Cf. Augusto Sainati, *La Settimana Incom. Cinegiornali e informazione negli anni '50*, Turin: Lindau, 2001. In Italy there were several competing newsreels, shown in the cinemas, before a film or between a double billing. *La Settimana Incom, Orizzonte Cinematografico, Cronache del mondo, Caleidoscopio Ciac, Cinemondo, Radar*. *La Settimana Inco* competed with the overtly rhetorical tone of the *Luce* newsreel. After the war, 50 per cent of the shares were purchased by a senator who was a member of the Centre Right Christian Democratic Party. Its newsreels provided an authoritative voice for the Right to replace the reformed *Luce* which had, after the fall of the Fascist dictatorship, swung to the Left, offering a pluralist platform of views right across the political spectrum. Cf. Mino Argentieri, 'Il 18 aprile 1948 e il cinema', in Ermanno Taviani (ed.), *Propaganda, cinema e politica 1945-1975, Annali 11*, Rome: Archivio Audiovisivo del Movimento Operaio, 2008, 58.

57 Guy Debord, *Society of the Spectacle*, Londton: Rebel Press, 2005, §3, 7.

58 The Marzabotto massacre became topical after a recent discovery of wartime archives, which had been hidden away half a century ago, in a government ministry, having been censored from cultural representation. Giorgio Diritti's film *L'Uomo che verrà* (2009) made sensitive use of recovered interviews to produce a sensitive reconstruction of events, mediated by a fictional treatment.

59 To a limited extent, this is beginning to happen today, as more and more important feature-length documentaries are made.

60 Zavattini, 'I cinegiornali liberi', (1967), in Tullio Masoni and Paolo Vecchi (eds), *Cinenotizie in poesia e prosa. Zavattini e la non-fiction*, Turin: Lindau, 2000, 173–81.

61 Zavattini, *ibidem*, 173–81; 173.

62 Zavattini, 'Conversazione prima,' *Cinema Documentario*, no. 1, April–June 1966, then in *Neorealismo ecc.*, 1979, 280–3.

63 Jacques Rancière, *The Politics of Aesthetics*, London: Continuum, 2010, 139. Also, Rancière, *Aesthetics and Its Discontents*, translated by Steven Corcoran, Cambridge: Polity, 2009.

64 Theodor Adorno and Max Horkheimer, *The Dialectic of Enlightenment*, London and New York: Verso, 2008 (1944), 120–67; 124.

65 Herbert Marcuse, *L'uomo ad una dimensione*, Turin: Einaudi, 1964.

Chapter 20

1 Zavattini, 'Conferenza economica del cinema italiano', in Mino Argentieri (ed.), *Neorealismo ecc.*, Milan: Bompiani, 1979, 188–92. Topics covered included government censorship, the dumping of American imports and the need for up-to-date legislation and regulation within the film industry.

2 Foot, *The Archipelago: Italy since 1945*, 130–3.

3 Zavattini, 'Un atto di coraggio, interviewed by Tommaso Chiaretti', *Mondo Nuovo*, 11 December 1960, later in *Neorealismo ecc.*, 1979, 224–9.

4 Zavattini, 'Posizione e funzione della cultura italiana negli anni della Resistenza', in *Neorealismo ecc.*, 1979, 278–9.

5 Zavattini, 'Contro il passato nel cinema' (1965), interviewed by Mino Argentieri, in Zavattini, *Neorealismo ecc.*, 1979, 268–9.

6 Zavattini, *ibidem*, 268–9.

7 Zavattini, *Sequences from a Cinematic Life*.

8 Zavattini, *Diario di cinema e di vita*, in *Straparole*, Florence and Milan: Giunti Editore and Bompiani, 2018, 10.

9 Zavattini, *ibidem*, 10.

10 Zavattini, 'Domande a Quattro Uomini di Cinema' (1967), in Di Bitonto, Ansano Giannarelli and Roberto Nanni (eds), *Una Straordinaria Utopia*, Rome: *Archivio Audiovisivo del Movimento Operaio*, 1998, n.p.

11 Peter Cowie, *Revolution! The Explosion of World Cinema in the 60s*, London: Faber and Faber, 2006, 199–205. 'Editorial: The Langlois Affair', *Cahiers du cinéma*, 200–1, April–May 1968, in Jim Hillier (ed.), *Cahiers du cinéma, Vol. 2, 1960-1968: New Wave, New Cinema, Re-evaluating Hollywood*, London: Routledge and Kegan Paul, by 'Editorial: The Estates General of the French Cinema', *Cahiers du cinéma* 202, June–July, in Jim Hillier (ed.), *Cahiers du cinéma, Vol. 2, 1960-1968: New Wave, New Cinema, Re-evaluating Hollywood*, London: Routledge and Kegan Paul, 1986, 309–10.

12 'Editorial: The Estates General of the French Cinema', *Cahiers du cinéma*, 202, June–July 1968, in *ibidem*, 309–10.

13 'Editorial: Changes in Cahiers', *Cahiers du cinéma*, 203, August 1968, in *ibidem*, 311–12; 311.

14 Cowie, *Revolution!*, 214. 'Editorial: Changes in Cahiers', in Hillier (ed.), *Cahiers du cinéma*, in *ibidem*, 311–12; 311.

15 Francesco Maselli, 'Le battaglie degli autori', in Antonio Medici, Mauro Morbidelli and Ermanno Taviani (eds), *Il Pci e il cinema tra cultura e propaganda 1959-1979*, Rome: Archivio Audiovisivo del Movimento Operaio e Democratico, 2001, 88–103; 97.

16 Maselli, *ibidem*, 94. The author remembers, with gratitude, Lorenzo Pellizzari's reading of the first version of this reconstruction in 2012, and acknowledges that he provided factual information about the Porretta Terme Film Festival, a mostly forgotten, if important, event.

17 A politicized student culture developed in the wake of new Marxist theorizing in *Quaderni Piacentini* and *Quaderni Rossi*, in the mid-1960s, expressing independent positions to the Left of the Italian Communist Party.

18 The Pesaro Film Festival was established by Lino Miccichè and Bruno Torri, in the wake of the *Mostra internazionale del cinema libero di Porretta Terme*, set up ten years earlier by Zavattini and others to create a space for alternative cinema in Italy and rival the hegemony of the Venice Film Festival. Mino Argentieri in conversation with author, Easter 2014. Cf. Documents presented by the Movimento Studentesco at Pesaro, in Faliero Rosati (ed.), *1968-1972. Esperienze di cinema militante*, Rome: Bianco & Nero, 1973, 26–31. Mino Argentieri, 'Un grande disegno riformatore', interview with Professor Antonio Medici, in Antonio Medici, Mauro Morbidelli and Ermanno Taviani (eds),

Il Pci e il cinema tra cultura e propaganda 1959-1979, *Annali* 4, Rome: Archivio Audiovisivo del Movimento Operaio, 2001, 77.

19 Mino Argentieri in conversation with author, Easter 2014. The party financed and produced documentaries through its film unit Unitelefilm.

20 Faliero Rosati, 'Documenti presentati nel giugno 1968 alla Mostra di Pesaro dai rappresentanti del movimento studentesco', in Rosati (ed.), *1968-1972*, 126–31.

21 Maselli, interviewed by author in Rome, Easter 2014.

22 Zavattini, 'Allargare l'area della conoscenza e verità', in Zavattini, *Neorealismo ecc.*, 285.

23 Zavattini, *ibidem*, 284. Maselli, 'Le battaglie degli autori', 97.

24 Maselli, *ibidem*, 93.

25 Zavattini, 'Allargare l'area della conoscenza e verità', 284–6.

26 *Bollettino dei Cinegiornali liberi*, March 1969, photographic copy reprinted in Bitonto, Giannarelli and Nanni (eds), *Una Straordinaria Utopia*. There can be no doubt that the meeting took place early in 1968. Cf. Battista, *Zavattini e l'altro cinema: i cinegiornali liberi*, Bologna University DAMS Course, unpublished undergraduate dissertation, supervised by Ansano Giannarelli, 1999, 158.

27 The footage edited by Giuseppe Ferrara and Michele Gandin formed *The Rome Free Newsreel no. 1. Is Cinema Over?* (1968) *Cinegiornale Libero di Roma, no. 1.*

28 Antonio Medici, in conversation with author, Easter, 2014. *Rome Free Newsreel no. 1. Is Cinema Over?* (*Il Cinegiornale Libero di Roma no. 1. Il cinema è finito?*) (1968). Cf. Giannarelli, *Zavattini Sottotraccia*, edited by Ansano Giannarelli and Aurora Palandrani, Rome: Effigi, 2009, 21.

29 Cf. Bertetto, cited in Roberto Nepoti, 'Il documentarismo militante', in Gianni Canova (ed.), *Storia del cinema italiano*, Vol. XI 1965/1969, Venice: Marsilio and Edizioni di Bianco & Nero, 2002, 328.

30 The references are to the dialogue in the film, restored and archived in AAMOD.

31 Peppino Ortoleva, *I movimenti del '68 in Europa e in America*, Rome: Editori Riuniti, 1998, 172.

32 Bellocchio went on to make *Matti da legare* (1975) with Silvano Agosti, Sandro Petraglia and Stefano Rulli. Cf. the screenplay written by Silvano Agosti, Marco Bellocchio, Sandro Petraglia, Stefano Rulli, *Matti da slegare*, Turin: Einaudi, 1976. The film shares Zavattini's enquiry film-legacy, as does the Free Newsreel *Apollon* (1969), made with the workers of the occupied print works by that name, *Contratto* (1970), or Pasolini's *12 December* (1972), made in collaboration with activists of the extra-parliamentary Left group *Lotta Continua*. All embrace Zavattini's theory of shadowing the real and coexistence with the filmed Other.

33 A contemporary account appeared in Faliero Rosati, 'Cinegiornali liberi', in Rosati (ed.), *1968-1972*, 6–15.

34 Ansano Giannarelli, Giannarelli, '"Altro" cinema e decentramento', interview with Antonio Medici, in Medici, Morbidelli and Taviani (eds), *Il Pci e il cinema tra cultura e propaganda 1959-1979*, 124.

35 Callisto Cosulich, 'Il '68 a Venezia: la XXIX Mostra e la contestazione. Documenti e testimonianze', in Cosulich (ed.), *'68 e dintorni. Bianco & Nero*, nos. 2–3, April–September 1998, 170–5.

36 ANAC, 'Documento dell'ANAC contro la XXIX Mostra di Venezia', 3 July 1968, in Callisto Cosulich, 'Il '68 a Venezia: la XXIX Mostra e la contestazione. Documenti e testimonianze', 157.

37 Cosulich, *ibidem*, 160.

38 Pier Paolo Pasolini, 'Perché vado a Venezia', *Il Giorno*, 15 August 1968, in *Saggi sulla politica e sulla società*, edited by Walter Siti and Silvia De Laude, Milan: Arnoldo Mondadori Editore, 1999, 168.

39 The films of Bernardo Bertolucci, Carmelo Bene, Liliana Cavani and Pasolini were selected for the Festival, despite being marginal to the mainstream. Pasolini asked the Director Chiarini to suspend the Golden Lion competition, until the new Festival statute was ratified. Pasolini, 'Perchè vado a Venezia', 163–9; 165. Pasolini's article is a response to Mino Argentieri's published in *Rinascita*, no. 32, 1968.

40 Giannarelli, *Zavattini Sottotraccia*, 59. For example, in 1958, Chiarini had co-scripted with Zavattini and Renato Nicolai the colour documentary *Sette contadini*, by Elio Petri, about the massacre of all seven Cervi brothers, assassinated by the Germans in November 1943.

41 Zavattini, *Io. Un'autobiografia*, 243–4.

42 Zavattini, 'Allargare l'area della conoscenza e verità', 286.

43 Zavattini, *ibidem*, 284.

44 Zavattini, *ibidem*, 285.

45 Maselli, 'Le battaglie degli autori', 97.

46 Pietro Germi, Telegram to Chiarini, 26 August 1968, in Cosulich, 'Il '68 a Venezia: la XXIX Mostra e la contestazione. Documenti e testimonianze', 188.

47 Carmelo Bene, 'Io difendo Chiarini', interview with Antonio Troisio, in *Momento Sera*, 5 August 1968, in Cosulich, 'Il '68 a Venezia: la XXIX Mostra e la contestazione. Documenti e testimonianze', 177–8.

48 The Italian Communist Party, its daily, *L'Unità*, the major Italian film journals, Lino Miccichè and the socialist paper *Avanti!*, the ARCI cultural network and the film club circles were also in favour.

49 Pasolini, 'Cosa è successo a Venezia', *Tempo*, 14 September 1968, in *Saggi sulla politica e sulla società*, 1110–15.

50 Zavattini, 'Allargare l'area della conoscenza e verità', 287–8.

51 Pasolini, 'Cosa è successo a Venezia', 1110–15.

52 Pirro, 'Contro le strutture', in Bollettino, Cinegiornali liberi, March 1969, photographic copy reprinted in Bitonto, Giannarelli and Nanni (eds), *Una Straordinaria Utopia*, 7–10.

53 Marialivia Serini, 'I tigrotti di Zavattini', *L'Espresso*, 1 September.

54 Pasolini, 'Per protestare posso solo stare a casa', *Il Giorno*, 28 August 1969. (Open letter to Ernesto Laura, the new director of the Venice Film Festival), in *Saggi sulla politica e sulla società*, 198. Pasolini, 'Cosa è successo a Venezia', 1110–15; 1111.

55 Pasolini, 'Cosa è successo a Venezia', 1111.

56 Pasolini, *ibidem*, 1114. 'Una forma di democrazia diretta assolutamente nuova per l'Italia e forse per l'Europa'.

57 Maselli, 'Le battaglie degli autori', 97.

58 Massimo Negarville, *Ombre Rosse*, 6 January 1969, cited in Enzo Lavagnini, 'Sale chiuse per immagini di piazza', in Italo Moscati (ed.), *1969. Un anno*

bomba. Quando il cinema scese in piazza, Venice: Marsilio Editori, 1998, 117–18.

59 Gianni Canova, 'La perdita della trasparenza. Cinema e società nell'Italia della seconda metà degli anni '60', in Canova (ed.), *Storia del cinema italiano*, 3–29. According to Ortoleva, this approach was adopted by other European filmmakers who questioned the organizational aspects within the industry, how labour is organized and work relations in creative teams. Cf. Peppino Ortoleva, 'Naturalmente cinefili: il '68 al cinema', in Gian Piero Brunetta (ed.), *Storia del cinema mondiale*, Vol. 1, Turin: Einaudi, 1999, 937.

60 In a short shot at Zavattini's home, in October 1968, Ugo Gregoretti, as president of ANAC, informs Zavattini of the association's official stand. The original is conserved in the AAMOD archive in Rome. *Zavattini e Gregoretti sui Cinegiornali liberi*, October 1968, https://www.youtube.com/watch?v=KGB WZ7M4s2M, accessed on 19 December 2018.

61 Lino Miccichè, *Cinema italiano, gli anni 60 e oltre*, Venice: Marsilio, 1995, 326.

62 For a straightforward explanation of forces of production and modes of production, cf. Karl Marx, 'Preface to A Contribution to The Critique of Political Economy', in Marx Engels, *Selected Works*, London: Laurence and Wisheart, 1991 (1968), 173–4. Marx distinguishes between the material, economic conditions of transformation and other forms, including artistic. This is where cultural politics intersects with economics. Stuart Hall's reading of Gramsci and the influence of the Birmingham School of Media has perhaps led to not giving enough weight to the economic relations, by privileging the idea of cultural hegemony. For *Dogme 95*, cf. Richard Kelly, *The Name of this Book Is Dogme 95*, London: Faber and Faber, 2000.

Chapter 21

1 Zavattini, 'Domande a Quattro Uomini di Cinema' (1967), n.p.
2 Zavattini, *ibidem*, n.p.
3 Zavattini, *ibidem*, n.p.
4 Renzo Bonazzi, Letter of 9 June 1968, in *Bollettino dei Cinegiornali Liberi*, no. 1, June 1968.
5 Zavattini, 'Al magnetofono di quest'estate agli amici reggiani' (1967), in Di Bitonto, Giannarelli and Nanni (eds), *Una Straordinaria Utopia*, n.p.
6 Zavattini, 'I cinegiornali liberi', in Di Bitonto, Giannarelli and Nanni (eds), *Una Straordinaria Utopia*, n.p.
7 Zavattini, *ibidem*, n.p.
8 Zavattini, 'Supplemento al Bollettino dei Cinegiornali Liberi no. 4. La Mostra di Pesaro e i Cinegiornali liberi'. The manuscript, with its handwritten corrections, is reproduced photographically in Di Bitonto, Giannarelli and Nanni (eds), *Una Straordinaria Utopia*, n.p.
9 Zavattini, *ibidem*, n.p.
10 Maselli, 'Le battaglie degli autori', 88–103; 92.

11 Zavattini, 'La Mostra di Pesaro e i cinegiornali liberi' (1970), in Masoni and Vecchi (eds), *Cinenotizie in poesia e prosa*, Turin: Lindau, 2000, 207–8.

12 Getino and Solanas, 'Towards a Third Cinema: Notes and Experiences for the Development of a Cinema of Liberation in the Third World', 33–58.

13 C. Mario Lanzafame and Carlo Podaliri, 'Zavattini and Africa: Traces and Research', in Ferraboschi (ed.), *Zavattini Beyond Borders*, 129–48.

14 Giannarelli, '"Altro" cinema e decentramento', interview with Medici, in Antonio Medici, Morbidelli and Taviani (eds), *Il Pci e il cinema tra cultura e propaganda 1959-1979*, 123–4.

15 Loris Gallico, cited in Lanzafame and Podaliri, 'Zavattini and Africa', 143.

16 Sarah Maldoror, Letter to Zavattini, 12 March 1968, cited in Lanzafame and Podaliri, 'Zavattini and Africa', 143.

17 Sarah Maldoror, *ibidem*, 143.

18 Sarah Maldoror, 'Lettera di Sarah Moldoror da Algeri', *Cinegiornale libero* no. 1, June 1968, 29, in Valeria Di Bitonto, Ansano Giannarelli and Roberto Nanni (eds) *Una Straordinaria Utopia: Zavattini e il Non Film. I Cinegiornali Liberi*, Rome and Reggio Emilia: Archivio Audiovisivo del Movimento Operaio e Democratico, 1998, n.p.

19 Sarah Maldoror, *Monamgabée* (1969), https://youtu.be/oenkyz4KBFw?list=P LbVYAox8eE48mBHv710eh12zT5zqmf6QQ, accessed 7 July 2020.

20 Faliero Rosati (ed.), 'Cinegiornali liberi', in *1968-1972*, 6–15. The article on Free Newsreels appeared in an early anthology of Italian militant cinema. It is accompanied by an appendix containing a partial catalogue and an estimate of thirty-five Free Newsreels in total.

21 Zavattini, 'I cinegiornali liberi', n.p.

22 Antonio Medici, 'Schede dei cinegiornali', in Masoni and Vecchi (eds), *Cinenotizie in poesia e prosa*, 136–7.

23 Ugo Gregoretti, 'Le incertezze del Pci', interview with Antonio Medici, in Medici, Morbidelli and Taviani (eds), *Il Pci e il cinema tra cultura e propaganda 1959-1979*, *Annali 4*, 162–73. Also, Ugo Gregoretti, 'Una classe operaia che non ha avuto eredi', interview with Antonio Medici, in Carlo Felice Casula, Antonio Medici, Claudio Olivieri and Paola Scarnati (eds), *Ciak, si lotta! Il cinema dell'Autunno caldo in italia e nel mondo*, *Annali 12*, Rome: Archivio audiovisivo del movimento operaio, 2011, 179–89. The factual basis for the following reconstruction is based on Gregoretti's direct testimonies in these interviews.

24 *Bollettino dei Cinegiornali Liberi* no. 2, March 1969, 20.

25 Battista, *Zavattini e l'altro cinema: i cinegiornali liberi*, Bologna University DAMS undergraduate degree course, unpublished dissertation, 1999, 136.

26 Battista, *ibidem*, 136.

27 Zavattini, Letter to Free Newsreels members, 22 October 1969, in *Cinenotizie in poesia e prosa*, 193–7; 195. The author acknowledges the pioneering work of Emiliano Battista. Cf. Battista, *Zavattini e l'altro cinema*.

28 Carlo Ruggiero, 'Apollon: La classe operaia va al cinema', *Rassegna Sindacale*, 17 December 2009, http://www.rassegna.it/articoli/2009/12/17/56351/apollon -la-classe-operaia-va-al-cinema, accessed 24 December 2019.

29 Nepoti, 'Il documentarismo militante', 329.

30 Zavattini and Ugo Gregoretti, 'Dibattito sull'*Apollon*', in Silvia Grasselli (ed.), *Apollon Contratto, due film di Ugo Gregoretti*, DVD booklet, Rome: Centro Studi Cinematografici, 2019, n.p.
31 Medici, 'Schede dei cinegiornali', 137.
32 In 1964, Grifi made the experimental *La verifica incerta*, a compilation film of 150,000 metres of offcuts of 1950s Hollywood discarded footage, and the painter Mario Schifano made cinematic portraits, avoiding montage altogether in *Carol + Bill,* and *Anna* (1965–7). Cf. Paolo Bertetto, 'Tutto, tutto nello stesso istante. Il cinema sperimentale', in Canova (ed.), *Storia del cinema italiano*, 314–25.
33 The estimate is made by Paola Scarnati in 'Effetti dei mutamenti', in Ansano Giannarelli (ed.), *Il film documentario nell'era digitale*, Rome: Ediesse, 2007, 110–11.

Chapter 22

1 Zavattini, *Non libro più disco*, in Zavattini, *Opere 1931-1986*, 848.
2 Founders included poets and scholars, such as Edoardo Sanguineti, Elio Pagliarani, Nanni Balestrini, Antonio Porta, Renato Barilli, Luciano Anceschi, Giorgio Manganelli' and Umberto Eco. Balestrini's later prose and Eco's *Open Work* (1964), based on writings first published in the mid-1950s, is probably the most interesting, in terms of experimental work. After Zavattini's death, Renato Barilli published an entry for Guglielmo Moneti's *Lessico zavattiniano. Parole e idee su cinema e dintorni*, Padua: Marsilio, 1992, 78–85, entitled 'Evento' ('Event'), and edited a catalogue of Zavattini's painting, entitled *Le opere e i giorni di Cesare Zavattini, Cesare Zavattini: una vita in mostra*, Vol. 2, Bologna: Edizioni Bora, 1997, containing his essay entitled 'Nostra pittura quotidiana', *ibidem*, 23–8. It is a pity none of the others could bring themselves to recognize Zavattini's contribution to poetry in dialect, to his literary Modernism and late Futurism in his experimental writing.
3 Forty years later, AAMOD has become a rare resource for the study of the visual history of the Italian working class, a store of materials which would have been lost, following the same fate as so many state television programmes. It is also a vibrant centre for independent documentary filmmaking, extending its remit to production and training, including filming and post-production, as well as being a research centre and library. It has also funded and published an important series of books on the documentary, film politics, Italian cinema and the PCI. Finally, in recent years, the Archive has restored many films, including *Giorni di gloria* (1945) (*Days of Glory*).
4 Zavattini, 'Archivio storico audiovisivo del movimento operaio' (1980), *Gli altri*, in Zavattini, *Opere 1931-1986*, 1791–4.
5 Zavattini, '25 March 1978', in Zavattini, *Io. Un'autobiografia*, 265.
6 Zavattini, *ibidem*, 267.
7 Zavattini, '17 December 1980', in *ibidem*, 268.
8 Zavattini, '17 December 1980', in *ibidem*, 269. By 'mythical truth' Zavattini was suggesting that the Italian status quo was so unbelievable as to contribute to the world of make-believe.
9 Vittorini, 'Una Nuova Cultura', 1.

10   Mario Verdone, Letter to Zavattini, 8 September 1982, Biblioteca Chiarini, Centro Sperimentale di Cinematografia di Roma. When it was consulted, the letter had only recently been donated and thus had not been archived. The author is grateful to Laura Pompei for drawing his attention to the Verdone correspondence.

11   Stefania Parigi, 'Cesare Zavattini: un lampo sul "caso Moro"', in Christian Uva (ed.), *Strane storie. Il cinema e i misteri d'Italia*, Soveria Mannelli: Rubbettino Editore, 2011, 79–87.

12   Foot, *The Archipelago: Italy since 1945*, 207–9.

13   The scenario was first published in Gambetti (ed.), *Zavattini mago e tecnico*, 311–19. Cf. letter to Lazar Wechsler, 29 May 1978, in Gambetti (ed.) *Zavattini mago e tecnico*, 1986, 309–10. The scenario later appeared in Christian Uva (ed.), *Strane storie. Il cinema e i misteri d'Italia*, Soveria Mannelli: Rubbettino Editore, 2011, 87–94.

14   Zavattini, 'Prove tecniche di *Telesubito*', in Alessandro Carri, *La televisione di Zavattini. L'idea e il progetto di Telesubito nelle parole e nelle lettere di Cesare Zavattini*, Reggio Emilia: Consulta librieprogetti, 2016, 31–51. The author would like to thank Giorgio Boccolari for bringing *Telesubito* to his attention.

15   Alessandro Carri, 'Zavattini e la televisione', in Carri, *La televisione di Zavattini*, 11–17.

16   Rachel Carson, *Silent Spring*, Boston and New York: Houghton Mifflin, 1962.

17   Nicola Dusi and Lorenza Di Francesco, 'Ligabue secondo Zavattini', Exhibition catalogue, *L'ossessione dello sguardo. Zavattini incontra Ligabue*, Reggio: Edizioni Recos, 2017, 21–9.

18   After the war, Zavattini's literary magic realism was all but forgotten. Italo Calvino's early attempts at copying Zavattini's *raccontini* are unknown until after his death, and, more importantly, the literary influence on Calvino was never acknowledged. There is also Gianfranco Contini's unjustified put-down in *Italie magique* (1946), an anthology of Italian poetry and prose, reprinted only in the 1980s. Perhaps Contini's slight in *Italie magique* explains why Zavattini hardly figures in the history of Italian literature. His pre-war comic, ironic, satirical, prose writing is now mostly forgotten, though his poems in dialect, *Stircarm in d'na parola* (1973), were appreciated by Pier Paolo Pasolini. Cf. Zavattini, *Stircarm in d'na parola*, Milan: Scheiwiller, 1973. Giovanni Raboni is right. As a writer, Zavattini has not been afforded his rightful public recognition, despite Elio Vittorini's early appreciation for his comic writing, and Giovanni Papini's too, for having transcended comedy altogether, to the point of recognizing him as a Modernist. Cf. Giovanni Raboni, 'Introduzione', in Zavattini, *Ligabue*, Milan: Bompiani, 2014, 17–16. As for Zavattini's experimental prose of, for example, *Non libro* (1970), it is much better than Edoardo Sanguineti's experimental writing or that of most of the members of the *Gruppo '63*, to which Sanguineti belonged.

Bibliography

Abruzzese, Alberto and Achille Pisanti (1984), 'Cinema e letteratura', in *Letteratura italiana*, Vol. 2, Produzione e consumo, Turin: Einaudi.

———— and Achille Pisanti and Giorgio Fabre (1979), 'L'industria culturale tra cinema e televisione', in Ezio di Monte and Andrea Fago et al. (eds), *La città del cinema. Produzione e lavoro nel cinema italiano 1930–1970*, Rome: Napoleone, 25–36.

Acevedo-Muñoz, Ernesto R. (2003), *Buñuel and Mexico. The Crisis of National Cinema*, Berkeley, Los Angeles and London: University of California Press.

Adorno, Theodor W. and Max Horkheimer (2008), *The Dialectic of Enlightement*, London: Verso [1944].

Agamben, Giorgio (2008), 'Che cos'è un paradigma?' in Agamben, *Signatura rerum. Sul metodo*, Turin: Bollati Boringhieri, 11–34.

Agee, James and Walker Evans (1988), *Let Us Now Praise Famous Men*, London: Violette Editions.

———— (1941), *Let Us Now Praise Famous Men*, Boston: Houghton Mifflin.

Agel, Henri (1955), *Vittorio De Sica*, Paris: Éditions Universitaires.

Agosti, Silvano, Marco Bellocchio, Sandro Petraglia and Stefano Rulli (1976), *Matti da slegare*, Turin: Einaudi.

Airoldi Namer, Fulvia (1979), *Massimo Bontempelli*, Milan: Mursia.

Aitken, Ian (2001), *European Film Theory and Cinema: A Critical Introduction*, Edinburgh: Edinburgh University Press.

Alba, Octavio (1955), 'Hoy llega a México el famoso Zavattini quien realizarà dos películas con Alazraki y Velo', *Cine mundial*, Mexico City, 24 June, 9.

Aldama, Luis (2004), 'Casa de las Américas', in Cordelia Chávez Candelaria, Arturo H. Aldama and Peter J. García (eds), *Encyclopedia of Latino Popular Culture*, Westport and London: Greenwood Press, Vol. 1 A-L, 111–13.

Alicata, Mario and Giuseppe De Santis (1941), 'Ancora di Verga e del cinema italiano', *Cinema*, Vol. VI, 130, 25 November, 314–15.

———— (1941), 'Verità e poesia: Verga e il cinema italiano', *Cinema*, Vol. VI, 127, 10 October, 216–17.

Alighieri, Dante (1980), *La Vita Nuova*, edited by Domenico De Robertis, Milan and Naples: Ricciardi Editore.

Almendros, Néstor (1960), Letter to Zavattini, 1 March 1960, ACZ E 2/7, fol. 40. Unpublished, in Italian.

Alonge, Giaime (1997), *Vittorio De Sica. Ladri di biciclette*, Turin: Lindau.

Álvarez, Gabriel Rodríguez (2007), *Cartas a México. Correspondencia de Cesare Zavattini 1954–1988*, Mexico City: Universidad Nacional Autónoma de México.

Amidei, Sergio in Franca Faldini and Goffredo Fofi (eds) (1981), *L'avventurosa storia del cinema italiano raccontata dai suoi protagonisti 1935–1959*, Milan: Feltrinelli.

Andreotti, Giulio (1980), 'Lettera aperta a Vittorio De Sica', in *Libertas*, in Lorenzo Quaglietti, *Storia economico-politica del cinema italiano 1945–1980*, Rome: Editori Riuniti [1952], 84.

———— (1952), 'Piaghe sociali e necessità di redenzione', *Libertas*, no. 7, 28 February.

———— (1947), 'Paure di registi', *Il Popolo*, 14 December, 1.

Andrew, Dudley (1976), *The Major Film Theories: An Introduction*, New York: Oxford University Press.

———— (1984), *Concepts in Film Theory*, New York: Oxford University Press.

Anon. (2015), 'Fornarina Fornaris', http://www.cubaliteraria.com//monografia/soci edad_nuestro_tiempo/revista.html, accessed 14 December 2015.

———— (2015), 'Fornarina Fornaris', *Ecu Red*, http://www.ecured.cu/index.php/ Nuestro _Tiempo_%28Revista%29, accessed 14 December 2015.

———— (2014), 'Una lunga storia', *Mostra Internazionale del Nuovo Cinema Pesaro*, http://www.pesarofilmfest.it/mostra-internazionale-del-nuovo-cinema-un a-breve-storia?lang=it, accessed 14 June 2014.

———— (1976), 'Sceneggiatura di Cesare Zavattini per il film *The Children of Sanchez*', *Gazzetta di Mantova*, Tuesday 28 December 1976, 11.

———— (1968), 'Documenti presentati nel giugno 1968 alla Mostra di Pesaro dai rappresentanti del movimento studentesco', in Faliero Rosati (ed.), *1968–1972. Esperienze di cinema militante*, Rome: Bianco & Nero, 1973, 26–31.

———— (1968), 'Editorial: The Langlois Affair', *Cahiers du cinéma* 200–201, April–May, in Jim Hillier (ed.), *Cahiers du cinéma, Vol. 2, 1960–1968: New Wave, New Cinema, Re-evaluating Hollywood*, London: Routledge and Kegan Paul, 307–8.

———— (1968), 'Editorial: The Estates General of the French Cinema', *Cahiers du cinéma* 202, June–July, in Jim Hillier (ed.), *Cahiers du cinéma, Vol. 2, 1960–1968: New Wave, New Cinema, Re-evaluating Hollywood*, London: Routledge and Kegan Paul, 309–10.

———— (1968), *Zavattini e Gregoretti sui Cinegiornali liberi*, October 1968, https:// www.youtube.com/watch?v=KGBWZ7M4s2M, accessed on 19 December 2018.

———— (1968), 'Editorial: Changes in Cahiers', *Cahiers du cinéma* 203, August, in Jim Hillier (ed.), *Cahiers du cinéma, Vol. 2, 1960–1968: New Wave, New Cinema, Re-evaluating Hollywood*, London: Routledge and Kegan Paul, 311–12.

———— (1961), [Interview with Zavattini], 'Fellini Tiene Ingenio … ¡Ma!', *El Mundo*, 9 January.

———— (1956), Draft contract in Italian, in 'Appunti e materiale vario raccolto durante il soggiorno messicano, 1955–1957', ACZ E 6/2, fol. 58.

———— (1955), 'La TV debe decir algo a la gente y no hacerla perder el tiempo', *Prensa*, 8 September.

———— (1955), 'Entrevista publica con Zavattini en la Sala Manuel M Ponce', *Novedades*, Mexico City, 22 August.

———— (1955), 'Zavattini, el monstruo', *Siempre!*, Mexico City, 20 August, 14.

———— (1955), Rubrica 'Lugares', in *Esto*, Mexico City, 26 July.

———— (1955), 'Llegada a Mexico del cineasta C. Zavattini', *Cine mundial*, Mexico City, 26 June.

———— (1955), '*Raíces* y el cine realista mexicano', in *Cineclub*, no. 3, Mexico City, June.

——— (1952), 'Rossellini e il Neo-realismo', in *Il Giornale di Vicenza*, 5 June.

Anreus, Alejandro, Leonard Folgarait and Robin Adèle Greeley (2012), *Mexican Muralism. A Critical History*, Berkeley, Los Angeles and London: University of California.

ANSA press agency (1953), 'L'opinione degli assenti', in *Cinema Nuovo*, no. 26, December, 399.

Aprà, Adriano (2012), 'Rossellini documentarista?', in Luca Caminati, *Roberto Rossellini documentarista. Una cultura della realtà*, Rome: Carocci Editore, 125–31.

——— (1995), 'Itinerario personale nel documentario italiano', in Lino Micciché (ed.), *Studi su dodici sguardi d'autore in cortometraggio*, Turin: Associazione Philip Morris and Progetto Cinema and Lindau, 281–95.

Aranzubia Asier (2011), 'Nuevo Cine (1961–1962) y el nacimiento de la cultura cinematográfica mexicana moderna', *Dimensió antropológica*, vol. 52, May-August, 101–21.

Argentieri, Mino (2008), 'Il 18 aprile 1948 e il cinema', in Ermanno Taviani (ed.), *Propaganda, cinema e politica 1945–1975*, *Annali 11*, Rome: Archivio Audiovisivo del Movimento Operaio.

——— (2001), 'Un grande disegno riformatore', in Antonio Medici, Mauro Morbidelli and Ermanno Taviani (eds), *Il Pci e il cinema tra cultura e propaganda 1959–1979*, *Annali 4*, Rome: Archivio Audiovisivo Del Movimento Operaio, 64–87.

——— (1995), 'Uno dalle mezze maniche da Pietroburgo a Pavia', in Lino Micciché (eds), *Il cappotto di Alberto Lattuada. La storia, lo stile, il senso*, Turin: Lindau, 57–68.

——— (1992), 'Giornalismo', in Guglielmo Moneti, Venice (ed.), *Lessico zavattiniano. Parole e idee su cinema e dintorni*, Venice: Marsilio.

——— (1974), *La censura nel cinema italiano*, Rome: Editori Riuniti.

Aristarco, Guido (1956), 'Il tetto di De Sica-Zavattini', *Cinema Universitario*, no. 4, December, 29–31.

——— (1955), *I fotodocumentari di Cinema Nuovo*, edited by Guido Aristarco, Milan: Cinema Nuovo.

——— (1954), Letter to Guevara, 2 June. ACZ Corr. A. 290/36. Photographic reproduction in Guevara and Zavattini, *Ese diamantino corazón de la verdad*, 23.

——— (1953), 'Più che una bandiera', *Cinema Nuovo*, no. 26, 31 December, 391.

——— (1953), 'Il mestiere del critico', *Cinema Nuovo*, no. 9, 15 April.

——— (1953), 'Ottimismo e pessimismo', *Cinema Nuovo*, no. 3, 15 January, 39.

Ascot, Jaime (1957), '*L'Anello*. Seconda continuità provvisionale. Osservazioni', ACZ, Sog. NR 8/5, fols 38–39. Unpublished manuscript.

Asier, Aranzubia (2011), 'Nuevo Cine (1961–1962) y el nacimiento de la cultura cinematográfica mexicana moderna', *Dimensió antropológica*, Vol. 52, May-August, 101–21.

Astruc, Alexandre (1948), 'Du stylo à la caméra et de la caméra au stylo', *L'Écran Français*, 144, 30 March.

Atienza, Juan García (1956), 'En busca del neorrealismo integral. Carlos Velo y ¡Torero!', *Cinema Universitario*, no. 4, December, 20–2.

——— (1955), 'Notas hacia la definición de un realismo cinematográfico español', *Cinema Universitario*, no. 2, October–December, 41–4.

——— (1955), 'Conversaciones con Giuseppe De Santis', *Objectivo*, no. 9, September–October, 25–31.

——— (1955), 'Te querre siempre. Remedios para familias mal avenidas', *Objectivo*, no. 9, September–October, 39–41.

Ayfré, Amédée (1954), 'Realismo umano, realismo cristiano', *La Rivista del Cinematografo*, no. 11, November.

——— (1952), 'Cinema e realtà', *Bianco & Nero*, no. 1, January, 6–21.

Badiou, Alain (2012), *Ethics. An Essay on the Understanding of Evil*, translated and introduced by Peter Hallward, London and New York: Verso.

——— (2007), '"Fidelity, Connection" and "Evental Sites and Historical Situations"', in Oliver Feltham (trans.), *Being and Event*, London and New York: Continuum, 232–9, 173–7.

——— (2007), *Being and Event*, translated by Oliver Feltham, London and New York: Continuum.

Baldacci, Luigi (1977), 'Note ai testi', in Luigi Baldacci, Milan (eds), Giovanni Papini, *Opere. Dal Leonardo al Futurismo*, Arnoldo Mondadori Editore, 760–3.

Baldelli, Pio (1965), *I film di Luchino Visconti*, Manduria: Lacaita.

Baldi, Alfredo (2017), 'Un anarchico al CSC', *Bianco & Nero*, nos. 588–9, May–December, 126–35.

Balduini, Consuelo (2013), *Miracoli e boom. L'Italia dal dopoguerra al boom economico nell'opera di Cesare Zavattini*, Reggio Emilia: Aliberti Editore and Archivio Zavattini-Biblioteca Panizzi.

Barbachano, Manuel (1957), Letter to Zavattini, 18 January, in *Cartas a México*, 115.

Barbaro, Umberto (1953), 'Il cinema di fronte alla realtà', in *Rivista del Cinema*, II, no. 6 June, 6–33.

——— (1953), 'I film. Stazione Termini', in *La Rivista del Cinema Italiano*, no. 6, June.

——— (ed.) (1950), *Il cinema e l'uomo moderno*. Atti del Convegno Internazionale di Cinematografia (Perugia 24–27 settembre), Milan: Le Edizioni Sociali.

Baranelli, Luca and Ernesto Ferrero (eds) (1995), *Album Calvino*, Milan: Arnoldo Mondadori.

Bardem, Juan Antonio, Juan Antonio Bardem, Basilio Martín Patino, Marcelo Arroita-Jáuregna, Joaquín de Prada, José Maria Pérez Lozano, Paulino Garagorri, Eduardo Ducay and Manuel Rabanal Taylor (1955), 'Boletín de las Primeras Conversaciones Cinematográficas Nacionales', *Cinema Universitario*, no. 1, January–March, 85–6.

———, et al. (1956), '¿Para qué sirve un film?', *Cinema Universitario*, no. 4, December, 24–5.

———, et al. (1953), 'Cannes, 1953', *Objectivo*, no. 1, June, 29–34.

Barnet, Enrique P. (1963), Letter to Zavattini, 10 June, ACZ E 2/7, 57. Unpublished.

Bartolini, Luigi (1946), *Ladri di biciclette*, Rome: Polin.

Barilli, Renato (ed.) (1997), *Cesare Zavattini: una vita in mostra*. Vol. 2, *Dipinti*, 1938–1988, Bologna: Edizioni Bora.

——— (1992), 'Evento', in Guglielmo Moneti (ed.), *Lessico zavattiniano. Parole e idee su cinema e dintorni*, Padua: Marsilio, 78–85.

Baroja, Pío Caro (1955), *El Neorrealismo cinematografico italiano, Prólogo y notas de Cesare Zavattini*, Mexico City: Editorial Almeda.

——— (1954), Letter to Zavattini, 13 February, in *Cartas a México*, 39.

Bartlett, Hall (1976), Letter to Zavattini, 25 September, ACZ Corr. 69/3, fols 7–8. Unpublished.

Battista, Emiliano (1999), *Zavattini e l'altro cinema: I cinegiornali liberi*, Bologna University DAMS Course, unpublished dissertation.

Baudelaire, Charles-Pierre (2010), *The Painter of Modern Life*, translated by P. E. Charvet, London and New York: Penguin Books.

Baudrillard, Jean (1988), 'Simulacra and Simulations', in Mark Poster (ed.), Jean Baudrillard, *Selected Writings*, Stanford: Stanford University Press, 166–84.

Baxendall, Michael (1990), *Painting and Experience in Fifteenth Century Italy: A Primer in the Social History of Pictorial Style*, Oxford: Oxford University Press.

Bazin, André (2013), *Qu'est-ce que le cinéma?* Paris: Les Éditions du Cerf.

—— (2013), 'L'Évolution du langage cinématographique', in *Qu'est-ce que le cinéma?* Paris: Les Éditions du Cerf, 63–80.

—— (2013), 'Voleur de bicyclette', *L'Esprit* 18, no. 161, November 1949, 820–32, now in Bazin, *Qu'est-ce que le cinéma*, Paris: Les Éditions du Cerf, 295–309.

—— (2013), 'Le réalisme cinématographique et l'école italienne de la Libération', *L'Esprit*, no. 141, January 1948, 58–83, now in Bazin, *Qu'est-ce que le cinéma*, Paris: Les Éditions du Cerf, 257–85.

—— (2013), 'Une grande œuvre: *Umberto D.*', in *Qu'est-ce que le cinéma?*, Paris: Les Éditions du Cerf, 331–5.

—— (2013), 'Vittorio De Sica: metteur en scène', in *Qu'est-ce que le cinéma?*, Paris: Les Éditions du Cerf, 311–29.

—— (1971), *What Is Cinema?* vol. 1, translated by Hugh Gray, Los Angeles and Berkeley: University of California Press.

—— (1954), 'En Italie', in André Bazin, J. Doniol-Valcroze, G. Lambert, C. Marker, J. Queval, and J.-L. Tallenay (eds), *Cinéma 53 à travers le monde*, Paris: Les Éditions du Cerf, 85–100.

—— (1953), *Vittorio De Sica*, Parma: Guanda.

Becchetti, Margherita (2014), 'Parma e l'Oltretorrente tra biennio rosso e biennio nero', *Centro Studi Movimenti* Parma, http://www.csmovimenti.org/agosto-1 922-barricate/, accessed 27 March 2018.

Bellos, David (2011), *Is That a Fish in Your Ear? The Amazing Adventure of Translation*, London: Penguin Books.

Beltrani, Alvaro (1955), 'No lo extrañe a Zavattini qe lo espere un mitotini', 'Flecha Neorrealista', *Novedades*, 21 August.

Benci, Jacopo (2011), 'Identification of a City: Antonioni and Rome: 1940–1962', in Laura Rascaroli and John David Rhodes (eds), *Antonioni Centenary Essays*, London: British Film Institute and Palgrave Macmillan, 21–63.

Bene, Carmelo (1968), 'Io difendo Chiarini', interview with Antonio Troisio', in *Momento Sera*, 5 August, in Callisto Cosulich, 'Il '68 a Venezia: la XXIX Mostra e la contestazione. Documenti e testimonianze', 177–8.

Benedetti, Benedetto (1953), 'Sviluppi del Convegno', *Cinema Nuovo*, no. 26, 31 December, 398.

Benjamin, Walter (1992), 'Theses on the Philosophy of History', in Hannah Arendt (ed.) and Harry Zohn (trans.), *Illuminations*, London: Fontana Press.

Berlanga, Luis García (1956), 'Cine italiano', *Cinema Universitario*, no. 3, May, 28–35.

Berger, John (2009), *About Looking*, London, Berlin and New York: Bloomsbury.

Bernal, Fernando (1959), Letter to Zavattini, 29 May, ACZ E 2/7, fol. 46.
Unpublished.

Bernardi, Sandro (ed.) (1985), *Si fa per ridere ... ma è una cosa seria*, Florence:
La casa Usher.

Bernardini Aldo and Jean A. Jili (eds) (1990), *Cesare Zavattini*, Paris and Bologna:
Centre Georges Pompidou and Regione Emilia Romagna.

Bernari, Carlo (1953), 'Esiste una crisi del neorealismo?', *Rinascita*, no. x.
December, 664–7.

Bertetto, Paolo (2002), 'Tutto, tutto nello stesso istante. Il cinema sperimentale',
in Canova (ed.), *Storia del cinema italiano*, vol. xi 1965/1969, Venice: Marsilio
and Edizioni di Bianco & Nero, 314–25.

Bertolucci, Attilio and Cesare Zavattini (2004), *Un'amicizia lunga una vita.
Carteggio 1929–1984*, edited by Guido Conti and Manuela Cacchioli, Parma:
Monte Università Parma.

Besas, Peter (1985), *Behind the Spanish Lens: Spanish Cinema under Fascism and
Democracy*, Denver: Arden Press.

Bessie, Alvah (1949), 'Letter to the Perugia Conference', in Umberto Barbaro
(ed.), *Il cinema e l'uomo moderno*. Atti del Convegno Internazionale di
Cinematografia (Perugia 24–27 settembre), Milan: Le Edizioni Sociali, 65–7.

Betti, Ugo (1971), 'La padrona', in *Teatro completo*, Bologna: Cappelli editore.

Beverley, John (2008), '*Testimonio*, Subalternity, and Narrative Authority', in
Norman K. Denzin and Yvonna S. Lincoln (eds), *Strategies of Qualitative
Inquiry*, Los Angeles, London, Delhi and Singapore: Sage Publications, 257–70.

Bhaskar, Roy (2008), *A Realist Theory of Science*, London and New York: Verso
[1975].

Bianchi, Pietro (1972), *Maestri del cinema*, Milan: Garzanti.

Birri, Fernando (2008), *La Escuela documental de Santa Fe*, Santa Fe, Argentina:
Editorial Documento del Instituto de Cinematografía de la Universidad
Nacional del Litoral.

—— (1997), 'Cinema and Underdevelopment', in Michael T. Martin (ed.),
*New Latin American Cinema. Vol. 1. Theory, Practices and Transcontinental
Articulations*, Detroit: Wayne State University, 86–94.

—— (1997), 'For a Nationalist, Realist, Critical and Popular Cinema', in Michael
T. Martin (ed.), *New Latin American Cinema. Vol. 1. Theory, Practices and
Transcontinental Articulations*, Detroit: Wayne State University, 95–8. Published
in *Screen* vol. 26, no. 3–4, 89–91.

—— (1986), 'Fernando Birri, The Roots of Documentary Realism', in Julianne
Burton (ed.), *Cinema and Social Change in Latin America. Conversations with
Filmmakers*, Austin: University of Texas, 1–12.

—— (1981), Postcard to Zavattini, 3 May, ACZ. Corr. 901/29. Unpublished.

—— (1960), Letter to Zavattini, 27 July, ACZ 901/14. On letter-headed paper:
'Universidad Nacional del Litoral. Instituto Social. Instituto de Cinematografia'.
In Spanish. Unpublished.

—— (1959), Letter to Zavattini, 22 June, ACZ 901/11. On private letter-headed
paper, with both Birri's private address and that of the Institute. In Spanish.
Unpublished.

—— (1958), *Tire dié*, 27 September, then in *La Escuela Documental*, 55–63.

—— (1958), Letter to Zavattini, 17 February, ACZ 901/10. In Spanish. Unpublished.

—— (1957), 'Como se estudia en el Centro Sperimentale de Roma', in *Punto y Aparte* 5. Santa Fe Argentina, September, poi in Birri, 'Organogramma 60', in Birri, *La Escuela documental de Santa Fe*, Santa Fe, Argentina: Editorial Documento del Instituto de Cinematografía de la Universidad Nacional del Litoral, 2008, 101–3.

—— (1957), 'Fernando Birri y 'El Techo' de De Sica', *El Hogar*, no. 2491, Buenos Aires, 30 August, 85.

—— (1957), Letter to Zavattini, 30 March, ACZ 901/7. On letter-headed paper: 'Universidad Nacional del Litoral. Instituto Social. Instituto de Cinematografia'. In Italian. Unpublished.

—— (1957), Letter to Zavattini, 9 March, ACZ 901/6. On letter-headed paper: 'Universidad Nacional del Litoral. Instituto Social. Instituto de Cinematografia'. In Italian. Unpublished.

—— (1957), 'Como se estudia en el Centro Sperimentale de Roma', in *Punto y Aparte* 5. Santa Fe, September.

—— (1957), Letter to Zavattini, 27 July, ACZ 901/9. Unpublished.

—— (1956), Letter to Zavattini and Vittorio De Sica, 19 May, ACZ 901/4. Unpublished.

—— (1956), *Fotodocumentalales*, Santa Fe, Argentina: Instituto de Cinematografia de la UNL-Instituto Social, 1956, cited in *La Escuela Documental*, 33–8.

—— (1956), Letter to Zavattini, 24 July, ACZ 901/5. In Italian. Unpublished.

—— (1956), Letter to Zavattini, 4 April, ACZ 901/3. In Italian. Unpublished.

—— (1955), 'Italia, Oggi. Quattro domande fatte da Fernando Birri e una confidenza in più'. ACZ 901/1. Unpublished.

—— (1955), Letter to Zavattini, 21 May, ACZ 901/2. In Italian. Unpublished.

Bisceglie, Pina et al. (eds) (1979) , *La città del cinema. Produzione e lavoro nel cinema italiano, 1930–1970*, Rome: Napoleone, 203–5.

Bo, Carlo (ed.) (1951), *Inchiesta sul Neorealismo*, Turin: Edizioni Radio Italiana.

Bolzoni, Francesco (1962), 'Zavattini e il film inchiesta', in *I misteri di Roma*, Rome: Cappelli Editore, 35–153.

Bono, Gianni (2003), 'Marc'Aurelio', in *Guida al fumetto italiano*, Milan: Epierre, 1251–2.

Booz, Mateo (1953), *Santa Fe. Mi país*, Santa Fe, Argentina: Castellví.

Bompiani, Valentino (2005), Letter to Zavattini, 26 February 1952, in Zavattini, *Cinquant'anni e più Carteggio con Valentino Bompiani*, edited by Valentina Fortichiari, in Zavattini. *Opere. Lettere*, Milan: Bompiani, 848.

—— (1973), *Via privata*, Milan: Mondadori.

—— and Cesare Zavattini (eds) (1931), *Almanacco Letterario Bompiani 1932*, Milan: Bompiani.

Bonazzi, Renzo (1968), Letter of 9 June, in *Bollettino dei Cinegiornali Liberi*, no. 1, 8–9.

Bontempelli, Massimo (1938), *Mia vita, morte, miracoli*, Milan: Bompiani.

—— (1929), 'Il nostro pudore', in Bontempelli, *Il neosofista e altri scritti. 1920–1922*, Milan: Mondadori.

—— (1929), *Il neosofista ed altri scritti. 1920–1922*, Milan: Mondadori. Borgna, Gianni (2013) *Profezia. L'Africa di Pasolini*, DVD Istituto Luce Cinecittà.

Borrelli, Armando (1953), 'Alcuni aspetti teorici del neorealismo', in *Rivista del Cinema Italiano*, II, no. 6, June, 34–42.

———— (1953), 'Naturalismo e realismo nel cinema italiano', *Rinascita*, X, no. 1, January, 41–44.

Bourke-White, Margaret (1937), *You Have Seen Their Faces*, New York: Viking.

Brancaleone, David (2019), *Zavattini, il Neo-realismo, e il Nuovo cinema latino-americano*, 2 vols, Parma: Diabasis.

———— (2014), 'Framing the Real: Zavattini and Neo-realist Cinematic Space as Practice', *Architecture, Media, Politics, Society*. In Proceedings of 'The Mediated City' Conference, London, Ravensbourne 1–3 April, http://architecturemps.com.

Brousil, Antonín Martin (1949), Perugia Conference Paper, in Barbaro (ed.), *Il cinema e l'uomo moderno*, 68–78.

Brunetta, Gian Piero (2015), *L'isola che non c'è. Viaggi nel cinema italiano che non vedremo mai*, Bologna: Cineteca di Bologna.

———— (2009), *Il cinema neorealista italiano. Da 'Roma città aperta' a 'I soliti ignoti'*, Rome and Bari: Editori Laterza.

———— (2009), *The History of Italian Cinema, A Guide to Italian Film from Its Origin to the Twenty-First Century*, Princeton and Oxford: Princeton University Press.

———— (2008), *Cent'anni di ciema italiano. Vol. 2. Dal 1945 ai nostri giorni*, Rome and Bari: Editori Laterza.

———— (ed.) (1999), *Storia del cinema mondiale. Vol. 1*, Turin: Einaudi.

———— (1985), 'La commedia e il lavoro di bottega', in Sandro Bernardi (ed.), *Si fa per ridere ... ma è una cosa seria*, Florence: La Casa Usher.

Brunetti, Argentina (1972), 'Con Cesare Zavattini. Ricognizione in Messico per *I figli di Sanchez*', *Il Progresso Italo-americano*, Sunday 9 January.

Bruni, David (2007), *Vittorio De Sica. Sciuscià*, Turin: Lindau.

Bueno, Salvador (1951), 'Hechos y Comentarios', *Revista Cubana*, 5, 38, January–June, 264–7.

Buiani, Gianfranco (1954), 'L'Italia d'Oltretorrente. La battaglia di Parma', *Cinema Nuovo*, III, no. 48, 10 December, 377–82.

Buffington, Robert M. (2004), 'Poniatowska, Elena', in *Mexico. An Encyclopedia of Contemporary Literature and History*, Oxford, Santa Barbara and Denver: ABC Clio, 399–400.

Buffoni, Laura (2004), *Documentario e memoria*, in Vito Zagarrio (ed.), *Utopisti, esagerati. Il cinema di Paolo e Vittorio Taviani*, Venice: Marsilio.

Burton, Julianne (ed.) (1986), *Cinema and Social Change in Latin America. Conversations with Filmmakers*, Austin: University of Texas.

———— (1986), 'Fernando Birri (Argentina) The Roots of Documentary Realism', in *Cinema and Social Change in Latin America. Conversations with Filmmakers*, Austin: University of Texas, 1–12.

———— (1981), 'Fernando Birri: Pioniere e Pellegrino', in Lino Miccichè (ed.), *Fernando Birri e la escuela documental de Santa Fe*, Pesaro: XVII Mostra Internazionale del Nuovo Cinema.

———— (1978), 'Revolutionary Cuban cinema', *Jump Cut*, no. 19, December, 17–20.

———— (1977), 'Individual fulfilment and collective achievement, an interview with T.G. Alea', *Cineaste* 8, 1.

Bustamante, Adolfo Fernandez (1955), 'Punto y Raya', *Hoy*, Mexico City, 6 July, 31–2.

Butler, Judith (2010), *Frames of War. When Is Life Grievable?* London and New York: Verso.

Caldiron, Orio (2002), *Cinema 1936–1943*, Rome: Fondazione Scuola Nazionale di Cinema.

——— (1975), *Vittorio De Sica*, Rome: Bianco & Nero.

Calendoli, Giovanni (1955), 'Neorrealismo: 1955', *Objectivo*, no. 9, September–October, 18–24.

Calvino, Italo (2000), *Lettere*, edited by Luca Baranelli, Milan: Arnoldo Mondadori.

——— (1995), 'Ricordo di Vittorio Metz', in Mario Basenghi (ed.), *Saggi. 1945–1985*, Vol. 2, 2900–2904.

——— (1994), 'Raccontini giovanili', in Mario Berenghi and Bruno Falcetto (eds), *Romanzi e racconti*, Vol. 3, Milan: Arnoldo Mondadori, 764–830.

——— (1951), Letter to Zavattini, 11 December, in Calvino, *Lettere. 1945–1985*, Turin: Einaudi, 2000, 330.

Camera dei deputati, *Atti della Commissione parlamentare, di inchiesta sulla miseria in Italia e sui mezzi per combatterla*, Rome: Camera dei Deputati, 1953. Now in Archivio Storico della Camera dei Deputati, http://archivio.camera.it /patrimonio/archivi_del_periodo_repubblicano_1948_2008, accessed 7 July 2017.

Caminati, Luca (2012), *Roberto Rossellini documentarista. Una cultura della realtà*, Rome: Carocci Editore.

Campanile, Achille (1924), *L'inventore del cavallo*, Rome: Fauro.

Canova, Gianni (2002), 'La perdita della trasparenza. Cinema e società nell'Italia della seconda metà degli anni '60', in Gianni Canova (ed.), *Storia del cinema italiano*, vol. XI 1965/1969, Venice: Marsilio and Edizioni di Bianco & Nero, 3–29.

Carpi, Michela (2005), 'Filmografia e Bibliografia', in Cesare Zavattini, *Dal soggetto alla sceneggiatura. Come si scrive un capolavoro: Umberto D.*, Parma: Monte Università Parma Editore, 217–30.

——— (2002), *Cesare Zavattini direttore editoriale*, Reggio Emilia: Biblioteca Palizzi-Archivio Cesare Zavattini and Aliberti Editore.

Carri, Alessandro (2016), *La televisione di Zavattini. L'idea e il progetto di Telesubito nelle parole e nelle lettere di Cesare Zavattini*, Reggio Emilia: Consulta librieprogetti.

Carson, Rachel (1962), *Silent Spring*, Boston and New York: Houghton Mifflin.

Cartier-Bresson, Henri (2005), 'The People of Russia', *Paris Match*, 29 February and 5 February, 38–43 in Mary Panzer, *Things as They Are: Photojournalism in Context since 1955*, London: Chris Boot and World Press Photo, 2005.

——— (1952), *Images à la Sauvette*, Paris: Tériade.

Casetti, Francesco (2015), *La Galassia Lumière. Sette parole chiave per il cinema che viene*, Milan: Bompiani.

——— (1994), *Teorie del Cinema. 1945–1990*, Milan: Bompiani.

Castro, Fidel (1977), 'Palabras a los intelectuales', in *Política cultural de la revolución cubana: documentos*, Havana: Editorial de Ciencias, 74–5.

Castello, Giulio Cesare (1962), *Cinema neorealistico italiano*, Turin: ERI.

Cavell, Stanley (1979), *The World Viewed: Reflections on the Ontology of Film*, Cambridge MA and London: Harvard University Press.

Césaire, Aimé (1950), *Discours sur le colonialisme*, Paris: Éditions Réclame.

Chanan, Michael (1997), 'Rediscovering Documentary. Cultural Context and Intentionality', in Michael T. Martin, *New Latin American Cinema. Vol. 1. Theory, Practices and Transcontinental Articulations*, Detroit: Wayne State University, 201–17.

—— (2004), *Cuban Cinema*, Minneapolis and London: University of Minnesota Press.

—— (1997), 'The Changing Geography of Third Cinema', *Screen*, 38.4, Winter, 372–88.

Chárraga, Tarisco ad Elvia Vera (2006), 'La presencia del Neorrealismo en América Latina: Cesare Zavattini en México', in *Quaderni del CSCI. Rivista annuale di cinema italiano*, Madrid: Istituto Italiano di Cultura di Barcellona, 129–40.

—— (1985), *Cesare Zavattini en México (Un documento para la historia del cine nacional)*, Mexico City: Universidad Nacional Autonoma de México. [Undergraduate dissertation].

Chiarini, Luigi (1956), *El cine en el problema del arte*, translated by Elsa Martina, Buenos Aires: Ediciones Losange.

—— (1954), 'Importanza di un convegno', in *Rivista del Cinema Italiano*, III, no. 3, March.

—— (1954), 'I film, la politica e la censura', in *La Rivista del Cinema Italiano*, no. 3, March, 48–52.

—— (1954), *Il film nella battaglia delle idee*, Milan: Fratelli Bocca Editori.

—— (1952), 'Spettacolo e film', II, no. 2, *Belfagor*, 31 March, and reprinted under the title 'Miscellanea', in *La Rivista del Cinema*, II, no. 6, June 1953, 76–88.

—— (1951), 'Discorso sul neorealismo', *Bianco & Nero*, XII, no. 7, July, 3–28.

—— (1951), 'Impossibilità di sintesi tra realtà e favola', *Cinema*, no. 62, 15 May.

—— (1949), *Il film nei problemi dell'arte*, Rome: Edizioni Ateneo.

—— (1949), 'Due congressi', *Bianco & Nero*, October, 3–6.

Chiodi, Pietro (1978), *Sartre and Marxism*, translated by Kate Soper, Hassocks, Sussex: The Harvester Press.

Cirillo, Silvana (2013), *Za l'immortale. Centodieci anni di Cesare Zavattini*, Rome: Ponte Sisto.

—— (2003), *Zavattini parla di Zavattini*, Rome: Bulzoni.

—— (ed.) (2003), *Una, cento, mille, lettere*, in Zavattini, *Opere. Lettere*, Milan: Bompiani.

Cirkov, Boris (1949), Perugia Conference Paper, in Barbaro (ed.), *Il cinema e l'uomo moderno*, 79–86.

Clark, Martin (1996), *Modern Italy 1871–1995*, 2nd edition, London and New York: Longman.

Clemente, Pietro (1999), 'I paesi di Qualcuno', in Pierluigi Ercole (ed.), with an essay by Marzio dall'Acqua *Diviso in due: Cesare Zavattini: cinema e cultura popolare*, Luzzara: Diabasis, 113–39.

Clifford, James (1993), *I frutti puri impazziscono*, Milan: Bollati Boringhieri.

Colombo, Cesare (ed.) (2003), *Lo sguardo critico: Cultura e fotografia in Italia 1943–1968*, Turin: Agorá.

Conti, Guido (2002), 'Il giovane Zavattini', in Guido Conti (ed.), Zavattini, *Dite la vostra. Scritti giovanili*, Parma: Guanda, 11–140.

Contini, Gianfranco (1992), *La letteratura italiana, otto-novecento*, Milan: Rizzoli.

———— (ed.) (1988), *Italia magica. Racconti surreali novecenteschi scelti e presentati da Gianfranco Contini*, Turin: Einaudi.

———— (1972), 'Introduction à l'étude de la littérature italienne contemporaine (1944) in Contini', *Altri esercizî*, Turin: Einaudi.

———— (1968)' *Letteratura dell'Italia unita 1861–1968*, Florence: Sansoni.

———— (ed.) (1946), *Italie magique. Contes suréels modernes*, translated by H. Breuleux, Paris: Aux Portes de France.

Corazzini, Sergio (1990), 'Desolazione del povero poeta sentimentale', *Piccolo libro inutile*, in Pier Vincenzo Mengaldo (ed.), *Poeti italiani del Novecento*, Milan: Arnoldo Mondadori Editore.

Correa, Miguel Ángel (1953), *Santa Fe. Mi País*, Santa Fe Argentina: Castellví.

Corwin, Sharon (2011), 'Constructed Documentary. Margaret Bourke-White from the Steel Mill to the South', in Sharon Corwin, Jessica May and Terri Weissman, *American Modern Documentary Photography by Abbott, Evans, and Bourke-White*, Berkeley and Los Angeles and London: University of California, 108–32.

Cosulich, Callisto (ed.) (1998), 'Il '68 a Venezia: la XXIX Mostra e la contestazione. Documenti e testimonianze', in Cosulich (ed.), '68 e dintorni. *Bianco & Nero*, nos. 2–3, April–September, 157–219.

———— (1961), '*Sedici anni a bagnomaria*', *La fiera del cinema*, no. 4, April.

Cosulich, Oscar (1997), 'Za soggettista di fumetti', in *Cesare Zavattini, una vita in mostra*, Bologna: Bora.

Cowie, Peter (2006), *Revolution! The Explosion of World Cinema in the 60s*, London: Faber and Faber.

Croce, Benedetto (2006), 'L'umorismo di Luigi Pirandello', *La Critica*, vol. VII, 20 May 1909, 219–23 now in Pirandello, *Saggi e Interventi*, edited by Ferdinando Taviani, Milan: Arnoldo Mondadori, 1571–72.

Cuba literaria (n.d.) http://www.cubaliteraria.com//monografia/sociedad_nuestro_tiempo/revista.html, accessed 14 December 2015.

Critchley, Simon (2002), *On Humour*, London and New York: Routledge.

Croce, Benedetto (1923), *Poesia e non poesia; note sulla letteratura europea del secolo decimonono*, Bari: Laterza.

Crovi, Raffaele (1999), 'Il mio Zavattini', in Pierluigi Ercole (ed.), *Diviso in due. Cesare Zavattini: cinema e cultura popolare*, Reggio Emilia: Edizioni Diabasis, 171–3.

Curti, Roberto (2011), 'Rediscovering Brunello Rondi', *Offscreen*, 15, no. 12, December, http://offscreen.com/view/rediscovering_brunello_rondi, accessed 28 October 2017.

Dam, Luis (1955), 'Close up semanal, 7 dias de cine', 'Cine' *Mañana*, Mexico City, 2 July, 60.

Davies, Charlotte Aull (2008), *Reflexive Ethnography*, London and New York: Routledge.

De Assis Guedes de Vasconcelos, Francisco (2008), 'Josué de Castro e Geografia da Fome no Brasil', *Cadernos de Saúde Pública*, 24, no. 11, Rio de Janeiro, November, https://www.scribd.com/document/417962678/Josue-de-Castro-e-a-Geografia-Da-Fome-No-Brasil, accessed 10 August 2020.

Debord, Guy (2005), *Society of the Spectacle*, translated by Ken Knabb, London: Rebel Press.

De Castro, Josué (2013), *Cinema 2. The Time-Image*, translated by Hugh
　Tomlinson and Robert Gaeta, London and New York: Bloomsbury [Fr. 1985].
───── (1961), ACZ D131/3, Letter to Zavattini, 22 May. In French. Unpublished.
───── (1961), Letter to Michael Altman, Co-Productions, 14 June, ACZ D133/1. In
　French. Unpublished.
───── (1961), Letter to Zavattini, 23 May 1961, ACZ D133/3. Unpublished.
───── (1961), Letter to Zavattini, 22 May 1961, ACZ D133/2. Unpublished.
───── (1954), *Geografia della fame*, Bari: Leonardo Da Vinci.
───── (1952), *The Geography of Hunger*, Boston: Little, Brown and Company.
Deleuze, Gilles (2012), *Cinema 1. The Movement-Image*, translated by Hugh
　Tomlinson and Barbara Habberjam, London and New York: Continuum [Fr.
　1983].
Del Fra, Lino (1954), 'Battezzata a Varese la poetica dei teologi', *Cinema Nuovo*,
　44, 10 October, 212.
Della Volpe, Galvano (1950), Perugia Conference Paper, in Umberto Barbaro (ed.)
　Il cinema e l'uomo moderno, 87–91.
De Martino, Ernesto (1955), 'Narrare la Lucania', [photographs by Arturo
　Zavattini, incorrectly attributed to Benedetto Benedetti] *Cinema Nuovo*, no. 59,
　377–84.
───── (1952), 'Realismo e folclore nel cinema italiano', *Filmcritica*, no. 19,
　December.
───── (1951), 'Note lucane: Il folclore progressivo', *L'Unità*, 28 June, 3.
───── (1950), 'Note lucane', *Società*, VI, no. 4, 650–67.
───── (1949), 'Intorno a una storia del mondo popolare subalterno', *Società*, V,
　no. 3, 411–35.
De Michelis, Cesare (1974), 'Solaria', in Armando Balduina, Manlio Pastore
　Stocchi and Marco Pecoraro (eds), *Dizionario Critico della Letteratura Italiana*,
　Vol. 3, Turin: UTET, 408–10.
De Prada, Joaquín (1955), 'El cine y la España tangible (Notas para una Escuela
　Española de Documental', *Cinema Universitario*, no. 1, January–March, 9–15.
De Santi, Gualtiero (ed.) (2009), *Ladri di biciclette. Nuove ricerche e un'antologia
　della critica (1948–1949)*, Atripalda: Quaderni di Cinemasud.
───── (2005), 'Postfazione. Un pensionato nel paese di Don Bosco', in Guido
　Conti (ed.), Zavattini, *Dal soggetto alla sceneggiatura. Come si scrive un
　capolavoro*, Parma: Monte Università Parma, 217–30.
───── (2003), *Vittorio De Sica*, Milan: Il Castoro-La Nuova Italia.
───── (2002), *Ritratto di Zavattini scrittore*, Reggio Emilia: Aliberti Editore.
───── (2019), 'Gabriel García Márquez in Za's Fantastic Mirror', in Alberto
　Ferraboschi (ed.), *Zavattini Beyond Borders*, Reggio Emilia: Corsiero Editore,
　201–12.
De Santis, Giuseppe (1997), 'Zavattini nel cinema italiano prima e dopo il 1940', in
　Giacomo Gambetti (ed.), *Cesare Zavattini: Cinema e vita, Atti del Convegno di
　Studi*, Bologna: Edizioni Bora, 23–36; 34.
───── (1983), 'Vi racconto come andò con *Roma, ore 11*', *Cinema Nuovo*, no.
　282, April, 32–5.
De Sica, Vittorio (2004), *La Porta del Cielo. Memorie 1901–1952*, Introduction by
　Gualtiero De Santi, Cava de' Tirreni: Avagliano Editore.
───── (1969), Interview by Armando Stefani, 'Per salvarmi dalle SS girai un
　Kolossal', T7, 6 July 1969, in *Il cinema ritrovato*, Cineteca di Bologna, http://

www.cinetecadibologna.it/evp_tenerezza_ironia_desica/programmazione/app_5 057/from_2013-07-02/h_1130, consulted 7 August 2018.

—— and Herbert List Zavattini (1968), *Napoli e i suoi personaggi*, Milan: Rizzoli.

—— (1954), 'Gli anni più belli della mia vita', *Tempo*, XVI, no. 50, 16 December, 18–22.

—— (1953), 'Perché avremmo dovuto separarci?', in Zavattini, 'Diario', *Cinema Nuovo*, II, no. 16, 1 August, 70, now in Orio Caldiron (ed.), *Vittorio De Sica*, Rome: Bianco & Nero, 1975.

—— (1952), 'Rassegna degli elementi letterari del film', *Copione*, 1, no. 1 January, 6–8.

—— (1948), 'Abbiamo domandato a Vittorio De Sica perché fa un film dal *Ladro di biciclette*', *La Fiera Letteraria*, 3, no. 5, 6 February, now in Orio Caldiron (ed.) *Vittorio De Sica*, Rome: Bianco & Nero, 1975, 258.

—— (1945), 'Sciuscià, Giò?', *Film d'oggi*, 1, no. 3, June, 4–5.

—— (1942), 'Volti nuovi nel cinema', in *Cinema italiano* XX, Rome: Edizioni di Documento, 39.

De Vincenti, Giorgio (1992), 'Utopia', in Guglielmo Moneti (ed.), *Lessico zavattiniano. Parole e idee su cinema e dintorni*, Padua: Marsilio, 295–302.

Di Bitonto, Valeria, Ansano Giannarelli and Roberto Nanni (eds) (1998), *Una Straordinaria Utopia: Zavattini e il Non Film. I Cinegiornali Liberi*, Rome and Reggio Emilia: Archivio Audiovisivo del Movimento Operaio e Democratico.

Didi-Huberman, Georges (2008), *Images in Spite of All. Four Photographs from Auschwitz*, translated by Shane B. Lillis, Chicago and London: The University of Chicago Press.

D'Lugo, Marvin (1991), *The Films of Carlos Saura*, Princeton: Princeton University Press.

Dolci, Danilo (2013), *Inchiesta a Palermo*, Palermo: Sellerio [1956].

—— (2013), *Banditi a Partinico*, Palermo: Sellerio [1955].

Ducay, Eduardo (1955), 'Fotodocumentales I: Objectivo Sanabria', *Cinema Universitario*, no. 1, January–March, 1955, 31–5.

—— (1953), 'La obra de Zavattini (Notas para una interpretación)', *Objectivo. Revista del Cinema*, no. 1, June, 9–19.

Dupin, Christophe (2006), *Free Cinema*, DVD booklet, London: British Film Institute.

Dusi, Nicola (2017), 'Introduzione. *Bellissima* tra carte d'archivio e conflitti estetici', in Dusi and Di Francesco (eds), *Bellissima tra scrittura e metacinema*, Parma: Diabasis, xi–xvii.

—— (2017), 'Scritture a confronto: *Bellissima* tra differenza e ripetizione, a partire da Zavattini', in Dusi, and Lorenza Di Francesco (eds), *Bellissima tra scrittura e metacinema*, Parma: Diabasis, 105–50.

—— and Lorenza, Di Francesco (eds) (2017), *Bellissima tra scrittura e metacinema*, Parma: Diabasis.

—— (2017), 'Ligabue secondo Zavattini' Exhibition catalogue, *L'ossessione dello sguardo. Zavattini incontra Ligabue*, Reggio: Edizioni Recos, 21–9.

Eco, Umberto (2015), *Dire quasi la stessa cosa. Esperienze di traduzione*, Milan: Bompiani.

—— (2015), 'Pirandello ridens', in Eco, *Sugli specchi e altri saggi. Il segno, la rappresentazione, l'illusione, l'immagine*, Milan: Bompiani, [1985], 352–65.

——— (2015), 'Ma cosa è questo campanile?' in *Eco, Sugli specchi e altri saggi. Il segno, la rappresentazione, l'illusione, l'immagine*, Milan: Bompiani, [1985], 366–78.

——— (1998), 'Campanile: il comico come straniamento', in *Eco, Tra menzogna e ironia*, Milan: Bompiani, 53–97.

Einaudi, Giulio (1952), Letter to Zavattini, 13 May 1952, ACZ E/37, 13.

Ellwood, Sheelagh (1995), 'The Moving Image of the Franco Regime: Noticiarios y Documentales, 1943–1975', in Jo Labanyi (ed.), *Spanish Cultural Studies: An Introduction*, Oxford: Oxford University Press, 201–3.

Engels, Frederic (1947), 'Tendentiousness and Individual Characters in Realistic art', Letter to Minna Kautskii, 26 November 1885 in Marx and Engels, *Literature and Art, Selections from Their Writings*, New York: International, 44–5.

Ercole, Pierluigi (ed.) (1999), *Diviso in due. Cesare Zavattini: cinema e cultura popolare*, Reggio Emilia: Edizioni Diabasis.

Evans, Peter (1995), 'Cifesa: Cinema and Authoritarian Aesthetics', in Jo Labanyi (ed.), *Spanish Cultural Studies: An Introduction*, Oxford: Oxford University Press, 215–22.

Faeta, Francesco and Giacomo Daniele Fragapane (eds) (2015), *AZ. Arturo Zavattini fotografo. Viaggi e cinema 1950–1960*, Rome: Contrasto.

Faeta, Francesco (2006), 'Il sonno sotto le stelle: Arturo Zavattini, Ernesto De Martino, "Un paese lontano"', in Francesco Faeta (ed.), *Fotografi e fotografie: Uno sguardo antropologico*, Milan: Franco Angeli, 113–39.

Fago, Andrea et al. (eds) (1979), *La città del cinema. Produzione e lavoro nel cinema italiano 1930–1970*, Rome: Napoleone, 25–36.

Faldini, Franca and Goffredo Fofi (eds) (1981), *L'avventurosa storia del cinema italiano raccontata dai suoi protagonisti 1935–1959*, Milan: Feltrinelli.

Falqui, Enrico (1933), Letter to Zavattini, 18 March, ACZ Corr. F512/6. Unpublished.

Fanfani, Amintore (1949), *Provvedimenti per incrementare l'occupazione operaia, agevolando la costruzione di case per lavoratori*, G.U. 7 March 1949, no. 54. Cf. http://www.edizionieuropee.it/LAW/HTML/15/zn38_07_00a.html#_ftn1, accessed 30 July 2017.

Fernandez, Henry, D. I. Grossvogel, Emir Rodriguez Monegal and Isabel C. Gómez (1974), '3/on 2 Desnoes Gutiérrez Alea', *Diacritics*, 4, no. 4 Winter, 51–64.'

Ferraboschi, Alberto and Laura Gasparini (eds) (2017), *Paul Strand e Cesare Zavattini. Un paese. La storia e l'eredità*, Milan: Silvana Editoriale.

——— (2017), 'Il cinema diventa libro: il progetto di *Italia mia* e *Un paese*', in Alberto Ferraboschi and Laura Gasparini (eds), *Paul Strand e Cesare Zavattini. Un paese. La storia e l'eredità*, Milan: Silvana Editoriale, 36–51.

Ferrara, Giuseppe (1957), *Il nuovo cinema italiano*, Florence: Le Monnier.

Ferrarotti, Franco (1992), *Mass media e società di massa*, Bari: Laterza.

Ferroni, Giorgio (1953), *Inchiesta sulla miseria*, Istituto Luce. Istituto Luce _ Inchiesta sulla Miseria _ Parte 1: https://www.youtube.com/watch?v=IkbApjfd9fc., accessed 14 December 2015.

Ferro, Hellen (1961), 'Cesare Zavattini en amable charla con Clarin', *Clarin*, Tuesday 10 January.

Flaiano, Ennio (1945), 'La porta del cielo', *Domenica*, no. 18, 6 May, now in *Lettere d'amore al cinema*, Milan: Rizzoli, 1978 and in Paolo Nuzzi and

Ottavio Iemma (eds), *De Sica & Zavattini. Parliamo tanto di noi*, Rome: Editori Riuniti, 1997, 70–1.

Fofi, Goffredo (1977), *Capire con il cinema. 200 film prima e dopo il '68*, Milan: Feltrinelli.

Foot, John (2018), *The Archipelago. Italy since 1945*, London and New York: Bloomsbury.

Ford, Alexander (1949), Perugia Conference Paper, in Barbaro (ed.), *Il cinema e l'uomo moderno*, 99–103.

Forgacs, David (2000), *David Forgacs, Rome Open City*, London: British Film Institute.

―――― (1988) (ed.), *An Antonio Gramsci Reader. Selected Writings, 1916–1935*, New York: Schocken Books.

Fornaris, Fornarina (n.d.) *Ecu Red*, http://www.ecured.cu/index.php/Nuestro _Tiempo_%28Revista%29, accessed 14 December 2015.

Fortichiari, Valentina (ed.) (1995), *Cinquant'anni e più ... Lettere 1933–1989*. Carteggio con Valentino Bompiani, Prefazione di Gaetano Afeltra, Milan: Bompiani.

Fortini, Franco (2018), 'Che cosa è stato il Politecnico', in *Dieci inverni (1947–1957). Contributi ad un discorso socialista*, Macerata: Quodlibet, 55–74.

Foucault, Michel (2007), *The Archaeology of Knowledge*, translated by A. M. Sheridan Smith, London and New York: Routledge [1969].

―――― (1998), *The Order of Things. An Archaeology of the Human Sciences*, London and New York: Routledge [1970].

Franchi, Rafaello (1931), 'Un umorista', *Il Lavoro*, Genoa, 28 April.

Frank, Robert (1959), *The Americans*, New York: Grove Press.

Freire, Paulo (2013), *Education for Critical Consciousness*, London, Delhi, New York and Sydney: Bloomsbury.

―――― (1996), *Pedagogy of The Oppressed*, translated by Myra Bergman Ramos, London: Penguin Books.

Gambetti, Giacomo (ed.) (1996), *Cesare Zavattini: cinema e vita*, 2 vols, Bologna: Bora.

―――― (ed.) (1986), *Zavattini mago e tecnico*, Rome: Ente dello Spettacolo.

Gamboa, Fernando (1955), Letter to Zavattini, 14 October, in *Cartas a México*, 78.

―――― (1955), 'Viajes de Cesare Zavattini y Fernando Gamboa en Mexico', Diary of journey by Cesare Zavattini and Ferdinando Gamboa in Mexico from 24 June to 15 July 1955 in ACZ, Sog. NR 2/1-5. Folder 4. Unpublished manuscript.

―――― (1955), Raquel Tibol, 'De los muros a las pantallas o Fernando Gamboa frente al cine y dentro del el' in 'México en la cultura', *Novedades*, Mexico City, 26 June, 4.

―――― (1954), Letter to Zavattini, 17 November, in Gabriel Rodríguez Álvarez, *Cartas a México*, 44 and ACZ Za Corr. G 111/1. On letter-headed paper 'Tele Producciones S.A.'

Gandin, Michele (ed.) (1956), *Il tetto di Vittorio De Sica. Dal soggetto al film*, Bologna: Cappelli Editore.

―――― and Enzo Sellerio (1955), 'Borgo di Dio', Aristarco (ed.), *I fotodocumentari di Cinema Nuovo*, Milan: Cinema Nuovo, 458–64.

Garagorri, Paulino (1953), 'Cesare Zavattini (Apuntes)', *Objectivo*, no. 1, June, 7–8.

García Escudero, José (1958), *Cine Social*, Madrid: Primera.

García Espinosa, Julio (1999), 'Memorie e ritorni', *Bianco & Nero*, LX, no. 6, novembre-dicembre, 58–62.

—— (1997), 'Towards an Imperfect Cinema', in Michael T. Martin, *New Latin American Cinema. Vol. 1. Theory, Practices and Transcontinental Articulations*, Detroit: Wayne State University, 197.

—— (1996), 'Recuerdos de Zavattini', in *Zavattini in Memoriam*, L'Avana: Cinemateca de Cuba, 3–9.

—— (1973), 'Por un cine imperfecto', Caracas: Rociante-Fondo Editorial Salvador de la Plaza.

——, in Augusto M. Torres and Manuel Pérez Estremera, 'Breve historia del cine cubano,' *Hablemos de cine* (Peru), 1969, cited in Michale Chanan, *Cuban cinema*, 163.

—— (1963), 'En Cuba el cine busca al público', *Cine cubano*, no. 13, August–September, 13–20.

—— (1955), Letter to Zavattini, 14 August, ACZ Corr. E 70/1. Unpublished.

—— (1954), 'El Neorrealismo y el cine cubano por Julio García Espinosa', ACZ E 3/1, fol. 27–46. Unpublished.

García Márquez, Gabriel (2002), 'Zavattini? Mai sentito', *Cine cubano*, no. 155, November, 32–3.

García Mesa, Héctor and Eduardo Manet (eds) (1960), 'Intervista a Zavattini', Stefania Parigi (ed.), *Bianco & Nero*, LX, no. 6, November–December, 104–14.

García Riera, Emilio (1994), *Historia documental del cine mexicano 1961–1963*, 2nd edition, Conaculta: Imcine, Universidad de Guadalajara.

—— (1974), *Historia documental del cine mexicano*, Mexico City: Era.

Germi, Pietro (1968), Telegram to Luigi Chiarini, 26 August, in Cosulich, 'Il '68 a Venezia: la XXIX Mostra e la contestazione. Documenti e testimonianze', 188.

Getino, Octavio and Fernando Solanas (1997), 'Towards a Third Cinema. Notes and Experiences for the Development of a Cinema of Liberation in the Third World', in Michael M. Martin (ed.), *New Latin American Cinema. Vol. 1. Theory Practices and Transcontinental Articulations*, Detroit: Wayne State University Press, 33–58.

—— (1997), 'Some Notes on the Concept of a "Third Cinema"', now in Michael M. Martin, *New Latin American Cinema. Vol. 1. Theory Practices and Transcontinental Articulations*, Detroit: Wayne State University Press, 99–107.

—— (1973), 'Hacia un tercer cine. Apuntes y experiencias para el desarrollo de un cine de liberación en el Tercer mundo', in *Cine, cultura y descorloización*, Buenos Aires: Siglo XXI. Now available online, https://cinedocumentalyetnolog ia.files.wordpress.com/2013/09/hacia-un-tercer-cine.pdf, accessed 30 December 2019.

—— (1969), Getino, Octavio and Fernando Solanas, 'Vers un troisième cinéma', *Tricontinental*, no. 3, Paris, October, 89–113.

Giannarelli, Ansano (ed.) (2009), *Zavattini Sottotraccia*, Rome: Archivio Audiovisivo Del Movimento Operaio, Edizioni Effigi.

—— (ed.) (2007), *Il film documentario nell'era digitale*, Rome: Ediesse, 110–11.

—— (2004), 'Il lungo cammino dell'inchiesta filmica', in Antonio Medici (ed.), *Schermi di guerra. Le responsabilità della comunicazione audiovisiva*, Annali 6, 2003, Archivio Audiovisivo del Movimento Operaio, Rome: Ediesse, 29–54.

—— (2001), 'Altro cinema e decentramento', interview with Antonio Medici, in Antonio Medici, Mauro Morbidelli and Ermanno Taviani (eds), *Il Pci e il cinema tra cultura e propaganda 1959–1979*, *Annali* 4, Rome: Archivio Audiovisivo Del Movimento Operaio e Democratico, 123–4.

——— (2000), 'Un cinema se ...', in Tullio Masoni and Paolo Vecchi (eds), *Cinenotizie in poesia e prosa. Zavattini e la non-fiction*, Turin: Lindau.

——— (1998), 'Un documento della nostra storia civile e cinematografica', in documento della (ed.), Mario Serandrei, *Giorni di gloria*, Rome: Bianco & Nero, Scuola nazionale di Cinema and Editrice il Castoro.

——— (1996), 'Zavattini e l'esordio sul set', in Giacomo Gambetti (ed.), *Cesare Zavattini: cinema e vita*, 2 vols, Bologna: Bora, 118–24.

Gili, Jean A. (1975), 'La naissance d'un cineaste', in Orio Caldiron (ed.), *Vittorio De Sica*, Rome: Bianco & Nero, 50–65.

Giménez, Manuel Horacio (1963), 'Apuntes del diario de filmación', in Mario Rodríguez Alemán, 'Neorrealismo argentino. Los Inundados', *Cine cubano* no. 11, Havana, June.

Ginsborg, Paul (1990), *A History of Contemporary Italy: Society and Politics 1943–1988*, London: Penguin.

Godard, Jean-Luc (2007), *Due o tre cose che so su di me. Scritti e conversazioni sul cinema*, edited by Orazio Leogrande, Rome: Minimum Fax.

——— and Youssef Ishaghpour (2005), *Cinema: The Archeology of Film and the Memory of a Century*, Oxford and New York: Berg.

Gómez, Juan Francisco Cerón (1999), 'El cine de Juan Antonio Bardem y la censura franquista (1951–1963): las contradicciones de la represión cinematográfica', *Imafronte*, no. 14. University of Murcia, 23–36.

Gómez, Manuel Octavio (1960), 'Jovenes cineastas opinan sobre Zavattini', *Cine cubano*, no. 1, 43.

Gonzáles Porcel, Lautaro (1955), 'Pero espere hasta mañana', *Ultimas noticias*, Mexico City, 29 June.

Gott, Richard (2004), *Cuba. A New History*, New Haven and London: Yale University Press.

Graham, Helen (1995), 'Pop Culture in the "Years of Hunger"' in Jo Labanyi (ed.), *Spanish Cultural Studies: An Introduction*, Oxford: Oxford University Press, 237–45.

Gramsci, Antonio (2011), *Prison Notebooks*, edited by Joseph A. Buttigieg and translated by J. A. Buttgieg and Antonio Callari, New York: Columbia University Press.

——— (1977), *Quaderni del Carcere*, Vol. III, edited by Valentino Gerratana, Turin: Einaudi.

——— (1971), *Selections from the Prison Notebooks*, edited by and translated by Quintin Hoare and Geoffrey Nowell-Smith, London: Lawrence and Wishart.

——— (1971), *Letteratura e vita nazionale*, Rome: Editori Riuniti.

Greenberg, Clement (1961), 'Avant-garde and Kitsch' (1939), in *Art and Culture*, Boston: Beacon Press.

Gregoretti, Ugo (2011), 'Una classe operaia che non ha avuto eredi', interview with Antonio Medici', in Carlo Felice Casula, Antonio Medici, Claudio Olivieri, and Paola Scarnati (eds), *Ciak, si lotta! Il cinema dell'Autunno caldo in italia e nel mondo*, *Annali* 12, Rome: Archivio Audiovisivo del Movimento Operaio, 179–89.

——— (2001), 'Le incertezze del Pci', Interview with Antonio Medici, in Antonio Medici, Mauro Morbidelli and Ermanno Taviani (eds), *Il Pci e il cinema tra cultura e propaganda 1959–1979, Annali 4,* Rome: Archivio Audiovisivo del Movimento Operaio, 162–73.

——— and Cesare Zavattini (2019), 'Dibattito sull'*Apollon*', in Silvia Grasselli (ed.), *Apollon Contratto, due film di Ugo Gregoretti,* DVD booklet, Rome: Centro Studi Cinematografici, n.p.

Gualtieri, Elena (ed.) (2005), *Paul Strand Cesare Zavattini. Lettere e immagini,* Bologna: Comune di Reggio Emilia-Biblioteca Panizzi and Fondazione Un Paese and Edizioni Bora.

Gubern, Román, Monterde, Pérez Peruchia, Esteve Riambau and Casimiro Torreiro (1995), *Historia del Cine Español,* Madrid: Catedra.

Guerra, Michele (2010), *Gli ultimi fuochi. Cinema italiano e mondo contadino dal fascismo agli anni Settanta,* Rome: Bulzoni Editore.

Guevara, Ernesto Che (1968), 'Cuba, Historical Exception or Vanguard in the Anti-Colonnial Struggle?' in Luis E. Aguilar, *Marxism in Latin America,* New York: Alfred A. Knopf, 172–9. Translated by Ernesto Che Guevara, 'Cuba, excepción histórica o vanguardia en la lucha anticolonialista', Verde Olivo, Havana, 9 April 1961, 22–9.

Guevara, Alfredo and Cesare Zavattini (2002), *Ese diamantino corazón de la verdad,* Madrid: Iberautor Promociones Culturales.

——— (2002), *Cuba mía,* in Alfredo Guevara and Cesare Zavattini, *Ese diamantin di corazón,* Madrid: Iberautor, 285–381.

Guevara, Alfredo (1976), 'Discurso pronunciado por el cro. Alfredo Guevara con motivo del inicio de la Semana de Cine Italiano en Cuba el 16 de diciembre. Estreno pelicula Amarcord', unpublished typescript. ACZ E 3/2, 2–4.

——— (1955), Letter to Zavattini, 6 December, ACZ Corr. G 583/5. Unpublished.

——— (1955), Letter to Zavattini, 13 June, in Guevara e Zavattini, *Ese diamantino corazón de la verdad,* 42–3.

——— (1955), Letter to Zavattini, 4 May, ACZ Corr. G 583/4. Unpublished.

——— (1955), Letter to Zavattini, 2 April, ACZ Corr. G 583/3. Unpublished.

——— (1955), 'Cuba', in 'Bollettino del Neo-realismo n. 1', *Cinema Nuovo,* no. 51.

——— (1954), Letter to Zavattini, 10 June, ACZ Corr. G 583, 2. Unpublished typescript.

——— (1954), 'Zavattini y Lattuada en Nuestro Tiempo'. Boletín de Cine 'Nuestro Tiempo' no. 5, Havana, February, 6–7; 11.

——— (1954), Letter to Zavattini, 5 February, in Guevara and Zavattini, *Ese diamantino corazón de la verdad,* 15–17.

——— (1954), 'Conferencia de Cesare Zavattini e Alberto Lattuada', ACZ E 3/2, fols 9–19. Typescript based on Guevara's notes and commentary.

Guillén, Nicolás (1951), 'Semanario Habanero. Noticia sobre Nuestro Tiempo', *El Nacional,* Havana, 19 February, in *Sociedad Cultural Nuestro Tiempo. Resistencia y acción.* Edited by Ricardo Luis Hernández Otero. Havana: Letras Cubanas, 2002, 205–8.

Guneratne, Anthony (2003), 'Introduction. Rethinking Third Cinema', in Guneratne, Anthony and Wimal Dissanayake (eds), *Rethinking Third Cinema,* New York and London: Routledge, 1–28.

Gusmano, Arianna (1990), 'Gino Saviotti', in Giorgio Inglese, Luigi Trento and Paolo Procaccioli (eds), *Letteratura italiana. Gli autori,* vol. 2, Turin: Einaudi. *Ad vocem.*

Gutiérrez Alea, Tomás (2006), 'Intervista con Cecilia Ricciarelli e Diego Malquori', in Cecilia Ricciarelli e Diego Malquori, 'Il Neorealismo cubano di Zavattini' in *Quaderni del CSCI. Rivista annuale di cinema italiano*, 142.

—— (1986), 'Beyond the Reflection of Reality', in Julianne Burton (ed.), *Cinema and Social Change. Conversations with Filmmmakers*, Austin: University of Texas, 115–31.

—— (1986), 'Non sempre sono stato un cineasta', in *Aspetti del cinema cubano*, Sulmona: Sulmona-Cinema '86, 98–9.

—— (1986), 'Intervista', *Paese Sera*, 11 November, ACZ. E 4/1.

—— (1986), 'Intervista', *Cineforum*, November ACZ E 4/1.

—— (1959), Letter to Zavattini, 14 October, ACZ E 2/7, fols 25–27. Unpublished. In Italian.

—— (1956), Letter to Zavattini, 27 May, ACZ Corr. A 101/2. Unpublished. In Italian.

—— (1955), Letter to Zavattini, 20 April, ACZ Corr. A 101/1. Hand-written in Italian. Unpublished.

—— (1954), 'Realidades del cine en Cuba por Tomás Gutiérrez Alea', ACZ E 3/1, 1–26. Unpublished.

Haaland, Toruun (2014), *Italian Neorealist Cinema*, Edinburgh: Edinburgh University Press.

Halliwell, Stephen (2002), *The Aesthetics of Mimesis: Ancient Texts and Modern Problems*, Princeton and Oxford: Princeton University Press.

Handler, Mario (1986), 'Starting from Scratch. Artisanship and Agitprop', in Julianne Burton (ed.), *Cinema and Social Change in Latin America. Conversations with Filmmakers*, Austin: University of Texas.

Hansen, Miriam Bratu (2012), *Cinema and Experience. Siegfried Kracauer, Walter Benjamin, and Theodor W. Adorno*, Berkeley, Los Angeles, London: University of California Press.

—— (1997), 'Introduction', in Siegfried Kracauer, *The Theory of Film. The Redemption of Physical Reality*, Princeton: Princeton University Press, vii–xlv.

—— (1993), 'The Skin and Hair: Kracauer's Theory of Film, Marseilles 1940', *Critical Inquiry*, 3, no. 19, Spring, 437–69.

—— (1991), 'Decentric Perspectives: Kracauer's Early Writings on Film and Mass Culture', *New German Critique* 54, Fall, 47–76.

Harvey, David (2000), *Spaces of Hope*, Edinburgh: Edinburgh University Press.

Henley, Paul (2013), 'Anthropology: The Evolution of Ethnographic Film', in Brian Winston (ed.), *The Documentary Film Book*, London: British Film Institute and Palgrave MacMillan, 309–19.

Hernández, Ricardo (ed.) (1989), *Revista 'Nuestro Tiempo'*. Prologue by Carlos R. Rodríguez, Havana: Letras Cubanas.

Hernández, Hosé (1960), Letter to Zavattini, 4 June 1960, ACZ E 2/7, fols 28–32. Unpublished typescript.

Hoffman, Michael E. (ed.) (1976), *Paul Strand. Sixty Years of Photographs. Profile by Calvin Tomkins. Excerpts from Correspondence, Interviews and Other Documents*, New York: Aperture.

Hont, Ferenc (1949), in Barbaro (ed.), *Il cinema e l'uomo moderno*, 105–10.

Hopewell, John (1986), *Out of the Past: Spanish Cinema after Franco*, London: British Film Institute.

Huberman, Leo and Paul Sweezy (1961), *Cuba. Anatomy of a Revolution*, New York: Monthly Review Press.

Huerta, Efraín (1955), 'Manuel Barbachano Ponce y Cesare Zavattini', *Aquí*, Mexico City, 25 June.

Husserl, Edmund (1989), *The Crisis of European Sciences and Transcendental Phenomenology: An Introduction to Phenomenological Philosophy*, Evanston: Northwestern University Press.

Inglese, Giorgio, Luigi Trento and Paolo Procaccioli (eds) (1990), 'Sebastiano Timpanaro snr', *Letteratura italiana. Gli autori*, vol. 2, Turin: Einaudi.

Isnenghi, Mario (1974), 'Piero Gobetti', in Armando Balduina, Manlio Pastore Stocchi and Marco Pecoraro (eds), *Dizionario Critico della Letteratura Italiana*, Vol. 2, Turin: UTET, 235–7.

Ivens, Joris (1960), 'Joris Ivens en Cuba', *Cine cubano*, no. 3 November, 22.

——— (1949), Perugia Conference Paper, in Barbaro (ed.), *Il cinema e l'uomo moderno*, 111–18.

Jameson, Frederic (1996), 'On Literary and Cultural Import-Substitution in the Third World. The Case of the Testimonio', in Georg M. Gugelburger (ed.), *The Real Thing. Testimonial Discourse and Latin America*, Durham and London: Duke University Press, 172–91.

——— (1991), *Postmodernism, or the Cultural Logic of Late Capitalism*, London and New York: Verso.

Jandelli, Cristina (2017), 'Cerchiamo un bambino distinto. La genesi di *Bellissima*', in Nicola Dusi and Lorenza Di Francesco (eds), *Bellissima tra scrittura e metacinema*, Parma: Diabasis, 81–98.

Johnson, William S., Mark Rice and Carla Williams (2000), *Photography from 1839 to Today*, George Eastman House, Rochester, NY, Cologne: Taschen.

Jordan, Barry (1995), 'The Emergence of a Dissident Intelligentsia', in Jo Labanyi (ed.), *Spanish Cultural Studies: An Introduction*, Oxford: Oxford University Press, 245–55.

Kant, Immanuel (1982), *Critique of Judgement*, translated by W. S. Pluhar, Indianapolis: Hackett.

Kelly, Richard (2000), *The Name of this Book Is Dogme 95*, London: Faber and Faber.

Kezich, Tullio (2007), *Federico Fellini. His Life and Work*, London and New York: I.B. Tauris.

Kinder, Marsha (1993), *Blood Cinema: The Reconstruction of National Identity in Spain*, Berkeley and London: University of California Press.

King, John (2000), *Magical Reels. A History of Cinema in Latin America*, London and New York: Verso.

——— (1999), 'Cinema', in Leslie Belhall (ed.), *Cultural History of Latin American Literature, Music and the Visual Arts in the 19th and 20th Centuries*, Cambridge: Cambridge University Press.

——— (1995), 'Latin American Cinema', in Leslie Bethell (ed.), *The Cambridge History of Latin America*, Vol. x. *Latin America since 1930: Ideas, Culture and Society*, Cambridge: Cambridge University Press, 455–18.

Koch, Gertrud (2000), *Siegfried Kracauer. An Introduction*, translated by Jeremy Gaines, Princeton: Princeton University Press.

—— (1991), '"Not Yet Accepted Anywhere": Exile, Memory, and Image in Kracauer's Conception of History', trans. Jeremy Gaines, *New German Critique* 54, Autumn, 95–109.

Kolker, Robert (1984), *Altering Eye*, New York: Oxford University Press.

Kracauer, Siegfried (2014), *History. The Last Things Before the Last*, Princeton: Markus Wiener Publishers [1969] with a Preface by Paul Oskar Kristeller.

—— (1994), *The Mass Ornament. Weimar Essays*, translated by and edited with an Introduction by Thomas Y. Levin, Cambridge MA and London: Harvard University Press.

—— (1997), *Theory of Film. The Redemption of Physical Reality*, Princeton: Princeton University Press [1960] with an Introduction by Miriam Bratu Hansen.

—— (1947), *From Caligari to Hitler: A Psychological History of the German Film*, Princeton: Princeton University Press.

Kramer, Victor A. (2001), *A Consciousness of Technique in 'Let Us Now Praise Famous Men'*, New York: Whitston Publishing Company.

Kriger, Clara (2003), 'La Hora de los hornos', in Paulo Antonio Paranaguá (ed.), *Cine Documental en América Latina*, Málaga: Signo y Imagen, 320–5.

Kristeva, Julia (1986), 'Word, Dialogue and Novel', in Toril Moi (ed.), *The Kristeva Reader*, Oxford: Basil Blackwell, 34–61.

Kuhn, Thomas S. (1962), *The Structure of Scientific Revolutions*, Chicago: Chicago University Press.

Labanyi, Jo (1995), 'Censorship, or the Fear of Mass Culture', in Jo Labanyi (ed.), *Spanish Cultural Studies: An Introduction*, Oxford: Oxford University Press, 207–14.

—— (1995), 'Literary Experiment and Cultural Cannibalization', in Jo Labanyi (ed.), *Spanish Cultural Studies: An Introduction*, Oxford: Oxford University Press, 295–8.

Lacan, Jacques (2006), *Écrits. The First Complete Edition in English*, translated by Bruce Fink in collaboration with Héloïse Fink and Russell Grigg, New York and London: W.W. Norton & Company [Fr. 1966].

Lacour, José André (1954), 'Il silenzio o la prigione', *Cinema Nuovo*, 44, 10 October, 213.

Lattuada, Alberto (1954), 'Una lettera', *La Rivista del Cinema Italiano*, no. 3, March, 46–7.

Laura, Ernesto G. (2000), *Le stagioni dell'Aquila. Storia dell'Istituto Luce*, Rome: Ente dello Spettacolo.

Lavagnini, Enzo (1998), 'Sale chiuse per immagini di piazza', in Italo Moscati (ed.), *1969. Un anno bomba. Quando il cinema scese in piazza*, Venice: Marsilio Editori, 117–18.

Lefèbvre, Henri (1991), *The Production of Space*, translated by Donald Nicholson-Smith, Oxford: Basil Blackwell.

—— (1991), *Critique of Everyday Life Volume 1*, translated by John Moore, London and New York: Verso.

Lévinas, Emmanuel (1988), *Totality and Infinity: An Essay on Exteriority*, translated by Alphonso Lingis, Pittsburgh: Duquesne University Press.

Lewis, Oscar (1969), 'Culture of Poverty', in Daniel P. Moynihan, *On Understanding Poverty: Perspectives from the Social Sciences*, New York: Basic Books, 187–220.

——— (1961), *The Children of Sanchez. Autobiography of a Mexican Family*, New York: Vintage Books.

Liehm, Mira (1984), *Passion and Defiance: Film in Italy from 1942 to the Present*, Berkeley: University of California Press

List, Herbert and Vittorio De Sica (1962), *Napoli*, Hamburg: Sigbert Mohn Verlag.

Lizzani, Carlo (1998), *Carlo Lizzani, Attraverso il novecento*, Turin: Bianco & Nero and Lindau.

——— (1954), 'Neorealismo e realtà italiana', *La Rivista del Cinema Italiano*, no. 3, March, 30–3.

——— (1945), 'L'Italia deve avere il suo cinema', *Il Politecnico*, no. 3, 13 October, 2.

Lonero, Emilio (1954), 'Note sul Convegno di Parma', *Rivista del Cinematografo*, XXVII, no. 1 January, 7–9.

López, Marisol (2016), 'Sanabria tiene carta: el rodaje de Ducay y Saura', *La Opinión de Zamora*, 18 November.

López, Ana Maria (1997), 'An 'Other' History. The New Latin American Cinema', in Michael T. Martin (ed.), *New Latin American Cinema*, Vol. 1, Detroit: Wayne State University Press, 135–56.

Luginbühl, Sirio and Raffaele Perrotta (1976), *Lo schermo negato. Cronache del cinema non ufficiale*, Brescia: Shakespeare.

Lukács, Georg (1972), 'The Zola Centenary' (1940) in Lukács, *Studies in European Realism. A Sociological Study of the Works and Writings of Balzac, Stendhal, Zola, Tolstoy, Gorki and Others*, London: The Merlin Press, 85–96.

——— (1970), *Writer and Critic and Other Essays*, edited by and translated by Arthur Kahn, London: Merlin Press.

——— (1970), 'The Intellectual Physiognomy in Characterization', in Arthur Kahn (ed. and trans.), Georg Lukács, *Writer and Critic and Other Essays*, London: Merlin Press, 149–88.

——— (1970), 'Narrate or Describe?' in Arthur Kahn (ed. and trans.), Georg Lukács, *Writer and Critic and Other Essays*, London: Merlin Press, 110–48.

Luis, Julio García (2008), *Cuban Revolution Reader. A Documentary History of Fidel Castro's Revolution*, Melbourne, New York and London: Ocean Press.

Lynch, Kevin (1960), *The Image of The City*, Cambridge, MA: MIT Press.

MacCabe, Colin (2011), 'Bazin as Modernist', in Dudley Andrew and Hervé Joubert-Laurencin (eds), *Opening Bazin: Postwar Film Theory and Its Afterlife*, Oxford: Oxford University Press, 66–76.

MacGaffey, Wyatt and Clifford R. Barnett (1965), *Twentieth Century Cuba*, New York: Anchor Books.

Malerba, Luigi (2005), 'Prefazione. Un mestiere zoppo', Zavattini, *Umberto D.*, in Guido Conti (ed.), Zavattini, *Dal soggetto alla sceneggiatura. Come si scrive un capolavoro*, Parma: Monte Università Parma, vii.

Malvezzi, Piero and Giovanni Pirelli (eds) (1952), *Lettere di condannati a morte della Resistenza italiana (8 settembre 1943-25 aprile 1945)*, Turin: Einaudi.

Manetti, Roberto and Marisa Mastellini (1955), 'Roma proibita', *Cinema Nuovo*, IV, no. 70. 10 November, 337–44.

Marcel, Gabriel (1947), *Existentialisme Chretien*, Paris: Plon.

——— (1991), *The Philosophy of Existentialism*, translated by Manya Harari, New York: Citadel.

Margulies, Ivone (2002), 'Exemplary Bodies: Reenactment in *Love in The City*', in Margulies (ed.), *Rites of Realism: Essays on Corporeal Cinema*, Durham: Duke University Press.

Martin, Michael T. (1997), *New Latin American Cinema. Vol. 1. Theory, Practices and Transcontinental Articulations*, Detroit: Wayne State University.

Martin, Gerald (2013), *Vita di Gabriel García Márquez*, Milan: Mondadori.

—— (1995), 'Latin American Narrative since c. 1920', in Leslie Bethell (ed.), *The Cambridge History of Latin America, Vol. x. Latin America since 1930: Ideas, Culture and Society*, Cambridge: Cambridge University Press, 129–222.

Martinelli, Renzo (ed.) (2007), *Domande agli uomini di Cesare Zavattini*, Florence: Le Lettere.

Marx, Karl (1991), 'Preface to A Contribution to The Critique of Political Economy', in Marx Engels, *Selected Works*, London: Laurence and Wisheart [1968], 173–4.

—— (1967), *Economic and Philosophic Manuscripts of 1844* in Marx, *Writings of the Young Marx on Philosophy and Society*, translated by and edited by Loyd D. Easton and Kurt H. Guddat, New York: Anchor Books, 282–337.

Maselli, Francesco (2001), 'Le battaglie degli autori', in Antonio Medici and Mauro Morbidelli and Ermanno Taviani (eds), *Il Pci e il cinema tra cultura e propaganda*, Rome: Archivio Audiovisivo del Movimento Operaio e Democratico, 88–103.

Masoni, Tullio and Paolo Vecchi (eds) (2000), *Cinenotizie in poesia e prosa. Zavattini e la non-fiction*, Turin: Lindau.

Massip, José (2002), 'Así hablava Zavattini', in *Cine cubano* 155, November.

—— (1999), 'Cronaca cubana', *Bianco & Nero*, LX, no. 6, November–December, 50–7.

—— (1960), Letter to Zavattini, 17 December, ACZ E 2/7, fol. 44. Unpublished.

—— (1955), Letter to Zavattini, 21 October, ACZ E 2/7, fol. 42. Unpublished.

—— (1955), Letter to Zavattini, 26 April, ACZ Corr. M 369 fol. 1. Unpublished

—— (1954), 'El mejor camino del cine: El realismo', *Boletín de Cine Nuestro Tiempo*, no. 4 Havana, January.

Masto, Raffaele (1936), 'I dolori di un giovane soggettista', *Cinema* no. 4, 25 August, now in Orio Caldiron (ed.), *Cinema 1936–1943*, Rome: Fondazione Scuola Nazionale di Cinema, 2002, 33–4.

Mastrostefano, Raffaele (2002), 'I dolori di un giovane soggettista. Colloquio con Zavattini', Cinema, I, 4, 25 August 1936 now in *Cinema 1936–1943. Prima del neorealismo*, edited by Orio Caldiron, Rome: Scuola Nazionale di Cinema, 33–4.

Mauro, Walter (1979), 'Reale e 'surreale' di Zavattini', in Gianni Grana (ed.), *Novecento. I contemporanei. Gli scrittori e la cultura letteraria nella società italiana*. Vol. 6, Milan: Marzorati Editore, 5435–40.

Mazzoni, Roberta (1979), 'Introduzione', in Cesare Zavattini, *Basta coi soggetti! a cura di Roberta Mazzoni*, Milan: Bompiani.

Medici, Antonio (2000), 'Schede dei cinegiornali', in Tullio Masoni and Paolo Vecchi (eds), *Cinenotizie in poesia e prosa. Zavattini e la non-fiction*, Turin: Lindau, 2000.

Melograni, Carlo (2008), *Architettura italiana sotto il fascismo. L'orgoglio della modestia contro la retorica monumentale 1826–1945*, Turin: Bollati Boringhieri.

Mendoza, Maria Luisa (1955), '¡El peligro in Hollywood!', *Cine mundial*, Mexico City, 22 August, 5.

Mengaldo, Pier Vincenzo (1990), 'Sergio Corazzini', in Mengaldo, *Poeti italiani del Novecento*, Milan: Arnolodo Mondadori Editore, 25–8.

Mercader, María (1979), in Pina Bisceglie et al. (eds), *La città del cinema. Produzione e lavoro nel cinema italiano, 1930–1970*, Rome: Napoleone, 203–5.

Merleau-Ponty, Maurice (1964), 'The Film and the New Psychology', in *Sense and Non-Sense*, translated, with a Preface, by Hubert L. Dreyfus and Patricia Allen Dreyfus, Evanston, IL: Northwestern University Press, 48–59.

—— (1948), *Sens et non-sense*, Paris: Les Éditions Nagel.

—— (1945), *Phénoménologie de la perception*, Paris: Gallimard.

—— (1945), 'La guerre a eu lieu', *Les Temps Modernes*, October, reprinted in Merleau-Ponty, *Sens et non-sens*, Paris: Nagel, 1948.

Mestman, Mariano (2012), 'From Italian Neorealism to New Latin American Cinema', in Saverio Giovacchini and Robert Sklar (eds), *Global Neorealism. The Transnational History of a Film Style*, Jackson: University Press of Mississipi, 163–77.

Mészáros, István (1978), Marx's *Theory of Alienation*, London: Merlin.

Micciché, Lino (2010), 'Il lungo decennio grigio', in Giorgio Tinazzi and Bruno Torri (eds), *Patrie visioni. Saggi sul cinema italiano 1930–1980*, Pesaro: Marsilio.

—— (2010), 'Oltre il '68, un sogno interrotto', in Giorgio Tinazzi and Bruno Torri (eds), *Patrie visioni. Saggi sul cinema italiano 1930–1980*, Pesaro: Marsilio.

—— (1995), *Cinema italiano, gli anni 60 e oltre*, Venice: Marsilio.

—— (ed.) (1995), *Studi su dodici sguardi d'autore in cortometraggio*, Turin: Associazione Philip Morris and Progetto Cinema and Lindau, 281–95.

—— (1990), *Visconti e il neorealismo. Ossessione, La terra trema e Bellissima*, Venice: Marsilio.

—— (ed.) (1981), 'Fernando Birri: Pioniere e Pellegrino', in *Fernando Birri e La Escuela Documental*, Pesaro: XVII Mostra Internazionale del Nuovo Cinema.

—— (1977), 'Introduzione al cinema cubano', ACZ E 4/1 [press cutting].

Micheli, S. (1992), 'Zavattini e i fumetti', in Guglielmo Moneti (ed.), *Lessico zavattiniano*, Venice: Marsilio, 92–7.

Minh-ha, Trinh T. (1992), *Framer Framed*, New York: Routledge.

Mogni, Franco (1960), 'Nuestro cine así, es un herramienta inútil' [Reportaje de Franco Mogni a F.B. durante la preparación de Los Inundados], *Che*, no. 0 and no. 2, Buenos Aires, 12 May and 11 October, reproduced in *Film ideal* n. 69–70, Madrid 1961. Then in Birri, *La Escuela Documental*, 159–60.

Moneti, Guglielmo (1999), '*Sciuscià* (e dintorni): Cesare Zavattini e la scrittura della realtà', in *Neorealismo fra tradizione e rivoluzione. Visconti, De Sica e Zavattini. Verso nuove esperienze cinematografiche della realtà*, Siena: Nuova immagine editrice, 65–7.

—— (1999), 'Ladri di biciclette: le visioni lungo la strada', in Moneti, *Neorealismo fra tradizione e rivoluzione*, Siena: Nuova immagine editrice, 93–138.

—— (ed.) (1992), *Lessico zavattiniano. Parole e idee su cinema e dintorni*, Venice: Marsilio, 142–55.

Montale, Eugenio (1925), *Ossi di seppia*, Turin: Gobetti Editore.

Monterde, José Enrique (1998), '*Cinema Universitario*', in José Luis Borau (ed.),
     Diccionario del cine español, Madrid: Alianza-Academia de las Artes y las
     Ciencias Cinematográficas de España-Fundación Autor, 227–8.
—— (1995), 'Continuismo y Disidencia', in Román Gubern, José Enrique
     Monterde, Pérez Peruchia, Esteve Riambau and Casimiro Torreiro (eds),
     Historia del Cine Español, Madrid: Catedra, 239–93,
—— (1991), 'Zavattini en España', in *Ciao Za*, Valencia: Filmoteca del la
     Generalitat.
Mora, Carl T. (2005), *Mexican Cinema: Reflections of a Society*, Jefferson, NC:
     McFarland and Company.
Moreieas, Alberto (1996), 'The Aura of Testimonio', in Georg M. Gugelburger
     (ed.), *The Real Thing. Testimonial Discourse and Latin America*, Durham and
     London: Duke University Press, 192–224.
Morley, Morris H. (1987), *Imperial State and Revolution. The United States and
     Cuba, 1952–1986*, Cambridge: Cambridge University Press.
Moscati, Italo (ed.) (1998), *1969. Un anno bomba. Quando il cinema scese in
     piazza*, Venice: Marsilio Editori.
Mota, Rosaria Lazrao Vazquez (1955), 'Notas Cortas', Supplement of 'La Afición
     en El Cine', *La Afición*, Mexico City, 28 June, 2.
Muñoz Suay, Ricardo (1994), 'Za e la Spagna', ACZ Carte rosse 125, fols 1–9.
—— (1956), 'Cine documental', *Cinema Universitario* no. 3, May, 37.
—— (1955), 'Una patética confesión *zavattiniana*', *Cinema Universitario*
     (Salamanca), no. 2, October–December.
—— (1955), 'Un material neorrealista', *Cinema Universitario*, no. 1, January–
     March, 19–25.
—— (1955), 'Carnet de notas Carta de Zavattini', *Cine Universitario*, no. 3, May.
—— (1955), 'Más notas sobre Zavattini', *Cinema Universitario*, no. 2, October–
     December.
—— (1955), Letter to Zavattini, 24 May, ACZ, Corr. M850/8. Unpublished.
—— (1955), 'El caballo de Troya: Zavattini y el Neorrealismo', *Objectivo*, no. 4.
—— (1954), '*Sobre Umberto D.*', *Objectivo*, no. 2, February, 6.
—— (1954), Letter to Zavattini, 17 January, ACZ, Corr. M 850/7. Unpublished.
—— (1953), 'En busca del tiempo vulgar', *Objectivo*, no. 1, June, 20–4.
—— (1953), Letter to Zavattini, 6 July, ACZ, Corr. M850/5.
—— (1953), Letter to Zavattini, 1 May, ACZ, Corr. M850/4. Unpublished.
—— (1953), Letter to Zavattini, 18 April, ACZ, Corr. M850/3. On letter-headed
     paper: 'Indice de Arte y Letras'.
—— (1953), 'Neorrealismo en el Palace', *Indice de Arte y Letras*.
Muscetta, Carlo (1976), 'Brancati e la censura' (1952) in Carlo Muscetta,
     Realismo, Neorealismo, Controrealismo, Milan: Garzanti.
Muscio, Giuliana (1999), 'Zavattini e Hollywood: tra mito e divulgazione', in
     Pierluigi Ercole (ed.), *Diviso in due. Cesare Zavattini: cinema e cultura popolare*,
     Reggio Emilia: Edizioni Diabasis, 135–46.
Muzii, Enzo (1953), 'Il cinema e la realtà, Zavattini. Tesi sul Neorealismo', *Emilia*,
     no. 17, November, 219.
Nagib, Lúcia and Chris Perriam and Rajinder Dudrah (eds) (2012), *Theorizing
     World Cinema*, London and New York: I.B. Tauris.
—— (2011), *World Cinema and the Ethics of Realism*, London and New York:
     Continuum.

Neher, Allister (2000), *Panofsky, Cassirer, and Perspective as Symbolic Form*, Montreal: Concordia University, Phd thesis.

Nelli, Piero (1957), 'Scritti relativi al Messico', [Interview for *Arte del Cinema*], in 'Scritti relativi al Messico', ACZ E7/4, 3 October, fols 3–12. Unpublished.

Nepoti, Roberto (2002), 'Il documentarismo militante', in Gianni Canova (ed.), *Storia del cinema italiano*, vol. xi 1965/1969, Venice: Marsilio and Edizioni di Bianco & Nero, 327–38.

Nichols, Bill (1991), *Representing Reality*, Bloomington: Indiana University Press.

Nicoletti, Giuseppe (1977), 'Cronologia', in Luigi Baldacci (ed.), Giovanni Papini, *Opere. Dal Leonardo al Futurismo*, Milan: Arnoldo Mondadori Editore, XLIV.

Nowell-Smith, Geoffrey (2013) [2008], *Making Waves. New Cinemas of the 1960s*, New York and London: Bloomsbury.

—— (2012), 'From Realism to Neo-realism', in Lúcia Nagib, Chris Perriam and Rajinder Dudrah (eds), *Theorizing World Cinema*, London and New York: I.B. Tauris.

Nuestro Tiempo (n.d.) http://www.cubaliteraria.com/monografia/sociedad_nuestr o_tiempo/articulos1.html, accessed 14 December 2015.

Nuzzi, Paolo and Ottavio Iemma (eds) (1997), *De Sica e Zavattini. Parliamo tanto di noi*, Rome: Editori Riuniti.

—— (ed.) (1997), *Cesare Zavattini: una vita in mostra*. Vol. 1, *Giornalismo, Letteratura, Cinema*, Bologna: Edizioni Bora.

Orgeron, Devin (2008), 'Visual Media and the Tyranny of the Real', in Robert Kolker (ed.), *The Oxford Handbook of Film and Media Studies*, Oxford and New York: Oxford University Press, 83–113.

Ortese, Anna Maria (1953), *Il mare non bagna Napoli*, Turin: Einaudi.

Ortoleva, Peppino (1999), 'Naturalmente cinefili: il '68 al cinema', in Gian Piero Brunetta (ed.), *Storia del cinema mondiale*, Turin: Einaudi.

—— (1998), *I movimenti del '68 in Europa e in America*, Rome: Editori Riuniti.

Otero, Ricardo Luis Hernández (ed.) (2002), *Sociedad Cultural Nuestro Tiempo. Resistencia y acción*, Havana: Letras Cubanas, 209–12.

Overbey, David (1978), *Springtime in Italy: A Reader on Neo-realism*, Hamden, CT: Archon Books.

Pagni, Silvia (2017), '*Bellissima*: sceneggiature a confronto', in Nicola Dusi and Lorenza Di Francesco (eds), *Bellissima tra scrittura e metacinema*, Parma: Diabasis, 99–104.

Palmer, Jerry (1994), *Taking Humour Seriously*, London and New York: Routledge.

Pancrazi, Pietro (1942), 'Io sono il diavolo', *Corriere della Sera*, 27 February.

Pandolfi, Vito (1954), 'Gli sceneggiatori del neorealismo', in *La Rivista del Cinema Italiano*, no. 3, March, 40–5.

Panofsky, Erwin (1991), *Perspective as Symbolic Form*, translated by Christopher Wood, New York: Zone Books [1927].

Papava, M. (1949), Perugia Conference Paper, in Barbaro (ed.), *Il cinema e l'uomo moderno*, 127–36.

Papini, Giovanni (1977), *Un uomo finito* in *Opere. Dal Leonardo al Futurismo*, edited by Luigi Baldacci, Milan: Arnoldo Mondadori Editore.

—— (1977), 'Sul pragmatismo. Saggi e ricerche 1903–1911', in Luigi Baldacci (ed.), *Opere. Dal Leonardo al Futurismo*, Milan: Arnoldo Mondadori Editore, 3–130.

—— (1937), Letter to Zavattini, 23 August 1937, in Silvana Cirillo, *Una, cento, mille, lettere*, in Zavattini, *Opere. Lettere*, Milan: Bompiani, 2002, 73–4.

Paranaguá, Paulo Antonio (2003), *Tradición y modernidad en el cine de América Latina*, Madrid: Fondo de Cultura Económica, 170–99.

—— (2003), *Cine Documental en América Latina*, edited by Paulo Antonio Paranaguá, Málaga: Signo y Imagen.

—— (2000), *Le cinéma en Amérique Latine: Le miroir éclaté: Historiographie et comparatisme*, edited by Paulo Antonio Paranaguá, Paris: Hatmattan, 36–42.

—— (1990), 'Le vieux rebelle et l'Amerique Latine: un compromis autour du néo-réalisme', in Aldo Bernardini and Jean A. Gili (eds), *Cesare Zavattini*, Bologna: Centre Pompidou and Regione Emilia-Romagna, 131–9.

Parca, Gabriella (ed.) (1959), *Le italiane si confessano*, Florence: Parenti Editore.

Parigi, Stefania (2012), *Neorealismo. Il nuovo cinema del dopoguerra*, Venice: Marsilio.

—— (2011), 'Cesare Zavattini: un lampo sul "caso Moro"', in Christian Uva (ed.), *Strane storie. Il cinema e i misteri d'Italia*, Soveria Mannelli: Rubbettino Editore, 79–87.

—— (2006), *Fisiologia dell'immagine. Il pensiero di Cesare Zavattini*, Turin: Lindau.

—— (2002), 'Dal cinema-varietà al cinema-verità', in Orio Caldiron and Stefania Parigi (eds), *Cesare Zavattini: parliamo dell'attore*, in *Bianco & Nero*, no. 6, November–December no. 6, 7–27.

—— (1999), 'L'Officina cubana', in *Bianco & Nero*, LX, no. 6, November–December.

Pascoli, Giovanni (1907), *Canti di Castelvecchio*, Bologna: Zanichelli.

Pascual, C. (1955), 'Tres revistas españolas de cíne', *Cinema Universitario*, no. 1, January–March, 64.

Pasolini, Pier Paolo (2010), 'La sceneggiatura come "struttura che vuol essere altra struttura"', *Empirismo eretico*, Milan: Garzanti [1972], 188–97.

—— (1969), 'Per protestare posso solo stare a casa', *Il Giorno*, 28 August, in Walter Siti and Silvia De Laude (eds), *Saggi sulla politica e sulla società*, Milan: Arnoldo Mondadori Editore, 1999, 198.

—— (1968), 'Lettera al Presidente del Consiglio', *Tempo*, 21 September, in *Saggi sulla politica e sulla società*, 1999, 1116.

—— (1968), 'Cosa è successo a Venezia', *Tempo*, 14 September, in *Saggi sulla politica e sulla società*, 1999, 1110–5.

—— (1968), 'Perché vado a Venezia', *Il Giorno*, 15 August, in Walter Siti and Silvia De Laude (eds), *Saggi sulla politica e sulla società*, Milan: Arnoldo Mondadori Editore, 1999, 163–9.

—— (1968), 'Ho cambiato idea per farla cambiare', *Il Giorno*, 22 August, in *Saggi sulla politica e sulla società*, Walter Siti and Silvia De Laude eds, Milan: Arnoldo Mondadori Editore, 1999, 170–4.

Paterson, Thomas G. (1994), *Contesting Castro: The United States and the Triumph of the Cuban Revolution*, New York and Oxford: Oxford University Press.

Patino, Basilio Martín (1955), 'Azorín', *Cinema Universitario*, no. 1, January–March, 2.

—— (1955), 'Nuestro cine', *Cinema Universitario*, no. 1, January–March, 4.

—— (1955), 'Cristo proibido', *Cinema Universitario*, no. 1, January–March, 2.

Payne, Stanley G. (1995), *A History of Fascism 1914–1945*, London: University College London Press.

Pedregal, Alejandro (2015), *Film and Making Other History. Counterhegemonic Narratives for a Cinema of the Subaltern*, Helsinki: Aalto University.

Pelizzari, Maria Antonella (2012), 'Un Paese (1955) and the Challenge of Mass Culture', *Études photographiques*, no. 30, http://etudesphotographiques.revues.org/3483, accessed 9 December 2015.

Pellizzari, Lorenzo (1997), 'Za soggettista e sceneggiatore', in Paolo Nuzzi (ed.), *Cesare Zavattini. Una vita in mostra*, Bologna: Edizioni Bora, 157–69.

——— (ed.) (1979), 'Una conversazione con il medesimo. Roma 24–25 marzo, 1962', in 'Zavattini nella città del cinema', *Cinema*, no. 20, July–September, 54–81.

Pérez, Louis A. (1995), *Cuba. Between Reform and Revolution*, New York: Oxford University Press.

Pes, Luca (2017), 'Storia critica nel film', in Roberto Mordacci (ed.), *Come fare filosofia con i film*, Rome: Carrocci Editore, 69–85.

Petraglia, Sandro and Stefano Rulli (1974), *Il Neorealismo e la critica. Materiali per una bibliografia*, Pesaro: Mostra del Nuovo Cinema.

Petri, Elio (1962), Letter to Zavattini, 1 April, ACZ, P344/3. Unpublished.

Piersantelli, Lorenzo (2013), 'Un'inchiesta sulla miseria in Italia', https://lpiersantelli.wordpress.com/2013/02/21/uninchiesta-sulla-miseria-in-italia/, accessed 22 April 2016.

Pina, Francisco (1956), 'Zavattini habla de Roma', in 'México en la Cultura', *Novedades*, Mexico City, 13 November, 6.

——— (1955), 'Un libro sobre el Neorrealismo', México en la Cultura, *Novedades*, Mexico City, 17 April, 4–5.

——— (1954), 'Cesare Zavattini, precursor del Neorrealismo', in México en la Cultura, *Novedades*, Mexico City, February, 4–8.

Pirandello, Luigi (2006), 'L'umorismo', in Ferdinando Taviani (ed.), *Saggi e Interventi*, Milan: Arnoldo Mondadori [1909], 775–948.

Pirro, Ugo (1983), *Celluloide*, Milan: Rizzoli.

——— (1969), 'Contro le strutture', in *Bollettino dei Cinegiornali liberi*, March, reprinted in Valeria Bitonto, Ansano Giannarelli and Roberto Nanni (eds), *Una Straordinaria Utopia*, Rome: Archivio Audiovisivo del Movimento Operaio, 1998.

Plunesrocelle, Raúl Segura (1955), 'Cesare Zavattini el extraordinario argumentista', *Zocalo*, 'Radar', Mexico City, 23 July.

Poniatowska, Elena (1961), 'Zavattini mío', *Palabras cruziadas*, Mexico City: Era.

——— (1958), 'Cesare Zavattini', *Revista de la Universidad de México*, Mexico City, 6 February, 20–23. http://www.revistadelauniversidad.unam.mx/ojs_rum/index.php/rum/article/view/7097/8335, accessed 22 April 2016.

Portelli, Alessandro (1985), *Biografia di una città. Storia e racconto: Terni 1830–1985*, Turin: Einaudi.

Prisco, Michele (1955), 'Il mio film ideale', in *Cinema Nuovo*, IV, no. 63, 25 July, 69–70.

Pudovkin, Vsevolod (1949), Perugia Conference Paper, in Barbaro (ed.), *Il cinema e l'uomo moderno*, 137–52.

Quaglietti, Lorenzo (1980), *Storia economico-politica del cinema italiano*, Rome: Editori Riuniti.

Quirk, Robert E. (1993), *Fidel Castro*, New York and London: W.W. Norton and Company.

Raboni, Giovanni (2014), 'Introduzione', in Zavattini, *Ligabue*, Milan: Bompiani, 7–16.

Rancière, Jacques (2016), *Film Fables*, translated by Emiliano Battista, London and New York: Bloomsbury.

——— (2014), *The Intervals of Cinema*, translated by John Howe, London and New York: Verso.

——— (2010), *The Politics of Aesthetics*, London: Continuum.

——— (2009), *Aesthetics and its Discontents*, translated by Steven Corcoran, Cambridge: Polity.

——— (2007), *The Future of the Image*, translated by Gregory Elliot, London and New York: Verso.

Randall, Margaret (2003), 'Women in the Swamps', in Chomsky, Aviv Barry Carr and Pamela Maria Smorkaloff (eds), *The Cuba Reader. History, Culture, Politics*, Durham and London: Duke University Press, 363–9.

Rathbone, Belinda (1995), *Walker Evans. A Biography*, London: Thames and Hudson.

Rascaroli, Laura (2009), *The Personal Camera: Subjective Cinema and the Essay Film*, London and New York: Wallflower Press.

Raschella, Roberto (1964), '*Tire dié*', *Tiempo de cine*, no. 3. Buenos Aires, October 1960, then in Birri, *La Escuela Documental*, 59–62.

——— (1960), 'Una fecha', Buenos Aires, 31 October 1958; Raschella, '*Tire dié*', *Tiempo de cine*, no. 3. Buenos Aires, October, then in Birri, *La Escuela Documental*, 59–62.

Rea, Domenico (1955), 'Gli allegri arcangeli', *Cinema Nuovo*, IV, no. 63, 25 July, 65–8.

Recanati, Amadeo (1955), Letter to Zavattini, 21 November, in *Cartas a México*, 91.

——— (1955), Letter to Zavattini, 14 October, ACZ Corr. Recanati R113/1. Unpublished letter.

Reid-Henry, Simon (2009), *Fidel & Che. A Revolutionary Friendship*, London: Hodder and Stoughton.

Renzi, Renzo (1954), 'Il neorealismo nei film di guerra', in *La Rivista del Cinema Italiano*, no. 3, March, 34–9.

——— (1953), 'S'agapò', *Cinema Nuovo* no. 4, 1 February.

Ricciarelli, Cecilia and Diego Malquori (2006), 'Il Neorealismo cubano di Zavattini', in *Quaderni del* CSCI. *Rivista annuale di cinema italiano*, Madrid: Istituto Italiano di Cultura di Barcellona, 129–40.

Riambau, Esteve (2014), 'The Clandestine Militant Who Would Be Minister and Cinema', in O. Ferrán and Gina Herrmann (eds), *A Critical Companion to Jorge Semprín. Buchenwald Before and After*, New York: Palgrave Macmillan.

Rich, B. Ruby (1997), 'An/Other View of New Latin American Cinema', in Michael T. Martin (ed.), *New Latin American Cinema*, Vol. 1, Detroit: Wayne State University Press, 273–97.

Robin, Régine (1992), *Socialist Realism. An Impossible Aesthetic*, Stanford: Stanford University Press.

Rodríguez Alemán, Mario (1963), 'Neorrealismo argentino. Los Inundados', *Cine cubano*, no. 11, Havana, June.

Rodríguez, Carlos Rafael (2002), 'Fragmentos del discurso por el XXX aniversario de la Sociedad Cultural *Nuestro Tiempo*', La Habana, 23 de marzo de 1982, in Ricardo Luis Hernández Otero (ed.), *Sociedad Cultural Nuestro Tiempo. Resistencia y acción*, Havana: Letras Cubanas, 307–16.

Román Gubern, José Enrique Monterde, Pérez Peruchia, Esteve Riambau and Casimiro Torreiro (1995), *Historia del Cine Español*, Madrid: Catedra.

Rondi, Brunello (1956), *Il Neorealismo italiano*, Parma: Guanda.

—— (1954), Letter to Zavattini, ACZ R/330.6. Unpublished.

Rondi, Gian Luigi (1954), 'Neorealismo, arte cristiana', *La Rivista del Cinematografo*, no. 1, 95–7.

Rosati, Faliero (1973), 'Cinegiornali liberi', in Rosati (ed.), *1968–1972. Esperienze di cinema militante*, Rome: Bianco & Nero, 6–15.

—— (1973), 'Documenti presentati nel giugno 1968 alla Mostra di Pesaro dai rappresentanti del movimento studentesco', in Rosati (ed.), *1968–1972. Esperienze di cinema militante*, Rome: Bianco & Nero, 26–31.

Rosenheim, Jeff L. and Douglas Eklund (eds) (2000), *Unclassified. A Walker Evans Anthology*, Berlin and New York: Scalo and Metropolitan Museum of Art of New York.

Rossellini, Roberto (2006), *Il mio metodo. Scritti e interviste*, edited by Adriano Aprà, Venice: Marsilio [1987].

—— (1956), 'Prefazione', in Brunello Rondi, *Il neorealismo italiano*, Parma: Guanda, 9–10.

—— (1952), 'Rossellini e il Neo-realismo', in *Il Giornale di Vicenza*, 5 June [Interview].

Rowe, Peter G. (1997), *Civic Realism*, Cambridge, MA: MIT Press.

Roy, Claude (1951), 'Réflexions sur *Miracle à Milan*', *Cahiers du cinéma*, no. 7, December.

Ruberto, Laura E. and Kristi M. Wilson (eds) (2007), *Italian Neorealism and Global Cinema*, Detroit: Wayne State University.

Ruggiero, Carlo (2009), 'Apollon: La classe operaia va al cinema', *Rassegna Sindacale*, 17 December, http://www.rassegna.it/articoli/2009/12/17/56351/a pollon-la-classe-operaia-va-al-cinema, accessed 24 December 2019.

Rushton, Richard (2011), *The Reality of Film. Theories of Filmic Reality*, Manchester and New York: Manchester University Press.

Sadoul, Georges (1949), Perugia Conference Paper, in Barbaro (ed.), *Il cinema e l'uomo moderno*, 153–70.

Sainati, Augusto (2001), *La Settimana Incom: cinegiornali e informazione negli anni '50*, Milan: Lindau.

Samugheo, Chiara and Domenico Rea (1955), 'I bambini di Napoli', in *Cinema Nuovo* IV, no. 63, 25 July, 57–64.

Sandoval, Jorge Piño (1955), 'Flecha en Zavattini' in 'Siga la flecha', *Novedades*, Mexico City, 27 August, 15; 21.

—— (1955), 'Projecto de cuestionario para entrevista publica al Sr. Cesare Zavattini', ACZ E 7/1, fol. 12. Unpublished.

Sanginés, Jorge (2003), 'Neorrealismo y Nuevo Cine Latinoamericano: la herencia, las coincidencias y las diferencias', in *El ojo que piensa. Revista virtual del Nuevo Cine Latinoamericano*, no. 0, Guadalajara, Jalisco, Mexico, August. https://www.scribd.com/document/47573974/JORGE-SANJINES -Neorrealismo-y-Nuevo-Cine-Latinoamericano-I-Parte, 10 August 2020.

—— (1997), 'Teoria y práctica de un cine junto al pueblo' (1979), translated as 'Problems of Form and Content in Revolutionary Cinema' now in Martin, *New Latin American Cinema*, 62–70.

Santos, Óscar Pino (1958), 'Las posibilidades de una industria cinematografica en Cuba: Consideraciones', *Carteles*, 30 November.

Santos, Mateo (1955), 'Cine', *Revista de revistas*, Mexico City, 3 April, 54.

Sartre, Jean-Paul (1955), 'El neorrealismo no es pesimista', *Cinema Universitario*, no. 1, January–March, 47.

—— (1948), 'La Nationalisation de la littérature' (1945), in *Situations* II, Paris: Gallimard, 40–1.

—— (1943), *L'Être et le néant*, Paris: Éditions Gallimard.

Savio, Francesco (ed.) (1979), *Cinecittà Anni Trenta: Parlano 116 Protagonisti Del Secondo Cinema Italiano (1930–1943)*, Vol. 3 (NAZ-ZAZ), Rome: Bulzoni.

Saviotti, Gino (1973), Letter to Zavattini, 6 December, ACZ Corr. S169/7. Unpublished.

Scarnati, Paola (2007), 'Effetti dei mutamenti', in Ansano Giannarelli (ed.), *Il film documentario nell'era digitale*, Rome: Ediesse, 110–11.

Scarpa, Cristina (1990), 'Sebastiano Timpanaro snr', in Giorgio Inglese, Luigi Trento and Paolo Procaccioli (eds), *Letteratura italiana. Gli autori*, Vol. 2, Turin: Einaudi. *Ad vocem.*

Schoonover, Karl (2012), *Brutal Vision. The Neorealist Body in Postwar Italian Cinema*, Minneapolis and London: Minnesota University Press.

Schultz, Victoria (1971), *Film Culture*, no. 52, Spring, 3.

Serini, Marialivia (1968), 'I tigrotti di Zavattini', *L'Espresso*, 1 September.

Sesti, Mario (1986), 'Cuba, schermi puntati sul mondo', *Paese Sera*, 11 November.

Shiel, Mark (2008), 'Imagined and Built Spaces in the Rome of Neorealism', in Richard Wrigley (ed.), *Cinematic Rome*, Leicester: Troubadour Publishing, 27–42.

—— (2006), *Italian Neorealism. Rebuilding the Cinematic City*, London: Wallflower Press, 63–79.

—— (2001), 'Cinema and the City in History and in Theory', in Mark Shiel and Tony Fitzmaurice (eds), *Cinema and The City. Film and Urban Societies in a Global Context*, Oxford and Malden, MA: Blackwell, 1–18.

Shohat, Ella and Robert Stam (1994), *Unthinking Eurocentrism: Multiculturalism and the Media*, London: Routledge.

Sica, Beatrice (2010), 'Massimo Bontempelli e *l'Italie magique* di Gianfranco Contini', *Bollettino '900*, 1–2, June–December, http://www3.unibo.it/boll900/n umeri/2010-i/, accessed 10 August 2020.

Sim, Stuart (1994), *Georg Lukács*, Hemel Hempstead: Harvester Wheatsheaf.

Siqueiros, David Alfaro (1951), *Siqueiros, por la vía de una pintura neorrealista o realista social en México*, Mexico City: Instituto Nacional de Bellas Artes.

—— , Diego Rivera, Xavier Guerrero, Fermín Revueltas, José Clemente Orozco, Ramón Alva Guadarrama, Germán Cueto and Carlos Mérida (2012), 'Manifesto of the Union of technical workers, painters and sculptors', El Machete, June 1924, in Anreus, Alejandro, Leonard Folgarait and Robin Adèle Greeley, *Mexican Muralism. A Critical History*, Berkeley, Los Angeles and London: University of California, 319–21.

—— et al. (2012), 'A call to Argentine Artists', *Crítica*, Buenos Aires, 2 June 1933, in Alejandro Anreus, Leonard Folgarait and Robin Adèle Greeley,

Mexican Muralism. A Critical History, Berkeley, Los Angeles and London: University of California, 330–2.

Skidmore, Thomas E. and Peter H. Smith (1997), *Modern Latin America*, Oxford and New York: Oxford University Press.

Smith, W. Eugene (1948), 'An Accident Interrupts His Leisure', *Life Magazine*, 20 September, 118–19.

Stam, Robert (2003), 'Beyond Third Cinema. The Aesthetics of Hybridity', in Anthony Guneratne and Wimal Dissanayake (eds), *Rethinking Third Cinema*, New York and London: Routledge, 31–48.

Skidmore, Thomas E. and Peter H. Smith (1997), *Modern Latin America*, Oxford and New York: Oxford University Press.

Steichen, Edward (1983), *The Family of Man*, Catalogue, New York: The Museum of Modern Art, 1983 [1955].

Steimatsky, Noa (2009), 'The Cinecittà Refugee Camp (1944–1950)', *October*, 128, Spring, 23–50.

Sterritt, David (ed.) (1998), *Jean-Luc Godard*. Interviews, Jackson: University of Mississippi.

Stieglitz, Alfred (2008), *Camera Work. The Complete Photographs 1903–1917*, Cologne: Taschen.

Stone, Rob (2002), *Spanish Cinema*, Harlow: Pearson Longman.

Strand, Paul (1949), Perugia Conference Paper, in Barbaro (ed.), *Il cinema e l'uomo moderno*, 171–9.

Szulc, Tad (1989), *Fidel. A Critical Portrait*, London: Hodder and Staughton.

―――― (1989), 'Fidel Castro's Years as a Secret Communist', *New York Times*, 19 October.

Taviani, Ermanno (ed.) (2008), *Propaganda, cinema e politica 1945–1975*, *Annali* 11, Rome: Archivio Audiovisivo del Movimento Operaio.

Taviani, Paolo and Vittorio (1990), Aldo Bernardini and Jean A. Gili (eds), *Cesare Zavattini*, Paris and Reggio Emilia: Centre Pompidou and Regione Emilia-Romagna, 158–9.

Thomas, Hugh (1986), *The Cuban Revolution*, London: Weidenfeld and Nicolson.

Tibol, Raquel (1955), 'Zavattini está mirando México' [Sunday supplement of 'México en la cultura'], *Novedades*, Mexico City, 21 August, 6–7.

―――― (1955), 'De los muros a las pantallas o Fernando Gamboa frente al cine y dentro de el', in 'México en la cultura', *Novedades*, Mexico City, 26 June, 4.

――――, Sebastiano senior [pre-1943], Letter to Zavattini ACZ Corr. T122/3 unpublished.

―――― (post-1930), Letter to Zavattini ACZ Corr. T122/2, unpublished.

―――― (1931), 'C.Z. *Parliamo tanto di me*', *Solaria*, September.

Tinazzi, Giorgio (1997), 'Cinema del pedinamento', in Paolo Nuzzi (ed.), *Cesare Zavattini. Una vita in mostra*, Bologna: Edizioni Bora, 193–6.

Thomas, Hugh (1986), *The Cuban Revolution*, London: Weidenfeld and Nicolson.

Todorov, Tzvetan (2009), *In Defence of the Enlightenment*, translated by Gila Wlaker, London: Atlantic Books.

―――― (2002), *Imperfect Garden. The Legacy of Humanism*, translated by Carol Cosman, Princeton and Oxford: Princeton University Press.

Tomkins, Calvin (1976), Michael E. Hoffman (ed.), *Paul Strand. Sixty Years of Photographs. Profile by Calvin Tomkins. Excerpts from Correspondence, Interviews and Other Documents*, New York: Aperture.

Torri, Bruno (1999), 'Cinema e rivoluzione', *Bianco & Nero*, LX, no. 6, November–December, 45–9.

Torricelli, Ugo (1946), 'Italia, case distrutte', *Domus*, no. 212, August, 30–1.

Tosi, Virgilio (2017), 'Come ho visto nascere *Un paese*', in Alberto Ferraboschi and Laura Gasparini (eds), *Paul Strand e Cesare Zavattini. Un paese. La storia e l'eredità*, Milan: Silvana Editoriale, 52–7.

—— (2016), 'Parliamo di Paul Strand e di Cesare Zavattini e del loro libro *Un paese* (1955)', *Il documentario. Il portale italiano sul cinema documentario*, June–September. http://www.ildocumentario.it/Virgilio_Tosi/Virgilio_Tosi_16.06 .htm, accessed 3 July 2017.

—— (2005), 'Postfazione', in Elena Gualtieri (ed.), *Paul Strand Cesare Zavattini. Lettere e immagini*, Bologna: Comune di Reggio Emilia-Biblioteca Panizzi and Fondazione Un Paese and Edizioni Bora, 257–61.

—— (1999), *Quando il cinema era un circolo. La stagione d'oro dei cineclub (1945–1956)*, Venice: Bianco & Nero and Marsilio.

Trasatti, Sergio (ed.) (1989), *I cattolici e il neorealismo*, Rome: Bulzoni and Ente dello Spettacolo.

Trotsky, Leon (1991), *Literature and Revolution*, translated by Rose Strunsky, London: RedWords.

Uva, Christian (ed.) (2011), *Strane storie. Il cinema e i misteri d'Italia*, Soveria Mannelli: Rubbettino Editore.

Vega, Jesús (1990), 'Cesare Zavattini: Alma del Neorrealismo', *Cine cubano*, 129, no. 1, 39–45.

Velo, Carlos (2003), 'Diàlogo sobre Cine Documental' (1986) in Paulo Antonio Paranaguá, (ed.) *Cine Documental en América Latina*, Málaga: Signo y Imagen, 477–90.

—— (1955), Letter to Zavattini, 7 November, in *Cartas a México*, 87–9.

Venè, Gian Franco (1976), *La Satira politica*, Milan: SugarCo.

Verdone, Mario (2009), 'De Sica 'ladro onorario'. Dalle biciclette ai clowns', *Il Progresso d'Italia*, 20 December 1948, now in Gualtiero De Santi (ed.), *Ladri di biciclette. Nuove ricerche e un'antologia della critica (1948–1949)*, Atripalda: Quaderni di Cinemasud, 139–41.

—— (1982), Letter to Zavattini, 8 September, Biblioteca Chiarini, Centro Sperimentale di Cinematografia di Roma. (No accession number).

Vergano, Aldo (1949), Perugia Conference Paper, in Barbaro (ed.), *Il cinema e l'uomo moderno*, 181–6.

Vertov, Dziga (1984), 'The Birth of Kino-Eye, 1924, *Kino-Eye*', in Annette Michelson (ed.), *Kino-Eye. The Writings of Dziga Vertov*, Berkeley, New York and London: University of California.

Vigorelli, Giancarlo (1954), 'Fine di un monopolio', *La Rivista del Cinematografo*, February 1954, cited in Sergio Trasatti (ed.) (1989), *I cattolici e il Neorealismo*, Rome: Ente dello Spettacolo, 99–108.

—— (1953), 'La seconda strada della cultura italiana', *Bianco & Nero*, xiv, December, 35–47.

Vila, Vicente (1955), 'Zavattini y el público', 'Cambio de rollo', *Diario Cine Mundial*, Mexico City, 29 August, 6.

Villa, Federica (2002), *Botteghe di scrittura per il cinema italiano*, Rome: Biblioteca di Bianco & Nero.

Vitti, Antonio (ed.) (2008), *Ripensare il neorealismo: cinema, letteratura, mondo*, Pesaro: Metauro.

Vittorini, Elio (1991), *Diario in pubblico*, Milan: Bompiani.

—— (1945), 'Una Nuova Cultura', *Il Politecnico*, no. 1, 29 September, 1.

—— (1954), 'La foto strizza l'occhio alla pagina', *Cinema Nuovo*, III, no. 33, 15 April 1954, 200–202.

—— (1931), 'Le Giubbe Rosse', in Valentino Bompiani and Cesare Zavattini (eds), *Almanacco Letterario Bompiani 1932*, Milan: Bompiani, 24–6.

—— (1931), 'Oggi, "Great Attraction!"', *Il Bargello*, 27 September.

von Moltke, Johannes (2016), *The Curious Humanist. Siegfried Kracauer in America*, Oakland, California: University of California Press.

—— and Kristy Rawson (eds) (2012), *Siegfried Kracauer's American Writings. Essays on Film and Popular Culture*, Berkeley, Los Angeles, London: University of California Press.

Ward, David (2010), *Piero Gobetti's New World. Antifascism, Liberalism, Writing*, Toronto and Buffalo and London: University of Toronto.

Waugh, Thomas (ed.) (1984), *Show Us Life: Toward a History and Aesthetics of Committed Documentary*, Metuchen, NJ: Scarecrow Press.

—— (1984), 'Introduction: Why Documentary Filmmakers Keep Trying to Change the World', *or Why People Changing the World Keep Making Documentaries*', in Thomas Waugh (ed.), *Show Us Life: Toward a History and Aesthetics of Committed Documentary*, Metuchen, NJ: Scarecrow Press, xi–xxvii.

Wayne, Mike (2001), *Political Film. The Dialectics of Third Cinema*, London: Pluto Press.

Webb, Barbara J. (1992), *Myths and History in Caribbean Fiction. Alejo Carpentier, Wilson Harris and Edouard Glissant*, Amherst: The University of Massachusetts Press.

Wilder, Gary (2015), *Freedom Time. Negritude, Decolonization and the Future of the World*, Durham and London: Duke University Press.

Williams, Gareth (1996), 'Fantasies of Cultural Exchange', in Georg M. Gugelburger (ed.), *The Real Thing. Testimonial Discourse and Latin America*, Durham and London: Duke University Press.

Williamson, Edwin (2009), *The Penguin History of Latin America*, London: Penguin.

Zampa, Luigi (1979), 'Gli attori del cinema italiano', in Pina Bisceglie, Ezio Di Monte, Amedeo Fago, Roberta Farina, Enzo Fiorenza, Giancarlo Guastini, Bruno Restuccia, Gianni Romoli, Franco Velchi and Silvia Vigia (eds), *La città del cinema. Produzione e lavoro nel cinema italiano, 1930–1970*, Rome: Napoleone, 284–5.

Zanetti, Livio (1953), 'Crescere è difficile', *Cinema Nuovo*, no. 26, December, 392–7.

Zavattini, Cesare (2021), *Selected Writings*, 2 vols, edited and translated by David Brancaleone, New York: Bloomsbury Academic.

—— (2018), *Diario di cinema e di vita*, in *Straparole*, Florence and Milan: Giunti Editore and Bompiani.

—— (2016), 'Prove tecniche di *Telesubito*', in Alessandro Carri, *La televisione di Zavattini. L'idea e il progetto di Telesubito nelle parole e nelle lettere di Cesare Zavattini*, Reggio Emilia: Consulta librieprogetti, 31–51.

—— (2014), *Ligabue*, Milan: Bompiani.

—— (2006), *Uomo vieni fuori! Soggetti per il cinema editi e inediti*, edited by Orio Caldiron, Rome: Bulzoni.

—— (2006), *México mío in Cesare Zavattini, Uomo vieni fuori! Soggetti per il cinema editi e inediti*, edited by Orio Caldiron, Rome: Bulzoni, 357–63.

—— (2005), *Cinquant'anni e più … Carteggio con Valentino Bompiani*, edited by Valentina Fortichiari, in Zavattini. *Opere. Lettere*. Milan: Bompiani.

—— (2005), 'Alcune idee sul cinema', in Guido Conti (ed.), Zavattini, *Dal soggetto alla sceneggiatura. Come si scrive un capolavoro: Umberto D.*, Preface by Luigi Malerba and Epilogue by Gualtiero De Santi, Parma: Monte Università Parma Editore, 4–23.

—— (2002), *Una, cento, mille, lettere*, edited by Silvana Cirillo in *Opere. Lettere*, edited by Silvana Cirillo and Valentina Fortichiari, Milan: Bompiani.

—— (2002), *Io. Un'autobiografia*, edited by Paolo Nuzzi, Turin: Einaudi.

—— (2002), *Dite la vostra. Scritti giovanili*, edited by Guido Conti with a Preface by Valentina Fortichiari, Parma: Ugo Guanda Editore.

—— (2002), 'Rodenstack & Co.', in Guido Conti (ed.), *L'Illustrazione*, 2 March 1929, Zavattini, *Dite la vostra. Scritti giovanili*, Parma: Guanda, 504–5.

—— (2002), 'La dimensión moral del neo-realismo', in Guevara and Zavattini, *Ese diamantino corazón corazón de la verdad*, 263–84.

—— (2002), *Neorealismo ecc.*, edited by Mino Argentieri, Milan: Bompiani.

—— (2002), 'Un atto di coraggio, intervista con Tommaso Chiaretti', *Mondo Nuovo*, no. 49, December 1960, now in *Neorealismo ecc.* Edited by Mino Argentieri, in Zavattini, *Opere*, Milan: Bompiani, 886–92.

—— (1999), 'Per una discussione con i non-impegnati', in Stefania Parigi (ed.), 'L'Officina cubana', *Bianco & Nero*, LX, no. 6, November–December.

—— (1999), 'Come si scrive una sceneggiatura' (1959), translated by Lia Ogno, *Bianco & Nero*, LX, no. 6, November–December, 102–3.

—— (1995), *Cinquant'anni e più, Lettere 1933–1989*, edited by Valentina Fortichiari, Milan: Bompiani.

—— (1991), *Cronache da Hollywood*, edited by G. Negri with a preface by Attilio Bertolucci, Rome: Lucarini.

—— (1991), *Opere (1931–1986)*, edited by Silvana Cirillo with an Introduction by Luigi Malerba, Milan: Bompiani, 809–903.

—— (1988), *Una, cento, mille, lettere*, edited by Silvana Cirillo with an Introduction by Walter Pedullà, Milan: Bompiani.

—— (1983), *La veritàaaa*, edited by Maurizio Grande, Milan: Bompiani.

—— (1978), Letter to Lazar Wechsler, 29 May 1978, in Gambetti (ed.), *Zavattini mago e tecnico*, 1986, 309–10.

—— (1979), *Neorealismo ecc.*, edited by Mino Argentieri, Milan: Bompiani.

—— (1979), *Diario cinematografico*, edited by Valentina Fortichiari, Milan: Bompiani.

—— (1979), *Basta coi soggetti!* edited by Roberta Mazzoni, Milan: Bompiani.

—— (1977), Letter to Lino Miccichè, 2 November, in Zavattini, *Una, cento, mille, lettere*, 329–30.

—— (1977), Letter to Hall Bartlett, 29 June, ACZ Corr. Bartlett 611, fol. 6a. Unpublished.

—— (1976), *Al macero*, edited by Roberta Mazzoni and Giovanni Negri, Turin: Einaudi.

—— (1974), *Un paese*, Milan: Scheiwiller.

—— (1973), Letter to Gino Saviotti, 14 November, ACZ Corr. S 169/9, unpublished.

—— (1972), Letter to Argentina Brunetti, 27 March, ACZ Corr. 69/3, fol. 5. Unpublished.

—— (1971), Letter to Massimo Ferrara, 18 September, ACZ Corr. 69/3, fols 1–2. Unpublished.

—— (1971), *Zavattini: Sequences from a Cinematic Life*, translated by William Weaver, New York: Prentice Hall.

—— (1970), 'La Mostra di Pesaro e i cinegiornali liberi', in Tullio Masoni and Paolo Vecchi (eds), *Cinenotizie in poesia e prosa*, Turin: Lindau, 2000, 207–8.

—— (1968), 'Domande a Quattro Uomini di Cinema', in Valeria Di Bitonto, Ansano Giannarelli and Roberto Nanni (eds), *Una Straordinaria Utopia, Zavattini e il non film. I cinegiornali liberi*, Archivio Audiovisivo del Movimento Operaio and Archivio Cesare Zavattini, Rome and Reggio Emilia: n.p., 1998.

—— (1968), 'I cinegiornali liberi', in Valeria Di Bitonto, Ansano Giannarelli and Roberto Nanni (eds), *Una Straordinaria Utopia*, n.p., 1998.

—— (1968), 'Supplemento al Bollettino dei Cinegiornali Liberi no. 4. La Mostra di Pesaro e i Cinegiornali liberi', in Valeria Di Bitonto, Ansano Giannarelli and Roberto Nanni (eds), *Una Straordinaria Utopia*, n.p., 1998.

—— (1968), *Zavattini e Gregoretti sui Cinegiornali liberi*, October, https://www.youtube.com/watch?v=KGBWZ7M4s2M, accessed on 19 December 2018. The original is conserved in the AAMOD in Rome.

—— (1967), 'Domande a Quattro Uomini di Cinema', in Valeria Di Bitonto, Ansano Giannarelli and Roberto Nanni (eds), *Una Straordinaria Utopia*, Rome: *Archivio Audiovisivo del Movimento Operaio*.

—— (1967), 'Al magnetofono di quest'estate agli amici reggiani', in Valeria Di Bitonto, Ansano Giannarelli and Roberto Nanni (eds), *Una Straordinaria Utopia*, n.p., 1998.

—— (1967), 'I cinegiornali liberi', in Tullio Masoni and Paolo Vecchi (eds), *Cinenotizie in poesia e prosa. Zavattini e la non-fiction*, Turin: Lindau, 2000, 173–81.

—— (1963), 'Il cinegiornale della pace', in Zavattini, *Neorealismo ecc.*, 236–41.

—— (1962), 'Produttori astuti, produttori onesti', in Valentina Fortichiari (ed.), Cesare Zavattini, *Diario cinematografico*, Milan: Bompiani, 1979, 374.

—— (1962), 'Il progetto del film', in Francesco Bolzoni, 'Zavattini e il film inchiesta' in *I misteri di Roma*, Rome: Cappelli Editore, 13–32.

—— (1962), Letter to Guevara, 12 October, ACZ Corr. G 583/25. Unpublished.

—— (1961), Letter to Josué De Castro, ACZ D 133, 23 May. Unpublished.

—— (1960), Letter to Valentino Bompiani, 7 March, in Zavattini, *Una, cento, mille, lettere*, 221–5.

—— (1960), *Color contra Color*, 24 February. 'Soggettini cubani', ACZ Sog. NR 27/6, fol. 19. Unpublished.

—— (1960), 'Reunion celebrada entre el. Sr. Cesare Zavattini y miembros de la ARTYC del día 15 de Enero de 1960 en las oficinas del Instituto Cubano del Arte e Industria Cinematograficos', transcription by Héctor García Mesa, ACZ E 3/2, 2–8. Unpublished.

—— (1960), 'Cuba 1960. Reportage-Intervista raccolta da Gianfranco Corsini', *Paese Sera*, 21 April–1 May (in 7 instalments).

—— (1959), Letter to Gutiérrez Alea, 1 November, ACZ Corr. E 2/5, 10–11. Unpublished.

—— (1959), Letter to Jaime García Ascot, 28 October, ACZ E 2/5, fols 15–16. Unpublished.

—— (1959), Letter to Alfredo Guevara, 2 January, ACZ Corr. E 2/4, 1. Unpublished.

—— (1958), Letter to Carlos Velo, 5 October, ACZ Corr. E/72, fol. 28. Unpublished.

—— (1958), Letter to Carlos Velo, 2 October, ACZ Corr. E/72, fol. 27. Unpublished.

—— (1958), '*México mío*, Nota di cose consigliabili', ACZ Sog. NR 20/3, fols 269–271. Unpublished.

—— (1957), 'Prime reazioni leggendo le 31 pagine della sceneggiatura di *México mío*', [Production annotations] ACZ Sog. NR 20/3, fols 256–264. Unpublished.

—— (1957), Letter to Fernando Birri, 10 May, ACZ Corr. B 901/25. Unpublished.

—— (1957), Notebook, in 'Appunti e materiale vario raccolto durante il soggiorno messicano, 1955–1957', ACZ E 6/2, fol. 35r. Unpublished manuscript.

—— (1956), 'Considerazioni su *México mío*', ACZ Sog. NR 20/3, 266. Unpublished manuscript.

—— (1956), 'Lettera da Cuba', in Elio Petri, *Roma ore 11*, Milan: Edizioni Avanti!, 13–15.

—— (1956), *México mío*, Rome, 22 September, ACZ Sog. NR 20/3, fols 238–250. Unpublished manuscript.

—— (1956), '*México mío*, Nota di cose consigliabili', ACZ Sog. NR 20/3, fols 269–271. Unpublished manuscript.

—— (1956), Letter to Birri, 16 November, ACZ 901/23.

—— (1956), Letter to Felipe Carrera, 29 January, ACZ E/72, fol. 52.

—— (1955), 'Nota relativa a una prima stesura per la necessità del deposito presso la Società Autori di *México mío*' [Production annotations] December, ACZ Sog. NR 20/3, fols 252c. 255. Unpublished.

—— and Paul Strand (1955), *Un paese*, Einaudi: Milan.

—— (1955), 'I fotodocumentari di Cinema Nuovo. 25 persone di Zavattini e Strand', *Cinema Nuovo*, 4, no. 53, 25, February, 137–44.

—— (1955), Letter to Alvaro Beltrani, 20 October, ACZ E/72, fols 19–20. Unpublished.

—— (1955), Letter to Alvaro Beltrani, 16 September, ACZ E/72, fol. 18. Unpublished.

—— (1955), Letter to Ascot, 14 October, in *Cartas a México*, 77.

—— (1955), 'La terra e la luna', *Il Contemporaneo*, 24 September, 1.

—— (1955), Letter to Gamboa, 16 September, ACZ E/72, fol. 3.

—— (1955), 'Tres peliculas de Zavattini en Mexico', Interview, 5 September, ACZ E 7/4, fols 1–2. Unpublished.

—— (1955), 'Appunti per la conferenza sul Messico', ACZ E 63, fols 1–53. Unpublished.

—— (1955), 'Appunti per la conferenza sul Messico', 'Primo taccuino. Dalla mia partenza da Roma al 4/7/55', ACZ E 6/1, fols 1–53. Unpublished.

—— (1955), 'Appunti per la conversazione del 24/8 Mexico D.F.', ACZ E 7/1, fols 1–12. Fol. 12: 'Projecto de cuestionario para entrevista publica'. Unpublished.

—— (1955), Notebooks concerning Mexican journeys, 'Primo taccuino. Dalla mia partenza da Roma al 4/7/55', ACZ E 6/1.

—— (1955), 'La hospidalidad mexicana', *Teleguia*, Mexico City, 18 August.

———— (1955), Letter to Guevara, 12 May, ACZ Corr. G 583/22. Unpublished.
———— (1955), Letter to Berlanga, 10 October, ACZ, Corr. B 749/16. Undated and unpublished typescript letter.
———— (1955), Letter to Berlanga, Rome, 21 March, ACZ, Corr. B 749/15. Unpublished typescript letter.
———— (1954), Letter to Francisco Pina, 22 December, ACZ Corr. P 424/5. Unpublished.
———— (1954), Zavattini, Ricardo Muñoz Suay, Luis García Berlanga, and 'Festival de cine', ACZ, Sog. no. 13/3. Published in Spanish, 1991. Unpublished in Italian.
———— (1954), 'Viaggio in Spagna', handwritten notebook, ACZ, fols 62–68.
———— (1954), Letter to Berlanga, ACZ, 749/11. Undated and unpublished typescript letter.
———— (1954), Letter to Berlanga, 6 September, ACZ Corr. B 749/12. Typescript. Unpublished letter.
———— (1954), Letter to Berlanga, 9 September, ACZ Corr. B 749/13. Typescript. Unpublished letter.
———— (1954), 'Epilogo', in Pío Caro Baroja, *El Neorrealismo cinematografico italiano*, 273–5.
———— (1954), 'Alcune idee sul cinema', in Cesare Zavattini, *Umberto D. Dal soggetto alla sceneggiatura: Precedono alcune idee sul cinema, Rivista del cinema italiano*. Milan and Rome: Fratelli Bocca Editore.
———— (1954), 'Il neorealismo secondo me', *La Rivista del Cinema Italiano*, no. 3, March, 18–26, reprinted in *Neorealismo ecc.*, 121–32.
———— (1954), '"Cine" en casa', *Objectivo*, no. 2, February, 5–6.
———— (1954), 'Zavattini habla de Cuba' [Partial translation into Spanish of: 'Cuba 1953. 31 dicembre 1953'], *Cinema Nuovo*, no. 27, 15 January, published in Nuestro Tiempo, Havana. ACZ, E 2/3.
———— (1954), Letter to Guevara, 25 May, ACZ Corr. G 583/20.
———— (1954), Letter to Francisco Pina, 22 December, ACZ Corr. P424/5. Unpublished.
———— (1954), Letter to Guevara, 21 June, ACZ Corr. G 583/21.
———— (1954), 'Cuba 1953. 31 dicembre 1953', *Cinema Nuovo*, no. 27, 15 January.
———— (1953), 'Cesare Zavattini racconta: è sempre valida la lezione Neo-realista', *Il Momento*, 24 December.
———— (1953), [interview], *Cine Mundial*, no. 295, 11 December.
———— (1953), 'Some Ideas on the Cinema', *Sight and Sound*, October 1953, 64–9. Translated by Pier Luigi Lanza. Then in Richard Dyer MacCann (ed.), *Film: A Montage of Theories*, New York: E.P. Dutton, 1966, 216–28.
———— (1953), 'Come spero di fare Italia mia', *Rassegna del film*, 2, no. 13, April, 21–9.
———— (1953), 'Come non ho fatto Italia mia', *Rassegna del film*, 2, no. 12, March, 21–8.
———— (1953), Letter to Einaudi, 30 October, ACZ Corr. E 87/113.
———— (1953), Letter to Einaudi, 27 February, ACZ Corr. E 87/110.
———— (1952), 'Un invito di Zavattini agli scrittori italiani', *Il Rinnovamento d'Italia*, Rome 4 August.
———— (1952), 'Alcune idee sul cinema', *La Rivista del Cinema Italiano*, 1, no. 2, December, 5–19.

—— (1952), 'Alcune idee sul cinema [Colloqui]', with author's handwritten corrections, ACZ 77/7, 10 May, fols 1–21. Typescript.

—— (1952), 'Biblioteca Nazionale', 10 May, *Italia mia*. Notes taken at National library in Rome, ACZ TV 2/1, fols 18–23; 24–59; 60–81. Unpublished typescript.

—— (1952), 'Regista e soggettista di fronte al personaggio', *Copione*, no. 1, January, 7.

—— (1952), 'Biblioteca Nazionale', 7–11 February, *Italia mia televisiva*, ACZ TV 2/1, Televisione, *Italia mia* 1, fols 77–81. Unpublished typescript.

—— (1952), 'Lavoro in biblioteca', Saturday 22–Monday 25 January 1952, ACZ, TV2, Televisione, *Italia mia* 1, fols 77–81. Unpublished typescript.

—— (1952), 'Regista e soggettista di fronte al personaggio', *Copione*, no.1, 1 January, 7.

—— (1951), 'Ciò che sta accadendo: questo è il cinema', [Zavattini interviewed by Pasquale Festa Campanile], *Il Momento*, Saturday, 8 December, 3.

—— (1951), 'La genesi della storia di Umberto D.', *Cinemundus* XXX, no. 13, 15 December.

—— (1951), 'Il cinema, Zavattini e la realtà', [Interview conducted by Pasquale Festa Campanile], *La Fiera Letteraria*, no. 47, 9 December, now in Zavattini, *Neorealismo ecc.*, edited by Mino Argentieri, Milan: Bompiani, 1979, 81–5.

—— (1951), *Roma, ore 11*, ACZ, Sog. R46/4, Copia C. Sceneggiatura. Fol. 1. Soggetto e sceneggiatura: G. De Santis, B. Franchina, R. Sonego, C. Zavattini. *Roma, ore 11*, ACZ, Sog. R47, Sceneggiatura (copia). *Roma, ore 11*, ACZ, Sog. R 47, U7/3 Documentazione. Interviews with the typists. 64 fols

—— (1951), 'Umberto D.', *Teatro Scenario*, IV, 15–16, 15 August.

—— (1951), 'Miracolo a Milano', *La Voce Repubblicana*, 7 July.

—— (1951), *Prima Comunione*, Screenplay, ACZ, Sog. R 45. Unpublished typescript with Zavattini's handwritten annotations.

—— (1950), 'Cinema italiano domani', in Gian Luigi Rondi and Alessandro Blasetti (eds), *Cinema italiano oggi*, Rome: Bestetti Editore-Edizioni d'Arte, now in *Neorealismo ecc.*, 74–6.

—— (1950), Letter to Géza von Radványi, 9 March, in Calderon (ed.), *Uomo vieni fuori*, 146.

—— (1950), Letter to Géza Radványi, 9 March, ACZ Corr. R 24/2. Part-unpublished.

—— (1950), 'Totò il Buono', *Il Momento*, 23 February.

—— (1950), 'Tu Maggiorani', 'Il grande inganno', ACZ, Sog. NR 29/2, fols 26–30. Typescripts.

—— (1950), 'Il grande inganno. Idea per un film di Cesare Zavattini', *L'Unità*, 11 January 1950, 2.

—— (1949), 'Lettera aperta', *L'Unità*, 5 January, now in *Neorealismo ecc.*, 1979, 369–70.

—— (1942), 'Imola, autunno 1942', in *Cinema*, reprinted in Giacomo Gambetti (ed.), *Cesare Zavattini: cinema e vita*, Bologna: Bora, 98–104.

—— (1940), 'I sogni migliori', *Cinema* v, no. 92, 25 April 1940, 252–3, now in Orio Caldiron (ed.), *Cinema 1936–1943*, Rome: Fondazione Scuola Nazionale di Cinema, 2002, 158–9.

—— (1940), 'Totò il Buono', *Cinema* v, no. 102, 25 September.

—— (1937), 'Bionda sotto chiave', *Tempo*, 111, no. 11, 21 September.

—— (1937), Zavattini, 'Charlot, Imola, 24 April 1937', in Giacomo Gambetti (ed.), *Cesare Zavattini: cinema e vita*, Bologna: Bora, 1996, 86–94.

———— (1934), 'Buoni per un giorno', *Quadrivio*, II, 43, 19 August.

———— (1933), Letter to Enrico Falqui, 9 October, ACZ Corr. F 512/99. Unpublished.

———— (1933), Letter to Alessandro Minardi, 12 February 1933, ACZ. Corr. M 890/179.

———— (1932), Letter to Enrico Falqui, ACZ Corr. F 512/88. Unpublished.

———— (1931), Letter to Falqui, November, ACZ Corr. F 512/74. Unpublished.

———— (1931), Letter to Falqui, October, ACZ Corr. F 512/70. Unpublished.

———— (1931), Letter to Enrico Falqui, ACZ Corr. F 512/72. Unpublished.

———— (1931), Letter to Enrico Falqui, ACZ Corr. F 512/71. Unpublished.

———— (1931), Letter to Enrico Falqui, ACZ Corr. F 512/70. Unpublished.

———— (1931), Letter to Enrico Falqui, ACZ Corr. F 512/64. Unpublished.

———— (1931), Letter to Falqui, ACZ Corr. 512/59, 22 January. Unpublished.

———— (1931), Letter to Alessandro Minardi, ACZ Corr. M890/167. Unpublished.

———— (1930), Letter to Alessandro Minardi, 4 October, ACZ. Corr. M 890/140. Unpublished.

———— (1930), Letter to Enrico Falqui, 21 August, ACZ Corr. F 512/48, Unpublished.

———— (1930), Letter to Alessandro Minardi, 17 February, ACZ. Corr. M 890/135. Unpublished.

———— (1929), Letter to Alessandro Minardi, ACZ Corr. M 829/71, 1 August. Unpublished.

———— (1929), Letter to Enrico Falqui, 23 November, ACZ Corr. F 512/36. Unpublished.

———— (1929), Letter to Enrico Falqui, 20 October, ACZ Corr. F 512/33. Unpublished.

———— (1929), Letter to Enrico Falqui, 10 July, ACZ Corr. F 512/30. Unpublished.

————, Luis García Berlanga and Ricardo Muñoz Suay (1991), *Cinco Historias de España y Festival de Cine*, Valencia: Filmteca.

———— (1954) *Festival de cine*, Madrid: Graficas Cine, 1954 [dated 11 December], *Festival de cine*, ACZ, Sog. 13/3.

———— and Paul Strand (1997), *Un paese. Portrait of an Italian Village*, translated by Marguerite Shore, New York: Aperture.

Index

CPSIA information can be obtained
at www.ICGtesting.com
Printed in the USA
LVHW041630220223
740134LV00004BA/89

9 781501 377358